ARIS AND PHILLIPS CLASSICAL TEXTS

EURIPIDES

Cyclops

and

Major Fragments
of Greek Satyric Drama

Patrick O'Sullivan and Christopher Collard

Aris & Phillips Classical Texts
are published by
Oxbow Books, Oxford

ISBN   hardback: 978-1-908343-35-2
ISBN   paper: 978-1-908343-77-2

A CIP record for this book is available from the British Library

This book is available from

Oxbow Books, Oxford, UK
Phone: 01865-241249; Fax 01865-794449

and

The David Brown Book Company
PO Box 511, Oakville, CT 06779, USA
Phone: 860-945-9329; Fax: 860-945-9468

or from our website

www.oxbowbooks.com

Printed and bound by CPI Group (UK) Ltd, Croydon, CR0 4YY

*Cover image: Amphora (type B) Side B: Return of Hephaestus.
Attributed to Group E, 540 BC (Cat. No. 42/57); James Logie Memorial
Collection, University of Canterbury, Christchurch NZ.*

CONTENTS

Contents

GENERAL EDITOR'S FOREWORD

I have begun the Foreword for all other volumes in the Euripides Series by emphasizing the poet's remarkable variety of dramatic subjects, ideas and methods. A different kind of variety is afforded by his *Cyclops*, which happens to be not only his one satyr-play which survives complete but also the only such survival from any poet. More on the matter is said in Preface I, in describing the special nature of this volume.

The volume is the nineteenth and last but one in the Series. There remains only *Iphigenia at Aulis*, and I am very pleased that James Morwood has offered to collaborate with me in the work, which is underway.

Oxford, April 2013   Christopher Collard

PREFACE I

This volume is a collection, incorporating texts from many authors as well as Euripides, some of them unidentified and without date. Soon after O'Sullivan accepted Collard's invitation to undertake *Cyclops* for the Euripides Series, we agreed that, since it is the only surviving complete satyr-play, it would be helpful to set beside it the major fragments of all satyric drama, at least in translation, for their mutual illustration; but it was quickly clear to us that only a much fuller treatment would be satisfactory. This volume is apparently the first such collection of satyric texts in English, and certainly the first with introductory and explanatory matter of any extent. We had as incitement and model the comprehensive German volume edited by R. Krumeich, N. Pechstein and B. Seidensticker, *Das griechische Satyrspiel* (1999); it contains the editors' own substantial contributions, and important illustrations; but it omits *Cyclops*. Our debt to it for the fragmentary plays, texts, translations and notes, and for its valuable studies of the entire genre, is very great.

Cyclops is presented in the style established for all complete tragedies in the Series; but the Series General Bibliography is replaced by one particular to this volume.

The fragmentary texts are set out as nearly as possible in the format employed for the two volumes of *Euripides: Selected Fragmentary Plays* (C. Collard, M. J. Cropp, K. H. Lee, J. Gibert, I 1995, II 2004):

> Introductory Note surveying the fragmentary remains and advising on our methods of presenting them, and including a bibliography categorized by both topic and ancient author;
> for each author and play (or single long fragment, attributable or not) a brief bibliography of significant items, under the headings *Texts etc.*, *Discussions* and, where appropriate, *Art*; an introductory description and discussion of the play-fragment(s); Greek text(s) and critical apparatus on the left-hand page, English translation and annotation, as concise as possible, on the right-hand page (these details are expanded in the Advice to Readers).

The volume ends with an Appendix of almost all other known-satyr plays, stating their extent in terms of testimonies and textual fragments, and where possible their likely content; an Index of Motifs and Characters; Addenda; and a General Index.

O'Sullivan took the first and final responsibility for the General Introduction and General Bibliography, and for *Cyclops* in its entirety, and Collard for the Fragments. Each of us read, annotated and contributed to the other's work. Most of our exchanges were necessarily through e-mail. The volume has been very long in preparation.

We and the publisher record our gratitude to the Curators of the James Logie Collection in the University of Canterbury at Christchurch for permitting the reproduction of the amphora (Cat. No. 42/57) which forms our cover illustration.

April 2013   Christopher Collard (Oxford)
                                          Patrick O'Sullivan (Christchurch, NZ)

PREFACE II

There are many people and institutions I am happy to thank for their support of this volume, which has been a long time in the making. I'm grateful to my collaborator and general editor of the Series, Christopher Collard, for inviting me to work on this project, for his contributions to this volume, and for reading and commenting on my own; we have often differed in our approach to the material, but I am indebted to him for his criticisms and encouragement at all stages, as much as for his patience. I would also like to thank the following institutions and bodies for their generous support: the Marsden Fund of the Royal Society of New Zealand for a major research grant in the earlier stages that was vital for setting out the work ahead (from 2003–5); the Fellows of Wolfson College, Cambridge, who elected me to a Research Fellowship in 2003; the College of Arts at the University of Canterbury for periods of study leave, and for a Research Grant which enable me to collaborate with my colleague, Robin Bond, on a full production of *Cyclops* staged in Christchurch in January-February 2008; this coincided with the 29th Meeting of the *Australasian Society for Classical Studies*, and confirmed my view that so much more can be gleaned from a dramatic text when put into performance, thereby greatly enhancing my own thinking about *Cyclops* and satyr drama overall. I am also grateful to the Centre for Classics and Archaeology at the University of Melbourne which hosted me for some of my sabbatical of 2008–9, during which I was also a Visiting Scholar at Ormond College.

The following individuals all deserve thanks for helpful dialogue and support in various ways. I am grateful to David Konstan and Pat Easterling, who both kindly read the General Introduction and made many helpful suggestions; their influence on my own work will be readily evident, but I alone am to be held responsible for any errors or oversights that remain. Over the years others were generous with ideas and input on various levels in correspondence and dialogue, such as Mark Griffith, Richard Seaford, Oliver Taplin, Michele Napolitano, Boris Nikolsky, Deborah Boedeker, Kurt Raaflaub, Nancy Worman, Andrew Morton, Andrew Wong (who read over the commentary on *Cyclops*) and my brother Neil. I'm also grateful to Greg Nagy, who hosted me at the Center for Hellenic Studies in Washington, DC in 2003, and to George Harrison, convenor of 'Satyr Drama: Tragedy at Play' at Xavier University in Cincinnati, Ohio in 2003, and editor of the volume that appeared as a result of that valuable meeting. Thanks also to the Staff of the Department of Greece and Rome in the British Museum who made material available to me for private viewing. Many thanks to Clare Litt and Tara Evans at Oxbow Books, who oversaw the transition of a very complex manuscript into a book; and to Val Lamb there, and Neil Leeder of the Ioannou Centre for Classics in the University of Oxford, for help with typesetting, fonts and formatting at earlier stages.

In the latters stages of this work Canterbury was hit by a series of devastating earthquakes, first in September 2010 with on-going aftershocks, then, with lethal and even more destructive force, in February 2011. In the wake of these devastating and tragic events the University of Canterbury and its Central Library were closed for an extended period, leading to restricted access to relevant materials and resources for months at a time; all this was followed by major aftershocks in June and December 2011, which caused further disruption to all aspects of life and work for people in Canterbury. Yet, throughout all of these major upheavals, I have enjoyed the love and support of my family – my wife Marita and children Zoe and Luke. It is a pleasure to thank them all here for providing me with, among other things, distractions of a different and far more welcome kind over the entire course of this project.

Christchurch, NZ, April 2013   Patrick O'Sullivan

GENERAL INTRODUCTION
TO EURIPIDES' *CYCLOPS*
AND
MAJOR FRAGMENTS
OF GREEK SATYRIC DRAMA

1. Satyr Drama: 'Tragedy at Play'

Of the three major dramatic artforms produced in the Greek world from the late sixth century BC onward – tragedy, comedy and satyr play – this last genre remains the most enigmatic for modern viewers and readers. This is due not least to the fact that we have only one complete satyr play, Euripides' *Cyclops*, which retells the famous Homeric story of Odysseus' blinding of the man-eating, one-eyed monster, Polyphemus. This play survives serendipitously intact as part of an alphabetical group of Euripidean plays in the Laurentian manuscript (L). By contrast, a combined total of thirty-two complete tragedies by Aeschylus, Sophocles and Euripides (and perhaps two anonymous authors[1]) have come down to us, and eleven comedies of Aristophanes have survived, along with substantial comic fragments from other authors. The relative abundance of tragedy and Old Comedy has understandably given these two genres a higher profile in studies of ancient Greek literature and performance culture, and Greek tragedies and Aristophanic comedies continue to be performed around the world to this day. For most of the last century it was standard for monographs devoted to Aeschylus, Sophocles and Euripides to neglect satyr plays altogether, or cast a cursory glance at them at best; *Cyclops* has been blandly dismissed as 'of little dramatic merit' and as having 'no real place in a study of Euripides' dramatic art'.[2]

But within the Classical period up to one quarter of the output of all tragic

---

[1] Issues concerning the authorship of *Prometheus Bound* and *Rhesus*, once ascribed to Aeschylus and Euripides respectively, continue to divide scholars and need not concern us here.

[2] So G. Grube (1941, repr. 1961), who devotes two perfunctory paragraphs to this play. P. Arnott (1961) dismisses the *Cyclops* merely as evidence of an 'overworked playwright'.

playwrights at the City Dionysia – the most important Attic festival held in honour of the god of theatre – was comprised of satyr plays.[3] Although poorly preserved, evidence for satyr plays can be found in significant fragments that have been preserved either in papyri or quotes from later authors from antiquity and beyond. It would therefore be a mistake to consider satyr-drama as inconsequential, and opinions dismissive of satyric drama are now deservedly unfashionable. In the nineteenth century some luminaries – notably outside the field of Classical scholarship – recognized the importance of satyr drama. Percy Bysshe Shelley, more famous for re-working 'Aeschylean' tragedy in his *Prometheus Unbound*, produced a translation of Euripides' *Cyclops* in 1819.[4] Moreover, recent decades have witnessed major scholarly interest in this dramatic medium,[5] which has also caught the creative attention of certain writers, and found its place on the stage again in performances, at least of *Cyclops*.[6]

From about the beginning of the fifth to the middle of the fourth century BC at the City Dionysia satyr dramas directly followed three tragedies as a more or less humorous postlude, written by the tragedians themselves.

---

[3]   Euripides' *Alcestis* of 438 BC was submitted in place of a satyr play, but still incorporated some of the themes of satyric drama: *e.g.*, an ostensibly happy ending, a disaster averted by the intervention of a wandering hero, (mildly) humorous elements involving gluttony and drunkenness; see A. P. Burnett (1971) 30–1, 44–5; D. Sutton (1971) 55–72, (1980) 180–92, esp. 180–4; Slater (2005) 83–101; L. P. E. Parker (2007) xx–xxiii; see also below §3.2. Comedies and tragedies were performed at the Lenaea from about 440 but there were no satyr plays (*I.G.* ii².2319); see A. W. Pickard-Cambridge (1988) 40–1.

[4]   Shelley (1819; eds A. and W. G. Galignani); the current scholarly controversies over the authorship of *Prometheus Bound* did not exist in Shelley's day and he would have considered it a work of Aeschylus.

[5]   Apart from commentaries by R. Ussher (1978) and R. Seaford (1984), other major contributions to the study of satyr drama include: D. Sutton (1980); G. Conrad (1997); N. Pechstein (1998); R. Krumeich, N. Pechstein and B. Seidensticker (1999 [=KPS (1999)]); P. Voelke (2001); M. Griffith (2002); P. Cipolla (2003); M. Napolitano (2003); the collection of essays edited by G. Harrison (2005); Paduano (2005); J. Gibert (2002) gives an overview of work done on satyr plays up to 2002.

[6]   Tony Harrison's *The Trackers of Oxyrhynchus* (1988), performed in Delphi, is an inventive treatment of Sophocles' satyr play *Ichneutae* (*Trackers*) re-cast as the discovery of the Oxyrhynchus Papyri by B. P. Grenfell and A. S. Hunt in 1898. Performances of *Cyclops* took place in Cincinnati, Ohio, in 2003, and in Christchurch, New Zealand, in 2008. Both performances coincided with academic conferences, with the Cincinnati performance being part of a scholarly colloquium on Greek satyric drama and its influence. Fuller details of these and performances of other Greco-Roman dramas can be found at *APGRD* (The Archive of Performances of Greek and Roman Drama) run by the Classics Faculty at Oxford University < http://www.apgrd.ox.ac.uk/>.

We know from inscriptional evidence (*IG* ii².2320) that by 341/40 BC this system had changed so that a satyr play was produced as prelude to the tragedies which would be part of a separate competition.[7] But the bulk of our material predates this new arrangement, and it has become standard to speak of classical satyr play as the fourth part of a 'three plus one' formula. We are told that Pratinas of Phlius was the first to compose satyr dramas – he is credited with 32 overall – and that he competed in Athens in the 70th Olympiad or 499–96 BC against Aeschylus and Choerilus (*Suda*, s.v. 'Pratinas').[8] These plays featured a chorus of part-animal (usually equine[9]), part-man followers of Dionysus known as satyrs, treated heroic myths in a burlesque fashion, and exploited the lechery, cowardice and buffoonery of the chorus of satyrs and their reprobate father Silenus for humorous effect. The antics of these figures are juxtaposed with more grand and heroic figures suited to the tragic stage, such as Odysseus in *Cyclops* (cf. Silenus' lampooning of Odysseus, esp. 96–105) or Cyllene in Sophocles' *Trackers*, who are therefore made to seem at times pompous or ridiculous. One recent critic presents this kind of drama as a virtual recipe along the following lines: 'take one myth, add satyrs, observe the result.'[10] The unsubtle insertion, as it were, of satyrs into heroic myths often dealt with by tragedy leads to a comedy of incongruity. Horace implicitly recognized this in speaking of Tragedy as a grand dame being reluctantly compelled to dance among the satyrs (*Ars Poetica* 231–3):

> *Effutire levis indigna Tragoedia versus,*
> *Ut festis matrona moveri iussa diebus,*
> *Intererit Satyris paulum pudibunda protervis.*

---

[7]   See Pickard-Cambridge (1962) 66; (1988) 72–3, 101–3, 107–111; E. Csapo and W. Slater (1994) 40–2; KPS (1999) 9 n. 49.

[8]   For more on the origins of satyr drama, see below §3.1. All references to fragments of tragedies and satyr plays come from *Tragicorum Graecorum Fragmenta* 5 vols (1971–2004) ed. B. Snell, vol. 1 (1971¹, 1986²); vol. 2 (1981); S. L. Radt, vol. 3: Aeschylus (1985); vol. 4: Sophocles, (1977¹, 1999²); R. Kannicht, vol. 5.1, 5.2: Euripides (2004) Göttingen.

[9]   Satyrs are sometimes addressed as 'goat' (Aesch. *Prom. F-K* F 207) or are considered 'like a goat' (Soph. *Trackers* 367); but such references could suggest more their buffoonish and lecherous behaviour than their physiognomy. In *Prom. F-K* they want to kiss fire on seeing it for the first time, and in *Trackers* the context is lecherous; they are masturbating in front of Cyllene, who also refers to their 'yellow beards' as another sign of their goatishness. On a kylix cup of *c.* 460 BC satyrs appear to imitate the movements of a goat and a bull (*LIMC* VIII.1 s.v. 'Silenoi' 75). For satyrs with goat-like faces and men dressed as satyrs with goat-like masks in fifth-century Greek art, see below n. 131.

[10]   F. Lissarrague (1990a) 236.

Tragedy, undeserving of babbling cheap verses,
Like a matron ordered to dance at festival time,
Feeling a little ashamed, will be among the wanton satyrs.

Satyr drama is the original 'straight-man, funny-man' brand of humour we know today.

Satyr play, for all its ostensible 'low-brow' elements, was a highly self-conscious and self-referential genre engaging with specific literary forms including epic and tragic poetry.[11] On this level, and as a humorous genre, satyr play would seem to share much with Old Comedy; but the case for this can be overstated,[12] notwithstanding the fact that we know of a number of comedies that feature a chorus of satyrs.[13] Satyr plays from the Classical period are distinct from Old Comedy in that they invariably keep to the realm of heroic myth and do not, as a rule, explicitly lampoon public figures and contemporary events as Old Comedy frequently did. Python's satyric *Agen* (F1), performed for Alexander in India, satirised his corrupt general Harpalus, and Lycophron's *Menedemus* (F 2–4) parodied the contemporary philosopher of that name. But these are exceptions from the late fourth and early third centuries BC, when satyr drama appears to come more directly under the influence of Old and Middle Comedy. As Isaac Casaubon established in a *tour de force* published in the early seventeenth century, Greek satyr plays of the Classical period are to be distinguished from comedy and satire, especially Roman satire.[14] Also in diction, metre and structure, satyr play is significantly closer to tragedy than to comedy,[15] and,

---

[11] For recent discussion, see R. Hunter (2009), esp. 56, whose treatment generally focuses on how *Cyclops* engages with Homer, especially *Odyssey* 9.

[12] Tanner (1915) saw a number of parallels between *Cyclops* and Cratinus' *Odyssês*. A. Katsouris (1999) 185 sees no real difference between the satyr chorus and the comic slaves of Aristophanes and Menander; cf. also N. Zagagi (1999).

[13] E.g. Cratinus' *Dionysalexandros*; for discussion of this and other comedies with satyr choruses, see I. Storey (2005) 201–18, who estimates that up to nine such plays were produced in the fifth and fourth centuries, beginning with the *Satyroi* of Ecphantides who first competed between 458 and 454 (*IG* ii².2325.49). Although Timocles wrote satyr plays such as *Lycurgus* and *Phorcides*, his *Icarian Satyrs* was almost certainly a comedy; see E. Constantinides (1969).

[14] I. Casaubon (1605 repr. 1989); see also C. A. van Rooy (1965) 124–85; for links between satyr play and Old and Middle Comedy, see KPS (1999) 9–11; C. A. Shaw (2010) and above, n. 12.

[15] A. López-Eire (2003) focuses on linguistic criteria which can be used to distinguish satyr play and tragedy, but in so doing also implicitly acknowledges that the two genres have much in common; see also the valuable discussions by Griffith (2005a) 166–72, (2005b), (2010)

despite its earthy concerns and folk-tale elements, is not altogether lacking in moments of pathos and even poignancy, for instance, Danae's plaintive speech in Aeschylus' *Net-Fishers* outlining her plight (F **47a 9–21), and the choral ode in *Cyclops* (356–74) denouncing the monster's cannibalism. As a genre, satyric drama has long been recognized as a hybrid; it was aptly dubbed in antiquity as 'tragedy at play' (Demetrius, *On Elocution* 169), a view reiterated by scholars today.[16]

Satyr play in the Classical period – what can be considered its 'heyday'[17] – was crucial to the overall experience of theatre at the City Dionysia, since the last onstage images and sounds seen and heard by Athenian audiences at the end of a day watching four dramas were invariably the final moments of a satyr drama. Aeschylus was considered the finest exponent of this genre in antiquity (Paus. 2.13.6–7; Diog. Laert. 2.133), which suggests a rather different side to the blimpish figure Aristophanes makes of him in the *Frogs*. It is likely that our view of the great tragedians, and indeed Greek drama generally, would be significantly different had more satyr plays survived. Tony Harrison, whose *Trackers of Oxyrhynchus* engagingly reworks Sophocles' satyric *Trackers*, goes further: 'With the loss of these plays we are lacking important clues to the wholeness of the Greek imagination, and its ability to absorb and yet not be defeated by the tragic.'[18]

Harrison's insight is valuable, certainly as far as satyr plays predating 341 BC are concerned. But satyr drama, or satyric performances, continued well into the Hellenistic and Roman imperial periods long after the 'three plus one' formula was abandoned.[19] The functions, appeal and performance contexts of satyr drama would inevitably change over time, and difficulties in understanding the genre from later periods are compounded by the almost complete lack of any remaining material. But satyr drama, whether in performance or surviving as a text to be read or recited, retained something of its popularity. Inscriptional evidence testifies to the longevity of the genre in performances at various locations such as Delos, Samos, Boeotia and

---

73–9; Seaford (1984) 44–8; KPS (1999), esp. 16–17.

[16]   Cf. also the view of the twelfth-century Byzantine scholar-bishop Eustathius in his *Commentary on Homer's Odyssey* (2.184.3 Stallbaum), that satyr drama is situated half-way between comedy and tragedy.

[17]   So Seidensticker (2003) 100.

[18]   Harrison (1990) xi; see above n. 6.

[19]   For discussion of satyr play in the Hellenistic era, see Sifakis (1967) 124–6; G. Xanthakis-Karamanos (1993).

Teos.[20] An epitaph composed by Dioscorides (*Anth. Pal.* 707 = *TrGF* 99 T 2.3–4) says that Sositheus, active in the third century BC and probably a native of Alexandria, led a revival of satyr drama worthy of Pratinas himself, the alleged inventor of the genre. The latest attested writer of satyr plays by name is Lucius Marius Antiochus of Corinth, who won with a production at Thespiae between AD 161 and 169 (*IG* vii 1773; *SEG* iii 334); performances involving satyrs seem to have continued until the third century AD.[21] Satyr plays and satyric performances took place outside the Greek world, including even in Rome, notwithstanding an infamous suppression of the Bacchic cult in 186 BC mentioned by Livy (39.8–19). Seaford therefore overstates the case when he says that satyr play remained virtually exclusively Greek 'no doubt' because it was inseparable from 'the thiasos of the satyrs in the religious imagination of the Greeks and in their public and private religious celebrations.'[22] T. P. Wiseman, rather, has argued that satyric performance of some kind, far from being an 'un-Roman' cultural product, was a living artform at the time of Horace, with Sulla and L. Pomponius credited with writing satyric comedies.[23]

Arguably the most important piece of visual evidence for satyr drama and satyric costumes of the Classical period is the Pronomos Vase of the late fifth century BC (Naples, Museo Nazionale 3240 = *LIMC* III.1 s.v. 'Dionysos' 835).[24] On this vase we see a large number of figures on different levels including Dionysus and a female figure (usually taken to be Ariadne), musicians (including the aulos-playing Pronomos), the chorus of a satyr play, and three actors, one of whom represents Heracles who faces an actor playing Silenus. This actor wears a costume covered in tufts of white hair and has a leopard skin draped over his shoulder; he holds a mask depicting the aged satyr as evidently balding, with a heavily furrowed brow and bushy white hair and beard. Of the eleven actors dressed as satyrs, most hold their masks while one, with mask on and hence *in propria persona*, seems to dance the satyric move known as the *sikinis*, described by Aristoxenus in the

---

[20]   For references, see Sifakis (1967) 26–7; Seaford (1984) 25–6; Csapo and Slater (1994) 46–7.

[21]   KPS (1999) 11.

[22]   Seaford (1984) 29–30.

[23]   Nicolaus of Damascus, a contemporary of Horace, writes that Sulla composed satyric comedies (*FGrH* 90 F 75 = Athen. 6.261c); for full discussion of this and other relevant evidence, see Wiseman (1988). Nicolaus' testimony possibly lies behind the story told by Plutarch that a satyr was captured and brought before the dictator (Plut. *Sulla* 27), just as Silenus was brought before Midas (Arist. F 44; cf. Hdt. 8.138).

[24]   This vase is now the subject of a monograph; see O. P. Taplin and R. Wyles, eds (2010).

fourth century BC (F 104, 106 Wehrli).[25] Once *in propria persona*, the satyr cannot keep still, a feature manifest in satyrs onstage; Euripides' monstrous Polyphemus gives this as the reason why he won't eat them, as he imagines they would continue to dance in his belly (*Cyc.* 220–1)!

The Pronomos vase continues to pose questions and problems for scholars.[26] One pertains to the number of these satyrs not including Silenus: eleven. It is known that at one stage the number of chorus members, or choreutae, was raised by Sophocles from twelve to fifteen (*e.g.*, *Life of Sophocles* T 1.4 *TrGF*); eleven-man choruses are unattested. It would seem, therefore, that Silenus on the vase is meant to be understood as coryphaeus, or chorus leader of a group of twelve, as opposed to being an independent actor free to go offstage as he does in some satyr plays (*e.g.* Soph. *Trackers* 209; Eur. *Cyc.* 174, cf. 589!). Conversely, Silenus may be a coryphaeus but with the freedom to come and go as actor, as he does in *Trackers* and *Cyclops*.[27] It is also conceivable that Silenus here is an actor, and that the painter has supplied eleven choreuts simply to give an impression of a satyric chorus, whose number in actual performance is more likely to have been fifteen rather than twelve in the light of Sophocles' innovation.

The satyrs are played by beardless young men in costumes which tell us much about the appearance of satyrs onstage, at least around the late fifth century. The satyrs each wear a furry loincloth with a short tail and a not exceedingly large erect phallus. Equine features of the satyrs are, however, much more in evidence in earlier Greek art, notably on the François Vase, an Attic black-figure volute krater of *c.* 570 BC (*LIMC* VIII.1 s.v. 'Silenoi' 22) and the earliest surviving image of satyrs in Greek art. On this vase they are denoted with an inscription ΣΙΛΕΝΟΙ, or 'silens'.[28] Of the many

---

[25] On the nature of this dance, see Athenaeus (600c–d), who cites Aristocles, and mentions the *pyrrhichê* as being like a satyric dance because it is danced quickly; for modern discussion, see Voelke (2001) 138–43, 149–57; Seidensticker (2010) 213–29, esp. 217–18; see also below *Cyc.* Comm. 37–40 and on Soph. *Trackers* n. 35, below.

[26] Griffith (2010) 47.

[27] Sutton (1980) 140, following Kaimio (1970) 158, makes this suggestion on the assumption that a Greek play could have a 'sub-coryphaeus' who would lead the chorus in the absence of the coryphaeus.

[28] From an early stage satyrs, who appear to be Peloponnesian in origin, have counterparts in the form of Attic/Ionic 'silens' or 'silenoi'; for discussion, see F. Brommer (1937) 2–5; id. (1940) 222–28; Hedreen (1992) 162–3. In Greek writings from the fifth century onward, there seems to be no palpable distinction between the idea of a 'silen' and a 'satyr', since the terms are used interchangeably (*e.g.*, Hdt. 7.26, 8.138; Xen. *Anab.* 1.2.13; *Symp.* 4.19; Plato *Symp.* 215b, 216c, 216d, 221d, 222d; Lysias fr. 34).

scenes on this vase, one depicts the Return of Hephaestus, a story told also by Alcaeus (F 349 L-P), and later to become the subject of a fifth-century satyr play by Achaeus (F 17), in which the god is brought back to Olympus under the influence of wine sent by Dionysus to be reconciled with his mother Hera. On the François Vase the satyrs are depicted as part of Dionysus' retinue, each with a long tail, horses' legs and a huge erect phallus, much like that belonging to the donkey carrying Hephaestus. But on the Pronomos Vase the satyrs' bestial characteristics have become more understated since, in addition to their smaller phalluses and shorter tails, the actors do not wear any kind of costume to give the impression of equine legs. That said, the satyrs on the Pronomos Vase with their exposed genitalia and virtual nudity comprise a significant contrast to the three actors on the vase who wear dignified and richly decorated costumes suited to tragedy. This contrast is further evident in the masks the satyrs wear, which depict them as snub-nosed, with bushy beards, enlarged pointed equine ears and heavy, sometimes furrowed, brows all of which give them a grotesque look; indeed, Aeschylus' satyr play *Sacred Delegates* (F **78a 13–15) gets comic mileage out of the conventional ugliness of satyrs which would frighten even their mothers.[29] Thus, the 'straight-man, funny-man' brand of humour of satyr play narratives is given visual form on the Pronomos Vase in the contrasting costumes and masks worn by the satyr chorus and by the actors.

2. Satyrs: Ambivalent Creatures for an Ambivalent Genre

If satyric drama is best designated as an ambivalent genre, this reflects the fact that satyrs occupy a similarly ambivalent status in the ancient Greek cultural imagination.[30] Both in art – predominantly vase painting of the sixth and fifth centuries BC – and in numerous passages of satyric drama, the hedonism, lechery and drunkenness of these creatures are readily evident. With some justification Edith Halls calls satyrs 'ithyphallic males behaving badly', and for François Lissarrague they are 'the anti-type' of the ideal

---

[29]   O'Sullivan (2000), esp. 360–3.

[30]   Further to the works cited in n. 5, see also Griffith (2005a), (2005b), (2008), (2010); for instance, Buschor (1943) and Brommer (1959). Among the more important studies of satyrs in Greek art of the last few decades are: Bérard (1989) 131–50; Lissarrague (1990a, 1990b, 1993); Hedreen (1992) who focuses largely on Attic black figure vases (esp. 125–78), but includes discussion of 'satyr play vases' of the fifth century (105–24); KPS (1999) 41–73; T. Carpenter (2005); A. Mitchell (2009) 150–234, 306–11.

male citizen of Classical Athens.[31] However, satyr plays and other sources including Herodotus (8.138), Plato (*Symp.* 216c–217a, etc.), Aristotle (F 44 Rose) and Plutarch (*Pericles* 5.3) reveal further aspects of these followers of Dionysus. Sometimes these include a certain wisdom, leading to gloomy insights into the nature of human existence; at other times satyrs are even linked to aspects of *aretê*, or 'excellence'.

2.1 The Satyr as Transgressor

The three habits of laziness, sex and drinking, which characterize so much satyric behaviour or preoccupations onstage, are conspicuous in the first three attestations we have of satyrs in Greek literature and art. The earliest extant literary reference comes from Hesiod, who dismisses them as 'worthless and useless for work' (Hes. F 10a.18 MW). Hesiod gives no physical description of the satyrs, nor is there any mention of Dionysus in the fragment, and it seems likely that the satyrs are understood as the sons of Iphthime and her sisters, who consort with the gods, including Hermes; but the god is not explicitly called their father.[32] This aversion to work remains a staple characteristic of satyrs, who nevertheless are compelled to carry out labours in some satyr plays. At the beginning of Euripides' *Cyclops* we hear the melodramatic Silenus who complains of the 'labours' he has performed for his natural master, Dionysus (1–9), and the tedious chores he must carry out for Polyphemus, his brutal overlord who keeps him and

---

[31]   E. Hall (1998), (2006); Lissarrague (1990a) 235.

[32]   In Nonnus' *Dionysiaca* (14.105–17) Iphthime is the mother of the Satyroi as well as the Nymphai and Kouretes. Hermes has connections with satyrs, apart from sharing with them an inclination towards ithyphallicism in the form of herms. As well as appearing in numerous satyr plays (*e.g.*, Soph. *Trackers*, *Inachus*; Eur. *Sciron*, *Syleus*; the *Omphale* plays of Ion and Achaeus; Astydamas II *Hermes*), Hermes appears with satyrs on numerous vases of the late Archaic and Classical period, *e.g.* the Berlin painter's splendid amphora (*LIMC* V.1 s.v. 'Hermes' 656 bis), and satyrs appear dressed as Hermes or at least wearing his attire (*LIMC* V.1 s.v. 'Hermes' 891 Douris). In fifth-century Attic vase painting Hermes is present at Dionysus' re-birth from the thigh of Zeus (*LIMC* III.1 s.v. 'Dionysus' 666); he also brings the infant Dionysus to Silenus (*LIMC* III.1 s.v. 'Dionysus' 686), a moment possibly enacted or alluded to in Sophocles' *Little Dionysus* (F 171–3); see KPS (1999) 253–5 for discussion. The statue, attributed to Praxiteles (Paus. 5.17.3), now in Olympia, of a youthful, athletic Hermes holding a bunch of grapes just out of reach of the infant Dionysus is another famous instance of the intimacy between him and the patron god of satyrs.

his sons enslaved on Sicily (23–35).[33] In literature we first hear of 'silens'[34] in the *Homeric Hymn to Aphrodite* (262–3), which refers to them indulging in another canonical activity or desire of theirs: having sex with nymphs. The return of Hephaestus on the François Vase in the company of Dionysus and the silens depicts a further preoccupation of these creatures: drinking, evidenced not least by the huge wine sack being carried by a silen whose ithyphallic state makes clear that other satyric thoughts are not far from his mind either.

In black-figure vase painting of much of the sixth century satyrs generally appear to be more bestial in their facial features, hairiness and equine legs.[35] However, with the advent of red-figure vase painting towards the end of the century, the satyrs lose their equine legs, which adopt human form, even though they retain their tails and the more or less grotesque characteristics of large pointed ears, snub noses, heavy eyebrows and often balding pates and heavily furrowed brows. It is possible that the modification of the satyrs' bestial features may reflect the appearance of satyrs onstage or other kinds of performance even if a link to a specific satyric performance, dramatic or otherwise, cannot be wholly established.[36] Certainly in the first quarter of the fifth century images of actors dressed as satyrs appear, affording a glimpse into these creatures as stage creations, evidenced perhaps most notably by the clear depiction of the actor's loincloth with attached erect phallus and tail.[37] And the appearance of satyrs in Greek art of the sixth and fifth centuries can tell us much about satyrs in the cultural landscape of Archaic

---

[33]   Elsewhere the satyrs are happy slaves of Dionysus (*Cyc.* 709), and worship of their god is seen as a presumably pleasant form of labour (Soph. *Trackers* 223–4); see also commentary on *Cyclops* (1n.).
[34]   See above, n. 28.
[35]   For a full study of silens in black figure vase painting, see G. Hedreen (1992).
[36]   G. Hedreen (1992) 125–78 distinguishes satyr plays *per se* and other satyric performances, *i.e.* of men dressed up as satyrs (105). Plato (*Laws* 815c) refers to people dressed as nymphs and satyrs as part of initiations and other rituals; cf. Hedreen (1992) 82, 87–88; Csapo and Slater (1994) 93. For images of satyrs accompanying Dionysus in a ship wagon that may reflect a Dionysian procession of the Anthesteria, see Pickard-Cambridge (1988) figs 12 and 13.
[37]   For such images, see KPS figs. 1b, 2a, 3a–b, 4a–b, 5a–b; on these and other images of onstage satyrs the equine legs are conspicuously absent. For ways of depicting satyr dramas on Greek vases with visual allusions to the satyric costume worn by the actors, see J. R. Green (1991); Hedreen (1992) 105–24, who notes that the presence of an aulos player in some satyric scenes indicates a performance is being portrayed. However, C. Bérard and C. Bron (1989) 143 argue that the presence of the loincloth does not always signify that a theatrical production is being depicted, and that this attire can occur in non-theatrical contexts.

and Classical Greece, even when there is no obvious connection between an image on a vase and a satyric performance.[38] The most conspicuous features of satyric activity on Greek vases of the sixth and fifth century tend to be these elements of play and energy with humour invariably present. Not only do buffoonery, lechery, heavy drinking, and incongruity continue to abound in such images, but for many images of satyrs on fifth-century vases, burlesque treatment of heroic figures and myths is prominent. These vases are thus on a similar footing to satyr drama.

The ithyphallic nature of satyrs in Greek art is a source for much visual and verbal humour.[39] The oversized nature of the satyr's phallus, however, is not a sign of hyper-masculinity, but, as Eva Keuls correctly notes, a sign of bestiality, and in the case of satyrs, a sign of lack of self-control.[40] A glance at the François Vase shows that the silens are literally more asinine than hyper-virile in their overendowed ithyphallic status, much like the donkey ridden by Hephaestus; this is confirmed by other features which the satyrs share with this animal, such as their equine legs and tails. An image of a different kind confirms the impression that huge genitals do not connote virility and potency. On an Attic red-figured pelike in the Villa Giulia (48238) Heracles is confronted by a figure called 'Geras' ('Old Age'), a diminutive, hunched, bald and decrepit figure whose enlarged testicles and penis hang limply between his legs. Such an image contrasts with the aristocratic ideal announced by the Stronger Argument in Aristophanes' *Clouds* (1011–20) where having a 'small prick' is announced as a desirable feature in contrast to a 'huge dick'.[41] It is true that Aristophanes lampoons much

---

[38] Mitchell (2009) 234 notes that 'there is no need to conjure up theatrical explanations to interpret the presence of satyrs in certain scenes.' Conversely, Hedreen (1992) 106 observes that there may well be images based on satyr play that give no indication that they were based on performance (with no obvious treatment of costumes, etc.), since such information could easily have been communicated verbally by the painter to the customer. E. Simon (1982) 139 suggests that some images on vases depict scenes from satyric drama even when no satyrs are portrayed.

[39] The sexual life of satyrs has attracted much attention in recent years; see, for instance, Lissarrague (1990a), (1990b), (1993); Keuls (1993) 65–97, 357–78; A. Stewart (1997) 187–92; Hall (1998), (2006); Voelke (2001) 211–59.

[40] Keuls (1993) 68; Stewart (1997) 189–91. K. Dover (1989) 127–9 points out that the oversized genitals of satyrs and other liminal figures depicted on Greek vases are presented as comical or ugly.

[41] Mitchell (2009) 118, also notes that Geras' physique in other respects has much in common with Homer's description of Thersites (*Il.* 2.216–19), infamously the 'ugliest man who came to Troy'.

in the Stronger Argument's character elsewhere, but the kind of physical aesthetic described at *Clouds* 1011–20 is reflected in countless idealized images of youths in Greek statuary and on vases, and occurs in other Attic literature, such as the comedies of Eubulus (F 11.2 K-A).[42] Silenus abuses his sons for their supposed cowardice by calling them among other things 'phalluses' (Soph. *Trackers* 151). Over-endowed satyrs, then, are better understood as grotesquely comical when depicted in Greek art rather than embodiments of enviable virility, especially when under the influence of their conspicuously erect phalluses. In such a state, masturbating satyrs are found on black-figure pottery, such as an amphora (Berlin 1761) and an aryballos by Nearchos (New York 26.49).[43] Likewise, satyrs onstage do the same thing, for instance, in response to the indignant Cyllene's long speech in defence of the infant Hermes (Soph. *Trackers* 366–8); masturbation is also the post-prandial diversion of choice for the monstrous Polyphemus in *Cyclops* (see *Cyc.* 327–8n.).[44]

Satyrs in sixth and fifth-century vase painting are also (in)famous for their attempts on female figures such as nymphs and maenads, evidence of their general lack of *sôphrosynê* (moderation, self-control).[45] On a red-figure cup by the Brygos Painter of c. 490 BC (London BM E65) satyrs molest even the messenger goddess Iris, and move with lecherous intent toward Hera, who is, however, flanked by Hermes and an advancing Heracles. Lechery abounds in satyric drama, and in *Cyclops*, for instance, prurient, misogynistic sentiments are expressed by the chorus, who fantasise about the gang-rape of Helen after the sack of Troy (179–87).[46] Aeschylus' highly fragmentary *Amymone* (F 13–14) seems to have told of a satyr's attempted rape of the nymph of the title who is 'saved' by Poseidon, only to have sex with the

---

[42] For discussion, see Henderson (1991a) 212.

[43] = Lissarrague (1990b) figs 2.4, 2.6; fig. 2.5 shows a satyr let down, so to speak, by his huge flaccid penis.

[44] Cf. Aesch. *Sacred Delegates* F **78a.29–36 (with n. 10) which could refer to satyrs' masturbating, resulting in their phalluses' becoming small and tapering in contrast to their usually excessive size; see W. Slenders (1992).

[45] Although satyrs like Marsyas could, however, be seen as embodying wisdom and *sôphrosynê* (Diod. Sic. 3.58–9). For discussion of *sôphrosynê* within aristocratic ethics, see H. North (1966); Dover (1974) 66–9; A. M. Radermaker (2005) *passim*.

[46] Cf. *Cyc.* Comm. 186–7n. Satyric violence of a different kind against women is attested elsewhere in Greek art. On a unique scene on a black-figure lekythos of c. 470–60 BC, which has become the name vase of the Bedlam Painter (Athens NM 1129), some satyrs torture a woman tied to a tree; see Osborne (1998) fig. 116.

god, willingly or otherwise.[47] There are times when the lecherous father of the satyrs, Silenus, indulges in absurd fantasies of rampant sex with nymphs (Eur. *Cyc.* 169–71; Achaeus, *Fates* F 28) or brags of his sexual exploits like some aged stud (Soph. *Trackers* 154–5); in Aeschylus' *Prometheus the Fire Kindler* (F 204b 4–5) the satyrs, perhaps led by Silenus as coryphaeus, even imagine that nymphs will be pursuing them! In Aeschylus' *Net-Fishers* (F **47a.57–67) Silenus menacingly fantasises about marrying Danae who had been washed up on the shore of Seriphos with the infant Perseus. Both he and his sons imagine that Danae is desperate for sex after having been at sea for so long, just as Euripides' satyrs see Helen as a nymphomaniac (*Cyc.* 181).

Hall's view of satyr drama as a hyper-male genre that implicitly encouraged violence against women begs the question that such satyric behaviour was endorsed by the dramatists and their audience, and that satyrs are masculine in some normative sense.[48] Satyrs are also at times cowards, simpletons and drunkards full of bluff and bluster; indeed, much has been written about satyrs as the comical 'anti-type' of the ideal citizen.[49] Evidence for satyrs' cowardice is found in their petty excuses for not helping Odysseus blind Polyphemus, confirming the hero's beliefs about them (Eur. *Cyc.* 635–50); Sophocles' *Inachus* seems to present them in a similar light (F **269c col. iii 35–47). In Aeschylus' *Sacred Delegates* (F **78c.48–55) they are frightened of what appears to be athletic equipment, or possibly fetters, which they would happily consign to one of their friends.[50] Elsewhere their father abuses them as cowards only to prove a bigger one himself on hearing Hermes' lyre music for the first time and bolting off in terror (Soph. *Trackers* 145–209); this drama, it has been argued, consistently undermines the masculinity of the satyrs.[51] In *Cyclops* Silenus toadies shamelessly to the monster, telling lies that endanger the life of Odysseus and his men (228–40). At times this cowardice is compounded by the satyrs' own bravado (Soph. *Inachus* F **269d; Eur. *Cyc.* 596–8) or specious boasts of their own heroic prowess

---

[47] The story is retold by later mythographers, such as [Apollod.] (2.1.4) and Hyginus (*Fab.* 169a); see also Sutton (1974c) for fuller discussion of the play.

[48] Hall (1998) 36 writes of satyr drama as a medium in which 'male sexual aggression was a phenomenon to be riotously celebrated'.

[49] Lissarrague (1990a), esp. 236. For modifications of Hall's view, see Voelke (2001) 411; Gibert (2002) 87–8; Griffith (2005) 166–72.

[50] For discussion of these 'playthings' (ἀθύρματα) and what they could be, see introductory discussion to Aeschylus' *Sacred Delegates* below p. 269.

[51] See E. OKell (2003).

(Eur. *Cyc.* 5–12) and overblown image of themselves and their fields of competence (Soph. F **1130). At such moments males in the audience are more likely to laugh at the satyrs rather than with them.[52]

Likewise the satyrs' drunkenness or over-reaction to wine is attested on sixth and fifth-century vaseware as in satyr drama, where once again Silenus is the culprit (*e.g.*, Eur. *Cyc.* 164–74, 431–4; cf. Soph. *Little Dionysus* F 171–2). Connected to this is the satyrs' bibulousness – a feature of satyric ogres such as Polyphemus (Eur. *Cyc.* 326–38, 417–26, 503–77, etc.) or Sositheus' Lityerses (*Daphnis or Lityerses* F 2.6–8); Heracles, a favourite hero of satyric drama, is also a glutton and big drinker (Eur. *Syleus* F 691; Ion, *Omphale* F 29–30; cf. also Eur. *Alc.* 747–72, 780–802, etc.). Indeed, the connection between satyrs and Heracles as bibulous gluttons is nicely encapsulated on an oinochoe of *c.* 470 BC (BM E 539), which parodies the myth of the hero's second last labour which involved retrieving the Apples of the Hesperides. Here a satyr, wielding a club and wearing a wine-sack in imitation of Heracles' lion-skin, approaches a tree encircled by a snake and bearing wine-jugs on its branches. The image also provides us with the comic incongruity of the cowardly satyr masquerading as the most formidable hero of all, rather like Dionysus whose impersonation of the hero reduces Heracles to uncontrolled laughter in Aristophanes' *Frogs* (38–172). The satyrs' transgressions – like those of the comically cringeworthy Basil Fawlty or Les Patterson – are reminders of what not to do. For all their lechery, satyrs are generally less threatening to female figures than, for instance, centaurs, whose monstrous violence is well attested in myth and art.[53] Satyrs' attempts on female figures on red-figure pottery end in inevitable failure.[54] Maenads fend them off easily enough with their *thyrsi*

---

[52]   Mitchell (2009) 309.

[53]   The Centauromachy, in which the Lapiths prevented the centaurs from raping the Lapith women, appeared on the west pediment of the temple of Zeus at Olympia, and on the metopes on the western façade of the Parthenon. The François Vase, our earliest known depiction of silens or satyrs in Greek art, is also the earliest known source for the Centauromachy in art and highlights the different natures of these two hybrid creatures: boozy, partying silens as opposed to violent, murderous centaurs. While the battle of Lapiths and centaurs is known as early as Homer (*Iliad* 1.262–68), Pindar (F 166 S-M) is the earliest extant source to mention the attempted rape as the cause of the conflict.

[54]   Gibert (2002) 85. Hall (2006) 146 cites two late examples of ancient beliefs that satyrs assaulted women, from Pausanias (1.23.7) and Philostratus (*Vit. Apoll.* 6.27); the latter refers to an apparition of a satyr said to have appeared in Ethiopia. Keuls (1993) 362 suggests that in scenes on Greek vases where satyrs' advances are not reciprocated, they are more intent on molesting rather than raping nymphs or maenads.

(ivy-wreathed staves) or fists, and at times the satyrs appear diminutive next to these more dignified female followers of Dionysus, adding to the absurd nature of the satyrs' desires and the unlikelihood of their fulfilment.[55] Just as the satyrs perennially avoid disaster however close they get to it, so, too, they never seem to be able to consummate their lust, thus remaining in a comical state of sexual excitation and frustration like the ithyphallic men in Aristophanes' *Lysistrata*. It seems that the rape of women in satyr play, if it took place at all, was carried out by figures such as Poseidon in Aeschylus' *Amymone* or Heracles in Euripides' *Syleus* (F 693; cf. [Apollod.] 2.1.4).[56]

Satyrs also lust after male figures, including the young Achilles (Soph. *Lovers of Achilles* F 157, etc.), and Heracles (Soph. F 756; cf. Achaeus F 26); in both cases the heroes, much like the maenads, would have no trouble in fending off the satyrs' ludicrous advances. Satyric homoeroticism appears on Greek pottery. On an Attic jug of *c.* 430 BC a satyr holding a cockerel – the standard gift from an *erastês* (older, male lover) to his *erômenos* ('beloved') – approaches a young robed boy somewhat aggressively.[57] Satyrs also show little discrimination with whom or what or how they attempt to satisfy their desires, but this does not mean that they are hyper-masculine sexual aggressors. Sometimes they will try to copulate with animals or each other; at other times they are penetrated anally or perform fellatio.[58] In a grotesque travesty of the Zeus-Ganymede myth the great lecher Silenus finds himself the victim of sexual violence in being dragged offstage to be raped by Polyphemus (*Cyc.* 582–89), and it is possible that the old satyr suffered a similar fate in Aristias' version of the same story.[59] In Euripides' *Cyclops*, Silenus' rape occurs immediately after the monster, in his drunken stupor, has leered at the chorus of satyrs, imagining them to be the Graces,

---

[55] *E.g.* the neck amphora by Oltos (Paris G 2) and pointed amphora by the Kleophrades Painter (Munich 2344). Sometimes the advances of satyrs appear to be welcomed by nymphs; see Hedreen (1994) pl. 1 (b) column krater by Lydos, *c.* 560; pl. 1 (c) amphora by the Amasis painter, *c.* 550; pl. 4 (a) Lip-cup by Oakeshott painter, *c.* 550. Hedreen interestingly suggests that the more fraught relations between satyrs and maenads on red-figure pottery may reflect certain plots in fifth-century satyric drama.

[56] See below on Eur. *Syleus* F 693 n. 11; Sositheus, *Daphnis*.

[57] *LIMC* VIII.1 s.v. 'Silenoi' 87.

[58] Lissarrague 1990b figs 219, 220; Stewart (1997) 187–91, *e.g.* fig. 122; for satyrs copulating with animals, see also *LIMC* VIII.1 s.v. 'Silenoi' 51 (amphora of mid-sixth century); ib. s.v. 'Silenoi' 52 (skyphos of *c.* 530/520 BC); ib. s.v. 'Silenoi' 55 (hydria of *c.* 540).

[59] The one surviving fragment of this play (= Aristias F 4) contains a close parallel to Eur. *Cyc.* 556–8; other parallels between the two plays may have existed; see A. Katsouris (1997) 3; KPS (1999) 219–20.

divine embodiments of female beauty, and thus making them potential effeminized victims of his lechery (*Cyc.* 581). The blurring of satyrs' sexual identity is further evident when they appear in drag on red-figure pottery.[60] Transvestite satyrs are likely to have appeared also in Ion's satyr drama *Omphale* in their usual role as slaves to some potentate, in this case a Lydian queen who gives orders to her 'girls' to bring out vessels for a symposium (F 20; cf. F 24, 25).[61] The very meagre fragments of Aeschylus' *Nurses* (F 246a-d) possibly featured a chorus of satyrs dressed as female nurses, and the same may be true of Sophocles' equally sparse *Little Dionysus* (F 171–2) and *Little Heracles* (F 223a–227).[62]

The composition of satyr plays could even be allegorized as a sexual encounter involving both 'active' and 'passive' sexual roles, as conventionally construed within Classical Athenian culture.[63] In Aristophanes' *Thesmophoriazusae* the tragedian Agathon, relentlessly pilloried for his effeminacy and sexual passivity, has just been theorizing that a poet should adopt the ways and habits of the kinds of dramas he is producing.[64] Aristophanes parodies this theory by showing that Agathon's 'effeminate dramas' are the result of the tragedian's own effeminacy (*Thesm.* 149–52). So, for Euripides' boorish kinsman, when it comes to producing

---

[60]   Brommer (1959) plate 118 (= fig. 69), 118a. Lissarrague (1990b) 60–1, notes the depiction of a satyr adopting 'a typically feminine pose', draping a fillet over a basket on a red-figure lekythos (= fig. 2.17); Voelke (2001) 66–71 aptly considers satyrs to be 'between masculine and feminine'.

[61]   Many have suggested that this drama featured a cross-dressing Heracles, consistent with images from fourth-century art in which Omphale appears in his lion-skin (*e.g.*, *LIMC* VII.1 45–50 s.v. 'Omphale'), and with the version told much later by Lucian (59.10); see Loraux (1990) 25; Maitland (2007) 277–8; see also below Ion, *Omphale* (p. 416).

[62]   The ancient *Hypothesis* to Euripides' *Medea* confirms that nurses of Dionysus are meant (= Aeschylus F 246a). For more on these three plays, see respectively KPS (1999) 197–202, 250–8, 266–9. If *Adespota* F 667a 'A Medea Play' is satyric, then the satyrs would be in drag, since they would comprise the chorus who are addressed as 'women' (F 667a. 113); see Sutton (1987) 9–60, and introductory discussion to *Adespota* F 667a below p. 491.

[63]   For discussion of this construction of sexual behaviour as centred on an active (= male penetrator) partner and a passive (= female/penetrated) partner, see Dover (1989) 81–91; D. Halperin (1990), esp. 266–9. See also J. S. Carnes (1998) esp. 109–14 who notes that Plato already deconstructs this antithesis in his *Symposium* in the speech given by Aristophanes on the mutual desire felt by the two separated lovers (whether male-male, male-female, female-female) to be reunited.

[64]   In *Acharnians* (410–13) Aristophanes makes a similar joke about Euripides, *mutatis mutandis*; cf. Euripides (*Suppl.* 180–3) and Aristotle (*Po.* 1455a30–32); cf. also Plato (*Ion* 535c–e).

satyr plays one should behave like satyrs; he tells Agathon that next time the playwright wants to compose a satyr drama (literally, 'do satyrs': σατύρους ... ποιῇς) the kinsman will (*Thesm.* 157–8): 'get right behind you with my hard-on (ἐστυκώς) and do [it] with you (συμποιῶ)'. Henderson is right to see *doubles entendres* in Aristophanes' use of ποιῇς and συμποιῶ here.[65] Satyr drama is an ambivalent medium sexually, since the production of satyr dramas is comically allegorized as involving both male sexual aggression and sexual passivity on the part of an 'effeminised male' – in this case Agathon, who is the butt of the joke in more ways than one. Aristophanes captures neatly the erotic ambivalence of satyrs. Sometimes they can be the object of sexual violence, as is Silenus in *Cyclops* (582–9) or, as certain vases show, they can appear in drag, or can become effeminized, like Agathon himself. Aristophanes implies that satyrs can fall into both camps as both perpetrators and recipients, even victims, of sexual activity.

Nor are inanimate objects safe from the advances of satyrs. Frequently on vases satyrs will combine drink and sex and will penetrate amphorae, or drink from wine sacks as if performing fellatio, or in their exuberance balance cups on their erect phalluses, as in the famous Douris psykter (BM 678) and elsewhere.[66] Masturbating satyrs are also widely attested in Greek art, as well as appearing in satyr drama (cf. Soph. *Trackers* 366–8).[67] Onstage and elsewhere, then, satyrs' sexual activity and desires take on many forms, and their inevitably unfulfilled lusting after female figures is just one of many outlets for their comical hyperactivity, which also at times sees them on the receiving end of violent or incongruous sexual advances. Satyrs are not primarily aggressively heterosexual, nor especially masculine in any straightforward normative sense for an ancient audience. Rather, these followers of Dionysus range in all directions for comic effect, especially as far as sexual activity is concerned.

2.2 More Positive and Paradoxical Features of Satyrs
These lecherous, buffoonish and incongruous qualities imply that satyrs are suitable objects of derision. Aristotle considers the depiction of inferior figures (χείρους) to be a hallmark of comedy, while tragedy depicts people generally better than we are (*Po.* 1448a16–18; cf. 1449a32–3, etc.). But on

---

[65] The translation is by Henderson (1991a) 158, who rightly sees in ποιῇς and συμποιῶ synonyms for βινεῖν ('fuck'); see also E. Stehle (2002), esp. 382–3.

[66] See, for instance, Attic cup, *c.* 520 BC (Palermo V651); Attic cup by Makron, *c.* 480 (Boston 01.8024).

[67] For discussion, see Dover (1989) 127–8; Lissarrague (1990b) 57, 61 and figs 2.4, 2.6.

the satyric stage and elsewhere there is more to satyrs than simply being comic exemplars of how not to behave. In his iconoclastic *Birth of Tragedy*, published in 1872, Friedrich Nietzsche saw in the satyrs a Dionysian wisdom and considered them embodiments of an idealized form of life free from the constraints, hypocrisies and pettiness of conventional values: 'For the Greek, the satyr expressed nature in a rude uncultivated state. ... the satyr was man's true prototype, an expression of his highest and and strongest aspirations. ... The satyr was sublime and divine ... .'[68] However romantic this may sound to jaded modern sensibilities,[69] Nietzsche was at least right to recognize that there is a more profound aspect to satyrs beyond their role as transgressors – comical or otherwise.[70]

Satyrs enjoy a special intimacy with Dionysus beyond that normally experienced by mere mortals. Writing in the fourth century BC, Theopompus (115 *FGH* 75c.3–4) notes that Silenus at least is 'less conspicuous than a god in nature, but superior to a man, since he was also immortal' (θεοῦ μὲν ἀφανέστερος τὴν φύσιν, ἀνθρώπου δὲ κρείττων, ἐπεὶ καὶ ἀθάνατος ἦν). If Silenus is immortal so, too, by implication are his sons, who may be considered 'minor divinities' as a result.[71] With one exception ([Apollod.] 2.1.2), dead satyrs are unattested in Greek myth, art and satyric drama. While some satyr plays are set in or near the Underworld, such as Aeschylus' *Sisyphus* (F 225–34), or Aristias' *Fates* (F 3), this does not require the satyrs to have died for them to be depicted there. Many satyr plays set partly or wholly in the Underworld will involve Heracles (*e.g.*, Soph. *Cerberus* F 327a, *On Taenarum* F 198a–e; Eur. *Eurystheus* F 371–80)[72] who would fit the mould well as the wandering hero who would release the satyrs from their gloomy subjugation if they were held captive there. The closest we get to dead satyrs onstage is when Silenus and his sons call down death on each other as the old satyr toadies to Polyphemus, falsely accusing Odysseus and his men of theft, while the chorus defend the new arrivals (Eur. *Cyc.* 228–40, 268–72). Apart from revealing dysfunctional family relations here, the joke

---

[68]   F. Nietzsche (1872, tr. F. Golffing, 1956) 52; see also chs 7 and 8.

[69]   G. F. Else (1939) 139 writes of the 'embarrassing problem' involved in the idea of a pre-tragic satyr play; (1965) 9–15; he dismisses Nietzsche's views on satyrs, citing with approval Hesiod's denunciation of them (Hes. F 10a.18 MW).

[70]   More nuanced views of satyrs and their abilities to function on many levels have been gaining ground; Lissarrague (1993) notes the ambivalence of satyrs' 'wildness'; see also Voelke (2001) esp. 211–59; Gibert (2002); Griffith (2005a) 172–86; Griffith (2010) 73–9.

[71]   For discussion, see Gantz (1993) 135–9.

[72]   See also Appendix: 'Index of Motifs and Characters', below.

may also be based on the audience's understanding that satyrs are, after all, immortal, thus rendering this exchange as one of bluff and bluster, typical of satyrs elsewhere (*e.g. Cyc.* 596, Soph. *Inachus* F ** 269d.21–22).

In Theopompus' account Silenus has a didactic role, explaining the physical nature of the earth to Midas, king of Phrygia; and the old satyr's status as a fount of wisdom occurs again when elsewhere Midas asks him 'what is best for mortals?' This famous encounter is alluded to by Herodotus (8.138) and Xenophon (*Anab.* 1.2.13), and told more fully by Aristotle (F 44 Rose) who ascribes to Silenus the following response, as gloomy as it is unexpected of a creature normally associated with hedonistic self-indulgence: '... the best thing for all men and women is not to have been born, and, after this, to die as quickly as possible...'. Such a remark equates with many choral utterances in Greek tragedy (*e.g.* Soph. *OT* 1186–96, *OC* 1211–1248), thereby implicitly underlining links between Silenus and his master, the patron god of tragedy.[73] A particularly notable, almost verbatim, parallel comes from the *Certamen Homeri et Hesiodi* (*Contest of Homer and Hesiod*). Our version of this fictitious encounter is dated shortly after the time of the emperor Hadrian (*Cert.* 33), but Nietzsche's hypothesis that it was traceable to the sophist Alcidamas and datable to the late fifth or early fourth century BC, has been confirmed by later papyrus finds dating from the third century BC (P. Lit. Lond. 191) and second century AD (P. Michigan inv. 2754).[74] In this account (*Cert.* 75–9) Hesiod challenges Homer with the same question Midas put to Silenus: '... above all else, what is finest for mortals?' The poet, considered the wisest of all the Greeks (Heraclit. 22 B 56 DK; Hdt. 2.53. etc.), gives the same response as the old satyr: 'Firstly, the best thing for mortals is not to have been born, but, once born, to pass through the gates of Hades as quickly as possible.'

---

[73] Easterling (2009) gives a valuable discussion of passages from tragedy and elsewhere which parallel Silenus' remark. David Konstan tells me that a Jewish wit is said to have remarked: "best never to have been born; but how many people do you know who have been so lucky?"

[74] Our version of the *Certamen* (240) refers to the *Mouseion* ('Literary Miscellany') of Alcidamas as a source for details of the death of Hesiod. For modern treatment of the date and authorship of the substance of the *Certamen* in the light of papyrological discoveries, see, *e.g.* N. J. Richardson (1981); N. O'Sullivan (1992) 63–6, cf. 79–105; West (1967) and (2003) 296–300. The general story of the alleged contest, and therefore the parallel between Homer's and Silenus' wisdom, may even be known as early as Heraclitus who preserves the story of Homer and 'the riddle of the lice' (Heraclit. 22 B 56 DK) which also occurs in the *Certamen* (321–38).

Further paradoxical elements ascribed to satyrs can be found in other sources which link them to intelligence and even self-control or σωφροσύνη. Plato's *Symposium*, which features a number of variably inspired speeches on the nature of desire, culminates in a boozy encomium of Socrates given by Alcibiades, who likens the philosopher to Silenus and Marsyas not only physically, but in his magical abilities to charm and beguile those around him as the satyrs were able to do (*Symp.* 215a–c, 216c–217a, 221d; cf. 222d).[75] Diodorus Siculus (3.58–9) in the first century BC writes of Marsyas as a devotee of the Great Mother, and sees him as embodying understanding (σύνεσις) and self-control (σωφροσύνη).[76] The motif of satyrs as teachers or carers of infants in some satyr dramas (*e.g.*, Aesch. *Net-Fishers*; Soph. *Little Dionysus*; cf. Eur. *Cyc.* 142–3, etc.) may playfully allude to their perceived wisdom as teachers or founts of wisdom elsewhere, as in the Silenus-Midas exchange mentioned by Aristotle (F 44). Silenus similarly plays the role of a fount of wisdom in Vergil's *Eclogue* 6, in a parallel noted by the fourth-century Vergilian commentator, Servius (Verg. *Buc.* VI 13; 26 = Theopomp. 115 *FGH* 75b). Here Vergil has the old satyr explain the origins of the cosmos and then proceed to sing of a number of well-known heroic myths to a couple of shepherds who have captured him in a cave. But Vergil praises Silenus' singing, which outdoes even that of Apollo and Orpheus (*Ecl.* 6.29–30). This perceived satyric wisdom occurs in satyr drama where it is given a typically humorous twist. A Sophoclean fragment has the satyr chorus bragging of their own wisdom, skills and knowledge, when apparently presenting themselves as suitors for the daughter of Oeneus (Soph. *Oeneus* F **1130); their fields of expertise range from astonomy, athletics, warfare (!), music and mathematics to ball-twisting and farting. While some have seen parodies of intellectual currents of the day and the speculations of Socrates and Hippias in particular,[77] we may also see the satyrs indulging in self-parody, given their reputation for wisdom in other contexts.

Griffith rightly notes that satyrs onstage rarely if ever make any profound or insightful utterances.[78] Had more satyric drama survived, however, we might well have evidence of wisdom and other sympathetic qualities on the part of

---

[75]   Alcibiades' speech has been dubbed a satyric drama; see F. Sheffield (2001).

[76]   As Wiseman (1988) 5 points out, Marsyas was important in Italian legend for his prophetic powers (Livy 25.12; Cicero *Div.* 1.89) and as eponymous founder of the Marsi (Silius Italicus 8.502–4, Pliny *HN* 3.108).

[77]   *E.g.* R. Carden (1974) 145–6; see also introductory discussion to Soph. *Oeneus* (= F **1130), below, and n. 8.

[78]   Griffith (2002) 202.

these paradoxical creatures. We find, for instance, their surprising, if short-lived, courage in standing up to Polyphemus in *Cyclops* (270–2). Elsewhere in the play the satyrs speak of the anti-Dionysian ogre Polyphemus as an ignoramus; they also consider their intended punishment of him as a form of 'education' (173, 492–3).[79] A satyric element even seems to have been considered an essential part of civic excellence or virtue (*aretê*) in the fifth century. Plutarch records a criticism of Pericles from one of the statesman's contemporaries, Ion of Chios. In criticizing Pericles for his aloofness and austerity, Ion, author of, among other things, satyr plays, demanded that (Plut. *Pericles* 5.4):

ὥσπερ τραγικὴν διδασκαλίαν ... τὴν ἀρετὴν ἔχειν τι πάντως καὶ σατυρικὸν μέρος.

like a tragic tetralogy, ... civic excellence/virtue should also always have some satyric component.

Although Plutarch disagreed with this assessment of Pericles,[80] Ion's view need not be dismissed as a glib aside. Instead, Ion's comment taps into widely held Greek views on the importance of combining the serious and playful for their moral value and intellectual soundness. W. K. C. Guthrie has demonstrated the philosophical value Plato placed on the idea of play (*Rep.* 7.536 b–c, *Tim.* 59 c–d, *Laws* 685a, etc.);[81] Agathon in Plato's *Symposium* acknowledges that his discourse on *erôs* has been given 'some part of it in playfulness and some in moderate seriousness' (τὰ μὲν παιδιᾶς τὰ δὲ σπουδῆς μετρίας: *Symp.* 197e).[82] Herodotus provides a fifth-century parallel to the importance of combining the serious with the playful in his portrait of the canny, successful sixth-century Egyptian pharaoh, Amasis. When some of his friends complained that he was not taking his role seriously enough, Amasis responded that if a man always devoted himself to seriousness (κατεσπουδάσθαι) and never allowed himself a share of play (παιγνίην), he would become mad or suffer a stroke (Hdt. 2.173).[83] The playfulness

---

[79] Cf. also *Cyc.* 678, the choral admonition to Polyphemus on the dangers of excessive drinking (!); Seaford (1984) 57–9 likens the downfall of Polyphemus to an initiation into Dionysian mysteries presided over by the satyrs.

[80] Cf. also Thucydides' glowing appraisal of Pericles (Thuc. 2.65.5–13).

[81] See Guthrie (1962–81) vol. 4, 56–9.

[82] While satyric elements have been identified in Alicibiades' speech in Plato's *Symposium* (above n. 75), we may see them elsewhere in the dialogue.

[83] Amasis prefaces his reply by noting that archers unstring their bows when not using them to ensure their increased utility, a comment which had become proverbial by Horace's time

of onstage satyrs, then, would not *always* make them figures of contempt for the audience; rather than making them the anti-type of a polis-based notion of excellence, satyric playfulness, at least in Ion's estimation, is one essential part of it.

Such views provide a salutory alternative to the puritanical dismissal of satyrs by Hesiod, which seems to have exercised an inordinate amount of influence on some modern scholarship.[84] The realization by other scholars, however, that satyrs onstage could be both sympathetic and transgressive in the eyes of the ancient audience offers a better account of these devotees of Dionysus and what ancient sources say about them.[85] Satyrs are a commonly imagined presence within the Attic polis, connected with many other civic rituals in honour of the god.[86] In the Classical period they are, perhaps, fringe-dwellers within the collective *Weltanschauung* and imagination of the Attic polis, rather than being completely antithetical to polis life and values. Satyrs, then, can be considered ambivalent creatures, operating on levels that put them between being human and animal, human and divine, adult and child, slave and free, naïve and sophisticated. In *Cyclops* and other dramas satyrs can display a number of these traits, sometimes simultaneously. As Pierre Voelke has noted, a satyr is a 'figure de l'intermédiare'.[87]

3. Aspects of Satyric Drama

3.1 Origins and Functions

The origins of satyric drama, like those of tragedy, remain obscure.[88] Ancient sources emphasise that satyric drama was linked to tragedy, even if the exact nature of these links eludes us today. Aristotle's famous pronouncement that tragedy was late in achieving its grandeur suggests that satyr drama predated tragedy. He writes of tragedy as developing 'because of the change from a satyric element' (διὰ τὸ ἐκ σατυρικοῦ μεταβαλεῖν) and says that tragedy's metre was firstly tetrameter because 'its poetry was satyric and more dance-like' (διὰ τὸ σατυρικὴν καὶ ὀρχηστικωτέραν εἶναι τὴν ποίησιν: *Po.* 1449a

---

(*Odes* 2.10.19).

[84] Above, n. 69.

[85] Above, n. 70.

[86] As Hedreen (2007) 150–95 shows, a number of vase-paintings from the sixth and fifth century may represent satyrs as 'practitioners of especially venerable or traditional forms of choral music' (186).

[87] See, esp. Voelke (2001) 53–90, esp. 61–71.

[88] For fuller discussion, see Sutton (1980) 1–13; Seaford (1984) 10–33; KPS (1999) 6–12.

19–23). But Aristotle nowhere identifies satyr drama as underlying tragedy, only 'a satyric element'. He may be alluding to the dithyrambs in which choruses of satyrs sang hymns in honour of Dionysus and from which he claims tragedy evolved.[89] In this context it is worth noting that Herodotus (1.23) mentions Arion of Methymna in Lesbos as an important innovator of dithyrambs, since the *Suda* (s.v. 'Arion') tells us that this poet flourished in the 38th Olympiad (628–24 BC) and that he 'first introduced satyrs speaking in metre'. In a work devoted to the world's first known actor, *On Thespis* (F 38 Wehrli), Chamaeleon, a pupil of Aristotle, mentions early poetic performances on Dionysiac themes called *satyrika*. According to Chamaeleon, who also wrote a book on satyr play (περὶ Σατύρων: F 37a–c Wehrli), over time these *satyrika* were supplanted by other myths and stories that became incorporated into tragedies 'when they (sc. the poets) no longer remembered Dionysus' (F 38 Wehrli). Although Chamaeleon seems to be developing his master's tersely expressed views a little further, the exact nature of these *satyrika* still eludes us.

These sources suggest that satyric performance of some kind predates tragedy. But other ancient sources assert that satyr-play came after tragedy had been established, for instance, Horace (*Ars Poetica* 220–24). Zenobius, author of a collection of proverbs and active at the time of Hadrian, mentions the famous phrase 'Nothing to do with Dionysus!' (Οὐδὲν πρὸς τὸν Διόνυσον) to explain the origin of satyr plays. According to this account, the crowd made this jeer at the poets' habits of producing tragedies on non-Dionysiac themes, which led to the introduction of satyr plays 'so that they (sc. the poets) might not seem to be forgetting the god' (ἵνα μὴ δοκῶσιν ἐπιλανθάνεσθαι τοῦ θεοῦ: Zen. *Prov.* 5.40). However, the waters get muddied here because Zenobius tells us that the poets 'introduced satyr plays as a prelude' (προεισάγειν), rather than as a 'postlude' to three tragedies throughout the fifth and for the first half of the fourth centuries BC. Possibly, Zenobius is working from a later source that refers to the presentation of satyr plays as a prelude, which we know to have begun by 341/40 BC (*IG* ii².2320). In any case, Zenobius' account sees the rise of satyr play as resulting from a need to restore a Dionysian element to Greek drama.

The appearance of satyrs in Attic vase painting from about 520 BC in scenes of apparently choral activity or in mythological scenes where one would not normally expect to see them has been cited as reflecting satyrs

---

[89] Seaford (1976) 209–221; (1984) 10–12.

onstage from around this time.[90] But even vases which depict the blinding of Polyphemus in the company of satyrs, such as the Richmond Vase, need not betray the influence of satyr dramas such as Euripides' or Aristias' *Cyclops*. Indeed, this ability of a painter to render the same story independently of a dramatic production is further evident in Pliny's account of a painting by Timanthes (active *c.* 400 BC) in which satyrs measure the thumb of the sleeping Cyclops (*HN* 35.74), a moment not depicted or alluded to in Euripides' version. While Timanthes may have known Euripides' drama, the painting betrays no direct influence of his version at least. Likewise, certain elements of the Inachus-Io story, dramatized by Sophocles in his satyric *Inachus* (F **269a–**295a),[91] appear on vases with satyrs included, *e.g.* Hermes about to slay Argus (*LIMC* V.I s.v. Io 56, 60). Such vases indicate, rather, that the painter was able to treat a well-known theme in a playful or burlesque manner, indicated by the presence of the satyrs, and could still remain independent of any playwrights.[92]

Then again, the putative reorganization of Attic dramatic festivals and the recording of victor-lists may be relevant here. This reorganization is inferred from reconstructed inscriptional lists, produced in the second half of the fourth century BC and known to modern scholarship as the *Fasti* (*IG* ii².2318).[93] One reconstruction has the list beginning in 502/1,[94] a

---

[90] Buschor (1943/5) 73, 82; Seaford (1984) 13; Hedreen (1992) 125–8. There are some links between satyrs in performance and padded dancers, or 'fat men' and komasts (revellers) which first appear on Corinthian vases by the late seventh century BC; for recent discussion, see T.J. Smith (2007), esp. 49–54; C. Isler-Kerényi (2007), esp. 87–92; Green (2007), esp. 102–5. Corinth seems to have been a centre of choral activity; Arion's dithyramb was probably performed at Corinth (Hdt. 1.23), and Pratinas, the alleged founder of satyr play, was a native of nearby Phlius; see also Hedreen (1992) 130–6; Csapo and Slater (1994) 90–5. Although E. Csapo and M. Miller (2007) 21 see komasts and satyrs as 'functionally equivalent', they deny that komasts are a type of satyr. Hedreen (2007) also sees significant iconographic differences between satyrs and komasts on Attic vases whereby the satyrs move in more orchestrated processions as opposed to the seemingly disordered antics of the komasts.

[91] For the scholarly controversies surrounding the genre of this play, see the introductory discussion to Sophocles' *Inachus*, below.

[92] T. Carpenter (2005), esp. 226–7.

[93] See Pickard-Cambridge (1988) 101–7.

[94] The case for 502/1 is made by E. Capps (1943) 10–11; see also P. Wilson (2000) 313 nn. 9–11. For full discussion of the ancient evidence for the organization of the dramatic festivals in Classical Athens, Pickard-Cambridge (1988) esp. 57–125, remains important; see also E. Csapo and W. Slater (1994) 103–85; Wilson (2000) *passim*. I. Storey and A. Allan (2005) 14–24 offer a brief overview.

date that has found favour with many scholars.[95] The following sequence, consistent with Zenobius' account, is therefore at least conceivable: (i) the traditional Dionysian subject matter of *satyrika* mentioned by Chamaeleon was superseded by tragedies on non-Dionysian themes – Zenobius (5.40) cites plays entitled *Centaurs* and *Ajax*; (ii) satyr plays were introduced either as a prelude to tragedies, or independently of them altogether, to restore Dionysian elements to drama; (iii) in the wake of the putative reorganization of around 502/1 satyr dramas became the fourth installment of the tetralogy;[96] (iv) satyr plays then returned to their status as a prelude or as separate pieces by 341/40 (cf. *IG* ii².2320). Such a scheme, though speculative, may illuminate aspects of satyric drama in the Classical period, namely its Dionysian elements, and its close connection to tragedy. Zenobius' account (5.40), however vague, bears witness to a need to preserve such elements and illustrates the link between tragedy and satyr play as dramatic genres initially part of a festival devoted to the one god.

Theories about the functions and effects of satyr drama have been mooted from antiquity to the present day.[97] One view claims satyr drama's role is to provide 'comic relief' or relaxation after three intense, emotionally complex tragedies. This is attested as early as Horace (*AP* 226), and occurs later in the writings of Diomedes (1.491 Keil), a grammarian of the fourth century, and in the *Lexicon* of Photius produced in the ninth century (s.v. Σατυρικὰ δράματα: Σ 502.13). In more modern times Richard Wagner, to whom Nietzsche dedicated the *Birth of Tragedy*, took the 'comic relief' theory for satyr play further when he invoked the genre to explain the initial function of his comic music-drama *Die Meistersinger von Nürnberg* (1868) and its relation to his earlier *Tannhäuser und der Sängerkrieg auf dem Wartburg* (1861). For Wagner, *Die Meistersinger* would be a satyric pendant to *Tannhäuser* – both operas feature singing contests – just as he understood that satyr dramas could playfully depict the heroic myths dealt with by tragedies.[98] Whether he realized it or not, Wagner was building on

---

[95] Wilson (2000) 13 writes: 'something approaching consensus sees the record begin in 502/1, though an earlier date is equally possible.'

[96] An exact date of 502/1 is not necessary for this hypothesis.

[97] Useful overviews can be found in the following works: Sutton (1980) 159–79; Seaford (1984) 26–33; KPS (1999) 34–39; Voelke (2001) 381–412; Griffith (2002) esp. 197–203.

[98] See *Wagners Gesammelte Schriften*, ed. J. Kapp (1914), vol. 1, 113 where Wagner discusses the *Die Meistersinger-Tannhäuser* nexus; elsewhere he refers to satyr drama as a 'notwendiges Zugeständnis' to follow tragedy (vol. 10, 216). As Sutton (1980) 201–2 notes, Wagner appears to have been the first to make this insight on the relation between satyr drama

the insights of Casaubon two and a half centuries earlier. The comic relief and satyr-play-as-parody theories have been reasserted in recent times by Sutton, who goes on to suggest that satyr plays make the world of tragedy look ridiculous, affected and, essentially, much ado about nothing.[99] While of some value, the 'comic relief' theory to explain satyric drama is chiefly relevant to those plays produced until 341/340 BC.

Indirectly related to this theory is the comic confrontation between the satyrs and solemn figures more at home in tragedy. This leads to a comedy of incongruity, where high-brow and low-brow characters collide in a fashion that has been compared to the comedy of the Marx brothers.[100] But in Seaford's view satyr drama was designed to restore what tragedy was deemed to have forsaken: the Dionysiac and ritual elements, whose importance was evident to Zenobius (5.40). Taking his cue from Nietzsche, Seaford locates the appeal of satyr play (at least in the Greek world) in the thiasos of the satyrs, which brings the audience into a pre-urban world of Dionysiac initiation, providing the comfort of communal joy and a release from the burdens and superficialities of civilisation.[101] This idea comes close to another view that satyr play involves a return to pre-polis, rustic values and privileges nature over culture, proposed by L. Rossi, F. Lasserre and Seidensticker; others, such as Lissarrague and Easterling, have likewise been correct to see that the 'wildness' of satyrs can hint at a deeper wisdom of sorts.[102]

Hall considers the sexual politics of satyric drama and sees the satyrs as embodiments of violence and misogyny.[103] Her analysis has value for bringing to light some of the gender implications of satyric drama: as something constructed by exclusively male authors and actors at a certain point in history; the world of the onstage satyrs could be seen as something

---

and tragedy. Wagner's admiration, bordering on obsession, for Greek tragedy, especially the dramas of Aeschylus – in contrast to those of Euripides – has been well documented, not least in the composer's own theoretical and autobiographical writings (*Mein Leben*, etc.); for an overview, see, Lloyd-Jones (1982) 126–42.

[99]   Sutton (1980) 165–6.

[100]   Sutton (1980) 159–79, esp. 162–5; cf. Seaford (1984) 29, who holds much the same view, but disputes Sutton's idea of satyr play as providing 'comic relief'.

[101]   Seaford (1984) 26–33, esp. 31–2.

[102]   Rossi (1972/89); Lasserre (1973); Seidensticker (2005). These views would seem to reflect the rural settings of so many satyr plays, which Vitruvius (5.6.9) saw as typical of the genre. See also Lissarrague (1993) 217–18; and Easterling (1997) 37–44, esp. 42–44, who aptly considers satyr play a 'show for Dionysus'.

[103]   Hall (1998) and (2006) 142–69.

of a boys' club. On her reading, satyr drama as a genre virtually encourages sexual violence against women, and reasserts a collective masculine identity among its audience after the supposedly feminising experiencing of tragedy; as a corollary of this view Hall claims that satyr play is a 'masculine' genre which assaults the 'feminine' genre of tragedy.[104] But this assumes an antithesis between the two genres that is belied by their connections in metre, diction, language and structure, recognized in antiquity and today.[105] Again, the satyrs, for all their lechery, are not an unequivocal embodiment of male heterosexual aggression; as has been discussed, they can evince homoerotic desires, be the victims of sexual violence and even appear in effeminized roles.[106] Moreover, such 'assaults' on tragedy, as Aristophanes's *Thesmophoriazusae* and *Frogs* show, are to be found much more readily in the world of Old Comedy and its relentless lampooning of figures such as Agathon and Euripides and their tragedies. It is true that paratragic elements in satyr drama can be found (Eur. *Cyc.* 689, etc.), but the obscenities of Old Comedy make the innuendos and *doubles entendres* of satyr drama look positively tame by comparison. As far as we can tell, satyr drama, for all its lewdness, seems to have abided by Horace's prescription that it avoid the obscenities of comedy (*AP* 245–7).

In its playful treatment of heroic myth and inevitable 'happy' (from the point of view the satyrs at least) ending, Seidensticker notes that the satyr drama offers a more optimistic and uncomplicated world-view than that found in tragedy. Rather than cancelling out the intensity of tragedies with their focus on death, suffering and destruction – or narrow avoidance thereof – Seidensticker argues that 'the light-hearted world of the satyr play appears much brighter against the dark background of tragedy.' Interestingly, he concludes: 'The contrasting juxtaposition of tragic and comic results in a mutual intensification.'[107] On this reading satyr drama is not so much an escape from the tragic – still less is it an assault on it – but rather gives scope to the audience's ability to engage with two different theatrical genres, or, as Harrison put it, 'to absorb and yet not be defeated by the tragic.'[108]

The various functions ascribed to satyr play need not be mutually exclusive of each other: provision of earthy humour; parody of tragic elements and

---

[104] See Hall (1998), (2006); Marshall (2000) 230 writes 'the satyr drama rapes an innocent and unsuspecting tragedy'; cf. R. Lämmle (2007) 372–7.

[105] Above, n. 15.

[106] See above, pp. 15–17.

[107] Seidensticker (2005) 49 n. 4.

[108] Above, n. 18.

heroic myth through a comedy of incongruity; celebration and/or parody of rustic or pre-polis values; assertion of polis values through the buffoonery of the satyrs as anti-types of the polis; restoration of Dionysian elements to theatre; reassertion of male identity and sexual aggression in the audience after three 'feminizing' tragedies. Perhaps, however, the one continuing thread through its various incarnations was the association of satyr drama with Dionysus. At least far as satyr play in the Classical era is concerned, Seidensticker well observes: 'At the moment when the naked, ithyphallic satyrs dance in the *orchêstra*, if not before, the festival god and his world once again move fully into the centre of the theater. In this sense, the satyr-play can rightfully be considered the high point of the tragic tetralogy performed in honour of the god.'[109] We would add that the tragic tetralogy during the classical period may be considered emblematic of Dionysus in still another way. If tragedy reflects the destructive side of the god with all the terrifying power, contradictions and complexities which his presence entails, satyr drama could reflect his more joyful and exuberant nature. The experience of the tragic tetralogy in classical Athens, in other words, could entail an ambivalence much like that embodied by the god himself, who in Euripides' *Bacchae* (860–1) announces that he is θεὸς | δεινότατος, ἀνθρώποισι δ' ἠπιώτατος 'to mortals the most terrifying and most benign god'.

3.2 Themes of Satyric Drama

A major aspect of satyr play is the recurrence of stock themes, characters and narratives.[110] Many of these entail folk-tale or romantic elements which involve the following: a happy ending after some danger is averted or, an ogre overthrown; a triumph against the odds in which the (inevitably male) hero has to use his pluck and wits no less than his strength in order to prevail; often a distant or exotic location; fantastic elements such as monsters or unnatural creatures; unheard of inventions; scope for earthy humor and irony, some of it even at the hero's expense, or resulting from the clash of urbane and unsophisticated characters; perhaps most significantly for satyr play, a relatively straightforward ethical framework in which the supremacy of the

---

[109] Seidensticker (2005); C. Calame (2010) 69 makes much the same observation; see also Easterling (1997) 37–44.

[110] See also P. Guggisberg (1947) 33–45; I. M. Fischer (1958); Seidensticker (1979) 243–7; Sutton (1980) 145–59; Seaford (1984) 33–44; Easterling (1997) 37–44; KPS (1999) 28–32; Voelke 378–81; Griffith (2008) 73–9; Griffith (2010); 'Index of Motifs and Characters' below pp. 509–12.

Olympians (especially Dionysus) is reasserted, the transgressor punished, and Greek values such as hospitality and friendship are upheld.[111] Such features are not unique to satyr play, and could apply to Homer's *Odyssey*, Old Comedy and other genres such as bucolic poetry and the novel.[112]

Euripides' *Cyclops* exemplifies these tropes with Odysseus punishing the cannibalistic giant Polyphemus and rescuing the satyrs who gleefully anticipate reunion with their god. Aristias' *Cyclops* testifies to the suitability of the story for the genre, and is likely to have been followed by the Euripidean version in general outline if not in detail.[113] Other satyr plays featured ogres guilty of similar crimes. Aeschylus' *Cercyon* (F 102–F *107) told of Theseus' encounter with the eponymous villain and how the young Athenian hero bested him in a wrestling match. Similarly, Sophocles' *Amycus* (F 111–12) told of Polydeuces' victory over the murderous boxer Amycus, king of the Bebryces who lived by the Black Sea; versions of the story told by Theocritus (*Id.* 22.1–134) and Apollonius (2.1–163) make clear Polydeuces' superior ethics as a Greek in addition to his boxing skills (esp. Theoc. *Id.* 22.131–4). In challenging travellers to physical contests to the death, Cercyon and Amycus will have been guilty of violating the law of *xenia* (hospitality), a precept sacred to Zeus (Homer *Od.* 9.266–71; cf. 9.479). A simple punitive ethic of transgression and punishment is likely to run through these and many satyric dramas, including Aeschylus' 'Justice' play (F 281a, esp. 17–19). In Euripides' *Sciron* one character, almost certainly Theseus, asserts: 'I tell you it is a fine thing to punish evil men.' (F 678); and in his *Syleus* it is said of or by Heracles himself that he is 'just to the just, but the greatest of all enemies on earth to the wicked.' (F 692).

---

[111]   S. Thompson (1946) remains a standard work on the folktale; see also G. Kirk (1970) 31–41, 202–13, and (1974) 30–7 for the relation of folktales to myths. On the idea of folktales and romantic elements and their relevance to satyr play, see A. P. Burnett (1971) 30–1, 44–5; Sutton (1980) 154–7, 185–7; Griffith (2002) 198–9, 201–2; (2010).

[112]   For links between satyr play as a genre and the *Odyssey*, see Sutton (1974b); Sutton (1980) 191–204 also discusses the influence of satyr play on other ancient and post antique literature; on links between satyr play and Old and Middle Comedy, see Zagagi (1999); Shaw (2010). Griffith (2005b) demonstrates links between the language of Sophocles' satyr plays and prose romances; elsewhere he discusses satyr drama as a 'middlebrow' genre anticipating much in the *Idylls* of Theocritus and novels such as Longus' *Daphnis and Chloe* (Griffith (2008) 73–81.

[113]   For discussion of the date of Euripides' *Cyclops*, see below §4.1. Aristias was the son of Pratinas and active from the 460s onward, making his *Cyclops* almost certainly predate that of Euripides.

Just as tragedy told the story of royal figures, so, too, could satyr play; and many villains on the satyric stage are foreign despots or Greek tyrannical figures, making them easy targets for the democratic Athenian audience. While the demonising of the barbarian Other on the tragic stage has been recognized for some time now,[114] it would appear that satyr drama could deploy similar motifs. The Egyptian pharaoh and title character in Euripides' *Busiris* (F 312b–315) conforms to a pattern of satyric villainy in his killing of strangers, and being a despot and foreigner. Busiris defies Zeus in conducting human sacrifice as we learn from [Apollodorus] (*Bibl.* 2.5.11; cf. Hdt. 2.45), just as Polyphemus carries out his cannibalism as a 'sacrifice' (Eur. *Cyc.* 334–46, 361–74). The pharaoh's villainy is thus likely to have been compounded in the eyes of the fifth-century audience, who would have enjoyed his destruction by Heracles.[115] Aeschylus dramatised the story of the Thracian king Lycurgus in a satyr play (F 124–6); as another non-Greek ogre, and with a hostility to Dionysus, known as early as Homer (*Il.* 6.130), Lycurgus was ripe for a downfall on the satyric, as well as tragic, stage.[116] Sophocles made hostility to Zeus the defining characteristic of the title character in his *Salmoneus* (F 537a–541a), who tried to impersonate the god, only to be brought down by the supreme deity. Another regal satyric ogre appeared in Euripides' *Eurystheus* (F 372–81), the infamously cowardly monarch who compelled Heracles to carry out his labours. Sositheus' *Daphnis or Lityerses* (F 1a–3) told the story of the Phrygian king, and bastard son of Midas, Lityerses – another foreign despot – who killed visitors after compelling them to partake in a reaping contest, until he challenged Heracles with predictable results. This play may have closely followed Euripides' *Reapers*, but it also seems to have much in common with his *Syleus*, in which Heracles triumphed over another ogre to whom he had become enslaved as a farmhand.[117] Achaeus' *Aethon* (F5a–11) told of Erysichthon who, as we learn from Callimachus (*Hymn Dem.* VI), defied Demeter in cutting down a tree sacred to her and was punished with insatiable ('burning') hunger only

---

[114] See, esp. Hall (1989).

[115] KPS (1999) 663–4 conjecture that Heracles appeared in up to thirty satyr dramas; see also Sutton (1980) 154.

[116] Polyphrasmon composed a *Lykourgeia* tetralogy in 467 BC (F 1; cf. *TrGF* vol. 1, T 3) which will have told of Lycurgus' downfall at the hands of Dionysus in tragedy and satyr play.

[117] For speculative links to Eur. *Reapers*, see, for instance, KPS (1999) 476; Voelke (2001) 23, 43; for arguably more concrete parallels with *Syleus*, see the introductory discussion to Sositheus below.

to die by consuming his own flesh; Achaeus, however, may have dealt with a different aspect of this grim story.[118]

What was the role of the satyrs in all this? The status of these satyric ogres as kings or overlords suggests that the satyrs were enslaved by them, just as they were enslaved by Polyphemus in Euripides' play (*Cyc.* 23–6, 79, 442, etc.); we learn, for instance, from [Apollodorus] (*Bibl.* 3.5.1) that Lycurgus enslaved satyrs as well as maenads. The theme of the liberation of the satyrs can be safely inferred from those plays featuring satyric ogres. Slavery has another function in satyr drama in linking the hero with the chorus. In Euripides' *Syleus* and *Eurystheus* Heracles and the satyrs have a common enemy in being slaves to the ogre; likewise, in *Cyclops* the chorus strike up a quick friendship with Odysseus when the hero understands the monstrous situation confronting them all and shares their desire for escape (Eur. *Cyc.* 176, etc.). The fact that the satyr chorus and hero are on the same side in these satyr dramas has important implications for how sympathetic the satyrs will be in the eyes of the audience.[119] Cowards and buffoons the chorus of satyrs may often be, as Odysseus readily sees (Eur. *Cyc.* 642), but as friends of the hero and followers of Dionysus there is no doubt about which side of the ethical divide they stand on; at no point does Odysseus plan to abandon the satyrs or even the treacherous Silenus. The satyrs' reunion with their god and the consequent bliss this brings will thus be a typical ending of these satyr plays, as with *Cyclops*. Interestingly, the satyrs will retain their servile status (Eur. *Cyc.* 709), but it will be under Dionysus, and such servitude will form a marked contrast to what they will have suffered at the hands of the now deposed ogre.[120]

There are times, however, when it seems that even this servitude will prove irksome to them. *Cyclops* begins with Silenus complaining of the 'labours' he has endured for the sake of Dionysus (1–10). In Aeschylus' *Sacred Delegates* (F **78a 23–36, F**78c 37–60) it appears that the satyrs

---

[118] Athenaeus (10.416b) tells us Aethon (= 'Burning') was another name for Erysichthon (= 'Earth Tearer'). We learn from Ovid (*Met.* 8.738–884) that to feed his appetite Erysichthon sold his shape-shifting daughter, Mestra, into prostitution, so that she could escape and be re-sold to other buyers in different form. According to Hesiod (F 43a.18–43 M-W), Sisyphus was a customer swindled by this arrangement, but when he complained, lost his case when Athena ruled against him. Achaeus' play may have told this more humorous side to the story, with the infamous trickster getting his come-uppance; but our fragments hardly indicate it; see Achaeus, *Aethon*, below p. 429

[119] Griffith (2002) 200 n. 14 lists examples of the satyrs as allies or helpers of the hero.

[120] On the 'slavish' nature of satyrs, see Griffith (2002).

are trying to escape from Dionysus who berates them for taking up athletics and abandoning his dance.[121] In Sophocles' *Trackers* Apollo promises the satyrs freedom and gold if they can find his stolen cattle; freedom from Dionysus may be meant here (63, 75, 77–8, 457). The satyrs refer to Apollo as the god who is our friend (θεὸς ὁ φίλος), calling on him to help with their 'labours' (*Trackers* 76–7), while Cyllene even refers to the satyrs' worship of their god as 'labours' (223–4).[122] If Dionysus is meant here, then we find satyr drama playing with one of its own motifs: here the satyrs desire to escape from their own patron god!

Connected to this theme of servitude is the idea of satyrs as labourers. Here again we see a comedy of incongruity whereby the satyrs take up menial tasks either under compulsion or not. *Cyclops* has Silenus cleaning out the monster's cave and depicts the chorus as none-too-successful herdsmen (41–62); in Sophocles' *Inachus* they were probably cowherds (cf. F **269c.8). Elsewhere in satyr plays the chorus are rustic or manual workers such as wood-gatherers (Soph. *Heracles* F 225) or smiths (Soph. *Pandora* or *Hammerers*). In Euripides' *Syleus*, like Heracles, they will have been slaves on the ogre's farm; in Euripides' *Reapers* and Sositheus' *Daphnis* they are likely to have been farm-labourers threatened by an overlord like Polyphemus (cf. Eur. *Cyc.* 203–19). On other occasions their work for others could be voluntary, in response to a call for help as in Aeschylus' *Net-Fishers* (F **46a.17–21), or even profitable, as in the promises of gold from Apollo in Sophocles' *Trackers* (4, 7–40; cf. 45–54). Both these calls for help are answered by the bumbling satyrs, who are motivated by a mix of goodwill, lechery and venality; Silenus is similarly on the make in *Cyclops* (*e.g.* 136; cf. 168–74, 179–87).

The satyrs' role as workers could takes some unusual forms, including possibly being servant 'girls' in Ion's *Omphale* (F 20; cf. F 24, 25) set in distant Lydia, but with an exotic queen instead of a brutal ogre as ruler. Euripides' *Sciron* tells of a brigand for whom the satyrs worked, this time by luring travellers between Athens and Corinth so that the villainous ogre could kill them. However, the satyrs may find their 'work' here more genial since, in a move that best illustrates their entrepreneurial skills, they set up

---

[121] A plausible supposition is that Dionysus is the interlocutor; see Lloyd-Jones (1956) 545 and Seaford (1984) 34. Lämmle (2007) 354 suggests that Dionysus appears precisely because of the satyrs' rebellious attitude. For fuller discussion and an outline of the problems in determining the action of this play and the identity of the interlocutor who has been identified as Sisyphus or Theseus, see Aeschylus' *Sacred Delegates* below p. 268.

[122] See introductory discussion to *Soph.* Trackers below.

a brothel, thus combining business and pleasure especially for Silenus in his role as pimp (F 674a–676),[123] which he may have reprised in Achaeus' *Aethon* and Python's *Agen*.[124] The latter tells of one of Alexander's generals, Harpalus, who siphoned vast amounts of money from campaign funds to spend on prostitutes – especially one called Pythionice – and had his achievements immortalised in a medium worthy of his endeavours. Sexual activity and desire are key motifs in satyric drama,[125] manifest in the satyrs' all-embracing proclivities. For onstage satyrs, these inclinations manifest themselves as ludicrous and prurient fantasies (*e.g.*, Aesch. *Net-Fishers* F **47a.57–67; *Prom. Pyrk.* F 204b 4–5; Eur. *Cyc.* 168–74, 179–87). Much of the sexually-based humour in satyr drama is thus likely to result from the inability of the satyrs to sate their desires, as seen in red-figure vase painting where they are easily rebuffed by thyrsus-wielding maenads.[126]

The satyrs' lechery is matched by their bibulousness, and wine is a conspicuous feature in many plays. In *Cyclops* it is essential for the blinding of the monster, but also in allowing for the antics of Silenus, from his first swig (156) until he is dragged into the cave by Polyphemus (582–9). Similarly, the monster drinks constantly (417–662), exhibiting a greed emblematic of satyric ogres and buffoons elsewhere. As Voelke suggests, in Aeschylus' satyric *Lycurgus* wine seems to have played a role in the downfall of the Thracian king, who, like Polyphemus, drinks it for the first time, we can be sure, to excess (F 124).[127] In the *Lycurgus* satyr dramas by Aeschylus and Polyphrasmon wine is likely to have stood for Dionysus himself, so that the god could be seen to be playing a direct role in the downfall of one of his enemies, as is the case with *Cyclops* (esp. 519–607).[128] Wine is associated with comic gluttony when Heracles defeats Syleus in an eating and drinking contest before dispatching him (Eur. F 691); in Sositheus' *Lityerses* (F 2.6–8) the eponymous ogre gorges and drinks to excess, much like the Euripidean Polyphemus. Wine also features in Ion's *Omphale*, where Heracles' famous

---

[123] A papyrus fragment summarizing the plot of *Sciron* tells us that the satyrs brought in 'revels with prostitutes' (P. Oxy. 2455; fr. 6 (T iia)).

[124] Prostitution may also have been involved in Aeschylus' *Sacred Delegates* which was set near Corinth (F **78a n. 10); NB Dionysus(?)' charge that the chorus have been squandering his money (F **78a.34–5). For *Aethon*, see above, n. 118; for Python's *Agen*, see below p. 448.

[125] Above, n. 39. For further references on sex as a motif in satyr drama, see Seaford (1984) 39 nn. 109–111; also 'Appendix: Sex, sexuality' below.

[126] Above, n. 55.

[127] See Voelke (2001) 190–1.

[128] See *Cyc.* Comm. 519–607n. below.

gluttony is again given full rein (Ion, F 20–22, 26–30); Easterling's suggestion that the hero's 'punishment' while in Lydia may have been a test of his powers of consumption is certainly plausible.[129] Wine is evident in Achaeus' *Omphale* (F 33), likely to have told much the same story as Ion's version; and it features again in his *Linus*, whose one fragment suggests a homoerotic and sympotic context (F 26); and Sophocles mentions the sympotic game of kottabos, where wine lees are thrown at a target, in his *Salmoneus* (F 537). Achaeus' *Hephaestus* tells of the god's return to Olympus under the influence of wine given him by Dionysus in the company of satyrs. A further satyric motif seems evident here, namely the preparation of a boorish guest for a symposium, as occurs in Ion's *Omphale* (F 21–7) and Euripides' *Cyclops* (519–75). Dionysus similarly prepares the smith-god for a feast (Achaeus, *Heph.* F 17); Hephaestus is no ogre, but, as an ungainly god, could easily be the source of humour in a sympotic context, as Homer makes him in the *Iliad* (1.597–600). In *Wasps* (esp. 1208–10) Aristophanes uses much the same motif when Bdelycleon inducts his oafish father, Philocleon, into the niceties of sympotic etiquette. In Sophocles' *Little Dionysus* (F 171–2) the satyrs preside over the invention of wine by the infant god with predictable results. The Delphians are lambasted for gluttony and venality in Achaeus' *Alcmeon* (F 12, 13). Conversely, in Lycophron's *Menedemus* (F 2) Silenus complains about the stinginess of the philosopher with his minimal servings of watered-down wine (cf. Ion, *Omphale* F 26; Eur. *Cyc.* 556, 558). Here the humour arises from seeing a bibulous glutton being denied, just as it does when we see lecherous satyrs fail to satisfy their desires.

Satyric encounters with inventions and more sophisticated aspects of polis culture are another recurrent feature. Lissarrague sees that the humour is predicated on the comically over-dramatized ignorance of the satyrs, whose behaviour is an example of what not to do; their transgressions provide the audience with an inverted anthropology of what it means to be a citizen of the polis.[130] Aeschylus (*Prom. F–K* F 207) has the satyrs wanting to kiss fire on seeing it for the first time, prompting Prometheus' famous warning: 'Goat, in that case you'll be mourning for your beard!' As in some red figure vases, satyrs are also present at what appears to be the creation of Pandora (Soph. *Pandora* or *Hammerers* F 482–6), whose presence will have excited their lechery and amazement; in Hesiod's account of her creation, Pandora's role as an artefact come to life is stressed (*WD* 60–3; *Th.* 571–2)

---

[129] Easterling (2007) 286.
[130] Lissarrague (1990a).

and even the gods are gripped by wonder on seeing her (Hes. *Th.* 588). Notable images of Pandora's creation with satyrs present occur in fifth-century art, but the date of Sophocles' play is unknown, making direct links between the two depictions hard to establish.[131] Satyric buffoonery with artworks and creations by Hephaestus may have featured in plays where the god would have appeared, such as Achaeus' *Hephaestus*. In the fuller remains of Aeschylus' *Sacred Delegates* (F **78a) the satyrs over-react to painted images of themselves which they admire not only for their beauty and life-like qualities, but which they realize are ugly enough to scare their own mother and any passing stranger.[132] Elsewhere in this play the satyrs show fear when presented with 'novel playthings' from the anvil and adze (F **78c.49–51).[133] Euripides' *Eurystheus* (F 372) similarly has a comic over-reaction, possibly by Silenus, to the life-like qualities of an artefact, this time ascribed to the craftsman Daedalus, who was the title character in a play by Sophocles which was possibly satyric (F 158–62).[134]

One of the satyrs' comic encounters involves their confusion and, in the case of their father, abject terror, on hearing the infant Hermes' lyre music for the first time (Soph. *Trackers* 131–220). In Sophocles' *Inachus* (F **269c 27–9) the chorus is startled by the pipe music played by Hermes again (!); in both these instances Sophocles seems to be divesting the satyrs of their role as accomplished musicians widely attested elsewhere.[135] In archaic and

---

[131] An Attic volute krater of *c.* 450 shows satyrs with small goat-like horns protruding from their foreheads, wielding hammers and dancing excitedly as a female figure appears to come up from the ground (= KPS fig. 10 a–b); the aulos player to the left suggests a depiction of a performance of this myth. An Attic calyx krater of *c.* 460 (BM E 467) shows Athena adorning a very static looking Pandora, while on the level below, men dressed as satyrs – they are wearing shorts and their faun-like masks have larger horns – dance in the presence of an aulos player, again suggesting a satyric performance. An Attic red-figure volute krater of *c.* 450 BC (Oxford, Ashmolean Museum G275) shows Epimetheus, 'husband' of Pandora, holding a hammer and watching as she rises from the ground; and an Attic white-ground plate of *c.* 450 (BM D 4) shows Hermes and Athena adorning a female figure called Anesidora, usually taken as another name for Pandora. Gantz (1993) 163–4 suggests the hammers are a means of summoning Pandora from the earth or way of releasing her from it.

[132] See introductory discussion to Aesch. *Sacred Delegates* below p. 270.

[133] *Ibid.*

[134] See below on Eur. *Eurystheus* F 372 n. 2; for the role of Daedalus in this and other satyr plays, see S. Morris (1992) 217–21.

[135] Although Lloyd-Jones (1996) 117 suggests on the basis of *Inachus* F 288 and F 295 that the satyrs presided as judges in the music contest between Hermes and Argus, which would imply that they are musical authorities of some sort. For satyrs as musicians, see Voelke (2001) 91–129, esp. 97–103, 127–9.

classical vase painting they are frequently depicted as playing the aulos and the lyre or barbitos; the amphora by the Berlin painter has a satyr holding a lyre in the company of Hermes himself! Satyrs also seem to have been associated with august rituals involving lyre playing and dancing.[136] In light of the satyrs' reaction to the lyre music in *Trackers*, however, Sophocles seems to be laughing at them again when they brag of their all-round expertise – which includes musical competence – in his *Oeneus* (F **1130.12).

Another common motif in satyr drama is athletics. At times this will be the means by which a hero may overthrow the villain of the piece, such as the wrestling match in Aeschylus' *Cercyon* or boxing in Sophocles' *Amycus*. Some titles imply that the satyrs are the athletes, *e.g.* Pratinas' *Wrestlers* or Achaeus' *Games*; an alternative title for Aeschylus' *Sacred Delegates* is *Isthmian Contestants* who are probably the satyrs. Images of satyr-athletes are known from fifth-century vase painting; the incongruity of the situation is evident in the figures dressed as Hellanodikai (judges or umpires) each holding a giant dildo, instead of a staff, as a symbol of authority.[137] Again the humour seems to be based on the idea of satyrs taking on something they are manifestly unsuited to. Their boasts in Sophocles' *Oeneus* include competence in events such as wrestling, running and boxing; they also boast of their biting and testicle-twisting powers (Soph. *Oeneus* F ** 1130.8–11). Athletics can be the object of criticism in satyric drama. The famous diatribe by an unknown speaker against athletes in the first of Euripides' *Autolycus* plays (F 282) was recognized by Athenaeus (10.413c) as an echo of criticisms made by Xenophanes (21 B F 2.11–24 DK).[138] The Euripidean fragment may be treated as another example of satyr play's ability to present serious or challenging ideas.

Much of the humour of satyr play is of incongruity and with it goes another regular feature, the setting in some distant, rural or exotic location, which Vitruvius (5.6.9) considered standard for the genre.[139] Aeschylus' *Net-*

---

[136] Hedreen (2007) 186; cf. also Pratinas' *Hyporchema* (F 3) in which the satyrs voice strong opinions on what they see as the intrusive role of the aulos in Dionysian worship, below pp. 242–47.

[137] See Brommer (1959) figs 59–60.

[138] While some doubt the satyric provenance of the speech – F. d'Angiò (1992); N. Pechstein (1998) 39–40, 114; cf. KPS (1999) 403 – most scholars view *Autolycus* A and B as satyr plays; see below introductory discussion to Euripides *Autolycus* A and B.

[139] The implications of foreign settings as the abode of some barbaric ogre, *e.g.* Busiris in Egypt, Amycus by the Black Sea, Lityerses in Phrygia, have been discussed above, pp. 29–31; see also *Cyc.* Comm. 20n. below.

Fishers and Sophocles' *Trackers* and *Inachus* are examples which some see as evidence for satyr play celebrating pre-polis values.[140] Sometimes these settings are fantastical, allowing for supernatural figures, monsters, shape-shifters or apparitions to become part of the drama. Aeschylus' *Proteus* was set probably on an island, featuring the minor sea-god who had prophetic and shape-shifting powers, rather like Silenus in Vergil's *Eclogue* 6. The *Glaucus Pontius* by Aeschylus told the story of a fisherman who became a sea god after eating a herb, and our fragments refer to his emergence from the sea (F 25e–26). Aeschylus' *Circe* tells of the Homeric sorceress who could transform men into animals (*Od.* 10.135–574); shape-shifting seems to have been a means by which Autolycus fooled those he stole from in Euripides' *Autolycus* B (cf. Tzetzes, *Chiliades* 8.435–8, 442–53). In Achaeus' *Aethon* Mestra probably would have been depicted or referred to as a shape-shifter; and Peleus speaks of his struggle to subdue the shape-shifting Thetis to make her his wife in Sophocles' *Lovers of Achilles* (F 150), which depicts the early life of the Homeric hero and is set in the cave of Chiron the centaur, or the distant island of Scyros, or both. The anonymous 'Atlas' play (*Adespota* F 655a) was set at the western extremity of the world where the Titan holds up the sky and fetches the Apples of the Hesperides for Heracles.[141]

Sometimes these settings will be more sinister, in or near the Underworld, as in Aeschylus' *Sisyphus* (F 225–34),[142] which tells of the famous trickster who cheated Death and was eventually punished with having to roll a stone up a hill eternally; this play also featured Sisyphus emerging from the Underworld carrying Death on his shoulders (F 227; cf. F 233). This rogue was the title character of another satyr play by Euripides – and probably another such play by Critias(?) (F 19) – and likely featured in Euripides' satyric *Autolycus* A and Achaeus' *Aethon*.[143] Other titles suggestive of an underworld setting include Aristias' *Fates*, which would have featured

---

[140] Above, n. 102.

[141] On an Apulian bell krater of *c*. 390–80 BC (= *LIMC* V.1 s.v. 'Heracles' 2687) satyrs steal the weapons of Heracles as he holds up the sky; they may have had this role in the play, but any direct links between this krater and F 655 remain very uncertain, not least because the play's date is unknown; see introductory discussion to *Adespota* F 655 below.

[142] Two titles concerning Sisyphus are accorded Aeschylus: *Sisyphus the Runaway* (*TrGF* 3.59 T 93b) and *Sisyphus the Stone-Roller* (as recorded by a scholiast on Arist. *EN* 1111a8–9); however, it is possible that one satyric play can be reconstructed; see the introductory discussion on Aeschylus, *Sisyphus* below, pp. 290–5.

[143] Above, n. 118. The genre of Sophocles' *Sisyphus* is not certain. Critias(?) (F 19) has been ascribed by some to Euripides as his *Sisyphus* play of 415 BC; see O'Sullivan (2012b) 167 n. 1.

spirits of the dead, and Sophocles' *Cerberus* and *On Taenarum*, the mountain through which Heracles descended to fetch the monstrous hound; Euripides' *Eurystheus*, about the king who set the hero this and other labours, would also have featured the Underworld as a setting or as part of the narrative background. Python's *Agen* was set near the tomb of the dead prostitute Pythionice in a region described as 'birdless' (F 1.2), a word used by Sophocles to describe an entrance to Hades (F 748). *Agen*, like Aeschylus' *Sisyphus* and *Glaucus Pontius*, seems to have involved a supernatural emergence, here of Pythionice from the Underworld, conjured up by the satyrs in another seemingly incongruous role, as Magi.

That satyrs could be figures of wisdom or learning – incongruously or otherwise – is another conspicuous feature of their collective onstage persona, evident in fifth-century art as well.[144] Related to this is their role as caregiver or even teacher of heroic or divine infants; Silenus' role as care-giver to Dionysus is well known, and he boasts about having discharged it in the satyric *Adespota* F 646a.12.[145] This motif, too, is combined with other common elements of satyric drama, such as the depiction of gods and heroes in infancy; in Aeschylus' *Net-Fishers* Silenus fancies himself as the foster father of the infant Perseus (F **47a.38–56). Aeschylus' *Nurses* may have dealt with the invention of wine by Dionysus,[146] as did Sophocles' *Little Dionysus*; and in Sophocles' *Trackers* the 'infant' god Hermes has already become a master thief. Sophocles' *Little Heracles* probably depicted the hero's strangling of the snakes sent by Hera, known also to Pindar (*Nem.* 1.35–72), in which he already displays the kinds of qualities he will exhibit throughout his life, much like the infant Dionysus and Hermes.

Youthful heroes will inevitably be beautiful, thus giving scope to another satyric motif, homoerotic desire. Achaeus' *Linus* deals with a later and more disturbing episode in Heracles' life, his slaying of his music teacher who punished him for poor lyre-playing. Whatever the satyrs' role here, there is evidence that they lusted after the young hero in a bibulous context (F 26), as they did in unnamed Sophoclean satyr play (F 756). Similar homoeroticism

---

[144] On a red-figure kalpis of *c.* 460 BC they appear as white-haired old men, evidently as mock-sages with long robes and staves, confronting the Sphinx (*LIMC* VIII.1 s.v. 'Silenoi' 160); Simon (1982) saw links here with Aeschylus' satyr play *Sphinx*, which parodied the Oedipus myth, and was part of his tetralogy on the house of Laius of 467.

[145] An Attic white-ground calyx krater by the Phiale Painter of *c.* 440 BC depicts Hermes entrusting the infant Dionysus to the care of Silenus; see also below Eur. *Cyc.* Comm. 141, 142–3nn.

[146] Cf. n. 62 above.

is evident in another play about a young hero and his education, Sophocles' *Lovers of Achilles* (F 153, 157). Although just what role the satyrs played in this drama is unclear, Sophocles emphasizes the young hero's extraordinary glance and its effects on the satyrs (F 157). The involvement of satyrs in dramas concerning the education and rearing of infants and youths may not just present them as comically ill-suited to such a nurturing role. It may also allude playfully to another side of satyrs attested outside satyric drama, namely their status as paradoxical founts of knowledge and wisdom, as evident in the gloomy wisdom Aristotle ascribes to Silenus (Arist. F 44), or in the didactic role the old satyr has in other writings by, for instance, Plato (*Symp.* 215a–c, 216c–217a, 221d), Theopompus (115 *FGH* 75c.1–2) or Vergil (*Ecl.* 6). Inverting their role as care-givers or teachers, satyrs may have been pupils as well. An anonymous drama, *Students* (*Mathêtai TrGF* 2, *Adesp.* 5g), evidently satyric, would seem to offer a good opportunity for the satyrs to be their usual rambunctious selves in a classroom setting, aggravating a (more or less) straight-laced or long-suffering teacher.[147]

Far from being mutually exclusive, the various tropes of satyric drama can co-exist within one play and satyrs can operate on many different registers within one drama. Euripides' *Cyclops* provides the most ample evidence of this, as the sole complete example of its kind. This drama not only engages with other literary, dramatic and mythic traditions, such as Homer and tragedy, it also playfully incorporates a number of concerns that loomed large in the political and philosophical culture of the day, and gives them the kind of treatment appropriate to a genre known for its combination of seriousness and earthy humour.

4. Euripides' Cyclops

4.1 Theories about the Date of the Play

The date of *Cyclops* is unknown. Some have used the criterion of thematic and verbal parallels with other plays of known dates and postulated, for instance, a date of the middle to late 420s to bring it in line with Euripides' *Hecuba*; this play features the blinding of Polymestor for his murder of Hecuba's son, entrusted to his care, and, like *Cyclops*, can be said to explore aspects of *xenia* and its violations.[148] Also citing thematic and verbal parallels, M.

---

[147] See Sutton (1974d) 121; cf. the survival and variants of this motif in television series, such as *Welcome Back, Kotter*.

[148] W. Arrowsmith (1956) 2 n. 1; Sutton (1980) 108–20, esp. 114–20. Kaibel (1895) 84–

Wright claimed that *Cyclops* must date to 412, the year in which Euripides' *Helen, Andromeda and Iphigenia among the Taurians* – his 'escape tragedies' – were produced.[149] Again, one can detect similar themes between *Cyclops* and these dramas such as escape from an ogre or monster, a distant setting, a happy ending, etc. But such parallels do not, however, constitute dating criteria. There is no reason why satyr plays had to follow the same themes as the preceding tragedies in detail, even if recognized as a genre that 'played' with tragedy. With the exception of some dramas by Aeschylus and Polyphrasmon, tragic 'trilogies' were not, as a rule, based around one unifying theme.[150] We need not expect any deep-running thematic unity to be continued in the satyr play which followed them. Nor is there any reason why Euripides' interest in such themes had to be confined to just one time of his career; he may have revisited these themes on different occasions. Parallels between *Cyclops* and other Euripidean plays can be more easily explained by the dramatically similar situations depicted in them. As R. Ussher has shown, verbal parallels can be found with many Euripidean dramas produced at different times; he establishes many parallels between *Cyclops* and other Euripidean plays such as *Ion, Trojan Women* and *Hecuba*, but rightly sees them as having no bearing on the date of the satyr play.[151] L. Paganelli suggested 414–13 as a date for the *Cyclops* on the basis of alleged historical allusions, such as the Sicilian expedition; and J. Duchemin, noting the negative image of Sicily in *Cyclops*, also linked the play to the Sicilian expedition but suggested the play was produced in 412, in the immediate aftermath of the disaster.[152] Even if such allusions could be firmly established, the Sicilian expedition could just as easily function as a *terminus post quem*, and the play could have been performed some years afterward.

---

5 inferred that *Hecuba* borrowed from *Cyclops* which he dated to the early 430s. Sutton (1980) 47–8 employs the same methodology to assert that Sophocles' *Trackers* was the satyr play accompanying *Ajax*. P. Maxwell-Stuart (1973) 399, asserts a date of 423 for Euripides' *Cyclops* without any discussion.

[149] M. Wright (2005) 54–5, for instance compares *Cyc.* 202 with *Andr.* F 125; and (2006) *passim*.

[150] *E.g.*, Polyphrasmon's tetralogy, *Lykourgeia*, in 467 (F 1; cf. T 3 Snell); Aeschylus did not always produce connected tetralogies; in 472 BC his satyric *Prometheus the Fire-Kindler* followed his tragedies which included the *Persians* (*TrGF* 3.48 T 55a); see also Gantz (1980).

[151] Ussher (1978) 197–9.

[152] L. Paganelli (1979) 135–9; J. Duchemin (1945) x.

Despite these difficulties, there is some consensus that *Cyclops* seems to come from late in Euripides' career, around 408 BC. Stylistic and metrical evidence, namely the high incidence of 'resolution' in Odysseus' iambic trimeters comparable with other Euripidean plays whose dates are known, has suggested this to some commentators. While aware that some metrical considerations are more telling than others, Seaford notes, for instance, that the frequency of resolution in Odysseus' diction in *Cyclops* occurs on average once every 3.8 trimeters, comparable to that in Euripides' *Helen* of 412 (3.6) and *Phoenissae* of 409 (3.9).[153] Close verbal parallels between *Cyclops* and plays of the late fifth century by Sophocles and Aristophanes have also been cited as dating criteria. Following Milman Parry's observation, Seaford takes *Cyc.* 222 as an allusion to Aristophanes' *Thesmophorizusae* 1105–6 (dated 411), itself a parody of Euripides' *Andromeda* (F 125).[154] He also notes the occurrence of the word ἀμφιτρής ('tunnelled, bored through on both sides') in *Cyc.* 707 and Sophocles' *Philoctetes* 19 (dated 409), a word not attested outside these two dramas.[155] He infers that Euripides is alluding to Sophocles here and that *Cyclops* is therefore a late play by and datable to c. 408. While it was once fairly common to assign *Cyclops* to Euripides' earlier years, most recent views date the *Cyclops* to the last decade of Euripides' life (between 415–406), for various reasons, some more cogent than others. Yet lack of certainty over the exact date of *Cyclops* is not a major hindrance to our understanding of its key themes and dramaturgy.

4.2 Euripides' Cyclops *as a Satyr Play: an Overview*

The most important literary precedent to Euripides' *Cyclops* is Homer's *Odyssey* book 9, just as the *Homeric Hymn to Hermes* was a major foundation for the *Trackers* of Sophocles.[156] Euripides' engagement with his Homeric model does not, however, simply entail a dramatization of the epic encounter between Odysseus and Polyphemus. Considerable differences between the two versions are evident, too, that are not just simply explained by the two

---

[153] Seaford (1982) *passim*, esp. 165; see also Seaford (1984) 48–51; cf. Ussher (1978) 204–212.

[154] M. Parry (1930) 140–1 put *Cyclops* at 409 and suggests that Euripides is answering Aristophanes' mockery of him with self-mockery.

[155] Seaford (1982) 168–72.

[156] The Homeric connections have been widely discussed; see, for instance, D. Ferrante (1960); Sutton (1974b); Seaford (1980) 51–9; Katsouris (1997) who discusses specific verbal parallels between Homer's and Euripides' versions; Napolitano (2003) 1–25; Paduano (2005) 1–37; Hunter (2009) 53–77.

different genres telling essentially the same story. Other treatments of this story in the satyr play by Aristias (F 4), and the comedies of Epicharmus (F 71–2 *PCG*) and Cratinus (F 143–57 *PCG*) are likely to have had some impact on Euripides as well.[157]

The play begins with a monologue by Silenus, an actor in this drama, as opposed to being a chorus member or coryphaeus (chorus-leader). The old satyr complains to his absent master of the dire situation he and his sons face as slaves of the brutal Cyclops and explains how they got there (1–40). In describing how the satyrs became lost when they were trying to rescue their master who had been kidnapped by pirates, Silenus encapsulates a number of important motifs for this and other satyric dramas (17–26):

> But then as we were sailing near Malea an easterly gale descending
> on the ship threw us onto this rock of Etna [20], where the one-eyed
> children of the sea-god, the Cyclopes who kill men inhabit their isolated
> caves. We were caught and are slaves in the house of one of them. They
> call the master we serve Polyphemus. And instead of Bacchic revels
> [25] we tend the flocks of a godless Cyclops.

Straightaway we encounter the motif of the enslavement of the satyrs by a monstrous overlord who is 'man-killing' and 'godless', here identified as Polyphemus. Schooled in Homeric epic, Euripides' fifth-century audience will have a general idea of what to expect of Euripides' *Cyclops* in light of *Odyssey* 9. But those expecting a close emulation of Homer may have been surprised to learn of the location of Euripides' drama on Sicily, an innovation possibly attributable to the Sicilian poet Epicharmus (F 70–2 *PCG*); in *Odyssey* 9 the home of the Cyclopes is never made clear.[158] Yet in the *Cyclops* the Sicilian location is made explicit fourteen times in a play of just over 700 lines (20, 60, 95 (twice), 106, 114 (twice), 130, 298, 366, 395, 599, 660, 703). By the fifth century Sicily had had a long history of sophisticated Hellenism, and as Thucydides (6.2–5) recognized, had been a cultural melting pot for centuries, home to Greek and non-Greek alike.[159]

---

[157]   The story is also treated by Philoxenus (F 816, 819 *PMG*) and in a dithyramb by Timotheus (F 780–3). The subject was popular in Archaic and Classical Greek Art (*LIMC* VIII.1 s.v. 'Polyphemos' I 16–18, 20; cf. I 40–44, 46, etc.).

[158]   Thrinakia, the island of the cattle of Helios (*Od.* 11.107), becomes associated with Sicily in the post-Homeric tradition (*e.g.*, Thuc. 6.2.2; Call. *Hymn* 3.57).

[159]   Willi (2008) explores many aspects of Sicily's cultural importance in the Greek world. Smith (2004) esp. 33–8 discusses what mainland Greeks are likely to have known of the place by the late fifth century.

But Euripides' drama presents the location as a barbaric dystopia, hostile to Greek religion and law, that is emblematic of the brutal nature of its natural inhabitants, the man-eating Cyclopes.[160] At the outset, Silenus speaks of their current location as 'this rock of Etna' (20) and the homes of the Cyclopes as 'isolated caves' (22). This lack of a civilized environment is consistent with the impious cannibalism of Polyphemus (30–1), who is acknowledged bitterly by Silenus as his current 'master' (34) in contrast to his natural master, Dionysus, whom he addressed at the outset of his speech.

Next comes the parodos, or the arrival of the chorus in the form of fifteen satyrs returning the monster's sheep which have been grazing. In their part as none-too-competent shepherds (cf. 49–51), the satyrs play the role of manual labourer as in other satyr dramas set in rural or distant locations, *e.g.* Aeschylus' *Net-Fishers*, Sophocles' *Trackers*, *Inachus*. The parodos (41–81), composed in lyric metres different from the spoken iambics of Silenus' prologue, extends much in Silenus' litany of complaints about their barbarous and backward location, notably the complete absence of Dionysus and his rites (63–6). Moroever, the chorus reminds the audience of certain motifs in the satyrs' condition: their enslaved state, role as forced labourers (64–81), and separation from their god, whose friendship with his entourage is emphasized in the epode or after-song (73–81):

> O my friend, O my friend (ὦ φίλος ὦ φίλε) Bacchus,
> where are you wandering, separated from your followers,
> are you shaking your golden hair? (75)
> I, your very own servant,
> am serf to the Cyclops,
> wandering in exile as a slave to this one-eyed monster,
> and wearing this miserable goat-skin cloak, (80)
> separated from your friendship (φιλίας).

Some have doubted the authenticity of lines (73–5) on stylistic and metrical grounds but they have been ably defended on the same grounds.[161] Either way, 'friendship' (*philia*) is important here in underscoring the satyrs' relationship to their god (81), and gains a certain poignancy as the satyrs allude to the absence of their god and his cult, immediately after their reference to 'the crags of Etna' (62). By the end of the parodos, then, we learn of the remoteness and harshness of the land and the man-eating, impious

---

[160] See O'Sullivan (2012a).

[161] For fuller discussion of the issues, see below *Cyc.* Comm. 73–5n.

monsters who inhabit it. With good reasons, the satyrs bemoan their plight, and their reluctance for work, however much it may tally with their natural disposition, takes on a more sympathetic aspect.[162]

When Odysseus and his men arrive, Silenus reiterates the brutality of the despotic monster and his homeland, described as 'hostile to strangers' and thus the Homeric law of hospitality (ξενία). In fact, Silenus even evinces some sympathy – destined to be short-lived – for the unsuspecting new arrivals (89–95):

> O unhappy strangers! Whoever are they? They have no idea what our master (δεσπότην) [90] Polyphemus is like, and that the land they have reached is hostile to strangers and that they have come, by an ill fate, right into the man-eating Cyclopean jaw. But quieten down so that we can learn where they've come from to be here at Sicilian Etna's rocky outcrop (Σικελὸν Αἰτναῖον πάγον).

The harshness of the environment here stands in contrast to Homer's description of the Cyclopes' land and the small island opposite from which Odysseus makes his ill-fated journey (*Od.* 9.105–41, 181–6). The Homeric Odysseus praises the Cyclopes' habitat, noting its fertility, its smooth and arable land, rich forests, fresh water springs and easy approach by sea with a natural harbour (*Od.* 9.131–7, 140–1). Homer's description is a precursor to the literary *locus amoenus* ('lovely place'), a motif found from Plato (*Phdr.* 230b) to Horace (*Odes* 3.4.6–8) and later still, and especially a feature of bucolic poetry; yet the landscape Euripides presents in his *Cyclops* is a stark and bleak contrast to the Homeric model.[163]

Odysseus appears, speaking dignified iambic trimeters even to the point of affectation at times (96–8), and is destined to play 'straight man' to the satyrs' 'funny man'. After Odysseus announces himself as 'the lord of the Cephallenians', Silenus brings the hero down to earth, calling him the 'shrill, relentless babbler', descended from Sisyphus (103–5), the infamous rogue who featured in some satyr dramas. Here the epic hero, praised by Homer for his oratorical powers (*Il.* 3.204–24, etc.), gets the satyric treatment.[164]

---

[162] Such sympathetic qualities of the satyrs have been well discussed by Griffith (2002) esp. 200; (2005) 172–86; (2010) 73–9.

[163] David Konstan refers me to P. Nieto (2000) who discusses the combined backward and idyllic features of Homer's Cyclopean world.

[164] Hostility to Odysseus in later poetry is widely attested, *e.g.* Pindar, *Nemean* 7, and Euripides may be alluding to it here; see below *Cyc.* Comm. 104n. Many have also tried to see the poet of the *Iliad* as hostile to the Ithacan hero; against this view, however, see Friedrich (2011). S. Montiglio (2011) sees Odysseus presented as a generally negative figure

Another significant difference between the Homeric and Euripidean accounts of Odysseus' arrival soon emerges. Homer has Odysseus, after he has escaped the Lotus-eaters, purposely set out for the land which has caught his interest, and which he does not yet know is inhabited by the Cyclopes; the hero sets out in one ship, having moored the rest of his fleet on an island nearby (*Od.* 9.170–6). Moreover, the Homeric Odysseus evinces a recklessness which endangers the life of his men by staying in the monster's cave, despite the urgings of his men to leave (*Od.* 9.220–30), an action which scholars see as an act of hybris or arrogance.[165] In *Cyclops*, by contrast, Odysseus is driven off course by a storm, just as the satyrs were, which underlines the shared precariousness of their situation, and puts hero and satyrs on something of an equal footing, as Silenus realizes immediately (108–10; cf. 17–22).

As Odysseus and the old satyr soon engage in a lengthy line by line exchange known as stichomythia (102–62), again the dismal plight of the satyrs and now Odysseus and his crew becomes clear: the land has no buildings and there are no people dwelling on it (115–118). These Euripidean Cyclopes are particularly backward, since in other traditions they were famous builders (Bacch. 10.77; Eur. *Tro.* 1088, etc.); but here they fall short of the human achievement of architecture, which was considered by fifth-century sophists such as Protagoras as fundamental to even a basic society (Pl. *Prot.* 322a). As was the case with the Cyclopes in Homer's account (*Od.* 9.112–15), there are no signs of civilization in terms of communal laws. Euripides' version goes beyond Homer to point out the backward nature of the Cyclopes' homeland in making clear that democracy is conspicuously absent from it (119–20), thus underscoring the political as well as physical distance of the dramatic locale from the fifth-century polis of its first production. Agriculture, viticulture – glossed as the domains of Demeter and Dionysus – are absent, too (121–4); the native inhabitants are relentless man-eaters (125–8).[166] Euripides thus develops the motif of liminal and distant setting of satyr plays to underscore the barbarism of Polyphemus and Cyclopes generally and to forge a bond of friendship at least between the chorus of satyrs and Odysseus who all desire

---

on the tragic stage, apart from exceptions such as Sophocles' *Ajax* and possibly his *Teucer* F **579a; she argues that the hero's 'rehabilitation' begins with Antisthenes' *Odysseus* and *Ajax* speeches (F 14–15 Caizzi) at the end of the fifth century.

[165] See, for instance, R. Friedrich (1991) esp. 25–6.

[166] Here again Euripides goes against the grain, as it were, of the historical Sicily, which was a prime centre of food production in the Mediterranean (Hdt. 7.158.4; Thuc. 6.20.4) and where the cult of Demeter was of great importance; see White (1964); Hinz (1998), esp. 55–167.

to escape from the island as soon as possible. While Vitruvius (5.6.9) is often quoted to show that typical settings of satyr plays tend to be in rustic and far off places, *Cyclops* makes clear that the satyrs are not always going to be at home in such environments.

After Odysseus gives Silenus wine in exchange for food from the monster's cave, the old satyr indulges in two of his favourite pastimes; excessive drinking and sexual fantasising (168–74). By this time a certain amount of good will has been established between Odysseus and the satyrs, couched in terms of friendship (*philia*), and the hero acknowledges the friendly relations that now exist between them (176). The chorus typically lower the tone with their own prurience and misogyny, thinking the Trojan war was essentially about the chance for a 'gang-bang' with Helen whom they call a 'traitor' and consider a nymphomaniac. After dismissing the entire race of women, the lechery of the satyrs gets the better of them here, and they collectively fantasise about having all the women of the world to themselves, thus comically recasting the bitter misogyny found in tragedy and elsewhere (179–87).[167] In other dramas the satyrs would appear to have lusted after Helen as well, including Sophocles' satyric *Helen's Marriage*, and Cratinus' comedy *Dionysalexandros* in which they appeared as the chorus.[168] Similarly, Aeschylus' *Net-Fishers* has Silenus and the chorus fantasizing that Danae is desperate for sex after such a long time at sea (F **47a.57–67).

But the real villain of the piece, Polyphemus, soon makes his appearance, barking orders to the terrified satyrs and making clear his hostility to Dionysus (203–5, 210–11):

CYCLOPS: Get out of the way! Make way! What's this? What's this idleness? Why are you performing a Bacchic revel? There's no Dionysus here, no castanet of bronze, no rattle of the drums! [205] ... What have you got to say for yourselves? What do you say? One of you will soon start shedding tears [210] courtesy of my club! Look upwards, not down!

The monster's opening words echo, but in the form of a brutal boast, the lament of the chorus that there is no Bromius and his cult on the island (63–4). Such hostility to Dionysus was a theme of many tragedies, Euripides'

[167] *E.g.* Hesiod's account of Pandora (*WD* 60–90; *Theog.* 571–90); Semonides F 7; Eteocles (Aesch. *Seven* 187–90, 256), Jason (Eur. *Medea* 573–5) and Hippolytus (Eur. *Hipp.* 616–50).
[168] Above, n. 13.

Bacchae being the most famous example.[169] Similarly, Sophocles' satyric *Salmoneus* told the story of that figure's attempt to displace Zeus, and Homer's *Odyssey* makes clear Polyphemus' rejection of Zeus and Olympian values (9.275–9). But the epic, of course, makes no mention of Dionysus in this context, while Euripides gives Polyphemus' hostility a satyric turn by making the monster, from his first utterance, an enemy of the deity. Inevitably, this anti-Dionysian antipathy makes Polyphemus an enemy not only of the satyrs, but of Odysseus, Zeus and Greek values explicitly (cf. *Cyc.* 320–3, 327–8, 338–42, etc.).

In what follows themes of loyalty, *philia* and family values are both overturned and played out.[170] Silenus proceeds to tell his outrageous lie that Odysseus and his men are not only thieves but intend to torture Polyphemus and sell him into slavery; the monster then decides to cook and eat the new arrivals, which Silenus cruelly endorses (232–52). Odysseus' straightforward account of events is denied by Silenus in an absurd, false and sycophantic oath, which culminates in his willingness to forfeit his sons' lives if he is forsworn (255–69). Such (ab)use of language puts Silenus on the same level of impiety as Polyphemus.[171] But the bonds of *philia* between father and sons become severed, at least temporarily, and those between the satyrs and Odysseus affirmed, when the chorus counter their father's false oath (268–72):

CHORUS: That's what *you* deserve. I myself saw you selling his property to the strangers. [270] If I'm telling lies, may my father die. (*To the Cyclops*) Don't wrong the strangers.

In other satyr dramas dysfunctional familial relations, mostly in the form of Silenus' abusing his sons, are found (Soph. *Trackers* F 145–68; Lycophron, *Menedemus* F 2), and have recurred in humour for millennia, from Aristophanes' *Wasps* to *Steptoe and Son*. But here, also of interest is the willingness of the satyrs to stand up to the monster directly and demand that he not harm the strangers. We see courage on the part of the satyrs here, even if later in the play they display their more predictable cowardice in backing out of Odysseus' plans to blind the giant (635–50). Silenus distorts *philia* by falsely claiming to love his sons so much (269 οὓς μάλιστ' ἐγὼ φιλῶ) and by siding with Polyphemus; yet the *philia* between Odysseus and the chorus is strengthened by the satyrs' stance against their father and the monster.

---

[169]   Cf. also Aeschylus' *Pentheus* F 183; *Bacchae* F 22; Iophon F 2; Xenocles F 1, etc.

[170]   See Ambrose (2005) for fuller discussion of this aspect of the play.

[171]   See Fletcher (2005) who argues that both characters pay the price for their false oaths and abuse of language.

In what may be considered the *agôn* or debate of the play (285–346) the cultural gulf that separates man from monster becomes clear. Odysseus speaks in terms of Olympian values, announcing firstly that he and his men are suppliants, as his Homeric counterpart does in referring to Zeus as protector of suppliants (*Od.* 9.270–1); Euripides' Odysseus invokes again the concept of *philia*, even describing himself and his men as 'friends' (φίλους) of the monster (287–8). From here he moves onto specious claims about how the Trojan War, denounced by Polyphemus as wasted on 'the most vile Helen' (281–2), had saved Greece from Trojan aggression and had benefited the monster as a supposed inhabitant of a land that is Greek (290–8). Many see Odysseus here using cynical and even comically inept arguments, representative of the supposed faults of the sophistic age,[172] but Euripides may just be playfully undercutting the rhetorical powers of this normally eloquent hero and giving him the satyric treatment again. But the hero's claims about the importance of the law or custom (*nomos*) of hospitality (*xenia*) put him on firmer ground ethically (299–311) and recall much of his Homeric counterpart's warning to the beast (*Od.* 9.266–71). Odysseus' tone is clearly more serious here, recalling motifs from tragedies, as he laments the deaths already caused by the Trojan War (cf. Aesch. *Ag.* 326–9, 430–57; cf. also Aesch. *Seven* 48). In language that recalls Silenus' description of the Cyclopes' impious and unholy ways at the outset of the play (30–1) he urges the monster to refrain from impious actions (309–11), just as the prophet Teiresias admonishes the maniacal Pentheus in the *Bacchae* (309). Odysseus finishes with a warning, pointing to the monster's inevitable fate, and marking a significant change in tone from the pleas which opened the speech.

Polyphemus sees through Odysseus' admittedly specious, or desperate, claims about the need to save Greece, but states that wealth and sacrificing to his belly, 'the greatest of gods', are most important to him (318–19, 334–8). He renounces the authority of Zeus (320–1), and even claims to rival Zeus' thunderings, not by impiously imitating the god, as did another another satyric ogre, Sophocles' Salmoneus (F 537–41a; cf. Diod. Sic. 6.7, etc.), but through the habit of masturbation.[173] The monster leads a life of excessive *autarkeia* or self-sufficiency which causes him to reject Olympian values (322–33) and concepts of *philia* which have characterised the interactions

---

[172]   Wilamowitz (1926) 21; Arrowsmith (1956) 2–8; Dougherty (1999); Worman (2002); cf. Ussher (1978) on 285–312; 187–94; cf. also Seaford (1984) 56. Sutton (1980) 121–2 offers a contrasting view, and Goins (1991) offers the best defence of the hero in the play, situating his actions in the context of ancient, especially satyric, ethics.

[173]   See *Cyc.* Comm. 327–8n.

among the satyrs, Dionysus and Odysseus.[174] In corruptions of language and ritual the monster allegorises 'Zeus' as nothing more than the ability to glut and pleasure oneself (336–7), and cruelly parodies the idea of *xenia* by saying he will offer it to his guests in the form of a bronze cauldron which will cook them as part of an implied sacrifice (342–6).

Many have seen Polyphemus here as a sophistic figure in his renunciation of laws (338–40) and conventional religion; Thrasymachus in Plato's *Republic* (338c–339a, etc.) is cited as a parallel, as is Callicles, who in Plato's *Gorgias* similarly attacks conventional ethics and law and argues for a 'greed is good' mentality (esp. *Gorg.* 482c-484d; 491e–492c).[175] But George Grote showed long ago that Callicles is no sophist or even an admirer of them (*Gorg.* 520a), and Guthrie has demonstrated that Thrasymachus does not endorse a supposed 'might is right' philosophy similar to Polyphemus' world-view.[176] Rather, Polyphemus is better understood as a parody of the tyrannical figure, who as a demonized stereotype in Attic literature embodies the same tropes as Polyphemus in *Cyclops* – greed, intolerance, sexual and other violence, contempt for law – albeit not in quite the same grotesque manners.[177] This is in fact consistent with Callicles' views since he advocates his 'greed is good' philosophy for those who can attain tyranny, *i.e.* tyrants (*Gorg.* 491e–492c). Polyphemus as tyrannical figure has good company in other ogres on the satyric stage: Aeschylus' Lycurgus, Sophocles' Amycus, Euripides' Busiris and Sositheus' Lityerses. Polyphemus' status as tyrannical ogre is central to his characterization in *Cyclops*, and he is often referred to negatively by the chorus

---

[174] Konstan (1990) 215, 216–17.

[175] W. Schmid (1896) 57; Wilamowitz (1926) 21–22; Duchemin (1945) 118; Lesky (1966) 401; Steffen (1971) 206, 211; W. G. Arnott (1972); Kovacs (1994), 56; Worman (2002) 103, 119, 121; cf. Seaford (1984) 52–3 who rightly sees the link to the Platonic Callicles, but does not call Polyphemus a sophist.

[176] Grote (1846) ch. 67, 344–50, esp. 347; see also Guthrie (1962) vol. 3, 102; Irwin (1995) 568–9; for discussion of Thrasymachus' views as a critical comment on what passes for 'justice' rather than a normative statement about how to enact it, see Guthrie (1962) 88–97; O'Sullivan (2005) 125–8.

[177] Berve (1967) 200 rightly referred to Polyphemus as a 'burlesk' tyrant without, however, developing the point. For full discussion, see O'Sullivan (2005) 119–59, esp. 128–59. The following tropes are all associated with tyranny in the following select instances: greed, especially for money (Aesch. *Ag.* 1619–24, 1628–32; Eur. *Pho.* 506, 439–40; Arist. *Pol.* 1311a1–11); brutality (*PV* 35, 324; Pl. *Rep.* 9.574e-575a), sexual violence (*PV* 736–7: Io's complaint about Zeus; cf. Danae in *Net-Fishers*; Hdt. 3.80.6; Eur. *Suppl.* 450–5); lawlessness or contempt for existing law (*PV* 149–50, 401–5; cf. 10, 222, 224–5, 305, 357, etc.; Hdt. 3.80.4–6; Eur. *Suppl.* 429–32); desire to enslave others (Arist. *Rhet.* 1393b5–22, referring to Stesichorus' warning to the citizens of Acragas of Phalaris' tyrannical ambitions).

as their 'master' (34, 90, 163, etc.) while they are his slaves (24, 78, 79, 442). The monster as slave-owning despot marks a key difference in his identity from his Homeric counterpart while still retaining much of the savagery of his epic incarnation. For the audience watching at the City Dionysia in democratic Athens, Polyphemus' tyrannical leanings would intensify his villainy.

The play now reaches its darkest moment as Odysseus' men are driven into the cave and the hero desperately calls on divine aid, invoking firstly Athena, then Zeus as god of hospitality, just as he is invoked in this role in the Homeric account (*Od.* 9.270–1). In a final tone of defiance Odysseus, unlike his Homeric counterpart, even entertains the possibility of the non-existence or irrelevance of the gods (354–55). It is a theme touched on by a number of Euripidean characters in moments of tragic despair (*Heracles* 1341; *Bellerophon* F 282, 286) and may have struck a chord in an age when skepticism about the nature of the divine is attested in the thought of some sophists such as Protagoras (80 B4 DK) and Prodicus (84 B5 DK). The challenge by a mortal to a god at the end of a scene occurs typically in late Euripidean dramas, too (*Hel.* 1093–1106; *IT* 1082–8, *Pho.* 84–7).[178]

The choral song which follows (356–74) dwells on the impiety and cruelty of the monster's cannibalism, and the revulsion the satyrs feel at the polluted meal. The tone of the satyrs' song is one of protest, disgust and despair all of which contrast strongly with malicious glee of Silenus who had earlier encouraged the Cyclops to eat the strangers (250–2, 313–15); the choral song is another instance of the ability of satyr drama to deal with serious emotion. Gluttony as a satyric theme now has moved from being merely crass to something darkly transgressive, and the chorus remind us again that the Cyclops is a native of Etna (366), underscoring the link between the monster and his monstrous habitat. Odysseus' re-emergence from the cave confirms their worst fears when they ask (377–8):

CHORUS: What is it, Odysseus? That most godless Cyclops hasn't really feasted on your dear companions, has he?

The chorus see the monster's crime as unholy and an affront to *philia* in the reference to the victims as Odysseus' 'dear companions'. Odysseus' long description of the monster's cannibalism (382–436), is the satyric counterpart to the typical 'messenger speech' in tragedy which describes often violent or spectacular off-stage action. The monster's impiety (396) and gluttony are stressed not least by reference to the vast size of his drinking vessels

---

[178]   Dale (1969) 183–4.

(388–91), typical of satyric ogres such as Lityerses who drinks from the same-size jar (Sositheus F 2.7–8). Unlike his Homeric counterpart, who eats his victims raw (*Od.* 9.289–92), the Euripidean Polyphemus is something of a transgressive gourmand, cutting the dead men's flesh, boiling it in his bronze cauldron (390–405; cf. 241–9), perhaps influenced by Cratinus' telling of the story in which the monster cooks his victims (F 150 *PCG*).[179]

But Odysseus' speech also forms a turning point in the play whereby the hero hits upon a way of punishing the Cyclops, escaping the island and re-uniting the satyrs with Dionysus. Interestingly, Homer emphasizes Odysseus' own thought processes in devising his revenge on the monster; it is a βουλή ('plan') that seems best to him (*Od.* 9.318, cf. 302). In Euripides' version the hero's escape plan is 'an idea sent from some god' (literally, 'something divine': τι θεῖον) that comes to him (*Cyc.* 411), and from here Dionysus is a more palpable presence in the play in the form of wine. The first step for Odysseus here will be to exploit the monster's unfamiliarity with wine by getting him drunk, thus making the god, often considered wine personified (Eur. *Cyc.* 156, 415; *Bacch.* 275–83, etc.), more central to the story. The 'wine motif' comes into play here as it did in other satyr plays such as Ion's *Omphale* and Achaeus' *Hephaestus*; but it is likely that the satyric Lycurgus, as depicted by Aeschylus (and possibly Polyphrasmon), forms the closest parallel as a slave-owning, anti-Dionysian ogre who tastes, and is defeated by, wine for the first time.[180] The major satyric themes, then, of the downfall of an ogre, escape from a distant locale and a return to Dionysian joy are all broached here, and this last aspect in particular is couched in terms of a three-way *philia* between Odysseus, the satyrs and Dionysus (433–8):

ODYSSEUS: But you – since you're still young – be saved with me and resume your old friendship with Dionysus, who's not like the Cyclops.
CHORUS: O dearest friend, if only we could see that day when we escape the godless presence of the Cyclops!

From here the revenge motif (*timōria*) becomes more conspicuous in the drama (441–2). It is not enough merely for Greeks and satyrs to escape; the old ethic of helping friends *and* harming enemies must be invoked (cf. Archilochus fr. 26 W; *Theognidea* 337–40). As Odysseus gradually reveals his plans to blind the Cyclops, the satyrs' enthusiasm grows excitedly (465; cf.

---

[179] Polyphemus may even resemble the Sicilian tyrant Phalaris, notorious by the time of Pindar (*Pyth.* 1.95–8) for roasting victims alive in his bronze bull; see O'Sullivan (2005) 132–4.
[180] See Voelke (2001) 190–1.

624–5), comparable perhaps to their over-reaction on seeing fire for the first time which they want to kiss (Aesch. *Prom. Fire-Kindler* F 207). Odysseus announces that he will rescue his men (whom he again calls 'friends'), the satyrs, and magnanimously and unhesitatingly includes Silenus, despite the old satyr's treachery earlier (466–8). As a somewhat comical sign of the *philia* between chorus and hero, the satyrs, full of bravado as elsewhere (cf. Soph. *Inachus* F 269d.22), declare their willingness to help blind the monster (469–71; cf. 483–5), and claim to be able to lift a hundred wagons if necessary (473–4) – a build-up that points only to their eventual cowardice (635–41). This pivotal scene, which began with an account of the horrors within the monster's cave, ends on an upbeat note, with an invocation of *philia*. Odysseus once again asserts, if somewhat pompously, the importance of *philia* to his own heroic identity and as a motivation for his actions (478–82).[181]

Now, in lyrics (483–518), the satyrs focus gleefully on wreaking revenge on the monster, who is derided for his tone deaf singing and ignorance, and whose punishment will be an education for him: 'let us educate (παιδεύσωμεν) him ... the ignoramus' (τὸν ἀπαίδευτον: 489–93; cf. 173). Interestingly, this may play on the idea of satyrs as instructors of sorts:[182] the monster, like his native Sicily, knows nothing of the joys of Dionysus whose worship involves dance, music as well as wine (63–72, 124; cf. 203–5). The intimates of this god will therefore be only too happy to let the ogre become acquainted with their deity if it means the downfall of their enemy. Compared to this beast, whose singing is as inept as his actions are deplorable, these satyrs are figures of elegance and refinement. Dionysian and erotic themes become more explicit in the satyrs' *makarismos*, or song of blessing, briefly describing activities of the typical reveller or *komast* in a general context of *philia*; this reveller embaces a 'dear male companion' (φίλον ἄνδρα), while an *hetaira* (girlfriend or courtesan) waits for him on the bed (495–502). A distorted version of this image becomes concrete in the appearance of Polyphemus, the supremely transgressive *komast*, who not only brags of his cannibalism and drunkenness, but is derided by the satyrs as a beautiful groom on his wedding night in the mood for love (511–18). A parody of Sappho has been detected earlier in the play (*Cyc.* 182–6), and here is possibly another in the sardonic 'compliments' of the satyrs

---

[181]   For discussion of the authenticity of these lines, see below *Cyc.* Comm. 480–2n.

[182]   Cf. their possible roles in, for instance, Aesch. *Nurses*; Soph. *Little Dionysus, Little Heracles*, Python, *Agen*.

which may be compared to compliments Sappho pays to the groom in her epithalamians, or wedding songs (cf. Sappho F 111–12, 115–16 L-P).[183] We also get a glimpse of the grotesquely comical Polyphemus as lover, a motif of later poetry, notably of Theocritus (*Id.* 6 and 11), and Ovid (*Met.* 13.740–897, esp. 750–68), and which may be reflected in the work of Euripides' younger contemporary, Philoxenus (F 816, 819 *PMG*).

In the lengthy stichomythia that follows Odysseus must keep the monster at home for his plan to work (521–69). Part of this involves educating Polyphemus in the niceties of the symposium, like Heracles in Ion's *Omphale* (F 21–7) or the title character in Achaeus' *Hephaestus* (F 17). Odysseus takes command of the situation early, speaking at times misleadingly (524, 526, 528) and preparing to use the trick of calling himself 'Nobody' (549), famous from Homer (cf. 672–5). All the while he plies the monster with drink glossed as 'the Bacchic one', a title of Dionysus; wine is presented to the Cyclops as the god himself (519–29, 575). The god who is the friend of the satyrs thus plays a crucial role in aiding Odysseus in his plan. The monster here comes under the influence of his foe in similar fashion to the way in which Pentheus in the *Bacchae* (811–46) falls under the sway of his destroyer, Dionysus.[184] Just as the deluded Pentheus imagines two suns in the sky (*Bacch.* 918), so, too, Polyphemus' state causes him to make errors of cosmic proportions (578–80). In making Silenus play Ganymede (582–9), the monster puts himself on the same level as Zeus, who famously loved the Trojan prince (Hom. *Il.* 20.232–5); the monster's delusion is consistent with his earlier hubristic claims to rival the supreme god (320–1, 328).[185] The monsters's rape of Silenus not only recalls the bizarre erotics that began the scene in the satyrs' parody of the Cyclops as lover (511–18); it is also a fittingly comical, if grotesque, way to bring the distorted *philia* between Polyphemus and the old satyr to its climax, so to speak.

In addressing the satyrs as 'sons of Dionysus, noble children' (590), Odysseus once more alludes, albeit metaphorically, to the implied presence of the god, who is certainly a better role model than their real father, who takes no further part in the play. Indeed, Silenus, as he appears in Sophocles' *Trackers*, is by far the most badly behaved of these ithyphallic males, and his onstage persona in *Cyclops* is in contrast to those other traditions that

---

[183]   See di Marco (1980) on *Cyc.* 182–6. For Polyphemus as failed *komast*, see Rossi (1971), and for parodies of sympotic behaviour in *Cyclops*, see R. Hamilton (1979)

[184]   An astute observation by Sutton (1980) 128.

[185]   Cf. also the Argive warrior Capaneus in tragedy, who is destroyed by Zeus' thunderbolt (Aesch. *Seven* 423–4; Eur. *Pho.* 1128–33).

ascribed a wisdom to him, preserved by, for instance, Plato (*Symp.* 215a–c, 216c–217a, etc.) or Aristotle (F 44; cf. Hdt. 8.138) or Vergil (*Ecl.* 6). Odysseus' encouragement of the satyrs collectively to act like 'a real man' (ἀνήρ: 595) will be as ineffectual as the satyrs' vain pledges of help (469–75, 596, 632–3). But before this joke on the perennial cowardice of satyrs is played out, we see them once again unite the themes of revenge, escape and reunion with their god, central to this and other satyr dramas. Odysseus prays to Hephaestus and the primordial deity, Sleep, with more heroic self-aggrandisement and another threat to downsize the status of the gods if aid is not forthcoming (599–607; cf. 353–55); then the chorus perform a short astrophic song joyfully anticipating the blinding of the monster, and finishing with another statement of their desire for their god (620–22). This desire is expressed with enough passion and evident noise to make Odysseus think they will wake the monster. This draws an angry rebuke from the hero who sees the chorus now as 'wild creatures' (θῆρες: 624–8), as Cyllene called them in Sophocles' *Trackers* (221–2). Like his Homeric counterpart, Euripides' Odysseus similarly can be harsh to sympathetic figures; the Homeric Odysseus threatens the aged Eurycleia with death, after she has recognized him by his scar and, in her astonishment, inadvertently risks revealing his identity before time (*Od.* 19.467–90).[186] As far as Euripides' satyrs are concerned, the dynamic of friendship between them and Odysseus ebbs and flows, and is about undergo another setback.

When the satyrs come up with – in some cases, literally – lame excuses for not helping blind the monster (635–41), Odysseus, as if invoking Hesiod, calls them 'worthless men and nothing as allies' (ἄνδρες πονηροὶ κοὐδὲν οἵδε σύμμαχοι: 642), something which he has long known (649). Here, then, the satyrs' status as the 'anti-types' of the citizen male, in Lissarrague's expression,[187] is all too clear, even if earlier they did stand up to the Cyclops, unlike their toadying father (270–2). Yet even in this situation Odysseus does not despair of them completely, and values their support which he sees as a source of courage for himself and his men, now called 'close friends' (653). In a neat paradox Odysseus looks to these creatures as a source of courage in the very moment of their most blatant cowardice.

While the last choral song (656–62) has presented scholars with various

---

[186] Compare also his words to Neoptolemus in Soph. *Philoctetes* (*e.g.*, 50–3, 74–8, 83–4, 108–9, 119–20).

[187] Lissarrague (1990a) 235.

problems metrically,[188] its general tenor is a clear exuberant cry for vengeance, a theme which has been steadily building since Odysseus first revealed his plan to them (437–8, 441–2, 464–5, etc.). The satyrs remind us again of the monster's crimes (658) and call for the blinding with a string of imperatives (656–7, 661) in asyndeton (*i.e.* without conjunctions) and in dochmiacs, a metre often associated with particularly emotive utterances. The blinded monster's reappearance and recognition of his own situation can be seen as a farce (663–709), in which the satyrs taunt their long-time tormentor with Odysseus' trick of Nobody (672–3). The satyrs' jokes with the name are certainly consistent with the Homeric hero's own mirth when he sees his trick take effect (*Od.* 9.413–14). The Homeric hero and Euripidean satyrs, it seems, have a similar sense of humour. This scene may also be considered as playfully invoking tragic norms ('paratragic') in being comparable to another Euripidean drama in which a blinded figure gropes around savagely to get back at his tormentors, as Polymestor does in *Hecuba* (1035–43, 1056–1126).

Some have seen the punishment of the beast as an act of gratuitous cruelty, but there is nothing to suggest we should pity Polyphemus.[189] While the Platonic Socrates may have been arguing that it is worse to commit wrong than to suffer it (Pl. *Gorg.* 469c, 475a–d, etc.), and tragedy may have been exploring the extent to which a punishment may exceed a crime (*e.g.*, Aesch. *Oresteia*; Eur. *Bacch.* 1348; cf. *PV passim*), no such qualms are evident in this play. In fact, the raging monster is even assimilated to the most terrifying threat to Olympian order, Typhon, who is imprisoned under Etna (Pindar, *Pyth.* 1.13–28; *PV* 363–72). More than once the chorus call for Polyphemus to be blinded, using cognates of the verb τύφω (to burn, consume in smoke), and remind us again that he is as violent as the volcano he inhabits in referring to him as 'the shepherd of Etna' (655–60), a reprise of their earlier description of him as the 'Cyclops of Etna' (366).[190]

---

[188] See, for instance, Dale (1981) 69; Kovacs (1994) 157; also *Cyc.* Comm. 656–62n.

[189] *E.g.* Arrowsmith (1956) 6 refers to the 'barbaric cruelty' of Odysseus' revenge, and refers to Polyphemus as a 'likeable buffoon who loathes war, understands generosity and tipsily "rapes" (*sic*) Silenus' (8); Ussher (1978) 191 writes: '... Odysseus proceeds to what can only be (as he himself well knows) a senseless outrage.' Neither in Euripides' account nor in Homer's does Odysseus express any remorse for his actions; in both instances he sees himself as an agent of justice (*Od.* 9.477–9; Eur. *Cyc.* 421–2, 693); cf. also Friedrich (1991); Segal (1992); C. Brown (1996).

[190] The chorus' words remind us of the brutal environment in which the play is set. Cf. also Ovid's conflation of the monster and his fiery, volcanic habitat (*Met.* 13.867–9; cf. 877).

Odysseus, moreover, reminds the Cyclops – and the audience – of the crimes committed by the monster which merited the punishment (693–5):

> You were bound to pay the penalty for your unholy feast. For a worthless thing it would have been for me to destroy Troy by fire, if I had not avenged the slaughter of my companions! [695]

Here Odysseus reiterates the impiety of the monster's crimes and the importance of *philia* as a motivating factor: indeed, avenging the murder of his companions even trumps his great triumph at Troy. The language here recalls 421–2, when Odysseus in the cave realizes that the drunken Polyphemus would 'soon pay his due' (δίκην δώσει τάχα) and the play has since then been leading up to this moment. This simple ethic of punishing wrongdoers occurs in other satyr dramas (cf. Aesch. 'Dike Drama' F 281a), and is evidently endorsed by Theseus, Athens' home-grown Heracles (Eur. *Sciron* F 678); it is emblematic of Heracles himself (Eur. *Syleus* F 692). In this case the punishment of the monster amounts almost literally to an 'eye for an eye', and this is enacted by Odysseus; and his final taunt 'go to hell' (κλαίειν σ' ἄνωγα: 701) recalls the monster's dismissal of Odysseus' pleas (κλαίειν ἄνωγα: 340).

Polyphemus' continued threats and prophecy about Odysseus' wanderings hardly mar the generally upbeat, if rather abrupt, ending of the play (703–7), spoken by the chorus (708–9):

> Well anyway, we're going to be fellow sailors with Odysseus here and from now on we'll be the slaves of the Bacchic god!

Homer's account ends the Odysseus-Polyphemus episode on a relatively sombre note, with Odysseus and his men shedding tears for their comrades slain by the monster, notwithstanding Odysseus' triumph and their escape (*Od.* 9.566–7). But this brief Euripidean couplet, in iambic trimeters as opposed to the anapaests which often conclude tragedies, has no hint of melancholy about it. It does, however, allude concisely to many important themes in the drama: friendship, slavery, the different master the satyrs have served, release from the monster and reunification with their god. The satyrs' self-professed status as Odysseus' fellow sailors is another nod to the *philia* they share with these Greeks. Paradoxically, the idea of slavery that had defined the satyrs' condition at the outset of the play (23–6, 78–81; cf. 442, etc.) emerges at the very moment of the satyrs' freedom. But now this 'slavery' is a byword for the friendship they enjoy with their god (73–5, 81, 435–6, 620–2, etc.), and stands in contrast to what they had endured under a despot living on the fringes of the Greek world.

Just as the final couplet refers with great economy to a number of important issues in the play, so the *Cyclops* as a whole, at just over 700 lines, can be said to encapsulate much of literary and dramatic significance.[191] In the play we not only find the tropes one would expect of a satyr play retelling a famous Homeric narrative, we also see Euripides incorporating a number of contemporarily significant elements in his work. Arguably the main theme of *Cyclops* is liberation from an ogre defeated by Greek hero who frees the satyrs and paves the way for reunion with Dionysus. Yet *Cyclops* also deals with issues such as hospitality and friendship (and transgressions thereof), impiety and its consequences. There is also a culture clash in which Greek values prevail over a creature who lives by greed and brute strength in a brutal, backward environment, and who would remind the audience of a debauched tyrant, especially offensive to Attic democratic sensibilities. Many such themes are common to other satyr plays, and in *Cyclops* they are approached with a mixture of seriousness and at times brutally bawdy humour. The satyrs make clear that Odysseus' heroic posturing at times cries out to be lampooned; but the play is not without its moments of pathos, and at all times the satyrs remain friends with Odysseus, just as they never despair of being reunited with Dionysus. It is significant that the chorus sympathise with the suffering of Odysseus and his men before the hero emerges as their saviour. In their comically transgressive but also sympathetic qualities the satyrs of Euripides' *Cyclops* are fitting embodiments of a medium that deftly combines the serious and playful.

---

[191] A truism of scholarship on ancient Greek drama is that all satyr plays were about this length; but this is based on the sole example of the genre to survive intact. The usual guess is that Sophocles' *Trackers* is of similar length to *Cyclops* on the basis of how far the action has proceeded in the extant papyri compared to the narrative progression of the *Homeric Hymn to Hermes*. Aeschylus' *Net-Fishers* could easily have gone well over 1,000 lines; the papyrus breaks off at line 832 (=F **47a.68), not long after Danae has arrived with her infant son on Seriphos. Aeschylus' *Sisyphus the Runaway* and *Stone-Roller* may be separate titles for just one play, which could have run to a similar length (see below pp. 293–4). The possibility that some satyr plays could be of similar lengths to tragedy should therefore not be ruled out.

GENERAL BIBLIOGRAPHY

In addition to this bibliography, see also the items for Fragments which appear on pp. 232–3 and under 'Discussions' in the introductions to each fragmentary play.

Titles of periodicals are abbreviated as in *L'Année Philologique.*

Allan, W. (2001) Euripides in Megalê Hellas: Some Aspects of the Early Reception of Tragedy, *G&R* 48, 67–86.
Ambrose, Z. P. (2005) Family Loyalty and Betrayal in Euripides' *Cyclops* and *Alcestis*: a Recurrent Theme in Satyr Play, in G. W. M. Harrison, ed. (2005), 21–38.
Arnott, P. D. (1961) The Overworked Playwright. A Study in Euripides' *Cyclops*, *G&R* 8, 164–69.
Arnott, W. G. (1972) Parody and Ambiguity in Euripides' *Cyclops*, in R. Hanslik, A. Lesky and H. Schwabel, eds, *Antidosis. Festschrift for W. Kraus*, Vienna. 21–30.
Arrowsmith, W. tr. (1956) *The Complete Greek Tragedies. Euripides* vol. II. Chicago.
Austin, C. and Reeve, M. D. (1970) Notes on Sophocles, Ovid and Euripides, *Maia* 22, 3–18.
Bain, D. (1985) Ληκύθιον ἀπώλεσεν: Some Reservations, *CQ* 35, 31–37.
Barrett, W. S. (1964) *Euripides. Hippolytos*. Oxford.
Bérard, C. and Bron, C. (1989) Satyric revels, in C. Bérard *et al.*, eds, *A City of Images. Iconography and society in ancient Greece*, tr. D. Lyons. Princeton, 131–50.
Bérard, C. (1990) Le Satyre Casseur, *Métis* 5, 75–87.
Berve, H. (1967) *Die Tyrannis bei den Griechen*, vol. I. Munich.
Biehl, W. ed. (1983) *Euripides. Cyclops*. Leipzig.
Biehl, W. ed. (1986) *Euripides. Kyklops*. Heidelberg.
Boardman, J. (1989) *Athenian Red Figure Vases. The Classical Period*. London.
Bond, G. W. (1981) *Euripides. Heracles*. Oxford.
Brommer, F. (1937) Satyroi, Diss. Munich.
Brommer, F. (1940) Σιληνοί und σάτυροι, *Philologus* 94, 222–28.
Brommer, F. (1959) *Satyrspiele. Bilder griechischen Vasen* (2nd edn). Berlin.
Brown, C. (1996) In the Cyclops' Cave: Revenge and Justice in *Odyssey* 9, *Mnemosyne* 49, 1–29.
Burkert, W. (1985) *Greek Religion*, tr. J. Raffan. Cambridge, MA.

Burnett, A. P. (1971) *Catastrophe Survived. Euripides' Plays of Mixed Reversal.* Oxford.

Buschor, E. (1943) *Satyrtänze und frühes Drama.* Munich.

Calame, C. (2010) Aetiological Performance and Consecration in the Sanctuary of Dionysos, in O. P. Taplin and R. Wyles, eds, 65–78.

Capps, E. (1943) Greek Inscriptions: A New Fragment of the List of Victors at the City Dionysia, *Hesperia* 12, 1–11.

Carden, R. (1974) *The Papyrus Fragments of Sophocles.* Berlin-New York.

Carnes, J. S. (1998) The Myth which is not One: Construction of Discourse in Plato's *Symposium*, in D. Larmour, P. Allen and C. Platter, eds, *Rethinking Sexuality. Foucault and Classical Antiquity.* Princeton, 104–21.

Carpenter, T. (2005) Images of Satyr Plays in South Italy, in G. W. M. Harrison, ed., 219–36.

Casaubon, I. (1605) De Satyrica Graecorum Poesi et Romanorum Satira, reprinted in Seidensticker (1989), 13–17.

Cipolla, P. (2003) *Poeti minori del dramma satiresco.* Amsterdam.

Collard, C. (2005) Colloquial Language in Tragedy: A Supplement to the Work of P. T. Stevens, *CQ* 55, 350–86.

Collard, C. (2007) *Tragedy, Euripides and Euripideans. Selected Papers.* Exeter.

Collard, C. and Cropp, M. J. (2008) *Euripides. Fragments I and II = Euripides VII and VIII* (Loeb Classical Library, Cambridge MA and London).

Collinge, A. (1989) The case of satyrs, in M. M. MacKenzie *et al.*, eds, *Images of Authority. Papers presented to Joyce Reynolds on the occasion of her 70th birthday.* Cambridge, 82–103.

Collinge, N. E. (1958/9) Some reflections on satyr-plays, *PCPhS* 5, 28–35.

Collins, D. (2004) *Master of the Game. Competition and Performance in Greek Poetry.* Cambridge, MA and London.

Conacher, D. J. (1967) *Euripidean Drama. Myth, Theme, and Structure.* Toronto.

Conrad, G. (1997) *Der Silen.* Trier.

Constantinides, E. (1969) Timocles' *Ikarioi Satyroi*: a reconsideration, *TAPhA* 100, 49–61.

Cornford, F. M. (1907) *Thucydides Mythistoricus.* Cambridge.

Csapo, E. (1986) A Note on the Würzburg bell-crater H5697 ('Telephus Travestitus'), *Phoenix* 40, 379–92.

Csapo, E. and Slater, W. eds (1994) *The Context of Ancient Drama.* Ann Arbor.

Csapo, E. and Miller, M. eds (2003) *Poetry, Theory, Praxis: the Social Life of Myth, Word and Image in Ancient Greece. Essays in Honour of William J. Slater.* Oxford.

Csapo, E. and Miller, M. eds (2007) *The Origins of Theater in Ancient Greece and Beyond. From Ritual to Drama.* Cambridge.

Dale, A. M. (1963) *Collected Papers.* Cambridge.

Dale, A. M. (1968) *The Lyric Metres of Greek Drama*. Cambridge.

Dale, A. M. (1981) *Metrical Analyses of Tragic Choruses. BICS* Supplement 21.2. London; also (1983) *BICS* Supplement 21.3. London.

d'Angiò, F. (1992) Euripide, *Autolico* Fr. 282 N2, *Dioniso* 62.2, 83–94.

Davidson, J. A. (1997) *Fishcakes and Courtesans. The Consuming Passions of Classical Athens*. London.

Davies, M. (1999) Comic priamel and hyperbole in Euripides, *Cyclops* 1–10, *CQ* 49, 428–32.

Denniston, J. (1949) *Euripides. Electra*. Oxford.

Diggle, J. (1969) Marginalia Euripidea, *PCPhS* 15, 30–35 (reprinted in *Euripidea* (1994), 5–33).

Diggle, J. (1971) Notes on the *Cyclops* of Euripides, *CQ* 21, 42–50.

Diggle, J. (1972) Euripides, *Cyclops* 511–18 (and other Passages) with a Note on *Elegiae in Maecenatem* I, 93–4, *Maia* 24, 345–8.

Diggle, J. ed. (1981) *Studies on the Text of Euripides. Supplices, Electra, Heracles, Troades, Iphigenia in Tauris, Ion*. Oxford.

Diggle, J. (1994) *Euripidea*. Leiden.

Dodds, E. R. (1959) *Plato. Gorgias*. Oxford.

Dodds, E. R. (1960) *Euripides. Bacchae* (2nd edn). Oxford.

Dougherty, C. (1999) The Double Vision of Euripides' *Cyclops*: An Ethnographic *Odyssey* on the Satyr Stage, *Comparative Drama* 33, 313–38.

Dover, K. J. (1974) *Greek Popular Morality*. Oxford.

Dover, K. J. (1989) *Greek Homosexuality*. Cambridge, MA.

Dover, K. J. (1993) *Aristophanes. Frogs*. Oxford.

Duchemin, J. ed. (1945) *Le Cyclope d'Euripide*. Paris.

Duchemin, J. (1968) *L'ΑΓΩΝ dans la Tragédie Grecque*, 2nd edn, Paris.

Easterling, P. E. (1994) Euripides outside Athens: a speculative note, *ICS* 19, 73–80.

Easterling, P. E. (1997a) A show for Dionysus, in P. E. Easterling, ed., *The Cambridge Companion to Greek Tragedy*. Cambridge, 36–53.

Easterling, P. E. (1997b) From Repertoire to Canon, in P. E. Easterling, ed., *The Cambridge Companion to Greek Tragedy*. Cambridge, 211–27.

Easterling, P. E. (2007) Looking for Omphale, in V. Jennings and A. Katsaros, eds, *The World of Ion of Chios. Mnemosyne Supplement* 288. Leiden, 282–92.

Easterling, P. E. (2009) Sophocles and the Wisdom of Silenus. A Reading of *Oedipus at Colonus* 1211–1248, in E. Karamalengou and E. Makrygianni, eds, Ἀντιφίλησις. *Studies on Classical, Byzantine and Modern Greek Literature and Culture*. Stuttgart, 161–70.

Edmunds, L. (1975) *Chance and Intelligence in Thucydides*. Cambridge MA.

Else, G. F. (1939) Aristotle and Satyr-Play, *TAPhA* 70, 139–57.

Else, G. F. (1965) *The Origin and Early Form of Greek Tragedy*. Cambridge MA.

Ferrante, D. (1960) Il *Ciclope* di Euripide ed il IX dell' *Odissea, Dioniso* 34, 165–81.

Fischer, I. M. (1958) *Typische Motive im Satyrspiel.* Göttingen.

Fletcher, J. (2005) Perjury and Perversion of Language in Euripides' *Cyclops*, in G. W. M. Harrison, ed. (2005), 53–66.

Flickinger, R. C. (1913) Tragedy and the Satyric Drama, *CPh* 8, 261–83.

Frazer, J. G. (1914–1917) *The Golden Bough. A Study in Magic and Ritual.* 12 vols. London.

Friedrich, R. (1991) The hybris of Odysseus, *JHS* 111, 16–28.

Friedrich, R. (2011) Odysseus and Achilleus in the *Iliad*: Hidden Hermeneutic Horror in Readings of the *Presbeia, Hermes* 139, 271–90.

Garland, R. (1990) *The Greek Way of Life. From Conception to Old Age.* Ithaca, NY.

Gantz, T. (1980) The Aischylean Tetralogy: Attested and Conjectured Groups, *AJPh* 101, 133–64.

Gantz, T. (1993) *Early Greek Myth. A Guide to Literary and Artistic Sources.* Baltimore and London.

Gauly, B. and Kannicht, R. eds (1991) *Musa Tragica. Die griechische Tragödie von Thespis bis Ezechiel. Ausgewählte Zeugnisse und Fragmente griechisch und deutsch.* Göttingen.

Ghiron-Bistagne, P. (1991) Le drame satyrique dans les concours dramatiques, *Dioniso* 61.2, 101–20.

Gibert, J. (2002) Recent Work on Greek Satyr-play, *CJ* 87, 79–88.

Goins, S. (1991) The Heroism of Odysseus in Euripides' 'Cyclops', *Eos* 79, 187–94.

Goldhill, S. (1990) The Great Dionysia and Civic Ideology, in J. Winkler and F. Zeitlin, eds (1990), 97–129.

Goldhill, S. (1997) The Audience of Athenian Tragedy, in P. E. Easterling, ed., 54–68.

Gomme, A. W., Andrewes, A. and Dover, K. J. (1970) *A Historical Commentary on Thucydides.* Vol. IV. Oxford.

Green, J. R. (1991) On Seeing and Depicting the Theatre in Classical Athens, *GRBS* 32, 15–50.

Green, J. R. (1994) *Theatre in Ancient Greek Society.* London.

Green, J. R. and Handley, E. W. (1995) *Images of the Greek Theatre.* London.

Green, J. R. (2007) Let's Hear it for the Fat Man. Padded Dancers and the Prehistory of Drama, in E. Csapo and M. Miller, eds, 96–107.

Griffin, J. (1998) The social function of Attic tragedy, *CQ* 48, 39–61.

Griffith, M. (2002) Slaves of Dionysos: Satyrs, Audience, and the Ends of the *Oresteia, ClAnt.* 21, 195–258.

Griffith, M. (2005a) Satyrs, Citizens, and Self-Representation, in G. W. M. Harrison, ed. (2005), 161–99.

Griffith, M. (2005b) Sophocles' Satyr-Plays and the Language of Romance, in I. J. F. de Jong and A. Rijksbaron, eds, *Sophocles and the Greek Language. Aspects of Diction, Syntax and Pragmatics.* Leiden-Berlin, 51–72.

Griffith, M. (2008) Greek Middlebrow Drama (Something to do with Aphrodite?), in M. Revermann and P. Wilson, eds, *Performance, Iconography, Reception. Studies in Honour of Oliver Taplin*. Oxford, 59–87.

Griffith, M. (2010) Satyr Play and Tragedy, Face to Face, in O. P. Taplin and R. Wyles, eds (2010), 47–63.

Grote, G. (1846) *A History of Greece*, London. Chapter 67.

Grube, G. (1941; repr. 1961) *The Dramas of Euripides*. London.

Guggisberg, P. (1947) *Das Satyrspiel*. Zurich.

Günther, H.-C. (2001) 4545. Euripides, *Cyclops* 455–71, 479–81, 484–96, in R. A. Coles *et al.*, eds, *The Oxyrhynchus Papyri*. Vol. LXVII. London, 16–18.

Guthrie, W. K. C. (1962–81) *A History of Greek Philosophy*. 6 vols. Cambridge.

Hall, E. (1989) *Inventing the Barbarian. Greek Self-Definition through Tragedy*. Oxford.

Hall, E. (1998) Ithyphallic Males Behaving Badly; or, Satyr Drama as Gendered Tragic Ending, in M. Wyke, ed., *Parchments of Gender: Deciphering the bodies of antiquity*. Oxford.

Hall, E. (2006) *The Theatrical Cast of Athens. Interactions between Ancient Greek Drama and Society*. Oxford, 142–69.

Halperin, D., Winkler, J. and Zeitlin, F. eds (1990) *Before Sexuality. The Construction of Erotic Experience in the Ancient Greek World*. Princeton.

Halperin, D. (1990) Why is Diotima a Woman? Platonic *Erôs* and the Figuration of Gender, in D. Halperin, J. Winkler and F. Zeitlin, eds (1990), 257–308.

Hamilton, R. (1979) Euripides' Cyclopean symposium, *Phoenix* 33, 287–92.

Harris, J. P. (2009) Revenge of the Nerds: Xenophanes, Euripides and Socrates *vs* Olympic Victors, *AJPh* 130, 157–94.

Harrison, G. W. M. ed. (2005) *Satyr Drama. Tragedy at Play*. Swansea.

Harrison, T. (1990) *The Trackers of Oxyrhynchus. The Delphi Text 1988*. London.

Hedreen, G. (1992) *Silens in Black-figure Vase Painting. Myth and Performance*. Ann Arbor.

Hedreen, G. (1994) Silens, Nymphs and Maenads, *JHS* 114, 47–69.

Hedreen, G. (2007) Myths of Ritual in Athenian Vase-Paintings of Silens, in E. Csapo and M. Miller, eds (2007), 150–95, with pls 43–67.

Henderson, J. (1991a) *The Maculate Muse*, 2nd edn. Oxford.

Henderson, J. (1991b) Women and the Athenian Dramatic Festivals, *TAPhA* 121, 133–47.

Hinz, V. (1998) *Der Kult von Demeter und Kore auf Sizilien und in der Magna Graecia*. Wiesbaden.

Howe, T. P. (1959) The Style of Aeschylus as Satyr-playwright, *G&R* 28, 150–65.

Hunter, R. (2009) *Critical Moments in Classical Literature. Studies in the Ancient View of Literature and its Uses*. Cambridge.

Hunter, V. (1973) *Thucydides. The Artful Reporter*. Toronto.

Irwin, E. (1974) *Colour Terms in Greek Poetry*. Toronto.

Irwin, T. (1995) Plato's Objections to the Sophists, in A. Powell ed., *The Greek World*. London, 568–90.

Isler-Kerényi, C. (2007) Komasts, Mythic, Imaginary, and Ritual, in E. Csapo and M. Miller, eds, 77–95.

Jouan, F. (1991) Personnalité et Costume du Choeur Satyrique, *Dioniso* 61.2, 25–37.

Kaibel, G. (1895) Kratinos' Ὀδυσσεύς und Euripides' Κύκλωψ, *Hermes* 30, 71–88.

Kaimio, M. (1970) *The Greek Chorus within the Light of the Number and Person Used*. Helsinki.

Kaimio, M. *et al.* (2001) Metatheatricality in the Greek Satyr-Play, *Arctos* 35, 35–78.

Kamerbeek, J. C. (1948) On the Conception of ΘΕΟΜΑΧΟΣ in relation with Greek tragedy, *Mnemosyne* 4.1, 271–83.

Katsouris, A. G. (1997) Euripides' *Cyclops* and Homer's *Odyssey*: An Interpretative Comparison, *Prometheus* 13, 1–24.

Katsouris, A. G. (1999) Comedy and Satyr Drama, *Dodone* 28, 181–207.

Katsouris, A. G. (2010) Echoes, Criticism and Parody of Socio-Political Phenomena and Literary Genres of Classical and Post-Classical Athens in Satyr Drama, *Athenaeum* 98, 405–12.

Keuls, E. (1993) *The Reign of the Phallus. Sexual Politics in Ancient Athens*. Berkeley.

Kilmer, M. F. (1993) *Greek Erotica on Attic Red-figure Vases*. London.

Kirk, G. S. (1970) *Myth. Its Meaning and Functions in Ancient and Other Cultures*. Berkeley and Cambridge.

Kirk, G. S. (1974) *The Nature of Greek Myths*. London.

Knox, B. M. W. (1977) The *Medea* of Euripides, *YCS* 25, 193–225.

Kokolakis, M. M. (1981) Homeric Animism, *MPhL* 4, 89–113.

Konstan, D. (1990) An Anthropology of Euripides' *Kyklōps*, in J. Winkler and F. Zeitlin, eds (1990), 207–27.

Kovacs, D. (1994a) *Euripides I*. Loeb Classical Library, Cambridge MA and London.

Kovacs, D. (1994b) *Euripidea*. Leiden.

KPS= Krumeich, R., Pechstein, N. and Seidensticker, B. (1999) *Das griechische Satyrspiel*. Darmstadt.

Lämmle, R. (2007) Der eingeschlossene Dritte: zur Funktion des Dionysos im Satyrspiel, in Bierl, Wesselmann, eds, *Literatur und Religion. Wege zu einer mythisch-rituellen Poetik bei den Griechen*. Berlin and New York, 325–86.

Lasserre, F. (1973) Le drame satyrique, *RFIC* 101, 273–301.

Lesky, A. (1966) *History of Greek Literature*, 2nd edn. (tr. J. Willis and C. de Heer), London.

Lissarrague, F. (1990a) Why Satyrs are good to represent, in J. Winkler and F. Zeitlin, eds (1990), 228–36.

Lissarrague, F. (1990b) The Sexual Life of Satyrs, in D. Halperin, J. Winkler and F. Zeitlin, eds (1990), 53–81.

Lissarrague, F. (1993) On the Wildness of Satyrs, in T. Carpenter and C. Faraone, eds, *Masks of Dionysus*. Ithaca and London, 207–220.

Lloyd, M. (1992) *The Agon in Euripides*. Oxford.

Lloyd, M. (1999) The Tragic Aorist, *CQ* 49, 24–45.

Lloyd-Jones, H. (1957) *Appendix*, in H. Weir Smyth, *Aeschylus II*. Loeb Classical Library, Cambridge MA and London, 523–603.

Lloyd-Jones, H. (1982) *Blood for the Ghosts. Classical Influences in the Nineteenth and Twentieth Centuries*. London.

Lloyd-Jones, H. (1990) *Academic Papers. Greek Epic, Tragedy, Lyric*. Oxford.

Lloyd-Jones, H. (1996) *Sophocles. Fragments = Sophocles III*. Loeb Classical Library, Cambridge MA and London.

López-Eire, A. (2003) Tragedy and satyr-play: linguistic criteria, in A. H. L. Sommerstein, ed. (2003), 387–412.

Luraghi, N. (1994) *Tirannidi Arcaiche in Sicilia e Magna Grecia*. Florence.

Maitland, J. (2007) Ion of Chios, Sophocles and Myth, in V. Jennings and A. Katsaros, eds, 266–81.

Mancini, A. (1899) Per la critica del *Ciclope* Euripideo, *RSA* 4, 3–16.

March, J. (1990) Euripides the Misogynist, in A. Powell, ed., *Euripides, Women and Sexuality*. London, 32–75.

Mancini, A. (1899) Per la critica del *Ciclope* Euripideo, *RSA* 4, 3–16.

di Marco, M. (1980) Una Parodia di Saffo in Euripide (*Cycl*. 182–6), *QUCC* 34, 39–45.

di Marco, M. (1991) Il dramma satiresco di Eschilo, *Dioniso* 61.2, 39–61.

di Marco, M. (2003) L'ambiguo statuto del dramma satiresco, in G. Arrighetti and M. Tulli, eds, *Letteratura e riflessione sulla letteratura nella cultura classica*. Pisa, 31–49.

di Marco, M. (2007) Il riso nel dramma satiresco, *Dioniso* 6 (n.s.), 168–79.

Marshall, C. (1999–2000) *Alcestis* and the Problem of Prosatyric Drama, *CJ* 95, 229–38.

Marshall, C. (2005) The Sophisticated *Cyclops*, in G. W. M. Harrison, ed., 103–17.

Mastronarde, D. ed. (1994) *Euripides. Phoenissae*. Cambridge.

Maxwell-Stuart, P. (1973) The Dramatic Poets and the Expedition to Sicily, *Historia* 22, 397–404.

Miller, S. (2004) *Ancient Greek Athletics*. New Haven and London.

Mitchell, A. G. (2009) *Greek Vase Painting and the Origins of Visual Humour*. Cambridge.

Montiglio, S. (2011) *From Villain to Hero. Odysseus in Ancient Thought*. Ann Arbor.

Morgan, K. ed. (2003) *Popular Tyranny. Sovereignty and its Discontents in Ancient Greece*. Austin.

Morris, S. (1992) *Daidalos and the Origins of Greek Art*. Princeton.

Napolitano, M. (2003) *Euripide. Il Ciclope*. Venice.

Nieto, P. (2000) Back in the Cave of the Cyclops, *AJPh* 121, 345–66.

Nietzsche, F. (1872/1956) *The Birth of Tragedy and the Genealogy of Morals*, tr. F. Golffing (1956), New York.

North, H. (1966) *Sophrosyne: Self-Knowledge and Self-Restraint in Greek Literature*. Ithaca, NY.

Oakley, J. H. and Sinos, R. H. (1993) *The Wedding in Ancient Athens*. Madison, Wis.

OKell, E. (2003) The 'Effeminacy' of the Clever Speaker and the 'Impotency' Jokes of *Ichneutae*, in A. H. L. Sommerstein, ed., 283–307.

Olson, S. D. (1988) Dionysos and the Pirates in Euripides' *Cyclops*, *Hermes* 116, 502–4.

Osborne, R. (1998) *Archaic and Classical Greek Art*. Oxford.

O'Sullivan, N. (1992) *Alcidamas, Aristophanes and the Beginnings of Greek Stylistic Theory*. Stuttgart.

O'Sullivan, P. (2000) Satyr and Image in Aeschylus' *Theoroi*, *CQ* 50, 353–66.

O'Sullivan, P. (2005) Of Sophists, Tyrants and Polyphemus: the Nature of the Beast in Euripides' *Cyclops*, in G. W. M. Harrison, ed., 119–59.

O'Sullivan, P. (2008) Aeschylus, Euripides and Tragic Painting: Two Scenes from *Agamemnon* and *Hecuba*, *AJPh* 129, 173–198.

O'Sullivan, P. (2012a) Dionysos, Polyphemos and the Idea of Sicily in Euripides' *Cyclops*, in D. Rosenbloom and J. Davidson, eds, *Greek Drama IV*. Oxford, 169–89.

O'Sullivan, P. (2012b) Sophistic Ethics, Old Atheism and 'Critias' on Religion, *CW* 105.2, 167–185.

O'Sullivan, P. and Wong, A. (2012) Odysseus the Athenian: Antisthenes, Thucydides and a Homeric Hero in an Intellectual Age, in *ASCS 33 [2012] Proceedings*: (ed. E. Anagnostou-Laoutides), 15pp. http://www.ascs.org.au/news/ascs33/O'SULLIVAN%20AND%20WONG.pdf

O'Sullivan, P. (forthcoming) *Cyclops*, in R. Mitchell-Boyask, ed. *The Blackwell Companion to Euripides*, Malden, MA & Oxford.

Paduano, G. (2005) *Euripide: Il Ciclope. Introduzione, traduzione e note*. Milan.

Paganelli, L. (1979) *Echi Storicho-Politici nel 'Ciclope' Euripideo*. Padua.

Paganelli, L. (1981a) *Euripidis Cyclopem cum apparatu critico edidit Leonardo Paganelli*. Bologna.

Paganelli, L. (1981b) Polifemo, Sileno e le Cariti (Eur. *Cycl.* 578–584), *Emerita* 49, 139–43.

Paganelli, L. (1989) Il dramma satiresco. Spazio, tematiche e messo in scena, *Dioniso* 59.2, 213–82.

Page, D. L. (1942) *Select Papyri III. Literary Papyri: Poetry*. Loeb Classical Library, Cambridge MA and London.

Page, D. L. (1955) *Sappho and Alcaeus. An Introduction to the Study of Ancient Lesbian Poetry*. Oxford.

Paley, F. A. (1857–1880) *Euripides*. 3 vols. London.

Parke, H. W. (1977) *Festivals of the Athenians*. London.

Parker, L. P. E. (2007) *Euripides. Alcestis*. Oxford.

Parry, A. M. (1981) *Logos and Ergon in Thucydides*. New York.

Parry, M. (1930) Studies in the Epic Technique of Oral Verse-Making. I. Homer and Homeric Style, *HSCPh* 41, 73–147.

Pearson, A. C. (1917) *The Fragments of Sophocles,* 3 vols. Cambridge.

Pechstein, N. (1998) *Euripides Satyrographos*. Stuttgart.

Pickard-Cambridge, A. W. (1962) *Dithyramb, Tragedy and Comedy* (2nd edn rev. T. B. L. Webster). Oxford.

Pickard-Cambridge, A. W. (1988) *The Dramatic Festivals of Athens* (3rd edn rev. J. Gould and D. M. Lewis). Oxford.

Plotnick, J. (1979) Horace on Satyr Drama, *CW* 72, 329–35.

Podlecki, A. (2005) Aiskhylos Satyrikos, in G. W. M. Harrison, ed., 1–19.

Pollitt, J. J. (1972) *Art and Experience in Classical Greece*. Cambridge.

Pritchard, D. (2012) Athletics in Satyric Drama, *G&R* 59, 1–16.

Raaflaub, K. (2003) Stick and Glue: The Function of Tyranny in Fifth-Century Athenian Democracy, in K. L. Morgan, ed., 59–93.

Radermaker, A. M. (2005) *Sôphrosynê: Polysemy, Prototypicality and Persuasive Use of an Ancient Greek Value Term*. Leiden.

Redondo, J. (2003) Satyric diction in the extant Sophoclean fragments, in A. H. L. Sommerstein, ed. (2003), 412–31.

Richardson, N. J. (1981) The Contest of Homer and Hesiod and Alcidamas' *Mouseion, CQ* 31, 1–10.

Rosenbloom, D. (2012) Athenian Drama and Democratic Political Culture, in D. Rosenbloom and J. Davidson, eds, *Greek Drama IV*. Oxford, 270–99.

Rossi, L. E. (1971) Il *Ciclope* di Euripide come κῶμος mancato, *Maia* 23, 10–38.

Rossi, L. E. (1989) Das Attische Satyrspiel, in B. Seidensticker, ed., 222–51.

Rossignol, J. (1854) Sur le rhythme d'un choeur du *Cyclope, RA* 11, 165–70.

Schmid, W. (1896) Kritisches und Exegetisches zu Euripides' Kyklops, *Philologus* 55, 46–61.

Schmidt, V. (1975) Zu Euripides *Kyklops* 120 und 707, *Maia* 27, 193–208.

Seaford, R. (1976) On the Origins of Satyric Drama, *Maia* 28, 209–21.

Seaford, R. (1981) Dionysiac Drama and the Dionysiac Mysteries, *CQ* 31, 252–75.

Seaford, R. (1982) The Date of Euripides' *Cyclops, JHS* 10, 161–72.

Seaford, R. ed. (1984) *Euripides. Cyclops*. Oxford.

Seaford, R. (1991) Il dramma satiresco di Euripide, *Dioniso* 61.2, 75–89.

Seaford, R. (1994) *Reciprocity and Ritual. Homer and Tragedy in the Developing City-State*. Oxford.

Seaford, R. (1996) *Euripides. Bacchae.* Warminster.

Seaford, R. (2003) Tragic Tyranny, in K. L. Morgan, ed., 95–115.

Segal, C. (1992) Divine Justice in the *Odyssey:* Poseidon, Cyclops and Helios, *AJPh* 113, 489–518.

Segal, C. (1997) *Dionysiac Poetics and Euripides' Bacchae* (expanded edn). Princeton.

Seidensticker, B. (1979) Das Satyrspiel, in G. A. Seeck, ed., *Das griechische Drama.* Darmstadt, 204–57.

Seidensticker, B. ed. (1989) *Das Satyrspiel*, Darmstadt.

Seidensticker, B. (2003) The Chorus of Greek Satyrplay, in E. Csapo and M. Miller, eds, 100–21.

Seidensticker, B. (2005) Dithyramb, Comedy, and Satyr Play, in J. Gregory, ed., *A Companion to Greek Tragedy.* Malden, MA and Oxford, 38–54.

Seidensticker, B. (2010) Dance in Satyr Play, in O. P. Taplin and R. Wiles, eds, 213–29.

Shaw, C. A. (2010) Middle Comedy and the 'Satyric' Style, *AJPh* 131, 1–22.

Sheffield, F. (2001) Alcibiades' Speech: A Satyric Drama, *G&R* 48, 193–209.

Shelley, P. B. (1819/1829) The *Cyclops:* A Satyric Drama. Translated from the Greek of Euripides, in A. and W. Galignani, eds, *The Poetical Works of Coleridge, Shelley and Keats. Complete in One Volume.* Paris, 245–53.

Sifakis, G. (1967) *Studies in the History of Hellenistic Drama.* London.

Simmonds, D. M. and Timberlake, R. R. eds (1927) *Euripides. The Cyclops.* Cambridge.

Simon, E. (1982) Satyr-plays on vases in the time of Aeschylus, in D. Kurtz and B. Sparkes, eds, *The Eye of Greece. Studies in the Art of Athens.* Cambridge, 123–48.

Simon, E. (1997) Silenoi, *LIMC* VIII.1, 1108–33.

Slater, N. W. (2005) Nothing to do with Satyrs? *Alcestis* and the Concept of Prosatyric Drama, in G. W. M. Harrison, ed., 83–101.

Slenders, W. (1992) Intentional ambiguity in Aeschylean satyr plays?, *Mnemosyne* 45, 145–58.

Slenders, W. (2005) λέξις ἐρωτική [erotic diction] in Euripides' *Cyclops,* in G. W. M. Harrison, ed., 39–52.

Slenders, W. (2006) The λέξις ἐρωτική in Sophocles' satyr-plays, in A. P. M. H. Lardinois *et al.*, eds, *Land of Dreams. Greek and Latin Studies in honour of A. H. M. Kessels.* Leiden, 133–45.

Smith, D. (2004) Thucydides' Ignorant Athenians and the Drama of the Sicilian Expedition, *SyllClass* 15, 33–70.

Smith, T. J. (2007) The Corpus of Komast Vases. From Identity to Exegesis, in E. Csapo and M. Miller, eds, 48–76.

Snell, B. (1953) Review of *The Oxyrhynchus Papyri, Part 20* by E. Lobel, E. P. Wegener and C. H. Roberts, eds, *Gnomon* 25, 433–40.

Snell, B. (1964) *Scenes from Greek Drama*. Berkeley and Los Angeles (revised edn as *Szenen aus griechischen Dramen*, Berlin, 1971).

Snell, B. (1979) Lekythion, *Hermes* 107, 129–33.

Sommerstein, A. H. ed. (2003) *Shards from Kolonos. Studies in Sophoclean Fragments*. Bari.

Sommerstein, A. H. ed. (2008) *Aeschylus. Fragments = Aeschylus III*. Loeb Classical Library, Cambridge MA and London.

Sommerstein, A. H. (2010) *Aeschylean Tragedy*, 2nd edn, London.

Stanford, W. B. (1939) *Ambiguity in Greek Literature*. Oxford.

Stanford, W. B. ed. (1947) *The Odyssey of Homer*. 2 vols. London.

Stanford, W. B. (1954) *The Ulysses Theme: A Study of the Adaptability of a Traditional Hero*, Oxford.

Steffen, V. (1971) The Satyr Dramas of Euripides, *Eos* 59, 203–26.

Stehle, E. (2002) The Body and its Representations in Aristophanes' *Thesmophoriazousai*: Where does the Costume End?, *AJPh* 123, 369–406.

Stevens, P. T. (1937) Colloquial Expressions in Euripides, *CQ* 31, 182–91.

Stevens, P. T. (1976) *Colloquial Expressions in Euripides*. Wiesbaden.

Stewart, A. S. (1997) *Art, the Body and Desire in Ancient Greece*. Cambridge.

Stinton, T. C. W. (1990) *Collected Papers on Greek Tragedy*. Oxford.

Storey, I. C. (2005) But Comedy has Satyrs Too, in G. W. M. Harrison, ed., 201–18.

Storey, I. C. and Allan, A. (2005) *A Guide to Ancient Greek Drama*. Malden, MA and Oxford.

Sutton, D. F. (1971) The Relation between Tragedies and Fourth Place Plays in Three Instances, *Arethusa* 4, 55–72.

Sutton, D. F. (1973) Supposed Evidence that Euripides' *Orestes* and Sophocles' *Electra* were Prosatyric, *RSC* 21, 117–21.

Sutton, D. F. (1974a) Sophocles' *Dionysiscus*, *Eos* 62, 205–11.

Sutton, D. F. (1974b) Satyr plays and the *Odyssey*, *Arethusa* 7, 161–85.

Sutton, D. F. (1974c) Aeschylus' *Amymone*, *GRBS* 15, 193–202.

Sutton, D. F. (1974d) A Handlist of Satyr Plays, *HSCPh* 78, 107–43.

Sutton, D. F. (1975) Athletics in the Greek Satyr Play, *RSC* 23, 203–9.

Sutton, D. F. (1980) *The Greek Satyr Play*. Meisenheim am Glan.

Sutton, D. F. (1984) Scenes from Greek Satyr Plays Illustrated in Greek Vase-Paintings, *AncW* 9, 119–26.

Sutton, D. F. (1987) *Papyrological Studies in Dionysiac Literature*. Oak Park ILL.

Tanner, R. H. (1915) The Ὀδυσσῆς of Cratinus and *Cyclops* of Euripides, *TAPhA* 46, 173–206.

Taplin, O. P. (1977) *The Stagecraft of Aeschylus*. Oxford.

Taplin, O. P. (1986) Fifth-Century Tragedy and Comedy: A Synkrisis, *JHS* 106, 163–74.

Taplin, O. P. (1993) *Comic Angels. And Other Approaches to Greek Drama through Vase-painting*. Oxford.

Taplin, O. P. (2007) *Pots and Plays. Interactions between Tragedy and Greek Vase Painting of the Fourth Century BC.* Los Angeles.

Taplin, O. P. and Wyles, R. eds (2010) *The Pronomos Vase and its Context.* Oxford.

Thompson, S. (1946) *The Folktale.* New York.

Trendall, A. D. and Webster, T. B. L. (1971) *Illustrations of Greek Drama.* London.

Turner, E. G. (1976) P. Bodmer XXVIII: A Satyr Play on the Confrontation of Heracles and Atlas, *MH* 33, 1–23.

Ussher, R. G. (1971) The *Cyclops* of Euripides, *G&R* 18, 166–79.

Ussher, R. G. (1974) Sophocles' *Ichneutai* as a Satyr Play, *Hermathena* 118, 130–8.

Ussher, R. G. (1977) The Other Aeschylus, *Phoenix* 31, 287–99.

Ussher, R. G. ed. (1978) *Euripides Cyclops. Introduction and Commentary.* Rome.

van Rooy, C. A. (1965) *Studies in Classical Satire and related Literary Theory.* Leiden.

Vernant, J.-P. and Vidal-Naquet, P. (1981) *Myth and Tragedy in Ancient Greece,* tr. J. Lloyd, New York.

Vian, F. (1952) *La Guerre des Géants. Le myth avant l'époque hellénistique.* Paris.

Voelke, P. (2001) *Un Théâtre de la Marge. Aspects figuratifs et configurationnels du drame satyrique dans l'Athènes classique.* Bari.

Wagner, R. (1914) *Richard Wagners Gesammelte Schriften,* 14 vols, ed. J. Kapp. Leipzig.

Walker, R. (1919) *The Ichneutae of Sophocles.* London.

Waltz, F. (1931) Le drame satyrique et le prologue du *Cyclope* d'Euripide, *L'Acropole* 6, 278–95.

Webster, T. B. L. (1967) *Monuments Illustrating Tragedy and Satyr Play. BICS* Supplement 20. London.

Werre-De Haas, M. (1961) *Aeschylus' Dictyulci: An attempt at reconstruction of a satyric drama, Papyrologica Lugduno-Batava.* Vol. 10, Leiden.

West, M. L. (1967) The Contest of Homer and Hesiod, *CQ* 17, 433–50.

West, M. L. (1982) *Greek Metre.* Oxford.

West, M. L. (1992) *Ancient Greek Music.* Oxford.

West, M. L. ed. and tr. (2003) *Homeric Hymns, Homeric Apocrypha, Lives of Homer.* Loeb Classical Library, Cambridge MA and London.

White, D. (1964) Demeter's Sicilian cult as a political instrument, *GRBS* 5, 261–79.

von Wilamowitz-Möllendorf, U. (1926) *Griechische Tragödien übersetzt.* Vol. III, Berlin.

Willi, A. (2008) *Sikelismos. Sprache, Literatur und Gesellschaft im griechischen Sizilien (8.–5. Jh. v. Chr.).* Basel.

Willink, C. W. ed. (1986) *Orestes.* Oxford.

Wilson, P. (2000) *The Athenian Institution of the Khoregia. The Chorus, the City and the Stage.* Cambridge.

Wilson, P. (2009) Tragic Honours and Democracy: Neglected Evidence for the Politics of the Athenian Dionysia, *CQ*, 58, 8–29.

Winkler, J. and Zeitlin, F. eds (1990) *Nothing to do with Dionysos? Athenian Drama in its Social Context*. Princeton.

Wiseman, T. P. (1988) Satyrs in Rome? The background to Horace's *Ars poetica*, *JRS* 78, 1–13.

Worman, N. (2002) Odysseus, Ingestive Rhetoric, and Euripides' *Cyclops*, *Helios* 29, 101–26.

Worman, N. (2008) *Abusive Mouths in Classical Athens*. Cambridge.

Wright, M. (2005) *Euripides' Escape Tragedies. A Study of Helen, Andromeda and Iphigenia among the Taurians*. Oxford.

Wright, M. (2006) *Cyclops* and the Euripidean Tetralogy, *PCPhS* 52, 23–48.

Wright, M. (2010) The Tragedian as Critic. Euripides and Early Greek Poetics. *JHS* 130, 165–84.

Xanthakis-Karamanos, G. (1993) Hellenistic Drama: Developments in Form and Performance, *ΠΛΑΤΩΝ* 45, 117–33.

Xanthakis-Karamanos, G. (1994) The *Daphnis* or *Lityerses* of Sositheus, *AC* 63, 235–50.

Xanthakis-Karamanos, G. (1997) Echoes of Earlier Drama in Sositheus' *Daphnis* and Lycophron's *Menedemus*, *AC* 66, 121–43.

Zagagi, N. (1999) Comic Patterns in Sophocles' *Ichneutae*, in J. Griffin, ed., *Sophocles Revisited. Essays in Honour of Sir Hugh Lloyd-Jones*. Oxford, 177–218.

Zuntz, G. (1963) *The Political Plays of Euripides*. Manchester.

Zuntz, G. (1965) *An Inquiry into the Transmission of the Plays of Euripides*. Cambridge.

COMMON ABBREVIATIONS

The names of Aesch(ylus), Soph(ocles), Eur(ipides) and Ar(istophanes) are often thus abbreviated; the titles of their plays are usually given in full in our play-introductions but often abbreviated in our notes. *Prometheus Bound* is treated as an inauthentic work of Aeschylus and his name is omitted before it.

Budé (1998–2004)	*Euripide (Edition Budé), Tome VIII, 4 parties*, ed. F. Jouan, H. Van Looy (Paris).
Denniston	J. D. Denniston, *The Greek Particles* (rev. K. J. Dover, Oxford, 1954²).
DK	H. Diels, W. Kranz, *Die Fragmente der Vorsokratiker* (Berlin, 1952⁶).
FGrH	*Die Fragmente der griechischen Historiker*, ed. F. Jacoby (Berlin, 1923–58).
IEG	*Iambi et Elegi Graeci*, ed. M. L. West (Oxford, 1989–91²).
LIMC	*Lexicon Iconographicum Mythologiae Classicae*, (1981–99) 9 double-vols, Zurich and Munich.
LSJ	H. G. Liddell and R. Scott, *Greek-English Lexicon* (rev. H. S. Jones, Oxford, 1940⁹, with a Revised Supplement, ed. P. G. W. Glate, 1990).
Nauck	A. Nauck (1889), *Tragicorum Graecorum Fragmenta*. Leipzig, 1889², reprinted with *Supplementum* by B. Snell. Hildesheim, 1964.
PCG	*Poetae Comici Graeci*, ed. R. Kassel, C. Austin (Berlin, 1983–).
PMG	*Poetae Melici Graeci*, ed. D. L. Page (Oxford, 1962).
Smyth	H. Weir Smyth, *Greek Grammar* (revised ed. by G. Messing, Cambridge MA, 1956).
TrGF	*Tragicorum Graecorum Fragmenta*, ed. B. Snell, R. Kannicht, S. L. Radt, 5 vols. (Göttingen, 1971–2004: Vol. 1, 1971¹, 1986²; Vol. 2, 1981; Vol. 3, 1985; Vol. 4, 1977¹, 1999²; Vol. 5, 2004). All vols contain Addenda, some to other vols.

ΚΥΚΛΩΨ

CYCLOPS

NOTE ON THE GREEK TEXT
AND CRITICAL APPARATUS

Text

The survival of *Cyclops* as the only complete satyr play by any poet is a secondary consequence of a remarkable accident. The principal medieval manuscript tradition of Euripides carries ten complete plays, including the almost certainly inauthentic *Rhesus*. A further nine plays, preserved in just one manuscript and its derivatives, descend from a very ancient edition which was arranged by titles alphabetically; it gives us most of those running from *epsilon* to *kappa*, the eight tragedies *Helen, Electra, Heraclidae (Children of Heracles), Heracles, Hiketides (Suppliant Women), Ion, Iphigenia at Aulis, Iphigenia in Tauris* – and the satyric *Cyclops*.

The one ms. of authority is L (see below, under Apparatus), written about 1320. Its master-mind was the accomplished late Byzantine scholar of Greek drama, Demetrius Triclinius. He revised the initial transcript against its now lost exemplar, and twice later made further corrections and conjectures, attempting for the first time since antiquity a metrical analysis and description of the lyrics.

The most important copy of L is P (below), long thought to derive from the same exemplar, since its text is so close and is known to have been written within a few years of L, and very probably in the same place. The great majority of manuscript experts, however, now accept the demonstration by G. Zuntz in 1965 that P was copied from L after Triclinius' first but before its subsequent interventions. P therefore has value only for preserving a few original readings of L where Triclinius later obscured or erased them; and for affording a few 'better' independent readings, whether by deliberate change or simple accident; and a few conjectures by subsequent revisers; in *Cyclops* these are very few indeed: see the Apparatus to lines 69, 181, 510, 514, 604.

A few other copies of L (not of P) survive, made around 1500 in Italy. The most important two are in Paris (below); they contain corrections or independent conjectures of value, about a dozen or so in *Cyclops*, at e.g. 52, 93, 172.

There are also partial texts of the play. Just one papyrus has been found, of the 4th Century AD (below); it has three small, very damaged fragments from twenty-five lines, which show a few differences from L. Lines, part-line or words from the play are found as quotations in other ancient writers: see the Apparatus at 104, 136, 333, 394, 410, 534, 654.

The first printed edition containing *Cyclops* was the famous Aldine *Euripides* of 1503 (below). The currently standard critical edition of Euripides is by J. Diggle (OCT, Vol. 1, 1984), on whose text and apparatus we have based our own in this volume. The most important individual editions equipped with introductory matter and full commentary are by R. Ussher (1978), R. Seaford (1984) and W. Biehl (1986).

Apparatus

The apparatus printed below the text omits many minor details, generally straightforward corrections of orthographic error in the manuscript tradition, and other small and long-accepted editorial corrections. Not all manuscript readings or editors' interventions and conjectures recorded are discussed in the commentary, especially when they are undisputed elements of the 'received text'; they are included simply for information. For a full and up-to-date apparatus see Diggle's edition.

Abbreviations

P. Oxy. =   Oxyrhynchus Papyri Vol. LXVII (2001) 16–18, No. 4545 (4th Century AD), ed. H.-C. Günther. Column i fr. 1 contains line-ends of *Cyclops* 455–71, column ii fr. 3 line-beginnings of 479–81 and fr. 2 line-ends of 484–96, all having a few letters only.

L =   Florence, Biblioteca Laurenziana 32.2 (1300–20 AD).

Tr1, Tr2, Tr3 =   Demetrius Triclinius, corrector of ms L; 1 = his corrections against L's exemplar; 2, 3 = his two subsequent revisions of L, chiefly his own conjectures.

P =   Rome, Vatican Library Palatinus graecus 287 (1320–25 AD), containing *Cyclops* 1–243 and 352–end (244–351 filled a folio now missing). A copy of L made after its corrections by Tr1 but before its revisions by Tr2, Tr3.

P2 =   corrections and conjectures by two later hands in P, of uncertain date.

apogr. Par. =   Paris, Bibliothèque Nationale grec 2817 or 2887 (both about 1500 AD): copies of L made after its revisions by Triclinius, with occasional corrections and (apparently) conjectures.

Aldine =   *Editio Aldina* (the 'Aldine Edition', published by Aldus Manutius, Venice 1503). The editor(s?) made a small number of minor corrections and conjectures.

*   each asterisk indicates a letter erased in a manuscript, and usually then overwritten, the original being now illegible.

< ... > = letter(s) or word(s) added, or lacunae identified, by scribes or editors.

[...] = letter(s), word(s), line(s) deleted by editors.

add(ed), beg(inning(s)), conj(ectured), del(eted), om(itted), punct(uated).

A colon separates details of individual readings or conjectures (letter, word, phrase or clause) in the numbered Greek line(s); a semi-colon separates such information from that relating to another place in the same line(s).

ΚΥΚΛΩΨ

ΣΙΛΗΝΟΣ ᾿Ω Βρόμιε, διὰ σὲ μυρίους ἔχω πόνους
νῦν χὤτ᾽ ἐν ἥβῃ τοὐμὸν εὐσθένει δέμας·
πρῶτον μὲν ἡνίκ᾽ ἐμμανὴς ῞Ηρας ὕπο
Νύμφας ὀρείας ἐκλιπὼν ᾧχου τροφούς·
ἔπειτά γ᾽ ἀμφὶ γηγενῆ μάχην δορὸς   (5)
ἐνδέξιος σῷ ποδὶ παρασπιστὴς βεβὼς
᾿Εγκέλαδον ἰτέαν ἐς μέσην θενὼν δορὶ
ἔκτεινα – φέρ᾽ ἴδω, τοῦτ᾽ ἰδὼν ὄναρ λέγω;
οὐ μὰ Δί᾽, ἐπεὶ καὶ σκῦλ᾽ ἔδειξα Βακχίῳ.
καὶ νῦν ἐκείνων μείζον᾽ ἐξαντλῶ πόνον.   (10)
ἐπεὶ γὰρ ῞Ηρα σοι γένος Τυρσηνικὸν
λῃστῶν ἐπῶρσεν, ὡς ὁδηθείης μακράν,
<ἐγὼ> πυθόμενος σὺν τέκνοισι ναυστολῶ
σέθεν κατὰ ζήτησιν. ἐν πρύμνῃ δ᾽ ἄκρᾳ
αὐτὸς λαβὼν ηὔθυνον ἀμφῆρες δόρυ,   (15)
παῖδες δ᾽ <ἐπ᾽> ἐρετμοῖς ἥμενοι γλαυκὴν ἅλα
ῥοθίοισι λευκαίνοντες ἐζήτουν σ᾽, ἄναξ.
ἤδη δὲ Μαλέας πλησίον πεπλευκότας
ἀπηλιώτης ἄνεμος ἐμπνεύσας δορὶ
ἐξέβαλεν ἡμᾶς τήνδ᾽ ἐς Αἰτναίαν πέτραν,   (20)
ἵν᾽ οἱ μονῶπες ποντίου παῖδες θεοῦ
Κύκλωπες οἰκοῦσ᾽ ἄντρ᾽ ἔρημ᾽ ἀνδροκτόνοι.
τούτων ἑνὸς ληφθέντες ἐσμὲν ἐν δόμοις
δοῦλοι· καλοῦσι δ᾽ αὐτὸν ᾧ λατρεύομεν
Πολύφημον· ἀντὶ δ᾽ εὐίων βακχευμάτων   (25)
ποίμνας Κύκλωπος ἀνοσίου ποιμαίνομεν.

1 ΣΙΛΗΝΟΣ add. Tr1: om. L
5 δ᾽ Heath
6 βεβὼς Kassel: γεγὼς L
13 <ἐγὼ> Tr2: <εὐθὺς> Diggle
15 λαβὼν] βεβὼς Diggle
16 δ᾽ add. Tr1: om. L; <ἐπ᾽> Seidler

CYCLOPS

Characters of the Play

        SILENUS, *father of the satyrs*
        CHORUS, *the satyrs captured by Polyphemus*
        ODYSSEUS
        POLYPHEMUS, *the Cyclops*

Scene: Outside the cave of Polyphemus. Silenus holds a rake and appeals to the absent Dionysus.

SILENUS: O Bromius, because of you I have had countless labours, now and when my body was in the strength of its prime. First, when you were driven mad by Hera, you left and abandoned your nurses the mountain nymphs; then, in the battle against the Earthborn Giants [5], positioned on your right side as shield-bearer, and smiting Enceladus right in the middle of his wicker shield, I killed him ... hang on – let me see, am I just saying what I saw in a dream? No, by Zeus! For I even displayed the spoils to Bacchus.

        But now I am enduring to the full a labour greater than those. [10] For when Hera roused the tribe of Tuscan pirates against you, so that you should be sold a long way off, <I myself> on learning this, set sail with my children, with the aim of finding you. Right on the stern, I myself took and steered the oared ship [15], and my boys sitting at the oars making the grey sea white <with> all their splashy rowing went in search of you, Lord. But then as we were sailing near Malea an easterly gale descending on the ship threw us onto this rock of Etna [20], where the one-eyed children of the sea-god, the Cyclopes who kill men, inhabit their isolated caves. We were caught and are slaves in the house of one of them. They call the master we serve Polyphemus. And instead of Bacchic revels [25] we tend the flocks of a godless Cyclops.

παῖδες μὲν οὖν μοι κλειτύων ἐν ἐσχάτοις
νέμουσι μῆλα νέα νέοι πεφυκότες,
ἐγὼ δὲ πληροῦν πίστρα καὶ σαίρειν στέγας
μένων τέταγμαι τάσδε, τῷδε δυσσεβεῖ (30)
Κύκλωπι δείπνων ἀνοσίων διάκονος.
καὶ νῦν, τὰ προσταχθέντ᾽, ἀναγκαίως ἔχει
σαίρειν σιδηρᾷ τῇδέ μ᾽ ἁρπάγῃ δόμους,
ὡς τόν τ᾽ ἀπόντα δεσπότην Κύκλωπ᾽ ἐμὸν
καθαροῖσιν ἄντροις μῆλά τ᾽ ἐσδεχώμεθα. (35)
ἤδη δὲ παῖδας προσνέμοντας εἰσορῶ
ποίμνας. τί ταῦτα; μῶν κρότος σικινίδων
ὅμοιος ὑμῖν νῦν τε χὤτε Βακχίῳ
κῶμος συνασπίζοντες Ἀλθαίας δόμους
προσῇτ᾽ ἀοιδαῖς βαρβίτων σαυλούμενοι; (40)

ΧΟΡΟΣ	παῖ γενναίων μὲν πατέρων	στροφή

γενναίων δ᾽ ἐκ τοκάδων,
πᾷ δή μοι νίσῃ σκοπέλους;
οὐ τᾷδ᾽ ὑπήνεμος αὔ-
ρα καὶ ποιηρὰ βοτάνα, (45)
δινᾶέν θ᾽ ὕδωρ ποταμῶν
ἐν πίστραις κεῖται πέλας ἄντρων, οὗ σοι βλαχαὶ τεκέων;

ψύττ᾽· οὐ τᾷδ᾽, οὔ; μεσῳδός
οὐ τᾷδε νεμῇ κλειτὺν δροσεράν; (50)
ὠή, ῥίψω πέτρον τάχα σου·
ὕπαγ᾽ ὦ ὕπαγ᾽ ὦ κεράστα
<πρὸς> μηλοβότα στασιωρὸν
Κύκλωπος ἀγροβάτα.

37 σικιννίδων Barnes   39 κῶμος Diggle: κῶμοι L
41 ΧΟΡΟΣ ΣΑΤΥΡΩΝ L; παῖ W. Dindorf: πᾷ δή μοι L
42 δ᾽ L. Dindorf: τ᾽ L   44 αὐλὰ Musgrave
47 πίστροις Boissonade
48 οὗ Casaubon: οὔ Tr1 in erasure: **L
52 ὕπαγ᾽ ὦ ὕπαγ᾽ ὦ apogr. Par.: ὑπάγω ὑπάγω L
53 <πρὸς> Wecklein; στασιωρὲ following Stephanus Wilamowitz
54 ἀγροβάτα Tr2: ἀγροβότα L

My sons, then, on the remotest hill slopes tend the young flocks of sheep, being young themselves, while I, remaining here, am ordered to fill the drinking troughs and sweep out the dwelling as the menial servant of this impious [30] Cyclops and his unholy meals. And now, my orders – I have to sweep out the house with this iron rake, so that I may welcome my absent master, the Cyclops, and his sheep in a clean cave.

A chorus of satyrs begins to enter through a side-entrance, driving sheep before them.

But now I see my boys driving the flocks here [35]. What's this? Are you really thumping away with dance-steps like those when you went to the house of Althaea, as a band of revellers and companions-at-arms of Bacchus, swaggering to the songs of lyres?   [40]

CHORUS:

Strophe
(addressing a ram) O son sprung from noble sires
and noble mothers,
tell me, by what path are you wandering towards the rocks?
Is there not a soft breeze and lush grass here   [45]
and swirling water from rivers
set aside in drinking troughs near the caves
where your bleating young are?

Mesode
Get on! Here! Here, won't you!
Graze on the dewy hill-side here, won't you?   [50]
Hey, I'll soon throw a stone at you!
Get a move on! Get a move on, you ram,
<to> the guardian of the fold that belongs to the Cyclops,
the shepherd who roams the wild.

σπαργῶντας μαστοὺς χάλασον·   ἀντιστροφή
δέξαι θηλὰς πορίσασ'   (56)
οὓς λείπεις ἀρνῶν θαλάμοις.
ποθοῦσί σ' ἀμερόκοι-
τοι βλαχαὶ σμικρῶν τεκέων.
εἰς αὐλὰν πότ' †ἀμφιβαίνεισ†   (60)
ποιηροὺς λιποῦσα νομοὺς
Αἰτναίων εἴσω σκοπελῶν;

οὐ τάδε Βρόμιος, οὐ τάδε χοροὶ   ἐπῳδός
Βάκχαι τε θυρσοφόροι,
οὐ τυμπάνων ἀλαλαγμοί,   (65)
οὐκ οἴνου χλωραὶ σταγόνες   (67)
κρήναις παρ' ὑδροχύτοις·   (66)
οὐδ' ἐν Νύσᾳ μετὰ Νυμ-   (68)
φᾶν ἴακχον ἴακχον ᾠ-
δὰν μέλπω πρὸς τὰν Ἀφροδί-   (70)
ταν, ἃν θηρεύων πετόμαν
Βάκχαις σὺν λευκόποσιν.
ὦ φίλος ὦ φίλε Βακχεῖε,
ποῦ οἰοπολῶν
ξανθὰν χαίταν σείεις;   (75)

ἐγὼ δ' ὁ σὸς πρόπολος
Κύκλωπι θητεύω

---

56 θηλὰς πορίσασ' Broadhead: θηλαῖσι σπορὰς L
57 οὓς Diggle: ἃς L
60 ἀμφιβαλεῖς Tr2: ἄν <σ>φι βάλοις Duchemin: ἀμφιλαφῆ Hartung
63 τάδε ... τάδε Aldine: τᾶδε ... τᾶδε (*i.e.* τᾷδε twice) L
66 after 67 Hermann
68 Νύσᾳ Musgrave: νύσσα P (and probably L: now illegible)
69 Ἴακχον Ἴακχον ᾠδᾷ Kassel (ᾠδαῖς Seaford)
70 πρὸς del. Wecklein
73 ὦ φίλος following Paley del. Seaford
74 ποῦ Wecklein: ποῖ L; οἰοπολῶν Nauck: οἰοπολεῖς L
75 <ποῦ> ξανθὰν Conradt; σείων Tr2
77 Κύκλωπι θητεύω Fritzsche: θητεύω Κύκλωπι L

Antistrophe
Loosen your full udders.   [55]
Receive those of the lambs whom you left in the chambers
and give them your teats.
Your bleating little children, who have slept
all day, are longing for you.
When †are you encircling† to your fold,   [60]
leaving the pastures where you graze
within Etna's rocks?

Epode
There is no Bromius here, no choruses either,
no thyrsus-wielding Bacchants,
no rapturous cries from drums,   [65]
no bright drops of wine
beside the rushing waters of springs.
Nor can I sing with the Nymphs on Nysa
the song "iacchos! iacchos!"
to Aphrodite, whom I pursued, flying along   [70]
with the white-footed Bacchants.
O my friend, O my friend Bacchus,
where are you, wandering, separated from your followers,
are you shaking your golden hair?   [75]

I, your very own servant,
am serf to the Cyclops,

τῷ μονοδέρκτᾳ δοῦλος ἀλαίνων
σὺν τᾷδε τράγου χλαίνᾳ μελέᾳ (80)
σᾶς χωρὶς φιλίας.

Σιλ.   σιγήσατ', ὦ τέκν', ἄντρα δ' ἐς πετρηρεφῆ
ποίμνας ἀθροῖσαι προσπόλους κελεύσατε.

Χο.   χωρεῖτ'· ἀτὰρ δὴ τίνα, πάτερ, σπουδὴν ἔχεις;

Σιλ.   ὁρῶ πρὸς ἀκταῖς ναὸς Ἑλλάδος σκάφος (85)
κώπης τ' ἄνακτας σὺν στρατηλάτῃ τινὶ
στείχοντας ἐς τόδ' ἄντρον· ἀμφὶ δ' αὐχέσιν
τεύχη φέρονται κενά, βορᾶς κεχρημένοι,
κρωσσούς θ' ὑδρηλούς. ὦ ταλαίπωροι ξένοι·
τίνες ποτ' εἰσίν; οὐκ ἴσασι δεσπότην (90)
Πολύφημον οἷός ἐστιν ἄξενόν τε γῆν
τήνδ' ἐμβεβῶτες καὶ Κυκλωπίαν γνάθον
τὴν ἀνδροβρῶτα δυστυχῶς ἀφιγμένοι.
ἀλλ' ἥσυχοι γίγνεσθ', ἵν' ἐκπυθώμεθα
πόθεν πάρεισι Σικελὸν Αἰτναῖον πάγον. (95)

ΟΔΥΣΣΕΥΣ   ξένοι, φράσαιτ' ἂν νᾶμα ποτάμιον πόθεν
δίψης ἄκος λάβοιμεν εἴ τέ τις θέλει
βορὰν ὁδῆσαι ναυτίλοις κεχρημένοις;
<ἔα·>
τί χρῆμα· Βρομίου πόλιν ἔοιγμεν ἐσβαλεῖν·
Σατύρων πρὸς ἄντροις τόνδ' ὅμιλον εἰσορῶ. (100)
χαίρειν προσεῖπα πρῶτα τὸν γεραίτατον.

Σιλ.   χαῖρ', ὦ ξέν', ὅστις δ' εἶ φράσον πάτραν τε σήν.

Οδ.   Ἴθακος Ὀδυσσεύς, γῆς Κεφαλλήνων ἄναξ.

Σιλ.   οἶδ' ἄνδρα, κρόταλον δριμύ, Σισύφου γένος.

Οδ.   ἐκεῖνος αὐτός εἰμι· λοιδόρει δὲ μή. (105)

86 ἄνακτας Tr2: ἄνακτα L
91 τε γῆν Jacobs: στέγην L
93 τὴν apogr. Par., Bothe: τήνδ' L; ἀνδροβρῶτα P2: ἀνδροβῶτα L; question-mark at line-end
F. J. Williams
99 <ἔα·> Wecklein
101 προσεῖπον Fix
104 punct. Kirchhoff; γόνον Scholia on Sophocles, *Ajax* 190
105 αὐτός L. Dindorf: οὗτος L

wandering in exile as a slave to this one-eyed monster,
and wearing this miserable goat-skin cloak,   [80]
separated from your friendship.

SIL: Be silent, my children, and order your attendants to herd the flocks into the rocky caves.

CHO: *(to the attendants)* Go on! But what's making you anxious, father?

SIL: I see a ship – a Greek ship – [85] and mighty oarsmen coming to this cave with someone who I suppose is their leader. Around their necks they carry empty containers – they must be wanting food – and pitchers for water. O unhappy strangers! Whoever are they? They have no idea what our master [90] Polyphemus is like, and that the land they have reached is hostile to strangers and that they have come, by an ill fate, right into the man-eating Cyclopean jaw. But quieten down so that we can learn where they've come from to be here at Sicilian Etna's rocky outcrop.   [95]

Odysseus and his men enter from the side.

ODYSSEUS: Strangers, would you tell us where we could find flowing river water to quench our thirst and if there is someone willing to sell food to sailors in need? <Hey>, what's this? We seem to have invaded the city of Bromius. I see a gathering of satyrs here in front of the cave. [100] I greet firstly the eldest.

SIL: Greetings, stranger, tell me who you are and what your country.

OD: Odysseus of Ithaca, king of the land of the Cephallenians.

SIL: I know the man, a shrill, relentless babbler, of the race of Sisyphus.

OD: I am that very man. No need to rub it in.   [105]

Σιλ.	πόθεν Σικελίαν τήνδε ναυστολῶν πάρει;
Οδ.	ἐξ Ἰλίου γε κἀπὸ Τρωϊκῶν πόνων.
Σιλ.	πῶς; πορθμὸν οὐκ ᾔδησθα πατρῴας χθονός;
Οδ.	ἀνέμων θύελλαι δεῦρό μ’ ἥρπασαν βίᾳ.
Σιλ.	παπαῖ· τὸν αὐτὸν δαίμον’ ἐξαντλεῖς ἐμοί. (110)
Οδ.	ἦ καὶ σὺ δεῦρο πρὸς βίαν ἀπεστάλης;
Σιλ.	λῃστὰς διώκων οἳ Βρόμιον ἀνήρπασαν.
Οδ.	τίς δ’ ἥδε χώρα καὶ τίνες ναίουσί νιν;
Σιλ.	Αἰτναῖος ὄχθος Σικελίας ὑπέρτατος.
Οδ.	τείχη δὲ ποῦ ’στι καὶ πόλεως πυργώματα; (115)
Σιλ.	‘ οὐκ ἔστ’· ἔρημοι πρῶνες ἀνθρώπων, ξένε.
Οδ.	τίνες δ’ ἔχουσι γαῖαν; ἦ θηρῶν γένος;
Σιλ.	Κύκλωπες, ἄντρ’ ἔχοντες, οὐ στέγας δόμων.
Οδ.	τίνος κλύοντες; ἢ δεδήμευται κράτος;
Σιλ.	μονάδες· ἀκούει δ’ οὐδὲν οὐδεὶς οὐδενός. (120)
Οδ.	σπείρουσι δ’ – ἢ τῷ ζῶσι; – Δήμητρος στάχυν;
Σιλ.	γάλακτι καὶ τυροῖσι καὶ μήλων βορᾷ.
Οδ.	Βρομίου δὲ πῶμ’ ἔχουσιν, ἀμπέλου ῥοάς;
Σιλ.	ἥκιστα· τοιγὰρ ἄχορον οἰκοῦσι χθόνα.
Οδ.	φιλόξενοι δὲ χὤσιοι περὶ ξένους; (125)
Σιλ.	γλυκύτατά φασι τὰ κρέα τοὺς ξένους φορεῖν.
Οδ.	τί φής; βορᾷ χαίρουσιν ἀνθρωποκτόνῳ;
Σιλ.	οὐδεὶς μολὼν δεῦρ’ ὅστις οὐ κατεσφάγη.
Οδ.	αὐτὸς δὲ Κύκλωψ ποῦ ’στιν; ἦ δόμων ἔσω;
Σιλ.	φροῦδος, πρὸς Αἴτνῃ θῆρας ἰχνεύων κυσίν. (130)
Οδ.	οἶσθ’ οὖν ὃ δρᾶσον, ὡς ἀπαίρωμεν χθονός;
Σιλ.	οὐκ οἶδ’, Ὀδυσσεῦ; πᾶν δέ σοι δρῷημεν ἄν.
Οδ.	ὄδησον ἡμῖν σῖτον, οὗ σπανίζομεν.
Σιλ.	οὐκ ἔστιν, ὥσπερ εἶπον, ἄλλο πλὴν κρέας.
Οδ.	ἀλλ’ ἡδὺ λιμοῦ καὶ τόδε σχετήριον. (135)
Σιλ.	καὶ τυρὸς ὀπίας ἔστι καὶ βοὸς γάλα.

116 ἔστ’ Schenk: εἴσ’ L
117 ἦ Kirchhoff: ἢ L
120 μονάδες V. Schmidt: νομάδες L
123 ῥοάς Reiske: ῥοαῖς L
129 ἦ Kirchhoff: ἢ L
131 δρᾶσον W. Canter: δράσεις L
136 βοὸς] Διὸς Athenaeus 14.658c

SIL:	Where have you sailed from to be here in Sicily?
OD:	From Ilion and the hardships at Troy.
SIL:	How did you get here? Didn't you know the way back to your fatherland?
OD:	Stormy winds brought me here headlong by force.
SIL:	Oh no! You are indeed suffering the same fate as befell me. [110]
OD:	So were you also driven here by force?
SIL:	Yes, as I was chasing pirates who had abducted Bromius.
OD:	What land is this and who inhabits it?
SIL:	The mound of Etna, the highest in Sicily.
OD:	But where are the city-walls and the fortifications? [115]
SIL:	There are none. The headlands are bereft of men, stranger.
OD:	Who occupies the land? A race of beasts?
SIL:	Cyclopes, who live in caves, not houses.
OD:	Whose subjects are they? Or is power shared among the people?
SIL:	They're loners; nobody is subject at all to anyone else. [120]
OD:	Do they sow Demeter's crop? Or what do they live on?
SIL:	On milk, cheese, and the meat of sheep.
OD:	Do they have the drink of Bromius, the streams of the grape-vine?
SIL:	Absolutely not. For that reason they inhabit a land where there is no dancing.
OD:	Are they kind to strangers and do they honour divine laws regarding strangers? [125]
SIL:	They say that strangers have the sweetest flesh.
OD:	What are you saying? Do they delight in killing and eating men?
SIL:	Nobody who has come here has not been eaten.
OD:	But where is the Cyclops himself? Inside his dwelling?
SIL:	He's gone away towards Etna, tracking down wild beasts with his dogs. [130]
OD:	Do you know, then, what you are to do, so we may get off this land?
SIL:	I don't know, Odysseus. But we'd do anything to help you.
OD:	Just sell us some bread, which we need.
SIL:	There isn't any, as I said, except for some meat.
OD:	Well, that's also a nice way of putting a stop to hunger. [135]
SIL:	And there's cheese curdled with fig juice, and cow's milk, too.

Οδ.	ἐκφέρετε· φῶς γὰρ ἐμπολήμασιν πρέπει.
Σιλ.	σὺ δ' ἀντιδώσεις, εἰπέ μοι, χρυσὸν πόσον;
Οδ.	οὐ χρυσὸν ἀλλὰ πῶμα Διονύσου φέρω.
Σιλ.	ὦ φίλτατ' εἰπών, οὗ σπανίζομεν πάλαι. (140)
Οδ.	καὶ μὴν Μάρων μοι πῶμ' ἔδωκε, παῖς θεοῦ.
Σιλ.	ὃν ἐξέθρεψα ταῖσδ' ἐγώ ποτ' ἀγκάλαις;
Οδ.	ὁ Βακχίου παῖς, ὡς σαφέστερον μάθῃς.
Σιλ.	ἐν σέλμασιν νεώς ἐστιν ἢ φέρεις σύ νιν;
Οδ.	ὅδ' ἀσκὸς ὃς κεύθει νιν, ὡς ὁρᾷς, γέρον. (145)
Σιλ.	οὗτος μὲν οὐδ' ἂν τὴν γνάθον πλήσειέ μου.
<Οδ.	>.
< Σιλ.	>.
Οδ.	ναί· δὶς τόσον πῶμ' ὅσον ἂν ἐξ ἀσκοῦ ῥυῇ.
Σιλ.	καλήν γε κρήνην εἶπας ἡδεῖάν τ' ἐμοί.
Οδ.	βούλῃ σε γεύσω πρῶτον ἄκρατον μέθυ;
Σιλ.	δίκαιον· ἦ γὰρ γεῦμα τὴν ὠνὴν καλεῖ. (150)
Οδ.	καὶ μὴν ἐφέλκω καὶ ποτῆρ' ἀσκοῦ μέτα.
Σιλ.	φέρ' ἐγκάναξον, ὡς ἀναμνησθῶ πιών.
Οδ.	ἰδού. Σιλ. παπαιάξ, ὡς καλὴν ὀσμὴν ἔχει.
Οδ.	εἶδες γὰρ αὐτήν; Σιλ. οὐ μὰ Δί', ἀλλ' ὀσφραίνομαι.
Οδ.	γεῦσαί νυν, ὡς ἂν μὴ λόγῳ 'παινῇς μόνον. (155)
Σιλ.	βαβαί· χορεῦσαι παρακαλεῖ μ' ὁ Βάκχιος.
	ἆ ἆ ἆ.
Οδ.	μῶν τὸν λάρυγγα διεκάναξέ σου καλῶς;
Σιλ.	ὥστ' εἰς ἄκρους γε τοὺς ὄνυχας ἀφίκετο.
Οδ.	πρὸς τῷδε μέντοι καὶ νόμισμα δώσομεν. (160)
Σιλ.	χάλα τὸν ἀσκὸν μόνον· ἔα τὸ χρυσίον.
Οδ.	ἐκφέρετέ νυν τυρεύματ' ἢ μήλων τόκον.
Σιλ.	δράσω τάδ', ὀλίγον φροντίσας γε δεσποτῶν.
	ὡς ἐκπιών γ' ἂν κύλικα μαινοίμην μίαν,
	πάντων Κυκλώπων ἀντιδοὺς βοσκήματα (165)

---

145 ἀσκὸς Radermacher: ἀσκὸς L
146–7 lacuna Nauck, Kirchhoff
147 νᾷ δὶς Blumenthal, Grégoire: †ναί· δὶς τόσον πῶμ'† Duchemin
148 τ' Reiske: γ' L
152 ἐγκάναξον Valckenaer: ἐκπάταξον L
153 ὀσμὴν] χροιὰν Kovacs: φυὴν Willink
164 ἐκπιών Kirchhoff: ἐκπιεῖν L

OD:	Bring them out. Market goods deserve to see daylight.
SIL:	And you, you'll give me in return, tell me, how much gold?
OD:	I carry not gold but the drink of Dionysus.
SIL:	Ah, yours are the dearest words! That's what we've needed for so long. [140]
OD:	And in fact Maron, the god's own son, gave me this drink.
SIL:	The one I myself once reared in these arms of mine?
OD:	Yes, the son of Bacchus, so you may understand more clearly.
SIL:	Is it in the hold of your ship or are you carrying it with you?
OD:	*(producing the wine-skin)* Here is the wine-skin that contains it, as you see, old man. [145]
SIL:	But this wouldn't even give me a mouthful.

<A lacuna of two lines here>

OD:	Yes; < > twice as much drink as flows from the wine-skin.
SIL:	Well, you really are speaking of a beautiful and pleasant spring – just what I like.
OD:	Do you want me to give you a taste of the wine unmixed, first?
SIL:	That's fair. For a taste calls for a sale. [150]
OD:	And look, I've even brought along a drinking cup with the wine-skin.
SIL:	Come on, pour it out and let it gurgle in so I can remember what it means to drink.
OD:	There, done! SIL: O wow! What a beautiful scent it has!
OD:	What? You saw that? SIL: No, by Zeus! But I'm smelling it!
OD:	Now taste, so that you don't just praise it in words alone. [155]
SIL:	O wow!! Bacchus is calling me over to dance! Yes! Yes! Yes!
OD:	Did it really gurgle down your throat beautifully?
SIL:	So that it reached the tips of my toes.
OD:	And what's more, we'll give you some money, too. [160]
SIL:	Just loosen the wine-skin. Let the gold be.
OD:	Now bring out cheeses and a young lamb.
SIL:	I'll do this, and not worry much about masters. I could go mad after drinking – yes, one cup – [165] swapping all the Cyclopes' flocks in

ῥίψας τ' ἐς ἅλμην Λευκάδος πέτρας ἄπο
ἅπαξ μεθυσθεὶς καταβαλών τε τὰς ὀφρῦς.
ὡς ὅς γε πίνων μὴ γέγηθε μαίνεται·
ἵν' ἔστι τουτί τ' ὀρθὸν ἐξανιστάναι
μαστοῦ τε δραγμὸς καί παρεσκευασμένου   (170)
ψαῦσαι χεροῖν λειμῶνος ὀρχηστύς θ' ἅμα
κακῶν τε λῆστις. εἶτ' ἐγὼ <οὐ> κυνήσομαι
τοιόνδε πῶμα, τὴν Κύκλωπος ἀμαθίαν
κλαίειν κελεύων καὶ τὸν ὀφθαλμὸν μέσον;

    <Χο.>   ἄκου', Ὀδυσσεῦ· διαλαλήσωμέν τί σοι.   (175)
    Οδ.   καὶ μὴν φίλοι γε προσφέρεσθε πρὸς φίλον.
    Χο.   ἐλάβετε Τροίαν τὴν Ἑλένην τε χειρίαν;
    Οδ.   καὶ πάντα γ' οἶκον Πριαμιδῶν ἐπέρσαμεν.
    Χο.   οὔκουν, ἐπειδὴ τὴν νεᾶνιν εἵλετε,
           ἅπαντες αὐτὴν διεκροτήσατ' ἐν μέρει,   (180)
           ἐπεί γε πολλοῖς ἥδεται γαμουμένη,
           τὴν προδότιν, ἣ τοὺς θυλάκους τοὺς ποικίλους
           περὶ τοῖν σκελοῖν ἰδοῦσα καὶ τὸν χρύσεον
           κλῳὸν φοροῦντα περὶ μέσον τὸν αὐχένα
           ἐξεπτοήθη, Μενέλεων ἀνθρώπιον   (185)
           λῷστον λιποῦσα; μηδαμοῦ γένος ποτὲ
           φῦναι γυναικῶν ὤφελ', εἰ μὴ 'μοὶ μόνῳ.
    <Σιλ.>   ἰδού· τάδ' ὑμῖν ποιμνίων βοσκήματα,
           ἄναξ Ὀδυσσεῦ, μηκάδων ἀρνῶν τροφαί,
           πηκτοῦ γάλακτός τ' οὐ σπάνια τυρεύματα.   (190)

---

166 ῥίψας Kirchhoff: ῥίψαι L
169 τ' ὀρθὸν Seidler: τοὐρθὸν L
170 παρεσκευασμένον Blaydes
171 ὀρχηστύς W. Canter: ὀρχηστύος L
172 <οὐ> Matthiae (and perhaps apogr. Par.): <οὐ>κ ὠνήσομαι Tyrwhitt
175 <Χο.> Tyrwhitt: om. L
177 and 179 Χο. Tyrwhitt: Σιλ. L
181 ἥδεται P?2: ἥδετε L
187 'μοὶ Bothe: μοι L
188 <Σιλ.> apogr. Par.: om. L; ποιμνίων Scaliger: ποιμένων L

exchange for it, throwing myself from the Leucadian rocks into the salt sea, drunk and relaxing my furrowed brows, just once. Since the one who drinks without enjoying it is mad. *(grabbing his phallus)* With drink it's possible to make *this* stand to attention. You can grab hold of breasts and lay your hands on bush all ready [170], and there's dancing to boot and a forgetting of woes. So shall I <not> kiss such a drink and tell that moron of a Cyclops – and his eye in the middle of his head – to go to hell?

Silenus goes into the cave.

<CHO>: Listen, Odysseus. We'd like to talk something over with you.   [175]
OD: Well, of course, since you come to me as friends to a friend.
CHO: Did you take Troy and Helen captive?
OD: Yes, and we sacked every house belonging to the sons of Priam.
CHO: So, when you had captured the young woman, did you all bang her, taking it in turns, [180] since she enjoys having sex with lots of partners anyway, the traitor. When she saw him sporting all that fancy trouser-equipment round his legs, and his gold necklace all around his neck, she was swept away, leaving behind [185] that excellent little fella, Menelaus. I wish that the race of women had never been created anywhere at all … except for me alone!

Silenus enters from the cave.

SIL: Look, here are the sucklings from the flocks for you, lord Odysseus, the nurslings of the bleating sheep, and abundant cheeses curdled with milk. [190] *(turning to Odysseus and his men)* Off with the lot of you!

φέρεσθε· χωρεῖθ' ὡς τάχιστ' ἄντρων ἄπο,
βότρυος ἐμοὶ πῶμ' ἀντιδόντες εὔίου.

οἴμοι· Κύκλωψ ὅδ' ἔρχεται· τί δράσομεν;

Οδ.   ἀπολώλαμέν τἄρ', ὦ γέρον· ποῖ χρὴ φυγεῖν;
Σιλ.   ἔσω πέτρας τῆσδ', οὗπερ ἂν λάθοιτέ γε.   (195)
Οδ.   δεινὸν τόδ' εἶπας, ἀρκύων μολεῖν ἔσω.
Σιλ.   οὐ δεινόν· εἰσὶ καταφυγαὶ πολλαὶ πέτρας.
Οδ.   οὐ δῆτ'· ἐπεί τἂν μεγάλα γ' ἡ Τροία στένοι,
εἰ φευξόμεσθ' ἕν' ἄνδρα, μυρίον δ' ὄχλον
Φρυγῶν ὑπέστην πολλάκις σὺν ἀσπίδι.   (200)
ἀλλ', εἰ θανεῖν δεῖ, κατθανούμεθ' εὐγενῶς
ἢ ζῶντες αἶνον τὸν πάρος συσσώσομεν.

ΚΥΚΛΩΨ   ἄνεχε πάρεχε· τί τάδε; τίς ἡ ῥᾳθυμία;
τί βακχιάζετ'; οὐχὶ Διόνυσος τάδε,
οὐ κρόταλα χαλκοῦ τυμπάνων τ' ἀράγματα.   (205)
πῶς μοι κατ' ἄντρα νεόγονα βλαστήματα;
ἦ πρός τε μαστοῖς εἰσι χὖπὸ μητέρων
πλευρὰς τρέχουσι, σχοινίνοις τ' ἐν τεύχεσιν
πλήρωμα τυρῶν ἐστιν ἐξημελγμένον;
τί φάτε, τί λέγετε; τάχα τις ὑμῶν τῷ ξύλῳ   (210)
δάκρυα μεθήσει. βλέπετ' ἄνω καὶ μὴ κάτω.
Χο.   ἰδού· πρὸς αὐτὸν τὸν Δί' ἀνακεκύφαμεν
καὶ τἄστρα καὶ τὸν Ὠρίωνα δέρκομαι.
Κυ.   ἄριστόν ἐστιν εὖ παρεσκευασμένον;
Χο.   πάρεστιν· ὁ φάρυγξ εὐτρεπὴς ἔστω μόνον.   (215)

193 continued for Σιλ. L. Dindorf: assigned to Οδ. L; Χο. οἴμοι ... ἔρχεται. Οδ. τί δράσομεν; Hermann, Paganelli
194 τἄρ' Hartung: γὰρ L
202 συσσώσομεν Schenk: εὖ σώσομεν L
203 ΚΥΚΛΩΨ Tyrwhitt: Σιλ. L: Χο. Duchemin: Σιλ. ἄνεχε πάρεχε. Κυ. τί ... ῥᾳθυμία; Biehl: Χο. and Κυ. Paganelli
204 οὐχὶ Διόνυσος Musgrave: οὐ διώνυσος (διόνυσος P) L
207 ἦ Hermann: ἢ L; τε L. Dindorf: γε L
212, 215, 217, 219 Χο. Tyrwhitt: Σιλ. L

	Move away from the cave as quickly as you can and give me a drink of Bacchus' wine in return. Oh no! The Cyclops is coming this way! What are we going to do?
OD:	Then we're done for, old man. Where can we to escape to?
SIL:	Inside the cave here, where you might well escape him. [195]
OD:	This is dangerous, what you say, to go into a trap.
SIL:	No, it's not dangerous. There are many places to hide in the cave.
OD:	No, not in there! Since Troy, I tell you, would groan very loudly if we are going to flee one man, when many times with my shield at the ready [200] I stood against a throng of Trojans beyond counting. But if I must die, I shall die nobly, or I shall live and preserve my good repute of old.

Enter the Cyclops by a side entrance.

CYCLOPS:	Get out of the way! Make way! What's this? What's this idleness? Why are you performing a Bacchic revel? There's no Dionysus here, no castanet of bronze, no rattle of the drums! [205] Tell me: how are my newborn lambs in the cave? Are they at the teat and are they running to their mothers' under-bellies? Has milk been drawn to fill the rush-made baskets for cheese? What have you got to say for yourselves? What do you say? One of you will soon start shedding tears [210] courtesy of my club! Look upwards, not down!
CHO:	See? My head is bent upwards towards Zeus himself, and I can see the stars and Orion.
CY:	Is my meal well prepared?
CHO:	It's here. Only may your gullet be well ready. [215]

Κυ.   ἦ καὶ γάλακτός εἰσι κρατῆρες πλέῳ;
Χο.   ὥστ' ἐκπιεῖν γέ σ', ἢν θέλῃς, ὅλον πίθον.
Κυ.   μήλειον ἢ βόειον ἢ μεμειγμένον;
Χο.   ὃν ἂν θέλῃς σύ; μὴ 'μὲ καταπίῃς μόνον.
Κυ.   ἥκιστ'· ἐπεί μ' ἂν ἐν μέσῃ τῇ γαστέρι   (220)
        πηδῶντες ἀπολέσαιτ' ἂν ὑπὸ τῶν σχημάτων.
        ἔα· τίν' ὄχλον τόνδ' ὁρῶ πρὸς αὐλίοις;
        λῃσταί τινες κατέσχον ἢ κλῶπες χθόνα;
        ὁρῶ γέ τοι τούσδ' ἄρνας ἐξ ἄντρων ἐμῶν
        στρεπταῖς λύγοισι σῶμα συμπεπλεγμένους   (225)
        τεύχη τε τυρῶν συμμιγῆ γέροντά τε
        πληγαῖς μέτωπον φαλακρὸν ἐξῳδηκότα.
Σιλ.   ὤμοι, πυρέσσω συγκεκομμένος τάλας.
Κυ.   ὑπὸ τοῦ; τίς ἐς σὸν κρᾶτ' ἐπύκτευσεν, γέρον;
Σιλ.   ὑπὸ τῶνδε, Κύκλωψ, ὅτι τὰ σ' οὐκ εἴων φέρειν.   (230)
Κυ.   οὐκ ᾖσαν ὄντα θεόν με καὶ θεῶν ἄπο;
Σιλ.   ἔλεγον ἐγὼ τάδ'· οἱ δ' ἐφόρουν τὰ χρήματα,
        καὶ τόν γε τυρὸν οὐκ ἐῶντος ἤσθιον
        τούς τ' ἄρνας ἐξεφοροῦντο· δήσαντες δὲ σὲ
        κλῳῷ τριπήχει, κατὰ τὸν ὀφθαλμὸν μέσον   (235)
        τὰ σπλάγχν' ἔφασκον ἐξαμήσεσθαι βίᾳ,
        μάστιγί τ' εὖ τὸ νῶτον ἀπολέψειν σέθεν,
        κἄπειτα συνδήσαντες ἐς θἀδώλια
        τῆς ναὸς ἐμβαλόντες ἀποδώσειν τινὶ
        πέτρους μοχλεύειν, ἢ 'ς μυλῶνα καταβαλεῖν.   (240)
Κυ.   ἄληθες; οὔκουν κοπίδας ὡς τάχιστ' ἰὼν
        θήξεις μαχαίρας καὶ μέγαν φάκελον ξύλων
        ἐπιθεὶς ἀνάψεις; ὡς σφαγέντες αὐτίκα

216 ἦ Tr1: ἢ L   219 ὧν Kaibel; 'μὲ Matthiae: με L
220 μ' Seidler: γ' L
227 μέτωπον Tyrwhitt: πρόσωπον L
234 ἐξεφοροῦντο Musgrave; σὲ Nauck: σε L
235 κατὰ W. Canter: κᾆτα (*i.e.* κᾆτα) L
236 ἐξαμήσεσθαι Duport: ἐξαμήσασθαι L
237 ἀπολέψειν Ruhnken: ἀποθλίψειν L
239 ναὸς Blaydes: νηὸς L
240 ἢ 'ς μυλῶνα Ruhnken: ἢ πυλῶνα L
243 ὡς apogr. Par.: ὦ (*i.e.* ᾧ) L

CY: And are the bowls full of milk?

CHO: So full that, if you want, you can drink a whole storage jar.

CY: Is it sheep's or cow's milk or mixed?

CHO: Whatever you like. Only please don't gulp me down.

CY: Of course not. Since you would kill me [220] with all your dancing, leaping around in my belly. Hey! What's this mob I see in front of my house? Are they robbers or thieves who have put into shore here? Anyway, I see my lambs here from my cave with their bodies all bound up together with twigs [225], and I see my baskets of cheeses jumbled everywhere, and the old man with his bald head and face all swollen up from a beating.

SIL: Ah me! Wretched me! The pains of my beating are burning me up!

CY: Who did this? Who has been pounding your head, old man?

SIL: These men did it, Cyclops, because I wouldn't allow them to carry off your things.   [230]

CY: Didn't they know that I am a god and am sprung from gods?

SIL: I told them this myself. But they continued to carry off your property and began to eat your cheese, although (I) wouldn't allow it, and to bring your sheep outside. And they boasted that they would bind you with a collar three cubits wide and in full view of that big eye of yours rip out your guts with brute force [235]; then they'd flay your back good and proper with a whip, then tie you all up and throw you onto the benches of their ship and sell you off to someone to heave rocks, or throw you into a mill-house.   [240]

CY: Really? *(to a follower)* Now then, you go and sharpen my cleaver, my knives and pile up a great bundle of fire-wood and set it alight – and

πλήσουσι νηδὺν τὴν ἐμὴν ἀπ' ἄνθρακος
θερμὴν διδόντες δαῖτα τῷ κρεανόμῳ,		(245)
τὰ δ' ἐκ λέβητος ἐφθὰ καὶ τετηκότα.
ὡς ἔκπλεώς γε δαιτός εἰμ' ὀρεσκόου·
ἅλις λεόντων ἐστί μοι θοινωμένῳ
ἐλάφων τε, χρόνιος δ' εἴμ' ἀπ' ἀνθρώπων βορᾶς.

Χο.	τὰ καινά γ' ἐκ τῶν ἠθάδων, ὦ δέσποτα,		(250)
ἥδιον' ἐστίν. οὐ γὰρ οὖν νεωστί γε
ἄλλοι πρὸς ἄντρα σοὺσαφίκοντο ξένοι.

Οδ.	Κύκλωψ, ἄκουσον ἐν μέρει καὶ τῶν ξένων.
ἡμεῖς βορᾶς χρήζοντες ἐμπολὴν λαβεῖν
σῶν ἆσσον ἄντρων ἤλθομεν νεὼς ἄπο.		(255)
τοὺς δ' ἄρνας ἡμῖν οὗτος ἀντ' οἴνου σκύφου
ἀπημπόλα τε κἀδίδου πιεῖν λαβὼν
ἑκὼν ἑκοῦσι, κοὐδὲν ἦν τούτων βίᾳ.
ἀλλ' οὗτος ὑγιὲς οὐδὲν ὧν φησιν λέγει,
ἐπεὶ κατελήφθη σοῦ λάθρᾳ πωλῶν τὰ σά.		(260)

Σιλ.	ἐγώ; κακῶς γ' ἄρ' ἐξόλοι'.	Οδ. εἰ ψεύδομαι.

Σιλ.	μὰ τὸν Ποσειδῶ τὸν τεκόντα σ', ὦ Κύκλωψ,
μὰ τὸν μέγαν Τρίτωνα καὶ τὸν Νηρέα,
μὰ τὴν Καλυψὼ τάς τε Νηρέως κόρας,
μὰ θαἰερὰ κύματ' ἰχθύων τε πᾶν γένος,		(265)
ἀπώμοσ', ὦ κάλλιστον, ὦ Κυκλώπιον,
ὦ δεσποτίσκε, μὴ τὰ σ' ἐξοδᾶν ἐγὼ
ξένοισι χρήματ', ἢ κακῶς οὗτοι κακοὶ
οἱ παῖδες ἀπόλοινθ', οὓς μάλιστ' ἐγὼ φιλῶ.

Χο.	αὐτὸς ἔχ'. ἔγωγε τοῖς ξένοις τὰ χρήματα		(270)
περνάντα σ' εἶδον· εἰ δ' ἐγὼ ψευδῆ λέγω,
ἀπόλοιθ' ὁ πατήρ μου· τοὺς ξένους δὲ μὴ ἀδίκει.

---

245 διδόντες Heath: ἔδοντος L (ἔ- in erasure: Tr?1)
247 εἰμ' ὀρεσκόου Stephanus: ἱμεροσκόου L
251 ἥδιον' Tr1: ἤδιον L; οὖν Reiske: αὖ L
252 σοὺσαφίκοντο Murray: τὰ σ' ἀφίκοντο L
258 τούτων Barnes: τούτω L
260 γ' ἐλήφθη Heath
261 γ' ἄρ' Kirchhoff: γὰρ L
265 θαἰερὰ Franke (τά θ' ἱερὰ Hermann): θ' ἱερὰ L

get a move on, will you? Since, once they're slaughtered, they'll soon fill my belly, giving me the dispenser of meat [245] a hot feast from the coals, and the rest will be boiled and cooked from the cauldron. Since I'm fed up with meat from the mountains: I have had enough of feasting on lions and deer, and I've been too long deprived of eating a man's flesh.

SIL: After one's usual diet, O master, [250] new food really is more pleasant. And recently other strangers haven't been arriving at your cave.

OD: Cyclops, listen also to us strangers in turn. We came from our ship near your cave wanting to make a purchase of food. [255] And this man sold these sheep to us, in return for a cup of wine, and after getting his drink, traded them to us, a voluntary seller to voluntary customers. There was no violence in any of this. But he speaks no truth in anything he says, since he was caught selling your things while your back was turned. [260]

SIL: Me? In that case – may you die a miserable death!

OD: If I'm lying.

SIL: By Poseidon, your own father, O Cyclops, by great Triton and Nereus, by Calypso and the daughters of Nereus, by the holy waves and the entire race of fishes, [265] I swear, O my most handsome little Cyclops, O my darling little master, that I really was not going to sell your things to these strangers. Otherwise may these miserable boys of mine, whom I love so dearly, die a miserable death.

CHO: That's what *you* deserve. I myself saw you selling his property to the strangers. [270] If I'm telling lies, may my father die. *(to the Cyclops)* Don't wrong the strangers.

Κυ.   ψεύδεσθ᾽· ἔγωγε τῷδε τοῦ Ῥαδαμάνθυος
        μᾶλλον πέποιθα καὶ δικαιότερον λέγω.
        θέλω δ᾽ ἐρέσθαι· πόθεν ἐπλεύσατ᾽, ὦ ξένοι;   (275)
        ποδαποί; τίς ὑμᾶς ἐξεπαίδευσεν πόλις;
Οδ.   Ἰθακήσιοι μὲν τὸ γένος, Ἰλίου δ᾽ ἄπο,
        πέρσαντες ἄστυ, πνεύμασιν θαλασσίοις
        σὴν γαῖαν ἐξωσθέντες ἥκομεν, Κύκλωψ.
Κυ.   ἦ τῆς κακίστης οἳ μετήλθεθ᾽ ἁρπαγὰς   (280)
        Ἑλένης Σκαμάνδρου γείτον᾽ Ἰλίου πόλιν;
Οδ.   οὗτοι, πόνον τὸν δεινὸν ἐξηντληκότες.
Κυ.   αἰσχρὸν στράτευμά γ᾽, οἵτινες μιᾶς χάριν
        γυναικὸς ἐξεπλεύσατ᾽ ἐς γαῖαν Φρυγῶν.
Οδ.   θεοῦ τὸ πρᾶγμα· μηδέν᾽ αἰτιῶ βροτῶν.   (285)
        ἡμεῖς δέ σ᾽, ὦ θεοῦ ποντίου γενναῖε παῖ,
        ἱκετεύομέν τε καὶ λέγομεν ἐλευθέρως·
        μὴ τλῇς πρὸς ἄντρα σοὺσαφιγμένους φίλους
        κτανεῖν βοράν τε δυσσεβῆ θέσθαι γνάθοις·
        οἳ τὸν σόν, ὦναξ, πατέρ᾽ ἔχειν ναῶν ἕδρας   (290)
        ἐρρυσάμεσθα γῆς ἐν Ἑλλάδος μυχοῖς·
        ἱερᾶς τ᾽ ἄθραυστος Ταινάρου μένει λιμὴν
        Μαλέας τ᾽ ἄκρας κευθμῶνες ἥ τε Σουνίου
        δίας Ἀθάνας σῶς ὑπάργυρος πέτρα
        Γεραίστιοί τε καταφυγαί· τά θ᾽ Ἑλλάδος   (295)
        †δύσφρον᾽ ὀνείδη† Φρυξὶν οὐκ ἐδώκαμεν.
        ὧν καὶ σὺ κοινοῖ· γῆς γὰρ Ἑλλάδος μυχοὺς
        οἰκεῖς ὑπ᾽ Αἴτνῃ, τῇ πυριστάκτῳ πέτρᾳ.
        νόμος δὲ θνητοῖς, εἰ λόγους ἀποστρέφῃ,
        ἱκέτας δέχεσθαι ποντίους ἐφθαρμένους   (300)

273 τῷδε W. Canter: τοῦδε L   274 μᾶλλον Kirchhoff: πολλὰ L
288 σοὺσαφιγμένους Radermacher: σοὺς ἀφιγμένους L
290 ναῶν W. Canter: νεῶν L
292 ἱερᾶς Kassel: ἱερεύς L: ἱερός apogr. Par.; ἄθραυστος Tr1: ἄθαυστος L
293 ἄκρας Seaford: ἄκροι L; ἤ apogr. Par.: οἵ L
295–6 lacuna Hermann
296 δύσφρονά γ᾽ Tr2: δύσφορά γ᾽ apogr. Par.: δύσφορον ὄνειδος Seaford, but as parenthesis
Diggle
297 κοινοῖ Seidler: κοινοῦ L
299 νόμος Musgrave: νόμοις L; εἰ Reiske: εἰς L

CY: *(to the chorus)* You're lying. As far as I'm concerned, I trust this man more than I would Rhadamanthys and I say he is more just, too. *(to Odysseus and his men)* But I want to ask you something. Where have you sailed from, strangers? [275] What country are you from? Which city reared you?

OD: We are Ithacans by birth, and we have come to your land from Troy, having sacked that city, since we were driven off our course by storms at sea, Cyclops.

CY: So are you the ones who went to avenge on the city of Troy, by the banks of Scamander, [280] the abduction of the most vile Helen?

OD: Yes, we are the ones who endured to the full that mighty labour.

CY: A shameful campaign, in that you sailed to the land of the Phrygians for the sake of one woman.

OD: It was the deed of a god. I don't blame any mortal for it. [285] But we, O noble son of the god of the deep, beg you as suppliants and are speaking freely: do not bring yourself to kill friends who have arrived at your cave, and make an unholy meal for your jaws. O lord, we protected your father and the sites of his temples [290] for him to occupy within the folds of Greece. The harbour of sacred Taenarus remains intact, so too the caverns of cape Malea, the rock of Sunium, that belongs to the goddess Athena, is safe with all its silver beneath, and safe are the sheltered places of Geraestus. We did not surrender Greece's cause [295] to Phrygians, †a senseless disgrace†. You also share in these things. For the land in whose folds you live – under Etna the rock that streams with fire – is Greek.

        But, if you turn your back on these arguments, there is a law among mortals, that you should receive those who have been languishing at sea as suppliants, [300] give them hospitality and provide them with

ξένιά τε δοῦναι καὶ πέπλους ἐπαρκέσαι,
οὐκ ἀμφὶ βουπόροισι πηχθέντας μέλη
ὀβελοῖσι νηδὺν καὶ γνάθον πλῆσαι σέθεν.
ἅλις δὲ Πριάμου γαῖ᾽ ἐχήρωσ᾽ Ἑλλάδα
πολλῶν νεκρῶν πιοῦσα δοριπετῆ φόνον   (305)
ἀλόχους τ᾽ ἀνάνδρους γραῦς τ᾽ ἄπαιδας ὤλεσεν
πολιούς τε πατέρας. εἰ δὲ τοὺς λελειμμένους
σὺ συμπυρώσας δαῖτ᾽ ἀναλώσεις πικράν,
ποῖ τρέψεταί τις; ἀλλ᾽ ἐμοὶ πιθοῦ, Κύκλωψ·
πάρες τὸ μάργον σῆς γνάθου, τὸ δ᾽ εὐσεβὲς   (310)
τῆς δυσσεβείας ἀνθελοῦ· πολλοῖσι γὰρ
κέρδη πονηρὰ ζημίαν ἠμείψατο.

Σιλ. παραινέσαι σοι βούλομαι· τῶν γὰρ κρεῶν
μηδὲν λίπῃς τοῦδ᾽· ἢν δὲ τὴν γλῶσσαν δάκῃς,
κομψὸς γενήσῃ καὶ λαλίστατος, Κύκλωψ.   (315)

Κυ. ὁ πλοῦτος, ἀνθρωπίσκε, τοῖς σοφοῖς θεός,
τὰ δ᾽ ἄλλα κόμποι καὶ λόγων εὐμορφίαι.
ἄκρας δ᾽ ἐναλίας αἷς καθίδρυται πατὴρ
χαίρειν κελεύω· τί τάδε προυστήσω λόγῳ;
Ζηνὸς δ᾽ ἐγὼ κεραυνὸν οὐ φρίσσω, ξένε,   (320)
οὐδ᾽ οἶδ᾽ ὅτι Ζεύς ἐστ᾽ ἐμοῦ κρείσσων θεός.
οὔ μοι μέλει τὸ λοιπόν· ὡς δ᾽ οὔ μοι μέλει
ἄκουσον· ὅταν ἄνωθεν ὄμβρον ἐκχέῃ,
ἐν τῇδε πέτρᾳ στέγν᾽ ἔχω σκηνώματα,
καὶ μόσχον ὀπτὸν ἤ τι θήρειον δάκος   (325)
δαινύμενος, εὖ τέγγων τε γαστέρ᾽ ὑπτίαν,
ἐπεκπιὼν γάλακτος ἀμφορέα, πέπλον
κρούω, Διὸς βρονταῖσιν εἰς ἔριν κτυπῶν.

301 πέπλους Blaydes: πέπλοις L
314 δὲ Lenting: τε L
316 τοῖς Tr2: τοῖ L
317 εὐμορφία Nauck
318 αἷς Paley: ἃς L
324 ἔχων Reiske: ἔχω L
325 (and in 324 ἔχω …) καὶ Boissonade: ἢ L
326 εὖ τέγγων τε Reiske: ἐν στέγοντι L
327 πέδον Musgrave: πλέων Kovacs

clothes, not that they should have their limbs pierced on beef-skewers and fill a belly and appetite like yours. The land of Priam has made Greece bereft enough as it is, having drunk many corpses' blood that was shed by the spear, [305] and has destroyed wives left without their husbands and made old women and grey-haired fathers childless. If you are going to put those that are left together into the fire and consume them in a cruel feast, where can one turn? But listen to me, Cyclops. Let go of this mad appetite, and choose what is holy [310] instead of what is unholy. Because wicked gains return punishment for many men.

SIL: I want to give you some advice. Don't leave behind a single morsel of this man's flesh. For if you bite off his tongue, you will become oh-so-smart and the best chatterer around, Cyclops. [315]

CY: Little man, wealth is god for the wise; the rest is all pompous and fine-seeming words. As for the sea-side capes where my father is set up in temples, I bid them 'good riddance'. Why did you put them in the forefront of your speech? But I don't tremble before the thunderbolt of Zeus, stranger, [320] nor am I convinced that Zeus is a mightier god than I am. Zeus isn't going to worry me for the future. As to why he doesn't worry me, hear this: whenever he sends the rain down from above, I have a water-proof shelter in this rock, and, dining on a roasted calf or some beast, [325] I lie on my back and give my belly a good soaking by drinking dry a storage jar of milk, and I bang my clothes, making enough noise to rival Zeus with his thunderings.

ὅταν δὲ βορέας χιόνα Θρήκιος χέῃ,
δοραῖσι θηρῶν σῶμα περιβαλὼν ἐμὸν   (330)
καὶ πῦρ ἀναίθων, χιόνος οὐδέν μοι μέλει.
ἡ γῆ δ' ἀνάγκῃ, κἂν θέλῃ κἂν μὴ θέλῃ,
τίκτουσα ποίαν τἀμὰ πιαίνει βοτά.
ἀγὼ οὔτινι θύω πλὴν ἐμοί, θεοῖσι δ' οὔ,
καί τῇ μεγίστῃ, γαστρὶ τῇδε, δαιμόνων.   (335)
ὡς τοὔμπιεῖν γε καὶ φαγεῖν τοὐφ' ἡμέραν,
Ζεὺς οὗτος ἀνθρώποισι τοῖσι σώφροσιν,
λυπεῖν δὲ μηδὲν αὑτόν. οἳ δὲ τοὺς νόμους
ἔθεντο ποικίλλοντες ἀνθρώπων βίον,
κλαίειν ἄνωγα· τὴν <δ'> ἐμὴν ψυχὴν ἐγὼ   (340)
οὐ παύσομαι δρῶν εὖ, κατεσθίων γε σέ.
ξένια δὲ λήψῃ τοιάδ', ὡς ἄμεμπτος ὦ,
πῦρ καὶ πατρῷον τόνδε χαλκόν, ὃς ζέσας
σὴν σάρκα διαφόρητον ἀμφέξει καλῶς.
ἀλλ' ἕρπετ' εἴσω, τοῦ κατ' αὔλιον θεοῦ   (345)
ἵν' ἀμφὶ βωμὸν στάντες εὐωχῆτέ με.

Οδ.   αἰαῖ, πόνους μὲν Τρωϊκοὺς ὑπεξέδυν
θαλασσίους τε, νῦν δ' ἐς ἀνδρὸς ἀνοσίου
ὠμὴν κατέσχον ἀλίμενόν τε καρδίαν.
ὦ Παλλάς, ὦ δέσποινα Διογενὲς θεά,   (350)
νῦν νῦν ἄρηξον· κρείσσονας γὰρ Ἰλίου
πόνους ἀφῖγμαι κἀπὶ κινδύνου βάθρα.

330 περιβαλὼν Tr1: περιλαβὼν L
333 Plutarch, *Moralia* 435b
336 τοὔμπιεῖν Reiske: τοῦ πιεῖν L; κἀμφαγεῖν Reiske
338 λυπεῖν Tr2: λιπεῖν L
340 <δ'> Barnes
341 γε Hermann: τέ L; σέ Fix: σε L
342 δὲ Fix: τε L; ἄμεμπτος Aldine: ἄμεπτος L
343 χαλκόν Jackson: λέβητά γ' L
344 διαφόρητον Scaliger: δυσφόρητον L: δυσφόρητος Seaford: δυσφάρωτον Barnes, Kovacs
345 τοῦ .... θεοῦ Blaydes: τῷ ... θεῷ (*i.e.* τῷ ... θεῷ) L
346 βωμὸν Stephanus: κῶμον L
349 ὠμὴν Reiske: γνώμην L
352 βάθη Musgrave

Whenever a northern wind from Thrace pours down the snow, I cover my body with the skins of wild beasts, [330] and get a fire blazing, and the snow is no worry for me at all. And the earth perforce, willy-nilly, brings forth grass and fattens my livestock. I don't sacrifice them to anyone except myself – not to the gods at all – but also to my stomach here, the greatest of divinities. [335] Since to drink and eat all you want every day and not cause yourself any grief – this is Zeus for folk who are sensible. Those who have established laws and complicated human life, can go to hell. <While> as for me, I won't stop short of gratifying [340] my desire by eating you. But as for hospitality, you'll have the following, so I'll remain blameless: fire and this ancestral bronze (cauldron), which, while it boils, will hold your chopped flesh nicely. But go inside, so that, standing around the altar of the god [345] within the cave, you may provide me with a feast.

OD: Ah! Ah! I have escaped ordeals at Troy and on the sea, but now have come to shore at a godless man's savage heart – no harbour at all. O Pallas, o mighty goddess born of Zeus, [350] come to help us now, now! For I have come to an ordeal greater than any I faced at Troy and am on the hard edge of danger. And you, Zeus, whose home is amongst the bright seat of the stars, protector of strangers, look upon these

σύ τ', ὦ φαεννὰς ἀστέρων οἰκῶν ἕδρας
Ζεῦ ξένι', ὅρα τάδ'· εἰ γὰρ αὐτὰ μὴ βλέπεις,
ἄλλως νομίζῃ, Ζεῦ, τὸ μηδὲν ὢν θεός.   (355)

Χο.   εὐρείας φάρυγος, ὦ Κύκλωψ,   στρ.
ἀναστόμου τὸ χεῖλος· ὡς ἕτοιμά σοι
ἑφθὰ καὶ ὀπτὰ καὶ ἀνθρακιᾶς ἄπο <θερμὰ>
χναύειν βρύκειν
κρεοκοπεῖν μέλη ξένων
δασυμάλλῳ ἐν αἰγίδι κλινομένῳ.   (360)

μὴ 'μοὶ μὴ προσδίδου·   μεσῳδ.
μόνος μόνῳ γέμιζε πορθμίδος σκάφος.
χαιρέτω μὲν αὖλις ἅδε,
χαιρέτω δὲ θυμάτων
ἀποβώμιος †ἂν ἔχει θυσίαν†   (365)
Κύκλωψ Αἰτναῖος ξενικῶν
κρεῶν κεχαρμένος βορᾷ.

†νηλὴς ὦ τλᾶμον ὅστις δωμάτων†   ἀντ.
ἐφεστίους ἱκτῆρας ἐκθύει δόμων,   (371)
ἑφθά τε δαινύμενος μυσαροῖσί τ' ὀδοῦσιν   (373)
κόπτων βρύκων   (372)
θέρμ' ἀπ' ἀνθράκων κρέα   (374)
<   >.

353 φαεννὰς Kassel: φαεννῶν L
355 ζεῦ Tr1: ?ζεῦς L
358–9 ἄπο <θερμὰ> χναύειν Hermann (ἄπο χναύειν Musgrave): ἀποχναύειν L; βρύκειν
Casaubon: βρύχειν L
360 κλινομένῳ Reiske: καινόμενα (-ό- Tr1: ?-ού- L)
361 'μοὶ Conradt: μοι L
362 γέμιζε Wecklein: κόμιζε L
365 ἂν ἀνάγει Jackson: ἂν παρέχει Wilamowitz; θυσία Hartung
370 δωμάτων del. Murray
371 ἐφεστίους ξενικοὺς ἱκτῆρας L: ξενικοὺς del. Bothe; δόμων] ξένους Kirchhoff
373 before 372 Hermann; μυσαροῖσί τ' Kirchhoff: μυσαροῖσιν (-ιν in erasure) L
372 βρύκων Casaubon: βρύχων L
374 Geg ἀνθρώπων θέρμ' L: ἀνθρώπων del. Hermann; lacuna after κρέα Hermann

things! For if you do not see them, then in vain are you worshipped,
Zeus, when you are nothing as a god. [355]

The Cyclops drives Odysseus and his men into the cave. Silenus follows.

CHO:

Strophe

O Cyclops, open up the mouth of your
wide gullet, since the limbs of your guests
are ready for you,
all boiled and roasted and <hot> from the coals
to munch, gnaw, tear in pieces,
as you lie back in your thick-fleeced goat-skin.   [360]

Mesode

Don't, I tell you, don't offer me any.
Alone, for yourself alone, fill up the hull of your ship.
Let me be rid of this dwelling!
Let me be rid of this
godless †sacrifice† of victims,   [365]
†which† the Cyclops of Etna †conducts†, as he rejoices in
the meat from his guests for food.

Antistrophe

†O cruel one! Pitiless is the one who in his home†   [370]
sacrifices suppliants come to the hearth in his home
and who feasts on them roasted and with polluted teeth,
tearing, gnawing
at their flesh hot from the coals.

<Some editors see a lacuna here>

Οδ. ὦ Ζεῦ, τί λέξω, δείν' ἰδὼν ἄντρων ἔσω (375)
κοὐ πιστά, μύθοις εἰκότ' οὐδ' ἔργοις βροτῶν;
Χο. τί δ' ἔστ', Ὀδυσσεῦ; μῶν τεθοίναται σέθεν
φίλους ἑταίρους ἀνοσιώτατος Κύκλωψ;
Οδ. δισσούς γ' ἀθρήσας κἀπιβαστάσας χεροῖν
οἳ σαρκὸς εἶχον εὐτραφέστατον πάχος. (380)
Χο. πῶς, ὦ ταλαίπωρ', ἦτε πάσχοντες τάδε;
Οδ. ἐπεὶ πετραίαν τήνδ' ἐσήλθομεν στέγην,
ἀνέκαυσε μὲν πῦρ πρῶτον, ὑψηλῆς δρυὸς
κορμοὺς πλατείας ἐσχάρας βαλὼν ἔπι,
τρισσῶν ἀμαξῶν ὡς ἀγώγιμον βάρος, (385)
καὶ χάλκεον λέβητ' ἐπέζεσεν πυρί. (392)
ἔπειτα φύλλων ἐλατίνων χαμαιπετῆ (386)
ἔστρωσεν εὐνὴν πλησίον πυρὸς φλογί.
κρατῆρα δ' ἐξέπλησεν ὡς δεκάμφορον,
μόσχους ἀμέλξας, λευκὸν ἐσχέας γάλα,
σκύφος τε κισσοῦ παρέθετ' εἰς εὖρος τριῶν (390)
πήχεων, βάθος δὲ τεσσάρων ἐφαίνετο, (391)
ὀβελούς τ', ἄκρους μὲν ἐγκεκαυμένους πυρί, (393)
ξεστούς δὲ δρεπάνῳ τἆλλα, παλιούρου κλάδων,
†Αἰτναῖά τε σφαγεῖα πελέκεων γνάθοις†. (395)
ὡς δ' ἦν ἕτοιμα πάντα τῷ θεοστυγεῖ
Ἅιδου μαγείρῳ, φῶτε συμμάρψας δύο
ἔσφαζ' ἑταίρων τῶν ἐμῶν, ῥυθμῷ θ' ἑνὶ
τὸν μὲν λέβητος ἐς κύτος χαλκήλατον

377 τεθοίναται Reiske: γε θοινᾶται L
380 εὐτραφέστατον Scaliger: ἐντρεφέστατον L: εὐτρεφέστατον P
382 στέγην Musgrave: χθόνα L
392 after 385 Paley, after 395 Hartung
387 ἔστρωσεν Pierson: ἔστησεν L
394 τἆλλα Scaliger: γ' ἀλλὰ L; κλάδων Scaliger: κλάδω (*i.e.* κλάδῳ) L and (-ῳ) Athenaeus 14.650a
394–5 lacuna Boissonade, 395–6 Fix
395 del. Diggle
397 Ἅιδου Stephanus: δίδου L
397, 399, 395 σφαγεῖον Αἰτναῖον γε, πελέκεως γνάθοις, 398 ... ῥυθμῷ τινι, 400 Seaford
398 θ' ἑνὶ Wilamowitz: τινι L
399 κύτος Aldine: σκύτος L

Odysseus enters from the cave.

OD: O Zeus, what am I to say, when I've witnessed such terrible things inside the cave [375] – things that are incredible, like stories but not like deeds of mortals?

CHO: What is it, Odysseus? That most godless Cyclops hasn't really feasted on your dear companions, has he?

OD: Yes, he spotted two and weighed them in his hands as they had the fattest, most well-nourished flesh.   [380]

CHO: O wretched man, how could you all go on enduring these things?

OD: When we entered this rocky dwelling, firstly he lit up the fire, throwing onto the wide hearth the trunks of a huge oak tree heavy enough for about three wagon loads, [385] then he put a bronze cauldron to boil on the fire [392]. Then he laid out on the ground a bed of pine tree leaves [386] near the fire's blaze. After milking the cows, he filled a bowl about as big as ten storage jars, pouring white milk into it, and he set next to it a cup of ivy wood about three cubits wide [390] and which looked to be four cubits deep, [391] as well as spits made of branches of thorny wood whose ends had been burnt in fire [393], but the rest smoothed with a sickle †and sacrificial bowls of Etna for the jaws of his axes†. [395] When everything was ready for that butcher from hell, so hateful to the gods, snatching up two men among my companions he cut their throats, and in one movement <*one line lost*> one of them into the bronze hollow of the cauldron. As for the other,

$$< \qquad\qquad\qquad >,$$
τὸν δ' αὖ, τένοντος ἁρπάσας ἄκρου ποδός, 　　　　　(400)
παίων πρὸς ὀξὺν στόνυχα πετραίου λίθου
ἐγκέφαλον ἐξέρρανε· καὶ †καθαρπάσας†
λάβρῳ μαχαίρᾳ σάρκας ἐξῶπτα πυρί,
τὰ δ' ἐς λέβητ' ἐφῆκεν ἕψεσθαι μέλη.
ἐγὼ δ' ὁ τλήμων δάκρυ' ἀπ' ὀφθαλμῶν χέων 　　　(405)
ἐχριμπτόμην Κύκλωπι κἀδιακόνουν·
ἄλλοι δ' ὅπως ὄρνιθες ἐν μυχοῖς πέτρας
πτήξαντες εἶχον, αἷμα δ' οὐκ ἐνῆν χροΐ.
ἐπεὶ δ' ἑταίρων τῶν ἐμῶν πλησθεὶς βορᾶς
ἀνέπεσε, φάρυγος αἰθέρ' ἐξανεὶς βαρύν, 　　　　　(410)
ἐσῆλθέ μοί τι θεῖον· ἐμπλήσας σκύφος
Μάρωνος αὐτῷ τοῦδε προσφέρω πιεῖν,
λέγων τάδ'· Ὦ τοῦ ποντίου θεοῦ Κύκλωψ,
σκέψαι τόδ' οἷον Ἑλλὰς ἀμπέλων ἄπο
θεῖον κομίζει πῶμα, Διονύσου γάνος. 　　　　　　(415)
ὁ δ' ἔκπλεως ὢν τῆς ἀναισχύντου βορᾶς
ἐδέξατ' ἔσπασέν <τ'> ἄμυστιν ἑλκύσας
κἀπήνεσ' ἄρας χεῖρα· Φίλτατε ξένων,
καλὸν τὸ πῶμα δαιτὶ πρὸς καλῇ δίδως.
ἡσθέντα δ' αὐτὸν ὡς ἐπῃσθόμην ἐγώ, 　　　　　(420)
ἄλλην ἔδωκα κύλικα, γιγνώσκων ὅτι
τρώσει νιν οἶνος καὶ δίκην δώσει τάχα.

399–400 lacuna (containing *e.g.* ἔρριψε) Diggle
401 στόνυχα Scaliger: γ' ὄνυχα L
402 διαρπάσας or διαρταμῶν Paley
404 τὰ δ' Heath: τάδ' L
406 κἀδιακόνουν W. Dindorf: καὶ διηκόνουν L
407 ἄλλοι Kirchhoff: ἄλλοι L
410 αἰθέρ' L and Athenaeus 1.23e: ἀέρ' Scaliger; ἐξανεὶς Porson: ἐξιεὶς L: ἐξανιεὶς Athenaeus
412 αὐτῷ τοῦδε L. Dindorf: αὐτοῦ τῷδε (*i.e.* τῷδε) L
413 ὦ παῖ Aldine
416 ἔμπλεως Dobree
417 <τ'> Barnes
419 καλῇ (*i.e.* καλῇ) Tr2: καλὸν L: καλὴ also L (or Tr1)
422 οἶνος following Herwerden Murray: οἶνος L

he seized him by his ankle, [400] dashed him against the sharp edge of a rocky stone and spattered his brains out. And †seizing down† their flesh with a savage blade he roasted them over the fire and threw their limbs into the cauldron to boil. In my misery, pouring forth tears from my eyes, I myself stood nearby [405] and was servant to the Cyclops. But the others like birds kept cowering in the recesses of the cave, and the blood was gone from their faces.

Then after glutting himself on the flesh of my companions, as he slumped back and let a deep belch from his gullet, [410] an idea sent from some god came to me. I filled a cup with Maron's wine here and offered it to him to drink saying this: "O son of the ocean god, Cyclops, see what sort of divine drink this is that Greece provides from the vine, the joy of Dionysus." [415] And he, full up with that most shameful meal, received it <and> drained it, knocking it back in one draught, and praised it, raising his hand: "Dearest of guests, you've given me a splendid drink to follow a splendid meal." When I realised that he was pleased by this [420] I gave him another cup, knowing that the wine would be his ruin, and that he would soon pay his due. Sure enough, he started singing, while I kept pouring out one

καὶ δὴ πρὸς ᾠδὰς εἶρπ'· ἐγὼ δ' ἐπεγχέων
ἄλλην ἐπ' ἄλλῃ σπλάγχν' ἐθέρμαινον ποτῷ.
ᾖδει δὲ παρὰ κλαίουσι συνναύταις ἐμοῖς   (425)
ἄμουσ', ἐπηχεῖ δ' ἄντρον. ἐξελθὼν δ' ἐγὼ
σιγῇ σὲ σῶσαι κἄμ', ἐὰν βούλῃ, θέλω.
ἀλλ' εἴπατ' εἴτε χρῄζετ' εἴτ' οὐ χρῄζετε
φεύγειν ἄμεικτον ἄνδρα καὶ τὰ Βακχίου
ναίειν μέλαθρα Ναΐδων νυμφῶν μέτα.   (430)
ὁ μὲν γὰρ ἔνδον σὸς πατὴρ τάδ' ᾔνεσεν·
ἀλλ' ἀσθενὴς γὰρ κἀποκερδαίνων ποτοῦ
ὥσπερ πρὸς ἰξῷ τῇ κύλικι λελημμένος
πτέρυγας ἀλύει· σὺ δέ – νεανίας γὰρ εἶ –
σώθητι μετ' ἐμοῦ καὶ τὸν ἀρχαῖον φίλον   (435)
Διόνυσον ἀνάλαβ', οὐ Κύκλωπι προσφερῆ.

Χο.   ὦ φίλτατ', εἰ γὰρ τήνδ' ἴδοιμεν ἡμέραν
        Κύκλωπος ἐκφυγόντες ἀνόσιον κάρα.
        ὡς διὰ μακροῦ γε †τὸν σίφωνα τὸν φίλον
        χηρεύομεν τόνδ' οὐκ ἔχομεν καταφαγεῖν†.   (440)

Οδ.   ἄκουε δή νυν ἣν ἔχω τιμωρίαν
        θηρὸς πανούργου σῆς τε δουλείας φυγήν.

Χο.   λέγ', ὡς Ἀσιάδος οὐκ ἂν ἥδιον ψόφον
        κιθάρας κλύοιμεν ἢ Κύκλωπ' ὀλωλότα.

Οδ.   ἐπὶ κῶμον ἕρπειν πρὸς κασιγνήτους θέλει   (445)
        Κύκλωπας ἡσθεὶς τῷδε Βακχίου ποτῷ.

Χο.   ξυνῆκ'· ἔρημον ξυλλαβὼν δρυμοῖσί νιν
        σφάξαι μενοινᾷς ἢ πετρῶν ὦσαι κάτα.

Οδ.   οὐδὲν τοιοῦτον· δόλιος ἡ προθυμία.

---

425 συνναύταις Aldine: σὺν ναύταις L, cf. 705
426 ἐπηχεῖ Barnes: ἐπήχει L
430 Ναΐδων Casaubon: δαναίδων L
436 ἀνάλαβ' οὐ apogr. Par.: ἀναλαβοῦ L
439–40 τὸν φίλον χηρεύομεν (or -ομαι) | σίφωνα τόνδε Diggle: (τὸν φίλον σίφωνα δὴ) | χηρεύομεν τόνδ' οὐκ ἔχοντα καταφυγήν Hermann
440 οὐκ Tr1: * L; καταφυγεῖν apogr. Par.
447 δρυμοῖσί Tyrwhitt: ῥυθμοῖσί L
448 κάτα apogr. Par.: κάτω L
449 ἡ προθυμία Musgrave: ἡ 'πιθυμία L

cup after another and warmed his innards with the drink. So he sings his cacophony next to my fellow sailors who are weeping, [425] while his cave resounds with it. Now I've come out quietly, because I want to save you and me, if you're willing. So tell me if you do or don't want to escape this monstrous man and live in the halls of Bacchus with the Naiad nymphs. [430] For your father inside has approved of it; but he's weak because he's been taking full advantage of the drink, caught in the cup as if in bird lime and is struggling with his wings. But you – since you're still young – be saved with me and resume your old friendship [435] with Dionysus, who's not like the Cyclops.

CHO: O dearest friend, if only we could see that day when we escape the godless presence of the Cyclops! For a long time now †my own siphon has been widowed and I've been unable to eat!†   [440]

OD: Well, hear the revenge I have for that utterly ruthless beast and the escape from your slavery.

CHO: Tell me! Because I would not more gladly hear the sound of the Asian kithara than that the Cyclops had been destroyed.

OD: He wants to go to his brother Cyclopes to a revel, since he is so pleased by this Bacchic drink.   [445]

CHO: I understand. You're raging to grab him when he's by himself in the woods to cut his throat or to push him down a cliff.

OD: No such thing. My purpose is to do this through cunning.

Χο.   πῶς δαί; σοφόν τοί σ' ὄντ' ἀκούομεν πάλαι.   (450)
Οδ.   κώμου μὲν αὐτὸν τοῦδ' ἀπαλλάξαι, λέγων
      ὡς οὐ Κύκλωψι πῶμα χρὴ δοῦναι τόδε,
      μόνον δ' ἔχοντα βίοτον ἡδέως ἄγειν.
      ὅταν δ' ὑπνώσσῃ Βακχίου νικώμενος,
      ἀκρεμὼν ἐλαίας ἔστιν ἐν δόμοισί τις,   (455)
      ὃν φασγάνῳ τῷδ' ἐξαποξύνας ἄκρον
      ἐς πῦρ καθήσω· κᾆθ' ὅταν κεκαυμένον
      ἴδω νιν, ἄρας θερμὸν ἐς μέσην βαλῶ
      Κύκλωπος ὄψιν ὄμμα τ' ἐκτήξω πυρί.
      ναυπηγίαν δ' ὡσεί τις ἁρμόζων ἀνὴρ   (460)
      διπλοῖν χαλινοῖν τρύπανον κωπηλατεῖ,
      οὕτω κυκλώσω δαλὸν ἐν φαεσφόρῳ
      Κύκλωπος ὄψει καὶ συναυανῶ κόρας.
Χο.   ἰοὺ ἰού·
      γέγηθα μαινόμεσθα τοῖς εὑρήμασιν.   (465)
Οδ.   κἄπειτα καὶ σὲ καὶ φίλους γέροντά τε
      νεὼς μελαίνης κοῖλον ἐμβήσας σκάφος
      διπλαῖσι κώπαις τῆσδ' ἀποστελῶ χθονός.
Χο.   ἔστ' οὖν ὅπως ἂν ὡσπερεὶ σπονδῆς θεοῦ
      κἀγὼ λαβοίμην τοῦ τυφλοῦντος ὄμματα   (470)
      δαλοῦ; φόνου γὰρ τοῦδε κοινωνεῖν θέλω.
Οδ.   δεῖ γοῦν· μέγας γὰρ δαλός, οὗ ξυλληπτέον.
Χο.   ὡς κἂν ἁμαξῶν ἑκατὸν ἀραίμην βάρος,
      εἰ τοῦ Κύκλωπος τοῦ κακῶς ὀλουμένου
      ὀφθαλμὸν ὥσπερ σφηκιὰν ἐκθύψομεν.   (475)

---

454 ὑπνώσσῃ Hermann: ὑπνώσῃ (*i.e.* ὑπνώσῃ) L: ὑπνωθῇ Dobree
455–71 and 484–96 very damaged line-ends, and 479–81 line-beginings, P. Oxy. 4545
456 ἐξαποξύνας Tr1: ἀποξύνας L [P. Oxy. defective]
458–9 βαλῶ | ... ὄμμα τ' Pierson: βαλὼν (β]αλων P. Oxy.) | ... ὄμματ' L [P. Oxy.]
461 end τ]ροχηλατει (*i.e.* -εῖ) P. Oxy.
468 ἀποστελῶ Tr?1: ἀποστέλλω L [P. Oxy.]
469 ὥσπερεὶ Reiske: ὥσπερ ἐκ L [P. Oxy.]
471 φόνου L [P. Oxy.]: πόνου Nauck
472 οὗ Reiske: ὃν L
473 ἀραίμην Matthiae: ἀροίμην L
475 ἐκθύψομεν Hertlein: ἐκθρύψομεν L

CHO: How, exactly? For a long time we've been hearing how clever you
        are!   [450]

OD: I intend to keep him from this revel by saying that he shouldn't give
        this drink to the other Cyclopes, but that he should keep it on his own
        and live in pleasure. When he falls asleep, conquered by the Bacchic
        god, there is a beam of olive in his cave, [455] whose point I'll sharpen
        well with this sword and place in the fire. Then, when I see it burning,
        I'll lift it up and thrust it hot into the middle of the Cyclops' eye and
        boil out his sight with the flame. And just as a man fitting the structure
        of a ship [460] drives the borer through back and forth with a couple
        of leather thongs, so I shall twist the fire brand around in the light of
        the Cyclops' eye and scorch out his pupil.

CHO: Wow! Wow! I'm happy, we're crazy about what you've come up
        with.   [465]

OD: And then I shall put you and (your) friends and the old man into the
        spacious hold of my black ship with its double bank of oars and send
        us away from this land.

CHO: Is there then some way I too could take hold of the brand that will blind
        the Cyclops' eye, [470] as if it were a libation to a god? I want to take
        part in this bloodshed.

OD: Yes – you'll have to. For the brand, which you must help take hold of,
        is massive.

CHO: I could carry the weight of a hundred wagons if we are going to smoke
        out – like a nest of wasps [475] – the eye of the damned Cyclops!

Οδ.   σιγᾶτέ νυν· δόλον γὰρ ἐξεπίστασαι·
χὦταν κελεύω, τοῖσιν ἀρχιτέκτοσιν
πείθεσθ᾽. ἐγὼ γὰρ ἄνδρας ἀπολιπὼν φίλους
τοὺς ἔνδον ὄντας οὐ μόνος σωθήσομαι.
καίτοι φύγοιμ᾽ ἂν κἀκβέβηκ᾽ ἄντρου μυχῶν·   (480)
ἀλλ᾽ οὐ δίκαιον ἀπολιπόντ᾽ ἐμοὺς φίλους
ξὺν οἷσπερ ἦλθον δεῦρο σωθῆναι μόνον.

Χο.   ἄγε τίς πρῶτος, τίς δ᾽ ἐπὶ πρώτῳ
ταχθεὶς δαλοῦ κώπην ὀχμάσαι
Κύκλωπος ἔσω βλεφάρων ὤσας   (485)
λαμπρὰν ὄψιν διακναίσει;   (486)

[ᾠδὴ ἔνδοθεν]

σίγα σίγα. καὶ δὴ μεθύων   (488)
ἄχαριν κέλαδον μουσιζόμενος
σκαιὸς ἀπῳδὸς καὶ κλαυσόμενος   (490)
χωρεῖ πετρίνων ἔξω μελάθρων.
φέρε νιν κώμοις παιδεύσωμεν
τὸν ἀπαίδευτον·
πάντως μέλλει τυφλὸς εἶναι.

μάκαρ ὅστις εὐιάζει   στρ. α
βοτρύων φίλαισι πηγαῖς   (496)
ἐπὶ κῶμον ἐκπετασθεὶς

480–2 del. Conradt, following an anonymous scholar: P. Oxy. has the initial letters of 480–1, and almost certainly had (those of) 482–3 also, since remnants of 484–96 follow in a further fragment
481 ἐμοὺς apogr. Par.: ἐμοῦ L: [P. Oxy.]
483–6, 488–94, 495–502, 511–18 assigned to semi-choruses by Tr2, cf. the distribution of 635–41
484 δαλοῦ Stephanus: δαλῶ (*i.e.* δαλῷ) L [P. Oxy.]; ὀχμάσαι Musgrave: ὀχμάσας L [P. Oxy.]
487 ᾠδὴ ἔνδοθεν L: ωιδη ε[P. Oxy.: deleted by most editors
490 κατακλαυσόμενος Hermann: τάχα κλαυσόμενος Fix [P. Oxy.]
491 χωρει (*i.e.* χωρεῖ) πετρ[(-ετρ[insecurely read) P. Oxy.: χωρεῖ γε L
492 νιν L (read uncertainly in P. Oxy.): νυν Diggle
492–4 κωμ[οις] | παιδευσωμεν [τον απαιδευτον] | παντως P. Oxy.
495 μακαρ (*i.e.* μάκαρ) P. Oxy., conj. Hermann: μακάριος L

OD: Now be quiet, all of you; for you know my ruse. When I give the order, obey its architects. I shall not save myself alone and abandon the men who are my friends inside. However, I could flee and I have emerged from the recesses of the cave. [480] But it would not be right for me to abandon my friends with whom I came here and be the only one saved.

CHO: Come on then, who is to be positioned first and who next to first
to hold fast and control the beam of the firebrand, thrusting it
into the Cyclops' eye and boring out his bright sight?   [485]

(singing from within)
Silence! Silence! For now the Cyclops
comes out from his rocky halls drunk,
trying to croon in charmless singing,
clumsy, tone-deaf and about to pay for it with tears.   [490]
Come now, let us educate him with our revels
the ignoramus;
he's certain to be blinded anyway.

Strophe A
Blessed is he who shouts the cry in honour of Dionysus, [495]
with the beloved streams of the grape-vine's cluster,
ready for a revel with sails spread

φίλον ἄνδρ᾿ ὑπαγκαλίζων,
ἐπὶ δεμνίοις τε †ξανθὸν†
χλιδανᾶς ἔχων ἑταίρας   (500)
μυρόχριστος λιπαρὸν βό-
στρυχον, αὐδᾷ δέ· Θύραν τίς οἴξει μοι;

Κυ.   παπαπαῖ· πλέως μὲν οἴνου,   στρ. β
γάνυμαι <δὲ> δαιτὸς ἥβᾳ
σκάφος ὁλκὰς ὣς γεμισθεὶς   (505)
ποτὶ σέλμα γαστρὸς ἄκρας.
ὑπάγει μ᾿ ὁ φόρτος εὔφρων
ἐπὶ κῶμον ἦρος ὥραις
ἐπὶ Κύκλωπας ἀδελφούς.
φέρε μοι, ξεῖνε, φέρ᾿, ἀσκὸν ἔνδος μοι.   (510)

Χο.   καλὸν ὄμμασιν δεδορκὼς   στρ. γ
καλὸς ἐκπερᾷ μελάθρων.
<   > φίλει τίς ἡμᾶς;
λύχνα δ᾿ †ἀμμένει δαῖα σὸν
χρόα χῶς† τέρεινα νύμφα   (515)
δροσερῶν ἔσωθεν ἄντρων.
στεφάνων δ᾿ οὐ μία χροιὰ
περὶ σὸν κρᾶτα τάχ᾿ ἐξομιλήσει.

501 λιπαρὸν Scaliger: λιπαρὸς L
502 τις Aldine
503 παπαπαῖ Hermann: πα πα πᾶ L
504 <δὲ> Tr2; ἥβᾳ following Lobeck (-ῃ) Diggle: ἥβης L
507 φόρτος Seymour: χόρτος L
510 ξεῖνε φέρ᾿ Tr2: φέρε ξέν᾿ P (L illegible)
512 καλὸς Scaliger: καλὸν L; ἐκπερᾷς Heath: ἐκπέρα Scaliger
513 τις Aldine
514 λίχνα Paley; ἀμμένει Tr1 or Tr2, and P: ἀμμέν** L
514–15 λύχνα σ᾿ ἤμμέν᾿ ἀμμένει (ἤμμέν᾿ ἀμμένει L. Dindorf) καὶ | ῥοδόχρως τέρεινα νύμφα
Seaford
515 χῶς (thus L)] κοὐ Paley
517 χροιὰ Barnes: χρόα L

embracing a dear male companion,
and on a couch
having †blonde† of a voluptuous girlfriend,   [500]
his glistening locks anointed with myrrh,
<and> he calls out: "Who will open the door for me?"

The Cyclops enters.

Strophe B

CY: O wow! I'm filled up with wine,
<but> I'm rejoicing with the feast's youthful zest.
Like a cargo ship my hull's loaded   [505]
up to the deck at the top of my belly.
This cheerful cargo leads me out
to the revel in springtime
to my brother Cyclopes.
Come on, come on, stranger, put that wineskin in my hands.
                    [510]

Strophe C

CHO: Giving a beautiful glance from his eyes,
he steps forth from the halls in beauty
<...> "Who loves me?"
Wedding torches †burning wait for your
flesh and like† a tender nymph   [515]
inside dewy caves.
But wreaths of no one colour
will soon be with you around your brow.

116   *Euripides:* Cyclops

Οδ.   Κύκλωψ, ἄκουσον· ὡς ἐγὼ τοῦ Βακχίου
           τούτου τρίβων εἴμ’, ὃν πιεῖν ἔδωκά σοι.   (520)
Κυ.   ὁ Βάκχιος δὲ τίς; θεὸς νομίζεται;
Οδ.   μέγιστος ἀνθρώποισιν ἐς τέρψιν βίου.
Κυ.   ἐρυγγάνω γοῦν αὐτὸν ἡδέως ἐγώ.
Οδ.   τοιόσδ’ ὁ δαίμων· οὐδένα βλάπτει βροτῶν.
Κυ.   θεὸς δ’ ἐν ἀσκῷ πῶς γέγηθ’ οἴκους ἔχων;   (525)
Οδ.   ὅπου τιθῇ τις, ἐνθάδ’ ἐστὶν εὐπετής.
Κυ.   οὐ τοὺς θεοὺς χρὴ σῶμ’ ἔχειν ἐν δέρμασιν.
Οδ.   τί δ’, εἴ σε τέρπει γ’; ἢ τὸ δέρμα σοι πικρόν; ·
Κυ.   μισῶ τὸν ἀσκόν· τὸ δὲ ποτὸν φιλῶ τόδε.
Οδ.   μένων νυν αὐτοῦ πῖνε κεὐθύμει, Κύκλωψ.   (530)
Κυ.   οὐ χρή μ’ ἀδελφοῖς τοῦδε προσδοῦναι ποτοῦ;
Οδ.   ἔχων γὰρ αὐτὸς τιμιώτερος φανῇ.
Κυ.   διδοὺς δὲ τοῖς φίλοισι χρησιμώτερος.
Οδ.   πυγμὰς ὁ κῶμος λοίδορόν τ’ ἔριν φιλεῖ.
Κυ.   μεθύω μέν, ἔμπας δ’ οὔτις ἂν ψαύσειέ μου.   (535)
Οδ.   ὦ τᾶν, πεπωκότ’ ἐν δόμοισι χρὴ μένειν.
Κυ.   ἠλίθιος ὅστις μὴ πιὼν κῶμον φιλεῖ.
Οδ.   ὃς δ’ ἂν μεθυσθείς γ’ ἐν δόμοις μείνῃ σοφός.
Κυ.   τί δρῶμεν, ὦ Σιληνέ; σοὶ μένειν δοκεῖ;
Σιλ.   δοκεῖ· τί γὰρ δεῖ συμποτῶν ἄλλων, Κύκλωψ;   (540)
Οδ.   καὶ μὴν λαχνῶδες γ’ οὖδας ἀνθηρᾶς χλόης.
Σιλ.   καὶ πρός γε θάλπος ἡλίου πίνειν καλόν.
           κλίθητί νύν μοι πλευρὰ θεὶς ἐπὶ χθονός.
Κυ.   ἰδού.
           τί δῆτα τὸν κρατῆρ’ ὄπισθ’ ἐμοῦ τίθης;   (545)
Σιλ.   ὡς μὴ παρών τις καταλάβῃ.   Κυ. πίνειν μὲν οὖν

520 πιεῖν apogr. Par.: πιὼν L
521 punct. mid-verse Nauck: τις θεὸς without punct. Ussher: 521 Οδ. θεὸς νομίζεται | 522 μέγιστος ... βίου Wieseler
525 οἴκους W. Canter: οἴνους L
526 τιθῇ Porson: τιθεῖ L
534 πληγὰς ... θ’ ὕβριν φέρει Athenaeus 1.36d   535 μεθύω μέν Reiske: μεθύωμεν L
541 Οδ. Mancini: Κυ. L; γ’ οὖδας Porson: τοῦδας L; ἀνθηρᾷ χλόῃ Kirchhoff
544 ἰδού add. Tr1: om. L
545 ὄπισθ’ ἐμοῦ Diggle: ὄπισθέ μου L; τίθης Tr2: τιθεῖς L
546 παριών Reiske; καταβάλη (*i.e.* καταβάλῃ) P2: καταλάβη (*i.e.* καταλάβῃ) L

OD: Cyclops, hear me, as I'm an old hand with this Bacchus, whom I gave
        you to drink.   [520]

CY: So who is this Bacchus? Is he acknowledged as a god?

OD: The greatest for men's enjoyment of life.

CY: Anyway, I belch him out with pleasure.

OD: Such is his divinity. He harms no mortal.

CY: But how can a god be happy to have a wineskin as his dwelling?
                                                                         [525]

OD: Wherever anyone puts him, there he goes easily.

CY: It is not fitting for the gods to cover their bodies in wineskins.

OD: Why, if he delights you? Or do you find the skin unpleasant?

CY: I hate the wineskin, but I love this drink here.

OD: Then stay where you are, drink and be merry, Cyclops.   [530]

CY: But shouldn't I give some of the drink to my brothers?

OD: No, because by keeping it yourself you'll appear all the more
        honoured.

CY: But giving it to my friends will make me more useful to them.

OD: A revel usually brings on conflict, insults and fighting.

CY: I may be drunk, but all the same nobody could lay a finger on me.
                                                                         [535]

OD: Listen, fella, a man who's drunk too much should stay at home.

CY: A man's a fool who doesn't drink and love a revel.

OD: No, but one who gets drunk and stays at home is wise.

CY: What should we do, Silenus? Do you think it's a good idea to stay?

SIL: I do; for what need is there of other banqueters, Cyclops?   [540]

OD: And, look, the ground and its flowery grasses are luxuriant.

SIL: And it's a fine thing to drink under the warmth of the sun. Now please
        set yourself down on the ground and lie on your side.

The Cyclops lies down.

CY: There, done! *(to Silenus)* Then why are you putting the wine bowl
        behind me?   [545]

SIL: So that no-one here may take it.

118   *Euripides:* Cyclops

κλέπτων σὺ βούλῃ· κάτθες αὐτὸν ἐς μέσον.
σὺ δ᾽, ὦ ξέν᾽, εἰπὲ τοὔνομ᾽ ὅτι σε χρὴ καλεῖν.
Οδ. Οὖτιν· χάριν δὲ τίνα λαβών σ᾽ ἐπαινέσω;
Κυ. πάντων σ᾽ ἑταίρων ὕστερον θοινάσομαι.   (550)
Οδ. καλόν γε τὸ γέρας τῷ ξένῳ δίδως, Κύκλωψ.
Κυ. οὗτος, τί δρᾷς; τὸν οἶνον ἐκπίνεις λάθρᾳ;
Σιλ. οὔκ, ἀλλ᾽ ἔμ᾽ οὗτος ἔκυσεν ὅτι καλὸν βλέπω.
Κυ. κλαύσῃ, φιλῶν τὸν οἶνον οὐ φιλοῦντα σέ.
Σιλ. οὐ μὰ Δί᾽, ἐπεί μού φησ᾽ ἐρᾶν ὄντος καλοῦ.   (555)
Κυ. ἔγχει, πλέων δὲ τὸν σκύφον δίδου μόνον.
Σιλ. πῶς οὖν κέκραται; φέρε διασκεψώμεθα.
Κυ. ἀπολεῖς· δὸς οὕτως.   Σιλ. οὐ μὰ Δί, οὐ πρὶν ἄν γέ σε
στέφανον ἴδω λαβόντα γεύσωμαί τ᾽ ἔτι.
Κυ. οἰνοχόος ἄδικος.   Σιλ. <οὐ> μὰ Δι᾽, ἀλλ᾽ οἶνος γλυκύς.
(560)
ἀπομακτέον δέ σούστὶν ὡς λήψῃ πιεῖν.
Κυ. ἰδού, καθαρὸν τὸ χεῖλος αἱ τρίχες τέ μου.
Σιλ. θές νυν τὸν ἀγκῶν᾽ εὐρύθμως κᾆτ᾽ ἔκπιε,
ὥσπερ μ᾽ ὁρᾷς πίνοντα χὥσπερ οὐκ ἐμέ.
Κυ. ἆ ἆ, τί δράσεις;   Σιλ. ἡδέως ἡμύστισα.   (565)
Κυ. λάβ᾽, ὦ ξέν᾽, αὐτὸς οἰνοχόος τέ μοι γενοῦ.
Οδ. γιγνώσκεται γοῦν ἄμπελος τἠμῇ χερί.
Κυ. φέρ᾽ ἔγχεόν νυν.   Οδ. ἐγχέω, σίγα μόνον.
Κυ. χαλεπὸν τόδ᾽ εἶπας, ὅστις ἂν πίνῃ πολύν.
Οδ. ἰδού, λαβὼν ἔκπιθι καὶ μηδὲν λίπῃς·   (570)
συνεκθανεῖν δὲ σπῶντα χρὴ τῷ πώματι.

550 ὕστατον Hermann
551 Σιλ. Lenting
553 Σιλ. L (self-correction, or Tr1): Οδ. L
554 σέ Diggle: σε L
555 οὐ Diggle: ναὶ L; φησ᾽ Chrestien: φὴς L
558 οὐ μὰ Δί᾽ Wecklein: ναὶ μὰ Δί᾽ L
560 οἰνοχόος (ᾠνοχόος) W. Canter: ὦ οἰνοχόος L; <οὐ> Hermann: L erased: ναὶ Aldine; οἶνος (ᾦνος) W. Canter: ὦνος (*i.e.* ᾦνος) L
561 ἀπομακτέον Cobet: ἀπομυκτέον L; σούστὶν ὡς Wilamowitz: σοι ὡς L: σοί γ᾽ ὅπως Tr1
564 end οὐκέτι Nauck
566 λάβ᾽ ὦ ... τέ μοι Dobree: λαβὼν ... γέ μου L
571 σπῶντα Casaubon: σιγῶντα L

CY:	You're wanting to steal some and drink it, more like. Put it down in the middle here. And you, stranger, tell me what name I should call you.
OD:	Nobody. And what favour shall I get and be grateful to you for?
CY:	I shall feast on you last after I've eaten all your companions. [550]
OD:	Well, Cyclops, that's a fine present to give to your guest.

Silenus drinks some wine, hoping to escape the Cyclops' notice.

CY:	Hey, you! What are you doing? Are you drinking the wine on the sly?
SIL:	No, but this wine here kissed me because I look beautiful.
CY:	You'll be sorry you love the wine that doesn't love you.
SIL:	No, by Zeus, since it says it's crazy for me because I'm beautiful. [555]
CY:	Pour the wine in and fill the cup, then just give it to me.
SIL:	I wonder how the mixture is. Come now, let me see…
CY:	You'll be my ruin! Give it as it is! SIL: No, by Zeus! Not until I see you wearing a crown and I've had a further taste.
CY:	The wine-pourer does me wrong! SIL: <No>, by Zeus! But the wine is sweet! [560] You have to wipe (your mouth), however, so you can have it to drink.
CY:	See, my lips and moustache and beard are clean.
SIL:	Now support yourself elegantly on one elbow and drink it down, just as you see me drinking – or not, as the case may be (*he drinks a large dose*).
CY:	You there! What are you up to? SIL: Sweetly down in one gulp! [565]
CY:	O stranger, take the wine and you be the wine-pourer for me.
OD:	Well, certainly my hands have some knowledge of the vine.
CY:	Come on, pour it in. OD: I'm pouring it. Just keep quiet.
CY:	That's a difficult thing you've said – for a man who's been drinking a lot.
OD:	There. Now take it and drink it all down and don't leave any. [570] Because when a man's knocking it back he should only be all spent when the drink is.

Κυ.	παπαῖ, σοφόν γε τὸ ξύλον τῆς ἀμπέλου.	
Οδ.	κἂν μὲν σπάσῃς γε δαιτὶ πρὸς πολλῇ πολύν,	
	τέγξας ἄδιψον νηδύν, εἰς ὕπνον βαλεῖ,	
	ἢν δ᾽ ἐλλίπῃς τι, ξηρανεῖ σ᾽ ὁ Βάκχιος.	(575)
Κυ.	ἰοὺ ἰού·	
	ὡς ἐξένευσα μόγις· ἄκρατος ἡ χάρις.	
	ὁ δ᾽ οὐρανός μοι συμμεμειγμένος δοκεῖ	
	τῇ γῇ φέρεσθαι, τοῦ Διός τε τὸν θρόνον	
	λεύσσω τὸ πᾶν τε δαιμόνων ἁγνὸν σέβας.	(580)
	οὐκ ἂν φιλήσαιμ᾽; αἱ Χάριτες πειρῶσί με.	
	ἅλις· Γανυμήδη τόνδ᾽ ἔχων ἀναπαύσομαι	
	κάλλιον ἢ τὰς Χάριτας, ἥδομαι δέ πως	
	τοῖς παιδικοῖσι μᾶλλον ἢ τοῖς θήλεσιν.	
Σιλ.	ἐγὼ γὰρ ὁ Διός εἰμι Γανυμήδης, Κύκλωψ;	(585)
Κυ.	ναὶ μὰ Δί᾽, ὃν ἁρπάζω γ᾽ ἐγὼ ᾽κ τῆς Δαρδάνου.	
Σιλ.	ἀπόλωλα, παῖδες· σχέτλια πείσομαι κακά.	
Κυ.	μέμφῃ τὸν ἐραστὴν κἀντρυφᾷς πεπωκότι;	
Σιλ.	οἴμοι· πικρότατον οἶνον ὄψομαι τάχα.	
Οδ.	ἄγε δή, Διονύσου παῖδες, εὐγενῆ τέκνα,	(590)
	ἔνδον μὲν ἀνήρ· τῷ δ᾽ ὕπνῳ παρειμένος	
	τάχ᾽ ἐξ ἀναιδοῦς φάρυγος ὠθήσει κρέα.	
	δαλὸς δ᾽ ἔσωθεν αὐλίων †ὠθεῖ† καπνὸν	
	παρευτρέπισται, κοὐδὲν ἄλλο πλὴν πυροῦν	
	Κύκλωπος ὄψιν· ἀλλ᾽ ὅπως ἀνὴρ ἔσῃ.	(595)
Χο.	πέτρας τὸ λῆμα κἀδάμαντος ἕξομεν.	
	χώρει δ᾽ ἐς οἴκους πρίν τι τὸν πατέρα παθεῖν	
	ἀπάλαμνον· ὥς σοι τἀνθάδ᾽ ἐστὶν εὐτρεπῆ.	

573 σπάσῃς Dobree: σπάση (*i.e.* σπάσῃ) L   574 βαλεῖ Musgrave: βαλεῖς L
575 ἐλλίπῃς Herwerden: ἐκλίπῃς (*i.e.* ἐκλίπῃς) L
581 end question-mark Wilamowitz
582 punct. after ἅλις Wecklein   583 κάλλιον ἢ Spengel: κάλλιστα νὴ L
586 τῆς Hermann: τοῦ L
588 πεπωκότι Scaliger: πεπωκότα L
589 Σιλ. apogr. Par.: om. L   590 Οδ. Tr1: L illegible
593 καπνὸν <πνέων> or <πνέων> καπνὸν, deleting ὠθεῖ, Diggle
594 κοὐδὲν Kirchhoff: δ᾽ οὐδὲν L
598 ἀπάλαμνον W. Canter: ἀπαλλαγμὸν L

CY:	Oh yes! How clever the wood of the grapevine is.
OD:	And if you drain a lot on top of a big meal, drenching your belly so it's no longer thirsty, the wine will send you to sleep, but if you leave some, Bacchus will make you parched. [575]
CY:	Wow! Wow! *(Takes a long drink)* I only just managed to swim out of that one! This is unmitigated delight! I think I see heaven borne along mingled with the earth. I'm gazing upon the throne of Zeus and the whole august majesty of the gods. [580] *(looking at the satyrs)* The Graces are tempting me. Wouldn't I like to kiss (them)? Enough! I shall get off more splendidly with Ganymede here than with the Graces. And I get a certain greater pleasure from boys than from females anyway.
SIL:	What? Am I Zeus' Ganymede, Cyclops? [585]
CY:	Yes, by Zeus, the one I myself am now seizing from the land of Dardanus.
SIL:	I've had it now, boys! I'm going to suffer something terrible!
CY:	Do you find fault with your lover and are you fastidious about one who's drunk?
SIL:	O woe is me! I'll soon see that the wine is very bitter now.

Polyphemus takes Silenus into the cave.

OD:	Come on now, sons of Dionysus, noble children! [590] The man has gone inside. Soon, relaxed in his sleep, he'll vomit the flesh from his shameless gullet. The brand is ready inside the cave, †it pushes out† smoke, and there's nothing left to do but burn out the Cyclops' eye. So be sure you act like a real man! [595]
CHO:	We shall have a heart of rock and adamant! Now hurry into the house before our father suffers something diabolical, since here things are ready for you.

Οδ.   Ἥφαιστ', ἄναξ Αἰτναῖε, γείτονος κακοῦ
λαμπρὸν πυρώσας ὄμμ' ἀπαλλάχθηθ' ἅπαξ,   (600)
σύ τ', ὦ μελαίνης Νυκτὸς ἐκπαίδευμ', Ὕπνε,
ἄκρατος ἐλθὲ θηρὶ τῷ θεοστυγεῖ,
καὶ μὴ 'πὶ καλλίστοισι Τρωϊκοῖς πόνοις
αὐτόν τε ναύτας τ' ἀπολέσητ' Ὀδυσσέα
ὑπ' ἀνδρὸς ᾧ θεῶν οὐδὲν ἢ βροτῶν μέλει.   (605)
ἢ τὴν τύχην μέν δαίμον' ἡγεῖσθαι χρεών,
τὰ δαιμόνων δὲ τῆς τύχης ἐλάσσονα.

Χο.   λήψεται τὸν τράχηλον
ἐντόνως ὁ καρκίνος
τοῦ ξενοδαιτυμόνος· πυρὶ γὰρ τάχα   (610)
φωσφόρους ὀλεῖ κόρας.
ἤδη δαλὸς ἠνθρακωμένος
κρύπτεται ἐς σποδιάν, δρυὸς ἄσπετον   (615)
ἔρνος. ἀλλ' ἴτω Μάρων, πρασσέτω,
μαινομένου 'ξελέτω βλέφαρον
Κύκλωπος, ὡς πίῃ κακῶς.
κἀγὼ τὸν φιλοκισσοφόρον Βρόμιον   (620)
ποθεινὸν εἰσιδεῖν θέλω,
Κύκλωπος λιπὼν ἐρημίαν·
ἆρ' ἐς τοσόνδ' ἀφίξομαι;

Οδ.   σιγᾶτε πρὸς θεῶν, θῆρες, ἡσυχάζετε,
συνθέντες ἄρθρα στόματος· οὐδὲ πνεῖν ἐῶ. (625)
οὐ σκαρδαμύσσειν οὐδὲ χρέμπτεσθαί τινα,
ὡς μὴ 'ξεγερθῇ τὸ κακόν, ἔστ' ἂν ὄμματος
ὄψις Κύκλωπος ἐξαμιλληθῇ πυρί.
Χο.   σιγῶμεν ἐγκάψαντες αἰθέρα γνάθοις.
Οδ.   ἄγε νυν ὅπως ἅψεσθε τοῦ δαλοῦ χεροῖν   (630)
ἔσω μολόντες· διάπυρος δ' ἐστὶν καλῶς.

604 ναύτας Tr2: ναῦς P (and probably L: now illegible)
610 ξενοδαιτυμόνος Hermann: ξένων δαιτυμόνος L
617 μαινομένου 'ξελέτω Hermann: μαινόμενος ἐξελέτω L
626 χρέμπτεσθαι Tr2: χρίμπτεσθαι L

OD: Hephaestus, lord of Etna, burn out your evil neighbour's bright eye and be rid of him once and for all. [600] And you, O Sleep, nursling of Black Night, come with unmitigated power to this beast, so hateful to the gods. And after his most noble labours at Troy do not destroy Odysseus himself and his men at the hands of a man who cares nothing for either gods or mortals. [605] Otherwise we will have to consider chance a divinity and the gods less than chance.

Odysseus goes into the cave.

CHO: The tongs will tightly
        throttle the neck
        of the guest-eater. For soon through the fire   [610]
        he will lose the pupil that brings him light.
        Already the firebrand is a burning coal
        and is hidden in the ashes, the mighty shoot   [615]
        of the oak tree. But let Maron come, let him do his work,
        let him take out the eye of the raging
        Cyclops, so his drinking may be his undoing.
        And I want to look on Bromius, whom I long for,   [620]
        who loves to wear ivy,
        and to leave the Cyclops' desolate land.
        Shall I come that far?

Odysseus enters from the cave.

OD: For the gods' sake, be quiet, you wild creatures, and keep still! Shut your mouths tight! I forbid anyone even to breathe [625] or blink or clear his throat in case the monster wakes up before the sight of the Cyclops' eye has been forced out by the fire.

CHO: We are silent and gulping our breath down through our mouths.

OD: Come on now, go inside and make sure you grab the brand firmly in your hands. [630] It is smouldering red-hot nicely.

Χο.   οὔκουν σὺ τάξεις οὕστινας πρώτους χρεὼν
    καυτὸν μοχλὸν λαβόντας ἐκκαίειν τὸ φῶς
    Κύκλωπος, ὡς ἂν τῆς τύχης κοινώμεθα;
Ημιχ.   ἡμεῖς μέν ἐσμεν μακροτέρω πρὸ τῶν θυρῶν   (635)
    ἑστῶτες ὠθεῖν ἐς τὸν ὀφθαλμὸν τὸ πῦρ.
Ημιχ.   ἡμεῖς δὲ χωλοί γ᾽ ἀρτίως γεγενήμεθα.
Ημιχ.   ταὐτὸν πεπόνθατ᾽ ἆρ᾽ ἐμοί· τοὺς γὰρ πόδας
    ἑστῶτες ἐσπάσθημεν οὐκ οἶδ᾽ ἐξ ὅτου.
Οδ.   ἑστῶτες ἐσπάσθητε;   Ημιχ. καὶ τά γ᾽ ὄμματα   (640)
    μέστ᾽ ἐστὶν ἡμῖν κόνεος ἢ τέφρας ποθέν.
Οδ.   ἄνδρες πονηροὶ κοὐδὲν οἵδε σύμμαχοι.
Χο.   ὁτιὴ τὸ νῶτον τὴν ῥάχιν τ᾽ οἰκτίρομεν
    καὶ τοὺς ὀδόντας ἐκβαλεῖν οὐ βούλομαι
    τυπτόμενος, αὕτη γίγνεται πονηρία;   (645)
    ἀλλ᾽ οἶδ᾽ ἐπῳδὴν Ὀρφέως ἀγαθὴν πάνυ,
    ὥστ᾽ αὐτόματον τὸν δαλὸν ἐς τὸ κρανίον
    στείχονθ᾽ ὑφάπτειν τὸν μονῶπα παῖδα γῆς.
Οδ.   πάλαι μὲν ἤδη σ᾽ ὄντα τοιοῦτον φύσει,
    νῦν δ᾽ οἶδ᾽ ἄμεινον. τοῖσι δ᾽ οἰκείοις φίλοις   (650)
    χρῆσθαί μ᾽ ἀνάγκη. χειρὶ δ᾽ εἰ μηδὲν σθένεις,
    ἀλλ᾽ οὖν ἐπεγκέλευέ γ᾽, ὡς εὐψυχίαν
    φίλων κελευσμοῖς τοῖσι σοῖς κτησώμεθα.
Χο.   δράσω τάδ᾽· ἐν τῷ Καρὶ κινδυνεύσομεν.
    κελευσμάτων δ᾽ ἕκατι τυφέσθω Κύκλωψ.   (655)

    ἰὼ ἰώ· γενναιότατ᾽ ὠ-
    θεῖτε σπεύδετ᾽, ἐκκαίετε τὰν ὀφρὺν
    θηρὸς τοῦ ξενοδαίτα.

633 καυτὸν following Scaliger (καυστὸν) Hermann: καὶ τὸν L
635–41 divided among two choral voices, and 640 beg. Οδ. (= L), Diggle: among three or four voices, other editors: 635, 637 semi-chorus L, 636 beg. Οδ. L (semi-chorus Musgrave), 638 Χο. before τοὺς L (del. Barnes), 640 mid-point Χο. Tr1 (?also L)
635 μακροτέρω Matthiae: μακρότεροι L: μακρότερον Musgrave: μακροτέραν Cobet
641 μέστ᾽ ἐστὶν Scaliger: μέτεστιν L; ἡμῖν Barnes: ἡμῶν L; κόνεος Musgrave: κόνεως L
642 ἄνδρες Matthiae
647 ὥστ᾽ Blaydes: ὡς L
654 κινδυνευτέον Scholia on Plato, *Laches* 187b

CHO: So won't you station those who are to be at the front end to take hold
           of the burnt pole and scorch out the Cyclops' eye, so that we can share
           in this success?

Chorus members speak severally, either in small groups or individually.

CHO. MEMBER(S) A:
           We're standing too far from the door to push the fire into his eye.
                                                                            [635]

CHO. MEMBER(S) B:
           Just now our legs have gone lame.

CHO. MEMBER(S) C:
           Then the same thing as you've suffered has happened to us. We've
           sprained our feet, just standing here … I don't know how.

OD: You've sprained your foot when you were standing still?

CHO. MEMBER(S):   Yes, and our eyes [640] have become full of dust and ash
           from somewhere.

OD: These are worthless men and nothing as allies!

CHO: Just because I pity my back and my spine and don't want to get beaten
           up and lose my teeth, is this cowardice? [645] Anyway, I know an
           incantation of Orpheus that's absolutely splendid, so that the brand
           will all by itself march up to his head and set the one-eyed son of the
           earth on fire.

OD: For a long time I knew you were like this by nature, but now I know it
           better. I'm going to have to use my close friends for this. [650] But, if
           there's no strength in your arm, then at least urge us on anyway, so we
           may get some courage for our friends through your urgings.

Odysseus goes into the cave.

CHO: We'll do this. We'll get a mercenary to run the risk for us. But may the
           Cyclops be consumed in smoke through our encouragement!   [655]

               O! O! Push it in most nobly,
               Hurry, burn out the eye
               Of the beast who dines on his guests!

τύφετ᾽ ὦ, καίετ᾽ ὦ
τὸν Αἴτνας μηλονόμον. (660)
τόρνευ᾽ ἕλκε, μή σ᾽ ἐξοδυνηθεὶς
δράσῃ τι μάταιον.

Κυ.　ὤμοι, κατηνθρακώμεθ᾽ ὀφθαλμοῦ σέλας.
Χο.　καλός γ᾽ ὁ παιάν· μέλπε μοι τόνδ᾽ αὖ, Κύκλωψ.
Κυ.　ὤμοι μάλ᾽, ὡς ὑβρίσμεθ᾽, ὡς ὀλώλαμεν. (665)
　　　ἀλλ᾽ οὔτι μὴ φύγητε τῆσδ᾽ ἔξω πέτρας
　　　χαίροντες, οὐδὲν ὄντες· ἐν πύλαισι γὰρ
　　　σταθεὶς φάραγγος τῆσδ᾽ ἐναρμόσω χέρας.
Χο.　τί χρῆμ᾽ ἀυτεῖς, ὦ Κύκλωψ; Κυ. ἀπωλόμην.
Χο.　αἰσχρός γε φαίνῃ. Κυ. κἀπὶ τοῖσδέ γ᾽ ἄθλιος. (670)
Χο.　μεθύων κατέπεσες ἐς μέσους τοὺς ἄνθρακας;
Κυ.　Οὖτις μ᾽ ἀπώλεσ᾽. Χο. οὐκ ἄρ᾽ οὐδείς <σ᾽> ἠδίκει.
Κυ.　Οὖτις με τυφλοῖ βλέφαρον. Χο. οὐκ ἄρ᾽ εἶ τυφλός.
Κυ.　πῶς φῂς σύ; Χο. καὶ πῶς σ᾽ οὖτις ἂν θείη τυφλόν;
Κυ.　σκώπτεις. ὁ δ᾽ Οὖτις ποῦ ᾽στιν; Χο. οὐδαμοῦ, Κύκλωψ.
(675)
Κυ.　ὁ ξένος ἵν᾽ ὀρθῶς ἐκμάθῃς μ᾽ ἀπώλεσεν,
　　　ὁ μιαρός, ὅς μοι δοὺς τὸ πῶμα κατέκλυσεν.
<Χο.>　δεινὸς γὰρ οἶνος καὶ παλαίεσθαι βαρύς.
<Κυ.>　πρὸς θεῶν, πεφεύγασ᾽ ἢ μένουσ᾽ ἔσω δόμων;
Χο.　οὗτοι σιωπῇ τὴν πέτραν ἐπήλυγα (680)
　　　λαβόντες ἑστήκασι. Κυ. ποτέρας τῆς χέρος;
Χο.　ἐν δεξίᾳ σου. Κυ. ποῦ; Χο. πρὸς αὐτῇ τῇ πέτρᾳ.
　　　ἔχεις; Κυ. κακόν γε πρὸς κακῷ· τὸ κρανίον
　　　παίσας κατέαγα. Χο. καί σε διαφεύγουσί γε.

659 τύφετ᾽ ὦ, καίετ᾽ ὦ Musgrave: τυφέτω καιέτω L
660 Αἴτνας Victorius: ἔτνας L　　661 μὴ ᾽ξοδυνη- | θεὶς apogr. Par.
664 αὖ Markland: ὦ L
668 τῆσδ᾽ Nauck: τάσδ᾽ L: ταῖσδ᾽ Kirchhoff
672 ἀπώλεσ᾽ Matthiae: ἀπώλεσεν L; <σ᾽> Battier
674 πῶς φῂς σύ Stinton: ὡς δὴ σύ L: ψεύδῃ σύ Diggle; σ᾽ οὖτις W. Canter: σύ· τίς σ᾽ L; W. Dindorf deleted this verse
677 κατέκλυσεν W. Canter: κατέκαυσε L
678 <Χο.> Reiske; οἶνος (ᾦνος) Camper: οἶνος L
679 <Κυ.> Reiske

O consume him in smoke! O burn
the shepherd of Etna!   [660]
Keep on twisting, keep on heaving it round, in case in his agony he
does something outrageous to you.

Polyphemus shouts from within.

CY: Ah! Ah! The light of my eye has been burned to charcoal!
CHO: A beautiful song of triumph! Sing it for me again, Cyclops.

Polyphemus comes to the mouth of the cave.

CY: Ah! Ah! Look how I've been assaulted! How I've been destroyed!
           [665] But you will never escape from this cave without paying, you
           nonentities! Because I'm going to stand in the cleft's opening here and
           block it up with my hands.
CHO: Why are you shouting, Cyclops?   CY: I am destroyed.
CHO: Well, yes, you do look ugly.   CY: And I'm in a pitiful state on top of
           all this.   [670]
CHO: Did you stumble right into the middle of the coals while you were
           drunk?
CY: Nobody has destroyed me.   CHO: So no one has wronged you.
CY: Nobody has blinded my eye.   CHO: So you are not blind.
CY: How do you mean?   CHO: And how could nobody make you
           blind?
CY: You're laughing at me. But Nobody, where is he? CHO: Nowhere,
           Cyclops.   [675]
CY: The stranger destroyed me – so you may understand correctly – that
           bastard, who gave me the drink and drowned me in it.
<CHO>:   Yes, for wine is powerful and hard to wrestle with.
<CY>:   By the gods, have they fled or are they staying in the cave?
CHO: They're standing here in silence occupying   [680]
           an overhanging rock.   CY: On which side of me?
CHO: On your right.   CY: Where?   CHO: Just near the rock itself.
           Have you got them?

The Cyclops hits his head on the rock.

CY: I've got worse on worse! Now that I've bashed my skull
           and I'm broken!   CHO: Yes – and now they're getting away from you.

Κυ.   οὐ τῇδέ πῃ, τῇδ᾽ εἶπας;   Χο. οὔ· ταύτῃ λέγω.   (685)

Κυ.   πῇ γάρ;   Χο. περιάγου κεῖσε, πρὸς τἀριστερά.

Κυ.   οἴμοι γελῶμαι· κερτομεῖτέ μ᾽ ἐν κακοῖς.

Χο.   ἀλλ᾽ οὐκέτ᾽, ἀλλὰ πρόσθεν οὗτός ἐστι σοῦ.

Κυ.   ὦ παγκάκιστε, ποῦ ποτ᾽ εἶ;   Οδ. τηλοῦ σέθεν

           φυλακαῖσι φρουρῶ σῶμ᾽ Ὀδυσσέως τόδε.   (690)

Κυ.   πῶς εἶπας; ὄνομα μεταβαλὼν καινὸν λέγεις.

Οδ.   ὅπερ μ᾽ ὁ φύσας ὠνόμαζ᾽ Ὀδυσσέα.

           δώσειν δ᾽ ἔμελλες ἀνοσίου δαιτὸς δίκας·

           κακῶς γὰρ ἂν Τροίαν γε διεπυρώσαμεν

           εἰ μή σ᾽ ἑταίρων φόνον ἐτιμωρησάμην.   (695)

Κυ.   αἰαῖ· παλαιὸς χρησμὸς ἐκπεραίνεται·

           τυφλὴν γὰρ ὄψιν ἐκ σέθεν σχήσειν μ᾽ ἔφη

           Τροίας ἀφορμηθέντος. ἀλλὰ καὶ σέ τοι

           δίκας ὑφέξειν ἀντὶ τῶνδ᾽ ἐθέσπισεν,

           πολὺν θαλάσσῃ χρόνον ἐναιωρούμενον.   (700)

Οδ.   κλαίειν σ᾽ ἄνωγα· καὶ δέδραχ᾽ ὅπερ λέγω.

           ἐγὼ δ᾽ ἐπ᾽ ἀκτὰς εἶμι, καὶ νεὼς σκάφος

           ἥσω 'πὶ πόντον Σικελὸν ἔς τ᾽ ἐμὴν πάτραν.

Κυ.   οὐ δῆτ᾽, ἐπεί σε τῆσδ᾽ ἀπορρήξας πέτρας

           αὐτοῖσι συνναύταισι συντρίψω βαλών.   (705)

           ἄνω δ᾽ ἐπ᾽ ὄχθον εἶμι, καίπερ ὢν τυφλός,

           δι᾽ ἀμφιτρῆτος τῆσδε προσβαίνων ποδί.

Χο.   ἡμεῖς δὲ συνναῦταί γε τοῦδ᾽ Ὀδυσσέως

           ὄντες τὸ λοιπὸν Βακχίῳ δουλεύσομεν.

---

685 τῇδέ πῃ Blaydes: τῇδ᾽ (*i.e.* τῇδ᾽) ἐπεὶ L

686 περιαγοῦ κεῖσε Nauck: περιάγουσί σε L

688 σοῦ Diggle: σου L

690 σῶμ᾽ W. Canter: δῶμ᾽ L

692 μ᾽ Nauck: γ᾽ L

694 καλῶς Dobree: ἄλλως Cobet; διεπυρώσαμεν Fix: διεπυρωσάμην L

701 λέγεις Paley

703 εἰς, del. τ᾽, Schumacher

704 σε Tr1: γε L

705 συνναύταισι Barnes: σὺν ναύταισι L

707 ποδί] πέτρας Kirchhoff

707–8 lacuna suspected by Diggle

CY:	Didn't you say, here somewhere, here? CHO: No. I said, right here.
	[685]

CY: Where, exactly?   CHO: Turn around that way, to your left.

CY: Ah! I am being laughed at! You're taunting me in my misery.

CHO: But not any more. Anyway, here he is in front of you.

CY: O utterly vile man, wherever are you?   OD: Far away from you,
           I'm keeping the body of Odysseus here in safety.   [690]

CY: What's that you said? You're changing your name and using a new one.

OD: The very one my father called me: Odysseus. You were bound to pay
           the penalty for your unholy feast. For a worthless thing it would have
           been for me to destroy Troy by fire, if I had not avenged the slaughter
           of my companions!   [695]

CY: Ah! Ah! An ancient prophecy is being brought to pass. For it said that I
           would have my sight made blind by you as you were sailing from Troy.
           But don't forget it also foretold that you also would pay the penalty for
           these actions, drifting over the sea for a great length of time.

                                                                      [700]

OD: Go to hell! I have done what I said. But now I am going to go to the
           shore and launch my ship over the Sicilian sea and to my homeland.

Exit Odysseus with his men by a side entrance.

CY: No way! Because I'm going to break off a piece of this rock, throw it
           at you and crush you, your sailors and all! [705] I'm going to climb up
           the hill, even though I'm blind, making my way on foot through this
           tunneled (cave) with its entrance on the other side.

CHO: Well anyway, we're going to be fellow sailors with Odysseus here and
           from now on we'll be the slaves of the Bacchic god!

Exit the chorus following Odysseus and his men.

FINIS

COMMENTARY

The Scene: all the action takes place in front of the cave of Polyphemus in Sicily, under Mount Etna. The door of the skênê *building functions as the mouth of the cave, and the* skênê *itself was probably painted to represent rocks and grass.*

1–40: Prologue: Silenus

Silenus enters from the *skênê* door and explains the background to the ensuing drama. This technique was already observed by the comic poet Aristophanes as a typical feature of Euripidean tragedies (*Frogs* 946–7), but is not unique to Euripides: cf. Aesch. *Ag.* 1–39. Although occasionally spoken in monologues by mortals principally involved in the action (*e.g. IT* and *El.*), such Euripidean speeches were often delivered by deities, as in *Alcestis, Hippolytus, Ion* and *Bacchae*; but in the former three the deities are only minor players, at least in terms of stage presence. In both the *Cyclops* and Euripides' *Bacchae* we have instances of introductory monologues delivered by immortals who are also chief players in the action to follow (for Silenus as immortal, see Theopompus 115 *FGH* 75c). Silenus complains to his patron god of his current plight as a slave to the brutal and godless Cyclops, Polyphemus (22, 26, 30–1, 34), deprived of Bacchic revelry (25), and of how he came into such a predicament (11–22). With such a preamble Euripides endows this satyr play with the common themes of the satyrs' subjugation by an ogre and isolation from Dionysus; see Gen. Intro., pp. 28–38. Their eventual rescue by a wandering hero will be a natural inference for the ancient audience in the light of the Odysseus-Polyphemus episode, familiar from Homer's *Odyssey* and treated by fifth-century dramatists such as Epicharmus (F 71–2 *PCG*), Cratinus (F 143–57 *PCG*), Aristias (*TrGF* 9 F 4), Philoxenus (F 816, 819 *PMG*) and in a dithyramb of Timotheus (F 780–3). It also featured widely in Archaic and Classical Greek art (*LIMC* VIII.1 s.v. 'Polyphemos' I 16, 17, 18, 20; cf. I 40–44, 46, etc.).

1 Bromius: 'the roarer' a title applied frequently to Dionysus in the play (also: 63, 99, 112, 123, 620), also found in Pindar (F 75.10), Aeschylus (*Eum.* 24) and elsewhere in Euripides (*e.g. Bacc.* 66). In the Homeric hymns, the god is ἐρίβρομος (*H. Hom.* 7.56, 26.1); he also roars when transformed into a lion (*H. Hom.* 7.45). His worship involves thunderous noise in *Homeric Hymn* 26.10, Ar. *Thesm.* 997–8; cf. also Ar. *Clouds* 313 and Eur. *Bacc.* 156, 546. These aspects of his persona are commensurate with the boisterous, exuberant nature of his worship. The significance of calling Dionysus 'Bromius' here and elsewhere (*e.g.* 63) gains irony and even poignancy since we are told a number of times that the cultic activity that his worship involved – including dance, percussive music and wine drinking – is starkly absent from Polyphemus' island (*e.g.*, 25–6, 63–81, 123–4, 203–5).

because of you ... countless labours: the satyrs are the servants, even the willing slaves, of Dionysus (*Cyc.* 23–6n. 709); Cyllene in Sophocles' *Trackers* refers to them as performing labours for the god as part of their worship (223–4). But here Silenus complains about his role as the god's servant. If the interlocutor at Aeschylus' *Sacred Delegates* (F **78a 23–36; 78c) is Dionysus, as plausibly suggested by Lloyd-Jones (1956) 545 and Seaford (1984) 34, at times the satyrs wished to escape even Dionysus; for full discussion of the satyrs as slaves of the god, see Griffith (2002) and (2005), esp. 176–85. In the *Cyclops* their relationship with the god is mostly characterized by φιλία ('friendship': 81, 176, 378, etc.) – in contrast to the brutal despotism they are subjected to under Polyphemus throughout the play. Despite Silenus' protestations to his patron god, the satyrs' separation from Dionysus is painful to them (63–75), and leads to an almost erotic desire to be reunited with him (620–3).

2 when my body was in ... its prime: a comically incongruous notion for the typically decrepit and debauched satyr, made all the more so by his appearance as a menial serf (28). On the basis of vase paintings, Seaford (2n.) suggests that Silenus may have 'aged' in the course of the fifth century. But Silenus, as the satyrs' father, will always be at least one generation older than the chorus (cf. 434). He reminisces similarly in Sophocles' *Trackers* (154–5); cf. also Aesch. *Net-Fishers* (F **47a, 821–2, esp. 830–2). The expression seems to recall, in mock-heroic fashion, the kind of utterances made by Nestor in the *Iliad* (*e.g.* 7.157; 11.670; 23.269).

3–4 driven mad by Hera: the story of Dionysus' madness is preserved by [Apollod.] (*Bibl.* 3.5.1) and Nonnus (32.38–152), and involved his coming into conflicts with Lycurgus, king of the Edonians, and Pentheus, king of Thebes. Euripides famously deals with the latter in his *Bacchae* of 406 BC or a little before, but earlier tragedians had dealt with the god's conflict with both kings. Aeschylus produced a *Semele* or *Hydrophoroi* (F 221–4 Radt), *Pentheus* (F 183) and *Bacchae* (F 22), and *Lycurgus* (F 124–6 Radt) was the title of an Aeschylean satyr-play that accompanied his tragedies *Edonians*, *Bassarids* and *Neaniskoi*. Interestingly, [Apollod.] (*Bibl.* 3.5.1) writes that Lycurgus enslaved Dionysus' maenads and satyrs. It seems very likely, then, that Aeschylus' *Lycurgus* involved the enslavement at least of these male followers of the god, thus anticipating the *Cyclops*. Iophon produced a *Pentheus* or *Bacchae* (*TrGF* <22> T 1a, F 2 Snell) and Xenocles I a *Bacchae* of 415 (*TrGF* <33> F 1 Snell). The story of each of these opponents of Dionysus is popular also in Archaic and Classical vase painting: *LIMC* VI.1, 309–19; VI.1, s.v. 'Lykourgos' I 12–14, 17, 19, 20, 26, 27; *LIMC* VII.1 s.v. 'Pentheus' 24, 39, 40, 41, 43–5, etc. Polyphrasmon's *Lykourgeia* tetralogy appeared in 467 BC (*TrGF* F 1; cf. T 3 Snell). We need not see here an allusion to any one of these plays specifically, but the brevity of the reference to Dionysus' madness sent by Hera implies that the tale and its consequences are well known.

3 mountain nymphs: the mountain in question is probably Nysa, where nymphs tended the infant Dionysus (*H. Hom.* 26.3–6; cf. also ib. 1–9 for Nysa as the god's birthplace). Mt. Nysa is mentioned by Homer (*Il.* 6.130–7) as the place where Lycurgus attacked the young god and his nurses; cf. also Aesch. *Prometheus the Fire Kindler* n. 3 and adesp. 646a nn. 7, 12.

battle: literally, 'battle of the spear', a common tautology in tragedy (Aesch. *Ag.* 438; Eur. F. 360.24, etc.), but also occurring in satyr drama where the satyrs similarly boast of their military prowess (Soph. *Oeneus* F **1130. 9–10). Silenus' overblown sense of his own heroics, hinted at in line 2, finds fuller expression here (5–8). Such implausible geriatric reminiscing features also in Soph. *Trackers* (154–60) where it is immediately followed by his running off in terror on hearing Hermes' lyre-music, which to him is unidentifiable noise (205–10). Dionysus famously took part in the battle against the Earth-born Giants (Gigantomachy), depicted not only on vases (*LIMC* IV.1 s.v. 'Gigantes' 193, 327, 365, 369, 375, etc.; also *LIMC* III.1 s.v. 'Dionysos' 613, 615, 618, etc.), but on the north frieze of the Siphnian treasury at Delphi. The role of Silenus and the satyrs in this conflict is less well established in the literary tradition; but they appear in this context on some early Classical vases; see (*LIMC* IV.1 s.v. 'Gigantes' 316). It has been suggested that their role in the Gigantomachy on vases from the late sixth and early fifth centuries may have been influenced by a satyr play; see Hedreen (1992) 70, 110; Vian (1952) 83–90.

6–7   on your right side as shield-bearer ... I killed him (*i.e.* Enceladus): Silenus fantasises about being a hoplite warrior, and Dionysus' 'right-hand man'. In hoplite formation the general practice was for the shield to be carried on the left arm of the man, who, standing to the right of his comrade, would thus protect him with his shield (Thuc. 5.71). Satyric mock-heroic warriors, including hoplites and peltasts, are depicted in black and red-figure vases (*LIMC* VIII.1 s.v. 'Silenoi' 130, 132, 154, 189, etc.); an Attic pelike of *c.* 500–490 depicts Dionysus donning a hoplite corselet while a satyr attends him, holding a helmet and thyrsus-cum-spear (*LIMC* III.1 s.v. 'Dionysus' 609). Silenus' boast about killing the giant Enceladus contradicts the usual version in art and literature whereby Athena slays him (Eur. *Ion* 209; [Apollod.] *Bibl.* 1.6.2; *LIMC* IV.1 s.v. 'Gigantes' 342, etc.).

8   hang on – let me see (φέρε ἴδω): for this as a colloquial expression, see Stevens (1976) 42; colloquialisms are common in the *Cyclops* (see 131, 174, 259, 340nn., etc.), as might be expected of satyric drama generally. The implausibility of the claim at 6–7 occurs even to Silenus, making his boast, temporarily at least, seem too outlandish even for him. The comic incongruity of the old satyr as elite warrior would not be lost on those among the audience who comprised Athens' hoplite army. For differing views as to the make up of the audience at Athenian dramatic festivals, see Goldhill (1997); cf. Henderson (1991b). **in a dream**: adverbial accusative in the Greek (cf. *IT* 518, etc.), not accusative governed by ἰδών ('I saw': literally, 'on seeing').

For ... even: translates ἐπεὶ καὶ, on which, see Denniston (1954) 296–7.   **displayed**

the spoils to Bacchus (literally, 'the Bacchic one'): dedicating the spoils of war to a god was a common practice for victors (*e.g.* Hdt. 8.121; Thuc. 2.84.4). Actors were known to dedicate masks to their patron god Dionysus after victory in the dramatic contests (Ar. F 130 *PCG*; see also Green (1994) fig. 3.17; cf. figs 3.18, 3.19). But Silenus' words are perhaps too brief here to be considered a 'metatheatrical' reference on the part of Euripides. Kaimio, *et al.* (2001) offers full discussion of such references in Greek satyr plays.

I am enduring to the full: Davies (1999) sees here the culmination of a comic and somewhat hyperbolic priamel – a poetic or rhetorical technique in which a series of alternative objects, ideas or topics is given before the real subject appears as the climax – from Silenus, and the verb adds a rather melodramatic touch. The verb ἐξαντλέω seems to be a favourite of Euripides (*e.g.*, *Medea* 79; *Suppl.* 838; cf. *Cyc.* 110); at 282 Odysseus uses it in a more heroic context for the ordeals at Troy.

11–12 Dionysus' (mis)adventures at sea are recounted famously in the seventh *Homeric Hymn* when he is kidnapped by pirates, who, with the exception of the helmsman, fail to recognize his godhead, like Pentheus and Lycurgus. This incident is recounted by Ovid (*Met.* 3.605–92), Nonnus (45.105–69) and [Apollod.] (*Bibl.* 3.5.3). The image by Exekias of the reclining Dionysus in a vine-laden boat surrounded by dolphins alludes to the same myth (*LIMC* III.1 s.v. 'Dionysos' 788). Seaford posits a connection here with the Attic ritual of the Anthesteria in which an image of Dionysus was carried through the streets on a ship laden with vines, but the monologue here explains how the satyrs ended up in Sicily.

13 **<I myself>**: translates the emphatic <ἐγώ> a conjecture by the corrector of L, Triclinius.

on learning this: Silenus presents himself as springing into action as soon as he hears of his master's predicament; consistent with this idea is Diggle's supplement <εὐθύς> ('immediately') in place of <ἐγώ>, although Triclinius' conjecture can stand.

set sail with my children: the satyrs later see themselves as fellow sailors of Odysseus (709), and sometimes appear as rowers in vase-painting (*e.g. ARV* 2nd edn., 134.3). The suggestion by Waltz (1931) 289–91 that this search for Dionysus was the subject of a satyr-play remains possible (cf. also Duchemin on 11–12).

14–17 The mock heroics underlying Silenus' image of his control of the ship continue here with resonances of epic and tragedy. **took**: translates the aorist participle λαβών, whose object seems to be the ship; some find the combination of 'took' with locative 'on the stern' awkward and Diggle (1969) 31 emended it to βεβώς (cf. 6 where βεβώς is Kassel's conjecture) to give the sense 'stationed on the stern'. Odysseus also describes himself as helmsman (*Od.* 9.177–80, etc.), indicating his role as captain. Euripides' words for describing how Silenus **steered the ... ship** – ηὔθυνον ... δόρυ – echo Aeschylus' ἴθυνεν δόρυ (*Pers.* 411); cf. Eur. *Helen* (1660). For δόρυ denoting 'ship', LSJ s.v. I; at *Odyssey* 9.384 δόρυ denotes a ship's timber. **oared**: translates ἀμφῆρες, lit. 'rowed on both sides'; at Thuc. 4.67.3 a cognate adjective, ἀμφηρικόν, describes a very small boat propelled by side-oars rather than over the stern (cf. below 468n.). The description of the satyrs' **splashy rowing** (ῥοθίοισι, literally 'dashing wave' or 'uproar') conveys the chaotic energy we would expect of them as oarsmen, making them comic counterparts to contemporary *thêtes* (hired rowers from the citizen body), while also recalling the rowing of Odysseus' men (*Od.* 12.472).

18–19   Malea: a headland in Laconia. Another parallel with the *Odyssey* can be found here; Odysseus likewise ends up in the land of Cyclopes when rounding Malea, but is driven off course by a northerly (*Od.* 9.80–1), instead of an easterly (ἀπηλιώτης ἄνεμος), as stated by Silenus here.

20   onto this rock of Etna: Homer makes no mention of Sicily as the Cyclopes' home, but Euripides repeatedly identifies it: *Cyc.* 62, 95, etc. (references to Etna); 95, 106, etc. (references to Sicily). This setting may have been invented by Epicharmus (F 70–2 *PCG*). Satyr plays were typically set in distant (from Greece) settings, often inhabited by ogres (*e.g.*, Aesch. *Lycurgus* F 124–6; Soph. *Amycus* F 111–12; Eur. *Busiris* F 312b–315; and Sosith. *Daphnis or Lityerses* F 1a-3); Euripides' *Cyclops* fits this mould. While Sicily was clearly recognized as a powerful and sophisticated part of the Greek world, here the description of the Cyclopes' homeland is an indication of their barbarism as ogres living on the fringes of the civilized world, as understood by the Atheno-centric audience and other mainland Greeks; for the implications of the locale for Polyphemus' characterization and for the idea of Sicily in the play more fully, see O'Sullivan (2012a) 169–89.

21–2   the one-eyed children of the sea-god, the Cyclopes who kill men: Poseidon is father of the Cyclopes also in Homer (*Od.* 9.412, 529) and, typically, of other menacing giants in Greek mythology, such as Antaeus (Pindar, *I.* 4.52ff) and Orion (cf. below 213n.). Two other ogres of Euripidean satyr-plays, Sciron and Busiris, are also sons of Poseidon (P. Oxy. 2455, F 6; [Apollod.] *Bibl.* 2.5.11). For discussion of these and other man-killing ogres in satyr-plays (*e.g.* Sositheus' *Daphnis or Lityerses*, F 2), see above Gen. Intro. pp. 28–31. **their isolated caves**: this extends the implications of the 'rock of Etna' where the Cyclopes live; on the wild and distant (from Athens) locales which frequently serve as the setting for satyr-plays, see previous note.

23–6   We were caught: ληφθέντες ἐσμὲν is periphrasis, involving a part of εἰμί and, here, an aorist participle (in this case the aorist passive participle of λαμβάνω); cf. 381, 635 below **slaves ... godless Cyclops**: these lines sum up the satyrs' situation and outline the character of the ogre of the piece. δοῦλοι ('slaves') in l. 24 is conceivably emphatic through enjambment. The status of the satyrs as slaves recurs in this drama (79, 442; cf. 709) and is common to satyr plays; see 1n. and on Eur. *Sciron* below, and *Index of Motifs* below. The description of Polyphemus and his murderous actions as 'godless' (ἀνόσιος) occurs throughout the play (26, 316–

21, 336–8, 348, 378, 438, 693); elsewhere he and his cannibalism are 'impious' (δυσσεβής: 30, 289). Homer similarly stresses the cruel and pitiless nature of the monster and his actions (*Od.* 9.272, 287, 295, 351, 368). Aeschylus emphasizes the horror and pity involved in Thyestes' unwitting cannibalism, referring to his meal in nautical terms as a 'pitiable freight' (*Ag.* 1221), and the chorus register their horror in recalling it (*Ag.* 1242–4). The same kind of nautical imagery will describe Polyphemus' anthropophagy ('eating of humans') later in the play (361–2, 505–7); The predicament of the satyrs is twofold (25–6): their slavery to such a monster is compounded by the absence of Bacchic revelry, their natural activity (cf. 38–40, 63–81); interestingly, the absence of wine is first mentioned, not by Silenus, but by the chorus (67) in the parodos (41–81).

27–8   Silenus sets himself apart from his sons, the chorus, in doing more domestic work as opposed to their pastoral labours. Silenus is the first actor to appear, as opposed to the coryphaeus, as is confirmed when he goes into the *skênê* building to fetch provisions for Odysseus (174), or is carried offstage by Polyphemus (589ff.).   **My sons ... tend the young flocks** (μῆλα νέα), **being young** (νέοι) **themselves**; Silenus' age also distinguishes him from the chorus, a contrast achieved by the polyptoton here of νέα νέοι. Nor is this the only contrast to emerge between father and sons (see below 268–9n., 270–2n.), and Polyphemus views him differently from the others (273–4), eventually taking a shine to the aged satyr in grotesquely comic terms (582–9).

29–30   **sweep out the dwelling**: στέγη in Greek, especially in tragedy (Aesch. *Ag.* 3, 518; Soph. *OT* 637, etc.), normally denotes the building represented by the *skênê*; *pace* Ussher 1978, Sophocles' use of it to denote a cave does not seem to be exceptional (*Phil.* 286, 298, 1262); cf. Euripides' *Antiope* (F 223.44). The audience may be meant to recall one of the labours of that great satyric hero, Heracles, which involved cleaning out the stables of Augeas, depicted on one of the metopes of the temple of Zeus at Olympia (*c.* 470–60 BC).

30–1   **this impious Cyclops and his unholy meals**: the implications of the man-killing (ἀνδροκτόνοι) Cyclopes (22) begin to emerge more clearly here, at least as far as Polyphemus is concerned, who has already been called 'godless' (26); see above 23–6n.

32   **my orders**: τὰ προσταχθέντα, an aorist neuter plural passive participle in the accusative case in apposition to the clause σαίρειν ... δόμους ('to sweep out ... the house'); cf. 296n.

33   **with this iron rake**: ἁρπάγη usually means 'hook', but is better understood here as 'rake'. As a theatrical prop it is a clear signifier to the audience of Silenus' menial status. In Sositheus' *Lityerses* (*TrGF* 1a), where travellers were forced to compete in a reaping contest, the satyrs, or at least Silenus, probably held sickles, again as an indication of their servile status (on *Lityerses*, see more fully below, pp. 456–61). There may be something paratragic in Silenus' lament, since to sweep out **the house** is understood as a typically servile duty in tragedy (Eur. *Hec.* 363, *Phaeth.* 56); cf. Eur.'s *Ion*, however, where the title character speaks proudly of his duties of sweeping the portico of Apollo's temple (102–43, 151–3, 181–3).

34–5   master … in a clean cave: Polyphemus has no slaves or attendants in the *Odyssey*, but in the *Cyclops* is a δεσπότης ('master') here and elsewhere (*e.g.* 34, 90, 163, 250; cf. 267). Given the references already to his murderous and godless disposition, δεσπότης is far from neutral here and carries overtones of brutality and harsh rule associated with tyranny, as it does in Herodotus (3.89) and Plato (*Laws* 859a; cf. *Statesman* 276e); for the idea of Polyphemus as a tyrannical figure in the play, see O'Sullivan (2005), and above Gen. Intro. pp. 46–50. Polyphemus thus stands in contrast to the satyrs' natural master, Dionysus, addressed shortly before as 'Lord' (ἄναξ: *Cyc.* 17). Polyphemus' demand that his cave – now denoted by the more usual ἄντρον – be kept clean for himself and his sheep (!) again sets him apart from his Homeric model and his filthy cave (*Od.* 9.329–30).

37–40   Silenus introduces the chorus as they make their way with the flocks along the eisodos (side-entrance) to the orchestra; some attendants appear, too (83; cf. 41–81 n.), either from the cave or with the chorus. The satyrs are typically boisterous, but Silenus' tone is one of surprise, given their current slavery and godless master, and the fact that they themselves lament their plight later in the parodos (63–81).

thumping … dance steps: κρότος σικινίδων. Aristoxenus tells us (F 104, 106, Wehrli) that the *sikinis* was the dance of satyr-drama; for discussion of ancient etymologies and speculations on its origins, see Seaford on *Cyc.* 37. The depiction of the actor in satyr-costume on the Pronomos vase in Naples seems to give a clear indication of its movements: head to the right, right hand on hip, left arm outstretched, weight on (ball of) right foot, left knee lifted high with toe pointing downward; for illustration and recent discussion, see Voelke (2001) pl. 3 and ib. 138–43; Seidensticker (2010); see also Soph. *Trackers* 35n. below.

39   band of revellers: Diggle (1971) 42 emends to κῶμος as a collective noun ('band of revellers') from L's plural κῶμοι ('bands'), his point being that satyrs only ever form one unified 'band'. The corruption probably arose from the adjacent plural συνασπίζοντες '**companions-at-arms**', which echoes Silenus' description of himself at *Cyc.* 5 as a 'shield-bearer'; see 6–7n. **Althaea:** Dionysus had an amorous encounter with Althaea, wife of king Oeneus (= 'wine-man'), who was the first to receive the gift of wine from the god ([Apollod.] *Bibl.* 1.8.1; Hyginus *Fab.* 129). Although no satyr play on this theme is known with certainty, such an episode would have lent itself well to satyric drama with its emphasis on wine and lechery. Sophocles' *Oeneus*, of which F **1130 is the sole certain remnant, may have alluded to or dealt with it. For discussion, see KPS 368–74.

swaggering: as Seaford notes, σαυλούμενοι connotes lasciviousness. The satyrs' movements evidently recall the kind of erotic κῶμοι (revels) they have participated in elsewhere with Dionysus; in Cratinus' *Dionysalexandros* (F 39–51 *PCG*) they accompanied the god in his attempts to seduce Helen; cf. also *Cyc.* 534 and Pratinas 4 F 3.7–9 (with nn.) for fights during a *kômos*, fuelled by erotic desire and/or wine. **songs of lyres**: although not the primary Dionysiac instrument, the lyre does appear in Dionysiac scenes: *e.g.* the Pronomos vase, and other satyric scenes, notably the amphora attributed to the Berlin Painter (*LIMC* VIII.1 s.v. 'Silenoi' 28c, 92, 93, 103, 104, 125, etc.); see also KPS: plates 15a, 15b, 28a. The double aulos ('pipe') is more usual with satyrs and revels, as early as the François Vase, the first extant depiction of satyrs (or 'silenoi'); see also *LIMC* VIII.1 s.v. 'Silenoi' 46a, 103, 104, 105a, 105b; KPS: plates 4, 6a, 7a, 10, 16; cf. R. Osborne (1998) fig. 80. For the instrument itself, see on Pratinas below, our introductory note and its n. 4.

41–81: Parodos: A chorus of fifteen satyrs enters with attendants (83) and possibly a token sheep or two (see Seaford 41–81n.). No further explicit reference is made to these attendants, and their identity is unknown. They cannot be other Cyclopes (cf. *Cyc.* 120); nor can they be satyrs who comprise the chorus. It is difficult to escape the conclusion that they are humans, even though Silenus tells Odysseus that all humans who arrive on the island get eaten (126–8); see also below 241–3n. They may have appeared solely as silent figures for dramatic convenience, and they are still onstage at 137 and 162. Here it seems likely that these helpers tended the sheep while the satyrs danced during the parodos. Evidently these attendants are lower in the pecking order than the satyrs, and Polyphemus would thus be a δεσπότης even without the satyrs as his slaves.

The satyrs sing what has been called by Seaford (1984) *ad loc.* the first extant bucolic song in European literature, but this genre is possibly known as early as Homer; cf. the herdsmen on Achilles' shield playing their pipes (*Il.* 18.525–6) before being ambushed. 'Lityerses', the ogre of a satyr play by Sositheus (*TrGF* 99 F 2–3), was also the name of a harvest song; and it is possible there may have been a similar song in Euripides' satyric *Theristae* or *Reapers*, which may well have told the same story (for discussion, see below, p. 446). In any event, pastoral is well-suited to many general themes of satyric drama, given the usually rural settings of satyr plays; but the song ends on a melancholy note. The satyrs' song begins with an address to the ram of the herd and orders to the ewes to suckle their young with references to the pastoral setting; the tone of this address vacillates from a playful grandiloquence (41–8) to frustration (49–52) to an almost sentimental wish to see the young lambs suckled (55–62). But their song overall finishes on a plaintive note in the epode (63–81), consistent with Silenus' prologue, as the satyrs lament their current plight as captives of a monster in a remote location isolated from their natural master. The epode thus emphasizes a number of themes important in the play: the absence of the kind of activity the satyrs associate with their worship of Dionysus, the friendship they usually enjoy with their god (now lost), and their current status as exiles at the foot of Etna and as slaves to an ogre. These motifs recur at significant points in the drama as wrongs which are eventually 'righted' by the play's end.

Structurally, the parodos is comprised of the following: a strophe (41–8); mesode, or a short astrophic 'midsong' (49–54); antistrophe identical to the metrical structure of the strophe (55–62); and epode, or aftersong (63–81). Metre is mostly aeolo-choriambic dimeters (*e.g.*, 41–8=55–62 in corresponsion) and anapaestic dimeters (50–1, 79–80) and anapaestic monometers (49, 74); for fuller analysis, see Dale (1968) 59, 130–77 (for aeolic choriambs generally), 215–16; for specific analysis of this ode and outline of the metrical scheme, see Dale (1981) 66–8; Ussher and Seaford.

41–42   son ... noble sires and noble mothers: The address referring to the 'noble' parentage of the ram constitutes a rather grandiloquent periphrasis, even if the satyrs mean it seriously; but cf. the Homeric Polyphemus' anthropomorphizing address to the ram of the flock after being blinded as κριέ πέπον, 'dear ram', which he thinks is lagging behind the rest of the sheep in sorrow for his master's blinded eye (*Od.* 9.443–60). **sprung from:** the Greek preposition ἐκ governing both nouns, but standing with the second, is a frequent trope (*e.g. Hcld.* 755–6, *IT* 886–7). [In 41 παῖ is Dindorf's emendation of the unmetrical πᾶ δή μοι of the ms, evidently caused by πᾷ δή μοι of 43, as Duchemin suggests.]

43   tell me: translates the ethic dative μοι, very common (*e.g. Cyc.* 206, 543); see Smyth §1486.

44–6   a soft breeze ... rivers: the satyrs at first attempt to entice the ram, using pastoral imagery associated with the motif of the *locus amoenus* ('lovely place'), a literary topos found in other genres: *e.g.*, Plato's *Phaedrus* (230b), and bucolic poetry of the Hellenistic era and beyond; cf. also Horace *Odes* 3.4.6–8. But Euripides uses similar imagery elsewhere, albeit briefly (*e.g.*, *Med.* 839–40). [Musgrave's emendation of αὔρα 'breeze' to αὐλά 'hall', is accepted by Duchemin to mean, in effect, 'a hall sheltered from the wind'. But this is not necessary, since ὑπήνεμος αὔρα, in meaning literally a 'breeze sheltered from the wind', amounts to a soft breeze; for further discussion, see Ussher and Seaford.]

47   drinking troughs: πίστραις is feminine in form, as usual; the neuter πίστρα in 29 is required by metre (and conjectured here by Boissonade: πίστροις).

48   where: translates οὗ, Casaubon's emendation; some editors (*e.g.*, Ussher, Paganelli) retain Triclinius' question οὔ, parallel with 44, which would give '... Do you not have your bleating young (here too)?'

49–51   Get on!: translates the blunt, onomatopoeic command ψύττα which the chorus almost spits out at the sheep; cf. the similarly inarticulate cries of the satyrs to each other (or their dogs) in Soph. *Trackers* F 314.176. The tone of the satyrs is now more imperious, then becomes pleading again: **Graze on ... here, won't you!:** For interrogative οὐ and future indicative in a brusque command expecting obedience, cf. *And.* 1067; see Smyth §1918. The satyrs' threat of stone-throwing (51) reflects their own frustration at failing to control the sheep, one of the menial tasks they must perform for which they are evidently ill-suited. **at you:** a variety of the partitive genitive, with ῥίπτω as at *Bacc.* 1096–7; see Smyth §1349.

52   **ram**: translates κεράστα, literally 'horned creature', which again seems to be a slightly grandiose way of referring to the sheep here (cf. 41–2n.).

53–4 **<to> the guardian of the fold**: (στασιωρὸν) Musgrave plausibly suggests that this refers to Silenus, since the old satyr is attendant of the fold (29–35); this interpretation requires Wecklein's supplement πρὸς, which would make the line a metrically acceptable paroemiac. [Wilamowitz suggested that the noun refers to the ram, and emended it to make it vocative (στασιωρὲ), a view endorsed by Kovacs (1994) 145–6.] **the shepherd who roams the wild**: Polyphemus is a hunter, even if not always successful (cf. 212–13, etc.). [Both μηλοβότα ('shepherd') and ἀγροβάτα ('who roams the wild') are Doric genitives in -α, typical of lyric; μηλοβότα may have led to the ms corruption to ἀγροβότα, which means 'a creature who feeds in the wild'. Triclinius emended to ἀγροβάτα (cf. also 658, below).]

55–62 This antistrophe is addressed to the ewes.

56–7 **give ... your teats**: [translates θηλὰς πορίσασ', Broadhead's emendation for the unmetrical and difficult θηλαῖσι σπορὰς of the ms 'receive (δέξαι) the young ones with your teats'; for this, admittedly doubtful, sense of σπορά, see LSJ s.v. II b. **whom**: Diggle emended L's ἃς to οὓς thereby restoring the masculine 'common' gender to the lambs, in line with 224, etc. **in the chambers**: (= θαλάμοι) another rather grandiose expression used by the satyrs, now for the cave's interior.]

60 **†are you encircling†** (= ἀμφιβαίνεις): L's verb is unmetrical and inappropriate in sense; Triclinius' emendation to ἀμφιβαλεῖς ('go round to') has generally not found favour because ἀμφιβάλλω (literally 'throw' or 'put around') does not elsewhere appear intransitively to denote motion, which is required to make sense of 61–2.

62 **Etna's rocks**: see 20n.

63 **no Bromius**: the epode (63–81) articulates more fully the satyrs' painful isolation from Dionysus and his rites, mentioned already by Silenus (25–6), who had addressed the god by the same title at the very beginning of the play (*i.e.* 1n.).

64–5 **thyrsus-wielding Bacchants** (thyrsi are ivy-wreathed staves typically carried by the devotees of Dionysus): these figures are frequently depicted in the company of the god and satyrs on Attic red-figure vase-painting, notably on the hydria by the Kleophrades painter (*LIMC* VIII.1 s.v. 'Mainades' 36); cf. also Eur. *Bacc.* 556–7, where the thyrsus appears again. **rapturous cries from drums** (= τυμπάνων ἀλαλαγμοί): these instruments resemble tambourines and in later fifth-century vase-painting are usually carried by Maenads. In the *Bacchae* (120–134), the chorus tell how this instrument was introduced into the cult of Dionysus by the Corybantes who received it from Rhea, mother of Zeus; at *Bacc.* 59 Dionysus calls drums his own invention and Rhea's. The verb ἀλαλάζω can refer to the cries of the bacchants themselves (*Bacc.* 1133) and the 'cries' of the drums suggest they are almost animated, fittingly enough for Dionysiac instruments, as if possessed by the god. The habit of endowing objects with an apparent life of their own is as old as Homer, who can speak of weapons as 'pitiless', 'shameless' or 'raging' (*e.g. Il.* 4.521, 5.661, 11.572–4, 13.501, etc); for discussion, see Kokolakis (1981). Similarly, Euripides can speak of parts of the body as if they have an energy or emotion of their own, *e.g., Hec.* 1128 when Polymestor wishes to lay his 'raging hand' on Hecuba; for animation of concrete objects elsewhere in Euripides, cf. *Hipp.* 807; *Hel.* 1352.

66–7   bright drops of wine: the Dionysian liquid *par excellence* is similarly spoken of as almost animated in being called χλωραί, suggesting brightness and freshness but also associated with physical and emotional life; thus it is applied to tears (Eur. *Med.* 906, etc.) and blood (*Hec.* 127; Soph. *Trach.* 1055); see Seaford's note ad loc. for more references, which suggest that χλωρός here means 'invigorating'. See Dodds' introduction to his commentary on the *Bacchae* for full discussion of still other kinds of liquids associated with Dionysus, apart from wine, such as blood, semen and sap in a young tree (1960: ix–xi); other liquids include milk, honey and water (cf. *Bacc.* 704–11). The invigorating brightness of the wine here also recalls its description in Homer as 'bright, gleaming' (αἴθοψ: *Il.* 4.259, etc.). The satyrs' enthusiasm for wine is, of course, also depicted widely in Greek art: *e.g.* the cup interior, *c.* 510 BC attributed to the Epeleios painter; Douris' psykter, *c.* 490 BC (= BM E768), the oinochoe depicting the satyric parody of Heracles and the Apples of Hesperides, *c.* 470 BC (= BM E539), etc.   **rushing waters of springs**: evocation of the god's boisterous, rural celebration through wine suits the life of satyrs generally, and here involves a brief description of a *locus amoenus* (see 44–6 n.). But here the satyrs are really lamenting the absence of such activity on Polyphemus' island, adding poignancy to their plight.

68   Nymphs on Nysa: see 4n. Nymphs, rather than maenads, are typically the companions of satyrs: cf. Soph. *Trackers* 223–8 and n. 39; and for full discussion, see Hedreen (1994). However, at *Cyc.* 72 the satyrs see themselves as the pursuers of bacchants, which the audience would likely understand as involving unsuccessful erotic attempts, as depicted on fifth-century vases, *e.g.* the Kleophrades painter's famous hydria of *c.* 480 BC; see 64–5n. Hedreen (1994) 58–65 shows that by the time of red-figure vase-painting, nymphs invariably fend off lecherous satyrs, in contrast to scenes of mutually amorous activity more readily found on black-figure vases, and suggests this may be due to satyr plays depicting maenads rebuffing their male counterparts. The choral reminiscences about such failed amorous encounters thus add a comic element to their longings here.

69–70   "iacchos! iacchos!": a song in honour of Dionysus (Hdt. 8.65), or another name for the god himself as Iacchos (Soph. F 959, Ar. *Frogs* 398); so taken by Kassel and Seaford who make iacchos the object of μέλπω and emend ᾠδὰν to become instrumental ᾠδᾷ (Kassel) or ᾠδαῖς (Seaford) 'with a song' or 'with songs' respectively.   **Aphrodite, whom I pursued**: it is perhaps surprising to find that the satyrs associate the song here with Aphrodite, but Dionysus is hardly excluded. Lecherous behaviour is typical of satyrs, especially under the influence of wine (*e.g.*,

163–74, 495–502), so the realms of the two deities combine easily. The reference to the goddess here is better understood as a personification of sexual activity, just as Dionysus is wine personified (*e.g.*, 415, 519–29), and Hephaestus fire personified (599–600); the satyrs are telling us they have had endured a forced abstinence from heterosexual activity (cf. 439–40). Sexual arousal induced, or increased, or diminished by alcohol is a perennial human experience and often a comic motif of western literature. After the murder of Duncan, the porter in *Macbeth* (Act II, Scene III) provides some light relief, satyric in spirit, in his earthy musings on the effects of alcohol 'which provoke the desire, but take away the performance'.

72 white-footed Bacchants: female skin is usually white in black-figure vase painting, and Greek poetry from Homer onwards, where 'whiteness' generally connotes femininity and beauty (*e.g. Il.* 1.55, 195, 208, etc. for Hera); it also suggests status and decorum in that girls of a certain class did not need to work outdoors and were covered up. Here 'white-footed-ness' is consistent with the Bacchants' being barefoot, as they are typically depicted in vase-painting; for discussion, see Irwin (1974, 111–29, esp. 123–6). Orestes is λευκόπους (*Anacr.* 9.4–5), possibly because, as Irwin suggests (1974) 126, in his frenzy he goes about barefoot like a Bacchant.

73–5 O my friend ... golden hair?: the important concept of friendship between Dionysus and his followers is broached here, and recurs to underscore their relationship with their god as well as with Odysseus and his men (81, 176, 378, 435–6, 437, 466, 478, 650–3; cf. 496–8), in contrast to the fear and loathing the satyrs feel for Polyphemus. [Some see problems in these lines and Diggle daggers them all. The textual problems, as well as those of metre, which has not been confidently identified, concern firstly, the coupling in ὦ φίλος ὦ φίλε of different forms, the nominative used as a vocative preceding the true vocative. The nominative can nevertheless function as a vocative, and ὦ φίλος occurs seven times in Euripides (*Andr.* 510, 530, 1204; *Supp.* 278; *Tro.* 267, 1081; *IT* 830), as Kovacs (1994b) 146, notes, who nevertheless emends to ὦ φίλος ὦναξ ('O my friend, my lord'). For the nominative as vocative elsewhere in satyric drama, cf. Aesch. *Prom. Fire-Kindler* F 207 (on which, see n. 9); Ussher also aptly compares *Il.* 4.189 (φίλος ὦ Μενέλαε); so L's reading may be right. Secondly, the form Βακχεῖε is rare, but it is paralleled in Aristophanes (*Thesm.* 987); L may again be right. Thirdly, there are two uncoordinated finite verbs in 74–5: οἰοπολεῖς ('are you wandering') and σείεις ('are you shaking?'). Nauck's conjecture οἰοπολῶν ('wandering') restores grammatical sense easily enough; also Wecklein's ποῦ, giving 'where (are you now)?' for L's incorrect ποῖ ('where to?'), fits in well with 81. The translation reflects both these emendations.] **are you shaking your golden hair?**: Elsewhere Dionysus shakes his hair (*Bacc.* 240) as do his male followers (ib. 185); head-shaking is typical of many maenads in red-figure vases (*LIMC* VIII.1 s.v. 'Mainades' 13, 30, 29, 144, etc.). The mention of Dionysus' hair as blonde or golden need not make him seem effeminate, even though the god is elsewhere described as effeminate (Eur. *Bacc.*

353, 455). ξανθός regularly describes Menelaus in Homer (*Od.* 4.76, 168, etc.), and is used for Achilles (*Il.* 1.197, 23.141) and Odysseus (*Od.* 13.399, 431).

76–81 Diggle (1971) 44–5 discusses the metre of the passage; line 77 has proved most problematic for editors. L has θητεύω Κύκλωπι (printed by, for instance, Murray, Paganelli and Paduano); but Diggle says *brevis in longo* (the final short iota in Κύκλωπι) 'is not to be tolerated' and prints Fritzsche's emendation Κύκλωπι θητεύω which gives an 'acceptable' iambic dimeter with spondaic contraction and is adopted by other editors (*e.g.*, Ussher, Napolitano); see also Seaford for further discussion.

76–9 your … servant … serf to the Cyclops … slave: under Dionysus the satyrs' servitude is characterized by friendship throughout the play (see above 73–5n.), just as Euripides' Ion can speak proudly of his servile duties of sweeping the portico of Apollo's temple (*Ion* 102–43, 151–3, 181–3); at *Cyc.* 709 the satyrs look forward to being slaves of the Bacchic god again. But under Polyphemus the satyrs endure a brutal despotism, which they complain about twice here. Sophocles' *Trackers* implies the servile state of the satyrs, who seem to be promised freedom by Apollo (62–3; cf. 75–8, 223–8), but whether this means freedom from Dionysus or a temporary master is not clear (see introductory discussion to Soph. *Trackers* below).

80 miserable goat-skin cloak: while satyrs occasionally seem to be goatish (Aesch. *Prom. Fire-Kindler* F 207; Soph. *Trackers* 367), they are much more equine in the Archaic and Classical periods in appearance. It is unlikely that that there is a reference here to the *perizôma* – the hairy shorts with phallus and tail attached, and an essential part of the costume of actors in satyr-plays, depicted on the Pronomos vase (cf. below 99–101n.); see also Hedreen (1992) 107–12. Rather, the chorus seems to be alluding to their abnormal and ungainly attire as a visual manifestation of their unnatural role as slaves to Polyphemus. As Seaford points out, there is a comic contrast here to the leopard-skins and fawn-skins they wear as part of their service of Dionysus (cf. Aesch. *Net-Fishers* F **46.790; Soph. *Trackers* 224–5 where Dionysus is their usual master); also, the Silenus-actor on the Pronomos vase wears a leopard skin over his costume. The satyric complaint is almost self-parodic in that these normally rustic, unsophisticated figures complain rather preciously of being made to wear rustic clothing.

81 your friendship: see 73–5n.

82–95 Silenus abruptly brings the parodos to an end and looks in the direction of the new arrivals, which heralds a new development in the drama. Descriptions of characters arriving along the eisodos, or the side entrance to the acting area and orchestra, are common enough in tragedy. This lengthy account of the arrival of Odysseus and his men not only adds to the anticipation of their presence, but, more practically for the theatre, allows them – and they are described as carrying buckets and containers (87–8) – time enough to get to the acting area. In Homer,

Odysseus brings twelve men with him (*Od.* 9.195); but in *Cyclops* their number is unspecified.

83 attendants: see above 41–81n.

85 a ship – a Greek ship: literally 'a hull of a ship of Greece'. This pleonasm is common enough (*e.g.* Aesch. *Pers.* 419; Eur. *IT* 742, 1345; cf. also *Cyc.* 118, 702).

86 mighty oarsmen: literally 'lords of the oar'. Silenus adds a grandiloquent touch to the information he gives in an almost paratragic manner, reminiscent of Aeschylus' heroising description of every Athenian oarsman at Salamis: κώπης … ἄναξ ('lord of his oar': Aesch. *Pers.* 378; cf. 383); in his *Telephus* (F 705 Kannicht) Euripides uses the comparable verbal expression κώπης ἀνάσσων. It is interesting to compare Silenus' words here to his otherwise mostly disdainful attitude to Odysseus and his men for the rest of the play.

87–8 In the *Odyssey*, Homer emphasizes Odysseus' own curiosity to the point of recklessness as the motivation for his arrival at Polyphemus' island and cave (*Od.* 9.172–6, 228–30). Euripides makes him a more reluctant traveller driven by necessity in the search for food and water (cf. also 96–8, 109).

89–93 These lines increase the sense of foreboding, further indicating that Polyphemus is every bit the transgressive monster of *Odyssey* 9, and thus a suitable ogre for a satyr play. **O unhappy strangers!** (ὦ ταλαίπωροι ξένοι): similar expressions of pity are found at Eur. *Medea* 990, 1057, *IT* 479; satyric drama could at times, even momentarily, broach the same emotions as tragedy. Silenus' sympathy for strangers is genuine (he also considers them unlucky: 92) but it is also relatively short-lived, in contrast to his more generous-spirited sons, *e.g.* at 381.

90–1 our master Polyphemus: here the monster's despotic nature (NB δεσπότης: 90) underscores his villainy. **the land … is hostile to strangers**: the location matches the character of its natural inhabitants, the Cyclopes (see 20n.). As in Homer, violations of hospitality characterize the behaviour of Polyphemus (*Od.* 9.259–80); Odysseus emphasizes that it is Zeus and the other gods who have avenged the monster's crimes against strangers (*Od.* 9.478–9). [For Jacob's emendation of L's στέγην ('dwelling') to τε γῆν ('and … the land'), accepted by Diggle, see Duchemin and Seaford; cf., however, Ussher, Biehl, Paduano who retain the ms reading. The essential point about the inhospitality of the Cyclops and his environs remains.]

92–3 the man-eating Cyclopean jaw: elsewhere in Euripides the adjective κυκλώπιος denotes gigantic, prehistoric architecture of what modern scholarship calls the Bronze Age, understood by the ancients to have been built by Cyclopes (*e.g.* Bacchylides 10.77; Eur. *HF* 15, 998; *Tro.* 1088; *El.* 1158; [Apollod.] *Bibl.* 2.2.1). Here the adjective is used literally to pun on both the size and the monstrous owner of such jaws. [Williams, cited in Diggle's OCT apparatus, suggests that 90–3 are a question to give: 'Do they have no idea that … Cyclops?' ἀνδροβρῶτα (= 'man-eating') is a correction by ms P of L's ἀνδροβῶτα.]

95 Sicilian Etna's rocky outcrop: see 20n. [As Seaford notes, πάρειμι ('be present') can be followed by simple accusative, here as elsewhere (*e.g.* 106, Eur. *El.*, 1278, *Bacc.* 5).]

96–8   Odysseus and his men probably, though not necessarily, enter from the opposite side to that used by the chorus.   **Strangers**: this is, of course, a conventional word of greeting, but Odysseus' first word is somewhat ironic given that Silenus has told us that the land is hostile to strangers (91) and its inhabitants are man-killing monsters (22).   **would you tell us**: Odysseus' language is polite with the optative and ἄν (on which, see Smyth §1830) and formal to the point of affectation in his use of periphrases, *e.g.* νᾶμα ποτάμιον: **flowing river water** (literally = 'a current of a river'). Despite Silenus' attempt to bring him down to earth (*e.g.* see below 104, 105, 314–5nn.), Odysseus mostly maintains a more dignified – if at times pompous – and heroic persona than is generally accorded him by many commentators; see Gen. Intro. p. 48.

99–101   **<Hey>, what's this?**: <ἔα·> is a supplement by Wecklein. As Ussher (who does not include Wecklein's supplement) notes, Odysseus' surprise as he gets a closer look at the satyrs is paralleled elsewhere by Euripidean characters (*Andr.* 896); see also Stevens (1976) 33. Also comparable is Eur. *Andromeda* F 125: Perseus' surprise on seeing Andromeda; and cf. Polyphemus (at *Cyc.* 222). **city of Bromius**: there is some irony in this remark, given that Silenus and the satyrs have told us that there is no Bromius or Dionysus present for them to worship in their current plight (25–6, 63). But to the sophisticated Odysseus, the sight of any satyr will naturally lead him to associations of Dionysiac worship, and it seems that the hero has seen enough satyrs to populate a small community.   **I greet...** (literally, χαίρειν προσεῖπα is: 'I addressed to greet') the aorist here is 'tragic', so-called 'instantaneous' or 'performative'; see Lloyd (1999). Fix emended to προσεῖπον, but editors print the aorist here in alpha, the first or weak aorist on stem εἰπ- (see Smyth p. 695). Again Odysseus is formal and polite, as befits his circumstances as a traveller in need of help. **the eldest**: that Silenus is conspicuously the older probably indicates that the actor playing him wore a mask with white hair attached as held by the actor on the Pronomos Vase (on the upper level speaking to the Heracles-actor); for an illustration, see Pickard-Cambridge (1962) fig. 85; see also above 2n.

102–62   This lengthy exchange is in stichomythia whereby each character speaks one line of dialogue in turn; also included are two lines of *antilabê* (a change of speakers within a line, *e.g.*, 153–4). The highly stylized question and answer format (esp. 102–31) occurs in all forms of Greek drama, but there are many colloquialisms in the following exchange (*e.g.* 149, 150, 152, 153, 154, 156), giving it a conversational tone; for general treatment of this form of dialogue, see, most recently Collard (2007) 16–30. Euripides uses it here to outline again the bleakness of the satyrs' situation: the remoteness and harshness of the environment; the man-eating monsters who inhabit the land (125–8); the lack of any of the accoutrements a Greek would expect of a civilised community: no buildings, communal laws, agriculture or viticulture (115–24); see more fully O'Sullivan (2012a). Odysseus and Silenus strike a deal: the old satyr will give the visitors food in return for wine which allows him to reveal his true colours and indulge in fantasies about a return to his old habits of drink and lechery (163–74). With some satyric lampooning of Odysseus' heroic posturing (104–5; cf. also 177–8), the exchange essentially establishes the goodwill between the hero and the satyrs (albeit short-lived in the case of Silenus), who all share a desire to escape as quickly as possible.

102   stranger: on the possible irony and foreboding of this word, see above 96–8n. **tell me who you are…** As Ussher notes, in immediately demanding to know the visitors' identity and origin, Silenus violates the heroic ethic of hospitality in Homer, just as the Homeric Polyphemus does (*Od.* 9.252). Contrast the Phaeacians in the *Odyssey*; Odysseus arrives at Alcinous' palace at *Od.* 7.132–5, and does not identify himself until *Od.* 9.19–20. However, Silenus is not on his home territory and it is conceivable that he may see in Odysseus' arrival a chance to escape.

103   Cephallenians: a name used by Homer for Odysseus' followers (*Il.* 2.631–2, *Od.* 20.210; cf. *Od.* 24.378). Sophocles' not altogether flattering portrait of the hero in *Philoctetes* of 409 BC likewise refers to him as Κεφαλλήνων ἄναξ ('lord of the Cephallenians': *Phil.* 264).

104   a shrill, relentless babbler: cf. *Rhes.* 499 where Odysseus is similarly called κρότημα (cf. Soph. F 913); see Collard (2005) 370. While Odysseus is praised for his powers of speaking in Homer (*e.g. Il.* 3.204–24), already by the *Odyssey* he is at times a long-winded liar, as even his patron goddess, Athena, tells him (*Od.* 13.291–301). Frequently unfavourable treatments in post-Homeric poetry are attested in Pindar (*Nem.* 7.20–6), and Euripides' *Hecuba* (218–437), and *Palamedes* (F 578–90 Kannicht), *Philoctetes* F 789c.§8, *Troades* (esp. 279–92), and Sophocles' *Philoctetes*; hostility may have set in already by the time of the *Cypria* of probably the seventh century BC (F 20 Davies), which tells of his murder of the innocent Palamedes. For full discussion of his various depictions, see Stanford (1954), esp. 91–117; more recently, S. Montiglio (2011) *passim*. **of the race of Sisyphus**: γένος functions as an accusative of respect to mean '(son) of Sisyphus by race' (cf. *Bacc.* 460, *Pho.* 125), or as a noun in apposition with ἄνδρα ('man') thus giving 'son of Sisyphus' (cf. *Her.* 888). Sisyphus was the notorious trickster, punished in the Underworld by having to roll a stone up a hill only to fail in every attempt (Homer *Od.* 9.593–600), who later became a symbol for Albert Camus' existential belief in the futility of human existence, *Le Mythe de Sisyphe* (1942). As something of a comic, incorrigible anti-hero, given to theft and trickery, he was a popular subject for satyr plays by, *e.g.*, Aeschylus (F 225–34; on which, see below), Euripides (*Autolycus* F 282–3; and F 673–4), possibly Sophocles (F 545: see p. 506) and (?)Critias (F 19; see below). Silenus' phrase here may be taken metaphorically, given that Odysseus' usual father was Laertes (*Od.* 9.19, 505), but in some accounts – at least according to his enemies – he was the bastard son of Sisyphus (Aesch. F

286; Soph. *Ajax* 189–90, *Phil.* 417, etc.). [The scholiast to Soph. *Ajax* 190 quotes the line with γόνον (lit. 'son'), but as Seaford notes, there is no reason to change γένος, notwithstanding the parallel of Eur. *IA* 1362.]

105   that very man: ἐκεῖνος αὐτός, cf. Ar. *Wealth* 82–3 where Chremylus uses the same expression somewhat incredulously of the dilapidated Plutus who replies dejectedly αὐτότατος ('my very self'), similar in tone to Odysseus' admission here. **No need to rub it in**: literally, 'don't abuse (me).' Silenus has just taken some gloss off Odysseus' grandiose persona (cf. 314–5), in an exchange that juxtaposes the heroic and comic. In *Od.* 9.20 the hero brags that his κλέος ('heroic renown', 'glory') reaches heaven; but Silenus turns such fame into a notoriety for deceit that has reached Sicily, thus puncturing his heroic pretensions somewhat. [αὐτός, which gives better sense, is L. Dindorf's emendation for L's οὗτος, which would give 'this is that man'.]

106   For πάρειμι, see 95n.

107   hardships at Troy: these hardships (πόνοι), which Odysseus mentions again (*e.g.* 282, 347, 351, 603), comprise a genuinely heroic counterpart to the 'hardships' which Silenus melodramatically complained about in the first line of the play.

110   Oh no! (παπαῖ): Silenus expresses a mixture of surprise and sympathy – the two need not be mutually exclusive – more in tune with his earlier response on seeing the strangers (cf. above 89–93n.), and a departure from his rather lame attempt at humour at 108. Now he identifies with the plight of the arrivals and even uses the same word – ἐξαντλεῖς (**you are indeed suffering**) – that he applied to his own sufferings; see above 10n.

112   Silenus alludes again to what brought him to Sicily in somewhat heroising terms, but Odysseus lets it pass. The audience has heard it before, and is spared what would no doubt be an embellished account of these events from the aged satyr.

114   The mound of Etna: Etna itself functions in synecdoche for Sicily (cf. 20n., etc.), but here 'mound' (ὄχθος) seems ironic in referring to the huge volcano; but ὄχθος occurs again at 706, and there as elsewhere can mean any hill, even the Athenian Acropolis (Eur. *Ion* 12).

115   Odysseus' apparently innocent question, following up his query at 113, taps into a major strand of Greek thought about human progress, since the invention of housing was amongst the first indications of even an emergent human society. Prometheus taught house-building to mortals who had previously lived in caves (*PV* 450–3, 469–71); in Soph. *Ant.* 359–60 house-building is one of many great human technical achievements. In Protagoras' myth of the origins of communities it indicates some level of human progress, albeit incomplete, even before the rise of politicized consciousness (Plato, *Prot.* 322a).

116   There are none (reading Schenk's ἔστι – the singular form required for the neuter plural subjects – for L's εἰσι): there is another possible irony here in that the

Cyclopes, famous for building monumental architecture (cf. above 92–3n.), live on an island without any buildings at all. **stranger** (ξένε): Silenus addresses Odysseus this way, even after learning the hero's name (103–5), implying that, as a stranger, Odysseus is likely to have a rough time whilst on the island; cf. above 91, 96–8 nn.

117 a race of beasts? (θηρῶν γένος): in his incredulity Odysseus inadvertently stumbles upon the right answer to his question about the native inhabitants of Sicily.

118 not houses: translates the periphrastic pleonasm οὐ στέγας δόμων (see 85n.). Silenus here implies that the inhabitants, as cave dwellers, do not comprise a civilized community (cf. 115 n.), as is confirmed also at 120. This recalls their habits mentioned already in Homer (*Od.* 9.112–15): 'They have neither assemblies for council, nor appointed laws, but they dwell on the peaks of lofty mountains in hollow caves, and each one is lawgiver to his children and his wives, and they take no account of each other.'

119 Whose subjects ...: literally, 'hearing/obeying whom?' (τίνος κλύοντες); for this use of κλύω (which functions as a synonym of ἀκούω in the next line), cf. Eur. *Bellerophon* F 286.11. **power shared among the people**: it seems odd to refer by implication to a δῆμος ('people' or 'citizen body') here, given that Odysseus has just been told that the inhabitants are cave-dwellers with no communal laws. The point may be to underline, by a rather slow process of question and answer, the vast difference between the lifestyle of these beasts and the culture of the Attic δῆμος, the play's first audience, for whom democracy and the related ideal of ἰσονομία ('equality before the law') were brandished as important political concepts (Hdt. 3.80.6; 83.1; 142.3; 5.37.2 [where it is opposed to tyranny]; Thuc. 2.37.1; Eur. *Suppl.* 429–62).

120 loners; nobody ... anyone else: the excessively self-contained lifestyle of each of the Cyclopes and consequent lack of communal activity is emphasized here in the threefold polyptoton (repetition of the same word in different cases) of οὐδείς. For the relevance of excessive *autarkeia* (self-sufficiency) to the *Cyclops* overall, see Konstan (1990). It is only under the influence of the wine which Odysseus gives him, that Polyphemus begins to think of his fellow Cyclopes; see 533n. [μονάδες is a now widely accepted emendation by Schmidt (1975), which develops 118, in place of of L's νόμαδες ('nomads'), which seems at odds with 121–2; but cf. Ussher, who retains the ms reading.]

121–2 In addition to lacking architecture of any type, the Cyclopes practice no agriculture (on which, see next note), even though here, as in Homer, they keep sheep and make cheese. Polyphemus tells us that the earth produces grass to fatten his livestock (332–3). The natives, in other words, have nothing to do with Demeter; here is another example of the reductive and distorted portrait Euripides gives of Sicily, which famously functioned as the bread basket of the ancient Mediterranean (Hdt. 7.158.4; Thuc. 6.20.4, etc.); for the importance of the cult of Demeter on Sicily, see White (1964) and Hinz (1998), esp. 55–167.

123–4   streams of the grape-vine: an appositional phrase with Βρομίου ... πῶμα. [Reiske's emendation ῥοάς is for L's ungrammatical ῥοαῖς, a scribal error likely influenced by the datives in 122.]   **no dancing**: dancing was about as important to the satyrs as drinking, and for them, there can hardly be one without the other. The absence of agriculture and wine signals an important difference not only culturally between the Cyclopes and mortals, but also in the relationship of each race to the gods. In the *Bacchae* (275–83) Teiresias posits Demeter's crop (cf. *Cyc.* 121) and the wine of Dionysus as the greatest goods for mortals. Both agriculture and wine were gifts bestowed on mortals by the Olympians – the former to Triptolemus ([Apollod.] *Bibl.* 1.5.2; cf. *H. Hom. Dem.* 2.470–9; Soph. F 539), the latter to king Oeneus, the 'wine-man' ([Apollod.] *Bibl.* 1.8.1; Hyginus *Fab.* 129; cf. above 39n.). Agriculture and wine are spoken of as gods – as Demeter and Dionysus, respectively – in fifth-century drama (*Bacc.* 275–83, 285; *Cyc.* 156, 415, 454) and philosophy (Prodicus 84 B5 DK); see Guthrie (1962–81) vol. 3, 226–49 for an overview of concepts of the divine in the age of the Sophists. The Cyclopes know nothing of such blessings, a fact which seems to underlie Polyphemus' disdain for the Olympians (see esp. 316, 318–19, 320–1, 327–8, 336–8nn.). Polyphemus' ignorance of wine puts him on the same uncivilized level as the centaurs who went berserk at the wedding of Pirithous when they got their first whiff of it ([Apollod.] *Ep.* 1.21–2). This led to the famous battle between Lapiths and Centaurs, depicted on such monuments as the west pediment of the temple of Zeus at Olympia and the metopes of the Parthenon, often seen as a battle between the forces of civilization and barbarism: *e.g.* Pollitt (1972) 81–3; Stewart (1997) 191–5; Osborne (1998) 172–3.

125–6   strangers: while the Cyclopes eat other kinds of food (122, 248–9), this exchange emphasizes their hostility to ξένοι, which Silenus has already mentioned (89–93, esp. 91). Again, Odysseus' unknowing question calls for an emphatic 'no', this time mentioning the man-eating habits of the monsters.

127   the ... flesh: βορά: although used twice in the fairly neutral sense 'food' or 'meat' for Odysseus and his men (88, 97), βορά frequently denotes the monster's vile appetite here and elsewhere (249, 254, 289, 367, 409, 416); twice this βορά is explicitly condemned; it is 'unholy' (289) and 'most shameful' (416).

128   Nobody ... has not been eaten: (οὐδείς) this clearly refers only to human travellers (as opposed to the monster's attendants; see above 41–81n.). The satyrs are, after all, immortal (Theopompus 115 *FGH* 75c, etc.), and not to Polyphemus' liking anyway (220–1). Does this line anticipate Odysseus' trick, made famous by Homer (*Od.* 9.364–7), of calling himself 'Nobody'? Although in Homer and later in the play (549) Odysseus calls himself Οὖτις, punning and word-play between the two negatives οὐ and μή (the first objective, the second subjective) is detectable already in Homer's account (*Od.* 9.405–6, 408, 410, 414, 422). Homer plays upon two 'nobodies': 'Nobody' οὖτις and 'nobody' μὴ τις and the etymologically distinct μῆτις 'ruse' (414, 422). Those familiar with the tale may have seen in Silenus' remark an ironic, even unintended, prophecy here. The pun in Homer was recognized long ago by Stanford (1939) 104–5 and 1964 on *Od.* 9.408.

130 Hunting with dogs carries with it aristocratic and heroic overtones at least in Homeric epic (*Il.* 9.533–49; *Od.* 19.428–66), but also occurs in satyric drama; see below on Soph. *Trackers* F 314 n. 35. Homer makes no mention of Polyphemus as hunter and dog-owner, but here this detail seems to give him a certain sophistication over his Homeric counterpart, even though in the play he remains bestial on other levels (cf. esp. 442, 602, 658). On the relative sophistication of Polyphemus, see, for instance, Seaford (1984) 51–9; cf. Marshall (2005).

131 Do you know ... what you are to do: Literally: 'Do you know what do...'. This translates the imperative δρᾶσον ('do'), Canter's emendation of L's δράσεις ('you shall do'); the question-mark is introduced because of the answer in 132 'I don't know. But ...'. L's reading, which also requires a question mark, is retained by some (Duchemin, Ussher, Paganelli, Biehl). But as Seaford notes, parallels to the emended text can be found elsewhere in Euripides (*e.g. Hec.* 225, *Ion* 1029, *IA* 725). Simmonds and Timberlake (1927) 131n. explain the emended construction as a change from indirect to direct speech; but it can also be understood as a colloquialism; see Stevens (1976) 36. For discussion of οἶσθ' ... ὃ δρᾶσον, see Diggle (1994) 500–1.

132 we'd do: δρῷημεν is an Ionic form; cf. *Hel.* 1010; *Alc.* 272; Smyth §460.

134–5 Meat is a staple of Homeric heroes (*Il.* 9.205–21; 24.621–7, etc.). In the diet of the Athenians of Euripides' day meat was not nearly as common as fish and cereals; for discussion, see Davidson (1998) 3–20. **nice ... hunger**: in the Greek these two words (ἡδύ, λιμοῦ) are juxtaposed to give the effect of an oxymoron as a result of hyperbaton, with predicative λιμοῦ advanced for emphasis.

136 cow's milk: The Greeks were not great drinkers of milk, and when Homer refers to milk, it is usually sheep's milk (*Il.* 4.434, etc.), rather than cow's milk as here; Homeric heroes usually drink wine (*Il.* 1.471–2, 9.706, 24.641–2, etc.). In the *Odyssey* Polyphemus has no cattle, only goats and sheep. That milk is Polyphemus' staple drink is the natural corollary of his ignorance of wine, and a further indication of his barbarism (see above 123–4n.). As Seaford notes, milk-drinking mostly had connotations of barbarism in Greek thought (*e.g. Il.* 13.5–6, Hes. F 150.15, Hdt. 1.216; Galen 6.765). [Athenaeus (14.658c) cites this line with Διὸς γάλα ('milk of Zeus', but the case for emending ms. L is generally not accepted. Διὸς γάλα might refer to the goat's milk that Zeus was fed as an infant by the nymph Amalthea (or goat of the same name) or the nymph Melissa on Mt. Ida in Crete (cf. [Apollod.] *Bibl.* 1.1.7).]

137 Bring ... out: ἐκφέρετε: as a plural imperative, this order can be only to the unidentified attendants of 83, because a chorus cannot enter the *skênê*. For similar 'anonymous' commands cf. *e.g. Hec.* 981, *Cretans* F 472e, 45–6; see Taplin (1977) 79–80 for Aeschylus. Silenus will act on it, too (163); this confirms his role as an independent actor, rather than being coryphaeus.

138   how much?: the word-order here – the postponement of πόσον ('how much') – emphasizes Silenus' venality (cf. 150, 160), which is evident in other satyr-plays and thus a trope of his characterisation, *e.g.* Soph. *Trackers* 51, 56, 78, 162, 208; cf. 456; in Eur. *Sciron* (F 675) the old satyr appears to act as pimp for some prostitutes.

140   the dearest words: cf. Eur. *Ion* 1488; Soph. *Phil.* 1290. The antecedent of οὗ is πῶμα (drink) of the previous line. **what we've needed**: a direct echo of οὗ σπανίζομεν which Odysseus used when asking for bread (133). Euripides incorporates a neat complement here: wine is to Silenus and the satyrs as bread is to civilized humans. Both are unknown to the Cyclopes.

141   Maron: a priest of Apollo and son of Euanthes in the *Odyssey*, who gave Odysseus wine (*Od.* 9.197–8); elsewhere he is also the grandson of Dionysus (Hes. F 238). This is the earliest extant description of him as the son of the wine-god; Satyrus gives him the same parentage as here (*FGrH* F 1.27). At Cratinus F 135 Maron is a metonymy for wine, like his father (cf. Cratinus F 146); and possibly also at *Cyc.* 412.

142–3   The one I ... reared: the wording evokes Silenus' well-known role as the carer of Dionysus in satyric drama (Soph. *Little Dionysus* F 171; cf. Aesch. *Net-Fishers* F **47a.770; *Adespota* F 646a.4–12) and art (*e.g.* Boardman 1989: fig. 126); cf. also statues of Silenus holding the infant god (*e.g. LIMC* VIII.1 s.v. 'Silenoi' 215, which is a replica in the Louvre, of a famous Vatican statue). But Odysseus' reply and reference to **the son of Bacchus** make it clear that Silenus has also reared Maron. Euripides is thus alluding to an episode otherwise unknown to us, but which may have been the subject of another satyr-play, as long ago suggested by Waltz (1931).

145   Here is the wine-skin ... it: the use of νιν (here = 'it') is rare for a neuter (πῶμα), but cf. Eur. *Bacc.* 289–90. [Radermacher's emendation ἀσκὸς (= ὁ ἀσκός 'the wine-skin') gives more force to the demonstrative ὅδε 'here' (literally 'this') than L's ἀσκὸς.]

146   Silenus' greed for wine – compounded here by his enforced abstinence during his time as Polyphemus' slave – matches the satyrs' more general exuberance for their favourite drink (cf. Sophocles' satyric *Little Dionysus* F 172).

147   The translation follows the text of Diggle who posits a lacuna here, following Nauck and Kirchhoff, while Duchemin's text daggers the first four Greek words. The problem is that ναί (**yes**) and δὶς τόσον πῶμα (**twice as much drink**) can only depend on a preceding but missing clause. However, Ussher and Seaford suggest that reading νᾷ (from νάω 'flow'), mooted by a number of scholars, apparently independently – Blumenthal, Grégoire, Levi, Cerri – removes the difficulty. The sense would thus be: 'there runs twice as much drink as flows from the wine-skin'. Odysseus might be saying that two parts of water are added for every part of wine (suggested by Cerri), or that the wine-skin will replenish itself twofold for every amount that Silenus drinks from it (suggested by Simmonds and Timberlake, who still nevertheless print ναί 'Yes'). This latter interpretation seems a plausible way of reading Odysseus' words, who is, after all, trying to strike a favourable deal for himself and his men, and it may be considered part of his 'sales pitch'; as we have learnt, the wine is of divine origin (141–3). But this reading would have more cogency if 147 began with an adversative in response to 146. These readings, then, must remain speculative; what does seem beyond dispute is that the reading of L here is too elliptical and abrupt after 146.

148 beautiful: the wine is spoken of in almost visual terms as καλός more than once in this scene; see 153n., 158n., below.

149 Literally: 'Do you want that I should give you a taste …?' This combines two questions 'do you want?' and a deliberative aorist subjunctive 'am I to give you a taste?' This paratactic idiom is colloquial; see Stevens (1976) 60.   **unmixed**: standard Greek practice was to mix wine either with honey or water (Ar. *Knights* 1187, etc.); more fully, see Davidson (1998) 20–69. Stronger drink here will affect Silenus all the more and give more scope for his comic and transgressive behaviour later in the play. In Lycophron's *Menedemus* (F 2.6–7) an enraged Silenus complains of his host's stinginess in serving watered down wine in small cups; cf. also Ion *Omphale* F 27 with n. and Achaeus, *Aethon* F 9, below. For word play and metaphorical uses of ἄκρατος, see below 576–7n. and 602n.

150 sale: cf. above 138n.

151 And look: translates the expression καὶ μὴν, which suggests that Odysseus produces the cup with a flourish, as if to entice the aged satyr further and increase his chances of getting a good return for the gift of wine.   **brought along**: translates ἐφέλκω (more literally) 'take in tow' (LSJ s.v. I); the cup is tied to the wine-skin (or Odysseus' belt) like a small boat towed by a ship.

152 Come on: φέρε followed by an imperative is colloquial; see Stevens (1976) 42; cf. above 8n.   **pour it out and let it gurgle in**: translates Valckenaer's emendation ἐγκάναξον, accepted by Diggle, of L's ἐκπάταξον ('hit' or 'knock'), retained by Duchemin and Ussher. The compound in ἐκ- more or less restricts the sense to 'out (of the skin)', and this seems acceptable only as a colloquialism. A good parallel for Valckenaer's emendation is Ar. *Knights* 105–6; but the ms reading can still be understood in the sense of 'hit' whereby the wine hits the cup when poured out; and as *lectio difficilior* L's reading still has some plausibility.   **so I can remember what it means to drink**: literally: 'so that I may remember, having drunk'. Here, the aorist participle πιών is coincident, but it could also be taken as a past 'by having drunk'; for discussion of such participles, see Barrett (1964) on *Hipp.* 289–92.

153–4 There, done! (ἰδού): a colloquial compliance (cf. 545); see Stevens (1976) 35–6.   **What a beautiful scent …** : ὡς is exclamatory (cf. also 577, 665); Smyth §2682. In the *Odyssey*, Maron's wine is described as having a 'sweet aroma' (*Od.* 9.210). But Silenus uses καλή, a word more usually associated with fine appearances (*e.g.* Aesch. *Sacred Delegates* F **78a 18; cf. ib. 12; LSJ refer it to 'outward form': s.v. καλός I). Seaford cites two instances of smell being spoken of in visual terms (Ar. *Birds* 1715–16; Alexis F 222.3–4). That a smell should be visible is paradoxical synaesthesia and is hardly sufficient reason to emend the text, as do Kovacs (χροιάν: 'colour') and Willink (φυὴν: 'form' or 'body'), for L's ὀσμὴν. The word seems to prompt Silenus' use of καλός ('splendid') at *Cyc.* 153 and Odysseus' question about 'seeing' the aroma, with εἶδες (**you saw**) emphatically placed first as if to underline his incredulity. The joke may work on another level: an incongruous, almost hyperbolic use of language by Silenus to express his excitement and anticipation; cf. his joy expressed at 159.   **What?** translates γάρ which can be used in abrupt questions to convey surprised recognition; see Denniston (1954) 78–9.

155   so that you don't …: ὡς ἄν + subjunctive in a purpose clause is rare in Attic prose, but occurs again at 634 (cf. Smyth §2201.a and b).   **in words alone**: the λόγος-ἔργον ('word-deed') distinction and interaction was famous in Sophistic thought (Gorgias 82 B3 DK, esp. 83–6; cf. [Aristotle] *On Melissus, Xenophanes and Gorgias* 979a11–80b 21), in Antisthenes (on which see O'Sullivan and Wong 2012) and in Thucydides' methodology as historian (1.20.3–22, etc; see Parry (1981)). It occurs in other Euripidean dramas (*e.g.*, *Alc.* 339; *El.* 893) and implicitly elsewhere in *Cyclops* (375–6 with n.) and other satyric drama (*e.g.* Soph. *Trackers* 152). It need not carry overtones of intellectual debate and speculation here at 155; Odysseus, rather, wants Silenus' appreciation of the wine to translate itself into action so that the old satyr gives generous amounts of food in return.

156–7   For satyrs, drink and dancing are inseparable; cf. 124n.

158   Did it really: Odysseus seems to be toying with Silenus; his question is here is ironic, as μῶν can sometimes expect a negative answer; cf. Latin *num*. But as Barrett (1964) on *Hipp.* 794 notes, Odysseus fully expects Silenus to react as he does to the wine and approves of it; the use of μῶν here suggests mock surprise.   **beautifully**: the play on καλός (cf. 148, 153) is kept up.

160–1   money: strictly speaking, an 'anachronism' – but one hardly likely to bother the audience – in that (a) the heroic age did not have any currency and (b) the mythical Sicily of the play has no people, and therefore no commerce, on it; cf. also *Sciron* F 675 for other anachronistic references to money in satyric drama. Odysseus' offer of money is probably a mere pretence (cf. 139), but perhaps was designed to ingratiate himself further with the old satyr.   **Just loosen the wine-skin**: the wine-skin has already been opened; now Silenus wants the wine to flow more freely from it. Silenus, a normally venal figure (cf. above 138n.), in rejecting Odysseus' offer of money, thus appears in his true colours as obsessed with the pleasures of drink, especially since he has begun drinking (155–9).

162   bring out: see above 137n.

163   masters: Ussher suggests that the plural δεσποτῶν can signify a single master, as at Eur. *Hec.* 557, and may refer to Polyphemus; conversely, as Silenus goes on to mention all the Cyclopes (165), it appears that these – including, of course, Polyphemus – are the masters he has in mind. The absence of an article, however, with δεσποτῶν may suggest that Silenus is thinking of masters generally.

164–6 I could go mad: ἂν ... μαινοίμην Silenus in his mania for drinking is hardly likely to be satisfied with 'one cup' of wine. The influence of Dionysus seems to be present on more than one level here, as cognates of μαίνομαι typically express the frenzy of Bacchic worship, evident in the etymology of the word *maenad* (Eur. *Bacc.* 32, 354, etc.); at *Bacc.* 130 the satyrs are themselves μαινόμενοι (but cf. 168n.). In his first appearance in Greek literature Dionysus is already μαινόμενος (*Il.* 6.132). Silenus' desire for drunkenness can be seen as a desire to be reunited with his god (cf. 124n.). **throwing myself** (ῥίψας): this intransitive use of ῥίπτω is paralleled at *Alc.* 897. **Leucadian rocks**: part of a promontory, off the west coast of Greece just north of Ithaca, and a place of execution for criminals who were thrown into the sea (Strabo 10.2.9). [While μαίνομαι can occasionally take infinitives in the sense 'rage madly to do something' (*e.g.*, *Il.* 16.75) it is far more often associated with participles; thus, Diggle prints Kirchhoff's emendations of ἐκπιών ('after drinking') for L's ἐκπιεῖν, and at 166 ῥίψας ('throwing') for L's ῥίψαι, which, like the aorist participle ἀντιδούς ('swapping'), is coincident with ἂν ... μαινοίμην (cf. above 152n.). But some editors, *e.g.*, Duchemin, Paganelli and Paduano, retain the infinitives.]

167 relaxing my furrowed brows: a unique usage of καταβάλλω here; Silenus' brow is furrowed because of his sufferings. Wine, as he tells us, leads to a forgetting of woes (172), an idea found elsewhere in Greek thought; for instance, in the *Cypria* (F 18 Davies) and Eur. *Bacc.* (280–3) wine is called the best antidote for sorrow. **just once**: in his comic enthusiasm, Silenus, normally a coward like his sons (Soph. *Trackers* 205–9; cf. *Cyc.* 635–45), claims he would be happy to die a criminal's death if he could sate his desire for drink 'just once', ἅπαξ. For parallels to the idea of attaining satisfaction by doing something 'just once', see Soph. *El.* 1483; Ar. *Wasps* 92; Solon F 33.6 (all cited by Seaford).

168 Since: translates ὡς, which here is 'elliptical' beginning a sentence, 'since, because, for ...'; for this colloquial use, see Stevens (1976) 48. **is mad**: μαίνεται. Here the word refers to those who are 'mad' in not enjoying wine as a gift of Dionysus (cf. 164n.). A destructive madness is a common affliction of those who refuse to acknowledge Dionysus properly, such as the Proetids (Hes. F 131–3M-W), the Minyads (Ovid. *Met.* 4.1 ff; Aelian *VH* 3.42) and Lycurgus (Soph. *Ant.* 955–65, esp. 959, 962); for Lycurgus, see also above 3–4n. The 'madness' of Dionysus' most famous opponent in tragedy, Pentheus in Euripides' *Bacchae*, is reiterated in the play; at *Bacc.* 325–6 Tiresias says to him, μαίνῃ ('you're mad'), because he 'fights the god'; cf. 301, 359; note also *Bacc.* 399–400, 887 and 999 where cognates of the verb μαίνομαι are used of divine opponents generally; and Cadmus' judgement at 1295.

169–71 These lines combine three cardinal satyric activities: drink, dance and sex, the last of which is uppermost, so to speak, in Silenus' fantasy here. For discussion of the sexual activity of satyrs, see Lissarague (1990b); Keuls (1993) 357–72; above Gen. Intro. pp. 9–17, and Index of Motifs.   **it's possible**: for ἔστι with infinitive (here, ἐξανιστάναι 'to make to stand to attention') cf. ψαῦσαι ('grab hold') at 171; *Hipp.* 705 (see also Smyth §1985).   **this**: τουτί is a more emphatic demonstrative than τοῦτο, and the deictic with final iota is not tragic; it occurs also in Soph. *Trackers* 114. Silenus grabs, or at least points to, his phallus, a conspicuous part of the satyric actor's costume (cf. Pronomos vase; KPS pls. 4, 5a–b, 28a–b; see also Lissarague 1990b figs. 2.4, 2.6, 2.23, 2.28 for satyrs grabbing their own penises; *LIMC* VIII.1 s.v. 'Silenoi' 117, 119).   **breasts**: satyrs groping female figures are widely depicted on vases (KPS pl. 29b, *LIMC* VIII.1 s.v. 'Mainades' 62, 64; 'Silenoi' 104, etc.), and they may have done so (or tried) in any number of satyr plays, *e.g. Net-Fishers*; Achaeus, *Fates* F 28; Soph. *Helen's Marriage* or *Pandora*.   **all ready**: translates παρεσκευασμένου, which Diggle considers corrupt; some emendations have been posited (see Duchemin; Seaford). Kovacs in his Loeb edition (1994a) prints Blaydes' conjecture παρεσκευασμένον, explaining elsewhere (1994b) 149 that he accepts it as neuter with ἐστίν understood; this would give (literally): 'it is ready...'. Ussher and Seaford more plausibly take the genitive participle with λειμῶνος (here='bush'; cf. κῆπος 'garden': Archilochus F 196a West) and tentatively suggest that it could refer to depilation (cf. Ar. *Thesm.* 591; *Lys.* 89). But, as λειμών connotes moisture as well as fertility (LSJ s.v. I), then the participle may refer to lubrication, natural or otherwise, in preparation for sex (cf. the *double entendre* at *Cyc.* 516: the nymph's 'cave' is moist: δροσερῶν ... ἄντρων). Such apparent readiness on the part of the female will seem unlikely here, but this is Silenus' fantasy after all; cf. other satyric fantasies of female sexual appetite (below 181–2n; *Net-Fishers* F**46c.59–61). And while it is true that red-figure scenes often show maenads resisting satyrs (*e.g.* the amphora by the Kleophrades painter of *c.* 490: *LIMC* VIII.1 s.v. 'Mainades' 36; the amphora by Oltos, *c.* 520: *LIMC* VIII.1 s.v. 'Mainades' 62), Hedreen (1994) has shown that black figure depictions more frequently show nymphs willingly accepting the advances of satyrs.

172   shall I <not> kiss: another example of Silenus' hyperbolic, almost erotic joy at being reunited with his beloved drink, paralleled elsewhere in the play (at 553 and 555 the wine 'kisses' Silenus; cf. 439–40) and in Greek art: *e.g.* Osborne (1998) 17–18; for depictions of satyrs' sexual play with drinking vessels, see the famous psykter by Douris (=BM E768); Kilmer (1993) figs R126, R 148. Plutarch (*Mor.* 2.86e) tells us that in Aeschylus' *Prometheus Fire Kindler* the satyrs want to kiss fire on seeing it for the first time but are warned they will mourn for their beards if they do (Aesch. F 207 with n. below). [The negative supplement <οὐ> by Matthiae, while requiring interrogative punctuation to follow it, is generally accepted (cf., however, Duchemin). κυνήσομαι should be retained over Tyrwhitt's <οὐ>κ ὠνήσομαι ('won't I buy?'), which also requires an interrogative to follow it.]

173   moron of a Cyclops (literally, 'the Cyclops' ignorance') such periphrasis recalls Homer's referring to the might of Hector (*Il.* 9.351), or Pindar referring to Heracles (F 29.4), but, appropriately for this drama, such grandiloquent expression is given a satyric spin and used to denote the stupidity of an ogre. Similar periphrases are also found at 580 ('the august majesty of the gods) and in Soph. *Trackers* 258. Polyphemus is ignorant of the pleasures of wine, and by corollary, the Dionysiac thiasos; elsewhere the chorus call him an 'ignoramus' (493) and the monster's boorishness and ignorance of sympotic etiquette are emphasized later in the play (519–75). Pentheus in the *Bacchae* similarly suffers from ἀμαθία (480, 490).

174   go to hell: translates the colloquialism κλαίειν κελεύων (literally: 'ordering him to cry'); as Stevens (1976) 15 notes, κλαίειν has the sense of 'smart for something'. The expression occurs in Aristophanic comedy (*e.g. Ach.* 1131, *Knights* 433), but not extant tragedy; cf. also below 340–1nn. and 701n. where κλαίειν appears with a similar verb of command (ἄνωγα). At 319 Polyphemus uses the milder expression χαίρειν κελεύω 'good riddance'. **eye in the middle of his head**: the position of μέσον is predicative, and does not refer to a middle eye. Silenus emphasizes the physical grotesqueness of the monster to show his disdain; his comment also anticipates – unwittingly from his perspective, but for the knowing audience at least – the blinding to come (cf. 458–9), as does the reference to 'crying' (κλαίειν).

175   talk something over: this reflects the prefix in the compound in the verb διαλαλήσωμέν, which is not necessarily pejorative in Euripides, while λαλεῖν can be so elsewhere in denoting 'chatter'; see below 313–15n. Tyrwhitt attributes this line to the chorus, while L leaves it unattributed. The satyrs want more than just a quick chat; their prurient reasons become clear at 179.

176   Well, of course ... friends to a friend: the theme of friendship (φιλία) is struck immediately between Odysseus and the satyrs, emphasised further by the particle μὴν ('well, of course'), which here, as Denniston (1954) 353–4 notes, expresses a favourable reaction to the words of the previous speaker; cf. above 73–5n.

177   take Helen captive (χειρίαν): for the predicative adjective so used, see *And.* 628; Smyth §1043.

179–80   you had captured (εἵλετε): there may be word-play following the appearance of 'Helen' in 177, alluding perhaps to Aeschylus' play on her name at *Ag.* 689–90 (where she herself 'captures', *i.e.* destroys); cf. also Eur. *Hec.* 442–3; *Tro.* 1213–14. **the young woman**: Helen is known to the satyrs in other dramas that deal with her marriage to Paris ten years earlier. In Sophocles' *Helen's Marriage* (F 181–4), the satyrs openly lusted after her, and she may have been onstage with them in Cratinus' comic *Dionysalexandros*. **all bang her**: compounds of κροτέω for sexual activity appear in Old Comedy; see Henderson (1991a) 171 n. 88 for refs. The satyrs' question implies that the Greeks went to war for the sole chance of having sex with her. This is not just a comic projection of the satyrs' own fantasies; it also deflates, in typical satyric fashion, the more 'heroic' and pompous reasons mooted for the Trojan war elsewhere in Greek tragedy, *e.g.* Eur.'s *Troades* (860–79), and later in *Cyc.* by Odysseus himself (285–312 below).

181–2   The satyrs consider Helen some sort of nymphomaniac. Apart from Menelaus and Paris, another of her 'husbands' was Deiphobus (*Little Iliad*, arg. 2; Eur. *Tro.* 959). Theseus abducted her as a child (Diod. Sic. 4.63.2; [Apollod.] *Ep.* 1.23–4), and in some accounts Achilles was her 'fifth husband' (Servius ad *Aen.* 1.34; Tzetzes, *On Lycophron* 143, 174; cf. also *Cypria* arg. 11).   **the traitor**: the satyrs take a predictably simplistic view of Helen's guilt, seemingly consistent with what Helen says about herself in the *Iliad* (3.180), and with views found in Alcaeus (F N 1, B10 L-P) and the chorus of Aeschylus' *Agamemnon* (esp. 403–8, 681–93); cf. Sappho (F 16 L-P) for a treatment different in tone. Elsewhere in Euripidean tragedies she is labelled 'traitor' (*And.* 630, *El.* 1028, *Hel.* 834, 931, 1148), but as early as Homer the question of Helen's guilt is an open one, with Priam blaming the gods for the war (*Il.* 3.162–5), as indeed does Odysseus in response to Polyphemus' attack on her (*Cyc.* 280–5). Euripides' lecherous chorus here have no interest in the issues raised by other treatments of Helen's story, such as Gorgias' *Encomium of Helen* (82 B 11 DK) which ostensibly portrays her as victim of one of four forces: the gods, erotic desire, Paris' violence, or his supposed rhetorical powers. Likewise the satyr chorus here would hardly countenance Helen's own defence speech which Euripides gives her in the *Troades* (914–65) and some of its claims: *e.g.* that the gods are to blame for the war, and that Hecuba, in ignoring baleful prophecies about Paris, is to be blamed for Troy's fall, and that Helen's own beauty saved Greece from a Trojan invasion.

182–4   The substance of these lines equates closely with those of Hecuba in the *Troades* who claims that Helen's arrogance and greed for Oriental splendour as much as lust led her to elope with Paris (987–97, 1020–22); di Marco (1980, 39–45) argues for a parody of Sappho F 22 (L-P). But Euripides incorporates some clever *doubles entendres* here to make the causes for Helen's elopement one and the same.   **fancy trouser-equipment** (θυλάκους τοὺς ποικίλους): Paris' attire is assimilated to the clothing of fifth-century Persians (Hdt. 5.49.3; Ar. *Wasps* 1087), but, as the cognate θυλάκη means scrotum (LSJ s.v. I; cf. Ar. *Frogs* 1203), a punning reference to sexual organs is inescapable here; see Henderson (1991a) 27.   **his neck**: in comedy αὐχήν can also mean penis (Ar. *Lys.* 681); see also Henderson (1991a) 114; cf. Sophocles' satyric F 756 where a lecherous satyr wants to throw his arms around Heracles' αὐχήν (possibly from his *Oeneus*; for discussion, see n. 2 on *Oeneus* p. 381 KPS 373–4). It is tempting to see another *double entendre* in the reference to Paris' αὐχήν here, notwithstanding the gold necklace around it, which identifies him as an exotic, richly attired barbarian.

185   she was swept away: by this passive ἐξεπτοήθη the satyrs do not intend to absolve Helen of responsibility any more than does Alcaeus' [ἐ]πτ[όαισε ('she fluttered'; F N 1.3 L-P, if correctly supplemented). In the *Troades* Hecuba claims that Helen's mind 'was made' Cypris, *i.e.* Aphrodite, at the sight of Paris (*Tro.* 988: ἐποιήθη), but, of course, still demands her death. Gorgias (*Hel.* 19) invokes much the same idea, when conversely claiming that Helen fell victim to the erotic nature of Paris' presence and is therefore to be exonerated.

185–6   that excellent little fella, Menelaus: di Marco (1980) 39–45 sees further parody of Sappho F 16.6–9 (L-P), especially her reference to Menelaus as ἄριστος where the tone is far more poignant than here. In the *Iliad* Menelaus is not small; at least he is broader than Odysseus when the two are standing, while the latter is more lordly when they are seated (*Il.* 3.180–1). That the satyrs have a fondness for this hero, expressed in a condescending diminutive (ἀνθρώπιον), seems apt (cf. Polyphemus' contemptuous ἀνθρωπίσκε to Odysseus at 316); diminutives are naturally rare in tragedy (but see Stevens (1976) 5 n. 12); see n. 12 on Critias (?) *Sisyphus* (?) F 19.39. Menelaus has comical elements about him as early as Homer, notably in his duel with Paris in *Iliad* 3 which he wins 'on points', but which ends only in his being cuckolded again (esp. *Il.* 3.426–48). While a competent fighter in the *Iliad*, he is in no position even to think about fighting Hector (*Il.* 7.109–19); and elsewhere in the *Iliad* he is compared to a mosquito (17.570–2). In the *Odyssey* he is upstaged by his wife (15.166–81), and in the *Troades*, for all his stated intentions, he is still in thrall to his wife, as Hecuba knows only too well, even as he makes lame attempts at humour about Helen's weight (1050–1). The failure of Menelaus' resolve to kill Helen on seeing her exposed breasts is known from Old Comedy (Ar. *Lys.* 155–6), and depicted in fifth-century art (*LIMC* IV.1 s.v. 'Helene' 260, 262, 264–6, 269–72, 274, 275, 277). In some traditions he is even considered a coward (implied at Aesch. *Ag.* 115; see Fraenkel's note ad loc.), and Apollo refers to him as a 'weak spear-fighter' (*Il.* 17.588), a description recalled in Plato's *Symposium* (174c); such qualities might further endear him to the chorus, whose own cowardice emerges readily enough in *Cyc.* (635–50).

186–7   This misogynistic topos is traceable to Hesiod in the accounts of Pandora's creation (*Th.* 571–90; *W&D* 60–90) and Semonides (F 7 *passim*, esp. 72, 96–7). Similar sentiments are expressed by a number of figures in tragedy: *e.g.*, Eteocles in Aeschylus' *Seven* (187–90, 256), Jason in Euripides' *Medea* (573–5) and Hipploytus (*Hipp.* 616–50), this last instance a particularly transgressive form of misogyny that is not only disturbing to one of Hippolytus' attendants (*Hipp.* 88–120), but earns the fatal wrath of Aphrodite. Such trenchant misogyny is comically recast by the hedonistic satyrs, who like to have their cake and eat it, too. The idea that Euripides was a misogynist is a running gag already in Aristophanic comedy (*e.g. Thesm. passim*), and has been the focus of much modern scholarship; for an overview, see, for instance, March (1990) 32–75.

188   flocks (ποιμνίων): translates Scaliger's emendation of L's 'shepherds' (ποιμένων) accepted by *e.g.* Duchemin, Ussher, Biehl, Paduano, which suggests 'creatures reared by shepherds' defined in 189 as 'lambs'.

189   lord Odysseus: Silenus' tone becomes more sycophantic now (cf. above 104), in the prospect of of making a decent exchange.

192   Although serious danger looms – Ussher sees urgency in the present imperatives (φέρεσθε, χωρεῖτε) – Silenus is still keen to make sure he gets his wine.

193–4   The ms attributes line 193 to Odysseus; Dindorf's attribution of it to Silenus is widely accepted. Hermann divided it between the chorus and Odysseus. Paganelli (1981) gives τί δράσομεν; ('what are we going to do?') to Odysseus, and divided 194 between Silenus and the chorus; Duchemin divided it between Silenus and Odysseus. But L's attribution need not be dismissed *tout court*, even though the evident alarm at 193 might seem uncharacteristic of Odysseus (cf. 198–202). He certainly expresses fear at 194 (the latter half at least is undeniably his words), and it is not uncommon for characters in tragedy and elsewhere to express alarm at shocking news, only to regain some element of composure or focus shortly afterwards; cf. the reaction of Eteocles to the news of Polynices' presence at the gate at which he himself is to fight (Aesch. *Seven* 653–7).

195–7   The advice to run into the cave, is, as Odysseus realizes, fraught with danger, but is necessary for the dramatic action to be consistent with the Homeric model. It need not be seen as malicious on the part of Silenus, despite his apparent glee at the prospect of Polyphemus' cannibalistic meal (250–1, 313–15).

198–202   Some sermonizing from Odysseus here, as he rehearses the heroic code of standing one's grounds against the enemy, which he enunciates and enacts himself when under pressure from hordes of Trojans (*Il.* 11.401–10); cf. *Il.* 17.90–112 when Menelaus allows discretion to be the better part of valour in similar circumstances (and which may be the source for the idea that he was a coward; cf. Aesch. *Ag.* 115, and above 185–6n.).   **if I must die … nobly** (εὐγενῶς): his concern to face death, if necessary, recalls Hector's resolve to fight Achilles and at least die 'not ingloriously' (μὴ ... ἀκλειῶς: *Il.* 22.304); on the theme and variants of καλῶς θανεῖν ('to die nobly') elsewhere in Euripides, see *Hec.* 329; *Hel.* 298; *Or.* 1152; *Erechtheus* F 361.

202   preserve my good repute of old: there is some irony here, since for Silenus, at least, Odysseus' renown conjures up a man of suspect ancestry and a relentless babbler (104), not the brave hero Odysseus announces himself to be. [Schenk emends L's εὖ σώσομεν to συσσώσομεν (lit. 'save together with my life)' to give better sense.]

203   Get out of the way! Make way! ἄνεχε πάρεχε, which seems formulaic, occurs at Ar. *Wasps* 1326 (cf. *Birds* 1720) and Eur. *Tro.* 308 where it introduces a wedding procession with torches; see Duchemin, Ussher, and Seaford for detailed discussion. L attributes this line to Silenus, Duchemin to the chorus; Paganelli divides it between the chorus and Polyphemus, and Biehl between Silenus and the monster. Attribution of 203 to Polyphemus (Tyrwhitt) is most likely; the bullying imperatives are well-suited both to his despotic nature, forcefully expressed here (and at 210) in the three tribrachs which express the monsters' impatience and anger, which are alluded to already by the satyrs and Silenus and become fully manifest as the play progresses (cf. 211).

204–5 Bacchic revel: the satyrs are not performing this at all; it is simply an inference which the ignorant Polyphemus makes as a result of seeing their **'idleness'**. Polyphemus' remarks on the absence of Dionysus and his cult brutally confirm what Silenus and the satyrs have already complained about (25–6, 63–81, esp. 63–5). Straightaway he emerges as another anti-Dionysian ogre to appear on the satyric stage, such as the Aeschylean Lycurgus (see above 3–4n.). Drums are instruments associated with the cult of Dionysus (see above 64–5n.; Eur. *Bacc.* 59, 156) and are depicted being played by maenads (Boardman 1989: figs 177, 229); drums were used in the worship of Cybele and Dionysus (Hdt. 4.76, Eur. *HF* 892), as were castanets (Eur. *Hel.* 1308; *H. Hom.* 14.3; Pindar, F 70b9–10; Hdt. 2.60).

206 Tell me: translates the ethic dative μοι (cf. 43n.).

207 L has γε, which is unparalleled in a question (Seaford); Dindorf emended to τε to make it co-ordinate with καί (here aspirated and elided before ὑπό). However, Duchemin, Ussher, Paganelli, Biehl all retain the ms reading.

208–9 Has milk … cheese? A slightly elliptical expression in the Greek; literally: 'has filling with cheeses been milked in ...?' The question is whether enough has been milked to produce sufficient cheese to fill the baskets after curdling.

210–11 shedding tears: cf. 490, 554 for other threats to make others cry (and 174n.). **my club**: Ussher sees a reference to stocks here, but it seems far more natural to see ξύλον as a club, the monster's weapon in Homer with which he is blinded (cf. *Od.* 9.319); s.v. ξύλον LSJ II.2. The club is the monster's weapon in many images on Greek pottery from the sixth century on; *e.g. LIMC* VIII.1 s.v. Polyphemus I 40–3, 46. In Eur. *Syleus* F 693 'club' is probably metaphoric for Heracles' penis (see n. 11 on p. 413), but the monster here need not be threatening the satyrs with rape, despite the fate of Silenus later (581–9). In any event, the use of violence by this monstrous despot (above 34–5n.) to control the satyrs reflects a motif concerning how tyrants rule (Plato, *Statesman* 276e); see also above 24n., and 442. **Look upwards, not down!** The satyrs are evidently cowering in fear; as it is likely that Polyphemus' costume noticeably increases the height of the actor wearing it, the order is for them to look him in his grotesquely single eye.

213 Orion: probably a reference to the giant himself rather than the constellation, despite the mention of stars. Here we may see a comic over-reaction of the satyrs to the fearsome prospect of their towering master, a hunter, like Orion, albeit one who has returned home empty-handed. The Orion reference is apt for the Euripidean Polyphemus for other reasons, too. Both are club-wielding giants and sons of Poseidon (*Od.* 11.572–5); both are violent and lecherous, since Orion's assaults on Merope and Artemis (Hesiod, F 148a) find their eventual parallel in Polyphemus' grotesque rape of Silenus (581–9). Both meet with the same punishment. Hesiod (F 148a) and

Servius (*Aen.* 10.763) mention Orion's blinding by Merope's father, Oinopion, a son of Dionysus. Seaford plausibly suggests that this episode may have been dealt with in Sophocles' satyric *Cedalion* (F 328–33). For discussion of *Cedalion*, see, more recently, KPS 344–8, esp. 344 n. 3 for other sources for this episode.

214 meal: ἄριστον is usually the morning meal, but can be a movable feast, as Ussher notes, citing Ar. *Birds* 788; also LSJ note that it could mean 'lunch' (Thuc. 4.90, Hdt., 3.26, etc.). Problems about the passage of time in the play disappear once we realize the satyrs need not be talking literally about seeing stars.

215 gullet: φάρυγξ: here a masculine, though more often feminine, *e.g.* 356; its gender not determinable at 410, 592. This becomes the focus for Polyphemus' cannibalism later in the play (356, 410, 592; cf. 608); the potentially comic glutton here emerges as something more sinister and malignant.

217 a whole storage jar: pithoi were large storage jars, many times the capacity of ordinary amphorae; the gluttony of the Cyclops is commensurate with his size; cf. also 327, 388. Lityerses, the ogre of Sositheus' satyr-play, *Daphnis or Lityerses*, has a similar penchant for bibulous excess in drinking down a pithos the size of ten amphorae (Sositheus, F 2.7–9; see n. 4).

218 sheep's or cow's: the Greek adjectives could refer to the neuter γάλα (216) or πίθος in the accusative. The relative ὃν (219), L's reading kept by Diggle, would suggest the latter is more likely.

220–1 dancing, leaping around: even though the satyrs have complained of the absence of dancing and other Dionysiac activities since their captivity (25–6, 63–81), Polyphemus seems to realise that dancing and constant movement are an essential part of their nature and makes a cruel joke from it. [L has no object expressed for ἀπολέσαιτε, resulting in Seidler's emendation of L's γ(ε) to μ(ε), commonly accepted].

222 The tone of ἔα (**Hey!**) here is one of resentment as well as surprise, while Odysseus' ἔα (99) is simply the latter; for both 'surprise' and 'unwelcome surprise', see Stevens (1976) 33 n. 81. Polyphemus is immediately hostile to the strangers in referring to them contemptuously as a 'mob': ὄχλος (cf. *Hec.* 607, *Her.* 527, etc; Plato, *Gorg.* 455a;).

223–5 Odysseus and his men have little chance in the wake of Polyphemus' reaction to their presence, more volatile than the comparatively restrained, but no less menacing, tone of his Homeric counterpart, who even tries to trick Odysseus into revealing the whereabouts of his ship (*Od.* 9.279–81). **Anyway** (γέ τοι): the expression is a livelier form of the more common γοῦν 'at any rate', and both particles combined can have a exclamatory force; see Denniston (1954) 550 (4), 551 (iii). Polyphemus goes on to leap from one wrong conclusion to another without directly addressing the strangers until 275. **bodies**: σῶμα (literally, in singular form 'body') here is an accusative of respect.

226–7 the old man ... beating: another wrong inference made by the Cyclops,

this time exploited by Silenus to escape the monster's wrath (228–34). It is typical
of the roguish satyr to side with whoever he thinks is in control. The objection
of Ussher on 224–30 that Silenus has not been drinking long enough to have a
ruddy complexion misses the point. Silenus is no ordinary imbiber, and we may
fully expect the effects of his sudden reacquaintance with his beloved drink to be
comically exaggerated. The actor may have put on another reddish mask on going
into the *skēnē*-building at 174, and he has certainly been onstage since 188.   **bald**:
φαλακρόν can also be a noun and mean tip of the penis or 'knob' (*Net-Fishers* F
**47a.24, and see note 12 below; Soph. *Trackers* 368, etc.); but here its proximity
to μέτωπον ('forehead') shows it is adjectival and means 'bald'; Silenus is bald
in almost all depictions of him in vase-painting.   **head**: translates Tyrwhitt's
emendation of L's πρόσωπον ('face') to μέτωπον ('forehead'), given Polyphemus'
reference to Silenus' κάρα ('head') at 229.
231   I am a god ... sprung from gods: With this remark, Polyphemus shows
that he is not an atheist, as many have asserted; see O'Sullivan (2005) 119–22.
In acknowledging the existence of the gods, but holding conventional religion in
contempt – including his father's temples (318–9) – the Cyclops is arguably an even
more transgressive figure; see also below 582–3n.
232   they continued to carry off: the imperfect ἐφόρουν implies that Odysseus
and his men wilfully ignored Silenus'protests; cf. also ἐξεφοροῦντο in 234.
233   although (I) wouldn't allow it (οὐκ ἐῶντος): μου is easily supplied from
232 ἐγώ, with ellipse of the 'subject' in the genitive absolute construction (Smyth
§2072).
234   This verse has a '3rd foot anapaest' so far unique in satyric drama; Musgrave
emends to ἐξεφροῦντο, but this gives it wrong sense ('let the sheep go out'): they
are tied up (225).
235   collar three cubits wide: collars were applied to dogs (Ar. *Wasps* 897) and
criminals (Xen. *Hell.* 3.3.11). Silenus' fiction tries to convey to Polyphemus that the
strangers view him as bestial as well as criminal; the huge size of the collar seems
to allude to his physical height, although the extent to which this was represented
visually (*i.e.*, in the actor's costume) remains unclear; cf. above 210–11n.   **in full
view of that big eye of yours:** [for κατά 'in the sight of', Canter's emendation for
L's impossible κᾆτα ('and next'), cf. Eur. *El.* 910. μέσον is again predicative (cf.
above 174n.); more literally the expression is 'the eye in the middle (of your head).']
237   flay: Ruhnken's emendation to ἀπολέψειν for L's ἀποθλίψειν, which means
'to squeeze'. The former seems more likely here unless the reference here is to
blood oozing from a whipped back, like juice from a grape; for this sense Seaford
cites Nicander F 86.
240   to heave rocks: putting Polyphemus to work in a quarry seems to be a grim
joke on the abilities of Cyclopes as builders of monumental architecture; cf. above
92–3n.   **mill-house**: Ruhnken's emendation to ἢ 'ς μυλῶνα for L's ἢ πυλῶνα. The

latter sense would seem to mean 'to knock down a gateway'; but the idea of being thrown into the mill after a beating is at least better attested in Greek thought (Lysias 1.18, Menander *Asp.* 245, *Hero* 3). Silenus' lie becomes more fanciful at every turn, including the implausibility that a disembowelled person (236) could be expected to perform hard labour.

241–3 Now then, you go ... will you?: for οὔκουν plus future indicative, see Denniston (1954) 435 and Smyth §2953.d; cf. also 632 below. To whom does Polyphemus address this gruff order? Ussher assumes Silenus. But the old satyr blithely remains onstage, and it is hardly likely that he would ignore a command from his brutal overlord, who does not repeat the command to him, despite his continuing presence. Also, the tone is out of keeping with Polyphemus' generally benign attitude to Silenus (229, 273–4, 539), even if this eventually manifests itself grotesquely later (581–9). The order may be addressed to one of the attendants mentioned at 83, as in the translation by Kovacs (1994a), who may have entered with the satyrs during the parodos (41–81n.).

243 Since (ὡς): see above 168n.

244–5 Unlike his Homeric counterpart, the satyric Polyphemus carves his victims up and cooks them, becoming a monstrous chef as in other versions of the tale (Cratinus F 143 *PCG*; Antiphanes F 132, 133 *PCG*); in the *Odyssey* he eats them raw (*Od.* 9.291–3). Here, this important difference endows the Euripidean monster with certain elements of sophistication amid all his savagery; for discussion of the form of sacrifice to himself that Polyphemus' meal takes (cf. 334–5), see Seaford 1984 and his introduction (pp. 51–9). **fill my belly**: Polyphemus is not only a typically gluttonous satyric ogre, but resembles the gluttonous athlete pilloried in another Euripidean satyr play, who is described as 'slave to his jaws and a minion to his belly' (*Autolycus* A F 282.5; see below p. 389). **me, the dispenser of meat**: κρεανόμος ('one who distributes the flesh of victims': LSJ, citing this passage). Simmonds and Timberlake translate it without explanation as 'my teeth', while Ussher sees it as 'with my knife', citing the sacrificial context; but the sacrifice is perverted. As Seaford notes, later passages in the play make it more likely that the reference is to Polyphemus, since the chorus refer to his activity of 'meat chopping' and 'dispensing' (359, 361). This gives rise to a new irony: instead of offering his guests food, this transgressive host eats his visitors, who thereby 'give' (διδόντες) their host a feast. [**giving** (διδόντες) is Heath's emendation for L's, ἔδοντος, a genitive participle in agreement with μου, implicit in the personal possesive ἐμὴν (cf. Eur. *Supp.* 921; Smyth §977). This genitive participle gives awkward sequence, meaning ... 'belly, as I eat my feast from the hot coals, to me as the dispenser of meat'.]

246 cauldron: later described as bronze (343, 392, 399), another sign of the monster's sophistication, albeit put to barbarous uses. For possible links to Phalaris, another Sicilian despot, infamous for his cruelty in roasting victims in a bronze bull (Pindar *Pyth.* 1.95–8), see O'Sullivan (2005) 132–4.

247 Since: translates ὡς, which is explanatory asyndeton; it could also be 'elliptical' here; see above 168n.

247–8 lions: the presence of lions in the Sicilian landscape again suggests the wild, uncivilised nature of the play's setting (see above 20n.). That Polyphemus eats these animals emphasises his savagery and brute strength. It is one thing to kill a lion as heroes like Heracles do; it is quite another to eat one. For the idea that one attains the characteristics of what one eats ('you are what you eat'), see below 313–15n.

249 too long deprived ... man's flesh: χρόνιος is idiomatically an adjective agreeing with Polyphemus, but here is translated as an adverb; cf. *And.* 84 (see also Smyth §1042). Here is an ominous confirmation, straight from the monster himself, of what Silenus and the satyrs have already mentioned of the Cyclopes generally (31, 92–3, 126,128); also, a grim counterpart to the satyrs' forced abstention from their natural drink, wine (140, 439–40).

250 after: for this meaning of ἐκ (*i.e.* 'following in change from'), see Smyth §1688. **O master**: Silenus continues to toady to the Cyclops, but there is some irony in calling him δέσποτης, albeit lost on the ogre (cf. 266–7) due to the negative connotations of δέσποτης in the play (see above 34–5n.); cf. also Silenus' disdain for 'masters' at 163. When at first currying favour with the civilized Odysseus, Silenus calls him ἄναξ (189), a title also reserved for Dionysus (17).

252 haven't been arriving at your: σοὺσαφίκοντο: Murray's conjecture for the unmetrical τὰ σ' ἀφίκοντο of L; this emendation gives better idiom but retains the sense of the ms; the crasis σοὺσ- is comprised of σοι and ἐσ- and recurs by conjecture at 288 and 561 with the enclitic following the third foot caesura (see West (1992) 26); and the dative is one of interest, not motion.

253 in turn: Odysseus' request to be heard ἐν μέρει might lead the audience to expect some sort of *agôn* (formal debate), so much a marked feature of many Euripidean plays (*e.g. Troades* 914–1032); before the *agôn* in *Hecuba* (1132–237) Agamemnon announces he will hear each speaker ἐν μέρει (1130); for this apect of Euripides' dramas, see Lloyd (1992). But this satyric *agôn*, which has no adjudicator, is postponed (285–346).

254 The asyndeton here, as Ussher notes, is continuative and explanatory of why Polyphemus should listen (see Smyth §2165a, 2167b).

255–8 Odysseus gives an accurate account of events, unlike the smooth talking chatterer he has been called earlier in the play; see above 104n. (cf. below 313–15n.). **voluntary seller ... no violence**: Odysseus invokes the ἑκών ... βίᾳ ('voluntarily' – 'by force') antithesis used elsewhere by Euripides (*Tro.* 373, *IA* 360); cf. the virtually identical ἑκών ... ἄκων ('voluntarily' – 'involuntarily') antithesis; *Hipp.* 319; *IT* 512; *Or.* 613, etc.

259–60 But he speaks ... back was turned: these statements are true, but, the latter is potentially problematic for Odysseus' case, as he bought the goods on the sly, knowing them to belong to Polyphemus (cf. 165). **no truth**: translates the colloquialism ὑγιὲς οὐδὲν (literally, 'nothing sound'); cf. Plato *Rep.* 10.603b 1–2; see also Stevens (1976) 26. **since he was caught**: translates ἐπεὶ κατελήφθη. The anapaest in the second foot is alien to tragedy; for similar departure from tragic metre, see 265n. The same translation comes from Heath's γ'ἐλήφθη, which removes the anapaest; it also uses the simple verb (λαμβάνω), as is usual with a participle in the sense 'caught (taking)', and is therefore preferable here to the compound (καταλαμβάνω).

261   In that case: translates Kirchhoff's emendation to γ' ἄρ(α) of L's γάρ which does not strengthen a wish on its own; cf. also the virtually identical expression κακῶς ὄλοιο 'may you die a miserable death' (without γάρ) at Aesch. *Sacred Delegates* F **78c col. I 2. **If I'm lying**: rather than simply repeating this curse back at Silenus, as the satyrs do at 272, Odysseus' rejoinder – completing the line – neatly undercuts Silenus' words by ostensibly agreeing with them with one obvious proviso. Cf. Chremylus' skeptical responses to the Old Woman's complaints in Ar. *Wealth* (1018–21); similarly, in the *Contest of Homer and Hesiod* Homer's improvisations undercut Hesiod's attempts to force him to complete a couplet that begins in a nonsensical way (*Contest* 9). This technique of agonistic exchange is one form of 'capping' which occurs when a participant in dialogue on a set theme responds to an opponent by cleverly modifying that thought or theme until one opponent is outmatched; for full discussion, see Collins (2004) *passim* who plausibly sees it operating in the *Cyclops* in 521–40, 669–75 and in the passage from the *Wealth* (see ib. 44–50), but neglects what appears to be a very blatant form of capping in *Cyclops* here.

262–5   The list of sea deities invoked by Silenus (although **Calypso** is not especially associated with the sea) begins, appropriately enough, with Polyphemus' own father, but continues in descending order of importance to end up with the most banal of sea creatures, in a comic anticlimax. As Seaford suggests, such an ending seems to parody oaths that finish with an invocation to 'all the gods' (*e.g.* Eur. *Med.* 746–7).

265   There is a second foot anapaest here (as at 334), on which see Denniston on Eur. *El.* 1141.

266–7   O my most handsome little Cyclops, O my darling little master (Κυκλώπιον ... δεσποτίσκε): an apostrophe as absurd as it is insincere, with diminutives – a linguistic form typical of satyric drama (*e.g., Cyc.* 185, 316) – addressed to a gigantic, one-eyed ogre; cf. the old satyr's contempt for the monster expressed earlier (173–4). In Achaeus' *Linus* F 26 the satyrs address Heracles in similar terms, but with a homoerotic intent absent from Silenus' remarks here.

268–9   may these miserable boys of mine: the joke seems to work on a number of levels. Satyrs are immortal (Theopompus 115 *FGH* 75c, etc.), so this wish is destined to remain unfulfilled, but this is hardly likely to be an issue for Silenus. The fact that he at least ostensibly puts his sons' lives on the line with this false oath and calls them κακοί ('miserable') undercuts any claims he makes to feeling affection for them as he does here. For the contempt the satyric father feels for his sons, cf. Soph. *Trackers* 145–68 (esp. 145–53); Lycophron, *Menedemus*, F 2; cf. also next note.

270–2 *you*: the view of Denniston (1954) 144 that αὐτὸς ἔχ(ε) literally means 'keep (the curse of 268–9) for yourself' is correct and suits the context well. It speaks volumes about Silenus' behaviour here that the satyrs are moved to defend Odysseus, even risking incurring the anger of their overlord. In Soph. *Trackers* (329–43, 371–403) they also stand up to Cyllene, a less threatening figure than Polyphemus, but fairly overbearing all the same. **If I'm telling lies**: recalls Odysseus at 261, and suggests the emerging friendship between him and the chorus of satyrs. **may my father die**: echoing their father, the satyrs give as good as they get. **Don't wrong the strangers** (or 'guests'): the preceding sentence referring to Silenus in the third person as 'my father' makes it more likely that the monster is addressed, as shown by his response in 273.

273–4 **Rhadamanthys** was a judge of the dead famous for his justice (Pindar, *Ol.* 2.75, *Pyth.* 2.73; Plato, *Laws* 624b). That Polyphemus offers such praise of the old satyr says more about the monster than it does about Silenus, by indicating the ogre's propensity to misconstrue things. Silenus' attitude to Polyphemus ranges from open hostility and contempt (see 23–35nn., 173–4nn.), to a deceptive obsequiousness (see 266–7n.), to attempts to steal the wine from him (552–3, 557–8, 565).

275–6 As is to be expected, Polyphemus' questioning here violates the heroic code of hospitality (cf. 102n.) as it does in the *Odyssey* (9.252–5).

277–9 The ellipse of the first person plural of εἰμί ('I am') in 277 is rare, but appears elsewhere in Euripides (*El.* 37), while that of the singular, in a similar formula of identification, occurs already at 103; see Smyth §945. Again, this is a straightforward version of events by Odysseus, consistent with what he told Silenus. Cf. the lie he tells Polyphemus in the *Odyssey* (9.281–6), albeit in response to a loaded question from the monster.

280–1 **went to avenge on the city of Troy**: μετέρχομαι takes the double accusative here (LSJ s.v. IV 2); here it constructs like other verbs of vengeance such as ἐτιμωρησάμην at 695. **the abduction**: translates ἁρπαγάς, a term often used in tragedy to refer to Helen's abduction (*e.g.* Aesch. *Ag.* 534). **the most vile Helen**: Polyphemus' verdict coincides with that of the satyrs (esp. 182), even though he has implied that she was a victim of rape in using ἁρπαγὰς (cf. Gorgias' verdict, esp. *Hel.* 6). That Helen, as one woman, is responsible for an entire war and its consequent destruction is repeated by the monster (283–4) and is a topos (Aesch. *Ag.* 62, 448, 800, 1455–7; Eur. *Tro.* 368–9, 781, 873–9; but cf. Gorgias *Hel.* 4; and above 181–2n.). Polyphemus' unmitigated misogyny (cf. the satyrs at 187) informs his antipathy to the war, rather than any sense of moral outrage at the sack of Troy (explored so in many tragedies) or the loss of life generally that resulted from the war.

282   endured to the full (ἐξηντληκότες): cf. 10n.

283   A shameful campaign in that you ... (στράτευμά γ᾽, οἵτινες ...): the relative
plural by sense rather than strict congruence is common enough with ὅστις 'marking
the character of a person, in that you ...'; see Diggle on *Phaethon* 160–2; Smyth
§2510.

285–346   Whether or not these speeches by Odysseus (285–312) and Polyphemus
(316–46) comprise a formal *agôn* or debate, this exchange between hero and monster
presents two world-views in sharp contrast to each other. On this level at least it differs
from the more typical of Euripidean *agônes* where attempts are made at justifying
past actions in the face of a lengthy accusation or denunciation (*e.g.*, *Hec.* 1132–
237; *El.* 1011–99; *Tro.* 914–1032). As might be expected of the hero famed for his
eloquence, Odysseus' speech works on a number of levels, beginning with appeals
to friendship and the rights of suppliants (288), before moving onto more specious
claims about the Trojan War and how it benefited Polyphemus as a 'Greek' (290–8).
Much of Odysseus' argument concerns the law (νόμος) of hospitality and respecting
suppliants which civilized people would be expected to uphold (299–311); his veiled
threat (312) suggests he realizes such claims will fall on deaf ears, nor is he mistaken.

The monster's detailed response attacks specific points raised by Odysseus (*e.g.*
316–19), but is based on an impious rejection of the authority of Zeus (320–1), and
of laws such as that of hospitality (ξενία) which are traceable to the god (338–40);
as long as the monster can enjoy physical comfort and gratification, nothing else
and nobody else matters (322–33, 340–1). The urgings of greed, indeed gluttony,
underpin the monster's world-view so much that he even makes them the basis of his
own theology of sorts (334–8). Such a response may well have struck the original
audience as surprisingly articulate, but Polyphemus' speech condemns him further
in showing that he acts out of conscious malice; his words will come back to haunt
him (see, for instance, 340, 701nn.). Many commentators have rightly seen parallels
between Polyphemus' *Weltanschauung* here and that of the Platonic Callicles, who
similarly argues for a 'greed is good' ideology (Pl. *Gorg.* 482c–4d; 491e–2c). This
connection need not make the Cyclops a sophistic figure, which has too often been
claimed; rather, his stated devotion to greed, lawlessness, violence and debauchery
(cf. 326–7) align him more closely with popular notions of tyrants as demonized
figures within Athenian culture; for full discussion, see O'Sullivan (2005) *passim.*
Odysseus' speech may be considered to uphold law (νόμος) on various levels (some
more plausible than others); Polyphemus, conversely can be seen to uphold nature
(φύσις), but only in so far as it serves his basest, most impious desires. An articulate
monster is still a monster, and a fitting ogre for satyric drama.

285   the deed of a god: the ascription of blame to the gods for the Trojan War is
as old as Homer (*Il.* 1.5; 3.164–5); cf. above 181–2n.). According to the *Cypria* (F
1) the war was a proto-Malthusian plan by Zeus to relieve Earth of excess human
population.

286–7   O noble son of the god of the deep: Odysseus tries to appeal to what he might consider Polyphemus' better nature and attempts to get him on side with reference to his parentage and calling him 'noble' (γενναῖε: 286) and 'lord', ἄναξ: 290). Given Poseidon's typical offspring, however, this may be a self-defeating ploy by Odysseus; cf. above 21–2n. Cf. Arist. *Rhet.* 1377b 21–8a 30 for discussion of the rhetorical techniques of cultivating good will in one's listeners and presenting oneself favourably to them.   **suppliants**: by identifying himself and his men as such, Odysseus puts a special obligation on Polyphemus to respect them, as one of Zeus' epithets was 'Protector of suppliants' (Aesch. *Suppl.* 347; Soph. *Phil.* 484; Eur. *Hec.* 345; Pherecydes F 114, etc.); a rejection of supplicant rights is therefore tantamount to an attack on Olympian and civilised values, consistent with Polyphemus' stated views elsewhere (320–1, 338–40, etc.).   **freely**: the implication is that Odysseus and his men deserve respect also as free men, and even as potential friends; cf. Eur. *Alc.* 1008 and see next note.

288–9   friends: Odysseus has good reason to invoke the concept of φιλία here, which already characterizes the relationship between Dionysus and the satyr chorus, as well as Odysseus, his men and the satyrs (again with the exception of Silenus; cf. above 73–4n., 176n.). Polyphemus' callous rejection of Odysseus' case thus involves a rejection of φιλία.   **unholy meal for your jaws**: this recalls Silenus' descriptions of Polyphemus' cannibalism (30–1; cf. 92–3).

290–91   we protected… : a specious claim as no part of Greece was under any threat from Troy; cf. also the implausibility of 295–6.   **temples**: Canter's emendation to ναῶν of L's νεῶν ('of ships'); 'the sites of ships' would mean, in effect, harbours. Although Odysseus goes on to mention the harbour of Taenarus (292), his point is that these places have been preserved as centres of worship of Poseidon.   **to occupy**: translates ἔχειν, a prolative infinitive nearing one of purpose (Smyth §2008).

292–5   sacred Taenarus: an old harbour town at the southern end of the Peloponnese, which had a temple to Poseidon (Strabo 8.5.1) and held a festival in honour of the god, called the Taenaria (Hesychius; *IG* 5.1.211.1). [L's ἱερεύς ('priest') is a manifest impossibility and a mere scribal error; an adjective is both needed idiomatically for Ταινάρου, and Kassel's emendation ἱερᾶς is an apt one (cf. e.g. *Med.* 825–6: ἱερᾶς / χώρας).] **caverns of cape Malea**: Malea was the easternmost of the promontories at the southern end of the Peloponnese; according to Pausanias (3.23.2), in the harbour beneath it was a statue of Poseidon, and a nearby cave seems to have been sacred to the god (Paus. 2.2.8; 8.7.2; 8.8.2; 8.10.4). [L's ἄκροι was emended to ἄκρας by Seaford, who takes it as referring not to the position of the cave or harbour inland, but to the cape itself, citing Paus. 3.23.2]. **rock of Sunium**: on the southern headland of Attica, the ruins of its temple of Poseidon are famously visible today, but one to Athena existed there in antiquity also (Paus. 1.1.1); reference to Athena does not add much to Odysseus' case, but Euripides would inevitably include it for the sake of his audience.　**silver**: nearby are remains of the important mines at Laurium.　**Geraestus**: a promontory in the south-east of the island of Euboea; like Sunium, this region was also sacred to Poseidon (Ar. *Knights* 559).

296　surrender: for this sense of δίδωμι, cf. *Od.* 24.65; Pindar, *Pyth.* 5.60; Pl. *Rep.* 574c. †**a senseless disgrace**†: translates δύσφρον᾽ ὀνείδη, which does not scan. Tricilinius emended to δύσφρονά γ ὀνείδη (printed by Duchemin and Ussher), but forms of δύσφορος have been put into the text to read δύσφορά γ ὀνείδη as in the Parisian apograph (printed by some editors), which literally translates as: 'intolerable disgraces'; Seaford (1975) conjectured δύσφορον ὄνειδος, ('an intolerable disgrace'), but reconstructed the Greek line to give the English sense 'We saved the Greek's cause, an intolerable disgrace for the Phrygians'. Diggle made the same conjecture, but with the two words as a parenthesis.

297–8　You ... share: translates Seidler's emendation to indicative κοινοῖ from the imperative κοινοῦ of L. Odysseus' rhetoric becomes more specious, perhaps goaded by a sense of desperation, given his interlocutor. Troy was no threat to Sicily, and no mythic tradition mentions Trojan plans to invade Greece (cf. the speciousness of Helen's arguments at Eur. *Tro.* 925–37!).　**the land ... under Etna ... is Greek**: although much of Sicily had long been considered part of the Greek world by the fifth century BC, the location is consistently presented in the play as a harsh, barbaric dystopia (20, 95, 622, etc.); for discussion, see Gen. Intro. pp. 42–4 and O'Sullivan (2012a *passim*). Odysseus' appeals to this Sicilian ogre are thus ironically undercut and may have resonated with the contemporary audience on various levels in the light of more recent historical events, *e.g.* the refusal of the Syracusan tyrants to help against the Persians (Hdt. 7.159; 7.161.3 – perhaps understandable in the face of the threat of Carthage). And, if the play has a late date (see Gen. Intro. pp. 39–41), the ruthless destruction of the Athenian forces in Syracuse, told with such pathos by Thucydides (7.75–87), would therefore be likely to undermine the idea of Sicily as a place of civilized Hellenic values as far as an Athenian audience was concerned.

299　But ... there is a law: Odysseus hopes that Polyphemus will act under the obligations imposed by law (νόμος, Musgrave's emendation for L's νόμοις, 'by mortal laws', which deprives the sentence of syntax), if he cannot be persuaded by Odysseus' **arguments** (λόγοι). Here Odysseus touches on the important contrast in Greek thought between persuasion and compulsion, but it would not suit his purposes here to start threatening the monster too openly. For other links between law and compulsion or oppression and contemporary debate on the issue, see Antiphon 87 F 44B DK A col. 2.26–30; Hippias in Pl. *Prot.* 337d–8b; cf. also the divergent views of the Anonymus Iamblichi 89 F 6.1 DK and Callicles in Pl. *Gorg.* 483–92.

300–3　Much the same law of hospitality (ξενία) is invoked by the Homeric Odysseus (*Od.* 9.266–71).　**suppliants** (ἱκέτας): in claiming this status (see above

286–7n.), Odysseus intends to increase the onus on Polyphemus of behaving in a civilized fashion, as the rights of suppliants were generally considered inviolate, and here overlap with those of ξένοι ('guests', 'strangers') as Odysseus and his crew are called (89, 252, etc.); for other equations of the rights of suppliants and strangers, see *e.g.* Aesch. *Suppl.* 191–6.

304–7 having drunk many corpses' blood ... fathers childless: Odysseus combines epic and tragic motifs of the carnage and suffering caused by war. For the focus on the loss of Greek lives at Troy and the consequent sorrow of parents and loved ones, see Aesch. *Ag.* 326–9, 430–57 (where it threatens to boil over into communal anger); Eur. *Hec.* 322–5, etc. For the earth drinking the blood of the slain, see Aesch. *Seven* 48, 734–8. Odysseus tries to present the Greeks as victims here, but such loss and waste is equally applicable to the Trojans (*Il.* 7.421–32, etc.); Priam's loss of so many of his children moves Achilles to 'pity his grey head and beard' (*Il.* 24.516; cf. 24.477–507). However, Polyphemus is unlikely to be moved by such considerations in the light of his earlier comment (283–4).

309–10 Odysseus' tone changes to being admonitory, so that his appeals are mixed with implied threats, a rhetorical technique recognized in the fifth century (cf. Gorgias 82 B 27 DK) and traceable to Homer, when the bard, Phemios, pleads for his life (*Od.* 22.344–53). **But listen to me, Cyclops:** ἀλλ' ἐμοὶ πιθοῦ, Κύκλωψ. Ussher pointed to the similarity between Odysseus' words here and those of Teiresias to Pentheus: ἀλλ' ἐμοί, Πενθεῦ, πιθοῦ: ('but listen to me, Pentheus': *Bacc.* 309); the expression ἀλλ' ἐμοὶ πιθοῦ occurs only four times in the extant Euripidean *corpus*. In both *Bacchae* and *Cyclops* not only is there a plea for correct religious observance (cf. *Bacc.* 309–13) but in each case a despotic or tyrannical figure is addressed; for Pentheus as tyrant, see *Bacc.* 43, 775–7; for Polyphemus as despot cf. above 34–5n.

311–12 return (ἠμείψατο): the aorist is gnomic (*i.e.*, one that makes a generally applicable or proverbial statement), which is appropriate for this sentiment, found elsewhere in Greek literature (Hes. *WD* 352; Soph. *Ant.* 311ff., esp. 326).

313–15 Silenus' gleefully malicious injunction here is counterpart to the choral interjections that occur in tragedies between the main speeches in a dramatic *agôn* (often these are neutral and conciliatory, *e.g. Alc.* 673–4, *Or.* 542–3; but cf. *Tro.* 966–8 for a passionate and partisan choral comment). Silenus has already spoken of Odysseus' garrulity (above 104n.), and his suggestion seems to reflect a belief held in some traditional cultures that one adopts the characteristics of what or whom one eats; see Frazer (1914–1917) vol. V ii, ch. 12. **oh-so-smart** (κομψός) can connote excessive ingenuity and subtlety (Eur. *Suppl.* 426); this latter sense is used of Odysseus by Diomedes (*Rhesus* 625). **the best chatterer**: λαλίστατος and its cognate λαλεῖν are almost always derogatory in fifth-century drama, denoting idle and incessant chatter (Eur. *Suppl.* 462), and contrasted with proper speaking (λέγειν) by Eupolis (F 91 *PCG*); Aristophanes presents Socrates and Euripides as chatterers

(*Frogs* 954; 1492; cf. 839). Silenus abuses his sons by calling them λαλίστατοι (Soph. *Trackers* 135, if Wilamowitz's supplement is correct), elsewhere the satyrs brag about their own powers of 'chatter' (λάλησις), Soph. ** F 1130.16 (and see n. 8); cf. above 175n. where the satyrs would like διαλαλεῖν to Odysseus about Helen.

316 Little man (ἀνθρωπίσκε): contemptuous in tone (cf. 185n. on ἀνθρώπιον and 266–7) and a play on Odysseus' size compared to the giant, likely brought out visually onstage (cf. above 210–11n.). **wealth is god for the wise**: there may be a parody of sophistic explanations of the divine espoused by, for instance, Prodicus (84 B 5 DK); but allegorising theologies are found as early as the sixth century BC, in Theagenes' readings of Homeric epic (8 F 2 DK), as well as other Euripidean tragedies (*Bacc.* 285, etc.). Polyphemus' obsession with wealth would have tyrannical overtones for the contemporary audience, as tyrants and greed (especially for money) frequently go together in ancient thought (*e.g.*, Aesch. *Ag.* 1633–9; Eur. *Suppl.* 450–1.

317 pompous and fine-seeming words: Polyphemus again seems to be on Callicles' wavelength, who dismisses conventional νόμος or law (Pl. *Gorg.* 492d); cf. Odysseus' invocation of laws at 299. Elsewhere in Euripidean tragedy characters dismiss ideas as mere show (*e.g. Antiope* F 16.2; *Andr.* 937, *Pho.* 470); at *Hec.* 131 the chorus, albeit for different reasons from those of Polyphemus, denounce Odysseus as a smooth-tongued liar. [L's εὐμορφίαι (emended to εὐμορφία by Nauck) may stand, as its plural form parallels κόμποι ('boasts'); the argument for singular εὐμορφία is perhaps the attachment of the genitive λόγων, but plural abstracts govern λόγων at *e.g. Bacc.* 266–7 ἀφορμαί, *Hec.* 250 εὑρήματα: such plurals usually mean 'instances of ...'.]

318–19 father is set up in temples ... 'good riddance': for the idiom χαίρειν κελεύω (literally, 'I bid fair well'), see Stevens (1976) 26. Polyphemus' dismissal of the worship of his father might seem odd in the light of 231, but the point is for him to be presented here as contemptuous of conventional religious and ethical precepts.

320–1 But I don't tremble ... Zeus: the monster's impiety becomes even more transgressive, putting him on the same level as the Argive warrior Capaneus – another giant – who openly defies Zeus' thunderbolt (Aesch. *Seven* 423–4; Eur. *Pho.* 1128–33), only to invite his own destruction (Eur. *Pho.* 1180–6: for an able defence of these lines, see Mastronarde (1994) 451–82; cf. also Soph. *Ant.* 131–7; Eur. *Suppl.* 496–90). In the probably satyric 'Atlas' play the Titan voices similar contempt for the power of Zeus (see below *Adespota* F 655 col. i Fr. A 15–18, and see n. 6). **stranger** (ξένε): Polyphemus' mentioning of this word underlines his rejection of ξενία, recalling the words of foreboding uttered earlier by Silenus (esp. 91).

322–3 Zeus ... for the future: the concentration on Zeus' weather in 323–31 and the equation of the monster's belly with Zeus (334–8) point to Zeus as the subject of μέλει. Zeus is also the unstated subject of ἐκχέῃ (cf. 320, 321; cf. also *Il.* 16.385 where Zeus χέει ὕδωρ). Here τὸ λοιπόν functions adverbially to mean 'for' or 'in the future', as it does at 709 and elsewhere in Euripides. In any event, it is clear for those who remember their Homer that the 'future' for Polyphemus will involve punishment, ultimately traceable to Zeus (cf. *Od.* 9.479), thus adding irony to the monster's remarks here.

324–5   The translation follows L's ἔχω 'I have' at 324, but also reflects Boissonade's emendation καί 'and' for L's ἤ 'or'. These readings are favoured by Seaford and noted by Diggle, who nevertheless prints 324 with Reiske's ἔχων 'having', and L's ἤ at 325). **beast**: translates δάκος, from the verb δάκνω ('bite'); it can signify a monster (*e.g.*, Aesch. *Seven* 558 where it signifies the image of the Sphinx on the shield of Parthenopaeus) or simply a wild animal (Eur. *Hipp.* 646). Euripides may wish to remind us that the Cyclops did eat lions (cf. 248).

326–7   **give … a good soaking**: translates Reiske's widely accepted emendation εὖ τέγγων τε of L's ἐν στέγοντι ('in a/the covering'), which gives only partial sense, as a noun would be expected. εὖ τέγγων seems to fit well with the gluttonous and uncivilized behaviour Polyphemus boasts about here; cf. also below 574n. Consistent with this are the monster's boasts about his capacity as a drinker at 327 and at 336–7; these are borne out later in the play (503–89). **a storage jar of milk**: amphorae were used in sympotic contexts for wine and water; here is a joke on the barbaric incongruity of using one for milk (cf. above 136n.). For gluttony as a satyric theme, see also Gen. Intro. pp. 33–4, and *Cyc.* 217, 338nn.

327–8   **I bang my clothes**: the general scholarly view sees here a reference to masturbation rather than farting, despite the reference to Zeus' thunderings: *e.g.*, Ussher (citing Catullus 32.10: *nam pransus iaceo et satur supinus / pertundo tunicamque palliumque*: 'For having dined, I'm lying back and I'm full, and I'm bursting through my tunic and bedclothes.'); Seaford (citing Catullus and Martial 11.16.5); Biehl (1986) 141; Henderson (1991a) 245; Slenders (2005) 46. Kovacs (1994b) 153–4 rejects any sexual innuendo here, but his reading depends on his own emendations including changing πέπλον to πλέων so that Polyphemus says '.... when I have drunk dry a full storage jar of milk, I beat on it, making a din to rival Zeus' thunder.' Musgrave's emendation πέδον 'ground' for πέπλον would mean Polyphemus is bragging about 'beating the ground' as if dancing loudly; but this is as coy as it is implausible, and the monster has already announced that there is no Dionysiac activity on the island, a key component of which is dancing (204–5). Moreover, for κρούω to denote sexual activity, see LSJ s.v. 8; also Henderson (1991a) 27, 171 for parallels in Old Comedy which support this reading (*e.g.* Eupolis, F 184 *PCG*, Aristophanes, *Knights* 1379, *Eccl.* 989, etc.). Although reference to the 'milk' that gives his belly a good soaking at 326 occurs before πέπλον κρούω, the drenching of the belly by this white liquid may still be a *double entendre* (given its proximity to the idea of masturbation), and could refer to ejaculation, as Henderson (1991a) 245, suggests; if the idea is 'drench his belly inside', one would expect σπλάγχνη ('innards'), which appears in this context at 424. Masturbation was often associated with slaves and satyrs (*e.g.* Soph. *Trackers* 366–8 and n. 64; cf. Aesch. *Sacred Delegates* F ** 78a.29–36 and see n. 10); see also Lissarague (1990b) 57, 61, figs. 2.4, 2.5, 2.6; Stewart (1997) 187–91. While his earlier claims to rival Zeus had made him comparable to the warrior-giant Capaneus (above 320–1n; cf. below 337n.), Polyphemus here reveals another aspect of his own self-sufficiency and impiety that descend to further sordidness. **to rival Zeus ... thunderings**: another satyric ogre, Salmoneus (Soph. F 537a–41a), attempted to do this, but in a rather different manner, by attaching bronze cauldrons to his chariot, only to suffer the inevitable punishment (Diod. Sic. 6.7; [Apollod.] 1.89; cf. Verg. *Aen.* 6.590–1; see also Appendix below, p. 506).

330–1 The participles περιβαλών (lit. 'throwing around') and ἀναίθων (lit. 'lighting up') are left without a first person singular verb to allow for the change in construction; they are thus 'hanging nominatives' (cf. Eur. *Hec.* 971; *Hel.* 290; *IT* 947; Smyth §3008e). This makes the impersonal μέλει (lit. 'it will be a concern for') the principal verb in the sentence. The verb περιβάλλω (lit. 'I throw round') stands here in the Greek idiom with the thing thrown round in the dative and the thing 'covered' in the accusative, *e.g. Or.* 372. [Triclinius corrected L's περιλαβών 'seizing round, grasping', an old transcriptional error in uncial letters.]   **no worry for me at all** (μέλει): 322–31 exemplifies ring-composition very evidently, with the order of 322 οὔ μοι μέλει ... 323 ἐκχέῃ reversed in 329 χέῃ ... 331 οὐδέν μοι μέλει.

332–3 perforce, will-nilly (literally, 'through necessity'): the idea of necessity (ἀνάγκη here) had become a personified concept in Presocratic philosophy of Parmenides (28 B 8.30 DK) and Empedocles (31 B 116 DK), but neither of these shows any indication of rejecting Olympian religion. In the *Troades* (886) Hecuba sees Zeus and Necessity as one and the same; but in Aristophanes' parody of Socrates' cosmology (*Clouds* 367, 377) Necessity does replace the supreme Olympian. Polyphemus admits the existence of Zeus and the other gods, but sees no reason to pay them honour. Here, Polyphemus emphasises necessity not for any philosophical reasons, but because it contributes to his own consumption and hoarding; ἀνάγκη not personified occurs elsewhere as the inevitable course of fate (*e.g. Hec.* 1295, cf. *El.*1301). The monster therefore sees himself, not as a beneficiary of the gods, but of something which compels the earth to provide for his livestock (cf. above 123–4n.).

334 For the second foot anapaest, see 265n.

334–5 Ussher wrongly takes these lines as evidence of Polyphemus' supposed atheism. Polyphemus is simply announcing that he does not sacrifice to gods whose existence he does not deny, but only to his belly; the impiety is compounded by his elevation of his belly to the role of supreme god. In his *Phoenissae* (506), Euripides has Eteocles deify tyranny in virtually identical terms as 'the greatest of gods'.

336–8 Since: translates the elliptical ὡς (on which, see 168n.). **for folk who are sensible** (ἀνθρώποισι τοῖσι σώφροσιν): Polyphemus posits, in effect, a redefinition of the cardinal Greek virtue of σωφροσύνη (lit., 'sound mindedness', 'moderation', 'self-control'), since he makes gluttony and self-indulgence prescribed behaviour. This is the opposite of what σωφροσύνη normally connoted in Greek usage (LSJ s.v. 2). For discussion of the concept in Euripides, see North (1966) esp. 68–84 and 76: 'the most common meaning is control of passion, appetite, or emotion'; see also Dover (1974) 66–9 and Rademaker (2005) *passim*. Polyphemus' rampant hedonism is echoed in the views of Callicles (Plato, *Gorg.* 491e–2c), but the latter still shows contempt for σωφροσύνη in any form at all and does not attempt to redefine it as does the monster here. **Zeus**: some of the more abstract or elevated notions of Zeus as an all-knowing and somehow inscrutable figure found in philosophy and tragedy (*e.g.*, Heraclitus 22 B 32 DK; Aesch. *Ag.* 160–6; Soph. *Tr.* 1278; Eur. F 877; *Tro.* 884–8.) are reduced by Polyphemus here to the most basic and rapacious levels of self-gratification. **every day**: for other less obviously impious doctrines of 'living for the day', see Eur. *Her.* 503–5 (with Bond's n.). [L's genitive τοῦ πιεῖν (336), emended to nominative τοὐμπιεῖν by Reiske, is widely accepted; the article in τοὐμπιεῖν is shared with φαγεῖν (but καὶ φαγεῖν is emended to κἀμφαγεῖν by Reiske) and λυπεῖν, and the article in τοὐφ' ἡμέραν is part of a fixed expression, *e.g.* Eur. *Phrixus* F 835.1.]

338–9 laws: Polyphemus' hedonism brings him on a collision course with νόμοι (laws), which he spurns for the sake of sating his desire to eat his hapless visitors (340–1). This contempt for νόμοι is consistent with Callicles' views (Pl. *Gorg.* 483b); see 317n., and above Gen. Intro., p. 49. **complicated**: in other contexts ποικίλλω can mean 'embroider' (Eur. *Hec.* 470), but the sense here is pejorative, as at Eur. *Suppl.* 187.

340–1 go to hell: κλαίειν ἄνωγα: a colloquialism, literally meaning 'I order <you> to cry' (ἄνωγα is a perfect with a present sense); it is a more emphatic version of κλαίειν κελεύων (174n; cf. below 701n.). **<While>**: translates the adversative δέ, which Barnes' posited after τὴν, and which is accepted by Ussher and printed by Diggle. But the text can stand without it, the resultant asyndeton adding emphasis to the monster's brutal statement. For the idea of asyndeton as the most effective in producing literary power or force (δεινότης) in ancient literary criticism, see Demetrius, *Eloc.* 269–71 (cf. 358–9 and 465nn.). **desire**: for ψυχή connoting appetite or desire, cf. Aesch. *Pers.* 841; Pl. *Rep.* 579b; Xen. *Cyr.* 8.7.4.

342 hospitality (ξένια, literally: 'hospitable things'): this responds to Odysseus' reference to ξένιά (301). Polyphemus again overturns traditional meanings and concepts (cf. 336–8 n.); his 'hospitality' will involve eating his guests, and in doing so he sardonically imagines himself a perfect host. A further irony is that instead of receiving a hot meal, as a ξένος would expect, Odysseus and his men will provide one themselves to their host. The Homeric Polyphemus sardonically announces his own notion of hospitality, not when stating his intention to eat Odysseus' men, but when saying he will eat the hero last, in return for his gift of the wine (*Od.* 9.369–70); cf. his parting guest-gift, ξείνια, of throwing a rock at Odysseus' ship (*Od.* 9.517).

343   this ancestral bronze (cauldron): translates πατρῷον τόνδε χαλκόν with Jackson's emendation χαλκόν of L's λέβητά γ' (dismissed as an intrusive and unmetrical gloss); as Seaford observes, Homeric Greek can be similarly elliptical in connoting 'cauldron' simply with 'bronze' (*Od.* 8.426). Bronze cauldrons were gifts from host to guests in the heroic world – Odysseus receives one from Alcinous (*Od.* 13.13–19); the normally benign function of such an object is again overturned here to become the instrument of Polyphemus' cannibalism. Why 'ancestral'? It seems unlikely that we should think of Poseidon here; perhaps it adds to the idea of Polyphemus as a debauched gourmand using his equivalent of the 'family silver'. There is no need to assume that the cauldron was onstage, despite the demonstrative τόνδε here. Demonstratives and deictic pronouns can be used for figures and objects not onstage, yet vividly present in the mind of the speaker; *e.g.* the Argive attackers with their shield-blazons in Aeschylus' *Seven* (*e.g.*, 395, 404, 492, 544, 595).   **while it boils**: translates the aorist participle of ζέω (literally, 'make hot'; here used intransitively to mean, in effect, 'become hot'), and is a coincident aorist participle with a verb in the future tense; see Barrett (1964) *Hipp.* 289–92n. The compound ἐπιζέω can be transitive as at 392 below (also *IT* 987).

344   chopped: translates διαφόρητον (literally: 'taken apart, broken'); for examples, see LSJ I.4. This is Scaliger's emendation, accepted by Diggle, Ussher (tentatively) and Paganelli, of L's δυσφόρητον ('hard to bear', described by Duchemin as 'malaisé à comprendre', who prints it anyway, as does Biehl). L's reading, in referring to 'flesh', is deemed nonsensical by Seaford who emends to δυσφόρητος to make the adjective agree with the bronze cauldron, which will thus be 'hard to wear'; Odysseus will 'wear' the cauldron (*i.e.* be put in it), but will not enjoy it. Kovacs (1994b) 155 along similar lines accepts Barnes' δυσφάρωτον ('ill-clad'), which he takes as a sardonic reference to the law invoked by Odysseus that suppliants should receive clothing from their hosts (300).   **nicely**: for καλῶς as a colloquialism, see Stevens (1976) 55; the adverb here has some irony in referring to instruments of the monster's heinous crimes; see also below 631n.

345–6   standing around the altar: the usual phrase for victims at an altar awaiting their sacrifice (cf. Aesch. *Ag.* 1036–8; Eur. *El.* 787–92, etc.). The 'altar' is an effective metaphor for the cauldron; just as a god receives gifts prepared at an altar, so too Polyphemus' belly, which he calls 'the greatest of gods' (335), receives gifts prepared in a cooking utensil. ['altar' is Stephanus' emendation to βωμὸν of L's κῶμον (revel)].   **of the god**: Blaydes' emendation to the genitive with βωμὸν. L's dative τῷ ... θεῷ (to mean 'in honour of the god') is accepted by many: *e.g.*

Duchemin, Ussher, Paganelli, Biehl, to be construed with εὐωχῇτέ με ('so that you can provide me with ...'). In any event, Polyphemus' cannibalism – the monster is referred to as a 'man' (see next n.) – will be yet more repugnant as a savage parody of a sacrifice to a god (cf. above 231, 334–5nn.). **within the cave**: the violence obviously has to take place offstage, and Euripides has to distinguish the interior 'altar' from the actual altar that stood in full view of the audience in the orchestra. **provide me with a feast**: cf. above 342n.

347–9 Odysseus' earlier heroic posturing (198–202) has dissipated, and the Greeks evidently go meekly into the cave. **godless man's**: much the same expression, 'a most godless host', is used of the murderous Polymestor in *Hecuba* (790) – one of many parallels between these two figures (see below 378, 681–8nn., 696–9n.) – and by the chorus in the *Bacchae* of Pentheus (613). Odysseus, like the satyrs (above 23–6, 30–1nn.), sees Polyphemus' crimes in religious terms; cf. also 289, 310–11, 605. Polyphemus, as a 'man', accordingly should behave like one, observing divine law and refraining from his intended feast (cf. also 429, 591, 602 with nn.). **no harbour at all**: translates ἀλίμενον, which develops the nautical sense of κατέσχον (cf. 223) and develops metaphorically the earlier reference to **ordeals ... on the sea** (πόνους ... θαλασσίους 347–8). [**savage heart**: reading Reiske's emendation ὠμὴν to agree with καρδίαν for L's γνώμην (which is accepted by many editors: *e.g.* Murray, Duchemin, Ussher, Paganelli, Biehl, Paduano) which would mean 'the mind and heart'; this would constitute a variant on the Homeric model, *e.g. Il.* 6.447 when Hector knows 'in his mind and in his heart' (κατὰ φρένα καὶ κατὰ θυμόν) that Troy will fall).]

350–2 Odysseus appeals to the goddess who supported him throughout the *Odyssey*. **born of Zeus**: this would remind the audience of the birth of their patron goddess from the head of Zeus, depicted famously on the east pediment of the Parthenon (cf. Eur. *Ion* 454–5). Odysseus' urgency is evident in the repetition of νῦν, as it was in his initial outburst αἰαῖ. This need not diminish his heroism; rather, it points to the savagery of the ogre he must face. **now, now!**: there is no parallel for doubled νῦν in extant Greek poetry; here the expression is very emphatic in Odysseus' of moment of desperation; but cf. double negative μὴ below (*Cyc.* 361); also *Trackers* 246 and n. 44. **hard edge**: translates βάθρα, which can mean the base or foundation of an altar (Eur. *Tro.* 16–17). βάθρα is an unparalleled metaphor for 'danger' and Musgrave conjectured βάθη ('depths'), so that Odysseus would be saying '(I have come to) the depths (of danger)'; cf. 'of troubles' (Aesch. *Pers.* 465; Eur. *Hel.* 303). But βάθρα is defensible in that Odysseus seems like a sacrificial animal brought to the base of an altar and is therefore close to, *i.e.* on the brink of, danger and death. This imagery is at least consistent with the language of sacrifice which Polyphemus has used for the imminent slaughter (345–6, cf. 334–5). At Eur. *El.* 608 ἐκ βάθρων means 'from the foundations (upwards)', referring to destruction.

353–5 **Zeus ... bright seat of the stars**: the supreme god is appealed to in similar terms (Eur. *Pho.* 1006). Odysseus ostensibly invokes Zeus in august terms as god of hospitality (cf. *Od.* 9.270–1) and in cosmic terms as a dweller among the stars; cf. Prometheus' appeal to cosmic agents to witness his own sufferings at the hands of Zeus (*PV* 1091–3). [φαεννὰς is Kassel's emendation for L's φαεννῶν: an example of enallage, with change from prime to secondary application of the adjective as at *Pho.* 84–5; *El.* 728.] **if you do not see** ... : underlying Odysseus' words is a more defiant tone – a manifestation of Odysseus' desperation, evident a few lines earlier (347, 351) – demanding of Zeus that he show himself worthy of such respect. Dale (1969) 183–4, sees the challenging tone of this prayer from a mortal to a god at the close of a scene as typical of Euripides' last plays (*e.g.*, *Hel.* 1093–106; *IT* 1082–8; *Pho.* 84–7). Odysseus voices a similar challenge just before the decisive action of the play (606–7n.). **in vain are you worshipped, Zeus, when you are nothing as a god**: this translates Triclinius' Ζεῦ for L's apparent Ζεύς. Another possible rendering of this reading would be 'in vain are you worshipped as a god, Zeus, when you are (as) nothing.' L's nominative would make Zeus the predicate of νομίζῃ and take θεός in apposition with τὸ μηδὲν, the predicate of ὢν to give: 'in vain are you worshipped as Zeus, when you are nothing as a god.' For other expressions of 'being nothing', cf. Eur. *Tro.* 613; *El.* 370; *Cyc.* 642, 667.

356–74 **Choral song**: The general tenor of this song is one of revulsion at the imminent cannibalism, and the satyrs, unlike their father (cf. 313–15), show their sympathy for Odysseus and his crew as strangers and suppliants (359, 365, 371) cruelly treated. The strophe (356–60) was probably sung while Polyphemus was driving Odysseus into the cave after the latter's brief soliloquy (348–55); in the mesode (361–7) and antistrophe (370–4) the satyrs' horror finds fuller expression. The metre is predominantly trochaic dimeters with some catalexis or truncation (which can involve either the suppression of the final syllable of a line, or syncopation between penultimate breve and final anceps/longum), also anapaestic and aeolic cola; for the full metrical scheme of this ode, see Ussher, Dale (1983) 221–2, and Seaford who tentatively posits corresponsion between 356–60 and 368–74 (as occurs elsewhere in the play, *e.g.* 41–8=55–62); Seaford also discusses whether or not 361–7 should be repeated, concluding that the case for repetition is not strong even if it might be dramatically apt. Simmonds and Timberlake and Duchemin reprint 361–7 after the antistrophe.

356–7 These lines evince a tone of foreboding, not endorsement of the cannibalism about to take place, and are in stark contrast to Silenus' malicious injunctions to Polyphemus (250–2, 313–15), which differ from his own complaints about the monster's cannibalism (22, 31). **wide gullet**: emphasizes the gluttony of the monster (as at 215), and physical grotesqueness of the cannibalism; his gullet is mentioned again in Odysseus' account of the bloody meal (410). **<hot>**: Hermann's supplement, made likely by 244–5 ('a hot feast from the coals', above) and 374 ('flesh hot from the coals'); the description of the cooked flesh here also recalls Cratinus' description of the same episode (F 150 *PCG*).

358–9   to munch, gnaw, tear in pieces: the three infinitives expressed in asyndeton χναύειν βρύκειν / κρεοκοπεῖν make the monster's actions more forceful and vivid to the audience's imagination. For the significance of asyndeton, see 340–1n; cf. 465n.

360   as you lie back: Polyphemus seems to adopt a quasi-symposiast pose as he does later in the play under instruction from Silenus (542–4, 563–4), as well as in the famous 'Richmond Vase' depicting his blinding (=*LIMC* VIII.1 s.v. Polyphemus I 24). [The translation reflects Reiske's emendation to κλινομένῳ of L's καινόμενα ('killed', *i.e.* 'dead' limbs: probably the result of reading an alpha instead of a lambda).]   **in your thick-fleeced goat-skin**: often translated as 'on your, etc.', but this would require ἐπί instead of ἐν. As Diggle (1971) 45–6 notes, ἐν refers to figures clothed *in* certain attire as occurs later at *Cyc.* 527 (cf. also Pindar, *Isthm.* 6.37; Hdt. 2.159.3; Soph. *Tr.* 613; Eur. *Bacc.* 249; and Diggle (1981) for further examples). That Polyphemus is to be imagined wearing his goat-skin is consistent with his bragging about throwing animal skins around himself to keep warm (330); also in the Richmond Vase he is partially clad in an animal skin.

361–2   In the mesode here (361–7) and antistrophe (370–4) the satyrs become more explicit in their denunciation of Polyphemus' actions, in keeping with their complaints in the parodos (esp. 76–81) and their own exhortations to Polyphemus not to harm the strangers (272).   **Don't ... don't**: note the double negative (μὴ ... μὴ...) for agitation and emphasis, brought out further with ἐμοί, and cf. Odysseus' desperate plea (351n.).   **Alone, for yourself alone**: these creatures of the communal thiasos realize the meal violates all notions of φιλία (friendship) which they cultivate with their god as well as Odysseus and his men (above 73–5n; 176n.). The monster has spurned this notion (288–9; cf. 340–1); the meal is thus another indicator of his self-sufficiency, manifesting itself here in isolation. This wish here also recalls their earlier complaint (74–5, 81) that their real master, Dionysus, has been forced to be on his own since the satyrs have become enslaved to their unnatural master, the Cyclops.   **fill ... ship**: introduces nautical imagery for the monster's inhuman gluttony; Polyphemus speaks of himself in similar nautical terms when emerging from the cave, drunk (505–6; cf. also 497). [**fill up**: Wecklein's emendation γέμιζε of L's κόμιζε 'convey'.]

363–4   Let me be rid (χαιρέτω): the satyrs' stated refusal of food voices their sympathy for Odysseus and his men and underscores the transgressive nature of Polyphemus' butchery, emphasized further in their desire to be rid of the monster's dwelling altogether, which is expressed in the anaphora (repetition) of χαιρέτω.

364–5   †sacrifice ... which ... conducts†: the phrase ἃν ἔχει θυσίαν is problematic because ἔχει is unmetrical here as an incomplete half-anapaest and has been variously emended: *e.g.*, παρέχει ('provide') Wilamowitz; ἀνάγει ('conduct') Jackson; also θυσίαν seems to have been attracted to the case of its relative, thus remaining, in effect, the nominative subject (cf. Eur. *Her.* 1163–4; Soph. *El.* 160; Aesch. *Seven* 553); Hartung posited θυσία. In either case θυσία would thus be the subject of χαιρέτω at 364 and be qualified by ἀποβώμιος to mean a sacrifice 'away from the altar', *i.e.* something that 'is, or ought to be, apart from altar(s) to the gods', *i.e.* 'godless' (LSJ s.v.) or 'impious' due to the nature of its **victims** (θυμάτων). Ussher keeps the transmitted text and takes ἀποβώμιος to qualify Κύκλωψ – who would thus become the subject of χαιρέτω – and retains θυσίαν as an accusative of respect to be taken with θυμάτων, and so renders: 'impious in the manner of his sacrificial offerings'. Despite the textual difficulties, the chorus clearly maintain the imagery of corrupted sacrifice broached already in Polyphemus' sardonic language and cruel threats (334–5, 345–6) and in Odysseus' desperate plea to Athena and Zeus (352).

366–7   Cyclops of Etna: for the significance of Polyphemus' Sicilian or 'Etnaean' nature in the play, see above 20n.   **the meat from his guests**: ξενικῶν/κρεῶν: another mention of the breach of ξενία ('hospitality') by the monster.

368–71   Pitiless (νηλής): the word used of the Homeric Polyphemus by Odysseus (*Od.* 9.287). Line 370 is unsound in metre. According to Murray, δωμάτων (here translated as 'in his home') should be deleted, while in 371 Kirchhoff wanted to substitute ξένους ('guests') for δόμων ('of his home').   **sacrifices** (ἐκθύει): this word highlights the impious nature of Polyphemus' crimes and puts him on the same level as another man-eating ogre from a Euripidean satyr play, Busiris, who conducted human sacrifice (Eur. *Busiris* F 312b–315).   **suppliants**: the satyrs' word pointedly corresponds with Odysseus' description of himself and his men at 287 and 300.

373–2   The lines are transposed in order to restore metrical corresponsion with 358, and with it the identical placing of the words βρύκειν in 358 and βρύκων in 372.   **with polluted teeth**: as another symbol of Polyphemus' impiety, his teeth are 'polluted' in eating suppliants and guests, as indeed his teeth presumably were before now (cf. 125–8, 249); this kind of graphic detail also recalls the reference to the monster's gullet (356).   **tearing, gnawing**: the asyndeton of these participles recalls that of the three infinitives in the strophe, evoking Polyphemus' gluttony (358–9 with n.).

374   Many editors after Hermann have posited a lacuna after this line; a whole verse is wanted to complete response with the strophe. Hermann deleted L's ἀνθρώπων before θέρμα to restore the metre (catalectic trochaic dimeter), the scribal error almost certainly caused by confusion with ἀνθράκων.

375–6   In Homer Odysseus has no opportunity (or narrative need) to leave Polyphemus' cave at any time before his actual escape because of the huge rock the monster places over the cave's entrance (*Od.* 241–2). Here a shocked Odysseus reappears and recounts in the manner of a messenger in tragedy events too violent and tumultuous to be depicted before the audience.   **O Zeus, what am I to say…?**:

λέξω here is a deliberative aorist subjunctive; Odysseus' expression is paratragic and identical to Talthybius' words to Hecuba as he contemplates with dismay the mutability of human fortunes (Eur. *Hec.* 488). Odysseus, known so widely as a powerful and effective talker here and especially in tragedy (104, 313–15nn.), is now at a loss for words to describe the horrors he has witnessed; what he does describe emulates the Homeric narrative (cf. 393–4n.). **like stories ... not like deeds**: in a further irony, he can only liken these events to μῦθοι, and in so doing he employs a variant on the well-known λόγος-ἔργον ('word-deed') antithesis and interaction; see 155n. The forebodings of the chorus in 356–74 will be shown to be well-founded.

377–8 The chorus understand instantly; μῶν ('**really**') need not be understood as 'nicely ironic', *pace* Ussher, who sees it in the light of 356–60, but misconstrues the tone of that passage. Here the particle has a tone of resignation or apprehension about it; see Barrett (1964) on *Hipp.* 794; the 'nicely ironic' tone is more evident at 158 (see with n.).   **most godless Cyclops**: the monster is on much the same level as Euripides' Polymestor and Pentheus (see above 347–9n.)   **your dear companions**: the expression φίλους ἑταίρους echoes Odysseus' words in Homer (*Od.* 9.63); the chorus see Polyphemus' crime as a violation of φιλία and religious sensibilities.

380 [**most well-nourished**: εὐτραφέστατον, Scaliger's widely accepted emendation of L's ἐντρεφέστατον, a superlative form of an otherwise unattested adjective ἐντρεφής, that would mean literally 'most nourished in a place'.]

381 **could you all go on enduring**: ἦτε πάσχοντες is periphrasis, involving a part of εἰμί and participle, for ἐπάσχετε, and seems to suggest prolonged suffering or endurance; for the combination, cf. above 23 and 635 below; Aesch. *Ag.* 1178; see also Smyth §1961.

382 **dwelling**: this translates Musgrave's emendation στέγην for L's inappropriate χθών ('land'); Odysseus is talking of the cave. At 29 Silenus refers to his chore of having to clean out Polyphemus' στέγας. However, cf. 118, where we are told that the Cyclopes do not have στέγας. Elsewhere in Euripides' dramas χθόνα can function as a synonym for 'home' (*e.g. Med.* 360), and, as Ussher (1978) notes, the formulation τήνδ' ... χθόνα as a verse-ending occurs elsewhere in Euripides (124, *Bacch.* 1043, *El.*, 111, cf. *Cyc.* 108).

383 **firstly he lit up the fire**: the entire preparations for the meal are carried out, not by any attendants (cf. 83n.), but by Polyphemus himself (383–94), as if to underline his enthusiasm for the impious feast.

385 **heavy enough for about three wagon loads**: ὡς literally, here: 'approximating to'; for this meaning, cf. 388; see also Smyth §2995. The rock that blocks the cave entrance in the *Odyssey* is too heavy for twenty-two wagons (*Od.* 9.214–2).

392 Paley, followed by Duchemin and Diggle, was the first to place this line here, which would seem to give a more straightforward sequence of events: the monster lights the fire and puts the cauldron on it. [Some scholars have suspected the order of

392 and 393 because they end in the same word, πυρί, but lines ending in identical or nearly identical forms (*i.e.* homoeoteleuton) are not rare in Euripides and their occurrence is not in itself a compelling reason for transposition. Like Hartung, Ussher transposes 392 after 395. But scholarly consensus has not been achieved; Simmonds and Timberlake, Paganelli and Biehl print the order of the ms.]

387   he laid out: ἔστρωσεν (aorist of στορέννυμι), Pierson's emendation of L's ἔστησεν ('he set up').

388–9   a bowl about as big as ten storage jars: Polyphemus' appetite for drink puts him on the same level as another satyric ogre, Lityerses in Sositheus' *Daphnis* (see F 2.7–8 and n. 4) who drinks from a pithos of the same dimensions, which is the only other occurrence of δεκάμφορον in extant Greek; cf. above 217n. We also see another aspect of Polyphemus' barbarism in that he uses a bowl, normally reserved for mixing wine at symposia, for milk drinking, on which see 136n.

390–1   a cup ... which looked ... deep: the cup (reading σκύφος as neuter, as at Eur. F 146.2) is the object of παρέθετο ('set next to') and βάθος ('depth') can be plausibly taken as subject of ἐφαίνετο ('looked'), to give literally 'and (its) depth looked (to be) of four (cubits)'; this makes better sense of τεσσάρων ('four'). The size of Polyphemus' ivy drinking cup, like that of the κρατήρ ('bowl'), underlines his own size and strength as well as gluttony (see previous note). At the same time, the description of the cup seems to recall in a primitive and parodic vein Homer's famous description of Nestor's elaborate golden cup in the *Iliad* (11.631–6), already well-known enough to become the subject of allegorising readings; for instance, Stesimbrotus (*FGrH* 107 F 23) in the late fifth century BC saw in Nestor's ability to handle the great cup an allegory of the old man's ability to hold his liquor. The monster is happy enough to drink from the much smaller cup in the company of Odysseus and Silenus (519–89), just as in the *Odyssey* he drinks from the cup the hero hands him, likewise made from ivy: κισσύβιον (*Od.* 9.346).

393–4   spits ... of branches: Odysseus' speech is quasi-Homeric in its attention to detail, and we may notice even here another contrast with a Homeric model. Achilles, in full accordance with heroic etiquette, prepares food for himself and Priam by roasting lamb on spits – ὀβελοῖσιν – (*Il.* 24.621–6). Here, the Cyclops prepares his own meal with ὀβελοί, but these are primitive wooden types like those used by the infant Hermes in his rustic dwelling (*H. Hom.* 4.121); Theophrastus (*HP* 1.3.2) also mentions that thorny wood is used for spits. [L's and Athenaeus' κλάδῳ was emended to κλάδων by Scaliger who also corrected the scribal slip γ' ἀλλά.

395   †sacrificial bowls of Etna ... axes†: Boissonade posited a lacuna before 395, while Fix posited one after 395. Diggle in his OCT apparatus prefers to delete this line, presumably because no prior mention has been made of σφαγεῖα (bowls to catch the blood of sacrificial victims) or axes. But, although considered by some to be corrupt, this line still conveys some interesting possibilities. The 'bowls' (*i.e.* cauldron) may be compared to the crater of Etna not just in terms of size, as

Duchemin and Ussher suggest (cf. also 'the Etna beetle' in Aesch. *Sisyphus* F 233 and n. 8; Soph. *Trackers* F 314.307), but also in the dangers each posed for human life; at Pindar, *Pyth.* 1.13–28 and in *Prometheus Bound* (363–72) the volcano's activity is attributed to the monstrous Typhon, struggling beneath its weight. The harsh and brutal connotations of the adjective Αἰτναῖος in the play (20, 62, 95, etc.) have been recently discussed (O'Sullivan 2012a; cf. above 366n.), and it is possible here that the bowls, in being 'Etnean' and put to a brutal use, may have become endowed with brutal characteristics themselves, just as the knife the monster uses is described as λάβρος 'savage' or 'violent' (403–4n.). Seaford suggested that the line be transposed after 399 then followed by 398 to give the following sequence of events: the giant throws one man into the cauldron, the 'sacrificial bowl', then grabs another by the ankle, etc. Seaford also suggests σφαγεῖον Αἰτναῖον γε 'the Etnean sacrificial bowl' in apposition with the cauldron.

396   hateful to the gods: θεοστυγεῖ (also at 602) can be both active and/or passive, *i.e.* hating and/or being hated by the gods; for the latter sense, cf. Lycurgus, another enemy of Dionysus, who was punished by Zeus and 'became hateful' (ἀπήχθετο) to all the gods (*Il.* 6.140). The active sense is also apt here, in the light of the monster's stated contempt for the Olympians, especially Zeus (316–21).

397   butcher from hell: Stephanus' emendation of L's δίδου to Ἅιδου is generally accepted, the corruption easily explained by reading the uncial alpha as a delta. For the metaphorical sense of Ἅιδου meaning 'hellish' cf. Aesch. *Ag.* 1115, 1235; Eur. *IT* 286–7; *HF* 1119; *Hec.* 1077. On the attributive genitive, see Smyth §1297–8.

398   and in one movement: translates ῥυθμῷ θ' ἑνί, Wilamowitz's emendation of L's ῥυθμῷ τινί. The emendation θ' ἑνί makes sense if we understand that the Cyclops is holding a man in each hand: one he throws into the cauldron; he then dashes the other's brains out on a rock. The use of the indefinite here lacks force ('in a movement'), while θ' ἑνί, in the position of emphasis at the end of the line, would nicely balance δύο in the same position immediately above. This would create a sequence of numbers for effect: (397) two; (398) one; (399) the one; (400) the other. Ussher plausibly cites Aesch. *Pers.* 462, 975 for similar expressions of 'one movement' or 'one rushing motion'; cf. also Eur. *Supp.* 94.

399   Diggle (1971) 48 posited a lacuna after this line to explain the absence of a verb governing τὸν μὲν in 399 and suggested that it contained ἔρριψε ('he threw'), but this is not reported in the apparatus to his OCT text.

400–2   This action recalls *Od.* 9.289–92, but the Homeric monster kills his victims by dashing them onto the ground, then devours them raw 'like a lion' after cutting them up. Duchemin suggests the account here may be influenced by Sophocles' description of Heracles' killing of Lichas (*Trach.* 779–82) by grabbing him by the foot and throwing him down a cliff; cf. also *Il.* 1.591 for the partitive genitive (Hephaestus thrown from heaven); Sositheus *Daphnis* F 3.1 and note 9; Smyth §1346.   †**seizing down**†: the sense of καθαρπάσας seems less satisfactory here than a verb of tearing or cutting apart as suggested by Paley (διαρπάσας or διαρταμῶν).

403–4 savage blade: the monster's equipment reflects its owner's character, and is spoken of in almost animated terms (LSJ λάβρος s.v. I, II.2), as are the weapons of war in Homeric epic which can be 'pitiless', 'shameless' or 'raging' (*e.g. Il.* 4.521, 5.661, 11.572–4, 13.501, etc.); see above 64–5n. Evidently an experienced cannibal (cf. 241–9), Polyphemus displays the culinary precision here of a meticulous butcher who distinguishes between various cuts of meat and cooks them accordingly; cf. the culinary detail of Polyphemus' cooking described by Cratinus (F 150 *PCG*). **to boil**: a prolative infinitive after a verb of motion as at 412; cf. above 257n., 290–1 n.

405–6 The significance of Odysseus' actions here is left unexplained, and is usually passed over by commentators. In the Homeric account he simply watches in horror and weeps with the rest of his men, gripped by helplessness (*Od.* 9.294–5). **In my misery, pouring forth tears ...**: there is nothing unheroic in such tears; the hero's first appearance in the *Odyssey* (5.81–4) has him weeping with longing to return home (cf. also *Od.* 8.522, etc.). In Euripides' version Odysseus' distress is palpable, but he retains his composure, and he distinguishes his response from the extreme, debilitating fear felt by his men (see next note.). **stood nearby**: this could be explained by Odysseus' wish to observe the Cyclops closely while hatching a plan to escape. **... was servant to the Cyclops**: cf. Silenus' complaint at 31 of being forced to be the monster's servant (διάκονος). But in what way was Odysseus Polyphemus' servant? The plan to ply the beast with wine does not occur to him until 411–12. [Note Dindorf's emendation to κἀδιακόνουν (with augment before preverb) for L's καὶ διηκόνουν (with augment following preverb) which is post-Classical; the alpha in διακονέω is long, and ancient.]

407–8 Euripides reworks *Od.* 9.236, which describes the fear shown by Odysseus' men, already in Polyphemus' cave, when they see the monster for the first time. **but the others ... kept cowering**: ἔχω in periphrastic expressions is found only with the aorist or perfect participle and expresses 'permanency' (*Med.* 33; *Hec.* 1013; see Smyth §1963) not just prolonged activity like εἰμί and the present participle at 381. **like birds**: cf. *Her.* 974; *And.* 1140.

410 deep belch: a virtual oxymoron as αἰθήρ typically denotes the upper air, the air of heaven as something bright and pure (*e.g.*, the realm of Zeus: Ar. *Frogs* 100; cf. ib. 892), but it can mean any air or vapour as at 629; and βαρύς here denotes something from the depths that is disgusting or noisome. The presence of αἰθέρα in Athenaeus' citation (1.23e) of this line protects it from Scaliger's conjecture of ἀέρα ('vapour, gas'). **gullet** (φάρυγξ): again, the focus of Polyphemus' monstrous gluttony (cf. 215, 356nn.).

411–12 idea sent from some god (literally, 'something divine'): Odysseus attributes his plan of action here to some god, while in the *Odyssey* his own θυμός ('heart' or 'mind') is emphasized as deciding his course of action. Firstly, it holds him back from killing the beast, as this would prevent their own escape (*Od.* 9.302); then he resolves to blind Polyphemus after getting him drunk, as this seems the best plan κατὰ θυμὸν ('according to my mind': *Od.* 9.318). **Maron's wine here**: see 141n. Odysseus has the wineskin onstage, a significant prop, as it will be crucial in the scene where Polyphemus is made more drunk in full view of the audience, as a prelude to the blinding offstage. **to drink**: prolative infinitive as at 290–1, 404, 561; cf. 257.

413 O son of the ocean god: recalls Odysseus' earlier imprecation to Polyphemus (286) when pleading for himself and his men to be spared. Odysseus would expect the monster to consider this address a compliment, despite Polyphemus' dismissal of his father's temples (318–19); yet Odysseus, in the light of his recent experiences, can use such a title again here to imply savagery on the monster's part, so typical of Poseidon's sons (cf. 21–2n.). [Diggle, citing Eur. *IT* 1230 and *Ion* 1619 as parallels (where Apollo is addressed as 'O son of Zeus and Leto': ὦ Διὸς Λητοῦς τ' Ἄπολλον), reads τοῦ for the Aldine's παῖ, on the basis that ὦ and the genitive of a bare or articular name is the idiom of invocation, rather than the explicit παῖ. But L's text is defensible.]

414 Greece: as Odysseus tries to entice Polyphemus with wine hitherto unknown to the monster (cf. 123–4), he implies that Greece is alien to Sicily, in contrast to his earlier somewhat specious claim that the land of Sicily was 'Greek' (297–8), which had fallen on deaf ears.

415 the joy of Dionysus: while γάνος means something bright or gleaming, appropriate for wine elsewhere (cf. *Cyc.* 67; Homer *Il.* 1.462, *Od.* 2.47, etc.), here it seems to connote something joyful as well (cf. Aesch. *Ag.* 579, 1392). Διονύσου could be a subjective genitive (*i.e.* wine is a gift from Dionysus), or 'Dionysus' could be simply a byword for wine itself; if the latter, god and wine are considered as one (cf. Prodicus 84 B 5; Eur. *Bacc.* 275–83; see above 123–4n., 141n.). At 519–29 the god is spoken of in the latter sense but called the 'Bacchic one' or 'Bacchus' as opposed to being explicitly called 'Dionysus' as here and at 139.

416–17 Polyphemus' man-eating habit is gluttonous – he is 'full up' with his meal; as Seaford notes, ἔκπλεως is a stronger word than ἔμπλεως (conjectured by Dobree), meaning just 'full'. This finds its natural corollary in his first cup of wine, which he drinks in one gulp. His consequently swift drunkenness in fact facilitates the monster's downfall, and is keenly exploited by Odysseus (420–4). **<and>**: Barnes' conjecture τ' restores the metre. **drained it … knocking it back**: σπάω and ἕλκω (the latter a coincident aorist participle; cf. 152n.) function as synonyms here to emphasize the monster's gluttony, evident also in ἄμυστιν ('in one draught'), an internal accusative of similar meaning to the verb ἑλκύσας.

418 raising his hand: Seaford interprets this gesture to Maron admiration, while Ussher says it indicates a request for another drink; the two meanings are not mutually exclusive. **'Dearest of guests…'**: this is the first time Polyphemus shows any inclination towards φιλία or ξενία in regard to his guests. But such a feeling is a distorted form of φιλία and ξενία, as it arises only as a result of his incipient inebriation and his expectation that his greed will be catered to; he still fully intends to eat his guests.

421 knowing that: ὅτι is a prepositive at verse-end, more common in Sophocles (*Aj.* 678, 792; *El.* 332, 426, 998, 1106, 1367, etc.) than Euripides (*e.g. Med.* 560).

422 would be his ruin: τρώσει (future of τιτρώσκω) literally 'wound, harm' seems to have a figurative meaning here. Polyphemus will be in a weakened state as result of his gluttonous drinking; the wine plays a decisive role in overcoming the monster. **pay his due** (δίκην δώσει): literally 'give justice'; Odysseus voices one of the key themes of satyric drama as he does again at 693: the meting out of punitive justice to an ogre; cf. Aesch. 'Dike Drama' F**281a; Eur. *Sciron* F 678; *Syleus* F 692, etc.

423–4 sure enough: as Denniston (1954) 249 notes, this usage of καὶ δὴ 'seems to combine the ideas of connexion and immediacy'. **started singing**: singing, as a natural consequence of drinking, is found in the *Odyssey* (14.464) and, more generally, in the genre of the σκολιόν ('drinking song'). See next note.

425–6 warmed his innards: cf. Ar. *Frogs* 844. **cacophony** (ἄμουσα): just as Polyphemus' sense of φιλία is grossly distorted, so, too, is his singing. He has already been denounced for his ignorance and boorishness (173) and will later be referred to as an ignoramus in need of education (492–3). Ussher and Seaford rightly see parallels with Heracles' singing in Eur.'s *Alcestis* (758–63); like Polyphemus, the hero is 'warmed' with wine (cf. Eur. *Alc.* 758). Cf. also Eur. *Syleus* (T iiia); Ion, *Omphale* F 22, below; and the gluttonous Lityerses' reaping song (Sositheus, *Daphnis* n. 1, below. In *Alc.* 760–1, Heracles howls a cacophony, but here, Polyphemus' deplorable singing adds insult to injury; for the monster's transgressions are far worse than Heracles' behaviour, which is not intended to upset the house of Admetus. **my fellow sailors who are weeping**: there seems to be a grim joke here in Euripides' expression; Polyphemus' singing, like his murderous actions, is another reason for the tears of the hapless sailors who are stuck in the cave, which resounds with the monster's cacophony.

427–8 The reference to the chorus is in both singular (σὲ, βούλῃ) and plural (εἴπατε, χρῄζετε); here the singular probably refers to the coryphaeus, the plural certainly to the chorus overall; but such a basis for the distinct uses of singular and plural is not always clear. The shift from singular to plural occurs unproblematically elsewhere (465, 476; cf. also 441–2), and the chorus can refer to their own actions in the plural (437–8, 444) or singular (447).

429 monstrous: translates ἄμεικτον. When applied to a person as here, literally it can mean 'incapable of mixing with others'. Polyphemus, like other monsters, such as centaurs (Soph. *Tr.* 1095), is therefore anti-social and savage (LSJ ἄμικτος, s.v. III) – another brief allusion to his inability to cultivate social relations or φιλία.

A direct corollary of this is the fact that he is, in the words of the chorus at 438, 'godless' (ἀνόσιος). However, ἄμεικτος also conveys the idea that one cannot 'mix it (*i.e.* fight) with' Polyphemus, just as Homeric and other warriors 'mix it' (μείγνυμι), *i.e.*, 'fight' in battle (*Il.* 15.510; Alcaeus F 330 L-P; Pind. *Pyth.* 4.212–13; cf. Soph. *OC* 1047, etc.); the two senses of 'monstrous' and 'unable to be fought' can easily co-exist.   **man** (ἄνδρα): although frequently called a 'beast' (442, etc.), Polyphemus is also called 'man' (also at 348, 591, 605; cf. 199) indicating that he is essentially an anthropomorphic monster (as opposed to Scylla, Hydra, etc.) and that his anthropophagy is essentially a form of cannibalism.

430   Naiad nymphs: this translates Casaubon's emendation of L's δαναίδων (most easily explained as a mistake due to dittography in ΑΔΑΝΑ) to Ναΐδων. Even though [Apollod.] (*Bibl.* 2.1.4) and Hyginus (*Fab.* 169a) mention a satyr's attempt on the Danaid Amymone, also the title of an Aeschylean satyr play (F 12–14 Radt; see also Appendix, below), the satyrs have no general connection with the Danaids; for satyrs and Naiads, cf. Pratinas F 3.4, below.

433–4   This rather elliptically expressed idea is that Silenus in his drunkenness flails his arms about in the same way as a bird caught by its feet in lime flaps its wings about – either uncontrollably or without achieving anything; but 'bird' does not appear in the simile, its presence being left to inference from 'lime' and 'wings'.   **struggling with his wings**: metrical phrasing and the logic of the simile make πτέρυγας an accusative of respect with ἁλύει which is only transitive in Oppian of the second century AD (*Halieutica* 4.195, 4.337); the subject of the verb is Silenus who is 'trapped' or 'caught' (λελημμένος) in his wine cup, and has already been described as 'weak' (ἀσθενὴς at 432). For liming in a simile for mental hopelessness, cf. Lucian, *Voyage to the Underworld* 14.

435–6   your old friendship: as Odysseus knows, the relationship between Dionysus and the satyrs is famously characterised by φιλία (thus he describes it as 'old'); cf. above 73–5n.

437   O dearest friend: φίλτατε is admittedly very common (Eur. *El.* 229, 345, etc.), but, given the numerous mentions of the φιλία between the satyrs and Odysseus earlier (see above 73–5n.), and the reiteration of the φιλία between Dionysus and the satyrs in the preceding line, it points again to the friendship between satyrs and hero.

438   godless presence of the Cyclops (ἀνόσιον κάρα): this periphrastic idiom (κάρα plus adjective and genitive of name) is usually honorific (*Or.* 475; cf. *Tro.* 661, etc.), but the reverse applies here, as at *Tro.* 1024; cf. also Dido's refers to Aeneas as: 'infandum caput', 'an unspeakable person/creature' (Vergil, *Aen.* 4.613).

439–40   †my own siphon ... to eat!† These lines are metrically at fault in three places (see below); in 440 the two finite verbs χηρεύομεν and ἔχομεν are uncoordinated, and καταφαγεῖν ('to eat up') is nonsensical. Apt sense can however be in part discerned. σίφων (lit. 'tube, 'pipe': LSJ I.a and b) makes a metaphor for 'penis', as almost certainly at Juvenal 6.310. It can stand here as accusative of respect with active χηρεύομεν (Seaford observes that the Middle would be idiomatic, as at *Alc.* 1089); thus, sexual abstinence has 'widowed' the satyrs' penis(es); for such frustration see the longings of 68–70, 169–70, 495–502. Seaford, emending the second half of 439, adds to the plausibility of this meaning by noting the satyrs' habits of confusing the pleasures of wine and sex as depicted on vases (to which we can add Osborne (1998) figs. 5, 89 [the latter =Lissarague 1990b: fig. 2.8, the psykter by Douris]); see also Kilmer (1993) figs. R126, R148; Voelke (2001) fig. 21. For the names of types of pottery as metonymy for male genitalia, see Ar. *Frogs* (1208, 1213, 1219, 1226, 1233, 1238, 1241), where Euripidean heroes, in losing their ληκύθιον ('little oil flask'), lose their manhood in all senses; see Snell (1979), and, for a different view, Bain (1985) who argues that no *double entendre* is meant; cf. Dover (1993) *ad loc.*, who inclines towards Bain's view.

An objection to the interpretation above is that the normal meaning of 439 διὰ μακροῦ is 'after a long time' (*IT* 480; *Pho.*1069) rather than 'for a long time' (*Hec.* 320 and *IA* 1399 are ambiguous). The latter has however been acceptable to some editors who in 440 adopt καταφυγεῖν 'to escape' (Paris apograph, for καταφαγεῖν) or καταφυγήν 'escape, refuge' (Hermann, but as part of further changes to the text); both the verb and the noun are made to depend upon ἔχομεν or some form of ἔχω '(we) are not able to, (we do not have an) escape'. This idea would expand upon 437–8; Hermann indeed conjectured '… our σίφων which has no refuge, no place to go', a transparent *double entendre*, on which Seaford comments 'an entirely satisfactory refuge would be provided by a nymph (68, 430)'. For detailed discussion of the difficulties here see Seaford especially; subsequently Biehl and Kovacs (1994b) 155–6.

[The metrical faults are: (1) in 439 the first syllable of σίφωνα is long where a short in the fourth foot is required; in 440 (2) the fourth foot in L consists of only two short syllables and (3) the fifth of a dactyl impossible in both tragedy and satyric. Cures for (1) have been sort in rearrangement of the words (*e.g.* Hermann, Diggle) and for (2) and (3) by conjecture (Hermann, cf. Seaford and Kovacs, much more adventurously: neither is cited in our apparatus).]

441–2   revenge: this brings on the next significant piece of action in the play: the punishment of the Cyclops, mentioned here again; see also 422n. Inflicting punishment on one's enemies was seen as a standard of behaviour going back to the Archaic age: Archilochus, F 126 W; *Theognidea*, 337–40; for discussion, see Dover (1974) 180–4. Goins (1991) cogently rebuts the views of those who find Odysseus' act gratuitous or presented in a negative light by the poet.

443–4   Asian kithara: Webster (1967) 18 sees a compliment here to the Milesian poet Timotheus; F 370 of Eur.'s *Erechtheus* of 422 BC refers to 'Asian music'. More to the point, however, is that Asia is the place from where Dionysus brought his cult and his music (*Bacc.* 64, 1168); the Phrygian aulos is part of the musical celebration of Dionysus when the 'raging satyrs' receive the tympanum from Rhea (*Bacc.* 128–30); cf. also lotus-pipe (*Bacc.* 160, etc.). **the Cyclops ... destroyed**: the satyrs, like Odysseus, are keen, not just to escape, but to wreak vengeance on Polyphemus (see previous note).

445–6 Ussher finds Polyphemus' desire to join in a revel (κῶμος) with his brothers 'a pleasing trait', but it seems likely that the monster's behaviour in such a context would be as transgressive as his cruel parody of the idea of hospitality or ξενία (342–4) and his own appalling singing (425–6; cf. Odysseus' warning to him on the potential violence of revels: 534). Nevertheless, Polyphemus' inclinations here form an interesting contrast to the generally solipsistic lifestyles of the Cyclopes (120; cf. *Od.* 9.112–15).

449 purpose ... through cunning: δόλιος ἡ προθυμία (lit., 'cunning intention'): this, as opposed to βία (strength), will be Odysseus' chief weapon against the monster, as it was in the *Odyssey* (9.282, 406, 408, 422). [Musgrave's emendation of L's ἐπιθυμία ('desire') cognates of which occur only twice elsewhere in extant Euripides, once in a sexual context (*Andr.* 1281; cf. *Alc.* 867). Conceivably, however, ἐπιθυμία may stand, so that Odysseus refers to his 'desire' to punish Polyphemus via deceit; such 'desire' may pick up the excited tone of satyrs who say to the hero 'you're raging' (μενοινᾷς) to punish the monster.]

450 exactly translates δαί: this colloquial particle (common in Aristophanes and absent from formal prose) functions as a semi-connective in a question motivated by what has preceded it (cf. *Hel.* 546); see Denniston (1954) 262–3. The satyrs want to know in detail how their monstrous oppressor will be overthrown. **For a long time ... clever**: Odysseus' reputation precedes him here in a way slightly more favourable than at 104. πάλαι could be taken with σοφός to mean that Odysseus has had a reputation for cleverness 'since the beginning' (*i.e.* all his life); cf. also 649 where the satyrs live up to their old reputation.

451 Duchemin suggests that the infinitive ἀπαλλάξαι depends on an assumed μενοινῶ, following the chorus' μενοινᾷς 'you're raging...' (448). But ἀπαλλάξαι is more easily explained as following on from προθυμία, so that the noun functions like a verb in taking the infinitive (*i.e.* προθυμία ἀπαλλάξαι = προθυμέω ἀπαλλάξαι) 'my desire/intent/purpose is to take him away...'; cf. *Tro.* 689. For the emendation προθυμία, see 449n.

454 conquered by the Bacchic god: νικώμενος is followed by a genitive of comparison (Βακχίου) and functions in the same way as ἡσσώμενος ('inferior'; cf. Smyth §2004; cf. also Eur. *Autol.* A F 282.5 where an athlete as is described as 'a minion to his belly': νηδύος ... ἡσσήμενος); the use of νικώμενος possibly continues the figurative language used for the effects of wine on the monster which will 'wound' or 'harm' him (see 421–2n.). As at 446, Odysseus' periphrastic way of referring here to wine in personified form as 'Bacchus' (literally, 'the Bacchic one') implies that Dionysus is present on more than one level (cf. 123–4), and has a direct hand in the defeat of the monster, as would be fitting, given Polyphemus' hostility to the god and his worshippers (esp. 203–11, and *passim*).

455 beam of olive: in the *Odyssey* (9.319–28) Odysseus blinds Polyphemus with the monster's club, which would have made a nice irony here: the instrument of the ogre's violence and oppression (211) is turned against him. The olive beam Odysseus uses here requires many to lift it (472), and his need of the satyrs' help in carrying this branch is exploited for comic potential later (635–41). In some depictions a beam, as opposed to Polyphemus' club, is also the intrument of his blinding (*LIMC* VIII.1 s.v. 'Polyphemos' I 18, 20, 31); on the Richmond Vase (*LIMC* VIII.1 s.v. 'Polyphemos' I 24) Odysseus and his men appear to be wielding a tree trunk over the sleeping giant).

456 sharpen well: translates ἐξαποξύνας which appears in Triclinius' text for ἀποξύνας in L; the compound with ἐκ, favoured by Euripides (see Zuntz (1965) 54), expresses thoroughness or completion.

457–9 At 454–7 the sentence proceeds more by vivid idiom and sense than by the expected syntax of a future indicative in the main clause after ὅταν + subjunctive; but here in 457–9 this normality does occur. [Pierson emended to βαλῶ ... ὄμμα τ᾽ for L's βαλὼν and ὄμματ᾽ (on the plural, see 462–3n.); but the asyndeton of L between the participles is perhaps defensible given that Odysseus is vividly outlining his revenge on the monster, which he extends in a simile, and is alluding to the decisive action of the play.]

460–1 And just ... leather thongs: the simile recalls the famous Homeric passage (*Od.* 9.383–6). Such an obvious reference here almost seems to break the dramatic illusion whereby the Odysseus of drama alludes to the Odysseus of epic. Likewise in Antisthenes' account of the *Judgement for the Arms of Achilles* (B XIX 12.14 Radermacher) Odysseus finishes his speech by saying how a future poet will depict the heroes, alluding again in heavy-handed fashion to specific Homeric passages and epithets which denigrate Ajax (*e.g. Il.* 7.219–23; 11.558–65), and present himself in a favourable light in describing him as πολύτλας ('much-enduring': *Il.* 8.97, *Od.* 5.171, etc.), πολύμητις ('of much cunning': *Il.* 1.311, etc.) and πολυμήχανος ('of many resources': *Il.* 2.173; *Od.* 1.205, etc.).

462–3 I shall twist ... Cyclops': the word-play and assonance between κυκλώσω and Κύκλωπος (cf. also 459) cannot be reproduced in English. **in the light of ... eye**: literally 'the eye that brings him light'; the monster's eye will be subjected to light in the form of scorching fire. Odysseus thus relishes the prospect of revenge on the monster with a pun and grimly ironic language. **pupil**: κόρας is plural, but must be translated in the singular for the Cyclops; at 617 and 673 the singular βλέφαρον ('eye') is used. On this issue even Homer nods, too, referring to the monster's 'eyebrows' (*Od.* 9.389).

465 I'm happy, we're crazy about ... : the satyrs' joy is predictably instantaneous and a little overstated (see also 624–5n.), expressed in asyndeton (cf. 341, 358–

9nn.), and change of person from singular to plural (cf. above 427–8n.). **what you've come up with**: literally, 'the discoveries, inventions' (τοῖς εὑρήμασιν). This is a typical reaction of the satyrs when confronting a εὕρημα (as here) for the first time, and a motif of satyric drama: *e.g.* Aesch. *Prom. Fire-Kindler* F 207 where the satyrs want to kiss fire on seeing it for the first time; Soph. *Trackers* and the satyric reaction on first hearing lyre music (131–209); see Gen. Intro. pp. 34–6, and Index of Motifs, below.

466 you: σέ ('you'), the singular here, refers to the coryphaeus. **(your) friends**: φίλους has no possessive adjective here, but its position between 'you' and 'old man' suggests that the satyrs are meant (cf. 176; cf. also 73–5n.), notwithstanding the fact that Odysseus also calls his men φίλοι ('friends': 478, 481) who are in the cave along with Silenus.

467 black ship: more Homeric resonance; ships are regularly black in Homeric epic (*e.g.*, *Il.* 1.141, 2.568, 24.780; *Od.* 2.430, 3.61, 21.39, etc.). The transitive aorist participle ἐμβήσας here takes two accusatives: the object embarked upon (Odysseus' ship) and the satyrs put onto it (see previous note); cf. Eur. *Hcld.* 845.

468 double bank of oars: this seems to give the best sense of διπλαῖσι κώπαις (cf. Lysias 1.9 where a two-storeyed house is called διπλόον οἰκίδιον) and would suggest that the ship to be imagined is a bireme with two levels of oars on each side; cf. also above 14–17n. on 'oared'.

469–70 as if it were a libation to a god: this translates Reiske's emendation ὡσπερεὶ for L's ὥσπερ ἐκ ('as from, after'); it is unfortunate that P.Oxy. 4545 (see 471n.) is defective here and cannot help with ὡσπερεὶ. Consensus on the precise meaning has not been achieved. Much of the obscurity arises from the terse combination of metaphorical (the libation) with concrete (the brand) elements; see the discussions by Duchemin, Ussher and Seaford (who suspects corruption). Reading with the ms ὥσπερ ἐκ to give: 'as if it were after a libation to the god'), the Cyclops may be envisaged as a sacrificial victim, over whom (or into whom) a libation has been poured with the wine given him by Odysseus. Conversely, the reference could be to the ritual of dipping a torch into holy water (χέρνιψ), which is then sprinkled over altar, onlookers and victim (Ar. *Peace* 959; Eur. *Heracles* 928–9). On this reading, Polyphemus' eye functions as the water into which the brand is plunged; cf. the words of the Homeric Odysseus who compares the act of blinding to a bronze-worker plunging hot metal into cold water (*Od.* 9.391–3). In any event, the sacrificial imagery is noteworthy: just as Polyphemus had earlier described his imminent slaughter of Odysseus' men as a sacrifice (334–5, 345–6), now the revenge will take this form. Sacrificial imagery is used to great effect to describe murder in some tragedies (Aesch. *Ag.*, esp. 1433; Eur. *Medea* 1054); see above 345–6n. **eye**: ὄμματα is a plural, but there is no problem here; consider our own expression that somebody has 'a good eye', meaning their sight generally (cf. above 462–3n.). 469–70 contain a rare example of ἔστιν ὅπως + optative with ἄν, thus disproving the view of Smyth §2552 that such a combination is not found in Attic; other Euripidean expressions come close to this formulation: see *Alc.* 52; *Or.* 638–9; *Her.* 186.

471   bloodshed (φόνου): Diggle prints πόνου (labour), Nauck's emendation of L's φόνου ('slaughter', 'bloodshed'); but the ms is quite defensible. L's reading is accepted by the first editor of P. Oxy. 4545 which contains the remains of *Cyc.* 455–71, 479–81, 484–96 (see app. crit.). But only the last two letters of 471 remain in the papyrus (lambda and omega), and even these are printed with sub-linear dots, so in its current state the papyrus does not confirm or contradict L's reading. In any event, φόνου has been widely accepted (by, for instance, Murray, Simmonds and Timberlake, Duchemin, Ussher, Paganelli, Biehl, Kovacs, Paduano) and is defensible on other grounds. φόνος need not always refer to actual killing, but can mean bloodshed or bloodletting (LSJ s.v. I.4). Even if φόνος does mean 'slaughter' here, its desire might be expected of the satyrs, whose enthusiasm for Polyphemus' punishment seems to know no bounds (cf. 464–5); Seaford notes the expression κοινωνεῖν φόνου ('take part in slaughter') elsewhere in Euripides (*Andr.* 915; *El.* 1048; *Or.* 1591). At *IT* 72 φόνος refers to blood spilt at an altar; a close verbal parallel is found in Porphyry (*On Abstinence* 2.29) in a similarly sacrificial context.

472   Yes – you'll have to: as Denniston (1954) 454 notes, γοῦν here signifies an affirmative response, indicating that Odysseus expects the satyrs to help him, which sets up the humour of their inevitable cowardice later (635–48). Odysseus' men are evidently still cowering in the recesses of the cave, weeping in fear (425–6; cf. 407–8), hence his reliance on the satyrs here and later (cf. 590–5); but he has 'to use his close friends', 650–1.   **brand ... massive**: see above 455n.

473–4   a hundred wagons: possibly a colloquial comparison; cf. the oak tree heavy enough for three wagonloads thrown by Polyphemus onto his hearth (385); the continued enthusiasm of the satyrs – creatures not known for their physical strength or courage – leads to them to exaggerate here; cf. their bluff and bluster later in *Cyc.* (596–8, 632–4) and elsewhere in satyric drama (Soph. *Inachus* F **269d.22). Audience recollection of such comments will add humour to the chorus' cowardly avoidance of action later in the play (635–41).

475   we are going to smoke out: ἐκθύψομεν, the future of ἐκτύφω, is Hertlein's emendation of L's ἐκθρύψομεν ('we shall break up'; see also 659n.).   **like a nest of wasps**: cf. the similar image in, for instance, Aristophanes (*Wasps* 457; *Lys.* 476; *Wealth.* 301).   **damned Cyclops**: literally 'Cyclops who will be destroyed terribly'; τοῦ κακῶς ὀλουμένου is a colloquial expression of abuse found elsewhere in Euripides (*Hcld.* 874) and comedy (cf. Ar. *Ach.* 865, *Ec.* 1076); for discussion, see Stevens (1976), 15.

476   be quiet, all of you: the plural imperative here (σιγᾶτε) is directed at the chorus as a whole; the singular ἐξεπίστασαι ('you know') is directed at the coryphaeus. (cf. 440–1, 435, 466).

477   its architects: while the metaphor is grandiose, it is worth noting that Odysseus refers to himself as a skilled craftsman only a few lines earlier (cf. above 460–1n.); more generally in Homeric epic Odysseus' skill as a craftsman is emphasized, *e.g.*, as shipwright (*Od.* 4.241–61), and even bed-maker (*Od.* 23.183–204), as well as when he is blinding the monster (*Od.* 9.383–93). The regular metaphor for someone who contrives a scheme is simple τεκτών, ('builder, carpenter, creator, deviser'), *e.g.* Aesch. *Ag.*153, 594; Eur. *Med.* 409. Interestingly, the τεκτών in either metaphorical or literal uses is frequently described as σοφός ('clever, skilled'), which also suits Odysseus here and more generally (*e.g.* Pind. *Pyth.* 3.113; Bacch. *Dith.* 6.6; Eur. *Med.* 409 [cf. *Alc.* 348]; Critias 43 F 19.34 [on which see below n. 10]; Ar. *Birds* 1154–5; Pl. *Prot.* 312c).

478–9 men who are my friends: Odysseus' actions are motivated by concerns of friendship (φιλία) here, and his heroism seems to be reasserting itself along Homeric lines compared to his despondency (347–55) after his altercation with the monster. At *Od.* 9.421 Odysseus' concern for his ἑταῖροι ('companions') is a strong motivating factor in his revenge on Polyphemus.

480–2 Seaford and Kovacs (1994a) follow Conradt and Diggle here in deleting these lines, while most editors accept them. The case for deletion rests on what some consider an oddness and ineptitude of style (*e.g.*, coordination of optative and ἄν with perfect indicative in 480); some commentators suspect the repetition of words from 478 in 481, and Seaford refers to what he sees as the 'lameness' of the sentiments. Such awkwardness may be consistent with Odysseus' somewhat stilted language (96–8n.) and heroic sermonizing earlier in the play (198–202). The beginnings of lines 480–1 appear in P. Oxy. 4545 (see 471n.), from which 482–3 are missing. Günther (2001) 18, who considers the lines 'most probably an interpolation', acknowledges that the papyrus shows that they were present in antiquity; it is possible to go further and say that Euripidean authorship of the lines is not ruled out either.

483–518 Choral song: Initially, the chorus focuses on the punishment of the monster in a metaphorical komastic (revel) setting (483–94), an idea which Polyphemus unwittingly develops in his desire to join a literal revel (κῶμος: 508). The strophe at 495–502 takes the form of a μακαρισμός, a song of blessing or thanksgiving, such as in the first strophe of the parodos of the *Bacchae* (72–87, esp. 72–4; cf. 902–12), which maintains an august tone throughout. Here the satyrs combine references to ritual Dionysiac utterances (εὐιάζει: 495) – cf. *Bacc.* 68, 1034 – with the more physical pleasures of sex and drunkenness; cf. Silenus' fantasy (168–74). But this need not be considered a parody of Dionysiac rites; such a combination of the mystic and hedonistic reflects the satyrs' own liminal status as devotees of the god with earthy and divine aspirations. Polyphemus staggers onstage (503–10), exuberant and bragging of his drunken state with thoughts of attending his first ever revel with his brother Cyclopes; typically of satyric gluttons (cf. Heracles in Eur. *Syleus* F 691; Ion *Omphale* F 21, 26, 29), the monster demands yet more wine.

At 511–18 the satyrs derisively serenade Polyphemus with a wedding song, presenting him, in effect, as a groom on his wedding night. A bizarre erotic tone emerges here, only to culminate in the intended rape of Silenus (582–9; see below 597–8n.). Euripides gives us here possibly the first treatment of the monster as would-be lover, if, as is likely, it pre-dates Philoxenus (*c.* 435–380 BC), poet of the earliest known version of the Polyphemus-Galatea story (F 816, 819 *PMG*), in which the monster is the unsuccessful and somewhat ludicrous suitor of the beautiful nymph, a theme which became famous in later poetry, *e.g.* of Theocritus (*Id.* 6, 11); see also Bion, (F 16); Moschus (*Ep. Bion.* 2); and Ovid (*Met.* 13.738–897; cf. Vergil *Ecl.* 9.39ff).

The metres are initially anapaestic dimeter with final line catalectic (483–94); but catalexis also occurs in 486 before the *parepigraphê* (stage direction) as well as in 494 at the end of the system. Anapaests are suitable here for the martial sentiments expressed in which the satyrs imagine the imminent blinding of the monster (cf. Eur. *Hcld.* 288–96 and [Eur.] *Rhes.* 379–87 which have martial language appropriately cast in anapaestic rhythm, imitative of marching). The satyrs' anapaests are followed by anacreontics, suitable for the erotic tone, in the three strophes (495–502, 503–10, 511–18), the second of which is 'sung' by the drunken Polyphemus. The sequence of three identical strophes is very rare in drama, and even more striking is that the central strophe is the one sung by the monster; one might expect the pair comprised of the first and third strophes to surround a lyric passage of a different character, probably free lyric; but the metre of Polyphemus' song is the same probably because it maintained the symposiast/erotic tone. Triclinius attributed 483–6 and 488–94 as well as the first and third strophes to semi-choruses; cf. the distribution of dialogue in 635–41.

483–4 The satyrs' excitement expresses itself in a repetition of πρῶτος ('first'). **to hold fast and control**: Musgrave's emendation ὀχμάσαι gives better logic to the scene: being positioned to hold, lifting, then driving (ὥσας: 485) the 'beam' into the monster's eye (for the infinitive with ταχθεὶς cf. 29–30). L's participle ὀχμάσας ('on holding fast') is the middle of three, in asyndeton – harsh perhaps, but appropriate to the action described (cf. 340–1n.). **beam** translates κώπην which most commonly means 'oar' or 'handle' and may thus continue the nautical imagery used elsewhere in the blinding (460–3).

485 **eye**: translates βλεφάρων, strictly speaking, a plural; see 462–3n.

487 *singing from within*: stage directions are rare in mss but can occasionally be found in tragedy (*e.g.*, Aesch. *Eum.* 117), comedy (Ar. *Thesm.* 129) and elsewhere in satyr drama (Aesch. *Net-Fishers* F **47a.29 and 39). Taplin (1977) 121–32 argues that such directions are not the words of the playwright but later additions to performance texts.

488–90 Polyphemus' charmless, drunken singing (ἄχαριν κέλαδον) has already been mentioned by Odysseus (see above 425–6n.), and now the satyrs derisively emphasize this as another of the monster's barbaric traits through the asyndeton of σκαιὸς ἀπῳδὸς (the former adjective: 'gauche' or 'ill-omened' (LSJ II.2); the latter: 'tone-deaf'). **and about to pay for it**: κλαυσόμενος (lit. 'about to weep'; see above 174n.): emendations were made by Hermann (κατακλαυσόμενος) and Fix (τάχα κλαυσόμενος: 'soon about to weep') to create climactic syntax with the three participles in asyndeton (cf. 483–5n.), but the last one in a different tense; Hermann's is perhaps preferable because τάχα seems otiose with the future participle (even though it stands with future indicatives at 518, 592).

492–3 As followers of Dionysus, the satyrs are accomplished revellers, musicians and singers; they are frequently depicted in this capacity on vaseware (above 40n.), and make boasts along these lines elsewhere in satyric drama (*e.g.* Soph. *Oeneus* (?) F ** 1130.12 [song] and 1130.15 [dance]). They thus know a bad singer when they hear one. **Come now let us educate** (φέρε ... παιδεύσωμεν): φέρε and subjunctive is colloquial; cf. above 8n. Diggle conjectured νυν for νιν, emphasizing the urgency of the satyrs' tone with φέρε. **revels** (κῶμοι): just as the punishment of the monster is glossed as a metaphorical education, it seems that 'revels' here has a similarly metaphorical usage, since later in the play it simply denotes the revel which Polyphemus hopes to have with his brothers and from which Odysseus keeps him (508, 534, 537), and at 497 κῶμος involves the earthy pleasures as conjured up in the satyrs' imagination. But the satyrs' metaphorical κῶμοι alluded to at 492 are apt, since they will provide a context for the downfall of Polyphemus, the self-proclaimed enemy of Dionysus and his worship. **the ignoramus**: significantly, Silenus has mocked Polyphemus' ἀμαθία before (173), when, as here, a komastic setting is being imagined. Given the centrality of μουσική to Greek education (Plato *Rep.* 398c–9d; *Laws* 812b–3a; Aristotle *Pol.* 1337b 23–b32; 1339a 14–41b 18), it is natural that the Cyclops' barbarous actions – most recent of which is his current cacophony – are seen to bring on a punishment glossed metaphorically as an education of sorts. The monster's 'education' by Odysseus (519–75), who inducts him into aspects of sympotic etiquette, is also comparable to that which the young sophisticate Bdelycleon imparts to his boorish father Philocleon in Aristophanes' *Wasps* (1122–64).

494 anyway: for this meaning of πάντως, cf. Hdt 5.111; Eur. *El.* 227 (with Denniston's note ad loc.); *Or.* 1163; Ar. *Thesm.* 984. For the explanatory asyndeton, cf. 683 and Smyth §2167.B.

495 Blessed is he...: likewise at *Bacc.* 902–12 the μακαρισμός recurs at a similar point in the action: it is followed by Pentheus' falling under the spell of Dionysus; here it is followed by Polyphemus' feeling the effects of wine, the first stage of Odysseus' plan to blind him (esp. 420–2).

496–7 with beloved streams: for πηγή describing Dionysus' constantly flowing wine, cf. Moschion 97 F 6.24–5; also *Cyc.* 123 (ῥοάς). φίλαισι πηγαῖς (496) is dative of instrument possibly going with the participle ἐκπετασθεὶς, but it could go with εὐιάζει ('shouts the cry in honour of Dionysus'); either way, the fact that these 'streams' are φίλαι ('dear, friendly, beloved') here expresses the precious closeness between Dionysus and his worshippers during such 'revels'; on the φιλία ('friendship') between Dionysus and the satyrs cf. 73–5n; Gen. Intro, *e.g.* p. 32.   **with sails spread**: ἐκπετασθείς, aorist passive participle of ἐκπετάννυμι (literally, 'spread out'), describes a person already 'spread out', who has laid himself on his back: the best parallel for which is Pind. *Isthm.* 3/4.65 ἀλωπήξ αἰετοῦ ἅτ ἀναπιτναμένα (the archaic form of πετάννυμι) ῥόμβον ἴσχει, ('like a fox on its back thwarting an eagle's swoop'). In the satyrs' choral song the person is simply reclining like a symposiast; he's already stationary, and so already 'embracing a male companion' (499).

498   embracing a dear male companion (φίλον ἄνδρ' ὑπαγκαλίζων): the participle can have erotic implications (cf. Soph. *Tr.* 540 for the cognate noun), and elsewhere satyrs reveal homosexual desires (Soph. *Lovers of Achilles* F 153, 157; F 756; Achaeus, *Linus* F 26, etc.) as well as heterosexual, which are also in evidence here at 500 (cf. also above 168–74, 169–71; cf. 186–7). For komastic satyrs arm in arm in Greek art, see, for instance, Carpenter, pl. 19B, and for satyric homosexual activity in art, see Lissarrague (1990b) 64–5 and fig. 2.28. Does the homosexual allusion point to Polyphemus' eventual rape of Silenus? Cf. 583–4n.

499–501   The text has been emended a number of times to account for (1) the metrical anomaly: τε is long before ξανθόν, whereas responsion requires a short, and a stichic anacreontic would not permit 3 longs; (2) ξανθόν ('blonde') and λιπαρόν ('glistening') qualify the same noun βόστρυχον ('lock of hair'); (3) there is no clear object of ἔχων ('having'). No consensus on how to construe the text has been achieved, but for a good overview, see Seaford. Although L's text is corrupt, there emerges a plausible picture of a more or less drunken komast, anointed with myrrh, and with glistening locks, embracing both his male friend, in the company of a girlfriend (ἑταίρα), and ready to partake in further pleasures of the κῶμος (reading Scaliger's λιπαρόν as the accusative semi-objective with the verbal adjective μυρόχριστος [on which, see Smyth §1598] in place of, L's λιπαρός).

502   Who will open the door for me? a clear *double entendre*, also found readily in Old Comedy (Ar. *Lys.* 309; *Thesm.* 424; *Eccl.* 989, etc.); see Henderson (1991a) esp. 27, 137, 138, 171. If the scene to be imagined is one of the satyr/komast reclining with both a male and female lover, the question becomes more telling. This meaning is not precluded by a likely allusion to the παρακλαυσίθυρον, the song by the lover outside his beloved's door (*e.g.*, Ar. *Eccl.* 962). For fistfights outside girls' doors, cf. Pratinas 4 F 3.7–9, below; cf. also 534n.

503–4   I'm filled … rejoicing: Polyphemus expresses his joy with γάνυμαι, which recalls Odysseus' description of the wine he proffered the monster as Διονύσου γάνος ('joy of Dionysus'; see above 415n.), the first part of his plan to subdue him; although the Cyclops feels at ease now, his undoing has already begun. The erotics of the choral song become steadily more emphatic now that Polyphemus appears. The monster's use of γάνυμαι may be a play on words to anticipate his amorous intentions later when Silenus plays the unwilling role of Ganymede to his Zeus (577–89). **<but>**: a conjecture by Triclinius likely made to restore metre. **with the feast's youthful zest**: Seaford compares Pindar, *Pyth.* 4.295; Polyphemus' *bonhomie* is made offensive by his gloating over his cannibalistic feast (δαιτὸς), and is exacerbated by the wine (cf. above, 416–17n.).

505–6   Like a cargo ship ... belly: the translation takes σκάφος as accusative of respect with γεμισθεὶς (literally, 'loaded up in respect of my hull'). The image is a vivid one, depicting him as a cargo ship of wine, unsteady on his feet in his drunkenness as a ship would be in rough seas. The monster's delight is all the more jarring to audience and satyrs, as he uses much the same nautical imagery for himself as the chorus used of him when they sang of their revulsion at his meal (361–7, esp. 362). The monster, extending the 'satyric glutton motif' to include cannibalism (cf. above 326–7n., and Gen, Intro., pp. 33–4), delights in what repelled the satyrs.

507   cheerful (εὔφρων), resembles the εὐφροσύνη of the wine-bowl at Xenophanes' symposium (21 B 1.4 DK); but the piety and high-mindedness of the poet-philosopher's prescriptive drinking party (esp. 21 B 1.13–14) could hardly be further from the monster's murderous self-indulgence here, so that the adjective εὔφρων conveys some irony. Polyphemus' increasing sense of joy and abandon will give his downfall more dramatic impact, and more pleasure for the satyrs and mortals onstage at least.   **cargo**: translates φόρτος, which continues the nautical imagery, is Seymour's emendation of L's χόρτος: 'fodder, produce'. Polyphemus imagines himself led or towed along like a ship by the wine which, in bestowing good cheer, is itself described in quasi-animated terms.

508–9   to the revel in springtime: the time of year of the City Dionysia, the occasion of the play's first performance, but the expression here need not be taken as an allusion to the festival.   **my brother Cyclopes**: it is a measure of the effect that the wine is having on him that Polyphemus, the great embodiment of extreme *autarkeia*, now feels the communal urgings of the thiasos (cf. also above 120n; 445–6n.).

510   Come on, come on (φέρε ... φέρε): a further indication of the monster's greed evident in this colloquialism; cf. 8 n., 152, 492, 568.   **stranger**: Triclinius emended L's now illegible reading to the Ionic ξεῖνε which occurs only here in the play (P has the Attic ξένε), possibly for the sake of metrical variation.   **put ... in my hands**: for this meaning of ἔνδος, cf. *IT* 167.

511–12   beautiful glance from his eyes ... in beauty: heavily sarcastic for the one-eyed monster – NB the plural reference to his eyes (462–3n.) ὄμμασιν – whose fearsome prospect turned the satyrs' faces away in fear (211); cf. also the comic obsequiousness of Silenus, which plays on a similarly incongruous notion (266–7; cf. 34–5, 174). For the καλόν/καλός repetition, cf. Ar. *Ach.* 253; *Peace* 1329–30, the latter in the context of a wedding song or 'hymeneal'. There is possibly here in *Cyc.*, as earlier (see 182–4, 186–7nn.), a parody of Sappho who also compliments the groom (F 111, 112, 115, 116 L-P); see Page (1955) 119–26 for Sappho's epithalamians ('wedding poetry'). The joke continues in that the monster has a lover's glance comparable to that of Helen herself who in Aeschylus' *Agamemnon* emits a 'melting glance from her eyes' (μαλθακὸν ὀμμάτων βέλος); cf. also Eur. *Tro.* 891–2. Noteworthy too, by way of contrast, are the 'spears' that the beautiful young Achilles emits from his eyes, filling the satyrs with lust for him (Soph. *Lovers* F 157, n. 11, below). The language of 511 works on another level in comically inverting the motif of the terrifying glare of warriors in epic (*Il.* 3.342, 23.815, etc.) or tragedy (Aesch. *Seven* 498; cf. *Sacred Delegates* 21), or monstrous images (*e.g.* *Il.* 11.37; [Hes.] *Shield* 160).

513   No supplement for the lacuna in the ms (revealed by incomplete responsion with 497) has received general acceptance.   **"Who loves me?"** The satyrs seem more likely to be attributing these words to Polyphemus, as they have just been speaking about him, rather than presenting it as one of their own utterances, as a complaint that nobody loves them. Heath and Scaliger conjecture ἐκπερᾷς ('you are coming out') and ἐκπέρα ('come out') respectively so that φιλεῖ τίς ἡμᾶς are simply the satyrs' own words and do not mock Polyphemus; but this would amount to the bizarre consequence of the satyrs' calling the monster beautiful and inviting him to 'love' them! While the lacunose state of the text urges caution, the idea of Polyphemus as an absurd lover is worth entertaining; it begins to appear in the poetry of Eur.'s younger contemporary Philoxenus and becomes a favourite theme for later writers (see above 483–518n.). We may also translate: 'Somebody loves me', with unaccentuated τις (Aldine edition) as Ussher does, who attributes the word to the satyrs and sees them alluding to Polyphemus' imminent amorous activity. Others (*e.g.* Diggle (1972) 345), retaining the interrogative form, suggest that the satyrs would be alluding to Polyphemus' own lecherous intentions towards them, citing 585–9. But Polyphemus' usual post-prandial diversion seems to have sufficed for him so far (327–8n.); moreover, this seems to lessen the impact of his intention towards Silenus, the grotesque humour of which is reinforced by its unexpectedness – at least from the satyrs' point of view – despite the allusion to homosexual activity in the satyr's komastic fantasy (see 498n.). Polyphemus has shown no such erotic interest in the satyrs, nor do the satyrs anticipate this possibility until their father is actually dragged into the cave (507–8). In keeping with their general disdain and loathing of the monster the satyrs seem here (511–13) to be mocking him in the most absurdly sardonic and incongruous terms they can think of: as a beautiful lover. But it is a joke that seems to backfire; Polyphemus' rape of Silenus takes place in a bizarrely erotic context that steadily builds up from here (see also 541n., 553–5n.).

514–15   The metre and sense of the obelised text are too corrupt for any restoration or explanation to command wide acceptance; the translation represents the text in L. For discussion, *e.g.*, Duchemin; Diggle (1972) 345–7 who despairs of making sense of the lines; Ussher accepts Paley's emendation κοὐ for L's χὡς to give: 'hostile (δαῖα) torches await your flesh and no soft nymph in dewy caves'. Seaford in his admittedly 'highly conjectural' restoration wishes to make the image less explicit, and would delete L's χὡς and δαῖα to give: 'Lighted torches await you, and (καί), a rose-coloured (ῥοδόχρως) tender nymph.' In any event, the nuptial imagery continues here with the mention of torches (λύχνα) and νύμφα ('bride' or 'nymph': LSJ s.v. I & II). The torch procession for the bride is referred to elsewhere in Euripidean drama (*Tro.* 308–50, etc.), and was one of the most conspicuous features of the marriage rite: see Garland (1990) 217–25; Oakley and Sinis (1993) *passim*. As the satyrs know Odysseus' plan to blind Polyphemus with a burning branch (451–65; 483–6), this short hymeneal emerges as a thinly veiled prophecy of the monster's imminent punishment with its reference to the torches which are δαῖα meaning both 'burning' and 'hostile'.

516–18 inside dewy caves: superficially this image has elements of a brief *locus amoenus* (cf. 44–6, 66–7nn.), but as nymphs are frequent sexual partners of satyrs (68n.), a *double entendre* is the more obvious point here; see 169–71n. and Henderson (1991a) 27. Silenus boasts of his youthful virility when in his prime through his manhood he left many memorials fashioned in nymphs' dwellings (Soph. *Trackers* 154–5). **wreaths**: these were worn by the groom (Plut. *Mor.* 771d), but also by symposiasts (Ar. *Ach.* 1091, *Eccl.* 133; cf. also Osborne (1998) figs. 72, 77, 92, etc.) of which Polyphemus wishes to become one **... of no one colour**: the implication is that such wreaths were of just one colour; but cf. Ar. *Birds* (159–61), and see Seaford for further refs. The satyrs seem to be dwelling graphically on the gore that will result from Polyphemus' wound; Ussher suggests the multi-coloured reference is to the flame of the fire; it could be to the flowers in the image (cf. 541), or all three.

519–607 In many ways this scene is the turning point of the play as Odysseus exerts control over the Cyclops. The early part of the scene is dominated by the exchange in stichomythia between hero and drunken monster (521–39). Again there is the much-stylized question and answer format, but, rather than being a frank exchange of information as earlier between Odysseus and Silenus (102–62), Odysseus' answers here must serve his purpose in keeping Polyphemus at home without arousing suspicion. The hero's answers are at times vague, misleading and designed to change the topic (524, 526, 528); and elsewhere he parries the monster's stated intentions to attend a revel with his fellow Cyclopes (530–8). Collins (2004) 44–6 sees much stichomythic 'capping' in the exchange whereby Odysseus even elicits from the monster an unwitting prediction of his own fate (535). Interestingly, it is Silenus who, for reasons most likely dictated by his desire to have more wine for himself, makes the decisive point that keeps Polyphemus at home (540). From here the comic antics come more into play with Silenus and Odysseus 'educating' the ogre into the niceties of sympotic etiquette, a likely satyric motif (cf. Ion 19 *Omphale* F 27; Achaeus, *Heph.* F 17); all the while the old satyr helps himself to the wine at every opportunity and inadvertently adds to the bizarre erotics of the scene that culminates in the threatened rape (541–65, 576–89). By this time, however, the monster's fate is sealed, as Odysseus confidently predicts when trying (vainly as it turns out) to recruit the satyrs into his plan to blind the beast (590–607).

519   this Bacchus (*i.e.* wine): literally, 'the Bacchic one', a periphrastic expression underscoring the link between Dionysus and his emblematic drink; for the conflation of Dionysus with wine, see 123–4 with n., 156, 415 with n., 575 with n; cf. also Moschion 97 F 6.24–5. As Sutton (1980) 128, observes, the Cyclops, like Pentheus in the *Bacchae*, gradually comes under the influence of his foe before his downfall; Dionysus entrances Pentheus (*Bacc.* 811–46) while Odysseus continues to ply the Cyclops with drink (*Cyc.* 519–75).

520   an old hand: translates τρίβων, a colloquialism; see Stevens (1976) 50.

521   This line is sometimes read as one question, with unaccentuated τις (Ussher, Paganelli), or has its second half (θεὸς νομίζεται) given to Odysseus (Wieseler, Duchemin) thus running on into 522; but such antilabê is extremely unlikely at the beginning of stichomythia.   **this Bacchus**: the monster knows nothing at least of Dionysus' emblem, the vine (cf. 123–4 with n.); this may be surprising given that Polyphemus has bragged about the absence of Dionysus and accused the satyrs of engaging in a Bacchic revel (see 204n.). But the apparent inconsistency may be explained by the fact that the monster has made no connection between wine – which he here calls 'the Bacchic one' – and the god he knows as 'Dionysus' (as he calls him at 204), despite Odysseus' description of wine as 'the joy of Dionysus' (415). Certainly the monster's ignorance of the debilitating powers of wine is essential for the ensuing plot; from here his 'education', as the satyrs have called it (492–3 wth n.), begins in earnest.

522   Odysseus' words are the corollary of the *Cypria* (F 18 Davies) and Eur. *Bacchae* (280–3) where wine is called the best antidote for sorrow; see above 167n.

524   He harms no mortal: anybody familiar with the story of Pentheus before Eur.'s *Bacchae* and of Lycurgus would know how destructive Dionysus can be (and cf. *Bacc.* 861–2: the god's admission of his own ambivalence); see 3–4n. for references to earlier treatments onstage of these opponents of the god. As part of his plan, Odysseus also uses the power of the wine to harm and overcome the monster (422, 454).

527   not fitting for the gods: Polyphemus, for all his contempt for the Olympians, still expects some dignity on their part at least in their appearance; although the wearing of skins is an indicator of servile status (cf. 80n.), the chorus describe their brutal 'master' (cf. 34–5n.) as doing this (360). In Ar. *Frogs* Aeschylus denounces the shabby attire of Euripides' tragic characters who he thinks should be dressed more in accord with their aristocratic status (1061–4). For other gnomic comments on how the gods should behave, cf. Eur. *Bacc.* 1348, also applied to Dionysus, and cf. the critiques of conventional theology by Xenophanes (21 B 11, 12 DK) who posits a more abstract notion of the divine (21 B 23–26 DK). **in wineskins**: for this meaning of ἐν, cf. above 360n.

528–9 Odysseus cuts short Polyphemus' elementary theological musings with a return to the pleasures of drink, thus playing to Polyphemus' likely capacity for it. **I love this drink here**: a more blunt statement than the almost erotic ecstasy Silenus exhibits, when reunited with the wine (172–3).

531 See 533n.

532 No, because: for this use of γάρ, cf. *Alc.* 147; see also Denniston (1954) 73. **you'll appear all the more honoured**: this appeal to τιμή (honour) would be more compelling to a Homeric hero (cf. Achilles, *Il.* 1.243–4, 355–6, etc.) or regal figure than a solitary Cyclops (cf. 120); but Odysseus has already addressed Polyphemus in terms befitting royalty (290). φαίνομαι without the participle of εἰμί recurs at 670 and elsewhere in Euripides: *Hipp.* 332 with the same adjective as here (τιμιώτερος: 'more honoured'); for φαίνομαι without the participle, see Smyth §2119.

533 my friends: as in his reference to his 'brothers' at 531, Polyphemus now feels communal urgings induced by the wine and wishes to join a revel (537; cf. also 445–6n.; 508–9). These sudden impulses fly in the face of the monster's disparagement of the idea of friendship (cf. 288n.), and in the solipsistic lifestyle of the Cyclopes generally (120n.).

534 See above 502n. Apart from Pratinas 4 F 3.7–9 and Eubulus F 94, a mythic example of violence after drinking is the attempted rape of the Lapith women by the Centaurs and the famous battle with the Lapith men that followed (123–4n.); this paradigmatic myth is recast in satyric terms in Polyphemus' drunken rape of Silenus (576–89). [Athenaeus (1.36d) offers a different version of this line: πληγὰς ὁ κῶμος λοίδορόν θ' ὕβριν φέρει ('the revel brings on blows, and abusive violence'), but none of these variants is considered superior to L's text.]

535 nobody: (οὔτις) *pace* Seaford, it does not seem too subtle to see here, as do Duchemin and Stanford (1954) 105, a reference to Odysseus' trick, famous from Homer onward, of using the name Nobody (cf. also *Cyc.* 550, 672–5). By now the monster, in his drunkenness, is beginning to fall into the trap set for him by the hero, and heavy-handed Homeric references have already occurred earlier in the play (*e.g.* 460–3). Here the joke may work on a paratragic level in that Polyphemus, like some tragic characters (*e.g.* Oedipus, Soph. *OT* 139–40, 249–52, 258–68), unwittingly voices an anticipation of his own fate.

536 Listen, fella: translates ὦ τᾶν, a colloquialism, which also occurs at Soph. *Trackers* 104; Odysseus refrains from addressing Polyphemus as a φίλος even ironically. But as Stevens (1976) 42 notes, ὦ τᾶν can convey impatience and condescension, both of which are well suited to Odysseus' tone here as he has been trying for some to persuade the boorish monster to stay at home.

538   No, but...: for this nuance of δὲ... γε, see Denniston (1954) 153. Polyphemus' desires to join in a κῶμος – natural enough for a Greek male under the influence of Dionysus – must be quelled for Odysseus' plan to work. But the monster is a travesty of a komast anyway; cf. 445–6n.

539   What should we do...? τί δρῶμεν, a common enough expression in moments of tragic crises, especially in Euripides (*e.g., Hipp.* 782, *El.* 967, *IT* 96, *Ion* 756; cf. Soph. *Phil.* 963); its appearance here suggests paratragic mock seriousness (cf. also its appearance in Soph. *Trackers* 104). Polyphemus' trust in Silenus is as comically ill-founded as it was earlier (273–4), when it came in the wake of the old satyr's outrageous lie (232–40). Silenus has not spoken since 313–15 and Polyphemus' address to him is a way for Silenus to be reintroduced into the action, so that the comic antics of his drinking can come into play, as well as his role as the victim of Polyphemus' lechery (after which he speaks no more in the play). From here until 575 the stichomythia involves an occasional third voice, a rarity.

540   Silenus' answer encourages the monster to stay and thus is consistent with Odysseus' plan to which he has agreed (431). But, independently of this, he may want the Cyclops to stay where he is simply so he can get more of the wine himself, as he does later (552–3, 560–1, 565).

541   L's attribution of this line to the Cyclops is accepted by most editors, but Mancini (1899) argued that it should be spoken by Odysseus; so also Diggle. To a large extent the issue of attribution depends on the nuances of καὶ μὴν ... γε (541). Although Ussher and Seaford take both expressions as implying assent (citing Denniston (1954) 157–9, 352), they draw different conclusions: Ussher follows the attribution in the ms to the Cyclops, while Seaford attributes it to Odysseus; if, as is plausible, Odysseus is the speaker, the particles suggest that his tone is one of further encouragement, rather than assent, as the plan to keep Polyphemus at home is Odysseus' (536, 538).   **the ground and its flowery grasses are luxuriant**: this expression is perhaps briefly redolent of the *locus amoenus* motif (cf. 44–6, 66–7, 516–18nn.), and certainly has erotic overtones reminiscent of epic and other dramatic poetry: cf. Zeus' making the ground soft with grasses and hyacinths immediately before having sex with Hera in the Διὸς ἀπάτη (Seduction of Zeus) episode in the *Iliad* (14.346–9); the water, grass and flowers and nymphs mentioned to which Aphrodite came from the Judgement of Paris (*IA* 1294–9; 1300); Chaeremon 71 *Oeneus* F 14; Io is bidden to await Zeus' advances in the flowery meadows where she is then turned into a heifer (Aesch. *Supp.* 538–42, etc.). Polyphemus has already been derided by the chorus as a grotesquely absurd lover (511–18), and this parodic symposium climaxes, so to speak, with a bizarre erotic encounter of its own (576–89).

543   please ... lie on your side: μοι is an ethic dative (cf. 43n.); the pose is that of the symposiast. Much of the humour of this scene depends on Silenus' moving around behind Polyphemus so he can drink on the sly (545–7). Polyphemus' posture here recalls the Richmond Vase scene of his blinding with satyrs on the right (*LIMC* VIII.1 I 24). Commentators have rightly drawn attention to the parallel in Ar. *Wasps* (esp. 1208–10) when son teaches father the niceties of symposium etiquette; but parallels to such instruction of a boorish or awkward figure in sympotic ritual can be found also in satyr drama (*e.g.* Ion, *Omphale* F 21–7; Achaeus, *Hephaestus* F 17).

544   There, done! (ἰδού): omitted by L:, but added by Triclinius; for this colloquialism, see 153n.

545   Then why (τί δῆτα): the particle with the interrogative expresses surprise here, even indignation; see Denniston (1954) 272; Smyth §2851.

546–7   here may take it: reading παρών καταλάβῃ (lit., 'being present, may take it') with L. Reiske emended to παριών ('going past'), but παριών creates a rare '2nd foot anapaest' (Seaford p. 45 n. 137), and, while P has καταβάλῃ 'spills it', L may just be right. Here the *antilabê* runs over to the next line (as at 558–9, 640–1, etc.); at 683 *antilabê* of just one word occurs. The attempts by Silenus to swindle Polyphemus out of the wine, and the monster's blunt recognition of this, followed by his gruff orders and impatience (cf. also 558, 560), undermine any suggestion, *pace* Ussher (on 226, 539–43), that there is anything 'touching' about the monster's attitude to the old satyr (cf. 273–4, 539nn.).

548–50   This allusion to the trick of Nobody (cf. 535n.), Odysseus' request for a 'gift' in return for the wine and the cruel nature of that 'gift', all follow in a very succinct manner the Homeric model (*Od.* 9.355–70), although here Polyphemus does not sardonically invoke ξενία (hospitality) as he had done earlier (342–3n.).   **last ... all your companions**: literally, ὕστερον is an adjective referring to Odysseus (σὲ) meaning 'later', and ἑταίρων ὕστερον can be taken as a genitive of comparison (cf. Ar. *Eccl.* 859; Smyth §1431); but the meaning is that Polyphemus will save Odysseus till last (as in Homer: see 342n.); Hermann altered to ὕστατον, presumably with this in mind.

551   Many editors accept L's attribution of line 551 to Odysseus, rather than Silenus (Lenting, Diggle). Coming from Silenus, it would be consistent with his earlier barbed comments (313–15); but it is difficult to see how even Silenus would encourage an action that would ruin his chance to get off the island, unless he is being ironic. In the ms attribution it is a sarcastic understatement from Odysseus, as well as drawing attention to the act as a violation of ξενία (hospitality); he is the ξένος a number of times (102, 548, 566, 676, etc.)

552   Hey, you!: the abrupt and colloquial οὗτος (see Stevens 1976, 37–8) from Polyphemus to Silenus may support the possibility that the old satyr spoke at 551. From 552–66 he toys with Polyphemus, and such antics would be effectively introduced with an interjection from him at 551, as it would turn the focus back from Odysseus to the old satyr.

553–4   this wine here kissed me: Silenus even describes the wine as having amorous feelings towards himself, as if the drink is somehow personified; cf. the satyric habit of making drinking vessels sexual objects (172–4n; cf. 439–40n.).   **wine ... doesn't love you**: Polyphemus continues the personification, as he goes on to do in his description of it as σοφός (572; cf. also 520–6).   **beautiful**: Silenus imagines himself (here and at 555) to be one of the καλός ('beautiful') boys so commonly depicted on sympotic vases and cups. The self-deluding vanity of a creature as ungainly as Silenus has been evoked earlier in the play (2n.), and recurs here as a motif of satyric humour: cf. Aesch. *Net-Fishers* (F **47a, 821–2); Soph. *Trackers* (154–5). In Aeschylus' *Sacred Delegates* a satyr describes his portrait as καλλίγραπτον ('beautifully painted': Aesch. F **78a12) and as depicting his καλῆς μορφῆς ('beautiful shape': F **78a 19); for discussion, see O'Sullivan (2000) esp. 360–3, and below on Aesch. *Sacred Delegates*. The comic incongruity of καλός applied to the old satyr recalls the satyr chorus' sarcastic description of the monster in the same terms (511–12 with n; cf. 583 the adverbial κάλλιον).

555   No: Diggle (1971) 48–9 emended L's ναὶ ('yes'); this reading thus has Silenus responding to Polyphemus' words: 'You'll be sorry' (κλαύσῃ: literally, 'you will weep'; see above 174n.). But L's text may be defensible as a response to Polyphemus' view that the wine doesn't love the old satyr, to give: 'Yes, by Zeus (the wine does love me!)'.

556–7   Silenus has no real interest in whether or not the wine is mixed (cf. above 149); here his delaying tactics allow for more visual play as the satyr helps himself to more drink, while the monster's impatience grows, exacerbated by his own greed in his demand that the drinking cup be full; cf. above 336–8n.

558   You'll be my ruin!: the translation assumes με ('me') after ἀπολεῖς, as in comedy's idiom (*e.g.* Ar. *Clouds* 93); see Stevens (1976) 11. But it is possible that τὸν οἶνον could be understood as the object, so that Polyphemus thinks the wine will be ruined, if mixed; so Ussher, who cites Polyphemus' words to Odysseus in Aristias' *Cyclops* F 4: ἀπώλεσας τὸν οἶνον ἐπιχέας ὕδωρ ('you will destroy the wine, pouring water into it'). But Silenus is simply using delaying tactics to drink more of the wine himself (559), and Polyphemus is already aware of the old satyr's tricks (546–7). In supplying 'me', the joke seems to work better in reflecting Polyphemus' increasingly hyperbolic desire for the wine; cf. also 576–83 for his exuberant, indeed hubristic, description of the wine's effects on him.   **as it is** (οὕτως): rather than 'without more ado' is colloquial (cf. *Alc.* 860), Stevens (1976) 56; so that ἀπολεῖς and οὕτως in tandem give a peremptory tone.   **No**: Wecklein's emendation for L's ναὶ ('yes') seems more plausible in this instance; it is difficult to see why the satyr would agree with the Cyclops on this point.

559   For wreaths worn at symposia, see 516–18n.

560   <No>: Hermann supplemented οὐ, but the Aldine text reads ναί ('yes'), which could add to the joke in that Silenus now brazenly admits to the tricks he is playing on Polyphemus (cf. 546), all for the sake of the wine.

561 **You have to wipe (your mouth)**: translates ἀπομακτέον, Cobet's emendation, the gerundive form of ἀπομάσσω. 'your mouth' is idiomatically not in the Greek, but here the sense of 'mouth' is required by 562 'my lips'. Cf. ἀπομαγδαλία, a crust the Greeks used to wipe their mouths or hands after a meal and then threw to the dogs (LSJ s.v. I): this is from the same root as (ἀπο)μάσσω 'rub', whence μᾶζα 'moulded' bread or cake (cf. Ar. *Peace* 1, 3, 4, 565, 853). But L's ἀπομυκτέον (from ἀπομύσσω 'remove the mucus') is accepted by some editors (Murray, Ussher, Paganelli, Biehl, Paduano); the idea of Polyphemus' mucus-ridden face would work well as another of his repulsive features to be imagined by the audience. It is also consistent with his own unsavoury habits he gloats about earlier (326–8); and other monstrous figures are also imagined as having mucus running down their faces, such as Achlys (an incarnation of Death and Darkness) on Heracles' shield ([Hes.] *Shield* 267).   **so you can have it to drink**: apart from here and one other instance (*Bacc.* 784) ὡς + future indicative of purpose is not attested in Euripides, and is generally much rarer than ὅπως (read here by Tricilinius); see Smyth §2203. [Wilamowitz's emendation σοὐστὶν (= σοι ἐστὶν) ὡς is metrical, although the copula is often omitted with both –τέος personal and -τέον impersonal; see Smyth §2151–2.]

562 **beard**: translates τρίχες, which usually means hair, but the reference here is to hair around the mouth.

563 See 543n. for other satyric and Aristophanic parallels to Silenus' instructions on proper sympotic behaviour.

564 **just as you see me drinking – or not ... be**: ἐμέ will be emphatic after enclitic με (cf. *And.* 752–4, cited by Seaford). [Nauck read οὐκέτι ('no longer') for L's οὐκ ἐμέ, which would give the sense that Silenus is urging Polyphemus to behave elegantly when he sees him drinking or 'no longer drinking'.] Diggle (1969) 33–4 interestingly suggests that Silenus dips his head into the 'bowl' so that he disappears from sight. But, while the language used for the drinking vessel in the play varies, mostly it is understood as a cup, rather than a bowl: ποτήρ (151), κύλιξ (164, 421, 433), σκύφος (411, 556); cf., however, κρατήρ (545); the only other instances of κρατήρ refer to Polyphemus' milk bowls including one as large as ten amphorae (216, 387). Alternatively, then, Silenus may lift the cup to his face with the same effect as would happen to a drinker from an 'eye cup' (κύλιξ). These vessels frequently depict Dionysian scenes on the interior, with two large eyes painted on the exterior which sometimes have a satyr's face between the eyes: see *e.g.* Osborne (1998) figs. 68–9. To an onlooker, the symposiast's face would be obscured behind the upturned cup as he drinks from it, his eyes replaced by those on the cup, and his ears by the handles; no painted eyes are mentioned on the cup here, but the effect of temporary 'invisibility', alluded to by Silenus, would be the same.

565 Literally: τί δράσεις 'what are you going to do?'; cf. the use of the present δρᾷς (552). Polyphemus here sees Silenus about to drink the wine; the satyr answers him after he has done so.   **one gulp**: Silenus' capacity for drink matches that of the monster (417, 558).

566–7 **for me**: μοι here is dative of advantage. Odysseus' role as οἰνοχόος ('wine pourer') gives him more control over Polyphemus' drinking. Silenus' drinking, when wine pourer, while providing some humour, could stand in the way of such plans in leaving insufficient wine to send Polyphemus off to a drunken sleep. Odysseus agrees to be wine pourer with cool understatement. **Well, certainly**: for this nuance of γοῦν, see Denniston (1954) 452. **some knowledge of the vine**: on the link between wine and civilization, cf. above 123–4.

569 **for a man**: it is impossible to know whether the omitted antecedent for ὅστις was τούτῳ ('this man': Ussher, Biehl) or τόδε, 'this thing, instance <of a man> who's ...' (Eur. *El.* 816; *Hel.* 942; Smyth §2510). **a lot** (πολύν): sc. οἶνον ('wine'); also at 573.
570 **drink it all down**: ἔκπιθι: the emphatic prefix ἐκ signifies completion, as elsewhere (456n.).
571 **Because**: for δέ functioning like γάρ, cf. *Alc.* 61; *Med.* 717; *Hipp.* 94; see also Denniston (1954) 169 with further refs. **when a man's knocking it back**: Casaubon's σπῶντα for L's σιγῶντα ('keeping silent') which is unmetrical; the emendation fits in well with Odysseus' instructions to the monster to drink all the wine. **only be all spent when the drink is**: literally 'die together with the drink'; the language here is striking; συνεκθνῄσκω – a *hapax legomenon* in Classical Greek – posits an identity of wine and drinker: another way of saying 'keep drinking till all the wine is gone.' Similar play on the identity of drinker and drinking vessel is evident in how one appears to others when drinking from an 'eye-cup' (564n.); drinker and cup merge as one as the wine (or Dionysus) is transferred from one vessel to another.
572 **how clever the wood of the grapevine**: no interpretation of ξύλον ('wood') so far offered seems completely convincing, given the lack of comparable uses of the word to cast any light on its appearance here. Some notable interpretations include: 'the living wood of the vine'; a periphrasis, *i.e.* just 'the vine' (Ussher, Biehl); possibly the 'club', *i.e.* 'the strength of the wine to kill you' (Seaford), or the wooden frame of the punitive 'collar' (cf. Ussher, citing Ar. *Clouds* 592), with a less drastic metaphor, *i.e.* to incapacitate merely. Either of the latter two is plausible only if we could be sure that Athenians used ξύλον in this allusive way. But it is difficult to see why Polyphemus would speak about the wine in such terms, since, for him at this stage, it is a purely a source of pleasure. Even as a statement of unintended irony, the language here is extraordinarily oblique; cf. the more straightforward allusive irony of 535 (with n.). On the other hand, literal 'wood' (= the vine) is paralleled by Anaxagoras 59 A 45.18 DK, where ξύλον is a constituent of a living δένδρον ('tree') together with its bark and fruit (cf. LSJ x. III), cf. literal Ἀργοῦς ξύλον ('timbers of the Argo': Aesch. *Argo* F 20; and LSJ II.1). In any event, again the grapevine is spoken of as somehow animated (cf. 507, 553–5), but not as the liquid embodiment of Dionysus as in 156, 415, 454, 519–27. Polyphemus evidently thinks of the wine as something to cater purely to his own greed (cf. 503–10, 523,

529, etc.); it would thus be easily incorporated into his idea of the good life earlier in which gluttony is the highest goal (esp. 336–8). But the wine is σοφός on another ironic level: more than just sating the monster's gluttony, it is an effective agent in his undoing orchestrated by Odysseus, a man also famous for being σοφός (450).

574 so it's no longer thirsty: ἄδιψον is a predicative-proleptic adjective which qualifies the object (here νηδύν: 'belly') of the verb (in this case the aorist participle 'drenching' τέγξας); see Smyth §1040b. Odysseus' encouragement of Polyphemus to 'drench his belly' ostensibly recalls the monster's boasts of doing this himself with his milk-drinking (326). But Odysseus seems to be referring to Polyphemus' stomach while it digests his huge, not to say hideous, meal (δαιτὶ ... πολλῇ: 573); cf. the modern colloquialism of drinking 'on a full (or empty) stomach'. Alcaeus refers to wine as drenching the lungs (F 347), presumably the result of anatomical ignorance, but it may refer to the experience of choking or gagging when one eats or drinks too quickly, which Polyphemus himself seems to allude to (577, 677). **the wine will send** (βαλεῖ): Musgrave's emendation of L's βαλεῖς ('you will fall', intransitive, a very rare use of the uncompounded verb; see LSJ A.III.1); the subject of βαλεῖ is the noun omitted with πολύν at 573 ('wine').

575 Bacchus will make you parched: another conflation of the god and his drink (see above 519n.). Odysseus seems to be saying that only drinking more than one's fill is proper tribute to Dionysus, although this is likely to be lost on the monster, who would still think that the 'Bacchic one' refers solely to wine and not Dionysus. Whether this really tells us something about Dionysus as a god who induces thirst is uncertain; but Apollo, as both healer and bringer of disease (*Iliad* 1), and Demeter, as goddess of and withholder of grain (and bringer of hunger at least to Erysichthon: cf. Achaeus' satyric *Aethon* F 6–10, below; Callimachus, *Hymn* 6), provide possible parallels (cf. 123–4n.). In any case, Odysseus is simply using any form of persuasion to get Polyphemus as drunk as possible, and the hero is not always candid with the truth (see 524n.).

576–7 I only just managed to swim ...: Polyphemus' 'near death' experience of almost drowning extends the reference to 'dying with the wine' (571) in almost literal terms; frequently the wine in drinking cups was likened to the sea with painted ships on the inside of the lip of the cup which would appear to float on the surface of the wine; cf. also the Homeric epithet of the sea as οἶνοψ (literally 'wine-faced', suggesting 'wine-coloured', or possibly 'wine-dark': *Il.* 23.316; *Od.* 2.421, 5.132), and the Cyclops has already compared himself to a ship (504–7; cf. 362). This is the monster's last swig of the wine and his enjoyment is now more emphatic here (ἰοὺ ἰού) than before (cf. παπαῖ at 572). Assuming Odysseus' instructions have been followed (570–1, 573–4), the wine has now been finished, leading to Polyphemus' desire for sex. **This is unmitigated delight!**: this refers not only to the intensity of Polyphemus' pleasure here, but may suggest that the wine is unmixed ('unmitigated') or ἄκρατος (cf. 149 when Silenus tastes it neat); for the same metaphorical language elsewhere for 'pure' 'pleasure' or 'desire', cf. Plato, *Laws* 793a; Soph. F 941. The monster does not seem to care either way (557–8), and unmixed wine would certainly aid Odysseus' plan to get the monster drunk as quickly as possible. Cf. 602 when Odysseus prays for Sleep, one of the effects of the wine, to come to the monster ἄκρατος or '(with) unmitigated (power)'.

578–80 Polyphemus' hallucination is comparable to that of another enemy of Dionysus who falls under the god's power, Pentheus (*Bacc.* 918–22).   **heaven ... mingled with the earth**: Seaford takes this to reflect beliefs about the cosmic, life-producing union of sky and earth (*e.g.*, Aesch. F 44; cf. Hes. *Th.* 126–58), but it seems more likely to indicate just how unhinged Polyphemus' mind has become, just like Pentheus' mind when he sees two suns in the sky (*Bacc.* 918) – an image of madness recalled in Vergil's description of the madness of Dido (Verg. *Aen.* 4.469–73). Earth combining with heaven is an impossibility elsewhere in satyric drama, *e.g.* Eur. *Syleus* F 687.   **the throne of Zeus and the whole august majesty of the gods**: the Cyclops has little trouble imagining or recognising the gods in his delirious state. The open contempt he showed for Zeus and *a fortiori* the Olympians (318–21) might seem tempered here, but his attitude is not one of a convert to Olympian religion; it simply spurs him on to further impious thoughts and actions.

581   Wouldn't I like to kiss (them)? the monster now seems to leer at the satyrs whom he imagines to be the Graces, (or possibly even the Olympians themselves with Silenus as Zeus). [The question mark inserted by Wilamowitz gives better sense than a simple statement; for the idiom οὐκ ἄν + optative as an interrogative wish, cf. Smyth §1824, cf. 2662. A number of editors read a semi-colon or full stop after φιλήσαιμι (*e.g.*, Paley, Murray, Duchemin, Ussher), but a connective such as γάρ would be needed to complete the sense if οὐκ ἄν φιλήσαιμι is read as a statement. If such punctuation nevertheless stands, Polyphemus is announcing that he does not wish to kiss the Olympians, adding a further comic strand to his impiety. If so, he would not be the only transgressor to harbour lecherous thoughts about the gods.] **Graces**: contemplation – albeit in a delusional state – of an attempt on divine figures like the Graces would put Polyphemus on a similar level to Ixion, father of Centaurs, who made an infamous attempt on Hera, and met with an equally notorious punishment, thereby becoming a paradigm of transgressive lust (apart from Aeschylus' probably satyric *Ixion* (F 90, 91), see also Pindar, *Pyth.* 2.21–48; Eur. *Pho.* 1185; *Ixion* T ii–iii; cf. *Pirithous* (Eur. or Critias?) F 5.7–15; cf. also Ixion in art; *LIMC* V.1 s.v. 1, 3, 9, 11–15, 17). On a kylix cup by the Brygos painter, *c.* 490 BC (= KPS fig. 29a-b), satyrs make a similar attempt on Iris, winged messenger of the gods, in the presence of Dionysus; on the reverse they even lecherously approach Hera (a parody of the Ixion myth?), who moves off, flanked by Hermes and Heracles.

582–3   Enough!: ἄλις with half-stop – Wecklein's punctuation – is a colloquialism, *e.g.* Eur. *Hel.*1581, *Philoctetes* F 791; see also Collard (2005) 367. **Ganymede**: his fame as the object of Zeus' desire is attested in early epic (*Il.* 20.232–5; cf. *H. Hymn* 5.202–4, etc.) and his abduction widely depicted in art, including an akroterion (roof-top sculpture) from Olympia, *c.* 470 BC (*LIMC* IV.1 'Ganymede' s.v. 56), and on various pots, which appropriately enough featured in sympotic contexts (*LIMC* IV.1, 12, etc.). Polyphemus' delusion here recalls his earlier hubristic claims in not fearing Zeus and rivalling him (320–1, 328). Now, in another context, he even imagines himself the supreme god in one of the Olympian's most famous encounters; for another satyric ogre's delusions of rivalling Zeus, see Soph. *Salmoneus* F 537–41a, and see above 327–8n. **I shall get off**: translates ἀναπαύσομαι which has sexual connotations elsewhere (Hdt.1.181.1; Machon 286; Athen. 603a; Plut. *Alex.* 2); see 583–4n. **more splendidly**: this translates Spengel's emendation to κάλλιον ἢ] of L's κάλλιστα νὴ, which, accepted by many editors (Murray, Duchemin, Ussher, Biehl), would give: 'By the Graces, … in the finest style.' But Polyphemus is dismissing heterosexuality for which the Graces may stand, so it hardly seems likely he would swear by them even in his drunken state. In any event, the monster's intent is clear enough.

583–4 boys: Polyphemus decides to indulge in a homosexual act on this occasion, but he is not devoid of heterosexual impulses; cf. his 'temptation' by the Graces (581). As Seaford notes, homosexual activity had aristocratic connotations (cf. Ar. *Knights* 735–40; Plato *Symp.* 181b); see Dover (1989) 142, 149–151. In Xenophon's *Hiero* (31–3) desire for παιδικά is seen as a natural impulse (ἐμφυέσθαι) in the tyrant. Polyphemus' longing for παιδικά puts him on a par also with certain barbarians (Athen. 603a); cf. 172–4, 492–3nn. for other allusions to his barbaric or uncivilised nature; elsewhere the same desire is displayed by satyrs themselves (Soph. *Lovers of Achilles* F 153).

585 What? for this meaning of γάρ, see 154n. Despite the fact that Odysseus is the οἰνοχόος ('wine-pourer') here (566), there is no suggestion he would ever be the object of Polyphemus' lust; he is never anything other than a potential meal for the monster (550). An erotic context has slowly been building up since 511–18, derisively at first, but inadvertently fuelled by Silenus' own words (at, *e.g.*, 553–5) which now come back to haunt him.

586 I myself am now seizing: reflects the particle γέ as qualifying ἁρπάζω. **from the land of**: translates ἐκ τῆς, reflecting Hermann's emendation of L's τοῦ, which, as the article qualifying Δαρδάνου, means that Polyphemus is stealing Ganymede from Dardanus; conceivably, this may stand. However, Ganymede was the son of Tros, Dardanus being his great-grandfather (*Il.* 5.265–7, 20.215–35). Also, ἐκ is not usually used with persons, and elsewhere in Euripidean drama ἐκ τῆς can have the same meaning 'from the land', since omission of the feminine noun γῆ is a very common locution (*Hcld.* 140, *Ion* 1297).

588 lover: ἐραστὴν: Polyphemus now grotesquely embodies the ideas of 511–

18 – however comically meant by the satyrs – and takes the role of the older or active lover. Silenus, as a result, is forced to play the role of the implicit ἐρώμενος ('beloved' or object of the lover's desire), an idea that has, with equal comic incongruity, been building up for some time (cf. 553–5, etc.); cf. the reference to the 'boys' in whom the monster takes pleasure. **fastidious about one who's drunk**: Scaliger's correction πεπωκότι of L's πεπωκότα (the accusative -οτα is a grammatical impossibility because an accusative with (ἐν)τρυφάω could be only an internal one); the indirect object of ἐντρυφᾷς is a dative of a person here, which is rarely attested with this verb until later Greek (*e.g.* Plut. *Them.* 18.5).

589   O woe … wine: there may be an untranslatable pun in οἴμοι … οἶνον. **I'll … see**: ὄψομαι here may be surprising and could stand as a synoynym for μαθήσομαι ('I'll learn') or γνώσομαι ('I'll find out'), but for 'seeing' as (later) full realization, see *e.g.* Eur. *Supp.* 731, 782–5; *Bacc.* 814–15 (with πικρός, as in *Cyc.* here); cf. also *Supp.* 945; *Hcld.* 415; *Med.* 1388.   **wine … very bitter**: for πικρός denoting objects seeming bitter in their after-effects, cf. Eur. *Med.* 399; *Hec.* 772, etc; this contrasts Silenus' earlier description of the wine as γλυκύς 'sweet' (560).

590   sons of Dionysus: Odysseus refers to the god by a different name now, rather than calling him 'the Bacchic one' when speaking to Polyphemus, perhaps to bring out an aspect of the god other than as wine personified. Here the hero is speaking somewhat loosely, but his purpose is to flatter the satyrs; their actual father Silenus (16, 269, etc.) is hardly an appropriate role model to be invoked (especially in the current circumstances!), compared to their patron god who was at least pre-eminent in the Gigantomachy (6–7n.).   **noble children**: this address takes the form of flattery, as the locution is mock-heroic or mock-solemn, as παῖδες and τέκνα often are, *e.g.* (Aesch. *Pers.* 402, Eur. *Cretans* F 471); cf. Homeric warriors described Greeks as 'offshoots of Ares' (*Il.* 2.663, 745, 3.147, etc.). But this appeal to the satyrs proves to be a groundless hope on Odysseus' part; he seems to have expected their cowardice all along (642, 649).

591   The man: see 347–9n., 429n., 605n.   **in his sleep** (literally, 'in the sleep'): the Greek article τῷ is surprising, as over-determined; perhaps 'the sleep which will follow his drunkenness' (455) is meant.

592   he'll vomit: in another close parallel to the Homeric account, Odysseus likewise mentions Polyphemus' vomiting (cf. *Od.* 9.372–4).   **from his shameless gullet** (ἐξ ἀναιδοῦς φάρυγος): as elsewhere, this part of the monster's body is the focus of Polyphemus' heinous gluttony (215, 356, 410), and is now qualified by a suitable adjective.

593   †it pushes out†: the indicative †ὠθεῖ†, which may have been corrupted by proximity of ὠθήσει in the previous line, is considered problematic because of the asyndeton with παρευτρέπισται ('is ready'). A participial phrase (*e.g.* καπνὸν <πνέων> 'emitting smoke') is arguably to be expected here; see Diggle (1969) 34–6, who conjectured καπνὸν <πνέων> or <πνέων> καπνὸν with ὠθεῖ deleted. However, some editors retain L's reading: *e.g.*, Paley (who suspects corruption), Duchemin, Paganelli and Biehl (who retains it as a parenthesis); the asyndeton is not entirely out of keeping with Odysseus' speech which aims to rouse the satyrs to action.

594–5 Here are two colloquialisms: (i) **there's nothing left to do**; (ii) **be sure**: in Odysseus' injunction, using ὅπως and the future indicative ἔσῃ (also 630; see also Collard (2005) 372) to the chorus on how to act collectively. These two colloquialisms together suggest excitement on the part of the normally cool Odysseus, and are dramatically apt as the play approaches the decisive action. **a real man** (ἀνήρ, literally 'a man'): the singular here possibly suggests that Odysseus is addressing the satyrs individually; on the use of the singulars and plurals for the chorus, see above 427–8n., 465n. ἀνήρ here has exactly the martial or heroic overtones which the satyrs typically fall short of, as Odysseus realises (642), and so its appearance here is comically incongruous, as satyrs can never be 'men' in the sense required here (cf. 590n.). The different nuances of the words are evident in Xerxes' despair at having many ἄνθρωποι but few ἄνδρες at the battle of Salamis (Hdt. 7.210–11); cf. also *Alc.* 957; *Phrixus* F 829, etc.

596 a heart (λῆμα): cf. the Theban defender Polyphontes who, in preparing for the oncoming battle, is αἴθων λῆμα ('fiery in his heart': Aesch. *Seven* 448; cf. also *IT* 609; *Hcld* 702); in their over-enthusiastic response (above 465n.) the satyrs put themselves on the same level with such figures, only to be deflated by their inevitable cowardice later (635–48). **rock and adamant**: here meant favourably (as at *Od.* 17.463) as a sign of the satyrs' courage; but 'rock' can be coupled with 'adamant' in a negative sense (Pind. F 33d*.8).

597–8 before our father suffers something: it remains unclear whether or not Silenus suffers this fate; he speaks no more in the play and there is no explicit indication whether in fact he goes into the cave with Polyphemus at 589, only a hint at 586. But the imminent threat of rape is probably sufficient for the grim humour, which would be more effective if the old satyr is in the cave, with the audience unsure of what, if anything, is going on. Ancient sources tell us that Solon enshrined the inviolability of a male citizen's body in law, proscribing male prostitution and enslavement (Demosthenes, 22.23–5; Aeschines, 1.17–19); for discussion, see Dover (1989) 33–4. Thus, Polyphemus' actions here would be not just a violation of the individual, but also an affront to Attic law; the satyric context, however, gives the scene an earthy, somewhat grotesque humour – at least for audiences used to Old Comedy (Ar. *Knights* 365, *Clouds* 529, etc.). Cf. the sexual humiliation of the victim on a famous oinochoe celebrating Cimon's victory over the Persians at Eurymedon (c. 466 BC) on which a Greek called 'Eurymedon' is about to sodomise a Persian who looks at the viewer in a gesture of helplessness with the word κύβαδε ('bending forward') written next to him; see Kilmer (1993) R1155. **diabolical** (ἀπάλαμνον): the rare enjambed word (this is its only attestation in all Greek drama and it is Canter's emendation for L's ἀπαλλαγμὸν) means literally 'without hands', but here could mean something like 'against which hands are useless', *i.e.*, 'something for which there is no remedy' (see below 662n.); cf. also Pind. *Ol.* 1.59, 2.63.

599–600 Hephaestus: while he had his forge on Etna (*Prometheus Bound* 366–7), there is no tradition of enmity between him and Polyphemus or any of the Cyclopes; in Callimachus (*Hymn* 3.46–8) and Vergil (*Aeneid* 8.416–23) the one-eyed giants work at his anvils. Here the reference seems to be to the god in his role as fire personified; Odysseus calls on the god to burn (πυρώσας) the monster's eye. As early as Homer Hephaestus embodies the power of elemental fire (*Il.* 2.426), especially in his battle against the river Scamander (*Il.* 21.342–82; cf. Ar. *Wealth* 660–1). His name in the fifth century also functioned as metonymy for fire itself (Theagenes 8 F 2 DK; Pindar *Pyth.* 1.25–6; Prodicus 84 B 5 DK), as did the names Demeter and Dionysus for grain and wine (123–4n.).

601 Sleep, nursling of Black Night: this follows Hesiod (*Th.* 211–12); Homer, makes Sleep the twin brother of Death (*Il.*16.672, 682) and the two are famously depicted as winged hoplites picking up Sarpedon's body on the column krater by Euphronius (*LIMC* VII.1 Sarpedon 4). Night, as a child of Chaos, is one of the primordial cosmic deities, and a figure to inspire fear (Hes. *Th.* 744–5, 758); like her father Chaos, she generates malignant incarnations associated with darkness; in Aeschylus Night is the 'black mother' of the Furies (*Eum.* 745, cf. 416; see also West, *Theogony* pp. 35–6). Elsewhere in Euripides Night is not only black (*El.* 54) or μελάμπεπλος ('black-robed': *Ion* 1150), she is mother of horrors such as Λύσσα ('Madness') that causes Heracles to kill his own family (*HF* 822); thus Sleep here, as child of Night, will be malignant for the monster in making him vulnerable to being blinded and plunged into a world of darkness.

602 unmitigated power: ἄκρατος here may deliberately recall Polyphemus' description of the χάρις ('delight') he experienced earlier in his drinking (577) of which Sleep is a natural consequence. Thus, the monster's excesses will bring on a punishment from agents, one of whom is described in the same terms as 'unmitigated' (see 577n.); both the wine and resultant sleep are necessary to the blinding, and the punishment will fit the crime, in keeping with satyric justice (see 421–2n., 693n.). **beast**: elsewhere Odysseus and the chorus speak of Polyphemus in such bestial terms (442, 658); but he is also referred to as a man (348, 429, 591 with n., 605). **hateful to the gods**: see 396n.

603 Odysseus invokes his heroic past again (cf. 198–200, 347–52, and later 694–5), this time as a rhetorical ploy for his prayer. **most noble labours**: the πόνοι at Troy to which he referred earlier (107) are now recalled but this time as a reflection of his heroism. His reliance on his heroic credentials does not preclude his dependence on and acknowledgement of divine help.

604 This portentous line is mock-epic in diction and its artificial word order – with second noun ναύτας ('sailors') interposed between attribute αὐτόν ('himself') and first noun Ὀδυσσέα ('Odysseus') – which cannot be rendered into clear English;

see Diggle (1994) 208 for parallels to this type of word order in Euripides.

605   man ... mortals: Odysseus' reference to Polyphemus, as a 'man', marks a contrast to his calling him a beast three lines earlier, but his point is that Polyphemus, as a man (which he has been called elsewhere, see 347–9n.), deserves punishment for his disdain of men and gods, like other transgressors (cf. 348, 429); for Odysseus' reference to the satyrs as θῆρες ('wild creatures'), see 624n.

606–7   Arguably a more telling example of the challenge from a mortal to a god than at 353–5 (see note).   **chance** (τύχη) has a neutral meaning as agent or cause beyond human control (*e.g.*, Archil. F 16 W; Pind. *Ol.* 14.15; Aesch. *Seven* 426); it can also be a personification or divinity (*e.g.*, *H. Hom.* 2.420; Soph. *OT* 977; *Trackers* 79; Eur. *Hec.* 786). In the late fourth century BC a cult of Tyche was established at Antioch, and Pausanias (6.2.6–7) tells us of a cult statue made in her honour by Eutychides, a pupil of Lysippus, for the Syrians on the river Orontes (c. 300 BC). The idea of τύχη dominating human affairs occurs in Talthybius' speech as he contemplates the fate of Hecuba (*Hec.* 488–91); and scholars have long recognized its treatment by Thucydides as a non-divine factor in determining some events in his history; see Cornford (1907) 97–108; Hunter (1973) 73–9; Edmunds (1975) *passim*.

608–23   In an upbeat interlude, the chorus expresses delight at the prospect of Polyphemus' imminent punishment, invoking 'Maron' as wine personified, which turns their thoughts to reunion with their natural master, Dionysus. The metre for this short, astrophic song comprises trochaic dimeters with catalexis and syncopation, dactylic cola, and iambic dimeters; but the colometry is uncertain, hence the irregular line numbering; Dale (1968) 46, and Ussher, for instance, take πρασσέτω ('Let him do its work': 616) with the next colon, while Seaford, following Diggle, argues that it fits better with the preceding trochaic rhythm. For fuller discussion and outline of the scheme, see Dale (1969) 42–6 and (1983) 223; Ussher; Seaford.

608–9   tongs ... throttle the neck: we need not take this image literally, at least as far as the tongs (καρκίνος) are concerned; Biehl saw the reference to the tongs as alluding to Odysseus' invocation of Hephaestus the smith-god at 599–600, but the god's name seems to be metonymy for fire. As Ussher observes, the satyrs hope that Polyphemus will 'get it in the neck' and the expression may thus be a folk saying; καρκίνος does not occur in tragedy but appears in Soph. *Trackers* (305), where it means 'crab', *i.e.* a creature that has tongs or pincers. LSJ (καρκίνος s.v. I) give two examples of proverbial usages of the word from Aristophanes (*Peace* 1083) and Herodas (4.44); cf. also *CPG* II.73.17. But the image need not be seen as a dead metaphor, since the monster's throat or gullet (φάρυγξ) has repeatedly been the symbol of his greed and cannibalism (215, 356, 410, 592) and now is a suitable focus for the punishment Odysseus will mete out to him.

610   of the guest-eater (ξενοδαιτυμόνος, Hermann's emendation of L's unmetrical ξένων δαιτυμόνος): the monster's violation of hospitality is recalled here (and again at 658). The chorus' anticipation of what Polyphemus is to suffer resembles the chorus' anticipation of Pentheus' punishment in the *Bacchae* (977–1022); immediately after Pentheus' departure, the chorus invokes the hounds of Lyssa to attack the impious king, and go on to rehearse his destruction, twice calling on 'sword-wielding' justice to pierce him in the throat: λαιμῶν διαμπάξ (*Bacc.* 992– 6=1011–15). Likewise, the satyrs look forward to the blinding of Polyphemus, who throughout the play has shown himself to be equally godless and lawless (*Cyc.* 26, 30–1, 348, 378, 438; cf. *Bacc.* 995–6, 1015–6). Pentheus is 'lawless' (ἄνομος: *Bacc.* 996, 1016), just as Polyphemus renounces law and Olympian religion (203–5, 316– 21, 338–40). For similar anticipations by a dramatic chorus of what will inevitably happen, cf. Eur. *Med.* 978–1001, *Hipp.* 765–75, although in each of these instances the chorus' tone is one of foreboding and dread rather than vengeful exuberance.

611   the pupil that brings him light: the satyrs' language recalls the grim irony of Odysseus at 462–3.

615   is hidden: the present κρύπτεται functions like a perfect, as at Eur. *Her.* 263 (see also Smyth §1886–7).   **mighty shoot / of the oak tree**: Odysseus has mentioned an olive beam as the weapon of Polyphemus' blinding (455), but the satyrs, who are hardly likely to be sticklers for detail, may simply be thinking of the beam's enormity; earlier it was called μέγας (472; see 455n.). On the Richmond Vase (*LIMC* VIII.1 s.v. Polyphemus I 24) Odysseus and his men appear to be wielding a tree trunk over the sleeping giant.

616   let Maron come, let him do his work: cf. the chorus' words in the (*Bacc.* 992–3=1011–12), gleefully anticipating the demise of Pentheus: ἴτω δίκα φανερός, ἴτω / ξιφηφόρος: 'let justice come manifest, let sword-wielding (justice) come!' Maron, like his father, Dionysus, is identified with wine itself (cf. 123–4, 415, 519– 29nn.).

617–18   the raging Cyclops: in what way is this sleeping monster μαινόμενος? Madness can denote the state of mind of worshippers of Dionysus (164n.), but Polyphemus is no proper follower of Dionysus, even though in his own grotesque way he partakes in a sort of revel of drunkenness and sex. But since 'madness' can refer to those who have spurned the god's proper worship, the participle aligns Polyphemus with figures such as Lycurgus and Pentheus (see 3–4, 168n.), and probably also refers to his own violent habits (203–11, 582–9, etc.). [Hermann's μαινομένου is a correction for ms. L, which gives μαινόμενος, thus making the rage Maron's; and L is unmetrical here).]

619   so his drinking may be his undoing: literally, 'so he may drink badly'; the adverb κακῶς, apart from alluding to the ill consequences that Polyphemus' drinking will have for him, could also have normative implications: the monster has drunk to excess and, as a travesty of a symposiast, committed acts offensive to religious and civic norms (cf. *Theognidea* 509 where the consumption of much wine is called a κακόν, 'evil'). However, there need not be any normative sense to the adverb at *Cyc.* 619, since Odysseus and the satyrs wanted him to drink, and the satyrs are great drinkers themselves; in Homeric epic and elsewhere in Euripides κακῶς need have no moral connotations (*e.g.*, *Il.* 5.164; Eur. *Hcld.* 450).

620–1   whom I long for: ποθεινὸν: as at Eur. *Hel.* 623, *Or.* 1045, ποθεινός need not have specifically erotic connotations, and no myth tells of erotic activity between the satyrs and their god (see 498n. for homosexual tendencies of satyrs). But the satyrs' desire to be reunited with Dionysus is passionately expressed, and there is a strong statement of the φιλία between the satyrs and their god, now addressed by his cult title **Bromius** (1n.) as Silenus had addressed him.   **who loves to wear ivy**: φιλοκισσοφόρος is a *hapax legomenon*, but the image is not so far from Pratinas F 3.16 where Dionysus is addressed as 'lord with ivy in his hair' (κισσόχαιτ' ἄναξ). The ivy wreath is a standard form of head-dress for Dionysus in art, especially when satyrs and maenads are engaged in a thiasos around him (cf. *Bacc.* 177, 205, 702, etc.); the imminent prospect of release now puts thought of cultic activity in the minds of the satyrs.

622   desolate land: ἐρημία is literally 'emptiness' or 'loneliness'. The Cyclops' land is 'empty' of the cult of Dionysus and all its pleasures (25–6, 63–81, 203–11, etc.); the satyrs' isolation from their natural lord has made them lonely as a result. Here is a further reiteration of the play's setting on the fringes of the civilized world, as conceived in Athenocentric minds, (see 20n).

623   Shall I come that far? literally, 'to such an extent': ἐς τοσόνδε without a following noun in the genitive occurs elsewhere in Euripides, *e.g. Pho.* 1449 (contrast Soph. *El.* 961). The only genitive one can supply from context is ἐρημίας which makes no sense here as the satyrs are anticipating joyful reunion with their god. The elliptical use of ἐς τοσόνδε and the satyrs' longing suggest that the chorus is saying something along the lines of: 'shall I ever reach such (an extent of) bliss?'

624   be quiet ... keep still: again, the satyrs' exuberance gets the better of them (465n.).   **wild creatures**: in contrast to his words of encouragement earlier (590n.) Odysseus' tone here is one of rebuke which underlines his role as a figure of ostensibly heroic or tragic status compared to these followers of Dionysus, whom he has elsewhere called 'friends' (φιλοί: 176, etc.). Cyllene, another dignified figure comically juxtaposed to satyrs onstage, likewise addresses them as θῆρες (Soph. *Trackers* 221–2; cf. 252); and their father, in a fine piece of hypocrisy, abuses them as κάκιστα θηρῶν (ib. 147) and κάκιστα θηρίων (ib. 153).

625–6   Shut your mouths tight! (literally, 'putting together the joints of your mouth'): ἄρθρα στόματος is a paratragic periphrasis reminiscent of Sophocles, *e.g.* Oedipus' eyes are described as ἄρθρα τῶν αὐτοῦ κύκλων (*OT* 1270, literally: 'the sockets of his own eyes'); Philoctetes refers to his own ankle as ποδὸς ἄρθρον (*Phil.* 1201–2 'the joint of his foot'). Odysseus' words here seem more emphatically stylized when followed by the more colloquial σκαρδαμύσσειν ('blink') and χρέμπτεσθαί ('clear throat': Triclinius' correction of L's χρίμπτεσθαι: 'to draw near'). Odysseus' anger here is consistent with his Homeric counterpart who responds in a similarly stern manner to those who, even unintentionally, might ruin his plans to wreak vengeance on his enemies, *e.g.*, his threats to the aged Eurycleia after she recognizes him by his scar (*Od.* 19.467–90); cf. also his words to Neoptolemus in Soph. *Phil.* (50–3, 74–7, 77–8, 83–4, 108–9, 119–20).

the monster: translates τὸ κακόν, used colloquially (cf. Ar. *Birds* 931 of an obnoxious person). But the word order leaves τὸ κακόν ambiguous, so that it could mean either 'the trouble, disaster' (abstractions can 'sleep' Eur. *Suppl.* 1147; cf. Eur. *El.* 41), or 'the monster' who should not be woken up; the 'Cyclops' only becomes explicit after the 'before' clause begins.

628   has been forced: a sense of contest or struggle (ἅμιλλα is emphasized here in ἐξαμιλληθῇ, a fairly popular word with Euripides, occurring six times in his extant *corpus*, with cognates occurring another 37 times. Willink (1986) on Eur. *Orestes* 38 seems to have considered the present tense of verb there to be middle (but active in force), rather than passive, and interprets 'has done battle with the fire'; but Euripides makes the passive sense of the uncompounded verb clear enough elsewhere (*e.g.*, Eur. F 812.2). ὄψις more likely depends on ὄμματος to give 'sight of the Cyclops' eye' (cf. *IT* 1167), as in the translation; but ὄμματος could also follow from the preposition ἐκ in ἐξαμιλληθῇ, to give: '... the sight has been forced from the Cyclops' eye by the fire.'

629   We are silent ... mouths: a rather grandiloquent response from the satyrs; cf. their pseudo-heroic claim (596). Here the satyrs, who neither eat nor drink in the play, gulp down αἰθέρα, in contrast to the gluttonous Polyphemus who belches αἰθέρα after his hideous meal (see 410n.).

630   make sure you grab: for ὅπως and future indicative, see 594–5n.

631   nicely: καλῶς, an echo of Polyphemus when describing the instruments of his cannibalism (see above 344n.); here, with equally colloquial tone, it is applied to the instrument of Odysseus' revenge.

632–4   So won't you ...?:   For οὔκουν plus future indicative, see above 241–3n. From here (until 641) the satyrs engage in predictable stalling tactics, in contrast to their zeal for the task earlier (469–71, 483–6). The joke, of course, is predicated on their perennial cowardice (cf. Soph. *Inachus* F **269c col. iii 32–47; *Trackers* 145–75), but Euripides is also playing with the dramatic convention that the chorus be continuously onstage from their first appearance (rare exceptions include, *e.g.*, Aesch. *Eum.* 234; Soph. *Ajax* 814). Aeschylus pushes the same convention to its limits when the chorus overhears the murder of Agamemnon and debates what to do next, including rushing in to intervene (*Ag.* 1343–71).

634   So that: For ὡς ἂν + subjunctive in a purpose clause, see above 155n. **success**: translates τύχη, which often has the neutral meaning of 'chance' or 'fortune' as an agent beyond human control (see 606–7n.); here the sense is more the idea of τύχη as a favourable outcome; cf. Theognis 130; Hdt. 7.10; Eur. *Hel.* 1409; Ar. *Birds* 1315, etc.

635–41 The exact attribution of these lines remains uncertain. Many editors (Duchemin, Biehl, Paganelli, Diggle, Kovacs) assign the lines to two semi-choruses. Diggle in his OCT apparatus argues for two such choral groups, giving 635–6, 638–9 and 640–1 to one (on the basis of the repetition of ἑστῶτες in 636 and 639, and καὶ ... γε at 640 as following on from 638–9) and 637 to the other. Sophocles' *Trackers* 176–202 has a similar problem of attribution in excited satyric lyric; 100–114 (ibid.) are clearly voiced by at least two chorus-members, and possibly more. In *Cyc.* 635–41 Ussher posits three individual speakers, Murray four, although the plurals would indicate that groups rather than indiviuals are speaking. Conceivably, several speakers would add to the comedy of the scene, so that the excuses seem to emerge randomly from a group of satyrs desperate to avoid any dangerous activity. Lines 638–9 need not necessarily be spoken by the same semi-chorus as 635–6; a new excuse is proffered for their inactivity.

635–6 too far: Matthiae emends to μακροτέρω as comparative adverb of place (Smyth §345a), while other editors posited different forms required for the meaning 'too far' (lit. 'further'): μακροτέραν (Cobet), μακροτέρον (Musgrave); L's μακροτέροι does not seem likely as μακρός is used of persons only when denoting height. **door**: this may be a metatheatrical reference; see Kaimio, *et al.* (2001); cf. also 667 below.

638–9 Then (= 'in that case'): for this meaning of ἆρα, see Denniston (1954) 45, s.v. (2). **we've sprained our feet**: the aorist passive of σπάω here literally means 'we have been dislocated' or 'wrenched'; for the accusative τοὺς ... πόδας, see Smyth §1748b (and cf. 663).

640–41 and our eyes: Barnes conjectured ἡμῖν for L's ἡμῶν to give the right idiom: dative of (dis)advantage. The position of the pronoun ἡμῖν, the third word in its line, is not emphatic, as Duchemin claims; contrast ἡμεῖς as emphatic first word in 635 and 637.

642 men: for the contrast with 'real men', ἄνδρες, which Odysseus hopes the satyrs will be, see 594–5n. By now, however, the satyrs have demonstrated their inability to fulfill what is expected of a male. The reading of L is correct here; ἄνδρες ('the men': Matthiae) destroys the sense, since the satyrs are not 'men' (ἄνδρες) in the normative sense of ἀνήρ at 595; here they are πονηροί ('worthless men'). **nothing as allies**: cf. 667n. Odysseus' verdict on the satyrs seemingly states the obvious, as he acknowledges (649); cf., however, the satyrs' willingness to stand up to the Cyclops (270–2). Odysseus' view here echoes that of Hesiod (F 10a.18 M–W), the earliest extant literary reference to satyrs, who calls them οὐτιδανοί and ἀμηχανοέργοι ('worthless and useless for work').

643 Just because: ὁτιή, more colloquial than ὅτι, is not attested in tragedy, but is common in comedy (Hermippus F 63.11; Eupolis F 305.2; Ar. *Ach.* 1062, etc.); its appearance in Aeschylus' 'Justice-play' (F 281a.9) suggests that that play is satyric.

644 lose my teeth: ἐκβαλεῖν literally means to 'throw out' (at *Cyc.* 20 it means 'throw off course'), but here the sense is 'shed' or 'lose'; cf. Solon F 27.1–2 (W)

645   this: αὕτη is attracted to the feminine as complement from the neuter subject, which is the clause from ὁτιή onwards.

646   incantation: literally an 'epode' ('song over' a person or thing; such were considered to have medicinal properties and psychosomatic effects (*Od.* 19.457–8; Gorg. *Hel.* 10, 14; Eur. *Hipp.* 478).   **Orpheus**: the satyrs want to take the efficacy of epodes further and charm an inanimate object, just as Orpheus and Amphion were said to do in attracting trees and rocks as well as animals through music (Eur. *IA* 1212–13: *Bacc.* 562–4; *Antiope* F 223.91–4).   **absolutely**: translates the colloquialism πάνυ (cf. Aesch. *Net-Fishers* F **47a.825; Soph. *Trackers* 105, etc; see Collard (2005) 366).

647   so that: ὥστ(ε), Blaydes's emendation (of L's ὡς), gives the regular syntax for Euripides in an infinitival consecutive clause (with πάνυ replacing the usual οὕτως); see Diggle (1981) 8, as at *Alc.* 358, *El.* 667. **all by itelf**: (αὐτόματον): cf. Eur. *IT* 1166; *Bacc.* 447.

648   son of the earth: while Polyphemus' father is emphasized as Poseidon in the play (21, 262, 286) and in the Homeric account (above 21–2n.), Hesiod makes the Cyclopes the offspring of Earth and Ouranos (*Th.* 139). In the choral reference to him as παῖδα γῆς Polyphemus becomes assimilated to the hubristic Earth-born giants who attempted to overthrow the gods, alluded to earlier in the play (5–9). The concept of being a 'son of the earth' thus connotes chthonic monstrosity; cf. other ogres and monsters such as Antaeus (ps. Apollod. 2.5.11), Typhon (Hes. *Th.* 821–2), the monstrous Argos (Aesch. *Supp.* 305), and others. Comparable, too, is the Euripidean Pentheus – a stated enemy of Dionysus, like Polyphemus (203–11, etc.) – whose earth-born nature is made explicit by the Bacchic chorus who call him the γόνον γηγενῆ of Echion (*Bacc.* 995–6, 1015–6; cf. 540–1); this kind of lineage would compound his villainy in the chorus' eyes (see also 608–10n for other links between Pentheus and Polyphemus). The satyrs' jibe at Polyphemus seems to be sardonic mockery of his portentous ancestry. Poseidon, too, is also associated with the earth in his capacity as the 'Earth-Shaker' or 'Earth-Encircler' (*e.g.*, *Il.* 7.45, 13.43, 15.173, 15.174; cf. Pindar *Pyth.* 4.33, etc.), so Polyphemus' status as a 'son of the earth' does not preclude this connection either.

649   For a long time (πάλαι): Odysseus' tone here is one of resignation, as the satyrs live up to their reputation (see 642n.). Cf. also 450: Odysseus similarly lives up to his reputation (for cleverness), which the satyrs have also known (πάλαι) and which excites them.

650   Odysseus' reluctance to use his men for the task may be explained by their traumatized state in the cave (407–8); in any case Euripides gets comic mileage out of the satyrs' mock-heroics (595–8, 629–48).   **close friends**: (οἰκείοις φίλοις): Odysseus reintroduces the theme of φιλία as a motivating factor for his actions (similarly at *Od.* 9.421–2) and for the support of the chorus. The fact that they are οἰκεῖοι underscores that they are fellow Ithacans, making the claims of φιλία here arguably stronger; cf. *And.* 986.

652–3   But … then at least: ἀλλ᾽ οὖν … γε introduces a more moderate suggestion, 'after concessive conditional clauses' (Denniston 1954, 444.6).   **some courage**: the command for such encouragement is more than a token gesture. Homer often stresses the emotional impact of speeches which rouse warriors to battle (*Il.* 4.414, 5.470, 792, etc.); cf. *Od.* 9.376–7, for Odysseus' words of encouragement to his companions. Gorgias (*Hel.* 14) emphasises the power of words to generate courage and banish fear or complacency as required.   **for our friends**: this command reiterates the φιλία mentioned at 650, and φίλων is enjambed, suggesting emphasis; in urging their friends the chorus now have something dramatically plausible to do while Odysseus goes back inside the *skênê* building.

654   mercenary … for us: literally 'will run the risk in the Carian'. Carians were known as mercenaries (Archilochus F 216 W; cf. Cratinus F 18 *PCG*) and their name became synonymous with vicarious involvement in danger, as Aelius Aristides explains (*Panath.* 163 Dindorf). Euripides perhaps alludes to a proverbial expression found later at *e.g.* Plato *Laches* 187b; *Euthyd.* 285c. In other words, the satyrs here will get someone else to confront the danger for them, just like anyone does who hires Carian mercenaries. For the preposition ἐν so used (apart from the Cratinus and Plato references), cf. Thuc. 2.35.1.

655   But may … be consumed in smoke (τυφέσθω): see 659–60n.

656–62   Duchemin follows the suggestion, made by Rossignol in 1854, that this short song follows the format of a nautical shanty, ultimately traceable to the κέλευσμα or call of the boatswain to the rowers to keep time. But there is nothing nautical about the song here, even though the satyrs later announce themselves as the συνναῦται (fellow sailors) of Odysseus (708). The song can be understood in the more basic sense of a κέλευ(σ)μα ('order, command') which not only appears in tragedy (Aesch. *Eum.* 235; Soph. *Ant.* 1219), but also in Odysseus' immediately preceding speech here (*Cyc.* 653, 655, cf. 652) and elsewhere in satyric drama (Soph. *Trackers* 231). The graphic nature of the imperatives (656–7, 659–60) plays out in words what is happening in the cave, so that the blinding is presented to the mind's eye of the audience through words, and quite possibly through some mimed action of the chorus itself (as was done in the production staged by staff and students from the University of Canterbury, NZ, in 2008).

Metrical problems in this last and shortest choral song are outlined by Dale (1981) 69, who says the colometry is doubtful overall; Seaford suspects the word-overlap between the choriambic dimeter at 656 and the dochmiacs of 657. Diggle's apparatus on 656–8 suggests a colometry of one iamb followed by two choriambic cola. Since ἐξοδυνηθείς in 661 forms a very rare brief colon (*e.g.* Aesch. *Seven* 152), Dale and Seaford suggest it could be divided as ἐξοδυνη|θείς to make line 661 a dochmius and choriamb followed by a pherecratean in 662, thus echoing the metre of 657–8; but Dale considers this a 'very dubious colon'. Kovacs (1994b) 157, prefers in 661 the (arguably improved) reading of the Paris apograph, μὴ 'ξοδυνη| θείς which omits σέ <'to you'>.

656–7 The triple imperative in asyndeton, like the double in 661, conveys the intensity of the chorus' emotion here emphasized in the two dochmiacs (cf. the four asyndetic imperatives at *Hec.* 62–3, if the text is authentic and not corrupt); cf. also Pratinas F 3.10–12. For imperatives from a chorus seeking punishment cf. *Bacc.* 977–1023; *Or.* 1302–10, esp. 1302–3.

658 the beast who dines on his guests: a reiteration of Polyphemus' crimes and his savage nature (esp. 302–3, 3411–4, 396–404). A Laconian skyphos of *c.* 550 BC (*LIMC* VIII.1 s.v. Polyphemus I 18) depicting the blinding of the Cyclops synoptically – with events happening over time compressed into one image – shows the monster holding severed limbs, as a visual reminder of his barbarity [for the Doric genitive in –α, see above 53–4n.].

659–60 consume him in smoke: cf. 475, 655; there may be an implicit conflation here with Polyphemus and Typhon, another infamous opponent of the Olympians, especially in the wake of two choral injunctions for Polyphemus to be destroyed, using τύφω. This cosmic monster, like Polyphemus in the play, has strong associations with Etna, ever since Zeus hurled it onto him after blasting him with a thunderbolt (Pindar, *Pyth.* 1.13–28; *PV* 363–72; [Apollod.] *Bibl.* 1.6.3); and Polyphemus' punishment is consistently spoken of in terms of burning or scorching, rather than blinding as such (456–63, 475, 599–600, 610–12, 627–8, 648, 655, 657, 659). **the shepherd of Etna**: see above 20n. and 366–7n. for the implications of the locale of the play. [L's ἔτνας is phonetic corruption].

661 keep on twisting, keep on heaving it ...: (τόρνευ' ἕλκε) as present imperatives imply sustained action. The language recalls Odysseus' own simile of a carpenter drilling through a ship's plank by spinning a borer with thongs (460–2) to describe how he will blind Polyphemus, itself an echo of *Od.* 9.383–6. The satyrs' choice of word does not have the pun contained in Odysseus' κυκλώσω (462).

662 something outrageous (τι μάταιον): μάταιος is used commonly of people who are wildly inappropriate or immoral, *e.g.* Theoclymenus (*Hel.* 918), Helen and Clytaemestra (*El.* 1064), rather than their actions (cf. *Med.* 450). Here the sense may denote 'irreverent, profane', (LSJ II); at Aesch. *Eum.* 337 it is used of the matricide. τι could refer to the instant physical destruction of Odysseus being roasted and eaten if he fails to kill Polyphemus; if so, then the expression recalls the idea of the appalling and sacrilegious nature of the monster's meals alluded to elsewhere (364–5, 416, etc., and later at 693). At the same time, the sense of μάταιον also recalls ἀπάλαμνον, which described the imminent fate of Silenus who was about to suffer something 'diabolical' or 'something for which there is no remedy' at the hands of the monster (see above 597–8n.); in the case of Odysseus, this does not, of course, mean rape, but rather the likelihood of death.

663–709 Polyphemus is blinded and eventually comes onstage where he is taunted by the satyrs in another exchange involving stichomythia and *antilabê*, or individual lines shared by two or more speakers (669–89; esp. 672–5, 681–6). The famous Homeric joke of 'Nobody' finally comes into play, this time as a result of the satyrs' deliberately misunderstanding the enraged monster's words (671–5). As Collins (2004) 47–8 suggests, it is a scene of paratragic anagnorisis in which the Cyclops' recognition of his own situation is reduced to farce by the satyrs, which may parody the tragic blinding and eventual appearance of the enraged Polymestor in *Hecuba* (1035–43, 1056–126). There is nothing to suggest that we should pity the Cyclops, whose crimes are outlined again by Odysseus when he finally identifies himself (690, 692) and refers to the monster's 'unholy feast' and 'murder of my companions' (693–5). Similarly, the hero's 'go to hell' (701) grimly recalls the monster at his most arrogant and menacing (340); the satyric ogre has been dealt satyric justice (see 421–2, 693nn; Gen. Intro. pp. 29–30, 51–2). Despite further threats from the defeated monster, echoing the actions of his Homeric counterpart, the play ends on a rollicking, if abrupt, note with the satyrs' upbeat rejoinder (708–9) that they will be Odysseus' fellow sailors and the self-professed slaves of their longed-for friend, Dionysus.

663 Polyphemus' initial outburst may have come from within the skênê-building, like Agamemnon's famous cries (Aesch. *Ag.* 1343, 1345), or Polymestor in Eur.'s *Hecuba* (1035, 1037), in which case there is some satyric parody of tragedy, or at least paratragic action, here. **the light of my eye**: for this accusative, see Smyth §1748b (and cf. 638–39n.); cf. also *Hec.* 1035 (Polymestor again). **burned to charcoal** (κατηνθρακώμεθα): cf. the description of Typhon as ἠνθρακωμένος ('incinerated') by the thunderbolt of Zeus (*Prometheus Bound* 372).

664 **beautiful song of triumph** (παιάν): conveys black humour elsewhere in Euripides (*e.g.*, *Tro.* 126); Seaford cites as parallels for the joyful reaction to cries of pain, *Her.* 751–2 and *Antiope* F 223.54. Polyphemus' cry is almost literally music to the ears of the chorus for whom it is a sign of Odysseus' success. While Odysseus and the satyrs had earlier described the monster's tone-deaf cacophony (423–6; 489–93), now there is a sardonic irony in their calling it καλός and their request to him to 'sing ... 'again' [Markland's emendation αὖ for L's ὦ].

665 Polyphemus is at the entrance to the cave now, if not before, and is wearing a bloodied mask. The re-emergence of Oedipus in the *OT*, whose self-blinding was graphically described by a servant (esp. 1268–79), also involved an actor wearing an altered mask; likewise Polymestor (*Hec.* 1056); cf. the 'forecast' of what his face will look like at (*Hec.* 1045–6, 1040).

666 **you will never escape**: οὔτι μή with aorist subjunctive (φύγητε) expresses strong denial for the future (Smyth §2755a); the expression is used by Polymestor to convey the same threat to his tormentor (*Hec.* 1039).

667 **without paying** (χαίροντες): normally 'rejoicing' but here in an idiom of 'impunity'; cf. esp. Eur. *Or.* 1592–3; *HF* 258; Ar. *Frogs* 843; Hdt. 3.69; cf. 9.106. The idiom is common (Smyth §2062.a), but it is not certain that is is truly colloquial, for it is very frequent in tragedy: *e.g.*, Eur. *Or.* (above); *Med.* 396, 398; Soph. *OT* 363; see Collard (2005) 366–7.   **nonentities** (οὐδὲν ὄντες): cf. *And.* 700. After his blinding the Homeric Cyclops similarly called Odysseus ὀλίγος τε καὶ οὐτιδανὸς καὶ ἄκικυς ('small and worthless and feeble'), unlike the man he expected would blind him (*Od.* 9.515); see also 642n., for Hesiod's similar verdict on satyrs.

667–8   in the … opening: literally, 'gates' (πύλαισι); the monster speaks of his cave as if it is a building of some stature; Silenus refers to it in architectural terms as a building (στέγας) and 'house' (δόμους); see above 29, 33, 635–6nn.   **cleft's … here**: this reflects Nauck's emendation τῆσδε qualifying φάραγγος (literally 'of this cleft'), for L's τάσδε, qualifying χέρας ('these arms'): while retained by some editors, L perhaps needlessly emphasizes the act of stretching rather than the precise location, which is important: the entrance-cleft, not mentioned before, rather than the whole cave (666).   **block it up** (ἐναρμόσω): literally, 'I will fit into'; cf. Eur. *Hipp.* 1189 (putting feet into footstalls); Lucian 79.11.4 9 (inserting a peg).

669   Why … ? τί χρῆμα; here means just τί; contrast 99 where it is an independent question, meaning 'What is it?' The feigned innocence of the satyrs is underscored in the colloquialism they use here; see Stevens (1976) 22. In 669–75 the chorus takes the role played by the other Cyclopes in Homer's account, who ask Polyphemus in all sincerity what his trouble is (*Od.* 9.403–6), in contrast to the satyrs' gleeful mockery here.

670   Well, yes: here γε is assentient and even exclamatory (Denniston (1954) 126–7); for φαίνομαι without the participle ὤν, see above 532n.   **ugly**: as Ussher notes, this use of αἰσχρός does not occur in tragic contexts; cf. Ar. *Eccl.* 705. Polyphemus' complaints are not evidence of compassion on the part of the poet, as Ussher claims; the monster's punishment would tally well with the audience's expectations of what usually happens to ogres in satyric dramas (Gen. Intro. pp. 29–30); see 421–2n. The satyrs' taunting of Polyphemus (*Cyc.* 669–88) contrasts with the sympathy, albeit brief, which the chorus in the *Hecuba* shows even for Polymestor, after which they hasten to remind him of his own crimes (*Hec.* 1085–6).

672–5   The trick of 'Nobody' is finally played out, its humour emphasized in four lines of *antilabê* (cf. 663–709n.), in which the satyrs deliberately misunderstand the monster's enraged words, as Euripides engages in word-play on Οὖτις (thrice), οὐδείς and οὐδαμοῦ.

673   has blinded my eye: τυφλοῖ is a vividly emphatic present tense (cf. Smyth §1887), just as the Homeric Cyclops (*Od.* 9.408) answers that Nobody 'is killing' (κτείνει) him. Here τυφλοῖ takes two objects 'me' and 'eye', one denoting the whole person, the other the part specifically affected; cf. *Or.* 545, *Tro.* 635; see Smyth §985.
674   How do you mean?: translates the conjecture πῶς φῂς σύ; by T. Stinton (1990, 290–1), which conveys some humour in allowing the satyrs another joke at

Polyphemus' expense who still takes at face value what the chorus is saying to him. Polyphemus' words here in the ms ὡς δὴ σύ; make little sense (cf. Eur. *Andromache* 235 where they introduce a complete clause); Diggle (1971) suggests they should be taken as an interrupted expression with σκώπτεις ('you're mocking'), but the καὶ πῶς in the satyrs' immediate rejoinder suggests that what precedes it – Polyphemus' utterance – must be complete; for καὶ πῶς denoting surprise (here feigned by the satyrs) or contempt, see Denniston (1954) 309–10. Stinton's conjecture has merit in being consistent with the satyrs' mocking tone, but no emendation commands assent, and elsewhere Diggle (1981) 38 n. 1 suggested ψεύδῃ σύ ('you're lying'); W. Dindorf deleted this verse.

677 bastard: μιαρός is another of many colloquialisms in this scene (cf. Soph. *Trackers* 197; Eur. *Sisyphus* F 673.2; and see Collard 2005, 369), which cumulatively give an overall effect of agitation and energy. **drowned** (κατέκλυσεν): Canter's emendation of L's unmetrical κατέκαυσε ('burned'); L's reading was a purely scribal slip, alpha for lambda in uncial. The image recalls Polyphemus' own exuberance in downing his last swig of the wine, which he 'only just managed to swim out of' (577); for κατέκλυζω in a simile, cf. *Or.* 343 (wealth), and in metaphor, [Aesch.] *Sept.*1078.

678–9 These two lines are unattributed in L, and therefore by implication (or omission) continued for Polyphemus, but 678 is very awkward in his mouth and 679 is then too abrupt; nevertheless Biehl accepts L. But the lines were plausibly given to the chorus and Polyphemus respectively by Reiske. **wine is powerful ... with**: the satyrs are not normally the sort of creatures to heed the dangers of excessive drinking, and their comic encounters with wine were a motif in other satyr dramas (*e.g.* Soph. *Little Dionysus*; cf. also *Oeneus* F 1130; Ion, *Omphale* F 20–30; Achaeus, *Hephaestus* F 17; cf. the complaints of Silenus in Lycophron, *Menedemus* F 2–4!); see also 123–4, 169–71nn. Coming from them, this self-satisfied, even sanctimonious, utterance has much comic irony; but it may also be considered one of the 'lessons' they teach the monster (cf. 492–3n.).

679–80 In another departure from Homer (cf. *Od.* 9.425–60) and one easily explained by its greater theatrical convenience, Euripides has Odysseus' men (and presumably Silenus) get past Polyphemus at the cave entrance rather than by clinging under his sheep. But the playwright finds further comic potential in this innovation. As Polyphemus attempts to chase Odysseus' men, the satyrs, having taunted him verbally, now let their revenge take the form of some farcical violence – inflicted vicariously, of course – again predicated on the monster's dim-witted insistence on taking what they say at face value.

681–2 occupying: translates λαβόντες (cf. Eur. *Supp.* 652; *IT* 962). Polyphemus' lunging and frantic questions about the whereabouts of his tormentors (also at 685–6) parallel the desperation of the blinded Polymestor in the *Hecuba* (1056–82, esp. 1065). The double change of speakers in one iambic trimeter is rare in extant drama

(Soph. *Trackers* 205 has three such changes; cf. also *Phil.* 753; Eur. *Alc.* 391; *Her.* 240), and conveys Polyphemus' agitated state and the satyrs' insistent mockery here (682).

682–3–4   Have you got them? (ἔχεις;): the continuation of the part-line 682 in just one word in the next verse is remarkable, but (a) it is syntactically separate and (b) it accommodates the theatrical time needed for the head-banging. Polyphemus' collision with the rock could be easily arranged by means of a stage property, or could have been mimed by the actor, again, exactly like the stumbling Polymestor (*Hec.* 1050, 1056–60, 1079–81); cf. also the half-heard steps of his persecutors (*Hec.* 1069).   **I've got worse on worse**: Polyphemus' remark is paratragic (similar wording at Eur. *Hipp.* 874).   **skull**: τὸ κρανίον is accusative object of παίσας (**Now that I've bashed**; cf. Eur. *El.* 688) and κατέαγα (perfect of κατάγνυμι: 'break', 'shatter', etc.) is used in a passive sense to mean literally 'I'm broken', just as ὀλώλα (strong perfect of ὄλλυμι) is frequently passive in sense (*e.g.* 665); conceivably, κρανίον could be accusative of respect (Ussher and Seaford point to *Ar.* Wealth 545), but this would leave παίσας unexplained. **Yes**: γε emphasizes καὶ: 'Yes, and ...'; see Denniston (1954) 157 (1) and 158 for the unusual separation of the particles here. Polyphemus has got a bump instead of the men – *and* they are now escaping him (cf. 666); the satyrs' γε is also assentient and conveys their enjoyment of the scene as spectators.

685   Didn't you say, here somewhere, here? this translates Blaydes' conjecture οὐ τῇδέ πῃ, τῇδ' εἶπας; which Diggle in his OCT and Seaford follow. Text and punctuation of 685 vary: Biehl and Ussher, for instance, keep L's οὐ τῇδ'ἐπεὶ τῇδ' εἶπας ('Not here, since you said, Here').

686   Turn around that way: The chorus need not be grouped altogether in this scene, but has probably spread out over the orchestra with individuals calling out instructions at random to confuse Polyphemus further. [This is Nauck's emendation περίαγου κεῖσε for L's senseless and unmetrical περίαγουσί σε. The middle form of the imperative has the literal sense of 'lead yourself around'.]

687   I am being laughed at: the laughter of one's enemies was a serious concern for heroic figures and was to be avoided virtually at all costs (*e.g.* Soph. *Ajax* 79, 379–82; Eur. *Medea* 797, 1049–51, 1354–7, 1362; see Knox 1977). Here such laughter contributes in no small way to Polyphemus' torment. Cf. also Polymestor's question to Hecuba about whether she is enjoying the outrage she has inflicted on him (*Hec.* 1257).

688   not any more: Seaford aptly compares *Hel.* 1230–1 for a similar rejoinder to κερτομεῖτέ με ('you're taunting me'), and notes that in both cases the charge of taunting is negated by the response, which introduces a new element in the exchange; in *Cyc.* this brings Odysseus into the action.

689   O utterly vile man (ὦ παγκάκιστε): common tragic abuse (Soph. *Ant.* 742; *Tr.* 1124; Eur. *Med.* 465; *Suppl.* 513, etc.), and is a more intense form of ὦ κάκιστε, also common in tragedy (Soph. *OC* 866; Eur. *Tro.* 943, etc.); neither term appears in extant comedy. Polyphemus' language is paratragic rather than colloquial here (cf. above 677n.). However the comparable expression ὦ πανοῦργε is found in comedy (Ar. *Ach.* 311), and in tragedy (Eur. *Hec.* 1257; *Hcld* 947).

689–90 I'm keeping the body ... in safety: there is a mild tautology in φυλακαῖσι φρουρῶ, perhaps as a form of emphasis; Biehl notes the same expression at *Rhes.* 764–5, of warfare (cf. also *IA* 1028; *Ion* 22). As in Homer's account, Odysseus does not begin his taunts until confident that he is beyond reach of the monster (*Od.* 9.475–9, 502–5, 523–5). [Canter's emendation σῶμα ('body') of L's nonsensical δῶμα ('home') is paralleled elsewhere in Euripides (*Her.* 435; *Hel.* 691; cf. *Cyc.* 527 where Pierson conjectured δῶμα); cf. also the periphrasis of δέμας ('body') + genitive of person (Eur. *El.* 1341; *Hec.* 724, etc.).]

692 me: Nauck's emendation με gives more regular and idiomatic word order (Diggle cites Eur. *El.* 264; *Ion* 324, 671 as parallels); L has γε which follows 691 with assent (the monster's observation that Odysseus is using a new name). **called me**: the imperfect of ὀνομάζω is idiomatic; in Eur. *Suppl.* 1218 ὠνόμαζε likewise expresses how Tydeus called his son Diomedes (cf. *IT* 1452; *Hcld.* 86).

693 Odysseus does not explicitly say here that Zeus and the rest of the gods punished Polyphemus, as in the Homeric account (*Od.* 9.479). But his reference to the monster's 'unholy meal', his consistent invocation of divine powers (350, 354–5, 599–602), and his attribution of his entire plan to τι θεῖον ('an idea sent from some god' 411) show that divine agency has played a big role in exacting justice from Polyphemus, in addition to the hero's own qualities demonstrated at Troy (cf. 603–5n.). In the *Odyssey* (9.302) the hero refers instead to ἕτερος θυμός ('a second thought') as the inspiration behind his decision to blind the monster. **You were bound**: ἔμελλες is similarly used in satisfied verdicts of those made to pay for their transgressions (Eur. *Med.* 1354; *HF* 1079). **to pay the penalty for your unholy feast**: the alliteration and hyperbaton of δώσειν δ' ἔμελλες ἀνοσίου δαιτὸς δίκας emphasizes the point (as at *Med.* 1298; *Bacc.* 489), which fits in well with the theme of swift, punitive justice evident elsewhere in satyric drama; see above 421–2n.

694–5 a worthless thing: this translates L's κακῶς, which makes clear sense as it is (Cobet conjectured ἄλλως 'in vain'). Dobree emended to καλῶς ('a fine thing'), accepted by Diggle, which has to be invested with irony to fit the context, and, even though this sense is not unparalleled (*e.g.*, Eur. *Med.* 504, 588), most editors accept the ms reading. Either way, in Odysseus' own words his revenge here trumps even his own glorious labours at Troy (603–5; cf. 347–52). **my companions**: Odysseus again alludes to the idea of φιλία – in the form of avenging his ἑταῖροι – as a motivating factor.

696–9 Polyphemus in the *Odyssey* describes the oracle at greater length (9.507–14) and makes a separate prayer to Poseidon to punish Odysseus (9.528–35); here the monster tells how the same oracle predicted Odysseus' further sufferings, rather than pray to his father for them. While Polyphemus has no prophetic powers of his own, his bitter recollection of the oracle is comparable to the vindictive prophecies by the blind and enraged Polymestor, similarly directed at his tormentor (*Hec.* 1259–73). In Euripides' *Heraclidae* (1026–44) Eurystheus is another defeated figure predicting at the end of the drama future events in the wake of his downfall.

697   by you (ἐκ σέθεν): (also *e.g. And.* 1275) an example of the ablatival suffix substituting for the genitive case-ending (cf. 689 τηλοῦ σέθεν).

698   But don't forget (ἀλλὰ καὶ ... τοι): the untranslatable particle τοι has 'threatening' overtones (Denniston (1954) 540) which we have tried to render in 'don't forget'.

700   drifting (ἐναιωρούμενον): literally, 'suspended', suggesting that Odysseus will have little if any control over the directions his journey takes; Euripides uses the same verb of Polydorus' ghost (*Hec.* 32), which is literally in the air, 'hovering'.

701–2   Go to hell! (κλαίειν σ' ἄνωγα): see 174n., 340n. This colloquialism echoes Polyphemus' contemptuous dismissal – κλαίειν ἄνωγα – of Odysseus' earlier arguments (338–40) and reinforces the sense of a transgressor getting his come-uppance.   **what I said**: Paley conjectured λέγεις ('you say') for L's λέγω on the basis that ἐγὼ δε (**But now I**) implies a different subject from the previous line; on this reading Odysseus would be referring to Polyphemus' words at 697–8. But the hero could easily be referring to his own words at 695 and L's reading may stand. λέγω here can mean 'I said'; the Greek present is idiomatic (Smyth §1885.a calls it the 'progressive perfect'); cf. also the chorus' words at *Hec.* 1047–8 δέδρακας οἷάπερ λέγεις; 'have you done what you said?', *i.e.* blinded Polymestor.

702–3   my ship (νεὼς σκάφος): for this pleonasm, see 85n. **over the Sicilian sea**: see above 20n. **and to my homeland**: this will, of course, be a long time coming for Odysseus, but there is no need to attach much dramatic irony to this remark. Notwithstanding Polyphemus' prophecies of hard times ahead and his threats of further violence, Odysseus' triumph dominates the mood of this last scene. By contrast, the recounting of the tale in the *Odyssey* ends with some foreboding (9.553–5) and on a sombre note, with Odysseus and his men mourning the loss of their companions (9.566–7) [Schumacher conjectured εἰς for L's ἔς τ' (cf. Eur. *El.* 1347). Zuntz (1963) 66, notes that the 'Sicilian sea' denoted the body of water between southern Italy, including Sicily and Greece, including Crete (Thuc. 4.24.5; Xen. *Oec.* 20.27). The idea behind Schumacher's conjecture, then, seems to be that Odysseus will sail on the Sicilian to sea to get home, as opposed to sailing it primarily to escape Polyphemus in the first stage of his journey home, which L's reading seems to suggest. However, L may stand and is accepted by Diggle.]

704–5   you (σε): an example of Wackernagel's Law, the advanced enclitic here separated by a complete sense-unit from its point of control.   **a piece of this rock**: πέτρας is a partitive genitive following a verb that affects the object only partially (Smyth §1341); Kirchhoff read the accusative here, in which case πέτραν = 'a whole rock' (cf. *Antiope* F 223.93).   **your sailors and all**: for αὐτός and dative in the common idiom to convey the idea of accompaniment, cf. *e.g. Med.*165; Smyth §1525 notes that the expression is common when the destruction of a person or thing is referred to. This action is clearly impossible to stage before the audience, so Euripides has Polyphemus announce his intention to hurl rocks at Odysseus and his men, to be consistent with the Homeric narrative (*Od.* 9.481–6, 537–42).

707   making my way on foot: similar expressions combining pleonastic ποδί with βαίνω (or compounds) are found in Euripides (*e.g.*, *Hec.* 1263; *El.* 489–90), but also in Sophocles (*Ajax* 1281), the lyric poetry of Stesichorus *PMG* 185.5) and Homeric epic (*Il.* 5.745); see also Schmidt (1975) 292–3; Diggle (1981) 36–7. [Kirchhoff nevertheless wanted to supply a noun, with πέτρας itself replacing ποδί (L's reading); Diggle preferred to suggest a lacuna after this line.]   **this tunneled (cave) with its entrance on the other side**: ἀμφιτρής literally means 'bored through on both sides' (ἀμφί + τετραίνω)', and qualifies (πέτρας) 'rock' inferred from 704; but this is too far away; the adjective has been substantivised here (examples in Smyth §1028). The monster's cave has another entrance which will give him access to a place from where he can hurl rocks at Odysseus and his men. The only other occurrence in extant Greek of ἀμφιτρής describes the cave of Philoctetes (Soph. *Phil.* 19), and has been taken by some as a dating criterion for the *Cyclops*; see above Gen. Intro., pp. 39–41. Because the word ἀμφιτρής appears both in Soph. *Phil.* and here in *Cyc.*, with their caves, its occurrence has been conjectured as having stood in the (much) earlier *Philoctetes* of Euripides, where, as in Sophocles' play, the existence of a rear-entrance is (even more) important: this is F 5 Mueller, mentioned by Kannicht in *TrGF* 5.830.

708–9   This choral couplet in iambic trimeters brings the play to a very abrupt end. We do not know whether other satyr dramas ended this way, as no other satyr play endings have survived. While anapaests usually conclude tragedies, the ending of Sophocles' *OT* (if genuine) and Euripides' *Ion* are in trochaic tetrameters; Barrett (1964) on *Hipp.* 1463–66 questions whether all the Euripidean tailpieces are genuine. In any case, the mood at the end of *Cyclops* is buoyant, and some important motifs in are alluded to here, namely friendship, slavery and the different natures of two masters the satyrs have experienced (see 23–6, 34–5, 73–5, 76–9, 435–6nn.).   **Well anyway ... fellow sailors**: δέ ... γε are often used in 'retorts and lively rejoinders' (Denniston (1954) 153); the satyrs thus give a riposte to Polyphemus' reference to Odysseus' fellow sailors (705). The satyrs' role as members of Odysseus' crew reasserts the φιλία between them and the hero and may recall 466–8. The present participle ὄντες ('being': 709) is probably 'dynamic' (cf. Smyth 2065) and its position at the beginning of the line implies emphasis and intensity, as does the identically placed pronoun ἡμεῖς ('we': 708); this is appropriate for the satyrs as they relish their newly won freedom.

709   we'll be the slaves of the Bacchic god: the satyrs' eagerness to resume this role indicates the joys of such 'servitude' (63–78, 620–3, etc.). The play ends on a note of mild ring composition and paradox, whereby slavery, emphasized in the satyrs' description of their plight at the outset (23–6, 78–81, cf. 442, etc.), resurfaces at the very moment of their escape. But this 'slavery' means a return to the joys of life under their natural master, Dionysus (cf. 429–30), and liberation from the brutal despotism of the Cyclops.

MAJOR FRAGMENTS
OF GREEK SATYRIC DRAMA

INTRODUCTORY NOTE

We offer here a Greek text and a modestly annotated translation of the more substantial fragmentary plays; of some single fragments of varying length important for satyric drama as a whole; and of some fragments interesting precisely because their attribution to the genre is disputed. They are set out roughly in the order of *TrGF*, that is, according to the approximate order of their poets' lifetimes; but useful hints, let alone evidence, are lacking for the date of almost every individual satyr-play or long fragment we include. Our chief purpose is to put beside the complete *Cyclops* examples of other satyric plots (in so far as they can be established) and of satyric themes, motifs, topics and styles in general.

Almost all the major fragments have been recovered on papyrus. Those of Aeschylus and Sophocles have transformed our knowledge of the satyric genre.[1] Many of their plays had earlier been known only from a very few book-fragments (or from titles alone) – a few more than ten plays of Aeschylus, a few more than fifteen of Sophocles. As to Euripides, however, our knowledge has hardly been increased at all. We still have barely one certain fragment from Pratinas' thirty-two plays known to antiquity, at least by title, although he was by repute the first great poet of the genre, perhaps even its inventor; and we have only scattered fragments from the seven or more of Achaeus, a contemporary of Sophocles and Euripides, also famous for his satyr-plays.

For example, without the papyri our texts of Aeschylus' *Sacred Delegates* would remain confined to one line and two single words (papyri add about 100 lines, many well-preserved), and of Sophocles' *Trackers* confined to two incomplete couplets and a single word (the one papyrus contains about 400 lines, many well-preserved). Papyri have yielded also the anonymous and unattributed fragments (*adespota*) with which our selection closes.

The numerous papyri with satyric testimonies and texts are listed in the General Index under 'Papyri'.

With regard to Euripides in particular: no papyrus fragment of substance has yet been found of his satyr-plays, and only one or two very fragmentary satyr-play 'hypotheses' ('introductions'): see on his *Autolycus A* and *B* and *Sciron*. Ancient scholars and writers could name only ten or eleven satyr-plays, *Autolycus A* and *B, Busiris, Epeus, Eurystheus,* the doubtful *Harvesters* (Greek *Theristai*), *Cyclops,* the doubtful *Lamia, Sisyphus, Sciron,* and *Syleus*.[2] Only for *Autolycus A* and *B, Eurystheus, Sciron* and *Syleus* are the fragments and indirect evidence extensive enough to be included in this volume; from each of the other plays only one or two fragments survive (*Busiris, Lamia, Sisyphus*), or none at all (*Epeus, Harvesters*), and there is almost no useful secondary evidence for any of them. Such poor survival may in the end reflect Euripides' possible lack of confidence or success in the genre, or even his dislike of it, whereas his older contemporaries Sophocles and Achaeus were accomplished in it, as indeed had been Aeschylus himself (Pausanias 2.13.6–7; Diogenes Laertius 2.133).[3] On the other hand we can at least surmise that Euripides was distinctive, though probably not original, in colouring the genre with contemporary references or immediacy (see, *e.g.*, *Cyc.* 316–41 and *Autolycus A* F 282).

During the fourth century satyric drama underwent a shift in status so that by 341 BC satyr plays were no longer a postlude to three tragedies (*IG* ii².2320); the pace of this shift cannot be traced, but it may already have been evident by the late 5th century and begun to influence Euripides' satyric dramas of that time. Whatever the facts, after the mid-4th Century, occasional compositions, perhaps not all meant for theatrical performance, are known from the years 320 to 270 and perhaps later, a period of attested revival; in our selection it is represented by the poets Python, Sositheus and Lycophron. For the earlier 4th century see Astydamas II and Chaeremon in our Appendix (p. 508 below). The *Adespota* which conclude our selection cannot be confidently dated.

Notes

[1] See most recently *e.g.* B. Seidensticker in KPS 3–4, 40 and in Csapo, Miller (2003) 100–1; G. W. M. Harrison in Harrison (2005) xiii–iv.

[2] For full information upon Euripides' plays see Pechstein, either his (1998) 19–38 or in KPS (1999) 399–402; cf. R. Kannicht in H. Becker and others (eds), *AHNAIKA. Festschrift ... C. W. Müller* (Stuttgart-Leipzig, 1996) 27 and S. Scullion in D. Cairns, V. Liapis (eds), *Dionysalexandros. Essays in honour of A. F. Garvie* (Swansea, 2006) 197–8.

[3] There is one firm indication that Euripides was willing from quite early in his career to disregard convention with satyr-plays. The ancient hypothesis ('introduction') to his tragedy *Alcestis* records it as the fourth play in his tetralogy of 438 BC; it therefore occupied the place regular for a satyr-play, making it in modern scholarly terminology a 'pro-satyric' drama. Indeed a later insertion into the hypothesis describes it as 'quite satyric', coupling it with the *Orestes* of 408 BC (whose place in its tetralogy is not known) in possessing happy endings typical rather of comedy; the 12th-century Byzantine scholar Johannes Tzetzes erroneously (on his own admission) included Sophocles' *Electra* with Euripides' *Alcestis* and *Orestes* as a 'satyric drama' (*Prolegomena on Comedy* XIa.151 Koster = Eur. T 221a *TrGF*). There is

an excellent recent evaluation of the *Alcestis* hypothesis, and of elements in the play itself which resemble those of satyric drama, by L. P. E. Parker, *Euripides. Alcestis* (Oxford, 2007) xix–xxiv, 47–9; cf. N. W. Slater in Harrison (2005) 83–101.

In the light of the *Alcestis* hypothesis there has been speculation whether other happily-ending plays of Euripides may have been pro-satyric, in particular the *Iphigenia in Tauris* and *Helen*. These two, and *Orestes*, date from the ten or so years within which scholars increasingly place the purely satyric *Cyclops*, although a few hold out for its older dating to the mid-420s (see Gen. Intro. pp. 39–41). The *Pirithous* (see our introductory discussion to Aeschylus' *Sisyphus* at (1)) , whose nature as a tragedy or a satyr-play is uncertain, and whose authorship is disputed between Critias and Euripides, has also been suggested as pro-satyric. For details of such speculation see Sutton (1980) 184–90 and C. W. Marshall, *CJ* 95 (1999–2000) 235 n. 21.

BIBLIOGRAPHY AND ABBREVIATIONS

(many items are included in the General Bibliography, pp. 59–71)

Budé (1998–2004) = *Euripide (Edition Budé), Tome VIII, 4 parties*, ed. F. Jouan, H. Van Looy (Paris).

Carden (1974) = R. Carden, *The Papyrus Fragments of Sophocles* (Berlin-New York).

Cipolla (2003) = P. Cipolla, *Poeti minori del dramma satiresco* (Amsterdam).

Chourmouziades (1974) = N. Ch. Chourmouziades, ΣΑΤΥΡΙΚΑ *(Satyrika)* (Athens).

Collard and Cropp (2008) = C. Collard, M. J. Cropp, *Euripides. Fragments I and II = Euripides VII and VIII* (Loeb Classical Library, Cambridge MA and London).

Conrad (1997) = G. Conrad, *Der Silen* (Trier).

Csapo, Miller (2003) = E. Csapo, M. Miller (eds) (2003), *Poetry, Theory, Praxis ... Essays in Honour of William J. Slater* (Oxford).

Csapo, Miller (2007) = E. Csapo, M. C. Miller, *The Origins of Theater in Ancient Greece and Beyond. From Ritual to Drama* (Cambridge).

Diggle (1998) = J. Diggle, *Tragicorum Graecorum Fragmenta Selecta* (Oxford).

Gallo (1992) = I. Gallo, *Ricerche sul teatro greco* (Naples).

Gantz (1993) = T. Gantz, *Early Greek Myth. A Guide to Literary and Artistic Sources* (Baltimore and London).

Gauly (1991) = B. Gauly, R. Kannicht (eds) and contributors, *Musa Tragica. Die griechische Tragödie von Thespis bis Ezechiel. Ausgewählte Zeugnisse und Fragmente griechisch und deutsch* (Göttingen).

Guthrie (1969) = W. K. C. Guthrie, *History of Greek Philosophy III* (Cambridge).

Harrison (2005) = G. W. M. Harrison (ed.) and contributors, *Satyric Drama. Tragedy at Play* (Swansea).

Kaimio (2001) = M. Kaimio and contributors, 'Metatheatricality in the Greek Satyr-Play', *Arctos* 35, 35–78.

KPS *or* Krumeich (1999) = R. Krumeich, N. Pechstein, B. Seidensticker (eds) and contributors, *Das griechische Satyrspiel* (Darmstadt).

Lämmle (2007) = R. Lämmle, 'Der eingeschlossene Dritte: zur Funktion des Dionysos im Satyrspiel', in A. Bierl, R. Lämmle, K. Wesselmann (eds), *Literatur und Religion. Wege zu einer mythisch-rituellen Poetik bei den Griechen* (Berlin-New York) 325–86.

Lesky (1983, 1972) = A. Lesky, *Greek Tragic Poetry* (New Haven and London, 1983; translation by M. Dillon of *Die tragische Dichtung der Hellenen*, Göttingen, 1972).

LIMC = *Lexicon Iconographicum Mythologiae Classicae,* 9 double vols. (Zurich and Munich, 1981–99).

Lloyd-Jones (1957) = H. Lloyd-Jones, *Appendix*, in H. Weir Smyth, *Aeschylus II* (Loeb Classical Library, Cambridge MA and London) 523–603.

Lloyd-Jones (1990) = H. Lloyd-Jones, *Academic Papers. Greek Epic, Tragedy, Lyric* (Oxford).

Lloyd-Jones (1996) = H. Lloyd-Jones, *Sophocles. Fragments* = *Sophocles III* (Loeb Classical Library, Cambridge MA and London).

Luz (2010) = C. Luz, *Technopaignia. Formspielerei in der griechischen Dichtung. Mnemosyne* Supplement 324 (Leiden-Boston).

Martina (2003) = A. Martina (ed.), *Teatro greco postclassico e teatro latino. Teorie e prassi drammatica* (Rome).

Morris (1992) = S. Morris, *Daidalos and the Origins of Greek Art* (Princeton).

Nauck (1889) = A. Nauck, *Tragicorum Graecorum Fragmenta* (Leipzig, 1889²), reprinted with *Supplementum* by B. Snell (Hildesheim, 1964).

Page (1942) = D. L. Page, *Select Papyri III. Literary Papyri: Poetry* (Loeb Classical Library, Cambridge MA and London).

Pearson (1917) = A. C. Pearson, *The Fragments of Sophocles,* 3 vols. (Cambridge).

Pechstein (1998) = N. Pechstein, *Euripides Satyrographos* (Stuttgart).

Seaford (1984) = R. Seaford, *Euripides. Cyclops* (Oxford).

Sommerstein (2003) = A. H. Sommerstein (ed.) and contributors, *Shards from Kolonos* (Bari).

Sommerstein (2008) = A. H. Sommerstein, *Aeschylus III. Fragments* (Loeb Classical Library, Cambridge MA and London).

Sommerstein (2010) = A. H. Sommerstein, *Aeschylean Tragedy,* 2nd edn (London).

Sutton (1980) = D. F. Sutton, *The Greek Satyr Play* (Meisenheim-am-Glan).

Taplin (1977) = O. P. Taplin, *The Stagecraft of Aeschylus* (Oxford).

Taplin (2007) = O. Taplin, *Pots and Plays. Interactions between Tragedy and Greek Vase-paintings of the Fourth Century BC* (Los Angeles).

TrGF = *Tragicorum Graecorum Fragmenta*, ed. B. Snell, R. Kannicht, S.L. Radt, 5 vols. (Göttingen, 1971–2004: Vol. 1, 1971¹, 1986²; Vol. 2, 1981; Vol. 3, 1985; Vol. 4, 1977¹, 1999²; Vol. 5, 2004). All vols. contain Addenda, some to other vols.

Trendall-Webster (1971) = A. D. Trendall, T. B. L. Webster, *Illustrations of Greek Drama* (London).

Voelke (2001) = P. Voelke, *Un Théâtre de la Marge. Aspects figuratifs et configurationnels du drame satyrique dans l'Athènes classique* (Bari).

West (1992) = M. L. West, *Ancient Greek Music* (Oxford).

Common abbreviations

The names of Aesch(ylus), Soph(ocles), Eur(ipides) and Ar(istophanes) are often thus abbreviated; the titles of their plays are usually given in full in our play-introductions but often abbreviated in our notes. *Prometheus Bound* is treated as an inauthentic work of Aeschylus and his name is omitted before it.

Titles of periodicals are abbreviated as in *L'Année Philologique.*

DK =	H. Diels, W. Kranz, *Die Fragmente der Vorsokratiker* (Berlin, 1952[6]).
FGrH =	*Die Fragmente der griechischen Historiker*, ed. F. Jacoby (Berlin, 1923–58).
IEG =	*Iambi et Elegi Graeci*, ed. M. L. West (Oxford, 1989–91[2]).
KPS, rarely Krumeich (1999) =	R. Krumeich, N. Pechstein, B. Seidensticker (eds) and contributors, *Das griechische Satyrspiel* (Darmstadt, 1999).
LSJ =	H. G. Liddell and R. Scott, *Greek-English Lexicon* (rev. H. S. Jones, Oxford, 1940[9]; with a Revised Supplement, ed. P. G. W. Glare, 1996).
PCG =	*Poetae Comici Graeci*, ed. R. Kassel, C. Austin (Berlin, 1983–).
PMG =	*Poetae Melici Graeci*, ed. D. L. Page (Oxford, 1962).
Smyth =	H. Weir Smyth, *Greek Grammar* (revised edn by G. Messing, Cambridge MA, 1956).

ADVICE TO READERS

1. General advice to those coming fresh to fragmentary texts, particularly through translation alone

The editing and interpretation and even more the appreciation of dramatic fragments are subject to variable factors.

First, papyri seldom present continuous text, let alone complete text. The stretches of text they do preserve are often wholly accidental in extent, because of the physical factors in their survival as separated and usually damaged pieces. Gaps in play-content between these pieces, and the dramatic order of the pieces, are often impossible to calculate. For the same reasons of physical damage, very few papyri survive with attribution to poet or play, let alone with indications of plot, context or speaking characters; these have usually to be inferred from the remains.

Second, papyri are continually reexamined. New readings are sometimes found and confirmed; new supplements, where text is damaged or lost, are constantly advanced; new textual conjectures appear frequently. A significant change in the text can affect (or be prompted by) the interpretation of a whole fragment or even play. Also, new papyri continue to appear. All this progress is irregular in being published, and sometimes advances are made independently of one another, so that an agreed 'state of the text' or 'received interpretation' is hardly, if ever, achieved.

Third, for some plays many if not all of the fragments are 'book-fragments', that is, they survive only as quotations (of greatly varying length) in other ancient authors or in ancient works of scholarship like commentaries (scholia), anthologies and dictionaries. The great majority of such fragments come with no dramatic context given, even if many are attributed to a particular poet or play, and sometimes to a play-character. Book-fragments, like papyri, are constantly being augmented, and some of those long known have their attribution reconsidered or changed.

The study of dramatic fragments is therefore in constant flux, at every level of engagement.

2. Advice upon using this selection

For a very few plays it is feasible to reconstruct or to hazard something at least of plot, characters and issues, built chiefly upon the fragments themselves and their sources, but occasionally upon other literary or secondary matter. It is seldom possible, let alone safe, to use evidence from art, almost exclusively vase-paintings, to 'reconstruct' satyr-plays (see R. Krumeich in KPS (1999) 41–4, 47–51, 56–61 and Taplin (2007) 33–5, cf. B. Seidensticker in *e.g.* Csapo and Miller (2003) 100–2 and T. H. Carpenter in Harrison (2005) 219–36); we nevertheless note interesting or suggestive illustrations which at least throw light on the mythological background of some plays and perhaps on the imaginations of some poets as well as painters. We attempt this expository work in our brief introductory discussions to each play or play-fragment, and in support we sometimes print shorter play-fragments or secondary evidence in translation alone.

We preface each play or unassigned fragment (*adespoton*, 'ownerless') with a bibliography giving:

> first, text-references from *TrGF*, now in universal and standard use;
>
> second (headed 'Text(s) *etc.*'), editions, part-editions, notes chiefly of a text-critical nature, commentaries complete or partial (some of which include translations);
>
> third (headed 'Discussions'), principal discussions of a general nature or of particular aspects (some of which may include texts or translations, in whole or part, for reference);
>
> fourth (headed 'Art'), a note of relevant works of art.

For all Greek texts we have relied heavily upon those in *TrGF*, and secondly on those in Diggle (1998) and KPS (1999) which we have edited or abridged in general conformity with the principles followed in this series by C. Collard, M. J. Cropp, K. H. Lee, J. Gibert in *Euripides. Selected Fragmentary Plays*, *I* (1995, corrected ed. 2009) and *II* (2004). In particular: normally only the principal sources for each fragment, and only significant textual information, are given in an *apparatus criticus*; full information must be sought from *TrGF*. For papyri we follow, like *TrGF*, the common practice of leaving it to inference that all readings, supplements or conjectures, and assignations of voice-parts, which are printed in the main text, except those otherwise attributed in the *apparatus*, originate with the first editor(s); we give their name(s) at the start in the form (*e.g.*) Sophocles, *Inachus* F **269c P. Tebt. 692 ed. A. S. Hunt, J. G. Smyly (1933) fr. 1. Throughout the volume, a single asterisk preceding a testimony- and fragment-number indicates that in *TrGF* it is ascribed to the play by conjecture (as *e.g.* Sophocles, *Inachus* F *271); a double asterisk indicates that it is ascribed by conjecture to the author (and sometimes therefore to both, as *e.g. Inachus* F **269c above); these asterisks appear chiefly in initial bibliographies and in the Greek texts and translations of the fragments, and are usually omitted in cross-references.

In our texts drawn from papyri single square brackets, [...], enclose gaps where text or letters are lost through physical damage; at beginnings and ends of lines a single square bracket, respectively] or [, marks off preceding or following loss of text. An in-line dot anywhere represents one letter calculated by editors to be missing, up to the number of five; we indicate greater numbers by *e.g.* '*6 let.*' or '*10–11 let.*', italicized, or where no number can be calculated, or minimal remnants of some letters are intermittent, we leave white space or state *e.g.* '*traces (of 6 let.)*' in italics. We do not reproduce, from *TrGF* or any other edition, (1) adscript iotas (sometimes lost from papyri in physical damage immediately following a long vowel); instead in the text we everywhere print iotas subscript, and in the *apparatus* adscript iotas only where necessary to full information; (2) nor do we reproduce under-line dots indicating insecurely read letters, because in computer-generated or -derived Greek texts they often appear to stand between letters, or to become confused with descenders; instead, we signal such uncertainties only in the *apparatus*, when most recent editors maintain doubts; where other factors, such as context, vocabulary or idiom, tend to confirm uncertain readings, and most editors are in agreement, we normally do not comment; similarly with letters or words conjectured within gaps ([...] above). Double square brackets, [[...]], enclose deletions made in the papyrus by a scribe himself. In both papyri and book-fragments, broken brackets, { ... }, enclose editors' deletions of text; pointed brackets, < ... >, enclose editors' conjectural additions to the text. We very seldom report editors' purely orthographic corrections.

In the *apparatus* throughout, as for *Cyclops*, a colon separates details of individual readings or conjectures (letter, word, phrase or clause) in the numbered Greek line(s); a semi-colon separates such information from that relating to another place in the same line(s).

In our translations, both of papyri and of book-fragments, we enclose between round brackets, (...), supplements standing either in the edited Greek text itself or in the *apparatus* alone, often with a question-mark to indicate uncertainty.

We use italics for information about the condition of the text, chiefly in damaged papyri; for necessary supplements of the English sense, also in round brackets; and for such pointers as 'stage-directions' where they may reasonably be inferred.

Line-numbers in the translation also appear between round brackets, and in the line, at intervals of five lines, *e.g.* (15), (55).

Numbered notes: for all plays and *adespota* notes are numbered continuously through the introductory discussions to the end of the translations. We include our infrequent comments on the Greek text in these notes.

Cross-references to other plays in our selection are made by name and fragment-number, or by 'introductory discussion to' followed by the name, often with the addition of a note-number, sometimes with the addition simply of 'above' or 'below'. Distinguish 'Introductory Note' with capitals (which you have just read) from 'introductory discussion' without capitals (to an individual play or fragment). We refer users to our Appendix and Index of Motifs (at the end of the volume) by these names alone.

A small amount of matter is deliberately repeated between plays, in the expectation that many users will consult only parts of it.

BIBLIOGRAPHICAL GUIDANCE
UPON THE FRAGMENTARY TEXTS

Editions. An outstandingly good comprehensive edition of all important satyric fragments is now available: Krumeich-Pechstein-Seidensticker (1999; KPS in Abbreviations); it has moreover splendid introductory chapters on the genre in its theatrical and literary aspects by B. Seidensticker (1–40) and on its representation in archaeological remains, especially vase-painting, by R. Krumeich (41–73); it offers introductions, the more important testimonies, Greek texts, translations and notes for individual plays; and it includes some important illustrations. P. Voelke has promised a commentary upon all the fragments. All the major fragments of Aeschylus, Sophocles and Euripides are included in the their Loeb editions, respectively Sommerstein (2008), Lloyd-Jones (1996), Collard and Cropp (2008); see also *Minor dramatists* below.

General surveys of the genre. The most accessible full reviews in English are Sutton (1980) and Seaford (1984) 1–44 (an authoritative account); briefer are P. E. Easterling in P. E. E. (ed.), *The Cambridge Companion to Greek Tragedy* (Cambridge, 1997) 37–44; Kaimio (2001) 68–75; I. C. Storey and A. Allan, *A Guide to Ancient Greek Drama* (Malden, MA and Oxford, 2005) 161–6; B. Seidensticker in J. Gregory (ed.), *A Companion to Greek Tragedy* (Malden MA and Oxford, 2006) 44–9. The collection edited by G. Harrison (2005) contains many reappraisals of *Cyclops* and other satyr plays reflecting recent scholarship: treatment of language and linguistic register, characterization and cultural context, satyrs in Old Comedy and art, links between Euripides' *Cyclops* and *Alcestis*. See also the two lengthy and wide-ranging papers of M. Griffith, 'Slaves of Dionysus: satyrs, audience and the ending of the *Oresteia*', *ClassAnt* 21 (2002) 195–258, at 195–237 (with bibl.), and 'Satyr drama (and its 'charms') – separate and in between', in M. Revermann, P. Wilson (eds), *Performance, Iconography, Reception. Studies in Honour of Oliver Taplin* (Oxford, 2008) 59–87, at 73–82.

Individual aspects of the genre. First, wide coverage is offered by B. Seidensticker (ed.), *Das griechische Satyrdrama* (Darmstadt, 1989; in German). Then: L. Paganelli, 'Il dramma satiresco. Spazio, tematiche e messo in scena', *Dioniso* 59.2 (1989) 213–82 (in Italian); papers by L. E. Rossi, F. Jouan, M. Di Marco, R. Seaford, P. Ghiron-Bistagne, I. Gallo in *Dioniso*

61.2 (1991) (all in Italian); G. Hedreen, 'Silens, Nymphs and Maenads', *JHS* 114 (1994) 47–69; M. Di Marco, 'L'ambiguo statuto del dramma satiresco', in G. Arrighetti, M. Tulli (eds), *Letteratura e riflessione sulla letteratura nella cultura classica* (Pisa, 2000) 31–49 (in Italian); B. Seidensticker, 'The Chorus of Greek Satyrplay', in Csapo, Miller (2003) 100–21; M. Di Marco, 'Il riso nel dramma satiresco', *Dioniso* 6 (2007) 168–79; G. Hedreen, 'Myths of Ritual in Athenian Vase-Paintings of Silens', in Csapo, Miller (2007) 150–95, with pls 43–67; Lämmle (2007) reviews the significance of the satyric Dionysus in Greek drama (in German); A. G Katsouris, 'Echoes, Criticism and Parody of Socio-Political Phenomena and Literary Genres of Post-Classical Athens in Satyr Drama', *Athenaeum* 98 (2010) 405–12; C. A. Shaw, 'Middle Comedy and the "Satyric" Style', *AJP* 131 (2010) 1–22. The excellent monograph by Conrad (1997, in German) offers interpretative and evaluative suggestions for *Cyclops*, and many fragmentary plays, although its emphasis is upon assessing the role of Silenus in them.

'Histories' of scholarly work on the genre are given in KPS (1999) 39–40 (literary) and 44–7 (archaeological); cf. M. Griffith (2002 above) at 197–203, 'Current views of the satyr-play', and J. Gibert, *CJ* 98 (2002–3) 79–88 (review article).

Aeschylus. R. G. Ussher, *Phoenix* 31 (1977) 287–99; Gallo (1992) 43–94 (in Italian); Sommerstein (2010) 235–40; A. Moreau, *Cahiers du GITA Montpellier. Université Paul Valéry* 14 (2001) 39–62; A. J. Podlecki in Harrison (2005) 1–19. Also: P. Yziquel, 'Bibliographie du drame satyrique eschyléen', *Cahiers ... Valéry* (above) 23–38 (185 items from the years 1918–2000).

Sophocles. S. L. Radt in *Entretiens XXIX. Sophocle* (Fondation Hardt, Geneva 1982) 190–4, 203–7 (in German; reprinted in H. Hofmann, A. Harder (eds) *Fragmenta Dramatica* (Göttingen, 1991) 82–5, 92–6 and in A. Harder *etc.* (eds), *'Noch einmal zu ...'. Festschrift ... S. L. Radt* (Leiden *etc.*, 2002) 266–70, 276–80); Radt includes a brief comparison between the satyric remains of the three major tragedians); P. Voelke in Sommerstein (2003) 329–54 (in French); M. Griffith, 'Sophocles' Satyr-Plays and the Language of Romance', in I. J. F. de Jong, A. Rijksbaron (eds), *Sophocles and the Greek Language. Aspects of Diction, Syntax and Pragmatics* (Leiden-Berlin, 2006) 51–72; W. Slenders, 'The λέξις ἐρωτική [erotic diction] in Sophocles' satyr-plays', in A. P. M. H. Lardinois and others (eds), *Land of Dreams. Greek and Latin Studies in honour of A. H. M. Kessels* (Leiden, 2006) 133–45.

Euripides. V. Steffen, *Eos* 59 (1971) 203–26 (in English); R. Seaford, 'Il dramma satiresco di Euripide', *Dioniso* 61.2 (1991) 75–89 (in Italian); Pechstein (1998) 10–18 (in German); Mastronarde (2010) 54–7; see also n. 2 below.

Minor dramatists. These are edited, annotated and assessed by Cipolla (2003; in Italian), who on 19–26 reviews the sources for these poets. Some of their fragments are surveyed by Gallo (1992) 95–106, and satyric drama after Euripides, in its transformation and shift in status, 107–23 (in Italian).

Satyric drama in the 4th Century and later. For the continuation of satyric outside Athens, with both new compositions and revivals over the period 3nd century BC to 2nd century AD, see the evidence gathered in *TrGF* 1².19–21 and 33–7, cf. 343; also B. Seidensticker in KPS (1999) 2, 9–12; A. Schachter, W. J. Slater, *ZPE* 163 (2007) 81–95. For texts from the later period see our (introductory discussions to) Python, *Agen;* Sositheus, *Daphnis*; Lycophron, *Menedemus;* and *Adespota* F 646a. We include also the possibly satyric *Adespota* F 655 (an 'Atlas' play) and F 667a (a 'Medea' play), and the almost certainly not satyric P. Köln 431.

Satyric motifs and features. Very useful collections and analyses have been made by Sutton (1980) 145–59; Seaford (1984) 33–44 and (index) 227–9; Paganelli (1989, above) 228–74; KPS (1999) 28–32 and (tabulation) 666–7; Cipolla (2003) 4–5; Voelke (2001: index, 443–54); and Harrison (2005: index, 283–95). We have drawn upon these for our own brief Index of Motifs at the end of the volume. Also, see M. Griffith on 'fantasy, identity and self-presentation' in Harrison (2005) 172–86, 194–8; and his concise survey of vocabulary and stylometrics *ibid.* 166–72, 192–4. Other studies of the language of satyric are by A. López Eire in Sommerstein (2003) 387–412 and J. Redondo *ibid.* 413–31; D. Cilia in P. Cipolla (ed.), *Studi sul teatro greco* (Amsterdam, 2006) 7–67.

Note

Many recent and important studies of satyric fragments have been made in continental Europe, above all in Italy. We fear that some of this work may not be readily available in English-speaking countries, and we are specially grateful to Prof. Luigi Battezzato (University of Piemonte, Vercelli) for securing us copies of the important papers in Martina (2003), before this volume at last became available in a British university library.

PRATINAS

(active from about 500 BC; birth and death not known)

Hyporchema

TrGF I².81–2 (4 F 3), 345; cf. 5.1105.

Text etc. U. von Wilamowitz, *Sappho und Simonides* (Berlin, 1913) 131–6; D. Campbell, *Greek Lyric Poetry* (London, 1967) 100–1, 403–5, cf. *Greek Lyric III* (Loeb Classical Library, Cambridge MA and London, 1991) 320–3; Sutton (1980) 7–12, 48–53; Gauly (1991) 50–3, 272–3; J. Schloemann in KPS 81–7; Voelke (2001) 117–25; Cipolla (2003) 52–61.

Discussions. H. W. Garrod, 'The Hyporchema of Pratinas', *CR* 34 (1920) 129–36; A. M. Dale, (from) 'Stasimon and Hyporchema', *Collected Papers* (Cambridge, 1968) 34–40 (orig. 1950) and (from) 'Words, Music and Dance', *ibid.* 166–8 (orig. 1960); Lloyd-Jones (1990) 227–30 (first publ. 1966); Chourmouziades (1974) 18–20; R. Seaford, 'The 'Hyporchema' of Pratinas', *Maia* 29–30 (1977–78) 81–94; B. Zimmermann, 'Ueberlegungen zum sogenannten Pratinasfragment', *MH* 43 (1986) 145–54, cf. his *Dithyrambos. Geschichte einer Gattung* (Göttingen, 1992) 124–6; Gallo (1992) 98–9; A. Melero, 'El hiporquema de Pratinas e la dicción satírica', in J.-A. López Férez (ed.) *Estudios actuales sobra textos griegos* (Madrid, 1991) 75–87; Conrad (1997) 29–30; Kaimio (2001) 35, 51–3; M. Napolitano, 'Note all' iporchema di Pratina', in A. C. Cassio and others (eds), *Synaulia. Cultura musicale in Grecia e contatti mediterranei* (Naples, 2000) 111–55 (with large bibl.); Voelke (2001, above) and in Sommerstein (2003) 330–1; Cipolla (2003) 38–9, 62–77; V. Nicolucci, 'Il dramma satiresco alla corte di Attalo I', in Martina (2003) 325–42, at 338–9; G. B. D'Alessio, '"Ην ἰδού: *Ecce satyri* (Pratina, *PMG* 708 = *TrGF* 4 F 3). Alcune considerazioni sull' uso della deissi nei testi lirici e teatrali', in F. Perusino, M. Colantonio (eds), *Dalla lirica corale alla poesia drammatica. Forme e funzioni del canto corale nella tragedia e nella commedia greca* (Pisa, 2007) 95–128, at 105–122 (with large bibl.); P. Redondo Reyes, 'Critica poética y unidad temático en Pratinas, frs. 1 y 5 Page. I.', *Myrtia* 22 (2007) 35–58 (not seen by us); P. A. Leven, 'New Music and its Myths: Athenaeus' Reading of the *Aulos* Revolution (*Deipnosophistae* 14. 616e–617f)', *JHS* 130 (2010) 35–47, at 38–9.

We include this piece, whose origin in satyric drama, or in drama at all, is still disputed, for its remarkable content.

Dale (1950, 1960, repeated in 1968) emphasized that Athenaeus, the source of the fragment, does not write of drama, but describes the piece only as a hyporchema (an imitative sung dance, a musical composition independent of drama); and this consideration has again been stressed by KPS 86. Because the singers of our piece insist on their closeness to Dionysus (vv. 2, 15–16) and on their dancing on the mountains among Naiads (v. 2; see n. 3 below), it is often inferred that the performers were a conventional, dancing chorus of 'satyrs'; but such language is also possible from a stationary dithyrambic chorus singing to honour Dionysus (note the explicit v. 15). Composition for the latter was argued by Wilamowitz, and after him by Lloyd-Jones (1990) and Zimmermann (1986); these two attributed the fragment's metrical and lexical features (especially the very long compound adjectives in vv. 12–13, 16), and in particular its near-technical polemic about pipe-music, to the later 5th century, and its authorship to an uncertainly attested poet of that time also named Pratinas who was subsequently confused with the earlier and famous one; this view was supported by R. W. Wallace in *HSCP* 101 (2003) 85, but Zimmermann later seemed more cautious (1992, 126 n. 27).

On the other hand, the old attribution to a satyr-play written by the great Pratinas of the early 5th century had been reasserted by Seaford (1978) and Sutton (1980); also Leven (2010). This Pratinas was celebrated as the first producer of satyr-plays, thirty-two being known to antiquity (*TrGF* 4 T 1, 6, 7; cf. our Appendix): thus, if this fragment is genuinely satyric, it is perhaps the earliest extant piece of European drama. Others argued that such a serious and intellectual tone was improbable in a conventional satyr-play such as Pratinas might have written, especially if the exiguous fragments are typical of his work (see Conrad (1997) 29–30 and KPS 84–5). Recent opinion has again been divided, *e.g.* in *TrGF* itself (see 1².345, and cf. Gauly (1991) 272 n. 9). Gallo (1992) 99 and Voelke (2001) 119–24 (and in Sommerstein (2003) 331) seem content with a loose attribution to choral lyric; Napolitano (2002) 140–1 and Cipolla (2003) 62–77 conclude that the piece is of uncertain origin.

Strong support for satyric origin has nevertheless again been voiced by Melero (1991) and particularly D'Alessio (2007). D'Alessio argues (a) that the deictic elements 'this' (v. 1) and 'Look, see this' (15), and the self-directed imperatives 'Strike!' (10) and 'Set fire!' (12) are characteristic of live theatre rather than simple lyric performance (D'Alessio 108–11, 113) and, moreover, comparable with the imperatives at Aeschylus, *Sacred Delegates* F 78a.4–5,

18–19; (b) that the location of the deplorably dominant pipe (4, 10–14) and inappropriate dances near Dionysus' altar, outraging it (1) rather than honouring it properly through singing (2–4) and dancing (15–17), indicate performance by a chorus who claim Dionysus as their own (2, 17; D'Alessio 111, 117); (c) that the association of this chorus with Naiads (2: see n. 3 below) points to satyrs as its dancing members, for their encounters with music are a constant of satyric drama (*e.g.* Sophocles, *Trackers* F 314.260–331, cf. our Index of Motifs) as of vase-painting (D'Alessio 115–16); and (d) that the metrical resolutions in the fragment (see next paragraph) closely resemble those of the excited lyrics at Sophocles, *Trackers* F 314.176–202 and *Inachus* F 269c.16–20 (D'Alessio 113, citing Garrod (1920) 134 for *Trackers* and Napolitano (2000) 137 for both passages).

It is likely then that the fragment, if dramatic, begins the formal entry of the satyr-chorus (parodos): note their surprised and irate excitement and the metrical transition from lengthy anapaests (1–2, already marked by syllabic resolutions) to freer mixed lyric of shorter periods, mostly dactylo-epitrite (3–17). The singers are angry that the pipe (*aulos,* see n. 2 below), noisy and penetrating, now aggressively dominates (1, 10–14) their tuneful sung dance (3–4), which it should merely accompany (5–6) in celebrating their divine

---

F 3 (Athenaeus 14.617b)

Πρατίνας δὲ ὁ Φλιάσιος αὐλητῶν καὶ χορευτῶν μισθοφόρων κατεχόντων τὰς ὀρχήστρας †ἀγανακτεῖν τινας† ἐπὶ τῷ τοὺς αὐλητὰς μὴ συναυλεῖν τοῖς χοροῖς, καθάπερ ἦν πάτριον, ἀλλὰ τοὺς χοροὺς συνᾴδειν τοῖς αὐληταῖς· ὃν οὖν εἶχεν κατὰ τῶν ταῦτα ποιούντων θυμὸν ὁ Πρατίνας ἐμφανίζει διὰ τοῦδε τοῦ ὑπορχήματος·

F 4

<ΧΟΡΟΣ>   τίς ὁ θόρυβος ὅδε; τί τάδε τὰ χορεύματα;
               τίς ὕβρις ἔμολεν ἐπὶ Διονυσιάδα πο-
               λυπάταγα θυμέλαν;
               ἐμὸς ἐμὸς ὁ Βρόμιος,
                  ἐμὲ δεῖ κελαδεῖν, ἐμὲ δεῖ παταγεῖν
                  ἀν' ὄρεα σύμενον μετὰ Ναϊάδων

patron Dionysus. Such advocacy by satyric performers of their own art when it is under threat is like that in *Adespota* F 646a.18–25: see our discussion there of these and other 'metatheatrical' passages; cf. Kaimio (2001) 38–53, esp. 51–3 on our fragment. The advocacy has analogies, however, both in the occasional self-referentiality of the chorus of Tragedy, especially the famous cry at Sophocles, *Oedipus* 896 'Why do I (join the sacred) dance?',[1] and in the often polemical parabases of Old Comedy (*e.g.* Aristophanes, *Frogs* 686–7 'it is right that the sacred chorus shares advising and instructing the city') which rupture the theatrical illusion; this is allowed by D'Alessio (2007) 117–21.

As to the pipe itself, satyrs frequently themselves play it on Archaic and Classical Greek vases (see *e.g.* D'Alessio (2007) 116). The satyr Marsyas famously revelled in the instrument after its inventor the goddess Athena discarded it, until his fatal contest with Apollo ([Apollod.] 4.2, cf. Herodotus 7.26.3). The 'attack' here, then, is not so much on the *aulos* itself, as on the dominant role it has assumed.

Note

[1] The classic discussion of this and comparable passages is by A. Henrichs, *Arion* 3 (1994–5) 54–111.

F 3 (Athenaeus 14.617b)
When hired pipe-players and choral dancers began to occupy the orchestras Pratinas of Phlius (was indignant? *lit.* †some were indignant†) that the pipers did not play to accompany the choruses according to tradition, but the choruses sang to accompany the pipers.[2] Accordingly he makes his anger plain towards those doing this, by means of this hyporchema:

[2] 'pipers': their instrument was a double pipe, with a deep and resonant tone, the *aulos* (v. 13); the two pipes, each played with one hand, came together in a single mouth-piece which held a single reed (v. 12): for the technical details, and differentiation from the post-Classical flute, see West (1992) 81–107; for the *aulos* generally, see P. Wilson in S. Goldhill, R. Osborne (eds), *Performance and Culture in Athenian Democracy* (Cambridge, 1999) 58–95, esp. 69–85; Leven (2010); for the *aulos* in Tragedy see A. Provenza, *RIFC* 137 (2009) 280–301, esp. 280 n. 1.

F 4
<CHORUS>   What is this din? What dances are these? What outrage has come to Dionysus' loud-sounding altar? Bromius is mine, *mine*! It is I who should sing his praise, it is I who should be loud, rushing over the mountains among Naiads, and keeping up like a swan a

οἷά τε κύκνον ἄγοντα
    ποικιλόπτερον μέλος.
τὰν ἀοιδὰν κατέστασε Πιε-
    ρὶς βασίλειαν· ὁ δ' αὐλός
ὕστερον χορευέτω·   (5)
καὶ γάρ ἐσθ' ὑπηρέτας.
κώμῳ μόνον θυραμάχοις τε
πυγμαχίαισι νέων θέλοι παροίνων
ἔμμεναι στρατηλάτας.
παῖε τὸν φρυνεοῦ   (10)
ποικίλου πνοὰν ἔχοντα·
φλέγε τὸν ὀλεσιαλοκάλαμον,
λαλοβαρύοπα <πα>ραμελορυθμοβάταν
ὑπαὶ τρυπάνῳ δέμας πεπλασμένον.
ἦν ἰδού· ἅδε σοι δεξιᾶς καὶ ποδὸς διαρριφά·   (15)
θριαμβοδιθύραμβε, κισσόχαιτ' ἄναξ,
<ἄκου'> ἄκουε τὰν ἐμὰν Δώριον χορείαν.

Athenaeus 14.617b–f
13 suppl. Bergk
14 ὑπαὶ Page: θυπα Athen.: θῆτα Hartung
17 suppl. Page

song of colourful flight.[3] Pieria's Muse established song as queen
– let the pipe perform the dance in second place, for it is a servant.
(5) Let the pipe wish to lead into battle only for the revel and
fisticuffs of drunken youths fighting at doors![4]

(*urging themselves on*) Strike the one (10) who blows like a
dappled toad![5] Set fire to the reed that wastes spittle when babbling
away with its deep voice, discordant and without rhythm, its form
fashioned beneath an auger's bore.[6]

(*invoking Dionysus*) Look, see this! Here are hand and foot flung
about in your honour![7] Triumphant one, dithyramb-praised![8] (15)
My lord with ivy in your hair, <listen,> listen to my Dorian sung
dance![9]

[3]   Cf. Pindar, *Isthmians* 5.63 'winged song'. Swans were credited with musicality, *e.g.* Eur.
IT 1104–5. The most evocative descriptions of Dionysus' ecstatic and loud celebration with
running and dancing on the mountains are in Eur. *Bacc.* 73–169; cf. also *Cyc.* 68–72, where
the satyrs complain that they cannot carry out their customary activity of celebrating the god
in the company of nymphs. Naiads, water-nymphs, are regularly associated with satyrs: see
e.g. Cyc. 430; Pindar fr. 156; Aesch. *Prometheus the Fire-Kindler* F 204b.4–8, 15–17; nymphs
generally *Cyc.* 68–72, 515; Soph. *Trackers* F 314.228; Voelke (2001) 218–25; further, G.
Hedreen, 'Silens, Nymphs and Maenads', *JHS* 114 (1994) 47–69 and in Csapo, Miller (2007)
150–95, at 169–76, with pls 55–61 (our fragment is discussed on pp. 150, 183–4).
[4]   'youths fighting at doors': those of desirable girls. For the drunken reveller outside the
'door' of his beloved, cf. *Cyc.* 496–502 and n., Ar. *Lys.* 309 and *Eccl.* 960–90, where 'door'
functions easily as a *double entendre*: see Henderson (1991) 27, 137–8, 171. For revels
typically leading to violence see, in satyr drama, Odysseus' warning to Polyphemus at *Cyc.*
534; it becomes a commonplace of comedy, *e.g.* Eubulus F 94.
[5]   'toad': the simile's point is the toad's insistent and resonant croaking.
[6]   For pipes bored cylindrically or conically see West (1992) 83. Hartung's conjecture gives
'Set fire to the hireling reed (cf. 'hired pipe-players' in F 3 from Athenaeus) that wastes ...
fashioned by an auger's bore.'
[7]   Possibly an allusion to the wild dance the *sikinis*: see n. 35 on Soph. *Trackers*.
[8]   Cf. 'Iacchus, triumphant, you – the leader of those here!', *Adespota* fr. 1027(d) *PMG*; cf.
our n. 11 on *Adespota* F 646a.15. Zeus addresses his infant son Dionysus with 'Dithyrambic
one!' at Eur. *Bacc.* 526. Cf. also Aesch. F 355 'It is fitting that the dithyramb with its mix of
voices (i.e. *from pipe and singers?*) should accompany Dionysus as his fellow-reveller.'
[9]   'Dorian': the fragment itself is in the Doric dialect usual for choral lyric, but the allusion
may be to the Dorian musical mode; Aristotle, *Politics* 8.1342a28–b17 commends its harmony
as 'manly', while condemning much pipe-playing as dissolute in character (vv. 7–14 here); in
our fragment, however, there is no mode contrasted with the Dorian, and there is no certain
polemic (D' Alessio (2007) 121–2). The satyrs in any case have a 'Doric' descent (first at
Hesiod F 10(a).17–19 M-W, where Dorus' descendants include the satyrs); the 'epitaph' of
Dioscorides praising Sositheus as reviver of satyric drama (see his *Daphnis*, introductory
discussion, first paragraph) writes of its 'Dorian Muse', *Anth. Pal.* 7.707.7.

AESCHYLUS

(active from about 500 BC; died 456)

Glaucus the Sea-god (*ΓΛΑΥΚΟΣ ΠΟΝΤΙΟΣ, Glaucus Marinus*)

TrGF 3.141–8 (F **25c–34), cf. 4².782–3.

Texts etc. E. Siegmann, *Philologus* 97 (1948) 59–62 (F 25e); Lloyd-Jones (1957) 529–30 (F 25e); R. P. Winnington-Ingram, *BICS* 6 (1959) 58–60 (F 25e.12–15); Diggle (1998) 2–3 (F 25e); A. Wessels, R. Krumeich in KPS 125–30; Sommerstein (2008) 22–33.

Discussions. Gantz (1993) 732–3; Voelke (2001) 295–7; A. Podlecki in Harrison (2005) 12.

Art. LIMC IV.1.271–3 ('Glaukos I') nos 1–16.

The play named just *Glaucus*, and as satyric, in the scholia to Theocritus 4.62 is the *Sea-god*, since Aeschylus' *Glaucus of Potniae* was the tragedy produced as part of his tetralogy in 472 BC which included the *Persians*. Other indications of satyric genre are the linguistic register of F 26 and F 34, and the tenor of Glaucus' story in Pausanias 9.22.5 and 7 (below). The book fragments are few (F 26–29, 31 and 34,[1] and there are scraps of two papyri (F **25c, the single word 'Euripus', **25d and **25e, the latter two below) – but they all fit Pausanias' outline well:

> (9.22.5) In Boeotia to the left of (the strait of) Euripus lies the mountain called Messapium, and beneath it by the sea the Boeotians' city Anthedon ... (7) by the sea is the so-called 'Leap of Glaucus'. He was a fisherman, and became a sea-god after he had eaten a herb, and to this day foretells the future: this is

---

F **25d

12 badly damaged lines put together from two vertically adjacent fragments, in which the following words are read:
    6 ἀνδρ[ῶν γε]ραιῶν, 7 *beg marks* ΧΟ[ΡΟΣ], 11 ἱππ[

P. Oxy. 2255 (2nd c. AD) ed. E. Lobel (1952) fr .12 col. ii (1–12) + fr. 13 (1–9)
6 supplemented by Snell

both a general belief and one held particularly by sailors who year in, year out give very many accounts of Glaucus' prophecy. While Pindar and Aeschylus learned this from the people of Anthedon, it did not come to Pindar to sing much of Glaucus' story,[2] although there was actually enough for Aeschylus to make a play of it.

Beside Glaucus himself (the eater of the immortality-conferring herb, F 28 and F 29), a herdsman had a speaking role (F 25e8). It was perhaps the only substantive one in addition to Silenus – unless Silenus was himself the herdsman, apparently as in Sophocles' *Inachus*[3] – and to the satyr-chorus (of whom however the fragments give no trace). The encounters of the herdsman and probably also of the satyrs with Glaucus as he emerged from the sea would provide action appropriately amusing, F 25e12–15, cf. the description of his strange appearance in F 26, 27 and 34 (see n. 5 below, Voelke (2001) 295–7); but how the plot developed, and what was the happy outcome, can only be guessed. Most of the sixteen works listed in *LIMC* show Glaucus as half-man, half-fish; but all are of uncertain allusion, and none is earlier than the 4th century BC

Satyrs' over-reaction to 'wonders', divine or cultural, seems to have been frequent in plays (see Gen. Intro. p. 34–6 and Index of Motifs).

Notes

[1]   F 25a (= fr. 32 Nauck) 'My body washed clean by fine bathing, I came to Himera on its steep cliffs' (approximate translation: text corrupt) is left unassigned to either *Glaucus* by Radt in *TrGF*; Sommerstein (2008) 22–3 now argues for its attribution to *Potniae*; similarly F 25b (= fr. 35 Nauck) 'two Pans, one the son of Zeus, the other of Cronus', a testimony. F 40 (= fr. 33 Nauck) belongs certainly to *Potniae*.

[2]   No wording survives from Pindar (see F 263 Snell-Maehler).

[3]   – and unless Silenus had a role similar to that in *Net-Fishers* (see the introductory discussion), an old suggestion shared by Sutton (1980) 22 and discussed inconclusively by Conrad (1997) 92. Apart from dramatic convenience, a menial role for him here too finds support from other plays, *e.g. Cyc.* 23–35, Eur. *Sciron* F 675.

F **25d (P. Oxy. 2255 fr. 12 col. ii + fr. 13)

12 very fragmentary lines, including these insecurely read words:

> 6 ... of (old?) men ... 7 CHO(RUS)   (*naming the voice-part*) ...
> 11 ... horse(s) ...[4]

[4]   6 '(old?) men', if a correct supplement, seems to herald the arrival in 7 of the chorus of satyrs; but they are not usually elderly, only their 'father' Silenus is (*e.g. Cyc.*2, 101). In art a few examples of white-haired satyrs are known (*LIMC* VIII.2.90, 96, 160), but on red-figure vases, notably the Pronomos Vase, Silenus is customarily differentiated from his sons by his white hair and decrepit physique (cf. *e.g.* Eur. *Autolycus B* T iv.449–50 'decrepit little old man').

F 25e

<ΒΟΥΚΟΛΟΣ> ....]αυτα μωρο[

.....]τιν' ἢ θύελ[λα

6 *let*.]. παύρουσ[

....]ν μὲν ἴσθι σ[

...]ν δ' ἔτ' ἐστὶ π[ί]στις ὀμμ[άτων   (5)

οὐκ ἀ]μβλυώσ<σ>ων οὐδὲ μὰψ αυ[

ἤθρη]σα δεῖμα καὶ περισπ..[

...].ς ἄγραυλός τ' εἰμὶ κἀπιχ[ώριος

ἀεὶ θ]αμίζων τῇδε Χαλκίδ.[

Μεσσ]απίου τ' ἄφυλλον ὑψηλὸ[ν λέπας   (10)

....]ναπι...βουσὶ φορ[βάσιν

ἔνθ]εν κατεῖδον θαῦμα.[

Εὐβο]ἲδα καμπὴν ἀμφὶ Κηνα[ίου Διὸς

ἀκτὴ]ν κατ' αὐτὸν τύμβον ἀθ[λίου Λίχα

κάμπτο]νθ' ἄπερ τέθριππον [(15)

P. Oxy. 2159 (2nd c. AD) ed. E. Lobel (1941)
2 θύελ[λαν Görschen
5 beg τούτ]ων Sommerstein; in π[ί]στις all letters except final ς are insecure; ὀμμ]άτων σαφής· Cantarella
6 beg οὐκ Diggle
7 περισπερ[χὲς Lloyd-Jones
8 beg ἴσθ'] ὡς Sommerstein; κἀπιχ[ώριος Siegmann
9 beg ἀεὶ Cantarella
10 Fraenkel
11 φορ[βάσιν Görschen
12 beg Görschen
13–14 Strabo 10.1.9 (= Aesch. fr. 30 Nauck)
14 αὐτὸν Strabo most mss.: αυτην P. Oxy., Strabo other mss.
15 κάμπτο]νθ' ἄπερ Diggle:]ντ' απερ P. Oxy.

F *26

ἀνθρωποειδὲς †θηρίον ὕδατι συζῶντ†

Phrynichus, *Sophistic Preparation* 6.1 de Borries; Photius α 1981 Theodoridis
ὕδατι συζῶν θηρίον West

F *27

δαῦλος δ' ὑπήνη καὶ γενειάδος πυθμήν

(*Etymologicum Genuinum* AB =) *Etymologicum Magnum* 250.4 Gaisford; Eustathius, *Iliad* 274.23, on Book 2.520; paraphrased in Pausanias 10.4.7

F 25e (P. Oxy. 2159)

<HERDSMAN> ... foolish ... or storm ... few ... Know (*imperative*) ... (Of this?) there is moreover (clear?) evidence (of) eye(s) ... (5) ... (not) dim-sighted nor ... in vain ... frightful things and (urgent?) ... (Know that?) I am a herdsman and (from the locality), frequently here in Chalcis ... Messapium's leafless height (10) ... grazing cattle ... I saw a wonder ... the curve of Euboea round the cape of Cenaean Zeus right by the tomb of the wretched Lichas ... (turning?) like a chariot and four ... (15) ...[5]

[5] The herdsman is terrified by his clear sight of Glaucus, emerging from the sea (cf. F 26, 27, 34; also the reaction of the speakers in Aesch. *Net-Fishers* F 46a.8–15 to the chest containing Danae and Perseus at sea). Mt. Messapium, located near the Euripus (named in the papyrus scrap F 25c: see introductory discussion), occurs in a 'geographical' narrative also at *Ag.* 292–3. Vv. 13–14 have something in common with Sophocles, *Women of Trachis* 237–8, 752–4; in 755–9 there Lichas is said to have given Heracles at Cenaeum the fatal shirt of Nessus, on the orders of Deianeira. The 'chariot and four' in 15 probably describes the 'wonder' of 12, Glaucus riding the waves just as the supreme sea-god Poseidon does (Homer, *Iliad* 13.23–21; Philostratus, *Imagines* 1.8).

F *26 (Phrynichus, *Sophistic Preparation* p. 6.1 de Borries)

... †a beast† in human form †living in the sea's waters†[6]

[6] Good sense, but unmetrical; West's rearrangement introduces a verse-end which breaks 'Porson's Law' (which for iambic trimeters in tragedy states that when a syllable that may be either long or short (*anceps*) is long in the third metron (fifth foot), it may not be immediately followed by the beginning of a new word; but this is tolerated in satyric, *e.g. Cyc.* 210.

F *27 (*Etymologicum Magnum* 250.4 Gaisford; Eustathius, *Iliad* 274.23, on Book 2.520)

... and thickly bearded on the upper lip and lower chin ...

F 28

ὁ τὴν ἀείζων ἄφθιτον πόαν φαγών

Anecdota Graeca I.347.20 Bekker; Photius α 409 Theodoridis

F *29

καὶ γεύομαί πως τῆς ἀειζώου πόας.

Anecdota Graeca I.347.25 Bekker; Photius α 409 Theodoridis

F 31

κᾆπειτ᾽ Ἀθήνας Διάδας παρεκπερῶν

Life of Aratus 1 p.77.3 Maass = p. 7.8 Martin

F 34

κόγχοι, μύες κὥστρεια

Athenaeus 3.86f

F 28 (*Anecdota Graeca* I.347.20 Bekker; Photius α 409 Theodoridis)
... the one who ate the imperishable herb giving eternal life ...

F *29 (*Anecdota Graeca* I.347.25 Bekker; Photius α 409 Theodoridis)
... and I try a taste of the herb giving eternal life.

F 31 (*Life of Aratus* 1 p.77.3 Maass = p. 7.8 Martin)
... and then, passing Diad Athens ...[7]

[7]   Diad Athens (*lit.* 'Athenae Diades') was a place on the island of Euboea.

F 34 (Athenaeus 3.86f)
... shell-fish, mussels and oysters ...[8]

[8]   Clinging to Glaucus' face, giving the appearance of a beard (F 27): so Plato, *Republic* 611d.

Net-Fishers (*ΔΙΚΤΥΟΥΛΚΟΙ*, *Dictyulci*)

TrGF 3.161–74 (F **46a–**47c), cf. 4².783.

Texts etc. R. Pfeiffer, *Die Netzfischer des Aischylos und der Inachos des Sophokles* (München, 1938) 3–22 (F 46a, b); Page (1942) 8–11 (F 46a); E. Siegmann, *Philologus* 97 (1948) 71–124 (F 47a); Lloyd-Jones (1957) 531–41 (F 46a, 47a); H. Werre-de Haas, *Aeschylus' Dictyulci* (Leiden, 1961); Gallo (1992) 78–92 (F 47a); Conrad (1997) 39–49 (F 46a, b, 47a); Diggle (1998) 5–9 (F 46a, 47a); A Wessels, R. Krumeich in KPS 107–24; W. B. Henry, *ZPE* 129 (2000) 13–14 (F 47a); Sommerstein (2008) 42–57.

Discussions. E. Fraenkel, 'Aeschylus: New Texts and Old Problems', *PBA* 28 (1942) 237–58, at 240–4; T. P. Howe, 'The style of Aeschylus as satyr-playwright', *Greece and Rome* 6 (1959) 150–65 (a general appreciation of the play); Chourmouziades (1974) 21–4, 45–6, 49–50, 59–60, 62–9; Taplin (1977) 418–20; Sutton (1980) 14–20, 137–9, *etc*.; M.R. Halleran, 'The speaker(s) of Aeschylus, *Diktyoulkoi* fr. 47a Radt (= P. Oxy. 2161) 821–32', *ZPE* 79 (1989) 267–9; Gantz (1993) 301–4; Conrad (1997) 31–55, 240–51; Voelke (2001) 177–80 (lyric structures), 232–5; M. Griffith, 'Forms of desire in Aeschylus' *Netfishers*', in Harrison (2005) 186–90, 198–9 (cf. A. Podlecki *ibid*. 9–11 and Z. P. Ambrose *ibid*. 25–6); Sommerstein (2010) 235–8.

Art. LIMC III.1.331–4 'Danae' nos 55–7 are all early 5th century Attic vessels showing Dictys with Danae and Perseus and the chest, in various postures; no. 67 of the same period (= Trendall-Webster (1971) II.3) shows Dictys leading Danae and the child Perseus away; nos 62–3 are surviving Roman murals. Cf. J. Oakley, *AJA* 86 (1982) 111–15.

The play's satyric nature and likely plot had been inferred from its title in an ancient catalogue, and from the character of three tiny lexicographic fragments: F 47 'a net's well-woven (mesh)', fr. 48 Nauck (now = F 47a.45) 'baby porcupines', and fr. 49 Nauck (now = F 47a.54) 'provide with feasts', before two papyri brought confirmation with their content, manner and vocabulary (F 46a, F 47a, below). These two are separated parts of one original papyrus roll; F 46a is a scene evidently near the play's start, and a line-number ('800') preserved at F 47a.36 indicates the place of this second fragment towards the play's end.

The plot was the recovery from the sea, by net-fishermen on the island of Seriphos (about 100 miles as the crow flies roughly east of mainland Argos), of Danae and her infant son Perseus; the island's name survives in the papyrus scrap F 47b. They had been cast adrift in a chest by her father Acrisius king of Argos, in a desperate attempt to thwart an oracle foretelling his death from a grandson; he had first shut up Danae underground to prevent access by any man, but Zeus had come to her in a shower of gold and impregnated her (these two sentences summarise [Apollod.] 2.4.1; Pherecydes 3 F 10.22–6 *FGrH* (= F 10.7–10 Fowler 280) has the rescue of Danae and Perseus by Dictys, and that 'he brought them up as he would were they his own kin').

In the prologue-scene the chest is found by Dictys, seemingly cast as an ordinary fisherman (his name means 'Mr. Net'). He is with Silenus in stichomythic dialogue, F 46a.1–6 (this identification is the most likely, but not agreed among scholars: *e.g.* Sommerstein (2008) 45 thinks of Dictys with another fisherman, because Silenus seldom enters without the satyrs; one example is Soph. *Trackers* F 314.45); one of them shouts for help from nearby farmers to recover the chest, 17–20. Help comes probably at once, in the form of the satyr-chorus; in lines 5–7 of the tiny F 46c they are already being urged not to let the net-ropes slip.

The middle of the action is wholly lost; but the substantial if damaged F 47a (68 lines) represents a crisis. Silenus and the satyrs claim Danae as their 'bride', 46–7, 57–8, 67; they assume her sexual readiness after being long 'without a man' at sea, 60–6; they ingratiate themselves with her child through extensive promises, 38–56, cf. 22–34, hoping to compel her submission (so they are cast both as lecherous and incongruously as tender towards infants, as often: see n. 11 below). Danae has already been terrified, however, foreseeing rape and even death, perhaps by suicide, 11–17; she has begged for help, 18 – but from whom? from Dictys? The first lines of this fragment (1–8) are so damaged that editors have assigned them either to him or to Silenus: both could describe themselves as prospectively 'an aged nurse' to Perseus, 6, and either might protest against the other's conduct, 1–5; but the wording more strongly suggests Silenus, given his manner later in the scene (Siegmann first, cf. esp. Gallo (1992) 86–8). Unfortunately the precise distribution of the voice-parts in 22–68 is an unresolved question (see n. 11 below). It seems therefore that the play's heart was a gradually enraged dispute between Dictys and Silenus (and satyrs) over the 'ownership' of woman and infant; and that before F 47a begins Dictys had been forced to abandon them to fetch further help. Because of the line-number 800 in this scene, and of general inference that satyr-plays seldom had a large number of lines, an ending must have followed the fragment quickly: a happy one for the castaways and Dictys, but disappointing for the satyrs, unless they were consoled merely with drunken revelry, or with a promise of leaving the island.[1]

For reconstruction of the play, and general evaluation of its character, see esp. Howe (1959), Werre-de Haas (1961) 72–5, Gallo (1992) 81–6, Conrad (1997) 33–9 and KPS 120–4. The stage-persons seem to have been just Dictys, Danae (with a live baby Perseus, almost certainly: the scene F 47a.22–56 would be flat without reactions to Silenus' miming and banter), and Silenus, the latter perhaps in his usual role as leader of the chorus of satyrs, rather than as distinctively individualised (see Conrad (1997) 49–52). It cannot be known whether Dictys' brother Polydectes, the island's king, appeared (see next paragraph); but it was probably to him that Dictys went for help in protecting the castaways. Two speaking actors, then, would have sufficed.

The story of Danae and Perseus was popular with dramatists. In Euripides' fragmentary *Dictys* (a tragedy), the action on Seriphos begins when Perseus is near adulthood (his tragedy *Danae* had ended with the casting adrift, it seems). Dictys has been protecting Danae and Perseus for many years from his brother Polydectes. When this man tries to 'marry' Danae, the young Perseus returns from Polydectes' challenge to fetch the Gorgon's Head and with it turns Polydectes to stone; Danae probably becomes Dictys' wife (and queen), and Perseus is promised the foundation of a new dynasty at Argos. This may have

---

F **46a

<A>	ξυνῆκ[ας	;
<B>	ξυνῆκα …[	
<A>	τί σοι φυλάσσω [	;
<B>	εἴ που θαλάσσης [	
<A>	ἄσημα· λεῖος πόν[τος	(5)
<B>	δέρκου νυν ἐς κευ[θμῶνα	
<A>	καὶ δὴ δέδορκα τῷδε.[	
	ἔα·	
	τί φῶ τόδ᾽ εἶναι; πότερα .[	
	φάλαιναν ἢ ζύγαιναν ἢ κ.[	
	ἄναξ Πόσειδον Ζεῦ τ᾽ ἐνά[λιε	(10)

PSI 1209 (2nd c. AD) ed. M. Norsa, G. Vitelli (1935²) fr. a. The papyrus was written almost certainly by the same hand as P. Oxy. 2161 = F 47a below. V. 10 (= fr. 343 Nauck) is apparently referred to, but not cited, by Pausanias 2.24.4.

The speakers are not certainly identified: some eds. have Dictys followed by Silenus; others, the converse.

10 ἄναξ insecurely read in PSI; γ᾽ Diggle

been, or resembled, the plot of Aeschylus' tragedy *Polydectes*, which is only a title to us. It is likely that *Net-Fishers* was the satyr-play concluding a tetralogy to which *Polydectes* belonged (see *TrGF* 3.118, Gallo (1992) 78–81, Conrad (1997) 53–4, S. E. Goins, *RhM* 140 (1997) 193–210 and Sommerstein (2008) 42); as in other Aeschylean tetralogies, the satyr-play made the myth amusing after the tragedies had drawn upon its stirring emotions. In *Net-Fishers*, then, it is probable that Silenus appeared as the comical counterpart of Polydectes, in lusting after Danae and posing a threat which is nevertheless averted – more or less amicably – by the play's end.

The mid-5th century comedian Cratinus' *Men of Seriphos* hammed (or exploited) the events on the island. The recovery from the sea of a chest containing an infant was common in myth (one version of the Oedipus-story has it); in Plautus' comedy *Rudens* ('*Rope*') a droll fisherman recovers a chest with important material contents (lines 906ff.). For the episode in art from the 5th Century onward see *LIMC* in 'Art' above.

Note

[1] Probably the play explained the presence of satyrs on the island, just as *Cyclops* 11–22 explains their presence on Sicily; in many plays they are found near sea-coasts (*e.g.* in both those plays and in Aeschylus' *Glaucus the Sea-god*: see Voelke (2001) 37–44).

F **46a (PSI 1209 fr.a)

On the shore of Seriphos; either Dictys or Silenus has seen the chest in the water but not yet identified it.

\<A\>	You get my meaning? ...
\<B\>	I get it ...
\<A\>	What do you want me to watch out for? ...
\<B\>	In case somewhere on the sea ...
\<A\>	No sign of anything! The sea (is) smooth ... (5)
\<B\>	Then have a look into the (crevices) ...
\<A\>	You can see that I'm looking ... this ... Hey! What should I call this? ... a whale? or a hammerhead shark? or ...? Lord Poseidon, and Zeus ruler of the (deep),[2] (10) ... (you're?) sending this up

[2] or '... Poseidon, Zeus of the deep' (Diggle); Pausanias 2.24.4 apparently refers to our v. 10 for Aeschylus calling Poseidon 'Zeus of the sea'.

[δ]ῶρον θαλάσσης πέμπετ[
..σοι θαλάσσης δίκτυον δ[
π]εφυκί{ω]ται δ' ὥστε μ' ἀγνο.[
......] ἔναιμον η[6 let.]εν[
.....].ε.ων νησαῖος ...[(15)
6 let.] ἐστι· τοὖργον οὐ χωρεῖ πρόσω.
..... β]οὴν ἵστημι τοῖσδ' ἰύγμασιν.
]πάντες γεωργοὶ δεῦτε κἀμπελοσκάφοι
]ε ποιμήν τ' εἴ τίς ἐστ[' ἐ]γχώριος
]οι τε καὶ μα[ριλ]ευτῶν ἔθνος   (20)
] ἐναντιωτάτης

13 in π]εφυκί[ω]ται the letters κιωτ are insecurely read; μ' ἀγνοε[ῖν Radt
14] ἔναιμον η[Pfeiffer:]εναιμονη[PSI, α insecure
15] γέρων νησαῖος Norsa-Vitelli
18–21 metre uncertain
20 μα[ριλ]ευτῶν Snell: μα[ρ]{ε}[ιλ]ευτων PSI, μα and second ε insecure

F **46b
centres of 12 lines, including
          1 ἄλγος, 2 Δίκτυν ο, 5 ὄμμα.[, 6 ποταιν[
          and 9 πρ]έσβυσ.[

PSI 1209 fr. b: see on F 46a

F **46c
3 badly defective lines, then:
          ].σδ[.] χώρας ποντ[ίας
          π]άντες τ' ἀγρῶσται κα[ὶ   (5)
          βοηδρομεῖτε κ[.]ν[
          σ]ε[ι]ρᾶς δὲ μὴ μεθῆ[σθε
          traces of one further line

P. Oxy. 2256 (2nd–3rd c. AD) ed. E. Lobel (1952) fr. 72; 8 badly damaged lines, written almost certainly by the same scribe as in F 47a (P. Oxy. 2161)

F 47
          δικτύου δ' εὐήτρια

Pollux 7.35

as a gift of the sea ... (your?) net ... of the sea and it's covered in seaweed so that I (don't recognise) ... with living blood in it ... of the island (?)³ ... (15) ... is ... This business isn't making progress! ... I'll start shouting with these cries for help! ... all you farmers and vine-diggers everywhere, come here! ... and if there's any shepherd in the place (20) ... and you folk who (burn charcoal)⁴ ... of the opposite-facing ...

---

³ 'old man of the island' Norsa-Vitelli, variously identified as the speaker himself (Dictys rather than Silenus), or by Pfeiffer as 'The Old Man of the Sea' (Proteus) in allusion.
⁴ For such rural folk in satyr plays cf. *e.g.* Soph. *Trackers* F 314.38–40 whose beginning resembles *Net-Fishers* here with the satyrs being summoned to engage in a shared task.

Some editors suspect a change of metre in 18 to trochaic tetrameters, others to iambic tetrameters.

F **46b (PSI 1209 fr. b)
centres of 12 lines, perhaps a further part of this scene, containing in 1 *the word* pain, *in* 2 *the name* Dictys, *in* 5 *a form of the word* eye *and in* 6 *of* unheard of, *and in* 9 *the word* old sir

F **46c (P. Oxy. 2256 fr. 72)
8 badly damaged lines, possibly also from this scene; 4–7 have:
... of the land by the sea ... all you countrymen and ... run and help ...! ... don't let go of the rope ...!⁵

---

⁵ Taplin (1977) 418 compares Ar. *Peace* 459ff. for a 'hauling-scene' (the goddess Peace is hauled out of her cave), but doubts whether there or in this much earlier scene of Aeschylus the theatrical wheeled trolley (*eccyclêma*) was used.

F 47 (Pollux 7.35)
... and a net's finely woven (mesh) ...

F **47a

col. i

<ΣΙΛΗΝΟΣ>	]..[.].αν καὶ θεοὺς μαρτύρομαι	(1) (765)
	].παντὶ κηρύσσω στρατῷ	
	] †πανταπασι† ἀποφθάρῃς	
	].ουσα πρόξενόν θ' ἅμα	
	]..ου με καὶ προπράκτορα	(5) (769)
	].ε μαῖαν ὡς γερασμίαν	
	].. ἠπίοις προσφθέγμασιν	
	] *traces* ς ἐν χρόνῳ μενεῖ.	
<ΔΑΝΑΗ>	]... καὶ γενέθλιοι θεοί	
	]..ας τάσδε μοι πόνων τιθείς·	(10) (774)
	τ]οῖσδε κνωδάλοις με δώσετε	
	]...γοισι λυμανθήσομαι	
	αἰχ]μάλωτος οὖσ' οἴσω κακά.	
	].αιγουν ἀγχόνην ἄρ' ἄψομαι	
	]ας τεμοῦσα κωλυτήριον	(15) (779)
	]ως μὴ ποντίσῃ τις αὖ πάλιν	
	]της ἢ πατήρ· δέδοικα γάρ.	
	]πεμπ' ἀρωγόν, εἰ δοκεῖ, τινα.	
	]εῖχες αἰτίας τῆς μείζονος	
	]ν δὲ πᾶσαν ἐξέτεισ' ἐγὼ	(20) (784)
	]ευς ἔλεξα. πάντ' ἔχει[ς] λόγον.	

P. Oxy. 2161 (2nd c. AD) ed. E. Lobel (1941), cf. most recently Henry (2000). The papyrus was written almost certainly by the same hand as PSI 1209 = F 46a, b. P. Oxy. has the Greek line-number 800 against col. ii. 36. There are identical in-built 'stage-directions' πόππυσμός in 29 (insecurely read) = 39 (securely).

1–8 <ΣΙΛΗΝΟΣ> Siegmann; <ΔΙΚΤΥΣ> Lobel

3 πανταπασι: σι insecurely read; αποφθαρης read in P. Oxy. by Henry (...φθαρης, conjecturing <μὴ> ... πάντ' ἅπαστ' ἀποφθαρῇς: μὴ παντάπασι φθαρῇς Lobel)

4 ουσα: ου insecure

8 μενεῖ Lobel: μενει P. Oxy

10 τιθείς Setti: τιθεις P. Oxy.

11 τ]οῖσδε Murray: οισδ insecure

13 οἴσω read in P. Oxy. by Coles (reported by Henry): ο.σα.ω P. Oxy. eds., with only ω secure

16 ὅπ]ως Siegmann, ω insecure

18 πρό]πεμπ' Siegmann; perhaps ὦ Ζεῦ, πρό]πεμπ' Lobel, Krumeich

19 μετ]εῖχες Lobel

20 τὴν ζημία]ν Lobel: δίκη]ν Pfeiffer

F **47a (P. Oxy. 2161)

From later in the play, towards its end. Danae and Perseus have long been revealed. Silenus (?) is triumphant; both Danae and (probably also) Dictys have become fearful of the satyrs' intentions, and he has apparently abandoned the castaways to fetch help. Then Silenus (?) exploits the infant's innocent delight in his colourful stage-phallus, so as to win Danae as 'wife'; he assumes her sexual frustration.

<SILENUS?>   ... and I call upon the gods to witness ... I proclaim to all people ... (so that?) you (i.e. *Danae or Perseus*) (do not?) perish (from total starvation?)[6] ... me your sponsor ... as well as your protector[7] (5) ... like an elderly nurse ... with gentle words of address ... will remain over time.

<DANAE>   ... and gods of my ancestors ... (putting?) these ... of ordeals on me. (10) ... and you will give me to these brutes ... I shall be abused ... as a prisoner I shall endure ... evil. ... I shall ... in that case fasten up a noose[8] ... devising prevention ... (15) ... (so that?) no ... or my father may ever drown me again. For I'm afraid! ... send[9] someone to help, please, (Zeus)! ... you had (a share in?) the greater responsibility ... but I have paid the whole (penalty?) ... (20) ... I have spoken; you have my whole speech.[10]

---

[6] 'from total starvation': in this reading and supplement (Lobel, Henry) the Greek neuter accusative plurals are both adverbial.

[7] 'sponsor' is the Athenian term for a citizen officially sponsoring and looking after an incomer from another city-state (it occurs four times in Aesch. *Supp.*, *e.g.* 919); the Greek word 'protector' is found only here, and some translate it as 'avenger' to avoid tautology (*i.e.* to trace and punish whoever maltreated Danae and Perseus).

[8] 'noose': suicide seemingly unavoidable to despairing women, *e.g.* those of Aesch. *Suppliant Women* 788 (who like Danae face being forced into an undesirable union) and of Jocasta at Soph. *OT* 1263.

[9] With editors' supplements, '(O Zeus,) send (forward) someone ...', Danae appeals naturally for help to Zeus, who impregnated her with Perseus (see introductory discussion).

[10] 'I have spoken ... my whole speech': the surprisingly forensic tone of 19–20 'responsibility ... (penalty?)' is here reinforced by a formulaic speech-ending, for which in Tragedy cf. *e.g.* Aesch. *Ag.* 582.

<ΣΙΛ.?>　　　]. γελᾷ μου προσορῶν
　　　　　　　].. ὁ μικκὸς λιπαρὸν
　　　　　　　μ]ιλτ[ό]πρεπτον φαλακρὸν
　　　　　　　]ειε[.] πάππας τις ἀρεσ-　　　　　　　(25) (789)
　　　　　　　]ωσ[.]. ποικιλονω-

remnants of 8 lines (27–34), including
　　　　　　　29 (793) *πο]ππυσμός (stage-direction)*
　　　　　　　and 31 (795)] ποσθοφιλὴς ὁ νεοσσὸς

col. ii < – >　εἰ μή σε χαίρω .[　　　　　　　　　(35) (799)
　　　　＇　　　ὄλοιτο Δίκτυς κρ[
　　　　　　　τᾶσδέ μ᾽ ἄγρας μ[

–　　　　　　ὦ φίντων, ἴθι δε[ῦρο·　　　　　　　　στρ.
between 802 and 804 ποππυσμός (stage-direction)
　　　　　　　θάρσει δή· τί κινύρῃ;　　　　　　　　(40) (804)
　　　　　　　δεῦρ᾽ ἐς παῖδας ἴωμεν ωσ.[
　　　　　　　ἵξῃ παιδοτρόφους ἐμά[ς,
　　　　　　　ὦ φίλος, χέρας εὐμενεῖς,
　　　　　　　τέρψῃ δ᾽ ἴκτισι κα[ὶ] νεβρο[ῖς
　　　　　　　ὑστρίχων τ᾽ ὀβρίχοισ[ι]　　　　　　(45) (809)
　　　　　　　κοιμάσῃ δὲ τρίτος ξὺν
　　　　　　　ματρὶ [καὶ π]ατρὶ τῷδε.

–　　　　　　ὁ πάππα[ς δ]ὲ παρέξει　　　　　　　ἀντ.
　　　　　　　τῷ μικκῷ τὰ γελ[οῖ]α
　　　　　　　καὶ τροφὰς ἀνόσους, ὅπως π[　　　(50) (814)
　　　　　　　ἀλδὼν αὐτὸς *traces*
　　　　　　　χαλᾷ νεβροφόνο[υ] ποδ[ὸς
　　　　　　　μάρπτων θῆρας ἄνευ δ[
　　　　　　　θῶσθαι μητρὶ παρέξεις

22–56 are variously distributed between Silenus, Chorus and/or Dictys by eds: P. Oxy. marks
voice-parts at 22, 38 (Henry), and 48; 22–56 Silenus, Siegmann; 22–34 Chorus, Lobel; 35–
56 Silenus, Lloyd-Jones: Chorus, Harrison: Dictys, Lobel
25 and 48 πάππας Diggle: παπας P. Oxy.
25–6 ἀρέσ- | κει Fraenkel
41 ὡς τ[άχιστα Fraenkel
43 εὐμενεῖς Setti: -ης P. Oxy.
52 νεβροφόνο[υ] Lloyd-Jones; ποδ[ὸς Lobel
54 θῶσθαι glossed by Hesychius θ 1024 Latte with θοινᾶσθαι, naming the play

<SIL.?>   (*singing*)[11] ... the little one is smiling as he looks at my bright-red
                 knob[12] ... some papa (is pleasing?)[13] ... (25) ... dapple-backed[14] ...
                 (*Silenus makes a clucking sound*) ... (30) ... the youngster loves a
                 little prick[15] ... If I don't rejoice in ... you ... (35) death to Dictys!
                 ... me of my catch here ...
(*change of voice-part? Strophe*)   O my little darling, come (here). (*Silenus makes
                 a clucking sound*) Be brave! Why are you grizzling? (40) Let's
                 go over here to my boys, (so?) you can come (at once?) to my
                 nurturing, kindly arms, my dear, and delight in martens and fawns
                 and baby porcupines[16] (45), and make three in a bed with your
                 mother and father here.
(*change of voice-part? Antistrophe*)   And papa will give the little one lots of fun
                 and healthy nourishment, so that (50) when you're grown up
                 yourself ... on hoofed foot that kills fawns you'll seize hold of
                 wild beasts without ... and provide your mother with feasts like

[11]   Silenus (?) appears to pick the baby up and dandle it (cf. 6); for satyrs elsewhere caring
for infants, see *e.g. Cyc.* 142; *Adespota* F 646a.7–12 below; Soph. *Little Dionysus* F 171;
Little Heracles F **223a, F 223b.
The voice parts of 22–68 cannot be securely established, nor the lyric metres of 22–34. 22–7
with their lyric teasing of the baby seem appropriate to Silenus as an individual. If Fraenkel
(1942) was right to identify 28–34 as anapaestic, the Chorus may well have uttered them;
Silenus would follow with 35–47, in which he alone might curse Dictys, 36; 'boys', 41, is
his frequent reference to the satyrs as a body; and the tone of 46–7 suits his leering style.
P. Oxy.'s voice-change at 48 suggests that the Chorus sang the antistrophe 48–56; if so, the
anapaests of 57–68 may begin from the Chorus, with Silenus voicing 63–8 (P. Oxy. marks
a voice-part at 63), again aptly to his prurience. The Greek metrical form shows that the
anapaests do not end at 68.
[12]   'knob': the word's commoner sense is 'bald head', *e.g. Cyc.* 227; but 'erection' is
confirmed by the explicit language of 31, cf. 66; similarly Soph. *Trackers* F 314.368 (see
our notes there) and Ar. *Clouds* 537–42 (Voelke (2001) 213, W. Slenders in Harrison (2005)
45–6, cf. *Mnem* 45 (1992) 155–8, and Kaimio (2001) 54 n. 72); an ambiguity at Soph. *Little
Dionysus* F 171.2–3 '(the baby Dionysus) brings his hand up to my ...' (that of Silenus).
[13]   'is pleasing', Fraenkel, *i.e.* to the baby.
[14]   'dapple-backed': theatrical (and artists') satyrs conventionally wore fawn-skins: cf. 44,
52 and Soph. *Trackers* F 314.225.
[15]   'little prick', a joke: Silenus' large theatrical phallus is meant: see n. 12 above.
[16]   As pets presumably, until the boy is mature enough to hunt for food-animals, 50–6.

κ]ηδεστῶν τρόπον οἷσιν   (55) (819)
ξύ]ντροφος πελατεύσεις.

< – ?>   ἀλλ᾿] εἶα, φίλοι, στείχωμεν ὅπως
γά]μον ὁρμαίνωμεν, ἐπεὶ τέλεος
καιρὸς ἄναυδος τάδ᾿ ἐπαινεῖ.
καὶ τήνδ᾿ [ἐ]σορῶ νύμφην ἤδη   (60) (824)
πάνυ βουλομένην τῆς ἡμετέρας
φιλότητος ἄδην κορέσασθαι.
< – ?>   καὶ θαῦμ᾿ οὐδέν· πολὺς ἦν αὐτῇ
χρόνος ὃν χήρα κατὰ ναῦν ὕφαλος
τείρετο· νῦν δ᾿ οὖν   (65) (829)
ἐ]σορῶσ᾿ ἥβην τὴν ἡμετέραν
...]ει γάνυται νυμφίον [ο]ῖον
...]σιν λαμπραῖς τῆς Ἀ[φ]ροδίτης ...

56 ξύ]ντροφος Henry (ἔ]ντροφος Harrison):]ντροπος P. Oxy.
57–68 (at 57 the metre changes from lyric to anapaestic, the latter suggesting the satyrs' readiness to march off in a body) are variously distributed between Chorus and Silenus by editors; in 63 P. Oxy. was thought to mark a voice-change: denied by Henry
67 νυμφιον read in P. Oxy. by Henry, with ιο insecure
68 χάρι]σιν Diggle

F **47b
scrappy centres of 9 lines in which the following words are clear:
     1]Σέριφον [*and* 4]παιδα καὶ γέρ[οντ
P. Oxy. 2255 ed. E. Lobel (1952) fr. 21

F **47c
     6 very damaged lines, with no significant word secure
P. Oxy 2255 fr. 20

your kinsmen, (55) whom you'll approach as a foster-brother.[17]

(*change of voice-part?*)   (But) come on now, my dears, let's all move off so we get the marriage going, since the moment for the rite commands (it) without speaking,[18] and I already see my bride here (60) absolutely wanting her fill and more or my love.[19]

(*change of voice-part?*)   And no wonder! She had a long time on the water in her ship without a man, fretting away; but now (65) she's looking at my manhood[20] ... she's happy with a groom such as ... in the brilliant (delights?) of Aphrodite ...

[17] 'on hoofed foot that kills fawns *etc.*': the text is too damaged for a secure translation; the idea may be that the adult Perseus will run as fast as horse-footed satyrs (as earlier Greek art usually depicted them: see Gen. Intro. p. 7). For fawns as source of satyrs' food and skins to wear cf. Eur. *Sciron* F 677 and n. 4. Note the slide from the baby as third person (49) into second (51–6).

[18] 'without speaking': a favourite Aeschylean trope, *e.g.* of a portrait *Sacred Delegates* F 78a.20; of stirred-up dust presaging a messenger *Seven* 82, *Suppliants* 180.

[19] An opportunity for stage-business: Silenus brandishes his 'manhood' (66: next n.; cf. 24 with n. 12), despite Danae's revulsion (60, cf. 11–12). His assumption of Danae's sexual readiness is taken to more prurient levels in the satyrs' view of Helen as some sort of nymphomaniac, *Cyc.* 179–81.

[20] Silenus brags of his sexual prowess and supposed desirability at Soph. *Trackers* F 314.154–5; if he is the speaker here (see n. 11), the incongruity of his claim to youthfulness would be emphasized through his padded costume and white hair (for the latter see n. 4 on *Glaucus* F 25d). 'manhood': the abstract noun 'youthful prime' is here concrete in sense, as notably at Ar. *Clouds* 976, of the imprint in sand of a seated youth's genitals.

F **47b (P. Oxy. 2255 fr. 21)

scrappy centres of 9 lines in which the following words are clear:
1 Seriphos, 4 child and old man

F **47c (P. Oxy. 2255 fr. 20)

letters and traces from 6 lines in which no significant word is secure

Sacred Delegates or Isthmian Contestants
(ΘΕΩΡΟΙ Η ΙΣΘΜΙΑΣΤΑΙ, Theori vel Isthmiastae)

TrGF 3.194–205 (F **78a–82), cf. 4².784–5.

Texts etc. Lloyd-Jones (1957) 541–56; W. Luppe, *Göttingische Gelehrte Anzeigen* 239 (1987) 32–4; Diggle (1998) 11–15 (F 78a, c); A. Wessels, R. Krumeich in KPS 131–48; W. B. Henry, R. Nünlist, *ZPE* 129 (2000) 14–16; W. B. Henry, *ZPE* 134 (2001) 12 (F 78c.41–53); Sommerstein (2008) 82–99.

Discussions. M. Untersteiner, 'Ι Θέωροι ἢ 'Ισθμιασταί', *Dioniso* 14 (1951) 19–33, 38–43; Chourmouziades (1974) 50–8, 69–71, 77–8, 194–8; Taplin (1977) 420–2; Sutton (1980) 29–35; Gallo (1992) 54–78; M. di Marco, 'Studi sul dramma satiresco di Eschilo I: Θέωροι ἢ 'Ισθμιασταί', *Helikon* 9/10 (1969/70) 373–422 and 'Sul finale dei 'Theoroi' di Eschilo', *Eikasmos* 3 (1992) 93–104; Morris (1992) 217–21; Green (1994) 45–6; W. Slenders, 'Intentional ambiguity in Aeschylean satyr plays', *Mnem* 45 (1992) 145–58, at 146–53; M. Stieber, 'Aeschylus' *Theoroi* and Realism in Greek Art', *TAPA* 124 (1994) 85–119, esp. 85–94; Y. Kawasaki, 'Aeschylus fr. 78a Radt', *Japanese Classical Studies* 43 (1995) 1–11 (résumé in *Forty Years of the Journal of Classical Studies* (Tokyo, 1998) 347–8); A. Melero, 'Notas a Los *Teoros* de Esquilo', in J.-A. López Férez (ed.), *De Homero a Libanio. Estudios actuales sobre textos griegos. II* (Madrid, 1995) 57–71; Conrad (1997) 56–86, 251–62; R. Krumeich, 'Die Weihgeschenke der Satyren in Aischylos' "Theoroi oder Isthmiastai" ', *Philologus* 144 (2000) 176–92; Kaimio (2001) 56–8, 60–2; P. O'Sullivan, 'Satyr and Image in Aeschylus' *Theoroi*', *CQ* 50 (2000) 353–66; D. Steiner, *Images in Mind. Statues in Archaic and Classical Literature and Thought* (Princeton, 2001) 45–50; Voelke (2001) 77–82, 283–8; C. Marconi, 'I *Theoroi* di Eschilo e le antefisse sileniche siceliote', *Sicilia Antiqua* 2 (2005) 75–93 (large bibl.); A. J. Podlecki in Harrison (2005) 13–14; D. Wiles, *Masks and Performance in Greek Tragedy* (Cambridge, 2007) 205–12; Sommerstein (2010) 238–9; D. M. Pritchard, 'Athletics in Satyric Drama', *G&R* 59 (2012) 1–16, esp. 10–11.

The alternative titles go back to late antiquity. Although accurate to the real and would-be roles of the satyrs in the play, the 'or' may reflect an ancient doubt, since both titles occur individually (see *TrGF* 3.58, on T 78.c6); but Gallo (1992) 68–9 suggests that there may have been another play titled simply 'Sacred Delegates'.[1] The papyrus fragments confirmed previous inference that the play was satyric from these titles alone and from three small lexicographic fragments: F 79 'old owl-dances', in which the dancers peered round like owls, from beneath raised hands (Kaimio (2001) 45); F 81 '*iambis*', apparently the name of a lively lyric form; F 82 'dirt and filth' (note also the colloquialism 'shower' at F 78a.71). The papyri also confirmed that the action was indeed set at the Isthmian Games (F 78a.30, 34; c.39, 58), and that a contrast of athletics with dancing (F 78a.33–6, 78.c.38–40) was a principal motif: see Melero (1995) 58, KPS 146–7.

The papyrus fragments are presumed to stand near the play's beginning. The satyrs have come to the Games, and to compete (F 78a.30 *etc.*, just cited), not primarily as sacred delegates or even simple spectators. As would-be contestants they have brought votive gifts to nail up in the regular way in Poseidon's Isthmian temple, hoping for the god's favour (F 78a.5–22); these are likenesses of themselves so realistic that they lack only a voice and would amaze their own mothers (13–17). The satyrs are however at once thwarted by their master Dionysus, from whom they have fled (F 78c.10), but who has pursued them (78a.23–7) and mocks their aspirations as athletes (29–36). The first column of F 78a ends here, but it seems certain from the matching of papyrus-fibres[2] that what had been thought to be the residual first column of F 78c in fact belongs to the now missing top of the second column of F 78a, as set out in the texts below. Together F 78c.1–6 and F 78a.61–72 reveal an altercation between satyrs and Dionysus: he appears to accuse them of breaking their oath of allegiance to him (78c.1 and note), but they complain of the harsh living which his service brings them (78c.5–7). He grows angry at their abuse of him for his unmanliness (F 78a.65–72: see n. 18 below). Then the second column of F 78c looks to continue this altercation, possibly at once: he rebukes the satyrs' abandonment of dancing, their proper activity in his service (78 c.37–40); he promises, they will suffer for it (41). When the satyrs refuse to leave Poseidon's temple (43–8), they are offered 'novel playthings' freshly made by a metal-smith (49–52); they reject them (53; see (2) below). The text then collapses into incoherence, and breaks off, but presumably the play proceeded through appropriate 'stage-business' to the satyrs' final reconciliation with – or submission to – Dionysus. Conrad (1997) 83–4 well observes that Dionysus must 'win' in the end, as in any satyr-play, because he 'needs' the satyrs, just as elsewhere the satyrs clearly need *him* (cf. *Cyc.* 73–81, 620–3 *etc.*); and even if they are rebellious, he will therefore show them mercy.

The fragments are colourful and suggestive, but leave many aspects of the play unclear, especially:

(1) The presence of the satyrs at the Isthmian Games is perhaps Aeschylus' invention, like their introduction by Sophocles in *Trackers* into the established mythology of Hermes and the invention of the lyre (see our introductory discussion); but 'athletic' satyrs had appeared perhaps earlier in Pratinas' *Wrestlers*, *TrGF* 1².81 (see our Appendix), and later appeared in Achaeus' *The Games*, 20 F 3–5 (below; cf. Euripides' *Autolycus A* F 282 which contains a lengthy denunciation of athletes, below). For satyrs and athletics, or satyrs as 'athletes', see Voelke (2001) 261–72, including representations in art (270 n. 29). Why the *Isthmian* Games, however? Gallo (1992) 63–8 considers at length the idea that the satyrs are shown abandoning their allegiance to Dionysus to serve another god, Poseidon, the deity *par excellence* of the Corinthian Isthmus, its temple and the Games (F 78a.22, 47; Xenophon, *Hellenica* 4.5.1–2; KPS 145). Kawasaki (1995), who supports a role in the play for Theseus, suggests that they came to the Isthmus directly after Theseus had freed them from slavery to the nearby ogre Sinis (or to Sciron: see Euripides' play, below); these two were dangers for travellers on the coastal road between Athens and Corinth.

(2) There may have been no very distinct individual role for Silenus (despite his possible lines at the truncated F 78c. col. ii.53ff.), only his common function as mouthpiece for the chorus (see Conrad (1997) 79–82) – but were there characters additional to Dionysus? A person unidentifiable from the surviving text is thanked for his help by the satyrs in F 78a.1–2: some have suggested that this may have been Sisyphus king of Corinth, that he was presented in the play as founder of the Isthmian Games (as recorded later by *e.g.* Pausanias 2.1.3), and that he may have returned in F 78c.49–62 to enforce the satyrs' compliance with 'the rules': so *e.g.* KPS 140 n. 40 (Sisyphus was a sly character well at home in satyric: see his Aeschylean name-play, below, and on Euripides, *Autolycus A* and *B*). Others, *e.g.* Kawasaki ((1) above), identify this person, again at both places, as Theseus king of Athens, for whom there is also a little supporting evidence in later mythography as founder of the Isthmian games (*e.g.* Plutarch, *Theseus* 11e) – for Theseus was in some myths a son of Poseidon, their patron-god. Most editors however judge the threatening tone of F 78c.49–62 much more apt for Dionysus (most recently Conrad (1997) 78–9; cf. Taplin (1977) 421–2 and Diggle (1998) 14); it is consistent with his anger in F 78a; the near-certain papyrological continuity from F 78a col. i into F 78c col. ii is a strong indication (see above). It would be surprising, however, if there were no further new character in the play, and at the least it seems likely that the

person speaking when F 78a begins would return to the action (see also (3) following). Marconi (2005) 77 views the identification of this person as an insoluble problem.

(3) What are the 'playthings' newly made from a smith's anvil, and therefore of metal (although an 'adze' is strictly a carpenter's tool), which the speaker of F 78c.49–51 'offers' to the satyrs, when they refuse to leave Poseidon's temple? If Dionysus is not the speaker, but *e.g.* Sisyphus or Theseus is ((2) above), then they would seem to be inducements to compete, 'toy' or even real javelins (Snell in a 1953 review of P. Oxy. 2162; Sutton (1980) 31–2; Melero (1995) 58; Pritchard (2012) 10, citing B. Seidensticker in Csapo and Miller (2003) 120) or 'toy' chariots (so, most recently, Kawasaki (1995), observing that some of the scholia on Ar. *Clouds* 28 attribute the invention of war-chariots to Theseus). Theseus appeared in another Aeschylean satyr play as an athletic hero (*Cercyon*: see our Appendix), who defeated the eponymous ogre in a wrestling match; does he urge the satyrs to take up athletics in *Sacred Delegates*? Lloyd-Jones (1957) 547–9 tentatively suggested Hephaestus, the artificer-god, as the maker of the playthings and as the speaker here (also as the unidentified speaker of F 78a.1–2: see (1) above); he thought of an episode related to the 'Return of Hephaestus', which Dionysus forced upon him (see Achaeus, *Hephaestus* F 16b, 18 below). If Dionysus is speaking, then the 'playthings' are probably fetters, threats real enough but disguised with ironic slyness (most recently Conrad (1997) 78 n. 219); note 'ankles' at the very end of F 78c, and see n. 26 on v. 54. Insofar as this wretchedly curtailed fragment permits interpretation, its wording suggests repression rather than encouragement (see esp. v. 41); and then the scene will begin to develop the satyrs' defiance (43–8) into the familiar motif of bravado collapsing into cowardice: KPS 140 n. 40, 148 (who nevertheless holds the threatening speaker to be Sisyphus).[3] Lämmle (2007) 354 observes that our play represents an extreme example in satyric drama of the tension between Dionysus' (usual) absence and presence: the satyrs' defiance prompts one of the god's few known stage-appearances in the genre.

(4) Dionysus' suppression of the satyrs raises a difficult question: what is this uncompromising behaviour of the god doing in a play-genre conventionally giving light relief to preceding tragedies? Is it nevertheless intended as a foil to tragedy's quite frequent depiction of this god as a ruthless destroyer of his human opponents? – such as in Aeschylus' Lycurgus-tetralogy, and in his separate Dionysus-tragedies *Bacchae*, *Xantriae* ('*Women Who Rend*', *i.e.* rend Pentheus), and *Pentheus* itself.

(5) Much recent opinion identifies the satyrs' votive gifts to Poseidon's temple as small tablets of wood or clay painted in their own likeness (F 78a.1, 6, 12): see KPS 142–4. Krumeich (2000) shows that such antefixes in front, or on the roof, of temples were apotropaic, menacing to rival contestants ('you're going to have to beat *me*').[4] Other interpretations, interdependent with those of statuary described at Aeschylus, *Agamemnon* 414–19 (the blank-eyed images of Helen), are that the votives are life-like statuettes (see Stieber (1994) 85–94; Steiner (2001)) or masks *e.g.* Green (1994), O'Sullivan (2000), Kaimio (2001), Wiles (2007) and, to our mind conclusively, Marconi (2005) 77–9, who also contends that on his visits to Sicily Aeschylus would have seen many satyrs in archaic temple-ornamentation and antefixes (81–91). Whatever their nature, the passage F 78a.5–17 has stirred great interest for its bearing on 'vividness' in the contemporary arts, for example when Aeschylus describes Iphigenia at her sacrifice and compares her eye-catching prominence in a painting (*Agamemnon* 242; O'Sullivan (2008)): see Stieber (1994) and O'Sullivan (2000), the latter arguing that Aeschylus offers 'a comically overdetermined response to (the satyrs') painted depictions' (p. 359), whereby the satyrs play games with the images' perceived powers to deceive and frighten onlookers; on contemporary aesthetic reactions see further Marconi (2005) 79–80. The first part of the play, then, involved a comic encounter with a cultural artefact, like that with fire in Aeschylus, *Prometheus the Fire-Kindler* or with lyre-music in Sophocles' *Trackers*.

F **78a

col. i   ὁρῶντες εἰκού[ς] οὐ κατ' ἀνθρώπους [
              ὅπῃ δ' ἂν ἔ[ρ]δῃς, πάντα σοι τάδ' εὐσεβῆ.
<XOPOΣ>   ἦ κάρτ' ὀφείλω τῶνδέ σοι· πρόφρων γὰρ εἶ.

P. Oxy. 2162 (2nd c. AD) ed. E. Lobel (1941) fr. 1(a) col. i
1–2 speaker unidentified
3–22 possibly three separate voices from the Chorus (Steffen)

Notes

[1] The translation of Greek *theoroi* as 'sacred delegates' (*the-* is 'divine') in the play-title is generally adopted, most recently by KPS and Sommerstein (2008); it rests chiefly upon referring Dionysus' incomplete words in F 78a col. ii.72 'for which I am gathering ...' to his intention that the satyrs should join the dancing at the Isthmian festival in his honour, and to his anger that they have exchanged practice for dancing with practice for athletic competition, F 78 a col. 1 33–4, 78c col. ii.37–40. Translation as 'spectators' is equally possible, however (see *e.g.* Lloyd-Jones (1957) 543, cf. Kaimio (2001) 60–2); it suits no less well the contrast with 'contestants' in the same latter two passages, and would go well with the satyrs' pretension to compete which is implicit in the portraits they first hang up in Poseidon's temple, F 78a col. 1–21 (see (5) above). The translation of the alternative title as *Isthmian Contestants*, rather than *Attenders of the Isthmian Games*, seems certain on the basis of these same passages. There is a similar difficulty in the wording of Achaeus, *The Games* F 3 'Do you mean (*to*?) spectators or competitors?

[2] So Henry and Nünlist (2000) 14–15, who also judge, again on papyrological grounds, that F 78c col. i offers iambic trimeters like F 78a col. ii, and not tetrameters as earlier editors had suggested. These difficulties had been most recently reviewed in KPS 146–8.

[3] These 'toys' (52) are unlikely to be *thyrsi*, the cut and wreathed wands emblematic of Dionysus' fertility, or metallic instruments of his worship, rattles, cymbals and the like (Voelke (2001) 103–11), which the satyrs have abandoned or ruined, F 78a.35–6. The latter were the 'toys' with which the infant Dionysus was lured and tricked to destruction: for the mythological tradition see M.L. West, *The Orphic Poems* (Oxford, 1983) 68–75, at 74, and O. Levaniouk, 'The Toys of Dionysus', *HSCP* 103 (2007) 165–202.

Slenders (1992) 151–3 suggests that 'toys', 'playthings' (50) and 'omen' (54, lit. 'bird', sometimes 'female genitals') may all have sexual allusion, and that Dionysus is tempting the satyrs in this way – but would satyrs resist such temptation (see 53 and 57)? Cf. nn. 10 and 14 below.

[4] See F 78a.21. The votives had first been identified as antefixes by E. Fraenkel, *PBA* 28 (1942) 245.

The play is set outside the temple of Poseidon (F 78a. col. i 18) at the Isthmus of Corinth, the site of the Games; the first fragment begins when the satyrs are finishing their thanks to an unidentified person for guidance how delegates or contestants (see n. 1 above) should hang up their votive gifts with due and ritual reverence (F 78a. col. i 2, 11–12, 19–22).

F **78a (P. Oxy. 2162 fr. 1(a) col. i)

< – > ... when they see portraits unlike men('s?) ... But however you act, all you do here (*will be*) in reverence.

<CHORUS> I'm truly much in your debt for this:[5] you've shown me favour!

[5] 'for this': a regular Greek causative genitive, Smyth § 1373a.

ἄκουε δὴ πᾶς, σῖγα δειθελειδ.[.].
    ἄθρησον εἰ.[..].[(5)
εἴδωλον εἶναι τοῦτ' ἐμῇ μορφῇ πλέον·
τὸ Δαιδάλου μ[ί]μημα· φωνῆς δεῖ μόνον.
two lines with only a few letters
    χώρει μάλα.   (10)
–   εὐκταῖα κόσμον ταῦτ[α] τῷ θεῷ φέρω,
    καλλίγραπτον εὐχάν.
< – >   τῇ μητρὶ τἠμῇ πράγματ' ἂν παρασχέθοι·
{ – }   ἰδοῦσα γάρ νιν ἂν σαφῶς
    τρέποιτ' ἂν αἰάζοιτό θ' ὡς   (15)
    δοκοῦσ' ἔμ' εἶναι, τὸν ἐξ-
         έθρεψεν· οὕτως ἐμφερὴς ὅδ' ἐστίν.

εἶα δὴ σκοπεῖτε δῶμα ποντίου σεισίχθο[νος
κἀπιπασσάλευ' ἕκαστος τῆς κ[α]λῆς μορφῆς .[
ἄγγελον, κήρυκ' [ἄ]ναυδον, ἐμπόρων κωλύτορ[α,   (20)
ὅ[ς γ'] ἐπισχήσει κελεύθου τοὺς ξένο[υς] φ.[
χαῖρ' ἄναξ, χαῖρ' ὦ Πόσειδον ἐπίτροπο[ς .]..[
<ΔΙΟΝΥΣΟΣ?>ἔμελλον εὑρήσειν ἄρ' ὑμᾶς, ὠγαθο[ί.
    οὐ τοῦτ' ἐρῶ σ'· 'οὐ δῆλος ἦσθ' ὁδοιπο[ρῶν·'
    αὐ[τὴ] κέλευθος ταῦτά μοι προσεν[(25)
    .....] ὁρῶντα τούσδε πλησ[ι]οσφ[
    .....].αυτα καὶ σαφῶς ἡγεῖτό μο[ι

4, 6 punct. Setti, 7 Fraenkel
4 δειθελειδ: δ, θελ and δ insecurely read in P. Oxy.
6 τοῦδ' Fraenkel
7 φωνῆς: ων insecure
10 χώρει Fraenkel: χωρει P. Oxy.: χωρεῖ Lobel
13 < – > and 14 { – } Lobel
14 νιν: ιν insecure
15 ἂν αἰάζοιτό Page: αξιαζοιτο P. Oxy.
19 end σ[αφῆ Page
20 ἐμπόρων Fraenkel, Dodds: εμπορον P. Oxy.
21 ὅ[ς] γ': o and γ insecure
23–36 <ΔΙΟΝΥΣΟΣ?> Murray
24 punct. Lloyd-Jones
25 προσεν[νέπει Lobel: προσεν[πεδοῦ (*i.e.* προσεμ[) Diggle
26].ρωντα P. Oxy.
27 αὐτὰ Lobel: ταῦτα Setti

(the unidentified speaker leaves and the satyrs address one another excitedly, mixing song and speech) Listen now, everyone, in silence ... *(lyric begins)* observe whether ... this image (5) is more *(like)* my own *(form)*.[6] It's a likeness by Daedalus![7] It lacks only a voice; *(two fragmentary lines)*. Come! Come on! (10)

— I'm bringing these prayerful gifts to the god to glorify him, a beautifully-painted votive!

< – > It would give my mother a hard time! If she saw it she'd turn and wail for certain, (15) thinking it's me, the son she raised – this one is so like me!

(speaking) Hey, all of you! Look at the house of the Earth-Shaker, the Ruler of the Sea,[8] and each of you nail up a (clear?) messenger of your beautiful form, a voiceless herald, one to keep away travellers (20), (which'll?) stop strangers on their way forward ... Hail, lord, hail, O Poseidon, protector ...

Dionysus (?) enters abruptly.

<DIONYSUS?> I was likely to find you in fact, my good men! I won't say this of you: 'You weren't obviously travelling.' Your journey itself (tells?) me this (25)[9] ... (seeing?) these ... (nearby ?) ... and led me clearly *(one fragmentary line)* when I saw your (little phalluses?),

[6] 6–7 'whether this image (seems to some degree) to be more ...' Kamerbeek. '*(like)*' completes apt sense, but the Greek expression hardly allows such a translation; the text is therefore insecure, but no convincing improvement has been found. It is possible that vv. 6–7 are spoken amid the lyric.

[7] Daedalus, the mythical constructor of figures that either did move or seemed to move, see and speak: see Eur. *Eurystheus* F 372 and n. 2.

[8] Poseidon: patron god of the Isthmian Games (F 78c.46–7); the temple (44) is his.
   The Chorus in 18–22 speak in lively trochaic tetrameters; cf. Aesch. *Sisyphus* F 227 n. 5.

[9] 'You weren't obviously travelling': taken to be, or to allude to, a colloquial saying. After Dionysus' address of his 'good men' (23) the rest of his speech is addressed to Silenus alone.
   23 at its end shows satyric breaking of 'Porson's Law': see on Aesch. *Glaucus the Sea-God* F 26, n. 6.
   In 25 Lobel's supplement means 'speaks this to me' and Diggle's '(confirms) this for me'.

6 *let.*].τα.δω[.]μη.[.]δωι πατ[
ὁρῶν μύουρα καὶ βραχέα τὰ φ[αλλί]α
ὡς ἐξέτριβες Ἰσθμιαστικὴν [....]ν   (30)
κοὐκ ἠμέλησας, ἀλλ᾽ ἐγυμνάζ[ου κα]λῶς.
εἰ δ᾽ οὖν ἐσῴζου τὴν πάλαι παρο[ιμία]ν,
τοὔρχημα μᾶλλον εἰκὸς ἦν σε.[.....]ειν.
σὺ δ᾽ ἰσθμιάζεις καὶ τρόπους και[νοὺς μ]αθὼν
βραχίο[ν᾽ ἀ]σκεῖς, χρήματα φθείρων ἐμὰ   (35)
κτέα[να 6–7 *let.*]ε ταῦτ᾽ ἐπηράνω πονων.

28 mid μη insecure
29 beg ορων insecure in P. Oxy.; end Maas, Reinhardt: θ[rather than φ[or π[read by Henry and Nünlist
30 [τριβὴ]ν Lloyd-Jones: [κόνι]ν Fraenkel
33 σ᾽ ἐπ[ισκοπ]εῖν Snell
36 κτέα[να Kamerbeek; ἐπηράνω πόνων conj. Lobel, who read επκρ- in P. Oxy., κ insecurely: επηρ- 'can now be seen in P. Oxy.' Henry and Nünlist

short as mouse-tails, as you trained for the Isthmian ...;[10] (30) and you weren't slack but exercising well. Now if you'd observed the old saying,[11] you'd likely be ... your dancing more.[12] But here you are, an Isthmian contestant, and you've learned novel ways to be training your arms,[13] wasting my money (35)[14] ... (*and*?) my possessions here when I'm a helper in your labours.[15]

[10] '(little phalluses)' is not a certain supplement (see the *apparatus*), but 'mouse-tails' make a clear reference to the way in which athletes tied up their foreskins, and thus jokingly belittles the over-large phalluses worn by stage-satyrs (cf. *e.g. Net-Fishers* F 47a.66, cf. 24?, 31?). Slenders (1992) 146–51 finds sexual allusions here in 'trained', 'Isthmian' and 'learning novel ways': 'Isthmus' can connote the female genitals. This, too, suggests a possible *double entendre* for how they have been 'training their arms'; and 'little phalluses' might comically explain why these normally large, ithyphallic 'organs' are now tapering like mouse-tails. See also nn. 3 above and 14 below.

In 30 'trained (hard?)' would translate Lloyd-Jones's supplement; Fraenkel's 'you trained (in) the Isthmian (dust)' would add a little colour.

[11] 'the old saying': something like 'keep to what you know' (Ar. *Wasps* 1431).

[12] In vase-paintings satyrs are most frequently depicted dancing vigorously to honour Dionysus: cf. *e.g.* F 78c.38 below; Soph. *Trackers* F 314.223–8; *Cyc.* 156; Kaimio (2001) 38–45; Voelke (2001) 131–82 and plates, with bibl. Snell's supplement gives 'You'd likely be (attending to) your dancing.'

[13] *E.g.* in wrestling, rather than in brandishing Dionysus' emblems (next n.) or, more likely, lifting wine-cups to drink (*Cyc.* 152): cf. the evocation of athletes' powerful arms and torsos at Achaeus, *The Games* F 4, below.

[14] Text and translation insecure. Our translation 'wasting my money' may suggest that the satyrs, given the likely sexual allusions in 29–30 (n. 10 above), have been overindulging themselves with the prostitutes for which Corinth at the Isthmus was famous: see Pindar F 122 (Snell); Chamaeleon F 31 Wehrli; also Eur. *Sciron* F 675 and n. 2, below. In an alternative translation, 'destroying my things ... (*and*?) my possessions', the two nouns have no certain connotation, but may refer to Dionysus' emblems which the satyrs have discarded (see F 78c.39–40 and introductory discussion n. 3) or (Sommerstein, 2008) to the satyrs' own persons.

[15] Line 36 is damaged at the start, but the end has now been confidently read by Henry and Nünlist. Together with 'labours', the word 'helper' suggests that the satyrs' acts of worship honouring Dionysus are meant (n. 12 above, cf. Soph. *Trackers* F 314.223–32), despite their complaint of hardship in his service at F 78c.4–7 (see introductory discussion). Satyrs' 'labours' are most commonly those of bringing up the infant Dionysus (*Adespota* F 646a.7–12 and nn. 7 and 10, below), or of aiding his survival (*Cyc.*1–14).

The pronoun μοι is supplied to dative ἐπηράνῳ from the adjective ἐμά: cf. μου supplied to genitive ἐῶντος at *Cyc.* 233 from ἐγώ at 232. See Smyth § 977.

F **78a col. ii

24 lines (37–60) lost at the top of the column; then 3 lines (61–3) with only a few letters, then:

<table>
<tr><td><ΔΙΟΝ.?></td><td>σάκει καλύψας [...]εν[</td><td></td></tr>
<tr><td></td><td>σπείρεις δὲ μῦθον τ[ό]νδε.[</td><td>(65)</td></tr>
<tr><td></td><td>καὶ ῥηματίζεις εἰς ἔμ' ἐκτρ..[</td><td></td></tr>
<tr><td></td><td>ὡς οὐδέν εἰμι τὴν σιδηρῖτι[ν</td><td></td></tr>
<tr><td></td><td>γύννις δ' ἄναλκις οὐδενειμ.[</td><td></td></tr>
<tr><td></td><td>καὶ νῦν τάδ' ἄλλα καὶ ποταιν[ι</td><td></td></tr>
<tr><td></td><td>ἔχθιστα πάντων τω[</td><td>(70)</td></tr>
<tr><td></td><td>πλύνεις τ' ἔμ' αὐτὸν [</td><td></td></tr>
<tr><td></td><td>ἐφ' ἣν ἀγείρω πλ[</td><td></td></tr>
</table>

P. Oxy. 2162 (see on F 78a col. i above) fr. 1(a) col. ii; from the 24 lines lost at the top of the column may come F ** 78b = P. Oxy. 2161 fr. 1(b); it has only letters from the centres of 12 lines
64–72 assigned to Dionysus by Murray, to Silenus by Terzaghi
66 ἐκτρέπ[ων Mette; end κότον Lloyd-Jones
67 end [ν τέχνην Lobel
68 οὐδέν εἰμ' (Cantarella) ἐ[ν ἀνδράσιν Reinhardt: οὐδ' ἔνειμ' ἐ[ν ἄρσεσιν Lloyd-Jones
69 ποταίν[ι' ἐγκαλεῖς Fraenkel

F **78c col. i

<table>
<tr><td>5–6 let.] ἔνορκόν ἐστί σο[ι] κα[...]φρονεῖν</td><td>(1)</td></tr>
<tr><td>5–6 let.] κακῶς ὅλοιο καὶ τ[6–7 let.]ε</td><td>(2)</td></tr>
</table>

14 damaged lines (3–16), in which the following can be read:

5]ουλον ἢ τρίδουλ[ον, 6]αξ δικα[, 7]ῳ τε κο[ίτ]ῳ καὶ κακαῖς δ[υσ]αυλίαις, 8 αἱ]εὶ παλαίοντ' οὐδὲν οἰκτ[[ε]]ίρε[ις ἐμ]έ, 10 φ]εύγων [, 11 π]ότερα παθών τι δε[, 12 πολλὰ

P. Oxy. 2162 (see on F **78a col. i) fr. 2(a) col. i
Snell suggested that F 78c col.i followed F 78a col. i directly (cf. Lloyd-Jones (1957) 542): confirmed now by Henry and Nünlist (2000) 14–15 (see introductory discussion). Division of these lines between speakers is likely, *e.g.* (Snell) 1–2 Dionysus?, 3–10 Silenus, 11–12 Dionysus, 13–16 Chorus.
The loss of all line-beginnings prevents identification of the metre: either iambic trimeters or trochaic tetrameters are possible.
5 δίδ]ουλον Steffen
6 ἄν]αξ Kamerbeek
7 κακ]ῷ Cantarella ('alone fits the space', Henry and Nünlist): σπαρν]ῷ Diggle; δ[υ]σαυλίαις: υλι insecurely read
8 beg Snell; end Radt, cf. Henry and Nünlist

F **78a (P. Oxy. 2162 fr. 1(a) col. ii)

<DION.?>   ... covering ... with a shield[16] ... you spread this story ... (65) and speechify, (turning your anger?) ... against me, that I am nothing at a blacksmith's (craft?), and as a gutless pansy I am nothing (among men?).[17] And now ... these further unheard-of things ... most hateful of all ... (70) and shower me – me! – with abuse ... for which[18] I am gathering ...

[16] 'shield': perhaps (Kamerbeek) an allusion to a particularly strenuous contest, a foot-race in full armour, the Hoplitodromos, with weapons carried, and introduced to Panhellenic festivals from c. 520 BC

[17] The taunt 'pansy' is hurled at the god by his human opponent Lycurgus in Aeschylus' tragedy *Edonians* F 61, a fragment cited by the scholia on Ar. *Thes.* 136, where the word also occurs: see commentators there, and on Eur. *Bacc.* 353, 453–9 (Pentheus' prurient remarks upon the god's 'effeminate appearance'). The cowardly and effete nature of Dionysus is a running gag throughout Aristophanes' *Frogs*, esp. 42–51, 461–500. Conversely, these lines may be spoken by the coryphaeus (chorus-leader) on behalf of the notoriously cowardly satyrs (see esp. Soph. *Trackers* F 314.145–68, spoken by, of all figures, Silenus! and Eur. *Cyc.* 635–9, 642, 649). There is a similar defensive tone in *Cyclops* when the satyrs make lame excuses for their inaction (643–8); and the reluctance of the speaker(s) here to take up the 'unheard-of things' is certainly consistent with the satyrs' rejection of the 'novel playthings' later in the fragment (F 78c col. ii 53, 55).

The articulation of the sense of 68 (we translate Reinhardt) is insecure: 'and (I am) a womanish coward and do not belong (among males)', Lloyd-Jones. In 69 Fraenkel's supplement 'And now (you charge me with) these further unheard-of things' might seem to suit the following abusive colloquialism 'shower me ... with'.

In 'at a ... (skill?)' the Greek accusative is 'adverbial', one of reference.

[18] 'for which', *i.e.* for 'dancing', probably: see n. 12 above, and introductory discussion (1).

F **78c (P. Oxy. 2162 fr. 2(a) col. i)

<DION.?>   ... you are bound by oath[19] ... to think ... Damn you, and ...!

Then: 14 damaged lines (probably part of a dialogue between Dionysus and the satyrs), in which some words are intermittently legible: 5 a slave (twice?) or three times over, 6 lord, just(ly?), 7 (evil or scanty?) bed and miserable lodgings, 8 (you always?) have no pity (for me as I struggle), 10 fleeing, 11 whether

[19] Compare Atlas reneging on his oath to Heracles in the 'Atlas' play, *Adespota* F 655.2–6, below.

278 Major Fragments of Greek Satyric Drama

δράσας, 13 θαρσῶν λεξ[, 14 ἱερῷ
20 lines are lost at the foot of this column

11 τι δε[ινὸν Fraenkel
13 λέξ[ον Kamerbeek

F **78c col. ii

<ΔΙΟΝ.?>   κοὐδεὶς παλαιῶν οὐδὲ τῶν νεωτέρω[ν   (37)
           ἑκὼν ἄπεστι τῶνδε διστοίχω[ν
           σὺ δ᾽ ἰσθμιάζεις καὶ πίτυος ἐστ[εμμένος
           κλάδοισι κισσοῦ γ᾽ οὐδ[α]μοῦ τιμη[(40)
           ταῦτ᾽ οὖν δακρύσεις οὐ καπνῷ [
           παρόντα δ᾽ ἐγγὺς οὐχ ὁρᾷς τα[
XO.   ἀλλ᾽ οὔποτ᾽ ἔξειμ᾽ ε[
           τοῦ ἱεροῦ και τι μο.[
           ταῦτ᾽ ἀπειλεῖς ε.[(45)
           Ἴσθμιον αντε[
           Ποσειδᾶνοσο[
           σὺ δ᾽ ἄλλοις ταῦτ[..]εμπε[
ΔΙΟΝ.   ....[.]α καινὰ ταῦτα μα[...]νειν φιλεῖ[
           ἐγὼ [φέ]ρω σοι νεοχμὰ [....] ἀθύρματα   (50)
           ἀπὸ [σκε]πάρνου κἄκμ[ονος ν]εόκτ[ιτα.
           τουτ[ὶ τὸ] πρῶτόν ἐστί σοι τ[ῶ]ν παιγ[νίω]ν.
XO.   ἐμοὶ μὲν οὐχί· τῶν φίλων νεῖμόν τινι.
ΔΙΟΝ.   μὴ ἄπειπε μηδ᾽ ὄρνιθος οὕνεκ᾽, ὠγαθέ.

P. Oxy. 2162 (see on F 78a col. i above) fr. 2(a) col. ii
37–62 divided between Dionysus and Chorus by most eds: 53, 55, 57, 59 Silenus Terzaghi
(see introductory discussion (2)); 49–52, 54, 56, 58, 60 Sisyphus and Theseus or Hephaestus
some eds (see (3)); P. Oxy. preserves voice-changes as far as 60
38 end χορῶν Lobel
40 γ᾽ Page: δ P. Oxy.; end τιμὴ]ν νέμεις Lobel
41 καπνῷ [δεδηγμένος Kamerbeek
47 e.g. Ποσειδᾶνος ο[or Ποσειδᾶν᾽, ὃς ο[eds
48 end ταῦτ[α π]έμπε[Snell
49 beg ἐπεὶ [τ]ὰ Barigazzi; μα[νθά]νειν φιλεῖ[ς Setti, Snell
52 beg τουτ[ὶ τὸ] Fraenkel, Siegmann; παιγ[νίω]ν Siegmann, π and ιγ insecurely read in P. Oxy.

suffering something (terrible?), 12 ... on doing many things, 13 ... have courage and (speak?), 14 ... (in the?) temple ...

F **78c (P. Oxy. 2162 fr. 2(a) col. ii)

<DIONYSUS> ... and no one among the old or the younger ones willingly keeps away from these (dances?) with their doubled lines;[20] but you're being an Isthmian contestant, and (garlanded) with twigs of pine you (do?) no honour at all to ivy.[21] (40) You'll be weeping therefore, and not (stung?) by smoke,[22] and you don't see ... [23] right here in front of you.

<CHO.> (*dancing and singing defiantly*) Well, I'll never leave the temple, and something (?) ... you threaten this ... (45) ... Isthmian ... (of?) Poseidon ... But (send?) these ... to others.

<DION.?>[24] (Since you?) like (learning?) these new things, I bring you ... novel playthings, (50) newly ·made from (adze) and (anvil). This (one here) is (the) first of your toys.

<CHO.> No, not for me! Give it to one of my friends![25]

[20] 'doubled lines': possibly a dance-formation common in Dionysiac celebrations; perhaps unique to satyr-choruses, Kaimio (2001) 41.

[21] 'pine': victory-wreaths of wild celery leaves were awarded to winners in the Isthmian Games, according to Pindar (*Ol.* 13.33, *Isthm.* 2.16, 8.64); but later sources say they were made of pine leaves (Paus. 8.48.2; Lucian, *Anacharsis* 9), consistently with what Aeschylus says here; cf. n. 13 on Euripides' *Autolycus A* F 282 below. Ivy was a ritual emblem of Dionysus' 'evergreen' fertility, and a wreath of it was a standard feature of the god in black-and red-figure vase-painting, just as he wears ivy in his hair: see Pratinas 4 F 3.16, *Cyc.* 620.

[22] 'weeping ... not ... by smoke': an everyday comparison for reaction to extreme physical suffering. Similarly, Polyphemus threatens to make the satyrs weep by means of his heavy club, *Cyc.* 210–11. 'Therefore' translates the idiomatic adverbial phrase ταῦτ' οὖν.

[23] The missing noun was perhaps the (ominous) 'playthings' of v. 50, and the words may be a threatening question, 'Don't you see ...?'

[24] It is most likely Dionysus who here continues his altercation with the satyrs, rather than another entrant who brings the 'novel playthings': see introductory discussion (3), and n. 27 below.

[25] 'Give it to one of my friends!': immediate cowardice from the satyr, who is quite willing for one of his friends to face what he himself finds terrifying; cf. Silenus' glib forswearing of his sons' lives (*Cyc.* 268–9): see also introductory discussion n. 3, at end.

ΧΟ.	τί δεῖ γανοῦσθαι τοῦτο; καὶ τί χρήσομαι;	(55)
ΔΙΟΝ.	ἥνπερ μεθειλ[.. τὴ]ν τέχνην ταύτῃ πρεπ[	
ΧΟ.	τί δ[ρ]ᾶν; τί ποιεῖν; [τοὺ]πίπλουν μ' οὐ[χ] ἀνδάν[ει.	
ΔΙΟΝ.	ξυνισθμιάζειν [.....] ἐμμελέστατον.	
ΧΟ.	φέρω[*about 17 let.*] ἐμβήσεται.	
ΔΙΟΝ.	ἐπισ[*about 17 let.*] βάδην ἐλ[ᾷ]ς.	(60)
< – ?>	.]ει[*about 19 let.*]φ.ρων σφυρά	
	traces of one further line	

55 τί δεῖ Lloyd-Jones: τιδη P. Oxy.
56 μεθεῖλ[ες Lobel; πρέπ[ει Kamerbeek
57 Nünlist (and Henry; οὐ[χ] ἀνδάν[ει Kamerbeek): in [τοὺ]π-,]π is more securely read in P. Oxy. than]τ

\<DION.?\>	Don't refuse it, my good man, don't – because of the omen![26]
\<CHO.\>	Why must I be delighted with this? And what shall I use it for?

(55)

\<DION.?\>	(It suits) exactly this skill (you've) taken up.
\<CHO.\>	To do what? For doing what? I don't like the equipment![27]
\<DION.?\>	For joining in the Isthmian games ... most suitable.
\<CHO.\>	... bring(ing?) ... will go on board (*or* mount?).
\<DION.?\>	... you will row (*or* drive?) at walking pace (60) ...
\< – ?\>	... ankles ...

---

[26] 'because of the omen': the point presumably lies in its threatening nature, probably that the mere sight of fetters should bring the satyrs to heel (English pun only! – but note 'ankles' in 61 after 'at walking pace' in 60), especially if they aspire to compete at running (cf. n. 17 above). In the Greek the double negative indicates urgent emphasis.

[27] The text of vv. 57–61 is badly or hopelessly damaged and its sense therefore eludes us, in particular the apparent references to going on board a boat (or a chariot?) (59) and rowing (60) – unless these are metaphors. In 57 the word read by Henry as 'equipment' is doubtful; earlier editors had tried to identify 'voyage' in it (the forms are very similar), in order to match those metaphors. Note however Lloyd-Jones's (1957) suggestion that it may be Hephaestus speaking with the satyrs here, trying to hitch a ride with them to avoid being taken back to Olympus (see introductory discussion (3)).

Prometheus the Fire-Kindler
(*ΠΡΟΜΗΘΕΥΣ ΠΥΡΚΑΕΥΣ, Prometheus Pyrkaeus*)

TrGF 3.321–8 (F *187a, **204a–**7a), cf. 4².787.

Texts etc. Lloyd-Jones (1957) 562–6 (F 204b), cf. (H. W. Smyth) 453–4 (F 205–7); Diggle (1998) 27 (F 204b); R. Germar, N. Pechstein, R. Krumeich in KPS 169–78; Voelke (2001) 274–6 (F 207); Sommerstein (2008) 210–21 (under *Prometheus the Fire-Bearer*).

Discussions. E. Fraenkel, 'Aeschylus: New Texts and Old Problems', *PBA* 28 (1942) 237–58, at 245–7; Chourmouziades (1974) 36–40; Gantz (1993) 154–8; Conrad (1997) 86–90, 267–8; Kaimio (2001) 38–40; Sommerstein (2010) 227–8; see also n. 1 below.

Art. Very many vase-paintings of satyrs with fire or torches in the company of Prometheus survive: *LIMC* VII.1.534–5 'Prometheus' nos. 4–22, esp. three from Attica of the late 5th century: no. 5, now published as KPS Plate 21a; no.13 = Trendall-Webster II.4 = J. Boardman, *Athenian Red Figure Vases. The Classical Period* (London, 1989) no. 181; no. 17 = KPS Pl. 21b. In general see KPS 175–7. Taplin (2007) 34 comments: 'it (is) quite plausible that these paintings were informed ... by the Aeschylus satyr play.'

This title is known for Aeschylus from Pollux 9.156 (*TrGF* 3.321) and from 10.64, the source of the book fragment F 205 (below). Of the other book fragments, F 187a (= fr. 206 Nauck, Sommerstein (2008) 18) is attributed in its source to Aeschylus 'in *Prometheus*', F 207b just to Aeschylus, and F 207 to Prometheus as its speaker. F 207a (a testimony: see below) and the papyrus-fragments F 204a–d are assigned by conjecture to this play rather than to *Prometheus the Fire-Bearer* (*ΠΡΟΜΗΘΕΥΣ ΠΥΡΦΟΡΟΣ, Prometheus Pyrphoros*). This latter play-title is known from an ancient catalogue (*TrGF* 3.59 T 78.14d) and from the attribution in their sources of the book fragment F 208 and the testimony F 208a; no other fragments are known. A few other book-fragments have at times been assigned to *Fire-Kindler* (esp. F 288 (below), F **451p) or to *Fire-Bearer* (esp. F 369), or to both (esp. F 312, 369, **451i).

In *TrGF* 3 Radt keeps the two plays and their fragments separate; we follow him and the majority opinion that *Fire-Kindler* was the play which in the medieval mss. of *Persians* (*TrGF* 3.48 T 55a) is recorded simply as *Prometheus*; and that this was the fourth play and by implication therefore the satyr-play in Aeschylus' tetralogy of 472 BC, which comprised *Phineus, Persians, Glaucus of Potniae, Prometheus*: for this opinion see M. Griffith, *Prometheus Bound* (Cambridge, 1982) 281–2; M. L. West, *Studies in Aeschylus* (Stuttgart, 1990) 71; A. Podlecki, *Aeschylus: Prometheus Bound* (Oxford, 2005) 27. In fact F 205 contains the only additional, but certain, indication of the play's satyric nature, an iambic trimeter from dialogue with a '4th-foot anapaest', a metrical licence impossible in tragedy.

Many scholars since D. Canter in the 16th Century, however, have lodged all the fragments under one title, *Fire-Bearer*: for the fullest and most recent argument see A. L. Brown, *BICS* 37 (1990), 50–6, followed by Sommerstein (2008) 210–13, (2010) 227–8. Brown claims that the satyr-play of 472 BC was so titled by ancient scholarship because in it Prometheus carries fire to men, rather than kindles it for them; and that *Fire-Kindler* in Pollux 9.156 and 10.64 (above) was an incorrect alternative title formed through association with Sophocles' tragedy *Nauplius the Fire-Kindler*.[1]

The content of the play related to Prometheus' theft of fire from the gods to give to man. Aeschylus perhaps constructed a meeting between Prometheus and the satyrs as he first approached men with his gift: they are astonished and delighted by fire and its novelty (compare their reactions to their portraits in *Sacred Delegates* F 78c col. ii, and to the sound of Hermes' lyre in Sophocles, *Trackers* F 314.243–331). They celebrate their hope for fire's benefits with song and dance (F 204b, the longer papyrus text: below); but they also risk being burned by it, or do get burned (F 207, included in a testimony):

> When the satyrs upon the first sight of fire wanted to embrace and kiss it, Prometheus said, 'Goat, in that case you'll be mourning for your beard!'[2] Fire burns the one who touches it, but it gives light and warmth and is the instrument of every craft ... (Plutarch, *Moralia* 86e = Aesop, *Fables* 467 Perry)

With this fragment cf. the start of F 187a (unassigned in *TrGF* except to a *Prometheus* trilogy; = fr. 206 Nauck, Sommerstein) 'Take good care the flare doesn't reach your lips: it's fierce!' (see n. 7 below; the rest of the fragment is irremediably corrupt).

While such a meeting between god and satyrs, possibly with live fire, could create amusing stage-business, it seems little enough to drive a whole play, even if Prometheus went on to recount the skills to which fire led (as in his description of this and his other gifts to men in *Prometheus Bound* 441–506). Accordingly the insecurely assigned F 207a (scholion on Hesiod, *Works and Days* 59: a testimony) is taken to reflect the play's later action (see KPS (1999) 177–8):

(Aeschylus) says that Prometheus took the jar of evils from the satyrs and, putting it beside Epimetheus (*his brother*), urged him not to accept anything from Zeus. Epimetheus disobeyed and accepted Pandora; but when he had this evil at his side, he then realised what he had been sent – whence in fact (*he is called*) Epimetheus (i.e. *'Afterthought'*).

The well-known story, what happened after Prometheus had stolen the fire, is told at Hesiod, *Works and Days* 54–95 (at *Theogony* 570–93 Pandora's disaster 'beyond control' for mankind is that she is model or image for the race of women, 572, 590, cf. *Works* 71).

While further stage-business with Pandora's jar and release of the evils from it would give the play a suitably chaotic ending, the testimony of F 207a prompts questions: how was it that Pandora's jar was in the hands of the satyrs before Prometheus had it to entrust to Epimetheus? Had the satyrs met her first, and she had foreseen that their curiosity and carelessness would be the easiest way to ensure release of the evils? Might Pandora have been a stage-character herself, whether speaking or mute? – quite possibly, since Sophocles' satyric *Pandora* or *Hammerers* (*Sphyrokopoi*, F 482–6) seems to have dealt with the creation of Pandora: in F 482 an unidentified person is instructed to 'begin first upon kneading the clay' from which to make her (unconfident attempts to link mid-5th Century Attic vase-painting to Pandora's creation are reviewed by KPS 378–9, with pl. 10 illustrating satyrs wielding hammers). Finally, however, one thing *is* clear: Prometheus has not yet been overtaken by Zeus' punishment.

F **204b

<ΧΟΡΟΣ>   (*the first verse of the ode is missing*)   (στρ.)

σία δέ μ' εὐμενὴς χορεύει χάρις
φ[α]ενν[ὸ]ν [
χιτῶνα πὰρ πυρὸς ἀκάματον αὐγάν.
κλυοῦσ' ἐμοῦ δὲ Ναΐδων τις παρ' ἐσ-
τιοῦχον σέλας πολλὰ διώξεται.   (5)

P. Oxy. 2245 (2nd c. AD) ed. E. Lobel (1952) fr. i col. ii; also col. i (F **204a: negligible) and col. iii (F **204c: below) and frs 2–12 (fr. 12 is F ** 204d: below); assigned to this play by E. Fraenkel, *PBA* 28 (1942) 246–7.

The responding ephymnia 6–8 = 15–17 suggest that 1–5 ~ 9–14 are strophe and antistrophe, but textual loss and damage and occasional metrical divergence (*e.g.* 4 beg ~ 13 beg) bar confidence.

The major fragment F 204b (below) is a most pleasing lyric composition in mainly iambo-trochaic metre (not rare in praise-hymns: see Voelke (2001) 274–6). It has an initially defective strophe but a complete antistrophe each with an identical refrain (vv. 1–17). It is possible that the fragment's last lines (vv. 18–26, very damaged), also lyric, are a continuation stretching, past ten lines now lost, into F 204c and d (12) (below; also very damaged), but no compositional structure is apparent from the remains.

There are also F 205 '... of flax, pitch and long cords of raw flax' (context uncertain; see n. 8 below); and, ascribed to the play by some, F 288 'I fear the stupid death of a severely scorched moth' (if authentic to the play, compare Prometheus' warning to the satyrs in F 207 and F 187a above), and F 369 'a mortal woman sprung from seed-stock fashioned with clay (*i.e.* Pandora)'.

We print here in both Greek and English only the longer papyrus fragments of *Fire-Kindler*, F 204 b and d, and after them the book fragments F *187a, 205 and 207.

Notes

[1] These issues are bound up with the unresolved questions whether Aeschylus (or another poet) composed an entire 'Prometheus' trilogy, including the surviving *Prometheus Bound* and the fragmentary *Prometheus Unbound* (*TrGF* 3.304–20, F 190–204), for *Prometheus the Fire-Bearer* has been claimed by some scholars as either the first or third play of such a trilogy: for the most recent discussions, see Griffith (1982) 281–2; West (1990) 51–72; R. Bees, *Zur Datierung des Prometheus Desmotes* (Stuttgart, 1992) 254–6; Podlecki (2005) 27–34; Sommerstein (2008) 210–13, (2010) 224–8.

[2] Translation not secure: see n. 9 on F 207 itself.

F **204b (P. Oxy. 2245 fr. 1 col. ii)

<CHORUS>   (*Strophe*) ... (Nysa's?)[3] benevolent favour makes me dance; ...
bright tunic beside the fire's tireless glow. One of the Naiads hearing
me will pursue me many times beside the hearth's gleam.[4] (5)

[3] 'Nysa' (Fraenkel's plausible conjecture): birthplace and haunt of Dionysus (*Il.* 6.132–3), evoked for its entire ambience or particularly for wine as the inspiration of dance: see *Adespota* F 646a and nn. 7 and 12.

[4] Conrad (1997) 88 nicely observes a reversal here of satyric convention: instead of satyrs chasing nymphs, the novelty of fire will make the nymphs chase them (an incidental benefit of Prometheus' gift, 12); cf. also the comic conceits of Silenus at *Net-Fishers* F 47a n. 20.

Νύμφας δέ τοι πέποιθ’ ἐγὼ　　　　　　(ἐφύμν.)
στήσει[ν] χορούς
Προμηθέως δῶ[ρ]ον ὡς σεβούσας.

καλ[ὸ]ν δ’ ὕμνον ἀμφὶ τὸν δόντα μολ-　　(ἀντ.)
πάσειν [.]ολ[...]ω λεγούσας τόδ’ ὡς　　(10)
Προμηθε[ὺς βρο]τοῖς
φερέσβιός ..[...].[]σπευσίδωρ[ος·
χορεύσειν .[6 let.]νι’ ἐλπὶς ὤ-
ρ]ίου χε[ί]ματ[ος ...]ερ.ιχ[..]..·

Νύμφ]ας δέ τ[οι] πέπ[ο]ιθ’ ἐγὼ　　　　(ἐφύμν.)
στήσε]ιν χορούς　　　　　　　　　　(16)
Προμ]η[θ]έως δῶρον ὡς σεβούσα[ς.

remains of 9 further lines, including the words

18 ποιμέν[.]ς πρέπειν, 19 νυκτιπλαγ[

to which F **204d fr.5.3

]ορχημα[

was joined by Lobel as

νυκτίπλαγ[κτον] ὄρχημα), 24]β[α]θυξυλο[

1 Νυ]σία (Νυ- ending the previous verse) Fraenkel; but σια is insecurely read in P. Oxy.
2 φ[α]εvν[ὸ]ν: the letters εν are insecurely read in P. Oxy.
9 καλ[ὸ]ν: αλ and ν insecure
10 beg to mid (]ω) largely insecure

F **204c *Some words but mostly a few letters from the beginnings of 29 lines, of which at least the first 12 were lyric; the following words are safely enough read*:

2 λειμων.], 3 χορευμασ[, 4 ἱερὰ δ’ ἀκτὶς σελ[, 5 τ]ηλέγνωτον,
6 ἀ[ν]τισέληνον

F **204c: P. Oxy. 2245 fr. i col. iii: see on F **204b above
4 Σελ[ήνης Görschen

(*Refrain*) The Nymphs, I do believe, will form dances[5] in honour of Prometheus' gift,

(*Antistrophe*) and they will sing a beautiful hymn about the giver ... telling how (10) Prometheus ... the bringer of life to mortal men[6] ... most eager donor. ... (*I have?*) hope ... they will dance and sing ... (*for?*) winter in season.

(*Refrain*) The Nymphs, I do believe, (15) will form dances in honour of Prometheus' gift.

Then come remains of 9 further lines, including the words:

18 shepherds (*or* shepherd's) ... stand out, 19 (dance?) that wanders in the night (?), 24 deep in a wood (?)

[5] 'dances': that is, sung dances, 9–10 (where the rare verb μολπάζειν has the same wide meaning as at Ar. *Frogs* 380: see the whole passage 370–90).

[6] 'bringer of life': alluding possibly not only to Prometheus' gift to men of skills which create a good life (*Prometheus Bound* 441–71, 476–506), but also to a myth-version attested only later in which he actually created mortals out of clay (see on Pandora in the introductory discussion), Ovid, *Met.* 1.82–8, Pausanias 10.4.4.

F **204c (P. Oxy. 2245 fr. 1 col. iii)

Some words but mostly a few letters from the beginnings of 29 lines, of which at least the first 12 were lyric; the following words are safely enough read:

2 meadow(s?), 3 dance(s?), 4 holy beam (of the Moon?), 5 known far and wide, 6 moon-like

F **204d   12

*7 damaged lines, of which 2–4 have the same metrical form as the ephymnion
in F 204b.6–8 = 15–17, and in which 2 has the particles* δέ τοι *placed
exactly as in 6 = 15 there; the following words can be read:*

> 3 πέλας πυρός, 4 μεθυ.[, (5]ορχημα[: *see on* F 204b.19), 6
> χιὼν δ' ἀριστιππο[, 7].όμβρου κ[.]ρα

P. Oxy. 2245 fr. 12: see on F **204b above
6 ἀρίστιππο[ς Snell
7 *e.g.* ἔκ] τ'ὄμβρου Mette; κ[ά]ρα Snell

F 187a

⟨ΠΡΟΜΗΘΕΥΣ?⟩   ἐξευλαβοῦ δὲ μή σε προσβάλῃ στόμα
         πέμφιξ· πικρὰ γὰρ †καὶ οὐ διὰ ζωῆς ἀτμοί†

Galen on Hippocrates, *Epidemics* 6, at 1.29; = fr. 206 Nauck
2 end: apart from the lack of sense, ἀτμοί is metrically at fault

F 205

         λινᾶ δέ, πίσσα κὠμολίνου μακροὶ τόνοι

Pollux 10.64

F 207

ΠΡΟΜ.   τράγος γένειον ἆρα πενθήσεις σύ γε.

Plutarch, *Moralia* 86e and elsewhere; other citations

F **204d (P. Oxy. 2245 fr. 12)

damaged beginnings of 7 lyric lines, in which the following words can be read:

> 3 near the fire, 4 drunk(en?), 5 dance, 6 snow splendidly horsed,[6] 7 (from?) rain ... (my head?) ...

[6]   *i.e.* snow imagined as a divine manifestation in the sky, 'white-horsed'.

F 187a Galen on Hippocrates, *Epidemics* 6, at 1.29)

<PROMETHEUS?>   Take good care that the flare doesn't reach your lips: it's fierce ... (*the rest of the fragment is corrupt*)[7]

[7]   'flare', cf. '(stormy) blast' *Prometheus Unbound* F 195.4; but others translate 'drop' (*e.g.* of boiling water – in this context?), citing 'drop of blood' Aesch. *Pentheus* F 183.

F 205 (Pollux 10.64)

> ... of flax, pitch and long cords of raw flax ... (*text insecure*)[8]

[8]   Perhaps materials for making torches or tapers, or, less likely, for binding up wounds. The context is indeterminable: if it relates to fire, it may describe its perpetuation once handed over by Prometheus: see *TrGF* 3. 327.

F 207 (Plutarch, *Moralia* 86e)

PROM.   Goat, in that case you'll be mourning for your beard![9]

[9]   Or 'In that case you'll be mourning for your beard like a goat!', or, as if a proverbial statement, 'In that case you'll be the goat mourning for his beard': the syntax is unclear. In whatever translation, 'goat' is derogatory: for satyrs' beards and goatish behaviour cf. Soph. *Trackers* F 314.367 and n. 63, and many vase-paintings.

Sisyphus (*ΣΙΣΥΦΟΣ*): one play or two?

TrGF 3.337–41 (F 225–34).

Texts etc. R. Germar, N. Pechstein, R. Krumeich in KPS 182–8; Sommerstein (2008) 232–9.

Discussions. H.Weir Smyth in Lloyd-Jones (1957) 457–60; Sutton (1980) 27–8; Taplin (1977) 428–9; Gantz (1993) 127, 174; Voelke (2001) 161, 297–8; A. J. Podlecki in Harrison (2005) 13; Z. P. Ambrose *ibid.* 27 and 36 n. 11; N. W. Slater *ibid.* 97 n. 12.

Art. *LIMC* VII.1.781–7 'Sisyphos I' nos 41 and 43, uncertainly identified as scenes of Hermes leading Sisyphus to the underworld, and no. 42, perhaps Sisyphus watching Zeus pursue Aegina (three Attic vessels of 470–440 BC); cf. KPS 186–7.

Sisyphus, an early king of Corinth, was a supremely crafty rascal, ideal for a satyr-play, as in Euripides' *Autolycus A* (below) and his *Sisyphus* (of unknown content). A two-word fragment alone survives of Sophocles' *Sisyphus*, but its genre is disputed, like that of Critias' (?) *Sisyphus* (?): see there. Sisyphus has been suggested as a character in Aeschylus, *Sacred Delegates* (above) and Achaeus' *Aethon* (below).

An ancient catalogue of Aeschylus' plays records a *Sisyphus the Runaway* (*ΔΡΑΠΕΤΗΣ*, *Drapetes*: *TrGF* 3.59 T 78.16a); and an ancient commentator on Aristotle, *Nicomachean Ethics* 1111a8–9 records for him a *Sisyphus the Stone-Roller* (*ΠΕΤΡΟΚΥΛΙΣΤΗΣ*, *Petrocylistes*: *TrGF* 3.63 T 93b) to which two book fragments are assigned by their sources (F 233–4); all eight other book fragments are attributed just to a *Sisyphus* (F 225–32). These perplexing testimonies divide opinions: Gantz (1993) 174 follows some earlier scholars in thinking that Aeschylus indeed wrote only one play (when the longer titles must be ancient alternatives, comparable in the catalogue T 78 with *e.g.* his *Sacred Delegates or Isthmian Contestants*). Other more recent scholars hold these longer titles to be trustworthy, and think of two plays (Sutton (1980), KPS 182, Podlecki in Harrison (2005) 13, Sommerstein (2008) 232–5); they point to secure analogies in T 78 for the titles which distinguish the three Prometheus-plays (there are many paired plays of Sophocles and Euripides). Yet other scholars remain undecided (*e.g.* Voelke (2001) 161 n. 72). The longer titles at least indicate that the mythological background to the play(s) was close to the story given by Pherecydes 3 F 119 *FGrH* (= F 119 Fowler

339; cited by the Scholia on Homer, *Iliad* 6.153 'Sisyphus ... who was the most gainful of men'):

> When Zeus abducted Aegina the daughter of Asopus ... by way of Corinth, Sisyphus (artfully?: *only one ms. of the scholia contains this adverb*) revealed her seizure to Asopus who was searching for her. In consequence he drew Zeus' anger down upon himself, and so Zeus sent Death for him. Sisyphus however perceived Death's approach, and confined him in strong bonds. In consequence it came about that no men were dying, until Ares (*two sources, Fowler; 'Hades' Jacoby*) set Death free and handed Sisyphus over to him; before Sisyphus died, however, he instructed his wife Merope not to send the customary offerings to Hades. Now after a time during which Sisyphus' wife sent no offerings, Hades discovered this and released Sisyphus to reprove his wife. When he had come to Corinth, however, he did not return (*to Hades*) until in old age (*he died. Therefore* [*these words supplemented by Jacoby*]) after his death Hades forced on him the rolling of a stone so that he should never again run away.

Alcaeus F 38a.5–10 had already told how Sisyphus was fated at Zeus' will to die twice, despite all his ingenuity in evading death for a first time. His punishment with the stone had already been fixed for mythology at Homer, *Odyssey* 11.593–600:

> I saw Sisyphus too suffering mightily, working at a gigantic stone with both arms. I tell you, he kept straining with hands and feet to push the stone up towards a summit, but just when he was about to get it over the top, its mighty weight kept turning him back; then the stone rolled down ruthlessly to the flat. Again and again he strove effortfully to push it; sweat streamed from his limbs, and dust rose in the air above his head.

The title 'Runaway' connotes Sisyphus' second escape from death, his release from the underworld by Hades and his intention not to return, just as 'Stone-Roller' connotes his final and inescapable punishment in Hades (see Pherecydes above). One fragment at least, F 225, may relate to, or perhaps narrate, his first 'escape', when he puts Death himself in bonds. F 226, a colloquial command, relates more naturally to a scene on earth than within Hades. F 227 and 233 suit Sisyphus carrying Death upon his back, and so presenting an unnaturally large or even monstrous shape, while two or three other fragments more likely fit Sisyphus' departure from Hades, an extraordinary event and spectacle (F 228, possibly 229 and 230). Whether all these incidents (and in effect most of the story as told by Pherecydes) could be contained within a single play, is linked with two further questions, (1) what the setting was of such a plot or plot(s), and (2) whether a single play (or each of two plays) was satyric.

(1) Setting(s). The binding of Death by Sisyphus when Death is sent for him, and then Death's release by Ares, imply a setting in the upper world, with both incidents dramatised, and with the underworld imagined 'off-stage', either nearby or far off; Death's reclaim of Sisyphus too seems suitable for the upper world. Whether or not the title *Stone-Roller* indicates a separate play, it entails a difficult problem: was Sisyphus's everlasting punishment merely forecast, or was he shown rolling his stone, and therefore in a scene set in the underworld itself? Or was this scene, and perhaps the play's whole action, placed at the border between the living and the dead worlds, close by an entrance to Hades? All the potential theatrical scenes in Pherecydes' story, from Death being sent for Sisyphus, could credibly take place there, with a fluidity of focus such as that discussed for Sophocles' *Lovers of Achilles*, below. Taplin (1977) 428–9 suggests that Sisyphus after his 'second' death might have been shown rolling his stone just as far as a mouth of Hades. For such 'liminal' settings cf. perhaps Python's satyric *Agen*, where the satyrs offer to conjure a ghost from a nearby entrance to the underworld; Aeschylus' *Ghost-Raisers* (*Psychagogi*), based upon Homer, *Odyssey* 11 in which Odysseus raises the spirits of the dead (the play is generally considered to have been a tragedy: *TrGF* 3.113–4, cf. Sommerstein (2008) 269 and our Appendix); and almost certainly Sophocles' satyric *On Taenarum* (the name of a Peloponnesian sea-cape with a cave held to be one of the entrances to Hades): for such settings see esp. Voelke (2001) 42. In fact an action set either in part or even wholly within the underworld itself may not be impossible, witness the *Pirithous* (disputedly attributed to both Euripides and Critias, and to both tragedy and satyric: *TrGF* 1².171–8 and Collard and Cropp (2008) II.636–57; both the fragments and the secondary evidence make its underworld setting clear).[1] See also the last paragraph of this introductory discussion.

(2) Satyric nature. The lexicographic book-fragments F 226 ('squint'), 227 ('country-mouse, oversized') and 233 ('beetle of Etna') give the strong impression that they are satyric in ethos and language; for the 'riddling' implied by F 227, see n. 53 on Soph. *Trackers* F 314.299–310. F 225 and 228–30 are only probably satyric, however, even if F 230 is an address to a dead person, even to Death himself, who is a speaking stage-figure in Euripides' *Alcestis* (a 'pro-satyric' play: on such status see n. 3 on our Introductory Note). The one-word lexicographic F 231 'mountain slopes', 232 '(ship's ?)

overseer' and 234 'flatteries' are not linguistically specific to any genre. Despite such indications from language the fragments themselves give no sure evidence of satyrs, and there are further cautions: Sisyphus' invariable depiction as a deceitful and cunning scoundrel might seem to confirm him out of hand as satyric, but Aristotle, *Poetics* 1456a19–22 implies that such characterisation of him was not incompatible with tragedy (see Radt in *TrGF* 4^2.415 on Sophocles' *Sisyphus*). Nor are returns from the dead necessarily satyric or comic: even if not 'shown' in tragedy, they are important dramatic fact, as in *e.g.* Sophocles, *Phaedra* (F 686) and in Euripides' *Heracles* (see also on Euripides' satyric *Eurystheus*, below); and there are not a few ghosts, *e.g.* Darius in Aeschylus' *Persians* and Clytemnestra in his *Eumenides* – and in his *Ghost-Raisers*. A last point: satyr-plays normally have happy endings (Introductory Note above, n. 3; introductory discussion to *Adespota* F 667a), but how would this story of Sisyphus bring happiness for himself? Only with either of his two escapes from death; and that could happen only in a 'first' play, for *Stone-Roller* implies an unhappy ending, of finality. Or might the happiness be solely that of the satyrs, released as so often from servitude (to Sisyphus) or, here, from Hades? At the same time, the punishment of Sisyphus would also suit what appears to be a likely theme in satyric drama: the cheater getting his come-uppance (*e.g.* Sisyphus outwitting his thieving opponent in Euripides' *Autolycus A*; cf. Hyginus, *Fables* 201), or being cheated by Erysichthon in Achaeus, *Aethon* F 6–11 below (see Gen. Intro. p. 30; also Sutton (1980) 149–50 for more examples).

In sum: if the generally favoured indication of the two longer titles, that there were separate plays, can be set aside, reconstruction of one play, satyric, is possible, but it requires a very crowded action; Sophocles' *Inachus* provides the only certain analogy (as for the length of such an action, Aeschylus' *Net-Fishers* had around 1,000 lines, for it is incomplete when its papyrus text runs out at 832 = F 47a.68). After a prologue-scene giving the background of Zeus' enmity against Sisyphus, successive scenes would promise amusement (a) when Death comes for Sisyphus (just as Death comes for Alcestis at the start of her name-play) and when Death is bound by Sisyphus (perhaps on stage: but Heracles' wrestling-victory over Death in *Alcestis* was off-stage); (b) when Ares releases Death, and Sisyphus must die for the first time, after instructing his wife to withhold grave-offerings; (c) when he returns from the underworld (as 'Runaway'), no doubt after a 'timeless' choral ode, but is almost immediately pursued by Death, whom he fails this time to thwart (there is no reason why Aeschylus should have used the story told by Pherecydes that Sisyphus lived to old age); finally (d), when he is hauled away a second time amid a description of the stone which awaits him, or even its representation (as Taplin suggests: (1) above). A double appearance by Death is quite credible, indeed would be aptly effective (cf. the likely reappearance of the disguised Hermes in Sophocles' *Inachus*, below).

What part might the chorus of satyrs have played, in a single play or in two, except their usual accompanying and often intrusive role? (Similar questions arise for their role in *e.g.* Aeschylus, *Glaucus the Sea-god* (above) and his 'Justice-play, F 281a; Sophocles, *Inachus*; Euripides, *Eurystheus*: all three below). Also, as rural and immortal beings, they might plausibly be near one of the entrances to the underworld, which are invariably in remote places.

Lastly, a wholly different and striking aspect of the play. The title *Stone-Roller* is given in one testimony (*TrGF* 3.63 T 93b, cf. a, c, d) in conjunction with four other plays of Aeschylus (*Women-Archers, Priestesses, Iphigenia* and *Oedipus*) in which it is said that he 'spoke in too meddlesome a way of the mysteries' (*i.e.* those of Eleusis). No fragment from any of these plays, and no secondary evidence other than that gathered in T 93, either illustrates or substantiates this statement. T 93b records too that Aeschylus

---

F 225

καὶ νίπτρα δὴ χρὴ θεοφόρων ποδῶν φέρειν.
λεοντοβάμων ποῦ σκάφη χαλκήλατος;

Pollux 10.77, with allusion at 7.40; the motif, if not Aeschylus' text, was known to Horace, *Satires* 2.3.21 *quo uafer ille pedes lauisset Sisyphus aere*, 'in what bronze (*vessel*) the famous trickster Sisyphus washed feet'; see n. 3 on the translation.

F 226

σὺ δ᾽ ὁ σταθμοῦχος εὖ κατιλλώψας ἄθρει ...

Pollux 10.20

was prosecuted for such an offence, but was acquitted when the court was reminded of his role at the battle of Marathon; T 93d argues that he could not have revealed anything consciously, only by accident, since he was not himself an initiate. Probably unconscious allusions in the plays are the reason why ancient scholars named as many as five, for after prosecution over one play Aeschylus would surely not have risked a second offence.[2] The testimony nevertheless gave support to argument both that *Stone-Roller* was set in the underworld, and that, whether there or in the upper world, the play's chorus comprised initiates (so Weir Smyth in Lloyd-Jones (1957) 457; cf. the initiates' chorus of Aristophanes' *Frogs*). Now *Frogs* crosses quickly from a beginning in the living world to a development in Hades, and it is therefore possible to think that *Sisyphus* had a similar, if theatrically notional, change of scene: see (1) above.

Notes

[1] We have been unable to see the treatment of such settings by D. F. Sutton, 'The Staging of Anodos Scenes', *RivStudClass* 23 (1975) 347–55 and M. Librán Moreno, ῞Οσα ἐν ῞Αιδου: tragedias y dramas satiricos ambientados en al inframundo', *Lexis* 23 (2005) 105–23.

[2] Latest discussion by Sommerstein (2008) I. xviii–xx and (2010) 9.

F 225 (Pollux 10.77)

> Now, water should be brought to wash feet that have carried a god! Where is the basin of hammered bronze, with its lion-base?[3]

[3] 'feet that have carried a god': Sisyphus carrying Death, cf. F 227 and introductory discussion. The allusion in Horace, *Satires* 2.3.21 implies that Sisyphus may have done the washing, and (KPS 188) that the 'trickster' may have washed Death's feet in order to disarm him before being seized; Sisyphus (or perhaps his wife Merope: Sommerstein, 2008) himself could even be the speaker. For such basins, often resting on a lion's paws, see M. J. Milne, 'A Greek Footbath in the Metropolitan', *AJA* 48 (1944) 26–63; and for treacherous foot-washing in a satyr-play cf. Euripides, *Sciron* T iib below. Possibly a feast or symposium is being prepared, with opportunity for satyrs' antics 'honouring' the guest: cf. *Cyc.* 519–75; Ion, *Omphale* F 20–7; Achaeus, *Hephaestus* F 17 (both plays below).

F 226 (Pollux 10.20)

> You, the master of the house! Take a good squint and look closely ...[4]

[4] Presumably addressed to Sisyphus in his house at Corinth; the expression 'take a good squint' suggests a satyr, perhaps Silenus himself, as the speaker.

F 227

ἀλλ᾿ ἀρουραῖός τις ἐστι σμίνθος ὦδ᾿ ὑπερφυής;

Aelian, *Natural History* 12.5.
ἀρουραῖος τίς some eds

F 228

<ΣΙΣΥΦΟΣ>   Ζαγρεῖ τε νῦν μοι καὶ πολυξένῳ <πατρὶ>
                  χαίρειν.

Etymologicum Gudianum MS d 578.9 de Stefani and *Anecdota Oxoniensia* 2.443.11
Cramer
<πατρὶ> Hermann: <λέγω> Hartung.

F 229 and F 230 are joined and confused in *Etymologicum Gudianum* MS
b ed. Cramer, *Anecdota Parisina* 4.35.18–21, and in ms. W 321.55–8 ed.
Sturz: separated and so edited (with corrections by earlier scholars) by
Boeckh and Bergk. F 229 is corrupt and unmetrical.

F 229

†καὶ θανόντων†, οἷσιν οὐκ ἔνεστ᾿ ἰκμάς.

Etymologicum Gudianum 321.55 Sturz

F 230

σοὶ δ᾿ οὐκ ἔνεστι κῖκυς οὐδ᾿ αἱμόρρυτοι
φλέβες …

Etymologicum Gudianum 321.58 Sturz: see on F 229

F 233

Αἰτναῖός ἐστι κάνθαρος βίᾳ πονῶν.

Scholia on Aristophanes, *Peace* 73

F 227 (Aelian, *Natural History* 12.5)

But is it some country mouse, so oversized like this?[5]

[5] Almost certainly a description of Sisyphus, emerging from the underworld, bent double and carrying Death in bonds: see Scholia on Homer, *Iliad* 6.153 and F 225. Some editors have interpreted differently: 'But which country mouse is so oversized?' – perhaps rightly (so KPS 185).

The metre is trochaic tetrameter: excitement? (see above on *Sacred Delegates* F 78a.18–22 n. 9).

F 228 (*Etymologicum Gudianum* 578.9 de Stefani)

<SISYPHUS>   Now I bid farewell to both Zagreus and (his) most hospitable (father).[6]

[6] Zagreus, *i.e.* 'Great Hunter', a cult-title of Dionysus in Orphism, identified here with Hades' son, but with Hades himself at Aesch. *Egyptians* F 5 (cf. G. Zuntz, *Persephone* (Oxford, 1971) 81 n. 5); cf. also Heraclitus 22 B 15 DK, who identifies Dionysus with Hades, if the text may be so interpreted. KPS 185 n. 5 suggests that this may be intended here, so that the twice-born Dionysus (for the myth see Gantz (1993) 112–13) may be named alongside one who is released from death. Hades is 'most hospitable' to the dead at *e.g.* Aeschylus, *Suppliants* 156–8.

The Greek is mocking; and the 'ethical' dative gives the sense 'I bid' to the idiomatic accusative and infinitive of the farewell (cf. Sappho fr. 155 Lobel-Page πολλά μοι τὰν Πολυανακτίδα παῖδα χαίρην, LSJ χαίρω III. 2.6, and *e.g.* Ar. *Lys.*1074; Smyth § 1486), but Hartung supplied the express verb 'I bid' where Hermann had supplemented 'father'.

F 229 (*Etymologicum Gudianum* 321.55 Sturz)

... †and (*of* ?) the dead†, in whom there is no blood.

F 230 (*Etymologicum Gudianum* 321.58 Sturz)

... but in you there is no vigour nor veins flowing with blood ...[7]

[7] F 230 may be addressed to Death while Sisyphus carries him (cf. F 227 and introductory discussion). Bloodless figures famously appear in Homer; the ghosts need blood in order to converse with Odysseus, *Odyssey* 11.95–6, 147–9 *etc.*

F 233 (Scholia on Aristophanes, *Peace* 73)

It (he?) is a beetle of Etna toiling mightily.[8]

[8] Said by the Scholia to describe Sisyphus labouring with the stone (as a dung-beetle rolls its ball, Ar. *Peace* 1–7); but cf. F 227 (and note), where Sisyphus carries Death (so A. C. Pearson, *CR* 28 (1914) 224). The line is probably from a stichomythic exchange as the satyrs(?) try to identify what they see, like F 227. For the colloquial comparison with a 'beetle of Etna' see Soph. *Trackers* F 314.307 and n. 57.

F 281a, b; **451n: from a 'Justice' (Δίκη, Dike) play

TrGF 3.380–4 (F 281a, b), 477–8 (F **451n) and 484 (F **451s6 and s10), cf. 4².788.

Texts etc. Fraenkel (1954 below) 63–75 (F 281a, b, 451n); Lloyd-Jones (1957) 573–81 (F 281b, 281a, 451n); Diggle (1998) 29–31 (F 281a only); A. Wessels in KPS 98–106; Sommerstein (2008) 276–87 (F 281a, b), 338–9 (F 451n).

Discussions. E. Fraenkel, 'Vermutungen zum Aetna-Festspiel des Aeschylus', *Eranos* 52 (1954) 61–75 (= *Kleine Beiträge* I.249–62); Lloyd-Jones (1990) 246–8 (orig. 1956, a review) and *The Justice of Zeus* (Berkeley, 1971²) 99–100; H.-J. Mette, *Der verlorene Aischylos* (Berlin, 1963) 187–91; Sutton (1980) 20–2 and 'A possible subject for Aeschylus' 'Dike' Play', *ZPE* 51 (1983) 19–24; P. Patrito, 'Sul 'frammento' di Dike', *Quaderni ... Dipartimento ... A. Rostagni* (Bologna, 2001) 77–95 (reference from *APh* 73 (2002) 8: unseen by us); L. Poli-Palladini, 'Some Reflections on Aeschylus' *Aetnae(ae)*', *RhM* 144 (2001) 287–325, at 313–15; Voelke (2001) 323–5; A. J. Podlecki in Harrison (2005) 15–16.

These badly damaged papyrus-texts have generated much speculation about the play and its occasion.[1] Aeschylus' authorship of F 281a is established by the coincidence of its line 28 with fr. 377 Nauck (attributed to Aeschylus in the scholia on Homer, *Iliad* 6.239). F **451n is judged by most editors to be from the same papyrus as F 281a, and by many to belong to the same play, perhaps to the same context.

The mythological background is found in Hesiod, *Works and Days* 252–62:

> Zeus has undying watchers, three times beyond number, of mortal men upon the bountiful earth, who keep watch on judgements and wrong deeds while clothed in mist and ranging all over the earth. And there is the maiden Dike, daughter of Zeus (as elsewhere in Aeschylus, *e.g. Choephori* 949), honoured and respected among the gods who live on Olympus; and whenever any man does her harm through crooked slander, straightaway she sits by her father Zeus the son of Cronus, and tells him the mind of unjust men, so that the people pay for the folly of princes who in their evil minds slant their judgements askew in crooked pronouncements.

In the main fragment, F 281a, the character Justice ('Dike') has evidently made a very recent entry: her presumably grand costuming as a goddess may have given theatrical life to the prompt but conventional questions about her name and prerogatives (14–29). She describes her role as Zeus' valued recording angel (8–13), a result of her assistance when he overthrew his father Cronus (who 'began' the violence, 6) to gain the throne of Olympus (1–7). To illustrate her powers she then starts a further narrative when (apparently; the text is damaged) she participated in the (apparently) 'just' suppression of a violent marauder (30–41); but here the papyrus breaks off. F 281b, six damaged lines which include the words 4 'I made a rhythm (*or* I brought into order)' and 6 'to be struck', may be a later part of this narrative. All editors agree that Justice is conversing with the Chorus (of males: F 281a.14); but that they are satyrs, and the play satyric, is positively suggested only by a word-form in 9 found at *Cyc.* 643 but not in tragedy,[1] and possibly by one in F 281b.4; but Sommerstein (2008) 277 judges that these indications are inconclusive.

A major role or name-part for an anthropomorphized 'abstract' divinity would be very unusual in tragedy: Lyssa ('Madness') has only a short part in Euripides, *Heracles*; similarly Death in his *Alcestis*, known to have been substituted for the satyr-play in his production of 438 BC (see n. 3 on our Introductory Note). Death may be addressed in Aeschylus, *Sisyphus* F 230 (above); and Death appears in *TrGF* 2.120 *Adespota* F 405, from a play of unknown nature and date. For 'abstract' play-titles and perhaps therefore play-characters compare also Sophocles' *Hybris*, *Momus* and *Eris* in our Appendix. This consideration strengthens slightly the likelihood of satyric nature for the play.

We cannot know: (1) The extent and importance of Justice's role. A minor rather than a major role (which would turn the play into a thorough-going 'morality') does seem probable, as also Justice's presence at play-end to resolve the issues, like the frequent 'saviour' roles of Heracles and Theseus in satyric drama. F 451n (below) is from a speech in praise of peace and its benefits, and would suit a reconciliation.

(2) If Justice's role was indeed minor, we cannot know whether the fragment(s) therefore derive from another more conventional but now lost satyr-play. Fraenkel (1954) advanced a much-discussed, but generally not accepted, suggestion that the scene in F 281a came from Aeschylus' tragedy *Women of Etna* (*TrGF* 3.126–30, 4².782). The poet is stated to have produced this play to help celebrate the Syracusan ruler Hiero's foundation of the city of Aetna in Sicily in the 470s, a ruler and a foundation which Pindar praised with strong hopes of their good and peaceable government, *Pythians* 1 (of 470 BC). While commendation of a peaceful prosperity in F 451n would fit

such programming, the title *Women of Etna* indicates a female Chorus; nor is it easy to suggest a motive for Justice.[2]

(3) Most frustratingly, we cannot be wholly certain who is the marauding son of Zeus and Hera in F 281a.31–5; if we did, we might hypothesize some at least of the plot, and the role of Justice. The god Ares, rampant in his field of warfare, is the most likely identification (Poli-Palladini (2001) 314 n. 93; Sommerstein (2008) 285 n. 5); the war god may well have appeared in Aeschylus' satyric *Sisyphus* (see our introductory discussion). Another son of Zeus and Hera, Hephaestus, was not capable of wildness, even if powerful. Heracles, a half-son of Zeus and no son of Hera, therefore does not qualify, any more than Ares' son Cycnus, whose violent story is told in [Hesiod], *Shield* 57–74, 325–476, or the ogre Sinis, a son of Poseidon. All

---

F 281a

<ΔIKH>	μακάρων .[	
	αυτη θεων[	
	2 lines with a few letters only	
	ἵζει δ' ἐν αὐτῷ [*then only traces*	(5)
	δίκη κρατήσας τῷδε.[	
	πατὴρ γὰρ ἦρξεν, ἀνταμ[	
	ἐκ τοῦ δέ τοί με Ζεὺς ἐτίμ[ησεν	
	ὁτιὴ παθὼν ημ[..].[	
	ἵζω Διὸς θρόνοισιν [....]ϊσμένη·	(10)
	πέμπει δέ μ' αὐτὸς οἷσιν εὐμεν[	
	Ζ[ε]ύς, ὅσπερ ἐς γῆν τήνδ' ἔπεμψέ μ' ..[	
	δ[έχ]εσθε δ' ὑμεῖς εἴ τι μὴ μά[την] λέγω.	
<ΧΟΡΟΣ>	τ[ί σ'] οὐ[ν προ]σεννέποντες εὖ κ[υ]ρήσομε]ν;	

P. Oxy. 2256 (2nd–3rd c. AD) ed. E. Lobel (1952) fr. 9 (a) and (b = F **281b below); the papyrus has many defective line-beginnings, and indications of voice-change survive only for vv. 15, 16, 17. For attribution to Aeschylus see on 28 below
5 αὐτῷ: the letters τω(ι) are insecurely read in P. Oxy.; *e.g.* [τοῦ πατρὸς θρόνῳ Lloyd-Jones
7 ἀνταμ[είψασθαι Görschen
8 *or* ἐκ τοῦδε
10 [ἠγλα]ϊσμένη Lobel
11 *e.g.* εὐμεν[ὴς πέλει Lobel
12 beg ζ[ε]υς insecurely read; end ευ[read and εὖ [φρονῶν or εὖ[φρόνως supplemented by Lobel
13 δ[έχ]εσθε Sommerstein: δ[έξ]εσθε Fraenkel

identifications proposed were reviewed by Sutton (1983); see also Voelke (2001) 323–5.

(4) What was the role, if any, of satyrs in all this? Did they harbour or even try to act on thoughts — as comically impious as they would be futile — of molesting Justice? They are not above attempting assaults on such august figures as Iris or even Hera herself in Greek art (*LIMC* V.1 s.v. 'Iris' 113, 117, 120; KPS Pl. 29a–b). Nothing in our fragments, however, sheds any light on their possible role in the action.

Notes

[1] ὁτιή: a word-form widely attested in Old Comedy, *e.g.* Ar. *Knights* 29, 34.

[2] The attribution and its problems have been discussed most recently by Poli-Palladini (2001) 313–15; cf. Sommerstein (2008) 276–9.

F 281a (P. Oxy. 2256 fr. 9 (a))

<JUSTICE>   ... of the blessed (*gods?*) ... myself (?) of the gods (?) ... (*two lines with a few letters only*) (*Zeus*) sits on the very (throne of his father?)[3] (5) after justly overcoming ... (in/by) this ... For his father began it, ... (to retaliate?) ... From that time (*or* As a result of that) Zeus honoured (me) ... because after his suffering ... I sit (in glory?) by the throne of Zeus (10). He sends me himself to those to whom (he is?) well-disposed, the very Zeus who has sent me to this land (out of good will?) ... (Welcome) me yourselves, unless I am speaking at all in vain.

<CHORUS>   (As what) then shall we rightly address (you)?

[3] The throne of Olympus, by which Justice sits (10); cf. Hesiod, *Works and Days* 453–500. For the parricidal Olympian successions see *e.g.* Aesch. *Ag.* 168–72.

<ΔΙ.>　　　Δίκην μ.[...]ον πρέσβο[ς] ἧς ε...ρο.[　　　　　　(15)
<ΧΟ.>　　　ποίας δὲ τ[ιμ]ῆς ἀρχ[*7 let.*].εισ.[
<ΔΙ.>　　　το]ῖς μὲν δ[ι]καίοις ἔνδικον τειν...ο[
<ΧΟ.>　　　*10–11 let.*].σα θέ[σ]μ[ι]ον τόδ' ἐν βρ[ο]το[ῖς.
<ΔΙ.>　　　τοῖς δ' αὖ μα]ταίοις *then only traces*
<ΧΟ.>　　　πειθοῦς ἐ]πῳδαῖς ἢ κατ' ἰσχύος τρόπο[ν];　　　(20)
<ΔΙ.>　　　γράφουσα] τὰ<μ>πλακήματ' ἐν δέλτῳ Διό[ς.
<ΧΟ.>　　　ποίῳ χρό]νῳ δὲ πίνακ' ἀναπτύσσει[ς] κακ[　;
<ΔΙ.>　　　*8 let.*]ῃ σφιν ἡμέρα τὸ κύριον.

　　　　　　　　　]εκτέα στρατῷ
　　　　　　　δ]έχοιτό μ' εὐφρ[όν]ως.　　　　　　　　　(25)
2 very damaged lines, with only a few central letters legible

　　　　　πό]λις τις οὔτε δῆμος οὔτ' ἔτης ἀνὴρ
　　　　　τοιάνδε μοῖραν π[αρ]ὰ θεῶν καρπουμένη.
　　　　　τέκμαρ δὲ λέξω τῷ τόδ' εὐδερκὲ[ς] φερε[..].[　　(30)
　　　　　ἔθρε[ψα] παῖδα μάργον ὃν τικτει [
　　　　　Ἥρα μιγεῖσα Ζηνὶ θυμοιδ[
　　　　　δ]ύσαρκτ[ο]ν, αἰδὼς δ' οὐκ ἐνῆ[ν] φρ[ον]ήματι·

17 end τείνω βίο[ν rejected by Lobel
20 πειθοῦς Pohlenz: πείθουσ' Collard
21] τὰ<μ>πλακήματ' Lloyd-Jones: ταπλ- P. Oxy.
22 κακ[οῖς rather than κακ[ῶν Lobel
28 οὔτε δῆμος ... ἀνὴρ (= Aesch. fr. 377 Nauck) Scholia on Homer, *Iliad* 6.239, Eustathius, *Iliad* 641.58.
29 καρπουμένη and punct. Diggle: -μενη[P. Oxy.: -μένη[ι *i.e.* -μένῃ Fraenkel: -μένη[ς Lloyd-Jones
30 no form of φέρω (*e.g.* φέρει[ς, φέρε[ι (= φέρῃ Middle), φέρει[ν Lobel) seems to give syntax: πρέπει Fraenkel
31 beg Lobel, but preferring ἔθρε[ψε]
32 θυμοιδ[or θυμωδ[(and *e.g.* θυμοίδ]η θέον) Lloyd-Jones

<JUS.>	As Justice, (whose authority) ... (15).
<CHO.>	What prerogative ...?
<JUS.>	For those who are just, I ... a just ...[4]
<CHO.>	... this ordinance among mortals.
<JUS.>	To the wicked, however, ...[5]
<CHO.>	Through (persuasion's?) spells,[6] or by means of strength? (20)
<JUST.>	(I write) their wrongdoings in Zeus' tablet.[7]
<CHO.>	And (at what time) do you unfold the tablet (for evil men?)?[8]
<JUS.>	... the day ... what is appointed for them. ... must be ... to the people; and ... (would welcome?) me kindly. (25) (*two very damaged lines*) ... (*no*) city or community or private man which enjoy[9] such a destiny from the gods. I will tell you proof by which (?) this ... clear to see.[10] (30) (I)[11] reared the rampant son whom Hera bore after lying with Zeus, an arrogant (?)[12] ... hard to control, with no mercy in his heart; ... the weapons of travellers

[4] 'I (prolong) a just (life)' Lobel – but he himself rejected this supplement.

[5] For this simple ethic, and its comparable formulation, in satyric drama see *Cyc.* 422, 693–5 with nn., cf. *e.g.* Eur. *Syleus* F 692, and *Sciron* F 678 'it is a fine thing to punish evil men'; in tragedy *e.g.* Aesch. *Choephori* 398. Pausanias 5.18.12 mentions an image of Justice throttling Injustice; cf. *LIMC* III.1.389 'Dike' no. 3. In Presocratic thought Dike is linked to the Erinyes, or avenging Furies and retribution (*e.g.* Heraclitus 22 B 94 DK, Parmenides 28 B 1.14 DK).

[6] Pohlenz's supplement 'by (persuasion's) spells' is attractive (alternatively '(Persuading them) by spells' Collard): it seems to anticipate the more explicit view of Gorgias in his *Encomium of Helen* that persuasion can take the form of spells, 82 B 11.10 DK.

[7] Like a recording angel, but such tablets are frequent in tragedy, *e.g. Prometheus Bound* 789 (metaphor) and esp. Eur. *Melanippe* F 506 (see M.L. West, *The East Face of Helicon* (Oxford, 1997) 561–2).

[8] '(for evil men)' preferred by Lobel to '(of their evil deeds)'.

[9] 'which enjoy': this is the sense intended by Diggle's nominative participle, agreeing formally with 'city' but applying to all three nouns. Fraenkel's dative participle and Lloyd-Jones's genitive depend for their syntax on free supplementation of a controlling noun in those grammatical cases in 27.

[10] No proposed restoration of this line convinces.

[11] The supplement '(I) reared ...' gives immediate and expected emphasis to Justice's own responsible action; '(Hera) reared ...' disappoints expectation and creates difficult Greek word-order, and Lobel seems to have been alone in preferring it. See Sommerstein (2008) 285 n. 4.

[12] 'irascible (god)', Lloyd-Jones.

8 *let.*].υκτα τῶν ὁδοιπόρων βέλη
8 *let.*].δως ἀγκύλαισιν ἀρταμῶν·   (35)
8–9 *let.*].ν ἔχ[αι]ρε κἀγέλα κακὸν
5 line-ends (37–41), *including*
37]ν στάζοι φόνος, 39]γον χέρα,
40]οῦν ἐνδίκως κικλήσκεται, 41]νιν ἐνδικ[.....].ος

34 μέλη Lobel
35 πίτυσιν ἀνα]ιδῶς Lobel (too many letters?)
36 beg καὶ τοῦτο δρ]ῶν Diggle
37 στα.[*i.e.* σταζ[οι P. Oxy. in margin, [ο]ζοι or [α]ζοι in text
40 beg Ἄρης] οὖν Sommerstein

F **281b

centres of 6 lines including the words
    4]ερρύθμιξα *and* 6 παίεσθαί

P. Oxy. 2256 (fr. 9(b)): see on F **281a

F **451n

9–10 *let.*].σ...ννῦσα μὴ σπείρειν κακ[
8? *let.*]ντ.τ' ἐστιν εἰρήνη βροτοῖς
8? *let.*].αινω τήνδε· τι[μ]ᾷ γὰρ πόλιν
ἐν ἡσύ[χοισ]ι πράγμασιν καθημένην·
δόμων τ' ἀέξει κάλλος ἐκπαγλού[μ]ενον   (5)
ἅ]μιλλαν ὥστε γειτόνων ὄλβῳ κρατεῖν·
.]δ' αὖ φυτεύειν, οἱ δ[ὲ] γῆς ἐπεμβολὰς
..]μῳ λέληνται δαΐας πεπαυμέ[νοι
σάλ]πιγγος, οὐδὲ φρουρί.. ἐξ *traces*
2 further lines (10–11) *with only a few letters*

P. Oxy. 2256 fr. 8, associated by Lobel with F 281a = fr. 9 (a) (see there), on papyrological gounds. Some other small fragments of 2256, with intermittent words legible but no useful bearing on the play, have been associated physically with fr. 9 (a): F **451s6 and s10 (*TrGF* 3. 484).
2 many letters insecurely read in P. Oxy.
3 θεὸν δ' ἐ]παινῶ Lloyd-Jones
4 ἡσύ[χοισ]ι: ησυ and ι insecurely read
5 ἐκπαγλου[μ]ένη Lloyd-Jones
6–7 text lost between these lines? Radt
7 επεμβολας P.Oxy. before correction, επεμπολας after it
9 φρουρίων Lobel, but the letters υρι are insecurely read

... jointing up (mercilessly?) by means of bent ....[13] (35) ... he was delighted and laughed (in doing this?) evil ...

then come 5 line-ends (37–41), including 37

(so that *or* whenever) blood dripped, 40 therefore he is justly called (Ares?), 41 just[14]

[13] Lines 34–5 defy restoration: if 'weapons' is correct, then Ares uses them *against* 'travellers'. Lobel's emendation 'limbs' complemented his reading and supplements in 35 'jointing up the limbs of travellers (mercilessly) by means of bent-over (pine-trees)', for he identified the rampant, murderous robber as Sinis, exterminated by Theseus (cf. n. 6 on Euripides' *Sciron* F 679), whose parentage does not fit here (see introductory discussion (3) here).

[14] 'justly called ... just': probably 'the etymologising of a proper name' (Lobel) – if so, apparently (and surprisingly) that of the rampant Ares; Sommerstein (2008) 284 conjectured the name's loss, from 'therefore Ares is ...' in 40.

F 281b (P. Oxy. 2256 fr. 9 (b))

words from the centres of 6 lines including

4 I made a rhythm (*or* I brought into order) *and* 6 to be struck

F **451n (P. Oxy. 2256 fr. 8)

... not to sow evil ... mortal men have peace ... I (praise?) this (goddess?),[15] for she honours a city engaging (quietly) in its affairs; and she increases the beauty of its houses that is admired (5) so as to surpass emulous neighbours in prosperity ... to plant, moreover, and they have eagerly undertaken hard work on the land[16] now they have given up war's trumpet, and .... not ... garrisons (*letters from two further lines*)

[15] Peace, often evoked for the benefits described in vv. 3–9, *e.g.* Eur. *Supp.* 488–91 and *Cresphontes* F 453.15–23.

[16] The text and translation of vv. 5–8 are most uncertain. In 5 'in magnifying it' (Lloyd-Jones) instead of 'that is admired' may well be right; in 7–8 'to plant' has no construction (one verse at least may be missing after 'prosperity': Radt), although its pairing with 'work on the land' is very plausible; and the translation 'have ... undertaken' is insecure.

SOPHOCLES

(active from about 470 BC; died 406/5)

Lovers of Achilles (*ΑΧΙΛΛΕΩΣ ΕΡΑΣΤΑΙ, Achillis Amatores*)

TrGF 4².165–70 (F 149–57a), 741–2; cf. 3.567.

Texts, etc. Pearson (1917) 1.103–9; Sutton (1980) 36–8 (F 149); Lloyd-Jones (1996) 58–63; Diggle (1998) 36 (F 149); S. Scheurer, S. Kansteiner in KPS 227–35.

Discussions. A. Carson, *Eros the Bittersweet* (Boston, 1986) 111–16; Gantz (1993) 580–2; Conrad (1997) 159–61, 286; Voelke (2001) 251–5; P. Michelakis, *Achilles in Greek Tragedy* (Cambridge, 2002) 172–8.

Very little is known about this play; its satyric nature is stated in the source of F 153.

The setting is disputed, either near Mt. Pelion in Thessaly (F 154 below), where the humane centaur Chiron was bringing up the young Achilles, son of Peleus the king of Phthia in Thessaly, or on the island of Scyros, where Achilles' mother, the goddess Thetis, hid the youth among girls, to prevent his going to fight at Troy, where it was his destiny to die. A fragmentary hypothesis of Aeschylus' *Women of Etna* (P. Oxy. 2257 fr. 1: *TrGF* 3.126) complicates this dispute, for it compares the two plays for their internal changes of scene: if the setting of *Lovers* was Thessaly, it is inferred that the scene moved between Peleus' palace and Chiron's cave on Mr. Pelion; if the setting (or a setting) was Scyros, the scene may have moved between, first, Thessaly, and second, Scyros: see further below.

As well as Achilles, two other speaking characters are named in the book-fragments; Achilles' father Peleus speaks F 150 (part of a narrative: see n. 5 there; F 151 is a prose paraphrase of another part of his account) and Phoenix speaks F 153: Peleus had brought him to Chiron for safety after Phoenix's father Amyntor had angrily expelled him for usurping his concubine, and he became Achilles' life-long mentor and friend (Homer, *Iliad* 9.434–95; cf. Euripides' tragedy *Phoenix*). Achilles was evidently portrayed as extremely handsome, attractive to men as well as women (his bodily form and looks were emphasized in Homer, *e.g. Iliad* 2.673–4, *Odyssey* 24.17–18), so that in the play he is on the verge of manhood, when 'the beard first appears, the most beautiful time of youth' (*Iliad* 24.347–8, of a young prince). He is already accomplished both in hunting (F 154, naming either him or one of his hounds) and in weaponry (F 156). Those who set the play on Scyros relate the armour described in F 156 to the incident in which Achilles' concealment among the girls, to keep him from going to Troy, was betrayed when his instinctive love of warfare responded to the sight of weapons or to the sound of a war-trumpet (the incident was almost certainly dramatized in Euripides' tragedy *Scyrians*, for which see *TrGF* 5.666).

Achilles' beauty drew the lust of the satyrs, the 'Lovers' of the play-title; Achilles may even have been shown flashing winning looks towards girls to which the satyrs however reacted (cf. F 157).[1] Here F 153 is difficult; Phoenix refers to the satyrs as having lost their 'darling boy'; Photius, the fragment's source, states that the Greek word, which is neuter in gender, was used of both females and males and that Phoenix speaks when the satyrs in sexual frustration are beginning to eye women (see n. 7). So those who set the play on Scyros think of Achilles' disguise as a girl and therefore his sexual ambiguity (*e.g.* KPS 233–4; more coarse comedy would result), but they must posit Phoenix's presence – and that of the satyrs – there, too. It is interesting that the satyrs lusted after another hero who also spent time as a cross-dresser, Heracles (Sophocles F 756, cf. Achaeus, *Linus* F 26), whose story as the apparently transvestite slave of Queen Omphale was told in at least two other satyric dramas, each entitled *Omphale*, by Ion and Achaeus (both in our selection below). For other examples of satyrs' undiscriminating sexuality see Seaford (1984) 38–9 and Lissarague (1990a); A. Dierichs, *Erotik in der Kunst Griechenlands* (Mainz, 2008) 30–42, esp. 38–42 and Pls. 18–31; cf. n. 1 below, Gen. Intro. pp. 9–17 and Index of Motifs.

Whether in Thessaly or on Scyros, or on both, the presence of the satyrs must be explained; and confinement to Thessaly is more likely, because a regular 'country' role for the satyrs is easier (here, affinity and association with the similarly unusual centaurs); their presence on an island such as Scyros is nevertheless possible, cf. Aeschylus' *Net-Fishers* which is set on Seriphos; cf. also Euripides' *Cyclops*. Their attraction to Achilles is one more of their unrealisable ambitions or 'quests' (Conrad (1997) 159), like their hope of securing Danae in *Net-Fishers* F 47a.57–68 or Deianeira in Sophocles' *Oeneus* F **1130; in both instances, they are disappointed (our F 153). Unfortunately, the few fragments give no idea of their other actions in the play.[2]

There is only one substantial fragment, F 149; its speaker cannot be identified, but was probably an observer of the passions stirred by Achilles (Peleus would be suitable, after his experience with Thetis, or Phoenix after his episode with his father's concubine), rather than the satyrs themselves.

Notes

[1]   For the play's strong erotic element see Voelke (2001) 251–5 and M. Griffith, 'Sophocles' Satyr-Plays and the Language of Romance', in I. J. F. De Jong, A. Rijksbaron (eds), *Sophocles and the Greek Language* (Leiden-Boston, 2006) 64–6; Griffith draws attention to the lengthy discussion of F 149 by the poet Carson (1986). Michelakis (2002) 174 observes that 'the satyrs who lay siege to the young hero' conform to Athenian practice, and that some vase-paintings show satyrs courting young men (*e.g.* his figs 4 and 5, on pp. 176–7).

Compare the explicit sexual relationship between Achilles and Patroclus in Aeschylus' tragedy *Myrmidons*, at F 135 and 136. When Ovid, *Tristia* 2.411–12 writes 'the author who

---

F 149

τὸ γὰρ νόσημα τοῦτ᾽ ἐφίμερον κακόν·
ἔχοιμ᾽ ἂν αὐτὸ μὴ κακῶς ἀπεικάσαι.
ὅταν πάγου φανέντος αἰθρίου χεροῖν
κρύσταλλον ἁρπάσωσι παῖδες εὐπαγῆ,
τὰ πρῶτ᾽ ἔχουσιν ἡδονὰς ποταινίους·   (5)
τέλος δ᾽ ὁ θυμὸς οὔτ᾽ ἀφεῖναί πως θέλει
οὔτ᾽ ἐν χεροῖν τὸ κτῆμα σύμφορον μένει.
οὕτω δὲ τοὺς ἐρῶντας αὐτὸς ἵμερος
δρᾶν καὶ τὸ μὴ δρᾶν πολλάκις προσίεται.

Stobaeus 4.20.46; 2–7 concisely paraphrased by Zenobius 5.58
1 τὸ γὰρ νόσημα Dobree: ἔρωτος γὰρ νόσημα Stobaeus; ἐφίμερον Arsenius: ἐφήμερον is read uncertainly in the mss. of Stobaeus
3 χεροῖν Stobaeus ms. B, conj. Scaliger: χερσὶν other mss. of Stobaeus
4 παῖδες εὐπαγῆ L. Campbell: παιδιαῖσαγῆ Stobaeus
6 θυμὸς Dobree: χυμὸς Stobaeus; οὔτ᾽ ἀφεῖναί πως θέλει Degani, Collard (Zenobius' paraphrase happens to use the infinitive ἀφεῖναι): οὔθ᾽ ὅπως ἀφῇ θέλει Stobaeus
7 μένει Pearson: μένειν Stobaeus
8 οὕτω δὲ Schneidewin, following Gesner: οὔτε Stobaeus
9 προσίεται Meineke: προίεται Stobaeus

portrays Achilles softened by love goes unharmed for diminishing brave deeds in his verse', he more likely refers to this celebrated and much-cited tragedy than to Sophocles' satyr-play; and it has been argued that Sophocles would not demean Achilles even in satyric (Conrad (1997) 161). For Achilles' glance with its 'spears', see n. 11 below.

[2] Unlocatable fragments: F 152 and F 155; F 157a is a one-word lexicographic fragment. Michelakis (2002) 173 reviews the problems of even notional reconstruction concisely; like some others he suggests that the satyrs had an educational role in the play towards Achilles (resembling their care given elsewhere to the infant or young Dionysus: see *e.g.* our n. 11 on Aesch. *Net-Fishers* F 47a.22; they are often portrayed as *paidagogoi*, 'tutors', on red-figure vases); but such a role was much more likely here for Phoenix (above).

F 149 (Stobaeus 4.20.46)

... for this affliction is a delightful evil;[3] I can give a pretty good picture of it. Whenever frost appears under a clear sky and boys seize well-frozen ice in two hands, at first they enjoy novel pleasures; (5) but in the end neither their heart is willing in any way to let the ice go nor does its possession remain to advantage in their hands.[4] So the same desire frequently pushes lovers into action and inaction.

[3] 'delightful (evil)': Arsenius' ἐφίμερον is widely accepted; it is uncertainly read in Stobaeus together with ἐφήμερον ('short-lived'), which was nevertheless printed by Nauck. The complex and intense experience of desire was often couched in oxymoron in Greek literature. Sophocles' 'delightful evil' here recalls Hesiod's description of the highly eroticized Pandora as a 'beautiful evil', *Theogony* 585, cf. *Works and Days* 66 where she excites 'painful longing'; Sappho famously described *eros* as 'bittersweet', F 130.2 *PMG* (cf. Carson 1986). Its effects are frequently expressed as an 'affliction', with the Greek word-root νοσ- used here, a metaphor from 'disease'; Gorgias, for instance, refers to Helen's desire (ἔρως) for Paris as a νόσημα (*Hel.* 19, 82 B 11 DK).

[4] The comparison between the inconstancy of love and of ice melting in the hands was perhaps already proverbial and certainly became so (*e.g.* Zenobius 5.58).

In vv. 6–7 we print a conjectural text. In 6 editors generally misgive Stobaeus' deliberative question ὅπως ... ἀφῇ in awkward dependence upon θέλει, a verb expressing will ('their heart is willing whether to let the ice go'), and they either obelize or emend the line; and in 7 many explain Stobaeus' infinitive μένειν either as dependent on 'is willing', with a difficult change of subject ('nor is their acquisition willing to remain'); or as upon 'to advantage' ('nor (is it) to advantage for their acquisition to stay'). In any interpretation 'to advantage' gives rather unconvincing sense; whence in conjecturing μένει '(nor does its possession) remain', Pearson nevertheless gave the Greek adjective σύμφορος the unparalleled meaning '(remain) solid'.

Lastly, in 6 Dobree's 'heart' for Stobaeus' 'liquid' is likely to be correct, for it admits 'emotion' to the comparison between love and ice, echoing 'desire' in v. 1 and anticipating its repetition in 8. Stobaeus' 'liquid' is however defended by E. M. Craik in Sommerstein (2003) 55–6, since the Greek word regularly in medical works describes any body-fluid, and the verb 'let go' in this line is both poetic and medical for 'emit, make to issue'; so Craik suggests it means both 'melt-water' and 'semen' (the verb is used of ejaculation at Archilochus F 196a.52 *IEG* West).

F 150

<ΠΗΛΕΥΣ>   τίς γάρ με μόχθος < ... > οὐκ ἐπεστάτει;
                λέων δράκων τε, πῦρ, ὕδωρ ...

Scholia on Pindar, *Nemeans* 3.60

F 152   ἢ δορὸς διχόστομον πλᾶκτρον·
              {δίπτυχοι γὰρ ὀδύναι μιν ἤρικον
              Ἀχιλλῇου δόρατος}

Scholia on Pindar, *Nemeans* 6.85
2–3 del. Casaubon, eds

F 153

ΦΟΙΝΙΞ   παπαῖ, τὰ παιδίχ', ὡς ὁρᾷς, ἀπώλεσας.

Photius Galeanus 369.4 Porson, other lexicographers

F 154   σὺ δ', ὦ Σύαγρε, Πηλιωτικὸν τρέφος ...

Athenaeus 9. 401c

F 155   γλώσσης μελίσσῃ τῷ κατερρυηκότι

Scholia on Sophocles, *Oedipus at Colonus* 481

F 156   ὁ δ' ἔνθ' ὅπλοις ἀρρῶξιν Ἡφαίστου τέχνῃ ...

Choeroboscus in *Grammatici Graeci* 4.1.415.6 Hilgard

F 150 (Scholia on Pindar *Nemeans* 3.60)

\<PELEUS\>   For what struggle did not attend me ...? Lion and serpent, fire,
water ... [5]

[5]   Part of Peleus' account how he pursued the ever-metamorphosing goddess Thetis before
he could take her as his destined wife.

F 152 (Scholia on Pindar, *Nemeans* 6.85)

or the two-edged point of the spear {for twofold pains inflicted
by the Achillean spear pierced him}.[6]

[6]   The 'spear' here is literal, not the metaphor of F 157 below (n. 11). Vv. 2–3 are generally
considered to belong to a second citation conflated with the first (v. 1).

F 153 (Photius Galeanus 369.4 Porson)

PHOENIX   Oh! You have lost your darling boy, as you see! [7]

[7]   'darling boy' is the term for the object of Polyphemus' homosexual lust at *e.g. Cyc.* 584;
while this may suggest that the satyrs courted Achilles unsuccessfully, such a scene would
produce much crude comedy appropriate to the genre.

F 154 (Athenaeus 9. 401c)

... and you, Boar-Hunter, raised on Mt. Pelion ...[8]

[8]   This could be addressed to Achilles or to one of his hounds.

F 155 (Scholia on Sophocles, *Oedipus at Colonus* 481)

... to him (?) who flowed with honey on his tongue ...[9]

[9]   Spoken perhaps by or about Phoenix, Achilles' mentor and the speaker of F 153, or the
eloquent Chiron in Thessaly; less likely, by or about Nestor on Scyros, suggested by KPS 234
(who cites Homer, *Iliad* 1.249 for his speech 'flowing more sweetly than honey').

F 156 (*Grammatici Graeci* 4.1.415.6 Hilgard)

... and he then ... in armour made unbreakable by the art of
Hephaestus ...[10]

[10]   The armour may be Achilles' first armour at Troy, which Patroclus puts on at Nestor's
suggestion (*Iliad* 11.798), and which Hector strips from him after his death (17.125, cf.
18.82–4 *etc.*); its description in 16.130–54 implies its divine origin. Or, 'armour' may allude
anticipatorily to the second, even more splendid weaponry which Achilles' mother Thetis
then asks Hephaestus to make for him (18.369–613).

F 157

ὀμμάτων ἄπο
λόγχας ἵησιν

Hesychius ο 736 Latte
ὀμμάτων ἄπο | λόγχας Casaubon, Blomfield: ὀμματοπάλογχα Hesychius; ἵησιν Nauck: φησίν
Hesychius

F 157 (Hesychius o 736 Latte)
    ... from his eyes he launches spears ...[11]

[11]   Achilles' glance with its 'spears' recalls the imagery of Aeschylus, whose Iphigenia shoots a 'piteous bolt' from her eye at those about to sacrifice her (*Ag.* 240), while the seductive gaze of his Helen is a 'melting glance shot from her eyes' (*Ag.* 742); in these latter two instances, the nature of the gaze reflects its impact on the onlooker (see P. O'Sullivan, *AJP* 129 (2008) esp. 173–87), and so here Achilles' glance engenders desire in others. 'Spears', like the armour of F 156 (cf. F 152), may, as Michelakis (2002) 175 notes, nevertheless suggest Achilles' future glory with this weapon; or the young hero's glance may also be comparable with the ferocious glance of the satyric Heracles in Euripides' *Syleus* F 689 below.

Inachus *(ΙΝΑΧΟΣ)*

TrGF 4².247–67 (F **269a–**295a), 745–6; cf. 3.569–70.

Texts etc. Pearson (1917) I.197–213 (F 270–95 only); Page (1942) 22–7 (F 269c, d, e); R. Pfeiffer, *Ein neues Inachos-Fragment des Sophokles* (Munich, 1958) (F 269a, b), supplementing and revising his *Die Netzfischer des Aischylos und der Inachos des Sophokles* (Munich, 1938) 23–62 (F 269c, d, e); Carden (1974) 52–93 (a delayed reaction to Carden by C. Pavese, *Dioniso* 61.1 (1991) 41–4: see also *Discussions* below); D. F. Sutton, *Sophocles' Inachus* (Meisenheim-am-Glan, 1979); Lloyd-Jones (1996) 112–35; Diggle (1998) 41–4 (F 269a, 269c); C. Heynen, R. Krumeich in KPS 313–43.

Discussions. W. M. Calder III, 'The dramaturgy of Sophocles' *Inachus*', *GRBS* 1 (1958) 137–55; N. E. Collinge, 'Sophocles' *Inachus*', *PCPS* 5 (1958–9) 32–5; C. Pavese, 'L'Inaco di Sofocle', *QUCC* 3 (1967) 31–50; Chourmouziades (1974) 75–6, 104–9; R. Seaford, 'Black Zeus in Sophocles' *Inachos*', *CQ* 30 (1980) 23–9; Sutton (1980) 48–54; S. R. West, 'Io and the dark stranger (Sophocles, *Inachus* F 269a)', *CQ* 34 (1984) 292–302; Gantz (1993) 198–202; Conrad (1997) 127–49, 277–84; Kaimio (2001) 41–2, 49, 58; A. L. Allan, 'Cattle-stealing in Sophocles' *Inachus*', in Sommerstein (2003) 309–28; Voelke (2001) 161–3, 168–70 (lyric structures), 244–50 and *passim*.

Art. LIMC V.1.356–8 'Hermes' nos 837–54, esp. 838 (= *ibid.* 653–4 'Inachos' no. 2) and 839 (= V.1.667 'Io I' no. 33 = Trendall-Webster (1971) II.6); *ibid.* 669 'Io I' nos 56 and 60; cf. Sutton (1979 above) pls 1–6.

This play is endlessly fascinating and frustrating to reconstructors, because papyrus fragments have at last provided a slightly firmer hold upon the plot, although they still give too little help with the long-known and numerous but almost wholly contextless book fragments;[1] and because the myth which provides the amusing plot was complex, variable and popular, but in this satyr-play paradoxically seems to become weighty in human and theological terms (as in its occurrence in the tragedy Aeschylus, *Suppliants* 291–315, 538–89, cf. *Prometheus Bound* 562–886): see esp. Conrad (1997) 146–9 on the difficulty of providing 'comic relief after tragedy' in this myth (he cites words of Sutton (1980) 164).

This last consideration had long frustrated confidence that the play was indeed satyric (see *e.g.* Calder (1958) and Collinge (1959)), because the single formal indication is a mutilated note of the voice-part at F 269a.46: χο followed by ρ, insecurely supplemented as XO<ΡΟΣ ΣΑΤΥ>Ρ<ΩΝ> 'Chorus of satyrs'. Weighty issues and genuine pathos are not, however, impossible for satyric drama: *e.g.* in *Cyclops* 347–436 Odysseus' desperate prayer to Zeus, the Chorus' revulsion at the cannibalism, and the hero's description of it; the piteous outburst in Aeschylus, *Net-Fishers* F 47a.9–21 of Danae who, like Io in *Inachus*, was another victim of Zeus' lust (but one could imagine the whole scene being played for laughs). Worth note too are satyrs depicted in scenes central to the Inachus-Io myth such as Hermes about to kill Argus, *e.g. LIMC* V.1.669 'Io I' nos 56, 60. Scholars, esp. Pfeiffer (1958) and after him Pavese (1967), Carden (1974) and Radt (*TrGF* 4, 1977), have instead inferred satyric nature from the characters, action and language revealed in the papyrus fragments: a mysterious 'dark stranger', described as a deceitful and injurious guest in Inachus' house (F 269a.22–9, 32–3; F 293 the single word 'crafty', see n. 1 at the end of this introductory discussion), but also as miraculous in his beneficence (F 275) and his transformation of Io (F 269a.36–42; F 279–80, cf. ?292, 295a); panicky stage-business from the chorus (F 269a.51–6, 269b, 269c.34–47); a mythic creature on stage, the many-eyed Argus (F 281a, cf. 281).

At the heart of the much-told myth (Sutton (1979) 1–8, Gantz (1993) 198–202, cf. *Prometheus Bound* 645–82, [Apollod.] 2.1.3) is Io, daughter of Inachus the king and eponymous river of Argos (F 284.1, cf. 270–1). Her beauty attracted Zeus' eye while she was (in many accounts, *e.g.* Aeschylus, *Suppliants* 291–3, [Apollod.]) a temple-servant of Hera, the patroness of Argos. Then, either Zeus abducted her but transformed her into a heifer, to disguise his *amour* and to protect her against Hera, or Hera tried to prevent the *amour* and herself transformed Io in this way. In either version Hera maddens the heifer-girl with a cattle-fly into endless running but also sets the multi-eyed and sleepless Argus over her as a 'cowherd'. Zeus frees her from Argus by having Hermes kill him (see below); but Io continues running frenziedly until she reaches Egypt, where Zeus restores her form by his touch and she bears him a son Epaphus ('The Touched One'). This man is to be the founder of a race which later returns to Argos and rules it, the Danaans (the return is the plot of Aeschylus' 'Danaid' trilogy which includes *Suppliants*; for this destiny see also *Prometheus Bound* 844–69).

Sophocles' play began with the abduction and transformation of Io. The orientating narrative prologue may have been spoken by Silenus (as in *Cyclops*); but since the chorus of satyrs in their entry-song greet Inachus (F

270, 271), the king is perhaps already on stage and therefore the more likely speaker (cf. KPS 341).

A marginal line-number in the first big papyrus fragment, F 269a (which tells of Io's abduction and transformation), shows that it comes already about 300 lines into the play; F 279 and F 295a describe the horns that have grown on Io's head, and probably come from this context. Whether there was a substantial scene preceding F 269a cannot be established, but a first appearance by Hermes has been regularly suggested; for his later entry at F 269c.23 is described as a return. In the latter part of this second big papyrus fragment Hermes has been suggested as one voice in the stichomythia 40–7 (but the attribution of voice-parts in F 269c as a whole remains speculative: see the Greek *apparatus*); in F 269d and e, separated and very damaged parts of the same papyrus, identification of speaker(s) is impossible, but Hermes is named as Zeus' 'lackey', d.22, e.2.

To add to these difficulties, one book fragment shows Hermes conversing with Iris, or at least in her presence (F 272): as the usual messenger of Hera she may have brought word that Hera was to set Argus over Io – and then Argus himself arrives, 'singing' (F 281a). Hermes may have made to kill him at once on Zeus' orders (implied in *Prometheus Bound* and [Apollod.]: above), but he may first have overcome him in a musical contest: F 269c.7–13 'pipe ... cow-stall ... fettered' have suggested to editors that Hermes is off-stage, playing the *syrinx* or Pan-pipes with which he tries to send Argus to sleep (see F 281 n. 31 below; at Ovid, *Metamorphoses* 1.671–721 Hermes with difficulty charms Argus to sleep by playing pipe-music, and then kills him); or that Argus himself appeared in this scene, only to be mistaken for Hermes (21–2). (Lloyd-Jones (1996) 117 adduces F 288 'a bean-casting juror' and 295 '(voting-)funnel' for the idea of the satyrs adjudicating the contest with a 'vote'; cf. Soph. *Trackers* F 314a.26 and, for in-play contests, *Adespota* F 646a.26–7 and n. 22.) Perhaps Argus fled, to pursue Io in her frenzy. For the play's presumably happy end see (1) below.

Some large features remain unclear. (1) Both papyri and book fragments yield little indication how important or how constantly present Inachus himself was, but as the title-character his concern must have been as much for his own destiny as for his daughter. At *Prometheus Bound* 645–68 oracles warn of his family's destruction if he does not sanction Io's union with Zeus, and Pausanias 2.15.4–5 writes that when Inachus 'chose' Hera as patroness for Argos, in preference to Poseidon the god of waters, the latter brought drought and dearth upon the land: see F 284, which some reconstructors put near the play's start, narrated by Inachus in the prologue-scene (the land's ancient prosperity may be recalled in F 278). Io's abduction would demoralise Inachus further; later he seems to be in angry protest at Hermes (F 269d.21–4; F 269c.28–33 has already shown criticism of Zeus' truthfulness and good faith). So the play's end probably told of the future nevertheless guaranteed by Zeus (and announced by Hermes?) both for Io, as his bedmate and mother of Epaphus, and for Inachus her suffering father, with the same promise of a dynasty and perhaps with immortalisation as the river.[2] The first, if uncomprehended, manifestation of such a destiny was Zeus' bestowal of miraculous plenty and wealth on the palace, F 273, 275, 283 (on F 273 and 283 see also (2) below), cf. F 274, 276 and 287.

(2) Io is abducted by a 'dark stranger' (F 269a.54, cf. 23, 45, 49), who thus in Greek morality commits a huge offence against his host Inachus (like the guest Paris abducting his host Menelaus' wife Helen, Aesch. *Ag.* 60–2, 399–402 *etc.*). It is not clear from the fragment whether this was Zeus himself in disguise: 'dark' is taken by some to allude to him as father of the 'dark-skinned' (Egyptian) Epaphus (*Prometheus Bound* 851; see *e.g.* Pfeiffer (1958) 37–9, Carden (1974) 63 and esp. West (1984) 293–8). Scholars have questioned such an unflattering on-stage portrayal of the great Olympian god, even in a light-hearted satyr-play, and many follow Seaford (1980) in identifying the stranger as the 'Zeus' of the Underworld, Hades-Pluto, presented here ambiguously as also Pluto the god of Wealth (F 273, 283)[3]; if the adjective 'dark' means not 'dark-skinned' but 'black', then Seaford's view is supported by numerous mentions elsewhere of an underworld Zeus, *i.e.* Hades: *e.g.* Homer, *Iliad* 9.457, Aesch. *Supp.* 158; cf. West on Hesiod, *Works and Days* 465. On the other hand, some identify the 'dark stranger' as Hermes, also in disguise, who later returns to make the future bright (see above; Calder (1958) 150 and Sutton (1979) 65 n. 54, cf. KPS 339; also the perplexing F 291 and n. 38); Hermes too has underworld associations, as escort of the dead to Hades (Aeschylus, *Choephori* 1–2 etc.); see n. 13 on F 269c.19. Whatever the truth, the mystery and excitement would have added to the spectators' enjoyment, especially if there was theatrical disguise.

(3) Last, what was the role or interest of the satyrs, except their invariable function in forming the chorus and creating 'atmosphere'? Because of the play's 'rustic' background (common in satyric, above all in *Cyclops* and Sophocles' *Trackers*), it is suggested that Silenus and chorus were working, perhaps involuntarily, for Inachus as cowherds; they are then appropriately present as commentators upon Io's transformation and upon the monstrous

Argus' arrival (note again Lloyd-Jones's suggestion that they adjudicated a singing contest, F 288, 295 above).[4] The fragments however give no evidence of the satyrs as 'slaves' or of their common reward at play-end with 'freedom'. Moreover, the action of the play is remarkably busy, and the parts of Inachus, Hermes (if not also Zeus himself), Iris and Argus provide enough stage-business to leave little for Silenus and the satyrs to do, and thus small importance for them – very differently from their major roles in e.g. *Cyclops* and other plays of Aeschylus and Sophocles (cf. KPS 343). Conrad (1997) 145–6 nevertheless judges that Silenus may have had a role independent of the satyrs.

A number of vase-paintings show scenes variously with Inachus, Io, Hermes and Argus, but are likely to have been inspired by the general mythographic tradition rather than Sophocles' play specifically: see *LIMC* and Sutton (1979) under 'Art' in the Bibliography.

F **269a
col. i
*first 6 lines lost, then 14 badly damaged lines (7–20) into which F **269b.2**
(the only line of the fragment's three which has more than letter-traces) is
perhaps to be restored:*]ς ἔχ' αὐτόν, ὦ ἰού ἰού;
then the ends of 8 lines (21–8):

          21 *traces* ἢ 'νθάδε, 22 *traces* τὸν θεοστυγῆ, 23 τὸν] ξένον
          νοῶ τίς ἦν, 24] θυρῶν τὸ πᾶν μύσος, 25]. ἐπῃνέθη καλά,
          26].ηυρέθη κακά, 27]. ἐξ ἐ[ν]ωπίων, 28] φηλώσας ἐμέ,
          then:

col. ii *(beginnings of 28 lines)*
<ΧΟΡΟΣ?>   ἀλλ' οἴχεται μὴν κἀστ..[
             τὰ σὰ σκοτώσας ὄμμ[ατα   (30)
             ταῦτ' οὐκέτ' ἴδρις εἰμ[ὶ] δειν[

P. Oxy. 2369 (1st c. BC) ed. E. Lobel (1956) fr. 1
23 οὐ lost earlier in the line Lobel
24 διὰ] θυρῶν Lobel; cf. 35
30–1 *e.g.* ὄμμ[αθ'· ἃ δέ σε δείν' ἔδρα] | ταῦτ' οὐκέτ' ἴδρις εἰμ[ὶ] δείν[' εἰ χρὴ καλεῖν *e.g.* (and
32 δεινά; ... punct.) Diggle

Notes

¹ *Inachus* has the largest number of book-fragments of any satyr-play, about 30; next is Ion's *Omphale*, with about 20. F 282 is the sole gnomic fragment, and impossible to locate; equally intractable are most of the very brief lexicographic fragments, which we translate here: F 280 'cow', F 289 'with darkening storm', F 292 'hair (dishevelled) by storm', F 293 'crafty' (lit. 'fox-like'), F 294 'up and down (metaphorical) or 'unwinnowed' (cf. F 276 'silos of barley'). F 285 is corrupt and incoherent; we do not print it.

² [Plutarch] (*On Rivers* 18.1.7–10 Müller) also tells that Inachus reviled Zeus for abducting Io and was punished by a madness so that he leapt into the river, which was renamed after him.

³ For Wealth ('Ploutos') named Pluto see Ar. *Wealth* 727 and scholia (the source of F 273); for the underworld Pluto as a euphemistic name (source of the earth's wealth) see Plato, *Cratylus* 403a.

⁴ Allan (2003) 314 mentions a myth that Argus killed a cattle-stealing satyr in Arcadia, but such a motif would only have complicated the plot. The mention is only incidental to Allan's otherwise careful study of the play, which includes an imaginative reconstruction, 316–28 (her title is unfortunately misleading).

The following first big papyrus fragment is already well into the play; its line 36 is numbered 300.

F **269a (P. Oxy. 2369 fr. 1)

6 lines (1–6) missing at the top of col. i, then 14 very fragmentary lines (7–20) into which the tiny F 269b is perhaps to be restored,

> 2 'Keep hold of him! Hey, go on, go on!'; *then:*

8 line-ends (21–8), perhaps the close of stichomythia between Chorus and Inachus:

> 21 ... (than *or* or) here, 22 ... the god-detested (*masculine*) ..., 23 ... I (do not) comprehend who (the) stranger was, 24 ... (through?) the doors (...?) that total pollution (*or* polluter), 25 ... (he?) was thanked ... good things, 26 ... (he?) was found ... bad things (*or* bad things were found), 27 ... away from the front, 28 ... after tricking me.

then the whole of col. ii, 28 line-beginnings (29–56):

<CHORUS?> Yes, he is gone, and ... after casting darkness over your eyes ... (30) ... I no longer understand ... these terrible things ...⁵

⁵ Diggle's supplement yields (30) '... your eyes (; but the terrible things he did to you –) I no longer understand (if I should call) these things terrible.' The highly poetic word here translated 'understand' is often used of (in)comprehensible events or prophecies; cf. conversely F 269c.16 and n. 12 'knowledgeable', from the same word-root.

<ΙΝΑΧΟΣ?>   εἰ δεινά; πῶς γὰρ οὔχ; ὁ....[
               σεμνὰς τραπέζας ἐν δόμοι[ς
               ὁ δ' ἀμφὶ χεῖρα παρθέν[ῳ
               Ἰοῖ δι' οἴκων οἴχεται σ.[(35)
               κόρης δὲ μυκτὴρ κρᾶτ.[
               ἐκβουτυποῦται κα..[
               φύει κάρα ταυρῶ[.].].[
               αὐχὴν ἐπ' ὤμοι[ς
               ποδῶν δὲ χηλ[αὶ   (40)
               κροτοῦσι θράν[
               γυνὴ λέαινα π.[
               ἧσται λινεργ[
               τοιαῦτα ..[
               ὁ ξεῖνος α..[(45)
ΧΟ.   ἄφθογγός εἰμ[ι
               2 lines with only a few uncertain letters
               ὁ ξεῖνος ουθυ...[
               ἄπιστα το.....[(50)
–   ἰώ, Γᾶ, θεῶν μᾶτερ
                   ἀξύνετ..[
                   ὁ πολυφάρμ[ακος
–   κάρβανος αἰθὸς ..[
–   ὁ μὲν ε.[(55)
–   ὁ δ' αἰολωπὸν α.[

34 end βαλὼν now lost Lloyd-Jones
35 end σ is insecure
36 P. Oxy. has the line-number 300 here
38 ταυρω[.].].[: τ and ρω are insecurely read in P. Oxy.: ταυρω[π]α.[, with ο above]α, *i.e.* correction to]ο, in either –ωπος or –ον, read and suggested by Pfeiffer
46–56 voice-part for Chorus marked in P. Oxy. for 46, with voice-change in 51, 54, 56 (and that for 49 deleted); see n. 9 on translation
51 [μᾶτερ is restored on the basis of Philodemus, *On Piety* P. Herc. 1428 fr. 3 and 428 II.11–13 Nardelli (A. Henrichs, *Cronache Ercolanesi* 5 (1975) 18)

<INACHUS?>   Whether they are terrible? Of course they are! The (one who) ... the sacred tables[6] inside the house ... He (threw?) his arm round the maiden Io and has gone off through the house ... (35). The girl's nostril ... (her) head ... has been formed into a cow's ... a (bull's?) head grows ... the neck on her shoulders ... hoofed feet ... (40) clatter on the floorboards ... a woman-lioness[7] ... sits ... (working?) linen[8] ... Such things ... the stranger ... (45).

CHO.[9]   I'm lost for words ...(*two very fragmentary lines*) ... the stranger ... unbelievable ... (50)

– (*singing*) O Earth, (mother) of the gods ...! ... incomprehensible ... the man with his great magic ...

– (*speaking*) ... dark stranger ...[10]

– (*singing*) The one ... (55)

– (*speaking*) The other ... (the ...?) with the glancing eyes ...

---

[6] 'sacred tables': altars polluted by the stranger's behaviour, 22, 24.

[7] 'woman-lioness': probably a comparison with the Sphinx (a scaly lioness with a young-girl's face) to illustrate a mixed creature such as the young girl Io has become with her horned head. West (1984) 299–302 however suggests that Io is (or had been) embroidering such a creature (see next note).

[8] '(working?) linen': at Ovid, *Art of Love* 1.77 Io wears linen.

[9] Vv. 46–50, 54 and 56 may be iambic trimeters spoken by the Leader, and 51–3 and 55 lyric responses by the rest of the Chorus.

[10] See introductory discussion (2), at end.

F **269c

col. i　15 *lines* (1–15), *mostly mere traces, but with these words legible:*

7] σύριγγο[ς] δὲ κλύω

(line-end; almost all letters insecurely read),

8 σ]ταθμου[, 13]ποδίζεται *(line-end);*
the end of the column is missing; then:

col. ii
<XO.?>

	πολὺ πολυιδρίδας
	ὅτις ὅδε προτέρων
	ὄνομ' εὖ σ' ἐθρόει,
	τὸν Ἀϊδοκυνέας
	σκότον ἄβ<ρ>οτον ὑπαί.　　　　(20)
<–>	τὸν Διὸς μὲν οὖν ἐρώτων ἄ[γγ]ελον, μέγαν τρόχιν,
	εἰκάσαι πάρεστιν Ἑρμῆν π[ρὸ]ς τὰ σὰ ψοφήματα.
<–>	αὐτὸν εἶπας, αὐτόν, ὅς μοι δεῦρ' ἀνέστρεψεν πόδα.
<–>	δευτέρους πόνους ἔοικας πρὶν μῦσαι κενοὺς ἐλᾶν.
<XO.>	ὠή· ἐσορᾷς;　　　　　　　　　(25)
	†ειστονα..† πόδ' ἔχειν·
	μανία τάδε κλύειν·
	σὺ γὰρ οὖν, Ζεῦ, λόγων
	κακὸς εἶ πίστεως

P. Tebt. 692 (2nd c. BC) ed. A. S. Hunt, J. G. Smyly (1933) fr. 1.
The divisions of the voice-parts are disputed among all editors.
20 ἄβ<ρ>οτον Fritsch
23 –ον ειπ- and ος μοι insecurely read in P. Tebt.
25 punct. as question Pfeiffer
28 end ων insecurely read
29 πιστεως insecurely read

F **269c (P. Tebt. 692 fr. 1)

col. i   *traces of 15 lines* (1–15), *with only these words partly legible:*
        7 but I hear a pipe, 8 cow-stall, 13 is fettered (?)[11]

col. ii

<CHO.?>   (*singing*) Very, very knowledgeable (parents had he?),[12] whoever
        of earlier men well called you by your name, you (here) under the
        divine darkness of the Cap of Hades.[13] (20)

<–>   (*spoken dialogue*) Yes, one may guess you are the messenger of
        Zeus' loves, the great runner, Hermes, from the noises you've
        made.[14]

<–>   Himself – you've said it! – himself!, who has turned back here
        towards me.[15]

<–>   You look to be bringing yourself fruitless work for a second time,
        before you can bat an eyelid![16]

<CHO.>   (*singing*) Oh, look! You see? (25) ... to keep your feet (away?);
        hearing these things is madness.[17] You're bad at (keeping?) your
        word, then, Zeus ...

[11] 'pipe ... cow-stall ... fettered': on the implication of these words for reconstruction see introductory discussion. In [Apollod.] 2.1.3 Argus is said to have bound Io to an olive-tree.

[12] 'knowledgeable': accusative case and plural of an adjective, its noun and controlling verb now lost from the previous column. Perhaps 'parents' are meant, for many seers and diviners descended in exclusive families. The wording of 16–18 resembles that of Aesch. *Ag.* 681–91, a play upon Helen's name (Greek *hel-* 'destroy').

[13] 'Cap of Hades': making the wearer invisible (the name Hades was sometimes etymologized as 'Invisible', *a-id-*), cf. F 272 n. 25 below; [Hesiod] *Shield* 226–7 describes it as 'having the dread darkness of night'. In some accounts Perseus wore it while killing the Gorgon. The distribution of the following voice-parts is mostly inferred by editors, who offer conflicting identification of the speakers.

    21–4 are trochaic tetrameters, suitable for the sudden anxiety; cf. Aesch. *Sisyphus* F 227 (a single line survives) and perhaps *Net-Fishers* F 46a.18–21 and n. 4.

[14] 'the noises you've made': at his entry or (Kaimio (2001) 49) those of his pipe, line 7, cf. 32 and n. 17.

[15] Possibly Hermes reenters here; cf. 34–5.

[16] Is this said to Hermes, who failed with a first attempt to send Argus to sleep (or to kill him)?

[17] The dochmiac metre of 27–9 underscores the satyrs' agitation: they are over-reacting to Hermes' music, as they do in Soph. *Trackers* F 314.138–220.

two fragmentary lines (30–1) ending with the word 31 πορπαφόρος; *rest of column missing; then:*

col. iii

	ψιθυραν μάλ' αἰολα[ν].	(32)
<–>	πάντα μηχανᾷ τὸ Δῖον ὡσ[	
<ΧΟ.?>	ἦ ῥα τάχα Διὸς αὖ,	
	Διὸς ἄρα λάτρις ὅδε;	(35)
	ἐπί με πόδα νέμει.	
	{ἔχε με· πόδα νέμει.}	
	†ἐμεχερακονιει†	
	μέγα δέος ἀραβεῖ.	
<–>	τῶν ἐναντίων τὸ τάρβ[ος	(40)
<–>	τοῦ κάτω Διὸς φαλαγγ[	
<–>	δωμάτων γ' εἰ μὴ ἀπελᾷ[	
<–>	ποῦ δὲ χρὴ πόδα στατίζε[ιν	
<–>	προστι...ς φόνον βλέπ[	
<–>	μη[8 let.]ωκ' ἀγῶνο[ς	(45)
<–>	μὴ λέγ' α... ἐκ κορύνης [	
<–>	οἴζομαι λα[7 let.]ριμ[	

traces of one further line; rest of column missing

32 -αν … -α[ν] P. Tebt.: grammatical case indeterminable
36 νεμεῖ Hunt, Smyly
37 added by a later hand in P. Tebt.: deleted by Maas
39 P. Tebt. may have intended a new voice for this line and positioned it incorrectly for 38
40 first ν and τι insecurely read in ἐναντίων
41 τοῦ (Pfeiffer) κάτω insecurely read
42 ἀπελᾷ[ς Hunt, Smyly
47 beg. οἰ[ ]ομαι insecurely read

two fragmentary lines (30–1) *ending with the word* 31 wearing a brooch; *the rest of col. ii is missing.*

col. iii

	(*end of spoken dialogue?*) ... very changeful whispering ...[18]
<–>	The ... of Zeus ... contrives everything like ...!
<CHO.?>	(*singing in sudden alarm*) Truly it's Zeus' – yes, Zeus' – servant here again so quickly. (35) He's moving towards me! {Hold me! He's moving!} (*corrupt and unintelligible line*) great fear is making my teeth chatter![19]

(*dialogue resumes*)

<–>	The fear of my enemies ... (40)
<–>	... the spider (?) of Zeus below ...[20]
<–>	Unless he (*or* you?) drive(s) ... from the house ...
<–>	But where should we stand our ground ...?
<–>	... is looking (?) (towards ...) death ...
<–>	(Don't?) ... of the struggle ... (45)
<–>	Don't speak ... from the cudgel ...
<–>	I'm wailing ...

    traces of one further line

[18] 'changeful whispering' (the syntax of the Greek words, here left unaccented, cannot be determined): probably that of Hermes' Pan-pipes (but that of Argus' pipes at *Prometheus Bound* 574–5); but Hermes was known as the 'Whisperer' because of his insidious and deceitful words (cf. Zeus in 28–9; he imbues Pandora with lies and deceit at Hesiod, *Works and Days* 67–8, 77–8). A statue of him with this name was a land-mark in Athens, [Demosthenes] 59.39.

[19] '(great fear ...) teeth chatter': more probably this, a colloquial phrase, than 'there's great terror in his rattling'. Satyrs' excessive fear is made 'comic' at *e.g.* Soph. *Trackers* F 314.145–68, *Cyc.* 635–49; cf. also their bluff and bluster at *Cyc.* 596–8, 632–4.

[20] 'of Zeus below': Hades: see introductory discussion (2). A threatening Egyptian at Aesch. *Suppliants* 886–7 is imagined as a nightmare spider.

F **269d (P. Tebt. 692: see on F **269c) fr. 2

Ends or near-ends of 13 very fragmentary lines (1–13) with only a few letters legible, then 14 further lines (14–27) in which the following words are read, some letters insecurely:

14] ἄρισ[τ]α δ' οὐ, 15]. ἐξηῦρον ὠμότητά τ[ε, 17] 6 *let.*
ἀλεύσομεν θο[*(most letters insecure),* 19] 7 *let.* ἡ φύσασα
γῆ, 20]οντι πείθεσθαι καλῶς, 21] ταῦτα· μὴ λέξῃς πλέω,
22 εἶ]πον Ζηνὸς αἰάξαι λάτρι[ν, 23] πάρεστιν Ἰνάχῳ λόγ[,
24] ὀλίγον ἰσχύεις ὅμ[ως

F **269e (P. Tebt. 692: see on F **269c) fr. 3

4 vestigial line-ends including the words

2 λάτριν *and* 3 καλῶς,

both with some letters insecurely read

F 270

XO.   Ἴναχε νᾶτορ, παῖ τοῦ κρηνῶν
         πατρὸς Ὠκεανοῦ, μέγα πρεσβεύων
         Ἄργους τε γύαις Ἥρας τε πάγοις
         κἂν Τυρσηνοῖσι Πελασγοῖς ...

Dionysius of Halicarnassus, *Antiquities of Rome* 1.25.2
4 κἂν Lloyd-Jones: καὶ Dionysius

F **269d (P. Tebt. 692 fr. 2)

Ends or near-ends of 13 very fragmentary lines (1–13) with only a few letters legible, then 14 further lines (14–27) in which the following words are read:

> 14 but not (the?) best, 15 I discovered (... and?) cruelty, 17 we shall be on guard against, 19 the earth that generated,[21] 20 to obey (... ?) well, 21 ... this: say no more!, 22 I (said) that Zeus' lackey (would?) cry in pain (*or* I (told) Zeus' lackey to cry in pain),[22] 23 it is (not?) possible for Inachus ... word, 24 you have little strength nevertheless.

[21] 'generated': *i.e.* bore Argus, probably, the earth being the mother of all and esp. monstrous creatures; but Argus appears in other mythology to have had human parents (*e.g.* Aesch. *Suppliants* 305).

[22] 'lackey': the word and cognates occur ten times in Sophocles, three in *Inachus* alone (also F 269a.35, 269e.2). Prometheus uses it contemptuously of Hermes in *Prometheus Bound* 966 (a play in which Io's story makes a whole episode, 589–886: see introductory discussion). In *Inachus* Hermes is also the 'great runner' (F 269c.21), similarly derogatory. If any part of F 269d.15–24 is spoken by the satyrs, such veering between bravado (here) and abject terror (see n. 19 above) is typical of them.

F **269e (P. Tebt. 692 fr. 3)

4 vestigial line-ends including the words

> 2 lackey, 3 well (*adverb*)

F 270 (Dionysius of Halicarnassus, *Antiquities of Rome* 1.25.2)

CHO. Inachus in your flow, son of Oceanus the father of springs, great in your power over the fields of Argos and the mountains of Hera, and among the Tyrrhenian Pelasgians ...[23]

[23] 'Hera': the patron goddess of Argos. 'Pelasgians': apparently immigrants to Argos from the Tyrrhenians who inhabited the island of Lemnos in the Aegean: see Philochorus 328 F 99–101 *FGrH*. This fragment and the next are anapaestic, appropriate to an intoned invocation.

'power over': the Greek datives 'fields' and 'mountains' are apparently controlled by the verb πρεσβεύων (LSJ I.1.c gives only this example, however), but they also construe as locative 'in'; in 4 the preposition ἐν 'among' (restored by Lloyd-Jones) is necessary to distinguish 'Pelasgians', persons from places.

F *271

<XO.>   ῥεῖ γὰρ ἀπ' ἄκρας
               Πίνδου Λάκμου τ' ἀπὸ Περραιβῶν
               εἰς Ἀμφιλόχους καὶ Ἀκαρνᾶνας,
               μίσγει δ' ὕδασιν τοῖς Ἀχελῴου
                         * * *
               ἔνθεν ἐς Ἄργος διὰ κῦμα τεμὼν   (5)
               ἥκει δῆμον τὸν Λυρκείου.

Strabo 6.2.4 (who states the interval after v. 4); ascribed to *Inachus* by Blomfield

F 272

ΕΡΜΗΣ   γυνὴ τίς ἥδε, συλὰς Ἀρκάδος κυνῆς

Scholia on Aristophanes, *Birds* 1203, cf.; Hesychius α 7273 Latte
συλὰς Pfeiffer: συληνὰς or κυλῆνας Scholia; κυνῆς Toup: κυνῆ or κυνὴ Scholia

F 273

               Πλούτωνος δ' ἐπείσοδος

Scholion on Ar. *Wealth* 727

F 274

               πάνδοκος ξενόστασις

Pollux 9.50

F 275

               πάντα δὲ ταῦτα πρὸς τῷ ἐν Ἰνάχῳ Σοφοκλέους ὅτε πάντα μεστὰ
               γίνεται τοῦ Διὸς εἰσελθόντος ...

Scholia on Aristophanes, *Wealth* 806–17: see n. 27 on the translation.
ὅτε scholia RE: ὅτι scholion V

F *271 (Strabo 6.2.4)

<CHO.>   For (Inachus) flows from the peak of Pindus and from Lacmus of the Perrhaebians to the Amphilochians and Acarnanians, and mingles with the waters of Achelous ... From here he cuts across the waves to Argos and comes to the people of Lyrceum.[24]

[24] In his commentary on Strabo 6.2.4 Radt attributes this 'geography' to Sophocles' equation here of the R. Inachus of N-W and W mainland Greece ('Pindus ... Achelous'), with the Inachus of Argos in the Peloponnese; Strabo is disputing the undersea and underground course of rivers, as mythical. N. Hammond, *Epirus* (Oxford, 1967) 458–9 believed that Sophocles drew the details here from Hecataeus. 'Lyrceum': eponymous city of Lyrcus, an ancient king of Argos.

The accumulation of proper names is typical of dramatic narratives or prophecies in order to suggest their veracity.

In the Greek in v. 5 διὰ ... τεμὼν is an example of tmesis (Smyth § 1650–1).

F 272 (Scholia on Aristophanes, *Birds* 1203)

HERMES   Who is this woman, the thief of the Arcadian cap?[25]

[25] The cap which conferred invisibility, called the 'cap of Hades' above, F 269c.19 and n. 13. The Aristophanes scholia say that the Arcadian cap had a distinctively local style resembling a broad-brimmed travelling hat; and they identify the 'thief' as Iris, and Hermes as the speaker.

F 273 (Scholion on Aristophanes, *Wealth* 727)

    ... and the approach of Wealth ...[26]

[26] Like F 283 (which follows it in the Scholion) cited to illustrate 'Pluto' as a half-colloquial diminutive of 'Ploutos', 'Wealth'; see introductory discussion (2) and n. 3.

F 274 (Pollux 9.50)

    ... an establishment for strangers welcoming to all ...[27]

[27] Cited by Pollux to illustrate the provision of such establishments in cities generally, but here perhaps referring to a special part of Inachus' palace.

F 275 (Scholion on Aristophanes, *Wealth* 806–17; a testimony)

    All this is close to Sophocles' *Inachus*, when everything becomes full after Zeus' entry ...[28]

[28] The scholion then extracts from *Wealth* 806–17 the words 'white barley-bread, flowery wine, fine olive oil, myrrh and figs; (*and vessels of*) bronze, silver and gold': for this plenty or 'Wealth' cf. F 273 and 283 and introductory discussion. The extent of Sophoclean wording reproduced by Aristophanes is not determinable.

F 276

σιροὶ κριθῶν

Scholia on Demosthenes 8.45

F 277　　　　ξανθὰ δ' Ἀφροδισία λάταξ
πᾶσιν ἐπεκτύπει δόμοις.

Athenaeus 15.668b

F 278

εὐδαίμονες οἱ τότε γέννας
ἀφθίτου λαχόντες
θείας ...

Scholia on Aristophanes, *Peace* 531; v. 1 Philodemus, *On Piety* P. Herc. 1609 IV.8 Gomperz

F *279

τραχὺς ᾧ χελώνης κέρχνος ἐξανίσταται.

Erotian κ 8 Nachmanson, ascribed to *Inachus* by Elmsley

F 281

ἐπιτήδειός γ' ἂν ἦν
τὴν τοῦ Πανόπτου διφθέραν ἐνημμένος
εἴπερ τις ἄλλος βουκολεῖν τὸν δήμιον.

Aristophanes, *Assembly-Women* 79–81, on which the scholia say that vv. 80–1 depend upon 'Argus and Io in Sophocles' *Inachus*'.

F 281a

Σοφοκλῆς ἐν Ἰνάχῳ καὶ ᾄδοντα αὐτὸν εἰσάγει.

Scholia on *Prometheus Bound* 574

F 276 (Scholia on Demosthenes 8.45)
    ... silos of barley ...

F 277 (Athenaeus 15.668b)
    The tawny wine-drops of Aphrodite's game sounded in the entire house.[29]

[29] The game of *kottabos*, played by (male) drinkers after dinner, aiming to hit a target with wine-drops, naming a lover and hoping to 'score' (see n. 11 on Achaeus, *Linus* F 26). Perhaps the 'dark stranger' (F 269a.54) interrupted it. 'tawny': in Epic the colour of wine is usually 'gleaming' (*Iliad* 1.462, *etc.*); at *Cyc.* 67 the satyrs yearn for wine's 'bright drops'. This and the next two fragments are lyric, and so probably sung by the Chorus.

F 278 (Scholia on Aristophanes, *Peace* 531)
    The men of that time were blest in owning an immortal, divine descent ...[30]

[30] Before the rule of Zeus, apparently, according to the second but damaged source P. Herc. 1609 (from Philodemus, *On Piety*).

F *279 (Erotian κ 8 Nachmanson)
    ... on which a rough excrescence (*like the shell*) of a tortoise rises up.[31]

[31] Io's transformation: either her horns or her hooves are being described, cf. F 295a.

F 281 (Aristophanes, *Assembly-Women* 79–81 and scholia)
    He'd be suitable, if any man would, to dress in the leather coat of the All-Seer and take in the public gaoler![32]

[32] Aristophanes exploits a scene from the *Inachus*: just as Argus ('the All-Seer') falls asleep to Hermes' music while wearing his outdoor leather-clothing and 'herding' the heifer Io, so the real-life Lamius (*or* -ias; named in Aristophanes vv. 76–7, not cited here), apparently the public gaoler, nods off and neglects his duties of guarding – but for his joke Aristophanes uses an ambiguous verb 'take in', both 'tend, husband cattle' and 'cheat, deceive'. In Sophocles' version Argus was therefore almost certainly costumed as a rustic shepherd, despite a mask showing his multiple eyes (F 269a.56; see introductory discussion).

F 281a (Scholia on *Prometheus Bound* 574)
    Sophocles in the *Inachus* brings on (Argus) actually singing.[33]

[33] Diggle (1998) suggested that F 269c.25–32 may be sung by Argus.

F 282

ἐπήνεσ᾽· ἴσθι δ᾽, ὥσπερ ἡ παροιμία,
ἐκ κάρτα βαιῶν γνωτὸς ἂν γένοιτ᾽ ἀνήρ.

Stobaeus 4.5.9 and one paroemiographer

F 283

τοιόνδ᾽ ἐμὸν Πλούτων᾽ ἀμεμφείας χάριν ...

Scholion on Ar. *Wealth* 727: see on F 273

F 284

πατὴρ δὲ ποταμὸς Ἴναχος
τὸν ἀντίπλαστον νομὸν ἔχει κεκμηκότων.

Hesychius α 5460 Latte
νομὸν Ellendt: νόμον Hesychius

F 286

πάντα δ᾽ ἐρίθων ἀραχνᾶν βρίθει.

Suda α 3750 Adler

F 287

ἐπίκρουμα χθονὸς Ἀργείας

Hesychius ε 4904 Latte; probably corrupt metrically

F 288

κυαμόβολον δικαστήν

Hesychius κ 4343 Latte; cf. F 295 (Scholia on Aristophanes, *Knights* 1150) κημός 'voting-funnel'

F 282 (Stobaeus 4.5.9)

> I'm grateful; but you are to know that, as the proverb has it, a man may become famous from a very small beginning.

F 283 (Scholion on Aristophanes, *Wealth* 727)

> ... my Wealth ... such, thanks to my blamelessness.[34]

[34]   Cf. F 273 and n. 25, and see introductory discussion (1) and n. 3.

F 284 (Hesychius α 5460 Latte)

> ... her father the river Inachus occupies the region which resembles that of the dead.[35]

[35]   'of the dead', *i.e.* bare, sterile: probably a reference to the time of extreme drought in Argos (see introductory discussion). 'region' is Ellendt's conjecture; the reading of Hesychius gives a difficult translation as '(has) tribute (that resembles *etc.*)', *i.e.* the same drought.

F 286 (Suda α 3750 Adler)

> Everything is full of labouring spiders.[36]

[36]   Lyric, probably from a praise of peace, a time when unused weapons were stored and attracted spiders (Eur. *Erechtheus* F 369.1), rather than an evocation of empty larders. Cf. the praise of peace in Aeschylus' 'Justice' play, F **451n.

F 287 (Hesychius ε 4904 Latte)

> ... a beating upon Argos' soil ...[37]

[37]   Almost certainly a description of dancing, probably the celebration of plenty's return (F 275) which was interrupted by the arrival of the 'dark stranger'.

F 288 (Hesychius κ 4343 Latte)

> ... a bean-(*i.e.* vote-)casting juror ...[38]

[38]   Cf. F 295 '(voting-)funnel' and for a possible context see Lloyd-Jones (1996) cited in the introductory discussion.

F 291

ἀναιδείας φάρος

Hesychius α 4321 Latte (see n. 39).

F **295a

στολοκρατές

Hesychius σ 1906 Hansen

F 291 (Hesychius α 4321 Latte)
                              ... robe of shamelessness ... [39]

[39]   Mysterious: the phrase is followed in Hesychius by a now irreparably damaged definition
and with allusion to Homer, *Iliad* 2.262 'cloak and tunic as coverings of the genitals' (of a dead
warrior). This seems to indicate an interpretation of F 291 as 'cloak for what it is shameless
to leave exposed', possibly a reference to the priapic satyrs; Pearson (1917) compares Soph.
F 360 (from an uncertainly titled satyr-play) '... I cover myself with my cloak here' (text and
translation insecure).
       Possibly, however, the phrase is a metaphor for the behaviour either of the 'dark stranger'
(F 269a.54) before he is identified or of Hermes wearing the 'Cap of Hades', F 269c.19–20.
If so, the phrase may be derogatory, just as Achilles in his clash with Agamemnon calls him
'cloaked in shamelessness', Homer, *Iliad* 1.149.

F **295a (Hesychius σ 1906 Hansen)
                              ... horn-stump-headed ...[40]

[40]   The transfigured Io: see on F 279.

Trackers (*IXNEYTAI, Ichneutae*)

TrGF 4².270–308 (F 314–*318), 747–53, cf. 3.570–2.

Texts etc. Pearson (1917) 1.224–70; R. Walker, *Sophocles' Ichneutae, with Notes ... Translation ... Introductory Chapters* (London, 1919: 664pp.!); Page (1942) 26–53; E. Siegmann, *Untersuchungen zu Sophokles' Ichneutai* (Hamburg, 1941); R. Carden, 'Notes on Sophocles' *Ichneutai*', *BICS* 18 (1971) 39–45; E. V. Maltese, *Sofocle, Ichneutae* (Florence, 1982 = *Papyrologica Florentina* 10; with 7 Plates of P. Oxy. 1174 and 2081); Lloyd-Jones (1996) 140–77 (cf. 'Notes on fragments of Sophocles', *SIFC* 12 (1994) 129–48, at 136–42 = (2005) 115–35, at 123–9); Diggle (1998) 45–63 (cf. 'Sophocles, *Ichneutae* (fr. 314 Radt)', *ZPE* 112 (1996) 3–17); S. Scheurer, R. Bielfeldt in KPS (1999) 280–312; A. Guida, 'Due varianti negli *Ichneutae* di Sofocle', *ZPE* 175 (2010) 5–8.

Discussions. G. Conflenti, *Il Ciclope, gli Ichneutae e il dramma satiresco* (Rome, 1932); U. von Wilamowitz, 'Die Spürhunde des Sophokles', *Kleine Schriften. I* (Berlin, 1935) 347–83 (orig. 1912); F. R. Walton, 'A problem in the *Ichneutae* of Sophocles', *HSCP* 46 (1935) 167–89; Chourmouziades (1974) 60–1, 72–99, 204–19; R. G. Ussher, 'Sophocles' *Ichneutai* as a Satyr Play', *Hermathena* 118 (1974) 130–8; S. L. Radt in *Entretiens XXIX. Sophocle* (1982), 203–6 (twice reprinted: details in our Bibliographical Guidance p. 239); Lesky (1983) 184–5 (= 1972, 257–9); Sutton (1980) 43–8; G. Martino, 'Chi è il δεσπότης dei satiri negli *Ichneutae* de Sofocle?', *Annali dell'istituto italiano per gli studi istorici, Napoli* 10 (1987/8) 11–26; Gantz (1993) 106; Conrad (1997) 95–126, 269–77; N. Zagagi, 'Comic Patterns in Sophocles' *Ichneutae*', in J. Griffin (ed.), *Sophocles Revisited. Essays ... Sir Hugh Lloyd-Jones* (Oxford, 1999) 177–218, esp. 208–11; Kaimio (2001) 42; Voelke (2001) 170–4 (lyric structures) and *passim*; E. OKell, 'The "effeminacy" of the clever speaker and the jokes of *Ichneutai*', in Sommerstein (2003) 283–308; Z. P. Ambrose in Harrison (2005) 28–30; N. J. Richardson, *Three Homeric Hymns. To Apollo, Hermes and Aphrodite* (Cambridge, 2010) 25–6.

Art. LIMC V.1.309–10 'Hermes' nos 241–57, esp. 246–8 (Hermes as infant or adult in various scenes with cattle, cave, satyrs *etc.*); 315 no. 310 (constructing the lyre).

There are substantial Addenda to *Trackers* at the end of the volume.

This is the longest continuous fragmentary text from any satyr-play; as such it affords the most important comparison with *Cyclops*. Furthermore, it contains the first 450 lines of the play (marginal line-numbers for 100, 200 (in erasure), 300 and 400 survive); and it is very probable that they make up at least a half of the whole (line-numbering is found also in the papyri at Aeschylus, *Net-Fishers* F 47a.36, and Sophocles, *Inachus* F 269a.36, both above). Although the text is almost everywhere damaged, and often badly, we not only have therefore a very good hold on the plot and characters, but can surmise their development for the rest of the play fairly confidently on the basis of another surviving (and complete) poetic text, the *Homeric Hymn to Hermes* (probably from the early or even middle 5th century). This is a strongly dramatized narrative of the same incident as in *Trackers* and was almost certainly Sophocles' chief poetic source (most easily accessible in the Loeb Classical Library volume *Homeric Hymns etc.*, ed. M. L. West (2003) 112–59; vv. 261–80 are cited below). It is frustrating that we so far have no evidence from which even to guess the date of Sophocles' play, and so to judge its closeness in time to the *Hymn*.

The scene is Mt Cyllene in Arcadia (v. 37), close to the eponymous nymph Cyllene's cave (a setting which is however not revealed until her entry at 221). In the developed 5th century theatre the cave would be represented by the central stage-door, as in *Cyclops* and in the *Philoctetes* of both Euripides and Sophocles.

In a prologue-speech Apollo describes the mysterious theft of his milk-cows and their calves, and his long search for them throughout Greece; loudly he promises any finder a reward of gold (1–44). He is overheard by the nearby Silenus, who eagerly undertakes the search if the reward can be not only of gold but also of the satyrs' 'freedom' (45–54; see further below). Apollo seems to guarantee both money and freedom before leaving (55–62).

The satyr-chorus join their father in his hopes of the reward (63–78), and Silenus orders them to begin hunting like hounds on a scent (79–99, esp. 81, 93, 97–8). At once they find hoof-marks, which confuse them because they point both forward and backward (100–23). Suddenly they (but not Silenus himself) hear a strange noise which frightens them (131, 143–4). Silenus denounces cowardice so false to his own brave triumphs of the past: it threatens their success now; he undertakes to direct their search from a central position if they will spread out (124–75). The satyrs dance and sing in self-encouragement until the noise recurs (176–202) – when it is Silenus who now flees in terror. They stamp the ground, to get attention from the unseen maker of the noise, who seems to be within the mountain (203–20).

In angry response Cyllene comes from her cave, incredulous at the satyrs' wild activity like that of yelling huntsmen (221–42). They sing an apology, and now politely describe the noise as a marvellous song (243–50, at 250); they wish to ask about its origin before telling Cyllene what they are hunting (251–61). She then narrates how she is tending a new child of Zeus (Hermes) for his mother (273 and n. 50, 267); he is a miraculous infant who at six days old has invented and now continually plays the musical instrument which produced the strange noise (262–89). Singing their astonishment, the satyrs are teased by Cyllene as she slowly reveals the instrument's nature (290–328): it is a tortoise-shell strung with cords, named a lyre by the child (312, cf. 327–8).

Because Hermes has used (cow-)leather in making the lyre (374–5, cf. 310, 314), the satyrs guess that he must be also the cattle-thief, but Cyllene defends him as a god and child incapable of such theft. She abuses the satyrs as young fools. Their altercation runs from 329 to at least 404 (the text becomes increasingly defective), and ends when Cyllene flounces off into the cave, for clearly 399–404 herald a challenge by the satyrs to her obstructiveness; they want to confront Hermes himself with their accusation. Lines 405–35 are completely lost, but the satyrs' words in 436–7 ('Come on, now ... in the interior') may indicate their intention to open up the cave; if so, it would require an assault on the closed stage-door, but they are forestalled, for then they appeal to Apollo (448, perhaps also to Pan: 438), and he reenters (451). Since his first lines include the words 'reward' (456) and 'free' (457), it is likely that he recapitulates his promise (to Silenus at 44–62) before learning that the cows are probably in Cyllene's cave. The papyrus ends at 459.

A meeting between Apollo and a slyly evasive Hermes like that which ends the *Hymn* seems certain to have followed quickly – perhaps Apollo was told of Hermes and called him out from the cave; it was surely the play's climax too. Vv. 261–80 of the *Hymn,* where Hermes deceitfully rejects Apollo's accusation of theft, are suggestive for the play:

Hermes answered Apollo in crafty words: 'Son of Leto, why this harsh speech, coming here in search of grazing cattle? I have not seen them, I have not inquired about them, I have heard no word of them from another. I could not be an informer, I could not take a reward for information. Nor do I look like a sturdy droving man: (265) this is not my work; other things have been first for my concern. Sleep is my concern, and my mother's milk, and to have swaddling round my shoulders, and warm baths. I wish that no one should ask the source of this accusation; it would be a great wonder indeed among the immortal gods, (270) that a new-born child should come in across a forecourt with grazing cattle! It is unseemly of you to speak of it. I was born only yesterday; and my feet are tender, and the ground hard under them. Yet if you wish, I will swear a great oath by my father's head: I promise you, I am neither myself responsible, (275) nor have I seen any other thief of your cattle, whatever the cows are; I only hear tell of them.' Such then were his words, and with frequent glances from beneath his brows he kept his eyes moving to look here and there, whistling away lengthily, holding Apollo's words of no account. (280)[1]

The differences between Sophocles' plot and the story in the *Hymn* may be due in part to influence from other accounts now lost, if not to Sophocles' own invention: these are principally that in the *Hymn* the precocious child Hermes has left his birth-cave in Arcadia and made the lyre before he steals Apollo's cows; that he drives them west of Arcadia (confusing their tracks as in the play) and leaves them there; that he takes the lyre to Mt Cyllene, when he returns to his birth-cave still inhabited by his mother Maia (and not by Cyllene the nymph who nurses him); that Zeus orders Apollo to recover the stolen cattle (see below); in particular, that Sophocles (later influencing [Apollod.] 3.10.2) has Hermes making the lyre at the cave itself with hides from the stolen cows – a clever dramatic device which engineers all the stage-business with the satyrs' search and fright at the underground noise – but they are not too terrified to follow the clues to finding the cows.

So in the missing end of the play Apollo was probably beguiled by the sound of the lyre (cf. *Hymn* 420–3, 434), and similarly accepted its gift as compensation for the cattle (*Hymn* 475–96) – but in the *Hymn* only after Zeus has ordered the reconciliation, 389–91, because while he has enjoyed Hermes' prevarication, he wants no further dispute between the two brothers, who are his own sons. After such a reconciliation between gods the satyrs would no doubt have danced and sung in celebration.[2] Almost certainly they got the gold as their reward – but if also their promised 'freedom', from what, or from whom? In other plays the satyrs are often in service or servitude to 'ogres', as in *Cyclops* and *Syleus*. The best suggestion for our play is advocated strongly by Lesky 1983, 185 = 1972, 258, cf. Siegmann (1941) 53–4, Seaford (1984) 34–5: they are in temporary service to Pan (again, note the possible occurrence of his name at 438), whose heartland Arcadia is, and with whom the satyrs had a natural affinity (see below; what survives of the papyrus does not however include any reason for the satyrs' presence in Arcadia). Most other scholars have identified the satyrs' 'master'

(224) as Dionysus, on the strength of Cyllene's assumptions in 223–8: see esp. Martino (1987/8) and Lämmle (2007) 353 n. 50.

One problem nevertheless attends this near-certain ending. Did anyone other than the chorus of satyrs witness the confrontation of Apollo and Hermes? An apparent Greek *sigma* in the margin of the papyrus after 458 has been read as the first letter of Silenus' name (or of 'satyr'), and as indicating a voice-part for him when he returns from his panicky flight (at 209). Indeed it seems likely that he would see the action out, given his earlier role, and he would want his share of the reward, even if he did nothing to earn it (cf. Conrad (1997) 119). His presence however would bring together on stage the maximum permitted number of speaking actors (three), playing Apollo, the emerging Hermes, and Silenus; that means, Cyllene does not return (unless replaced by a mute), in order for her actor to be available to play Hermes. Fr. 26 of the papyrus (F 314a.26) is interesting here, the single word 'adjudication' (if correctly interpreted): might Silenus have swashbuckled himself into this role between the two gods, with the amused tolerance of Apollo? It has been suggested that he and the satyrs acted similarly in adjudicating Argus' singing at the end of Sophocles' *Inachus*: see introductory discussion there, on F 288 and 295.

Because of the extent of the papyrus, and with the aid of the *Hymn*, the play's form and temper are clearly visible: theft of the cows narrated, search for them begun and taken to the brink of recovery, reward for the finders, and reconciliation of robbed with robber. This straightforward movement is delayed by Silenus' cowardice, the riddle of the lyre's noise, and the stand-off between satyrs and Cyllene (see Conrad (1997) 122).

The play's uncomplicated character as a pure amusement has prompted suggestion that it was an early composition, in this respect resembling the manner of Aeschylus in *Net-Fishers* and *Sacred Delegates* (see towards the end of this introductory discussion). It is as playful as the *Hymn*, which concentrates upon the child Hermes' inventive mischief and slyness. Zagagi (1999) traces many analogies in the play for themes and scenes from comedy, both Old and New Greek, and Roman, *e.g.* elderly men offering help (45–50), bargaining (51–53), boasting (79–92); searching compared with that of dogs hunting (93–123, 207–36); door-scenes (210–43); riddling (284–328); see also nn. 22 and 23 below.

Of significance to our appreciation not just of the play but also of the entire satyric genre is the unusually sustained contrast between Silenus and the satyrs. It is rare among satyric remains; Conrad's exposition is valuable, (1997) 120–6. Similarly in *Cyclops* the satyrs favour Odysseus, while their lying father toadies to the monster (232–40, cf. 313–15 – in fact the father and sons curse each other, 261–72); cf. also the old satyr's abuse of his sons at Lycophron, *Menedemus* F 2. Commoner is a contrast between uninhibited satyrs, beings out of time, and ordinary, 'civilised', mortal men (see esp. Seaford (1984) 5–6, 32–3; Gantz (1993) 135–9; KPS 17–23; B. Seidensticker in Csapo and Miller (2003) 120). Silenus is full of greed, bluster and cowardice (205–9, cf. *Cyc.*1–8, 163–74 *etc.*), giving a negative picture of his own species (Conrad (1997) 124: see vv. 148–9, 152, 158, 161). The satyrs are eager and enterprising; and their energy and success come from their suitability as creatures of the wild (147, 221) to be 'trackers, hunters' (81, 93–123, 166–202, 231–2) – even if Cyllene abuses them for having taken up this work instead of their normal duty of celebrating Dionysus (223–9). Nevertheless Silenus at play-end may well have reasserted his dominance over the satyrs as their father (cf. the early 75, 142, 153–68) if, as seems probable (above), he returns at play-end to claim Apollo's reward and their 'freedom': he and they come from a world of such moral inconsequence.

Sophocles' writing is everywhere apt to scene and character: Apollo's indignant narrative (1–44); Silenus' eagerness for success (45–63, 79–99), followed by his hypocritical abuse-cum-encouragement of the satyrs (124–75); the satyrs' excitement and energy (64–78, 100–23, 176–202, 210–20, 329–37; all lyric) and then their amazed curiosity (243–50 = 290–7; lyric); lastly, Cyllene's passage from incredulity at finding the satyrs 'hunting', through her tolerant but teasing narrative of the lyre's invention, to angry disappearance (221–404) when the satyrs accuse Hermes of the theft (329–38 = 371–9, lyric again). Two of the longer speeches have caught critics' attention. Cyllene's measured language (especially in 262–89) is set off by the satyrs' constant tumble of words (cf. *e.g.* Lesky (1983) 184 = (1972) 258). Silenus' tirade against his satyr-sons (145–68, prepared in his 124–30, 132–5) outdoes even Comedy's capacity for sustained abuse, *e.g.* Ar. *Peace* 182–4; it is boldly related by OKell (2003) to other hunting and sexual imagery in the play; she argues an interconnection, through its clever rhetoric, between contemporary Athenian views of sexual deviance, effeminacy, and both the reality and the image of slavery. Zagagi (1999) 203–4 sees the rhetoric as parody of urban style in the mouth of the rustic Silenus.

The play's lyric passages compare in their brevity with those of *Cyclops*: free, astrophic lyrics at 64–78, 177–202, cf. *Cyc.* 608–23, 656–62; strophic systems 243–50 = 290–7, 329–38 = 371–9, cf. *Cyc.* 41–8 = 55–62 (followed by an epode, 63–80), 355 -60 = 370–<5>, 495–502 = 503–10 = 511–18 (preceded by anapaests, 483–94); see Voelke (2001) 170–4. This similarity seems to suggest that both Sophocles and Euripides abandoned the more extensive and perhaps archaic lyrics of Aeschylus in satyr-plays, *e.g.* astrophic *Net-Fishers* F 47a.22–56 (followed by anapaests, 57–68).

It is particularly interesting to compare how Sophocles in this play and Euripides in his *Cyclops* adapted tales from the epic tradition, Sophocles from the *Hymn* and Euripides from Book 9 of the *Odyssey*. A narrative and dramaturgical comparison between the two plays was made early on by Conflenti in her short monograph (1932, with a résumé of still earlier such judgements at p. 5 n. 1). In a valuable wider comparison of the two plays Radt (1982) traces the unfavourable 'aesthetic' reaction to *Trackers* immediately after its publication in 1912, and how this has gradually changed to the detriment of *Cyclops*; like many other readers, he observes how the lighter, inconsequential ambience of Sophocles' play resembles much of Aeschylus' *Net-Fishers* and *Sacred Delegates*, in which three plays the greater role of the chorus may well be more typical of older satyric drama; and he suggests that Euripides' major innovation in the genre was the treatment of real-life, contemporary issues (*e.g. Cyc.* 316ff. on materialism) which are rare in Sophocles and Aeschylus: on this topic see n. 8 on Sophocles, *Oeneus* F 1130 and especially the end of our introductory discussion to Python's *Agen*.

Walton (1935) argued that the play should be read in association with *IG* II. 1651 (early 4th century BC). This Piraeus inscription mentions hounds and hunters and sacrifices to Hermes and Apollo; Walton speculated about a connection between such ritual and Sophocles' play and posthumous heroization as 'Dexion' – but under this name the playwright is usually associated with the cult of Asclepius (*TrGF* 4^2.57–8 T 67–71).

It is notable and pleasing that *Trackers* was itself adapted in 1988 by Tony Harrison for his 'satyr-play' *The Trackers of Oxyrhynchus*, first performed at Delphi before moving to the National Theatre in London, and published in

London (1990, rev. 1991); Harrison was dramatising an 'epic' recovery of modern times, not of cows but of the play's papyrus text, by B. P. Grenfell and A. S. Hunt. The Archive of Performances of Greek and Roman Drama in Oxford records other productions of Harrison's play in England, Austria and Denmark since 1990; and it lists ten apparently 'straight' productions of Sophocles' text, in the original or in (supplemented) translation, from the first, amazingly early one of 1913, in Halle, Germany (in translation: see Addendum), until 2001, in the Czech Republic, Italy, England, USA and Greece.

Other fragments of the play: on F 314a.26 see above; on F 316 and F 318 see n. 2 below.

Notes

[1] The later mythographer [Apollod.] (3.10.2) also recounts the story: Apollo himself traces the cows and is led to the cave on Mt. Cyllene; Hermes is forced to admit the theft. While tending the cows he had also made himself a herdsman's pipe. Apollo covets this as well as the lyre, and in a further negotiation secures it in return for giving Hermes his emblematic golden wand and the skill of divination.

The *Hymn* is the earliest 'aetiology' of the lyre's invention (*e.g.* vv. 25, 46). In (the damaged) *Trackers* 312 we read only '(Hermes) calls ... the lyre', and there is no hint of an etymology in the *Hymn* – just as there is no 'aetiology' dependent upon Hermes' invention of the *syrinx* at *Hymn* 512, or upon Apollo's gift of the wand (*rhabdos*, 529).

For the relation between *Hymn* and *Trackers* see also the end of this introductory discussion and Richardson (2010) 25–6, with bibl.

[2] The lexicographic book-fragment F 316 has the uncompounded verb ῥικνοῦσθαι cited from the play and glossed 'to be bent over in all manner of shapes' and 'to be so bent in an unseemly dance'. The former is hard to relate to the surviving text, unless at a line-end missing from 96–8 where Silenus uses also a different verb for 'bend over', and there is no room for it in the almost completely preserved 125–8, where Silenus mocks the satyrs' bending over while searching; nor does Cyllene use it in the latter sense in describing their 'sudden turns of madness' when she likens them to excited hunters approaching their prey, 229–32, 237–8. Even more confusingly, at 302 the compound verb καταρρικνοῦσθαι describes the 'shrivelled' appearance of Hermes' tortoise-shell.

The book fragment F 318 has the single word 'cow-thief', describing Hermes.

F 314

col.i

\<ΑΠΟΛΛΩΝ>

The play begins with 12 now very fragmentary lines, including the words
4 ἐ]πεσσύθ[ην *at mid-line, and from line-ends* 7 ἀγγέλλω [β]ροτο[ῖς,
8 ὑπισ]χνοῦμαι τελεῖ[ν, 9 ἀ]πόπροθεν, 10 δύσ]λοφον φρενί, 11 β]οῦς
ἀμολγάδας, 12 πορτίδων, *then:*

ἄπα]ντα φρ[οῦδα *7 let.*]ν ἰχνοσκοπῶ
λαθ]ραῖ᾽ ἰόν[τ.....βου]στάθμου κάπης
...]νῶς τεχνη.[..... ἐ]γὼ οὐκ ἂν ᾠόμην   (15)
οὔτ᾽ ἂ]ν θεῶν τιν[᾽ οὔτ᾽ ἐφημ]έρων βροτῶν
δρᾶσ]αι τόδ᾽ ἔργ[ον οὐδὲ] πρὸς τόλμαν πεσεῖν.
[.....]᾽ οὖν ἐπείπερ [..]θον ἐκπλαγεὶς ὄκνῳ
σκοπ]ῶ, ματεύω, παντελὲς κήρυγμ᾽ ἔχων
θεοῖ]ς βροτοῖς τε μηδέν᾽ ἀγνοεῖν τάδε.   (20)
ἀκολο]υθίᾳ γὰρ ἐμμανεῖ κυνηγετῶ·
.....]ων δ᾽ ἐπῆλθ[ο]ν φ[ῦ]λα τ[οῦ] παντὸς στρατ[οῦ

P. Oxy. 1174 (late 2nd c. AD) and (remnants of vv. 127–30) P. Oxy. 1175 (similarly dated) fr.
46 ed. A.S. Hunt (1912) and (remnants of vv. 149–51, 379–83, 435–8) P. Oxy. 2081 (2nd c.
AD) (a) ed. Hunt (1927). Our text depends upon Hunt as re-edited both by Radt in *TrGF* 4².
275–308 and 571–2, and by Diggle (1998) 45–63; we do not distinguish between the original
and the correcting hands in the papyrus; and we ignore matters of orthography. P. Oxy. 1174
has occasional, often damaged, marginal glosses or variant readings attributed mostly to
Theon (probably the Alexandrian scholar of Hellenistic poetry insecurely dated around the
1st century BC; but the papyrus would be the only evidence of his work upon tragedy). There
are 36 tiny separated fragments of P. Oxy. 1174 which yield only one significant word, F
314a fr.26 below.
13 beg ἄπα]ντα Wilamowitz
14 λα[θρ in marg. Theon, whence λαθ]ραῖ᾽ Hunt; ἰόν[τα τῆλε βου]στάθμου Wilamowitz
17 οὐδὲ] Vollgraff
18 [ἦλ]θον Siegmann, but θ is insecurely read in P. Oxy.; ὀκνῶ Degani
19 σκοπ]ῶ Walker
21 ἀκολο]υθίᾳ Wilamowitz, from a probable gloss on this passage by Photius α 787
Theodoridis ἀκολουθία· ἡ ἀκολούθησις· Σοφοκλῆς (Soph. F 990 = fr. 1067 Pearson); ἐμμανεῖ
Bignone: εμμαν[[ε]]ις P. Oxy.

F 314

Characters of the play: Apollo, Silenus, Chorus of Satyrs, Cyllene *(a mountain-nymph),* Hermes.
Scene: Mt. Cyllene in Arcadia. A cave-entrance leading underground is represented by the stage-backdrop (the skênê*) and its (closed) central door. Apollo enters from the side.*

<APOLLO>   *The first 12 lines of the god's prologue-speech are very fragmentary, but include the words*

4 (I) have come rushing, 7 I proclaim to mortal men, 8 I (promise) to fulfil, 9 from afar, 10 (hard) for my heart (*to bear*), 11 milking-cows, 12 of heifers. *Then:*
... all are gone ... I am looking for their tracks which go unseen (far from?) the cows' stall and manger ... (by?) skill. I would not have thought (15) that anyone (either) of the gods (or of mortal) men would have (done) this deed (or even) entered upon its audacity. ... so, since I (have come?) dismayed and fearful,[3] I'm (looking), I'm seeking, making an authoritative edict[4] to (gods) and mortals that none is to be unaware of these things. (20) For I'm hunting in mad (pursuit); and ... I've approached the tribes of all peoples.

[3]   'dismayed, I'm in fear' Degani.
[4]   'edict ... that': in the Greek κήρυγμ' ἔχων acts like κηρύσσων in controlling the accusative and infinitive, here in an indirect command; cf. *Ajax* 606 ἐλπίδ' ἔχειν = ἐλπίζειν.

then traces of 1 line (23), then 4 lines missing (24–7), then remnants of 5 line-ends (28–32) including the words

30 Θεσσαλῶν, 31] Βοιωτίας τε γ[ῆς, *then:*

col. ii *first line (33) lost, then centres of 5 lines (34–8) including the words*

34 Δωρικο[, 36]ηκω, 37 Κυλ]λήνης, 38 χῶρον, ἐς δ᾽ ὕλ[ην, *then:*

> 6 *let.* ποι]μὴν εἴτ᾽ ἀγρωστη[
> μαριλοκαυ]τῶν ἐν λόγῳ παρ[ίσταται　　　　　　　(40)
> εἴτ᾽ οὖν ὀρ]είων νυμφογεννή[τ
> Σατύρω]ν τίς ἐστι, πᾶσιν ἀγγέλ[λω
> τὸν φ]ῶρα τοῦ Παιῶνος ὅστις α[
> ....]. τὸ χρῆμα, μισθός ἐσθ᾽ ὁ κε[ίμενος.

<ΣΙΛΗΝΟΣ>　ἐπεὶ] θεοῦ φώνημα τὼς ἐπέκλυον　　　　　(45)
> βοῶ]ντος ὀρθίοισι σὺν κηρύγμασ[ιν,
> σ]πουδῇ τάδ᾽ ἢ πάρεστι πρεσβύτῃ [τελῶν
> σ]οί, Φοῖβ᾽ Ἄπολλον, προσφιλὴς εὐε[ργέτης
> θέλων γενέσθαι τῷδ᾽ ἐπεσσύθην δρ[ό]μῳ,
> ἤν πως τὸ χρῆμα τοῦτό σοι κυνηγ[έ]σω.　　　　(50)
> τ[ὸ] γὰρ γέ[ρα]ς μοι κείμενον χρ[υ]σο[σ]τεφὲς
> μά[λι]στ᾽ ἐπ[.....]αισ[..]ρόσθεσ.[7 *let.*]ν.
> παῖδας δε.[..]ς ὅσσοισι *traces*
> .[6 *let.*]᾽ [.]ν εἴπερ ἐκτε[λ]εῖς ἄπε[ρ] λέγεις.

36] ἥκω Wilamowitz
38 ὕλ[ην Terzaghi
39 ὡς εἴτε ποι]μὴν Hunt; ἀγρωστή[ρων τις ἢ Wilamowitz
40 μαριλοκαυ]τῶν Wilamowitz, restored from glosses in Photius μ 114 Theodoridis and Hesychius μ 285 Latte; παρ[ίσταται Wilamowitz: πάρ[εστι νῦν Vollgraff
41 εἴτ᾽ οὖν Diggle; ὀρ]είων Wilamowitz
42 Σατύρω]ν Diggle
43 τὸν φ]ῶρα Wilamowitz, ω insecure
44 end ε[insecure
45 ἐπεὶ] Diggle; θεοῦ] Maltese
47 end [τελῶν Diggle
50 ἤν Diggle: ἄν P. Oxy.: similarly 74, 171
53 παῖδας δ᾽ ἐμ[οὺ]ς Hunt

16 fragmentary or missing lines (23–38), including the words 30 of the Thessalians, 31 and of (the land of) Boeotia, 34 Dorian,[5] 36 I have come (?), 37 of Cyllene,[6] 38 country-place, but into (the wood?). *Then:*
... (if some) shepherd or farmer ... (*or*) charcoal-burner (is nearby) while I speak,[7] (40) (or yet) any (of the mountain Satyrs)[8] born of nymphs, I proclaim to all that (for?) whoever ... (the thief) from Apollo Healer ... the thing (?),[9] there is the reward (laid down).

Silenus enters in haste.

<SILENUS>   (When) I heard the voice (of the god crying out) (45) like this with loud proclamations, I came with such haste as an old man has, (with) this (purpose), wanting to be your friendly benefactor, Phoebus Apollo, running at this pace in case I can somehow hunt this thing down for you. (50). For ... the gold-wreathed prize fixed for me ... very much ...;[10] and ... (my?) sons ... with (their?) eyes ... if you will indeed fulfil just what you say.

[5] 'Thessalians, Boeotia, Dorian *(i.e.* Peloponnesian)': Apollo is listing the places in which he has searched throughout Greece (22).

[6] 'Cyllene': both the mountain and its nymph.

[7] 'shepherd, farmer, charcoal-burner': with Apollo's call for help to nearby countrymen compare that of Dictys at Aeschylus, *Net-Fishers* F 46a.17–21: in both places the joke is that instead of useful aid the callers get inept satyrs, described by Hesiod F 10(a).18 as 'hopeless at work'; note too the inability of the satyrs to control the sheep at the start of *Cyclops*, 41–62.

[8] '(... Satyrs)': Diggle's supplement is persuasive in the light of a similar and abrupt identification of the satyrs at *Cyc.* 100; for 'nymphs' as their mothers see *Oeneus* F 1130.7.

[9] 'the thing': syntax obscure – and meaning disputed, although the imprecise word recurs in 50. Suggested: the mystery of the cattle (the 'situation', A. López Eire in Sommerstein (2003) 411), the search for them (the 'business'), or the reward promised as 'laid down' and named as gold, 51.

[10] 'gold-wreathed' may mean no more than 'golden', for the prize is simply so described in 78. Silenus is always out for gain, selling his master's cheese or lambs for wine (or gold) at *Cyc.* 134–74, esp. 138, or pimping in Eur. *Syleus* F 675.

<ΑΠ.>   *9 let.*]ωσω· μοῦνον ἐμπ[έδου τ]άδε.   (55)
<ΣΙ.>   *12 let.*]οι· σὺ δ᾽ ἐμπέδου [....]ν.
<ΑΠ.>   τ.[*10–11 let.*]ρων ὅστι[ς] ἔ[σ]θ᾽· ἐτ[οῖμ]α δ[έ.
     letters from 2 lines (58–9), then:

col. iii   *first line (60) lost, then traces of a second (61), then:*

<ΣΙ.>   τί τοῦτο; πῶ[ς *15–16 let.*]εις;
<ΑΠ.>   ἐλεύθερος συ[*16–17 let.*]ων.

ΧΟΡΟΣ ΣΑΤΥΡΩΝ   ἴθ᾽ ἄγε δ[*16–17 let.*
     πόδα βά[*16–17 let.*]ν   (65)
     ἀπαπαπ[αῖ *13–14 let.*
     ὢ ὤ, σέ τοι [*16–17 let.*
     ἔπιθι κλωπ[*15–16 let.*
     ὑπόνομα κ[*16–17 let.*
     διανύτων ὁ[*15–16 let.*   (70)
     πατρικὰν γῆρ[υν *11–12 let.*
     πῶς πᾷ τὰ λάθρι[α *9–10 let.*
     κλέμματα ποσσι[*10–11 let.*
     εἴ πως, ἢν τύχω, πο.[*9–10 let.*
     πατρί τ᾽ ἐλεύθερον β[..]..μετ[.]   (75)
     ξὺν ἅμα θεὸς ὁ φίλος ἀνέτω
     πόνους, προφήνας ἀρίζηλα
     χρυσοῦ παραδείγματα.
ΣΙ.   θεὸς Τύχη [κ]αὶ δαῖμον ἰθυντήριε,
     τυχ[ε]ῖν με πράγους οὗ δράμημ᾽ ἐπείγεται,   (80)
     λείαν, ἄγραν, σύλησιν ἐκκυνηγέσαι
     Φ[ο]ίβου κλ[ο]παίας βοῦς ἀπεστερημένο[υ.
     τ]ῶν εἴ τις ὀπτήρ ἐστι[ν] ἢ κατήκοος,
     ἐ]μοί τ᾽ [ἂ]ν [ε]ἴη προσφιλὴ[ς] φράσας τόδε
     Φοίβῳ τ]᾽ ἄνακτι παντελὴς εὐεργ[έ]της.   (85)

55]ωσω insecurely read: δ]ώσω conj. Siegmann
62 πῶ[ς Siegmann
64 ΧΟ(ΡΟΣ) ΣΑΤΥ(ΡΩΝ) in marg. P.Oxy.
65 βά[σιν τε Hunt: P. Oxy. has τα ιχν(η) in marg.
72 λαθρι[α νυχια 'or a kindred word' originally in P. Oxy., as inferred by Hunt from δ]ιανυχ(ια) in the margin attributed to Theon
73 ποσσὶ Hunt
74 voice-change marked in P. Oxy.
84 φράσας Wilamowitz: δρασας P. Oxy.   85 παντελὴς Pearson: προστελης P. Oxy.

\<AP.\>	... I will (give it?); just (ensure) this! (55)
\<SI.\>	... and you ensure ...!
\<AP.\>	... whoever he is; all's (ready). (57)
	4 defective lines (58–61), then:
\<SI.\>	What's this? How ... (you?) ...? (62)
\<AP.\>	(You'll be?) free ...[11]

Apollo leaves; the CHORUS *of satyrs rushes in, singing and dancing freely.*[12]

CHORUS	*beginnings of 12 lines (64–75):*
	Come on, there! ... foot (and step?) ... (65) ... Here, what the ... ! (*some of them collide at once in surprise*) Hey, it's you ... ! Come on, ... the thief ... underhand[13] ... achieving (*or* hastening) ... my father's voice ... (70) How, where ... the unseen (night-time?) theft ... on foot (?) ... in case somehow, if I succeed, ... and for my father ... free ... (75).
	Let the god who is our friend be with us and help[14] complete our labours, now he's offered us splendid examples of gold!
SI.	O Fortune, goddess and divinity guiding us! (*Grant*) I may succeed in the business upon which I run eagerly,[15] (80) to track down the booty, the prey, the plunder, the stolen cows that Phoebus has had taken from him. If there is anyone who has seen or heard of them, and tells me, he'll be my friend (and) a perfect benefactor (to Phoebus). (85)

[11] Apollo repeats the promise of freedom in 457; cf. also 75 and 164.

[12] This seems to be the Chorus' initial entry, unless they came in with Silenus at 45. The metre of the free lyrics in 64–78 has not been identified. See Addendum.

[13] 'underhand': if correctly so translated, metaphorical; lit. 'mined below, underground'.

[14] In the Greek ξύν is adverbial ('(be) together with (us)'), Smyth § 1638, cf. Pearson (1917) 2.298 on Soph. *Phaedra* F 679; and ἅμα ('help') goes closely with the verb ἀνέτω (this verb is a variant form of ἀνύτω, 70).

[15] 'Fortune': personified; cf. the n. on *Cyc.* 606–7, where an appeal to her is made in desperation, and Eur. *IA* 1136 'O fate my mistress, and fortune, and my divinity!' '(*Grant*) I may etc.': bare accusative and infinitive of a prayer (*e.g.* Soph. *OT* 190; cf. on Aesch. *Sisyphus* F 228 n. 6); sometimes a verb for 'grant' is expressed. 'upon which': in the Greek an objective genitive regular with verbs of desire or eagerness, Smyth § 1349.

letters from one line, then:

col. iv

letters from 4 lines (87–90), the last 3 containing excited cries by the Chorus, then:

<ΣΙ.>   φησίν τις .[;   (91)
              ἔοικεν ἤδη κ[
              ἄγ᾽ εἶα δὴ πᾶς ..[
              ῥινηλατῶν ὀσμ[
              αὔρας ἐάν πῃ πρ[*16–17 let.*   (95)
              διπλοῦς ὀκλάζω[ν *16–17 let.*
              ὕποσμος ἐν χρῷ .[*14–15 let.*
              οὕτως ἔρευναν καὶ π[*10–11 let.*
              ἄπαντα χρηστὰ κα[ὶ *10–11 let.*]λειν
<ΧΟ.>   θεὸς θεὸς θεὸς θεός· ἔα [*9–10 let.*   (100)
              ἔχειν ἔοιγμεν· ἴσχε, μὴ ..ρ[...].τει.
—   ταῦτ᾽ ἔστ᾽ ἐκεῖνα· τῶν βοῶν τ[ὰ] βήματα.
—   σίγ[α]· θεός τις τὴν ἀποι[κία]ν ἄγει.
—   τί δρῶμεν, ὦ τᾶν; ἢ τὸ δέον [..].νομεν;
—   τί; τοῖσ[ι] ταύτῃ πῶς δοκεῖ; — δοκεῖ πάνυ· (105)
              σαφῶ[ς γ]ὰρ αὔθ᾽ ἕκαστα σημαίνει τάδε.
              ἰδοὺ ἰδού·
              καὶ τοὐπίσημον αὐτὸ τῶν ὁπλῶν πάλι[ν.
              ἄθρει μάλα.
—   αὔτ᾽ ἐστὶ τοῦτο μέτρον [ἐ]κμε[μαγ]μ[έ]νον. (110)
—   χ[ώ]ρει δρόμῳ καὶ τα[*10–11 let.*].ν ἔχου
remnants of 1 line ending with]μενος

col. v

           ῥοίβδημ᾽ ἐάν τι τῶν [*6 let.*]. οὖς [

91 τις; punct. Radt: τις ἢ [… ; Hunt   94 ὀσμ[αῖσι Hunt
99 χρησθαι in marg. Theon, whence χρῆσται (*i.e.* χρὴ ἔσται) and 98 ἐρευνᾶν (Wilamowitz) Vollgraff
102 punct. von Blumenthal
104]ηνομεν read in P. Oxy. by Hunt: [ἐξ]ήνομεν Wilamowitz
106 σαφῶ[ς Carden: σαφη[read in P. Oxy. by Hunt
108 επισιμωμο( )νι( ) *i.e.* ἐπίσιμον μό(νος) Νι(κάνωρ) *or* Νί(κανδρος) read (with some letters uncertain) in P. Oxy. marg. by Hunt
110 [ἐ]κμε[μαγ]μ[έ]νον Pearson: cf. 146
113 οὖσ[*i.e.* οὖς [read in P. Oxy. by Hunt; between this line and 114 P. Oxy. has ροιβδος, probably a gloss on the rarer form ῥοίβδημα

5 very damaged lines, including further cries by the Chorus, then:

\<SIL.\>	Does anyone say ...? (91) ... seems already ... Come on, everyone ... tracking (by scents?) ... the breeze in case somehow ... (95) ... bending over double ... following the scent right up close ... in this way a search (*or* to search) and ... everything good,[16] and ...
\<CHO.\>	(*exclaiming excitedly in two or more groups*) The god, the god, the god, the god![17] Look there! ... (100). Seems like we have him! Stop, don't ...
–	Here they are! The hoof-prints of the cows!
–	Be quiet! Some god is leading our expedition.[18]
–	How are we doing, my friend? (Were?) we (achieving?) what's needed?
–	What? What do the ones over here think? (105)
–	They think (so?), absolutely – for every single thing here is a clear indication. See! See! And the actual imprint of their hooves, again! Take a good look!
–	This is their actual size, (moulded off)! (110)
–	Off you go at a run and keep ... (*a very fragmentary line*) ... if any whistling[19] of the ... (to?) ... (ear?).

[16] 'good': Theon's apparent variant reading χρῆσθαι ('to use'?) led to Vollgraff's χρῆσται '(99) it will be necessary ... (98) to search everything.'

[17] 'The god ...!': there is, however, no article in the Greek; possibly the satyrs attribute their discovery to Apollo; see the next note.

[18] 'god': Apollo again, most likely (100), and here invoked as patron of colonists sent overseas (Thucydides 6.3.1: Apollo Archegetes, 'Leader of Beginnings'), for 'expedition' translates the usual word for a colony so established; the satyrs mean that they are well away from their usual haunts.

[19] 'whistling': the noise made by herdsmen (Homer, *Odyssey* 9.315): cf. 160.

—   οὐκ εἰσακούω ...[....]στου φθ[έγγ]ματος.
　　　　 ἀλλ᾽ αὐτὰ μὴν ἴχ[νη τε] χὠ στίβος τάδε   (115)
　　　　 κείνων ἐναργῆ τῶν β[ο]ῶν μαθεῖν πάρα.
　　　　 ἔα μάλα·
　　　　 παλινστραφῆ τοι ναὶ μὰ Δία τὰ βήματα
　　　　 εἰς τοὔμπαλιν δέδορκεν· αὐτὰ δ᾽ εἴσιδε.
　　　　 τί ἐστι τουτί; τίς ὁ τρόπος τοῦ τάγματ[ος;   (120)
　　　　 εἰς τοὐπίσω τὰ πρόσθεν ἤλλακται, τὰ δ᾽ αὖ
　　　　 ἐναντί᾽ ἀλλήλοισι συμπ[επλεγ]μένα·
　　　　 δεινὸς κυκησμὸς εἶχ[ε τὸν βοη]λάτην.

<ΣΙ.>　 τίν᾽ αὖ τέχνην σὺ τήν[δ᾽ ἄρ᾽ ἐξ]ηῦρες, τίν᾽ αὖ,
　　　　 πρόσπαιον ὧδε κεκλιμ[ένος] κυνηγετεῖν   (125)
　　　　 πρὸς γῇ; τίς ὑμῶν ὁ τρόπος; οὐχὶ μανθάνω·
　　　　 ἐχῖνος ὥς τις ἐν λόχμῃ κεῖσαι πεσών,
　　　　 ἤ] τις πίθηκος κύβδ᾽ ἀποθυμαίνεις τινί.
　　　　 τ]ί ταῦτα; ποῦ γῆς ἐμάθετ᾽; ἐν πο[ί]ῳ τόπῳ;
　　　　 σ[η]μήνατ᾽· οὐ γὰρ ἴδρις εἰμὶ τοῦ τρόπου.   (130)
<ΧΟ.>　 ὗ [ὗ] ὗ ὗ.
<ΣΙ.>　 τ[ί 8 *let.*] τίνα φοβῇ; τίν᾽ εἰσορᾷς;
　　　　 τ[ί 8 *let.*]ις; τί ποτε βακχεύεις ἔχων;

118 ναὶ μά Δία τὰ βήματα printed by all eds, but most letters are insecurely read
120 τάγματ[ος: also πραγματος marg. P. Oxy.
122 συμπ[εφυρ]μένα Pearson
129 τόπῳ Wilamowitz: τροπωι P. Oxy.

– I don't hear ... voice! But here, I swear, are the actual tracks and path (115) of the cows, clear to make out! Hey, what's this? Their hoof-prints have been turned round, by Zeus! You can see they face backwards! Have a close look at the things! What is this, here? What kind of arrangement is this? (120)[20] The prints in front have been changed to go backwards, with the others (tangled?) together in opposite directions.[21] A weird confusion took hold of (the cow)herd!

At this moment a mysterious noise is heard, which causes the hunting satyrs suddenly to bend low to the ground, as if it came from there.

<SI.>   *Now* what's this technique you've invented here, eh? Just what is it, with your tracking in a sudden new way bent over like this (125) to the ground?[22] What kind is this way, of yours? I just don't understand. You're lying down there like a hedgehog in a bush, or you're bent over and farting at somebody like a monkey![23] What *is* this? Where on earth did you learn it? In what sort of place? Explain! I've no knowledge of this way! (130)

<CHO.>   (*in alarmed excitement*) Hu-u! Hoo! Hu-u! Hoo!

<SI.>   What ...? Who is it you fear? Who is it you're looking at? What ...? Why ever go on with this frenzy? ... are you wanting to discover

---

[20] 'arrangement': P.Oxy. in its margin appears to offer a variant 'business'.

[21] 'The prints ... directions': wording which echoes the *Homeric Hymn* 77–8. For the insecure supplement '(tangled?)' Pearson suggested 'muddled'.

[22] Zagagi (1999) 188–98 points particularly to the similarity of this searching-scene, modelled on hounds, with the Furies' search by scent for the blood-tainted Orestes at Aesch. *Eum.* 244–54.

[23] 'hedgehog in a bush': a folk-comparison. For a hedgehog doubled up (but when hiding) see Ion of Chios, *Phoenix* F 38.2–4. Zagagi (1999) 198–204 compares especially Strepsiades' astonishment at the pupils of 'Socrates' bent over while examining the earth at Ar. *Clouds* 184–93.

Monkeys farting: behaviour perhaps suggested by observation in Athens itself; monkeys were kept as pets (see Diggle's commentary on Theophrastus, *Characters* 5.9). The colloquial comparison may reflect a common image; *LIMC* VI.1 56 'Kirke' no. 57 is a bell-crater of about 460 BC depicting a satyr in ape-form bent over and apparently farting in front of Circe. This interpretation of the crater has nevertheless been disputed, a doubt recently strengthened by zoologists' observation that monkeys do not in fact fart at one another (information we owe to Dr. Andreas Antonopoulos (formerly) of Exeter University, from his proposed commentary on the play). Further, 'farting' is also disputed as the translation here of a verb elsewhere unattested whose etymology suggests rather the meaning 'getting very angry'.

For farting in satyr-drama cf. 168 and n. 33 below

α[*9 let.*]. κέρχν[ο]ς ἱμείρει[ς] μαθεῖν
τ[ί *6 let.*] σιγᾶθ', οἱ πρ[ὸ] τ[οῦ] λ[αλίστ]ατοι;   (135)

1 line (136) from the Chorus with only its first letter preserved (of about ten), then:

<ΣΙ.>	τ[*8–9 let.*]ναπονος[...]εισεχων. (137)
<ΧΟ.>	ἄ[κουε δή.

col. vi

<ΣΙ.>	κα[ὶ] πῶς ἀκούσ[ω μηδεν]ὸς φωνὴν κλύων;
<ΧΟ.>	ἐμ[ο]ὶ πιθοῦ. (140)
<ΣΙ.>	ἐμ[..]δ..[*8–9 let.*].ῶς ὀνήσετε.
<ΧΟ.>	ἄκουσον αυτ[.]...[ν, πά]τερ, χρόνον τινὰ
	ο]ΐῳ 'κπλαγέντες ἐν[θάδ'] ἐξενίσμεθα
	ψόφῳ, τὸν οὐδε[ὶ]ς π[ώπ]οτ' ἤκουσεν βροτῶν.
<ΣΙ.>	τί μοι ψ[ό]φον φοβ[εῖσθε] κα[ὶ] δειμαίνετε, (145)
	μάλθης ἄναγνα σώ[μα]τ' ἐκμεμαγμένα,
	κάκιστα θηρῶν ὀνθ[ί' ἐ]ν [π]άσῃ σκιᾷ
	φόβον βλέποντες, πάν[τα] δειματούμενοι,
	ἄνευρα κἀκόμιστα κἀνε[λε]ύθερα
	διακονοῦντες, [σώ]ματ' εἰ[σ]ιδ[ε]ῖν μόνον (150)
	κα[ὶ γ]λῶσσα κα[ὶ] φάλητες; εἰ δέ που δέῃ,
	πιστοὶ λόγοισιν ὄντες ἔργα φεύγετε,

135 σιγαθ' οι προ του Theon: σιγ]ατ' ω πρ[P. Oxy; end Wilamowitz
137 the letters εισ are insecure:]εις ἔχων Hunt
141 ἐμ[οὶ] Diehl; οὐδα]μῶς Hunt
142 νῦ[ν, πά]τερ Carden
143 κπλαγεντες marg. Theon, with attribution to Ar(istophanes) or Aul: πλαγεντες P. Oxy.; εξενισμεθα marg. Theon: εξ[.].γισμεθα P. Oxy.: ἐξ[ω]ρyίσμεθα Hunt: ἐξ[η]γίσμεθα Siegmann: ἐξ[η]γίσμεθα Walker, Guida
146 εκμεμαγμενα 'Ar(istonicus)' in P. Oxy. (see on 143): -μενοι P. Oxy.
147 ὀνθ[ί' ἐ]ν Walker
150 [σχή]ματ' Tammaro
152 πιστοὶ all eds, but πιστ is insecurely read

... millet(?)?[24] Why ... are you silent, who were so very talkative before? (135)

(2 lines yielding nothing securely intelligible)

\<CHO.\>	(Listen, do!)
\<SI.\>	And how am I to listen when I hear (no one's) voice?
\<CHO.\>	Do as I say! (140)
\<SI.\>	... you'll be (no) help (at all?) (to *me*?)!
\<CHO.\>	Listen ... (now), father, for a while, to the sort of noise that has terrified and baffled us here – one that no mortal ever yet heard![25]
\<SI.\>	Why (are you) frightened and terrified of a noise, (145) tell me? – you're unholy bodies, moulded out of wax,[26] the worst of animal (dung), seeing a fright[27] in every shadow, terrified at everything, spineless and disorganized and gormless assistants, mere bodies (150) to the eye, and mouths[28] and phalluses! In an emergency anywhere,[29] you say you're loyal but you avoid action

[24] 'millet': kept in underground 'silos' (of barley: *Inachus* F 276*)*, so that the satyrs might well bend over (125, 128) to look for it: so Lloyd-Jones (1996). He and Pfeiffer took the Greek word as a rare form identical with another word of different meaning, either an 'excrescence' (Io's horns, *Inachus* F 279), which here would be an unusual outcrop of rock, or a rasping throat-sound, which would refer to that of cowherds (cf. 'whistling' 113 and n. 19); it cannot be the underground noise heard by the Chorus, for they do not tell Silenus they can hear it until 138.

[25] 'baffled': the apparent meaning of Theon's marginal reading; also 'enraged' (Hunt), 'possessed' (as if by magic, Siegmann), 'confounded' (Walker, an unattested verb-form, but advocated by Guida).

The Greek article τὸν serves as relative pronoun, a usage and metrical licence rare in dramatic dialogue but common in lyric (Diggle (1994) 466–7) and much of Greek poetry (Smyth § 1105).

[26] 'wax': used on writing-tablets, but also for modelling, ointments, tapers and so on; here it denotes 'softness' on the part of the satyrs.

[27] 'seeing a fright': possibly an ironic word-play, for the same Greek words elsewhere mean 'glaring terror' (*e.g.* the rampaging warrior Hippomedon at Aesch. *Seven* 498).

[28] 'mouths': cf. Hesiod, *Theogony* 26 '(shepherds) mere bellies'. Mouths here may indeed stand for the satyrs' gluttony, but also their ceaseless chattering: see on *Oeneus* F 1130.16. OKell (2003) 284–8 however relates 'mouths' to oral sex, an activity of satyrs in some vase-paintings (*e.g.* Lissarague (1990) 81 fig. 2.28). As to 'bodies': the reading [σώ]ματ(α) is now accepted by all editors, but V. Tammaro, *Eikasmos* 15 (2004) 57 has suggested [σχή]ματ(α) 'mere shapes', as at Eur. *Erechtheus* F 360.27.

[29] In the Greek conditional clause the absence of ἄν from the subjunctive is a poetic archaism, cf. 220: see Smyth § 2327.

τοιοῦ[δ]ε πατρός, ὦ κάκιστα θηρίων,
οὗ πόλλ' ἐφ' ἥβης μνήματ' ἀνδρείας ὕπο
κ[ε]ῖται παρ' οἴκοις νυμφικοῖς ἠσκημένα,　　　　(155)
οὐκ εἰς φυγὴν κλίνοντος, οὐ δειλ[ο]υμένου,
οὐδὲ ψόφοισι τῶν ὀρειτρόφων βοτῶν
π]τήσσοντος, ἀλλ' α[ἰχ]μαῖσιν ἐξει[ρ]γασμένου
ἃ] νῦν ὑφ' ὑμῶν λάμ[πρ' ἀ]πορρυπαίνεται
ψ]όφῳ νεώρει κόλακ[ι] ποιμένων π[ο]θέν.　　　　(160)
τί] δὴ φοβεῖσθε παῖδες ὣς πρὶν εἰσιδεῖν,
πλοῦτον δὲ χ[ρ]υσόφαντον ἐξαφίετε,
ὃν Φοῖβος ὑμῖν εἶπε κ[ἀ]νεδέξατο,
καὶ τὴν ἐλευθέρωσιν ἣν κατήνεσεν

col. vii

ὑμῖν τε κἀμοί· ταῦτ' ἀφέντες εὕδετε.　　　　(165)
εἰ μὴ 'νανοστήσαντες ἐξιχνεύσε[τε
τὰς βοῦς ὅπῃ βεβᾶσι καὶ τὸν βουκόλο[ν,
κλαίοντες αὐτῇ δειλίᾳ ψοφή[σ]ετε.

<ΧΟ.>　　πάτερ, παρὼν αὐτός με συμποδηγέτε[ι,
ἵν' εὖ κατείδῃς εἴ τίς ἐστι δειλία·　　　　(170)
γνώσῃ γὰρ αὐτός, ἢν παρῇς, οὐδὲν λέγω[ν.
<ΣΙ.>　　ἐγὼ πα[ρ]ὼν αὐτός σε προσβιβῶ λόγῳ,
κυνορτικὸν σύριγμα διακαλούμεν[ος.

156 δειλουμενου 'Ni(cander) *or* Ni(canor)' marg. P. Oxy.: δουλ- P. Oxy.
161 τί] Körte

– and that with a father like me, you worst of creatures, who in his prime through his manhood left many memorials fashioned in nymphs' dwellings![30] (155) He hasn't turned to flight, he hasn't been cowed, nor quailed at noises from mountain-grazing cattle, but done feats of weaponry whose brilliance you now tarnish – at a new-fangled soothing noise from herdsmen somewhere! (160)[31] (What) can you be frightened of before you see it, like children, and why are you letting go of the wealth in the form of gold that Phoebus spoke of and undertook to give you, and the freedom he promised you *and* me?[32] You're dozing if you let this slip! (165) If you're not going to come back and track down where the cows and the herdsman have gone, you'll be sorry when you're letting out noise from sheer cowardice![33]

<CHO.> Father, do come with me and lead me yourself, to find out clearly if there's any cowardice here. (170) For if you come you'll know for yourself that you're talking nonsense!

<SI.> I'll come with you myself and bring you over by argument! I'll call to you everywhere like a huntsman whistling on his hounds.

[30] Translation and reference uncertain: the description of the 'memorials' as 'fashioned' suggests that they were material reminders of courage in war or hunting; 'manhood' (154) and 'weaponry' (158, lit. 'spears', cf. Ar. *Lysistrata* 985) support this interpretation, which is maintained in 156–7. But why 'nymphs' – for satyrs usually mention them in the anticipation or celebration of sex, *e.g.* Aesch. *Net-Fishers* F 47a.60, cf. 66–7; *Prometheus the Fire-Kindler* F 204b.1–5, 6 = 15, *Cyc.* 68–72, cf. 515. Satyrs do speak of nymphs as their kin (228, cf. 41, *Cyc.* 4), but satyrs' 'memorials fashioned' and left in their dwellings would most appropriately be erotic remembrance-gifts, in the form of the graffiti or painted vessels common in real life (Ar. *Wasps* 98–9, cf. KPS 299 n. 34) – rather than the resulting babies.

[31] Silenus has heard nothing strange himself, and accuses the satyrs of terror at the ordinary noises of cattle and their herdsmen (167).

[32] At 56–63, cf. 51. On the whole speech 145–68 see the introductory discussion p. 341 and Addendum at the end of the volume.

[33] 'letting out noise': farting in terror (so, most recently, A. López Eire in Sommerstein (2003) 411), or worse (*e.g.* in Comedy Ar. *Knights* 1057, *Frogs* 308, 479); satyrs pride themselves on their farting at Soph. *Oeneus* F 1130.15–16 below. An older but much less vigorous translation was 'when you die noisily, and your cowardice with you': see Pearson (1917), Page (1942), and D. Bain's discussion of the passage at *SIFC* 13 (1995) 182–9. '... sorry' is lit. '... shedding tears', a colloquial idiom for suffering physical punishment. So Silenus' meaning may just be to threaten the satyrs with a strong beating, as Polyphemus threatens with similar language at *Cyc.* 210–11; cf. also the threat by the satyrs' interlocutor (Dionysus?) to them in Aesch. *Sacred Delegates* F **78c.4.

ἀλλ᾽ εἴ [ἐ]φίστω τριζύγ᾽ εἰς οἶμον βάσιν·
ἐγὼ δ᾽ ἐν [ἔ]ργοις παρμένων σ᾽ ἀπευθυνῶ.   (175)

<XO.>   ὒ ὒ ὒ, ψ ψ, ἃ ἇ. λέγ᾽ ὅ τι πονεῖς.
                    τί μάτην ὑπέκλαγες, ὑπέκριγες,
                    ὑπό μ᾽ ἴδες; ἔχεται
                    ἐν πρώτῳ τίς ὅδε τρόπ[ῳ;
                    ἔχῃ. ἐλήλυθεν, ἐλήλ[υθεν.   (180)
                    ἐμὸς εἶ, ἀνάγου.
                    δευτέρῳ τίς ὅδε .[.....].της;
                    ὁ Δράκις, ὁ Γράπις, [*5–6 let.*
                    Ο]ὐρίας, Οὐρίας, αδ[*6 let.*]κεις
                    παρέβης· μεθυ[*10–11 let.*   (185)

2 damaged lines giving no clear sense, but with ἔποχον ἔχει *beginning* 187,
then:

                    στίβος ὅδε νέο[ς *11–12 let.*
                    Στράτιος, Στράτ[ιος *traces*
                    δεῦρ᾽ ἕπου· τ[ί]δρ[ᾷς;   (190)

col. viii

                    ἔνι β[ο]ῦς, ἔνι πόνο[ς.
                    μὴ μεθῇ, Κρ[ο]κία[ς.
                    σ]ὺ τί καλ[ὸ]ν ἐπιδ[
                    ὅδε γ᾽ ἀγαθὸς ὁ Τρέ[χις

174 τριζύγ᾽ εἰς Wilamowitz, οἶμον Lloyd-Jones: τριζυγης οιμου P. Oxy.
176–202 some eds divide into parts for chorus-members alone, others between Chorus and Silenus
180 ἔχῃ Walker: εχει P. Oxy.
185 Μεθυ[Robert
188 ὅδε νέο[ς Rossbach: οδενε.[P. Oxy.
190 τ[ί] δρ[ᾷς; Robert
191 πόνο[ς Diehl
192 Κρ[ο]κία[ς Robert
194 Τρέ[χις Robert

On with you then, go and stand where the three paths meet,[34]
while I stay where the action is and direct you on your way. (175)

The Chorus spread out and caper excitedly in imitation of 'hunters'.[35]

<CHO.>   (*crying out inarticulately and then abusing one another harshly;*
                 lyric) Say what your trouble is! Why the useless shouting,
screaming, scowling at me? Who's this caught at the first turn?
You're caught! He's here, he's here! (180) You're mine: off to
the pen! Who's this at the second ...? Dracis there, Grapis ...
Ourias, Ourias ... You've missed your way! ... drunk (?) ... (185)
(*two damaged lines with no clear sense, but including the words*
has (him?) caught (?)) Here's a fresh track ...! Soldier, Soldier,
... chase over here! What (are you doing)? (190) There's a cow
here, there's work here! Don't let go, (Saffron?)! What good ...
you ...? He's good, (Runner?) here! He's chasing as usual. (195)

---

[34] 'where the three paths meet': our 'fork in the road'. In the theatre, this point would be in front of the still undisclosed cave of Cyllene (221), so that (ironically) Silenus points the satyrs exactly to the source of the noise.

     'Go and stand': in the Greek of 174 βάσιν is an internal accusative (acting like a cognate noun) with ἐφίστω, lit. 'halt your step'.

[35] Some eds accordingly divide 176–202 into different voice-parts; others think that the satyrs call variously to one another or to dogs, for some of the names suit one or the other (Dr Antonopoulos (see n. 23) suggests that 'Dracis' may mean 'Grasper' or 'Grabber', and 'Ourias' 'Mountain-Bred' (cf. 41) or 'Long-Tail'; 'Grapis' is almost certainly 'Wrinkly', and 'drunk' in 185 may be 'Drinky'). Walton (1935) esp. 167–9 suggested that the satyrs wore canine costumes, but Zagagi (1999) 189 n. 26 is rightly sceptical; it would be enough for the satyrs to mimic hounds while tracing the hoof-prints (cf. their posture at 125). At 181 a captured cow seems to be addressed, 'off to the pen' being a gaoler's command to a prisoner, and perhaps also at 197 (see n. 36); presumably these animals were left to imagination. Some eds think that Silenus too has a part in the lyric shouting, when names are called at 183 or 189, or fear of failure voiced at 198 'Pretty soon ...', addressed to a satyr. These lines are severely damaged, and we have printed a number of plausible if unverifiable supplements to give an idea of very lively stage-business.

     For the lyric form and metre of this passage, and its possible relation to the excited dance known as the *sikinis*, see *Cyc.* 37–40 and n., Kaimio (2001) 44–5 and 51–3 (on Pratinas 4 F 3.15 p. 247 above), Voelke (2001) 170–2 and M. Griffith in Harrison (2005) 170–1 – but no explicit words for dancing survive throughout 176–202 or in Cyllene's reaction to the satyrs movements and noise in 221–3, 229–31 and 237–40.

κατὰ νόμον ἔπετα[ι.   (195)
ἐφέπου, ἐφέπου μ.[
ὁπποποῖ· ἃ μιαρέ, γε[
ἢ τάχ' ὁπόταν ἀπίῃ[ς
ἀπελεύθερος ὢν ολ.[
ἀλλὰ μὴ παραπλακ[(200)
ἔπ[ι]θ' [ἔ]πεχ' εἴσιθ' ἴθι [
τ[ὸ] δε πλάγιον ἔχομ[εν.

πάτερ, τί σιγᾷς; μῶν ἀληθ[ὲς εἴπομεν;
οὐ[κ ε]ἰσακο[ύε]ις; ἢ κεκώφη[σαι *4–5 let.* ;   (204)
<ΣΙ.>   ἔα. <ΧΟ.> τί ἔστιν; <ΣΙ.> οὐ μενῶ. <ΧΟ.> μέν', ε[ἰ]
                                                          θέλεις.
<ΣΙ.>   οὐκ ἔστιν. ἀλλ' αὐτὸς σὺ ταῦθ[' ὅπῃ θέλεις]
          ζήτει τε κἀξίχνευε καὶ πλού[τ
          τὰς βοῦς τε κα[ὶ] τὸν χρυσὸν *traces*
          μὴ πλεῖστ[ον] ἔτι .[*traces*] χρόνον.
<ΧΟ.> *7 very damaged lines* (210–16), *possibly divided between two voices
of the Chorus, in which these words are read:*

          210 ἀλλ' οὔ τι μ[ὴ, 211 οὐδ' ἐξυπελθ[εῖ]ν and σαφῶς, 212
          εἰδῶμεν ὅς[τις], *then lyric* 213 ἰώ, 214 φθέγ[γμ' ἀφύσεις,
          (col. ix) 216 δ]όμοισιν ὀλβίσῃς, *then again speech:*

          ὁ[..]ῦ φαν.[..]αιτοισιν. ἀλλ' ἐγὼ τάχα
          φ[έρ]ων κτύ[π]ον πέδορτον ἐξαναγκάσω
          π[η]δήμασιν κραιπνοῖσι καὶ λακτίσμασιν
          ὥ[σ]τ' εἰσακοῦσαι κεἰ λίαν κωφός τις ἦ.   (220)
<ΚΥΛΛΗΝΗ> θῆρες, τί [τό]νδε χλοερὸν ὑλώδη πάγον
          ἔν[θ]ηρον ὡρμήθητε σὺν πολλῇ βοῇ;
          τίς ἥδε τέχνη; τίς μετάστασις πόνων,
          οὓς πρόσθεν εἶχες δεσπότῃ χάριν φέρων,

200 παραπλάκ[ηθι Rossbach   202 τ[ὸ] δέ Hunt: τ[.]δε P. Oxy.
203 ἀληθ[ὲς εἴπομεν Wilamowitz   204 punct. and ἢ Radt: η P. Oxy
206 both οπηι θελεις and οπηι δυναι marg P. Oxy.
207 *e.g.* πλού[του κράτει Radt
209 πλεῖστ[ον]: -ιστ- in P. Oxy. insecurely read
214 φθεγγμα αφυσ[.]ις marg. (ἀφύσεις Hunt, as a variant reading for ἀφύξεις) and φθεγ[in
text P. Oxy.: ἀφήσεις or ἀπύσεις Vollgraff
224 εἶχες Wilamowitz: ειπες P. Oxy.; φέρων; punct. Diggle

Chase him hard, chase him hard ...! Oh, no! Ah, you loser ...![36]
... Pretty soon, when you go away ... restored to freedom ... But
don't (wander?) off ... (200) Go on! Keep at it! Go in! Go ...! But
we've got the flank ...!

The strange noise apparently recurs, and the Chorus return to speech.

Father, why the silence? (We spoke) the truth, didn't we? Can't
you hear or have you gone *deaf (a word missing)*?

<SI.>   (*alarmed*) Oh! There!

<CHO.>   What is it?

<SI.>   I'm not going to stay!

<CHO.>   Stay, please! [37](205)

<SI.>   Impossible! But you go on yourself with this search as you wish (*or
            where or as you can*), and track things down and (get?) rich(es?),
            both the cows and the gold ... not for very much longer!   (209)

Silenus runs off in fright.

<CHO.>   *7 very damaged lines possibly divided between two voices,
            including (speaking)* 210 But there's no way ..., 211 nor sneak
            off *and* clearly, 212 (*so that*) we may know who ... , (*singing*) 213
            Oh, ...! ..., 214 ... you'll utter a word ..., 216 (so?) you may count
            (me?) happy (in?) my house.
            (*speaking*) (*the first words yield no sense*) but I'll quickly (217)
            bring in noise to make the ground ring, with rapid jumping and
            stamping, to force anyone to hear us even if he's really deaf!
                                                                    (220)

The nymph Cyllene comes out abruptly from the cave.

<CYLLENE>   You beasts of the wild, why have you invaded this grassy, wooded
            hillside, the home of wild things, with this loud shouting? What's
            this technique?[38] What's the change from the work you had before
            in pleasing your master, when you were always drunk with wine
            and had fawn-skins slung round you (225)? – and you balanced a

---

[36] 'loser!': translated as a rebuke to a fellow-satyr rather than as a curse upon an escaping
cow, when *e.g.* 'blighter' would be appropriate. The word, lit. 'polluter, polluted', is a
colloquial metaphor for one who brings disaster, *Cyc.* 677.

[37] 'Oh!' ... 'Stay, please' (205): division of a single dialogue-verse into four voice-parts is
exceedingly rare, but Sophocles has it in his tragedy *Philoctetes* 753, a moment of comparable
tension. For three voice-parts see *Cyc.* 682 and n.

[38] 'technique': cf. Silenus' question at 124; it is the word which the satyrs use to boast of
their abilities and activities at Soph. *Oeneus* F 1130.8.

ὕποινος αἰεὶ νεβρίνῃ καθημμέν[ο]ς　　　　　(225)
δορᾷ χερ[ο]ῖν τε θύρσ[ο]ν εὐπαλῆ φορῶν
ὄπισθεν ἠΰίαζες ἀμφὶ τὸν θεὸν
σὺν ἐγγόνοις νύμφαισι κὠπαδῶν ὄχλῳ;
νῦν δ' ἀγνοῶ τὸ χρῆμα· ποῖ στροφαὶ νέαι
μανιῶν στρέφουσι; θαῦμα γάρ· κατέκλ[υ]ον　　　　　(230)
ὁμοῦ πρέπον κέλευμά πως κυνηγετ[ῶ]ν
ἐγγὺς μολόντων θηρὸς εὐναί[ου] τρο[φ]ης

4 badly damaged lines (233–6), including the words 233 ὁμοῦ and φωρ[,
234 γλώσσης and κλοπὴν, 235 αὖθις, 236 κηρυγμα[, then:

καὶ τ[α]ῦτ' ἀφεῖσα ... ποδῶν λακ[τισμα　　　　　(237)
κ]λη[δὼ]ν ὁμοῦ πάμφυρ[τ]' ἐγειτν[ία

then 4 further badly damaged lines, with many letters insecurely read (239–
42), end the column: 239 ...] ταῦτ' ἂν ἄλλω[ς traces, 240 ....]ων ἀκο[ύ]σασ'
ὧδε παραπεπαισμέν[ων, 241 letters and traces, ending ὑμᾶς νοσεῖν, 242
letters and traces, ending ἃ]ν οὐ τιθεῖτ' ἀναιτίαν.

col. x
ΧΟ.　　　　　νύμφα βαθύζωνε, παῦ[σαι χόλου　　　　　στρ.
　　　　　　　τοῦδ'· οὔτε γὰρ νεῖκος η[
　　　　　　　δά[ο]υ μάχας οὔτ' ἀξενο[　　　　　(245)
　　　　　　　γλ[ῶ]σσ' ἂν μάταιός τ[
　　　　　　　μή με μὴ προψαλ[άξῃς

225 ὕποινος read in P. Oxy. by Maltese
226 φορῶν Diggle: φερων P. Oxy.
228 κὠπαδῶν Maas: καιποδων P. Oxy.: καἰπόλων Steffen
229 νεαι read in P. Oxy. by Carden
230 half-stop after γάρ Hunt: no stop, but half-stop after κατέκλ[υ]ον eds; κατήλυθεν marg
Theon
237 λακ[τίσμασιν or λακ[τίσματος Hunt
238 as supplemented by Hunt, but Diggle in particular shows that the first two words must
remain wholly insecure as both reading and supplement
242 ἃ]ν οὐ τιθεῖτ' read in P. Oxy., the first 6 letters insecurely, by Diggle:]νετιποειτ' (i.e.]ν
ἔτι ποεῖτ'), the first 5 letters insecurely, read by Hunt.
243 νύμφα Diggle: νυμφη P.Oxy., cf. 329; παῦ[σαι χόλου Murray
244 ἥ[κω φέρων Diehl
245 οὔτ' Diggle: ουδ P. Oxy.
247 προψαλ[άξῃς (and deleting the second μή) Diggle

thyrsus easily in your hand, and would shout the Bacchic cry close behind the god, together with your family nymphs and a throng of followers.[39] Now, I don't understand the thing! Where are these sudden turns of madness whirling you? It's astonishing! I heard (230) a clear command rather like that of hunters approaching a wild beast's young in its lair ... (232)

4 badly damaged lines (233–6), *with some words legible but not all securely:*

233 together ... thief (?), 234 of a voice ... theft, 235 again, 236 loud call, *then:*

237 abandoning (*or* emitting?) these ... (thumping(s?)) of feet, 238 (shouting?) (together?) ... confused(ly?)[40] was in the neighbourhood ...; *then:*

239 ... these (I?) would otherwise ... 240, ... on hearing such crazy ..., 241 that you are sick ..., 242 ... you would not count (me?) ... innocent.[41]

CHO.   (*singing; strophe*)[42] Deep-girdled nymph,[43] ... leave off this (anger?); for (I?) neither (come with?) a quarrel for hostile fighting nor ... an unfriendly ... (245) ... a reckless tongue would ... No, no,[44] don't assail me ... but readily ... (*to*) me ... in this

[39] 'family nymphs': cf. 'sons of nymphs' above, 41 and n. 8. At *Cyc.* 63–72 the satyrs themselves miss these customary rites in honour of Dionysus during their separation from him.

'followers': Maas's conjecture; Steffen's 'goatherds' is close to P. Oxy.'s lettering, but identifies Dionysus' 'followers' too narrowly.

[40] 'loud call ... (thumping(s?)) of feet': 218–20; similarly of the satyrs' boisterous arrival at *Cyc.* 37–40.

In the Greek of 237 the fem. nom. participle 'abandoning *or* emitting' has no clear noun of reference (hardly the insecurely read 'shouting' in 238); and it is equally difficult to take it as syntactically 'hanging' (Smyth § 2148c), of Cyllene herself, who is the person 'hearing' in 240. In 238 'together' also is a wholly insecure reading.

[41] In 239 the readings and translation are uncertain; in 242 'innocent' is feminine gender and so must refer to Cyllene herself, cf. her protest at 251–7; Hunt's reading means '(What) will (?) you do (to an) innocent ...?'

[42] The responding lyric antistrophe is 290–7; iambic and cretic rhythm.

[43] 'Deep-girdled': apologetic flattery here (cf. 258 and n. 46); but in Homer and early poetry (*e.g. Iliad* 9.594) it is a conventional description of a richly dressed (and therefore) superior woman of any age; again in 270 (of a goddess).

[44] In the Greek the doubled negative expresses alarm, cf. *e.g. Ajax* 190. Diggle however deleted the second negative to secure approximate metrical responsion with 294.

ἀλλ᾽ [εὐ]πετῶς μοι πρ[
μ᾽ ἐν [τ]όποις τοῖσ[δε
στως ἐγήρυσε θέσπιν αὐδά[ν.　　　　　　(250)

<KY.>　　ταῦτ᾽ ἔστ᾽ ἐκείνων νῦν [
καὶ τοῖσδε θηρῶν ἐκπύ[θοιο
ἀλκασμάτων δ[*traces*
νύμφης· ἐμοὶ γὰ[ρ *traces*
ὀρθοψάλακτον εν[*traces*　　　　　　(255)

ἀλλ᾽ ἥσυχος πρόφαινε καὶ μ[*traces*
ὅτου μάλιστα πράγματος χρείαν ἔχεις.

<XO.>　　τόπων ἄνασσα τῶν[δ]ε, Κυλλήνης σθένος,
ὅτου μὲν οὕνεκ᾽ ἦλθ[ο]ν, ὕστερον φράσω·
τὸ φθέγγμα δ᾽ ἡμῖν τοῦ[θ᾽] ὅπερ φωνεῖ φράσον　　(260)
καὶ τίς ποτ᾽ αὐτῷ δι[α]χαράσσεται βροτῶν.

<KY.>　　 ὑμᾶς μὲν αὐτοὺς χρὴ τάδ᾽ εἰδέναι σαφῶς
ὡς, εἰ φανεῖτε τὸν λ[ό]γον τὸν ἐξ ἐμοῦ,
αὐτοῖσιν ὑμῖ[ν ζ]ημία πορίζεται·
καὶ γὰρ κέκρυπτ[αι] τοὖργον ἐν [θ]ε[ῶ]ν ἕδραις,　　(265)
Ἥραν ὅπως μ[ὴ πύ]στ[ι]ς ἵζετα[ι] λόγου.
Ζ[εὺ]ς γ[ὰρ] κρυφ[αίως εἰς στέ]γην Ἀ[τ]λαντίδος

2 badly damaged lines (268–9), the first presumed to contain the genitive
Μαίας *and the second ending with* φίλας

col. xi

　　　　7 *let.*] λήθῃ τῆς βαθυζώνου θεᾶς　　　　(270)
　　　　7 *let.*].ς δὲ παῖδ᾽ ἐφίτυσεν μόνον·
　　　　8 *let.*] χερσὶ ταῖς ἐμαῖς ἐγὼ τρέφω·
　　　　μητρὸς γ]ὰρ ἰσχὺς ἐν νόσῳ χειμάζεται·
　　　　κἄδεσμ]α καὶ ποτῆτα καὶ κοιμήματα
　　　　πρὸς σπ]αργάνοις μένουσα λικνῖτιν τροφὴν　　(275)

249 τοῖσ[δε eds
250 omitted by the first hand, added by the second, in P. Oxy.
252 ἐκπύ[θοιο (Hunt) πλείον᾽ ἂν Lloyd-Jones (μᾶλλον ἂν Hunt)
260 τουτο πως φωνει marg. Theon in P. Oxy.
267 κρυφ[αίως εἰς Diggle; ἐς στέ]γην Wilamowitz
268 Μαίας supplemented and differently located by eds in this line
272 beg τοῦτον δὲ] Wilamowitz: βρέφος δὲ] Diggle
274 κἄδεσμ]α Bucherer: κἄδεστ]ὰ Wilamowitz

	place ... uttered a divine voice.[45] (250)
<CYL.>	Now this is ... than that ... and if you hunt with these ... (you'll) find out (more than from?) feats of strength ... (against *or* of?) a nymph. For to me ... a loudly-plucked (?)[46] ... (255); but calmly reveal and ... what matter is your particular need.
CHO.	Queen of this place, mighty Cyllene,[47] I shall say later why I have come; but tell us just what this voice is that sounds, (260) and whoever of mortal men is tearing us apart us with it.[48]
CYL.	You should understand clearly, that if you reveal what I say, there's punishment provided for yourselves: for the matter is kept hidden where the gods have their seat, (265) so that no (news) of the story may reach Hera. Zeus (*came*) secretly (to the dwelling?) of Atlas' daughter ...[49] (*two badly damaged lines including the name* Maia *and the word* loving *or* dear) ... in secret from the deep-girdled goddess (270) ... he fathered a single son ... I'm nursing (him) in my arms, for (his mother's) strength is buffeted by storms of sickness. His (food)[50] and drink and bedding, (as well as) his swaddling, his cradle-care, (275) – these I stay and

[45] 'divine voice': of the as yet unidentified lyre, 260–1, 284 *etc.* The papyrus text of 248–9 appears to have had words divided at the end of both lines, 250 beginning with the end of an adverb; editors suggest a sense like 'but readily (tell) me (who) in this place uttered ... (agreeably) a divine voice'.

[46] 'loudly-plucked': 'plucked' translates insecurely the verb with this secure meaning at 329 (while at 247 it means securely 'assail') – for only in 284ff. does Cyllene reveal that the mysterious noise is the 'voice' of the lyre. So Zagagi (1999) 212 n. 84 asks whether this adjective should not rather be translated as 'fingered erect': Cyllene is then already reprimanding the satyrs for their sexual arousal in front of her, and 366–8 will repeat her indignation.

[47] 'Mighty Cyllene': lit. 'might of Cyllene', periphrasis typical of high poetry to describe such grand figures as Hector, *e.g. Iliad* 9.351 or Heracles, *e.g.* Pindar F 29.4; 'Queen' has similar epic pedigree. The anomalous register of these words leavens the satyrs' temporary abasement before the nymph.

[48] 'tearing me apart', lit. 'scratching': with frustration, to know what it is.

[49] Maia, a nymph (whose name almost certainly stood in the damaged 268): Hermes' conception by Maia (and birth in the cave itself) secretly from Zeus' wife Hera begin the *Homeric Hymn* (see introductory discussion). Such secrecy about Zeus' paramours is good satyric fodder: see *e.g.* the introductory discussion to Aesch. *Sisyphus*.

[50] 'His (food)' (both Bucherer and Wilamowitz) seems inescapable but is resisted by some editors on the ground that the baby is barely six days old (279) – but he grows miraculously (281–2). His cradle-care (275) also echoes the *Hymn* (21) verbally.

ἐξευθ]ετίζω νύκτα καὶ καθ᾽ ἡμέραν.
.... α]ὔξεται κατ᾽ ἦμαρ οὐκ ἐπεικότα
.....]στος, ὥστε θαῦμα καὶ φόβος μ᾽ ἔχει.
οὔπω γ]ὰρ ἐκτὸν ἦμαρ ἐκπεφασμένος
.....]ς ἐρείδει παιδὸς εἰς ἥβης ἀκμήν,   (280)
κἀξορ]μενίζει κοὐκέτι σχολάζεται
βλάστη·] τοιόνδε παῖδα θησαυρὸς στέγει.
Ἑρμῆς δὲ] τοῦ[νομ]᾽ ἐστὶ τοῦ πατρὸς θέσει.
12–13 let. φ]θέγγμα μηχανῇ βρέμ[, *then:*

*damaged beginnings and ends of 13 lines (285–97), including, from the end
of Cyllene's speech, the words* 285 *end* ἡμέρᾳ μιᾷ, 286 *end* ἐμηχ]ανήσατο,
287 *beg* ἐξ ὑπτίας, 288 *beg* τοιόνδε, 289 *beg* ἔμμεστον *and end* παῖς βοῆς;
then, from the antistrophe 290–7 *responding with the strophe* 243–50 *above,*
290 *beg* ἄφραστ[, 292 θηρευμ[, 293 φώνημ[, 297 (col. xii) *end* πορίζειν
τοιάνδε γῆρυν.

<KY.>   μή νυν ἀπίστει· πιστὰ γάρ σε προσγελᾷ θεᾶς ἔπη.
<XO.>   καὶ πῶς πίθωμαι τοῦ θανόντος φθέγγμα τοιοῦτον βρέμειν;
<KY.>   πιθοῦ· θανὼν γὰρ ἔσχε φωνήν, ζῶν δ᾽ ἄναυδος ἦν ὁ θήρ.
                                                        (300)
<XO.>   ποῖός τις ἦν εἶδος; πρ[ο]μήκης, ἢ ᾽πίκυρτος, ἢ βραχύς;
<KY.>   βραχύς, χυτροίδης, πο[ι]κίλῃ δορᾷ κατερρικνωμένος.
<XO.>   ὡς αἰέλουρος εἰκάσαι πέφυκεν ἢ τὼς πάρδαλις;
<KY.>   πλεῖστον με[τ]αξύ· γογγύλον γάρ ἐστι καὶ βραχυσκελές.
<XO.>   οὐδ᾽ ὡς ἰχνευτῇ προσφερὲς πέφυκεν οὐδ᾽ ὡς καρκίνῳ;
                                                        (305)

277 *beg* παῖς δ᾽] Radt
278 ἄπαυ]στος Pearson
279 οὔπω γ]ὰρ Wilamowitz
281–2 κἀξορ] and 282 βλάστη] lost in P. Oxy.: supplied from Athenaeus 2.62f
282 τ[ρε]φει marg. P. Oxy., a variant for στέγει
283 Ἑρμῆς δὲ] and τοῦ[νομ]᾽ (with -ου- insecurely read in P. Oxy.) Diggle
284 βρέμ[ον Hunt
285–96 beginnings restored here (from attachment to col. x) by Siegmann, to the ends of
284–95 already by Hunt
298 νυν Wilamowitz: νῦν Hunt
302 τροχοιδη[ς marg. P. Oxy.
303 πάρδαλις Diggle: πορδαλις P. Oxy.
304 in πλεῖστον the letters -ιστο- are insecurely read in P. Oxy.

(set in order) night and day. ... grows improbably day by day ... so that I'm held by wonder and fear. For though it's (not yet) the sixth day[51] since he manifested himself, ... he's pushing towards a boy's peak bloom, (280) and his growth is shooting up with no more delay. Such is the boy this treasure-house hides (*or* nurtures)! (Hermes) is his (name),[52] at his father's giving. ... voice (thundering?) by a device ...

12 very fragmentary lines, including, from the end of Cyllene's speech, the words

285 in one day, 286 he (devised), 287 from an upturned ...[53], 288 such a ..., 289 full of loud sound ... the boy, *and (from the antistrophe 290–7 responding with the strophe 243–50 above)* 290 inexpressible, 292 hunt (*or* prey: *noun*), 293 voice, 297 to produce such a voice;

then dialogue resumes:[54]

<CYL.>   Now don't be so disbelieving! When the words of a goddess smile their greeting, they may be believed!

<CHO.>   And how am I to believe that such a voice resounds from the dead (creature)?

<CYL.>   Believe it! In death the creature obtained a voice, while in life it was voiceless.[55] (300)

<CHO.>   What kind of appearance did it have? Elongated? Rounded? Short?

<CYL.>   Short, pot-shaped, with a dappled hide, and shrivelled.

[51] 'sixth day': the 'next day' in the *Hymn* (273).

[52] 'Hermes ... his (name)': it was variously 'etymologized' in antiquity, 'explaining' the god's association with messages and their carriers (he was Zeus' messenger), with good luck, and with inventive deception (the last is here in point); see *e.g.* Eur. *Autolycus A and B*, introductory discussion.

[53] 'an upturned ...': a dead creature (299), a tortoise-shell, the 'solution' to Cyllene's riddling answers as far as 310, and possibly named explicitly in the damaged 324. Part of a riddling exchange on this same invention of the lyre survives from the Roman Pacuvius' *Antiopa* as fr. IV Ribbeck (= fr. I D'Anna), and may originate therefore in Euripides' *Antiope* (see *TrGF* 5.278, Collard and Cropp (2008) I.172). For riddles and the like in satyric drama see introductory discussion (2) on Aeschylus, *Sisyphus* and on his *Sphinx* in our Appendix; cf. Seaford (1984) 41. In tragedy the most accomplished – but doomed – riddle-solver is Oedipus.

[54] The metre of the spoken dialogue ensuing in 298–324 is iambic tetrameter, rare outside lyric verse; another example is Ion, *Omphale* F 20 (a single line), cf. possibly also Aesch. *Net-Fishers* F 46a.18–21 and n. 4. Voelke (2001) 164–5 suggests that this metre was related to the near-incantatory style of question-and-answer exchange such as we have here.

[55] Cf. the *Hymn* 38, Hermes addressing the still-living tortoise, 'if you die, then you'll sing very well!'; cf. 328 below.

<KY.>   οὐδ' αὖ τοιοῦτ[ό]ν ἐστιν· ἀλλ' ἄλλον τιν' ἐξευροῦ τρόπον.
<XO.>   ἀλλ' ὡς κεράστ[η]ς κάνθαρος δῆτ' ἐστὶν Αἰτναῖος φυήν;
<KY.>   νῦν ἐγγὺς ἔγν[ως] ᾧ μάλιστα προσφερὲς τὸ κνώδαλον.
<XO.>   τ[ί δ' αὖ τὸ] φων[οῦ]ν ἐστιν αὐτοῦ, τοὐντὸς ἢ τοὔξω,
       φράσον.
<KY.>   *9 let.*]λο[.. φ]ορίνη σύγγονος τῶν ὀστρέων.   (310)
<XO.>   *about 16 let.*]νε[...]. πόρσυνον, εἴ τι πλέον ἔχεις.
<KY.>   *about 21 let.*]υν δ' αὖ λύραν ὁ παῖς καλεῖ.

ends of 12 lines (313–24), *3 ending the dialogue and including the words*
       313 κτέανον, 314 δέρμα, 315 ὧδ[ε] κλαγγάνει;
then the first lines of a speech by Cyllene,
       316 ξενήλατ' ἄξύλ' ἀρτίγομφα διατ]όρως ἐρείδεται,
and from the end of
       317]πλεκτας[;
then 7 further very scrappy line-ends (318–24) including
       318 κόλ]λοπες, 320 καθ]αμμάτω[ν;
then Cyllene's speech continues:

col.xiii

    καὶ τοῦτο λύπη[ς] ἔστ' ἄκεστρον καὶ παραψυκ[τ]ήρ[ιο]ν
                                  (325)
    κείνῳ μόνον, χα[ί]ρει δ' ἀθύρων καί τι προσφων[ῶν μέλος·
    ξύμφωνον ἐξα[ί]ρει γὰρ αὐτὸν αἰόλισμα τῆς λ[ύ]ρας.
    οὕτως ὁ παῖς θανόντι θηρὶ φθέγγμ' ἐμηχανήσατ[ο.

310 φ]ορ{ε}ίνη Marx ({ε} Page); τῶν ὀστρέων Wilamowitz: τῶν ὀστράκων Hunt: τωστρακρεων P. Oxy.; (συγγονους) ωστρα[marg. Theon
311 in πλέον the letters –λεο- are insecurely read
316 Walker, restored from Pollux 10.34 (who names the play) ἐνήλατα ξύλα τρίγομφα διατόρως ἐρείδεται (διάτορος ερειται δε mss. of Pollux, corr. Bethe)
320 καθ]αμμάτω[ν Schenkl
326 ἀθύρων Bucherer: αλυιων P. Oxy.: ἀλύων Hunt; μέλος Wilamowitz
327 half-stop after ξύμφωνον P. Oxy.: del. Maas

\<CHO.\>	Is it to be imagined like a cat or like a panther?[56]
\<CYL.\>	Very different from both: it is round and short-legged.
\<CHO.\>	And not like a weasel, nor like a crab? (305)
\<CYL.\>	No, not like that either. Find some other sort!
\<CHO.\>	Then it must be like the Etna horned beetle in nature?[57]
\<CYL.\>	Now you nearly know what the creature is most like.
\<CHO.\>	(Well, what part) of it has the voice, the inside or the outside? Tell us!
\<CYL.\>	... the shell, akin to oysters. (310)
\<CHO.\>	... provide (us) ..., if you have anything further.
\<CYL.\>	... and the boy, moreover, calls ... a lyre.

3 fragmentary lines conclude the dialogue, including the words
313 (a/the) possession, 314 skin, 315 resounds like this;
then come the first lines of a speech by Cyllene,
316 Firmly fixed pegs, not made of wood, are bored and pierced through[58]
and 317 ... woven ...;
then 7 further very fragmentary line-ends, including
319 pegs *and* 320 knots,
before she continues:

And this is his only remedy and consolation when upset. (325) He enjoys playing[59] with it and singing (a melody?) to it; for the lyre's shifting tone in harmony with him transports him. This is how the boy devised a voice for a dead creature.

[56]   In the Greek the infinitive εἰκάσαι is explanatory ('to imagine, to compare (with)') and its active voice idiomatic, as at *e.g.* Eur. *Bacchae* 1078; Smyth § 2012.d.

[57]   The 'Etna horned beetle' occurs also in satyr-drama at Aesch. *Sisyphus* F 233 (perhaps also as part of a riddling identification: see n. 53 above) and Soph. *Daedalus* F 162, signifying an unfamiliar, frightening creature – or a large one, *e.g.* in comedy at Ar. *Peace* 73. For 'Etna' as metaphor for abnormal size cf. Achaeus 20 F 42 (probably satyric), where huge 'Etna' snails cause amazement, and see n. on *Cyc.* 395.

[58]   Walker's text, justified and explained by Diggle (1996) 11–12. The pegs 'not of wood' were made from reed, supporting cross-pieces to which to attach the strings, as at *Hymn* 47–8; cf. Soph. F 36 'the reed of the lyre'. See West (1992) 61–2.

[59]   'playing with it' Bucherer; 'its excitement' Hunt (adjusting P. Oxy.), defended by some editors. Hermes' delight in his own music is prominent in the *Homeric Hymn*, esp. 420–6, 455. Sophocles goes further, alluding to the psychological effects of music with 'remedy and consolation' (325), much as Gorgias describes odes and incantations as banishing grief (*Helen* 10, 82 B 11 DK); and with 'enjoys' (325) and 'transports' (327) Sophocles presents music almost as a 'beguilement of the soul', ψυχαγωγία, applied to the powers of rhetoric by *e.g.* Plato, *Phaedrus* 261a8, and of visual art by Xenophon, *Memorabilia* 3.10.6.

XO.   <ὀμ>οψάλακτός τις ὀμφὰ κατοιχνεῖ τόπου,   στρ.
             πρεπτὰ <δ' ἤ>δη τόνου φάσματ' ἔγ- (330)
                 χωρ' ἐπανθεμίζει.
             τὸ πρᾶγμα δ' ᾧπερ πολεύω βάδην,
             ἴσθι τὸν δα[ί]μον', ὅστις ποθ' ὃς
                 ταῦτ' ἐτεχνάσατ' – οὐκ ἄλλος ἐστὶν κλ[οπεὺς
             ἀντ' ἐκείνου, γύναι, σάφ' ἴσθι.   (335)
             σὺ δ' ἀντὶ τῶνδε μὴ χαλε-
                 φθῇς ἐμοὶ <μη>δὲ δυσφορήσῃς.

<KY.>   9 let.]νησε· τίνα κλοπὴν ὠνείδισ[ας;
<XO.>   9–10 let. πρέσ]βειρα, χειμάζειν [
<KY.>   15–16 let.   ]ντα φιλήτην κ.[(340)
<XO.>   16–17 let.   ]αν αὐτῇ τῇ κλο[πῇ.
<KY.>   17–18 let.   ε]ἴ γε τἀληθῆ λέ[γεις.
<XO.>   17–18 let.   τ]ἀληθῆ λέγ[ω.

5 *very fragmentary line-ends* (344–8), *including the words*

                 345 βοῦς πάνυ, 346 καθήρ[μ]ο[σεν, 347 τεμών,

followed by 3 now missing lines (349–51), *then* (col. xiv) *further line-ends:*

             10–11 let.] ἄρτι μανθάνω χρόνῳ   (352)
             9–10 let. ἐγχ]ασκοντα τῇ 'μῇ μωρίᾳ
             9–10 let. ο]ὐδέν, ἀλλὰ παιδιᾶς χάριν.
             11–12 let.]ν εἰς ἔμ' εὐδίαν ἔχων   (355)
             11–12 let.]μ' ἤ τι κερδαίνειν δοκεῖς
             11–12 let.]χαζε καὶ τέρπου φρένα·
             10–11 let. ὄ]ντα τοῦ Διὸς σαφεῖ λόγῳ
             10–11 let.]ων ἐν νέῳ νέον λόγον·
             7 let. οὔτε] πρὸς πατρὸς κλέπτης ἔφυ   (360)

329 <ὀμ>οψάλακτος von Blumenthal; ὀμφὰ Diggle: ομφη P. Oxy.
330 <δ' ἤ>δη Diggle
332 ᾧπερ πολεύω Diggle: οὗπερ (*i.e.* ὅπερ) πορευω P. Oxy.
337 δυσφορήσῃς Diggle: δυσφορηθῇς P. Oxy.
339 πρέσ]βειρα Wilamowitz
358 ὄ]ντα Wilamowitz, Murray
360 οὔτε] πρὸς and 361 beg οὔτ(ε) space μ]ήτρωσιν Wilamowitz

The Chorus dance and sing (strophe).

CHO.   A fine voice (which accompanies) the plucking spreads over the place, (and) brilliant images of tone (330) (already) bloom[60] upon the land. But as to the business on which I'm pacing around,[61] you are to know that whoever the god is who devised these tones – none other than he is (the thief), lady;[62] know this for certain! (335) Do not be angry with me in response, and do (not) take it badly!

Stichomythic dialogue begins; only line-ends survive at first.

<CYL.>   ... What theft are you blaming him for?

<CHO.>   ... to cause (you?) distress, my lady.

<CYL.>   ... a swindler ... (340)

<CHO.>   ... theft and all.

<CYL.>   ... if you are speaking the truth.

<CHO.>   ... I speak the truth!

5 very fragmentary line-ends, including the words

          345 cows *and* absolutely, 346 fitted *(verb)*, 348 after cutting,

followed by 3 now missing lines. At some point in them Cyllene *has begun a long speech.*

<CYL.>   .... now at last I understand ... that you (are scoffing at) my stupidity ... nothing, but for fun. ... be at ease as far as I'm concerned (355) ... or if you think to profit at all ... and delight your heart. ... (who) by definite report (is) Zeus' son ... youthful talk in one newly born. ... (neither?) was he born a thief on his father's side (360)

[60] 'bloom': the metaphor for music we know in 'anthem'. In 329 'over the place' is a Greek genitive of extent, Epic in character, *e.g. Iliad* 2.785; Smyth § 1448.
[61] 'But as to ... around': an accusative of respect in the Greek; see Smyth § 1601c.
[62] In the Greek the pleonastic comparison 'no other instead of' is idiomatic, *e.g. Ajax* 444. *Trac.*1255–6.

10–11 let. μ]ήτρωσιν ἡ κλοπὴ κρατεῖ.
9–10 let.]ις ἐστι, τὸν κλέπτην σκόπει
7 let.]αρπον †τουδετουπαναι† δόμος
...]ει γένος, πρόσαπτε τὴν πονηρίαν
πρὸ]ς ὄντιν' ἥκει· τῷδε δ' οὐχ οὕτω πρέπει.   (365)
ἀ[λλ'] αἰὲν εἶ σὺ παῖς· νέος γὰρ ὢν ἀνὴρ
π[ώγ]ωνι θάλλων ὡς τράγος κνηκῷ χλιδᾷς.
παύου τὸ λεῖον φαλακρὸν ἡδονῇ πιτνάς·
ο]ὐκ ἐκ θεῶν τὰ μῶρα καὶ γέλοια χρὴ
χ]ανόντα κλαίειν ὕστερ', ὡς ἐγὼ γελῶ.   (370)

365 πρὸ]ς Wilamowitz
366 εισι P. Oxy.
367 κνηκῷ Wilamowitz: κα.κωι P. Oxy.: κνήκῳ Hunt, who read κνικωι in P. Oxy.
369 εἰς θεοὺς Wilamowitz; λοια χρη rewritten in P. Oxy.
370 υστερωιτεγωγελω in the line, υστερωσεγω marg. P. Oxy· ὕστερ'; ὡς ἐγὼ λέγω preferred
by Hunt

(nor?) does thieving prevail ... (among?) his mother's people. ... is ... look for the thief, ... (*nothing intelligible*) house ... (his) birth-line, attach the crime (to) whomever it comes home; but it's improper to attach it like this to *him*! (365) You've always been a child, however: now you're new to manhood you're rampant like a goat with a flourishing yellow beard![63] Stop making that smooth knob longer in pleasure![64] It's wrong to blurt out stupid and ridiculous things, and to suffer for them later at the gods' hands, to make me laugh.[65] (370)

[63] 'goat ... beard': cf. Aesch. *Prometheus the Fire-Kindler* F 207 and n. 'Yellow' is a conjecture (P. Oxy. is insecurely read), but the sexual reference is unmistakable and prepares for 368 (see next n.). Hunt had read the word as 'thistle', as 'you're rampant with a flourishing beard like a goat (*feeding rampantly*) on thistles'.

[64] 'making ... longer': by masturbating (cf. *Cyc.* 327–8), with a play on the two senses of φαλακρόν as 'bald head' (*e.g. Cyc.* 227) and 'end of an erect *phallos*'; here the latter sense is even more blatant than at Aesch. *Net-Fishers* F 47a.24 (see n. 12 there): so Voelke (2001) 213, with reference to Ar. *Clouds* 537–42, cf. M. Griffith, *ClassAnt* 21 (2002), 224 n. 103, W. Slenders in Harrison (2005) 43, 45–6. The sense of the Greek verb translated as 'making longer' is unparalleled, but may be a colloquial usage otherwise unattested; all recent editors offer a similar translation. The same action is caught in a single verb in Sophocles' satyric *Momus* F 423 'pull back your foreskin' (a lexicographic fragment without context), and again in unmistakable play upon the two senses of φαλακρόν at Herodas, *Mimiamb* 6.76 '(a woman) stroking his ...'. See also n. 65.

There are vase-paintings of satyrs masturbating: see Dover on Ar. *Clouds* 675, referring especially to *LIMC* VIII.1.1121 'Silenoi' no. 116; Seaford (1984) 135 on vv. 170–1; F. Lissarague, 'The Sexual Life of Satyrs', in D. J. Halperin, *et al.* (eds) *Before Sexuality* (Princeton, 1990) 53–81 at *e.g.* 57, with Figs 2.4 and 6; and OKell (2003) 293–6. For the stage-action cf. Aesch. *Net-Fishers* F 47a.23–4, 61, 66 and nn. 12, 19 and 20.

[65] If the papyrus' text of 369–70 is correct (its translation is also insecure), Cyllene seems to dismiss both foolish words (353–7) and offensive behaviour (366–8) as improper attempts to amuse her. Editors are in strong doubt and many emend, esp. the end of 370, *e.g.* '... later: this is what I say' (Hunt's preferred text); for a recent discussion see W. Luppe in S. Gödde, Th. Heinze (eds), *Skenika ... Festschrift .... H.-D. Blume* (Darmstadt, 2000) 87–9. A passage in Ar. *Clouds*, 537–42, links crude physical humour involving red-tipped stage *phalloi* 'to create laughter for lads' (539) with 'dirty jokes' (542), so that our 370 'to make me laugh' may well be correct, a kind of metatheatrical allusion. For the comic incongruity, in which the satyrs' deference towards Cyllene quickly lapses into typical satyric crudity, cf. *Cyc.* 175–87, where Odysseus' boasts about sacking Troy are followed by the satyrs' asking him about Helen's supposed nymphomania.

<XO.>   στρέφου λυγίζου τε μύθοις, ὁποίαν θέλεις   ἀντ.
         βάξιν εὕρισκ᾽ ἀπόψηκτον· οὐ
           γάρ με ταῦτα πείσεις,
         <ὅ>πως τὸ χρῆμ᾽ οὗτος εἰργασμένος
         ῥινοκόλλητον ἄλλων ἔκαρ-   (375)
           ψεν βοῶν που δοράς [ἢ] ἀπὸ τῶν Λοξίου.
         μ]ή με τᾶ[σδ᾽ ἐ]ξ ὁδοῦ βίβαζε·

the two final lines of this antistrophe are lost from the top of col. xv

---

col. xv

The first 2(–3?) lines are missing, including the last 2 of the antistrophe (not numbered by eds) and the first (378), apparently spoken by Cyllene, *of a resumed, mostly stichomythic exchange between her and* Chorus; *then come very damaged and partly dislocated line-beginnings (379–96), with some words legible:*

     379 <XO.?> γυνη[, <KYΛ.?> 380 μανιων.[, 381 ὦ παμπονη[ρ, 382 .]..αι τάχ᾽ ὀργα[, <XO.> 383 τ]ἀληθὲς and 390/385 ὁ] παῖς κλοπ[, <KYΛ.> 391/386 τ[ά] τοι πονη[ρ, <XO.> 392/387 κακῶς ἀκου[, <KYΛ.> 393/388 εἰ δ᾽ ἔστ᾽ ἀλη[θ;

then, after traces of 394/389 *and* 395–6:

<KY.>   πο[λ]λαὶ βόες νέμουσι τ[(397)
<XO.>   π[λ]είους δέ γ᾽ ἤδη νῦν [
<KY.>   τ[ί]ς, ὦ πόνηρ᾽, ἔχει; τί πλε[
<XO.>   ὁ παῖς ὃς ἔνδον ἐστὶν ἐγκεκλῃ[μένος.   (400)
<KY.>   [τὸ]ν παῖδα παῦσαι τοῦ Διὸς [
<XO.>   π[α]ύοιμ[᾽ ἄ]ν[, εἰ] τὰς βοῦς τις ε[
<KY.>   ἤδη με πνίγεις καὶ σὺ χα[ὶ βόες σέθεν.
<XO.>   ...]λεισε..[...]υ[. ἐ]ξελαυν[(404)

374 <ὅ>πως Wilamowitz, Murray; χρημα ουτος Theon: χρηματουτες P. Oxy.
375 ἔκαρ | ψεν read in P. Oxy. by Carden, ἔκλε | ψεν by Hunt
376 [ἢ] Wilamowitz
390/385–394/389: Diggle restored the separated tiny fragments of 390–4 to the beginnings of 385–9
397 πο[λ]λαὶ Siegmann: πάλαι Carden, reading πα]λαι in P. Oxy.
400 ὃς Wilamowitz, Murray: τοδ᾽ P. Oxy.: οδ (*i.e.* ὅδ᾽) its second hand
401 end *e.g.* [κακῶς λέγων Hunt

<CHO.>   (*singing; their antistrophe responds with 329–37*) Bend and twist in your speech,[66] invent whatever polished talk you want: you'll not persuade me that the maker here of the thing with hide-glue[67] dried (375) skins from any cows except those of Loxias![68] Don't try to move me off this road!

The two final lines of the antistrophe are lost.

Then come 17 line-beginnings (378–96) from a fresh exchange between Cyllene *and* Chorus, *including*

> 379 <CHO.> lady (*not vocative*), <CYL.?> 380 madness(?), 381 You utter scoundrel!, 382 quickly ... angry (?), <CHO.> 383 the truth *and* 390/385 the boy ... theft *or* thief, <CYL.> 391/386 the villainy (, I tell you?), <CHO.> 392/387 evil repute, <CYL.> 393/388 if it is true;

then, after traces of 394/389 and 395–6, come fuller line-beginnings:

<CYL.>   Many (?) cows are grazing ...[69]
<CHO.>   Yes, but more already now ...
<CYL.>   Who has them, you scoundrel? What ...?
<CHO.>   The boy who is shut up inside. (400)
<CYL.>   Stop (abusing?) the son of Zeus!
<CHO.>   I'd stop, if someone ... the cows!
<CYL.>   You and your cows are choking me already!
<CHO.>   ... bring (them) out ...

[66] 'bend and twist in your speech': terminology from wrestling illustrates manipulation of language; Pindar, *Nemeans* 4.93–6 applies the metaphor to poetic craft; Protagoras (80 B 1 DK) and Thasymachus (85 B 7 DK) wrote handbooks on combative rhetorical techniques with titles borrowed from wrestling. The satyrs' challenge in such terms to Cyllene implies a near-sophistic argument between them: see esp. 342–3, 352–7, 364–5.

[67] 'hide-glue': hide, horn and hooves (and other parts) of cattle have been primary ingredients of carpenter's glue until modern times. 'dried': read in P. Oxy. by Carden (1971) 44–5, who adduced *Homeric Hymn* 124 '(Hermes) stretched hides' (on a rugged rock), *i.e.* to prepare them for making the lyre; 'stolen' read by Hunt.

[68] 'Loxias': Apollo, invoked at 448 under this name. While its etymology as 'The Oblique, Slanting One' seems certain (Apollo as the giver of such oracles), it is often used indiscriminately, in any context, as here.

[69] 'Cows have long been grazing ...' Carden.

col. xvi *entirely and the first three lines of* col. xvii (= 405–34) *are lost.* 435–58 *are the extremely damaged beginnings of 24 lines.* 435–450 *appear to be lyrics from the Chorus, with alternate marked voice-parts surviving at* 436, 443 *and* 446; *they include the line-beginnings* 436 ἄγ' εἶα νυ[ν, 437 μυχῷ σκ[, 438 παν'.[*(probably* Πᾶν'.[*)*, 443 ἰοὺ ἰοὺ[, 448 ὦ Λοξία, δε[, 450 τῶν [β]οῶ[ν.

A voice-part ΑΠΟΛΛΩΝ *is marked at* 451; *his words include*

456 μισθο.[*and* 457 ἐλευθερο[.

In the left margin of 452, *which begins* βο[, *is written* π]ελεθοις βοων *attributed to Theon, but eds believe this note to relate to the text of the lost col. xvi.*

Below 458 *the single letter* σ *is insecurely read in the margin, supplemented as* Σ[ΙΛΗΝΟΣ by Siegmann.

F 314a fr.26

]βραβευμ[

P. Oxy. 1174 (see on F 314) fr. 26

F 316

ῥικνοῦσθαι

Photius Galeanus I.489.1 Porson (= Suda ρ 166 Adler)

F *318

βοόκλεψ

Athenaeus 9.404b, attrib. 'Hermes in Sophocles'

Column xvi is wholly lost from the papyrus, as are the first 3 lines of column xvii (numbered as 405–34)*, but against* 452 *of this column the words* cow dung *are written in the margin and may be a variant reading which relates to the lost column. Then follow the beginnings of 24 lines, the last of the papyrus* (435–58)*, in which* (436–50) *the Chorus urge themselves on, perhaps to enter the cave*

(436–7 'Come on then now ... in the interior ...', 443 'Hurrah, hurrah ...!').

The name of Pan *may occur in* 438; *then the satyrs invoke* Loxias (*Apollo,* 448)*, who appears at once* (451)*, pat on the mention of* the cows (450); *his opening lines include the incomplete words* 456 reward *and* 457 free.[70] *It is possible that Silenus, who had run away at* 209*, also returns suddenly, at the beginning of the first missing line.*[71]

[70]   Cf. Apollo's promise to Silenus, at 63–5.
[71]   A marginal *sigma* is unconfidently read in the papyrus here; it has been taken as the first letter of a voice-part for Silenus.

There are three one-word fragments:

F 314a fr.26 (P. Oxy. 1174 fr. 26)
            adjudication

On the possible significance of this word, see the introductory discussion.

F 316 (Photius Galeanus I.489.1 Porson)
            to be bent over *or* to perform an unseemly dance

Meanings given or suggested in antiquity.

F *318 (Athenaeus 9.404b)
            cow-thief

i.e. Hermes. For both F 316 and F 318 see the introductory discussion n. 2.

Oeneus (ΟΙΝΕΥΣ)

TrGF 4².636–8 (F **1130), 774; cf. 3.589.

Texts etc. Page (1942) 166–71; Carden (1974) 135–46; Lloyd-Jones (1996) 418–21; Diggle (1998) 77–8; R. Krumeich and N. Pechstein in KPS 368–74.

Discussions. P. Maas, *Kleine Schriften* (München, 1973) 50–3 (first publ. 1912); R. Pfeiffer, *WS* 79 (1966), 65–6; Sutton (1980) 57–8; Gantz (1993) 432–3; Conrad (1997) 154–9, 284–6; Voelke (2001) 261–3.

Art. LIMC VIII.1.915–16 'Oineus I' nos 1–12 (early 6th to 4th century depictions of Oeneus and Deianeira, and the fight between Achelous and Heracles, none with secure relevance to Sophocles, whether to *Women of Trachis* or to *Oeneus*); no. 10 = IV.1.835 'Herakles' no. 1682 = Trendall-Webster III.2.11. See also n. 1 on our introductory discussion to Ion's *Omphale*.

The sole certain remnant of this play is P. Oxy. 1083 fr. 1, published in 1911 (F 1130). P. Oxy. 2453, published in 1962, proved to be written by the same hand as 1083, and confirmed Maas's suspicion (of 1912) that 1083 was from an anthology of play-texts. The total of some sixty or so fragments comprised by the two papyri includes more than one play-title; these not only convinced Maas that Sophocles was the author, but the lexical register of some words, and fragmentary voice-parts 'Ch(orus of s)aty(rs)' opposite v. 6 and of ']oeneus' opposite v. 19, pointed to Hunt's ascription of 1083 fr. 1 to a satyric *Oeneus* as correct; and it is now almost everywhere accepted: Carden (1974) 136–7; Radt in *TrGF* 4².637; Lloyd-Jones (1996) 418–19; Conrad (1997) 154; KPS 368–9; cf. Diggle (1998) 77 'perhaps'.[1] Of the other fragments of 1083, the attribution to *Oeneus* also of fr. 2 (= F **1131, 9 damaged line-centres) and fr. 3 (= F **1132, a mere scrap), is no more than a possibility, advanced on the ground of physical similarity with fr. 1. F *321, F 717 and F 732, three lexicographic scraps of uncertain attribution, have also been suggested for the play.

The plot was Oeneus' dilemma: who should marry his daughter Deianeira? He resolved it by proposing a wrestling-match between her initial and persistent suitor the river-god Achelous and a subsequent rival the hero and demi-god Heracles; and the latter was victorious. This is told succinctly by the Scholia on Homer, *Iliad* 21.194 (= Pindar, *Dithyramb* II, fr. 249a):

> After Heracles had gone down to Hades to get Cerberus, he met Meleager the son of Oeneus; when Meleager entreated him to marry his sister Deianeira,

on his return to the daylight he hastened to Aetolia, to Oeneus. Coming upon Achelous, the neighbourhood river, wooing *(text insecure)* Deianeira, Heracles wrestled Achelous, who was in the form of a bull. After actually wrenching off one of his horns, he took the maiden.

(Cf. Bacchylides 5.165–75 and Sophocles, *Women of Trachis* 1–27, 497–530; Gantz (1993) 432–3; D. A. Secci, 'Ovid, *Met.* 9.1–97: Through the Eyes of Achelous', *G&R* 56 (2009) 34–54).

Sophocles turned this mythical contest between appropriately divine and semi-divine opponents into opportune fun with satyrs. He perhaps presented the wooing of Deianeira as 'open to all-comers', and the satyrs' aspiration to her hand (F 1130.6, 17–18) as ludicrous, like their ambitions to have Danae in Aeschylus' *Net-Fishers* and Achilles in Sophocles' *Lovers of Achilles* (see introductory discussions there; compare too the public announcements which begin *Net-Fishers* and *Trackers*, and to which the satyrs respond, enthusiastically but disruptively). The satyrs may have come then on their own initiative (as they do their own thing with athletic competition when sent by Dionysus to the Isthmian Games in Aeschylus' *Sacred Delegates*), arriving probably long after Achelous has made his suit known to Oeneus but before Heracles appears (F 1130.19–20?): that would match the sequence in the Homeric Scholia (where Meleager, dead in Hades, might well 'know' about the future of Achelous).

No doubt the collapse of the satyrs' suit once Heracles came was an amusing episode, especially if they 'challenged' him, buffoons confronting the greatest of heroes;[2] in satyric drama his abnormal status and strength are usually exerted for good ends but often create chaos, *e.g.* in Euripides' *Eurystheus* and *Syleus* and the Omphale-plays of Ion and Achaeus (all in this volume below). After the satyrs' failure, there seems little for them to have done except to report Heracles' victory over Achelous (KPS 373–4) and to dance in celebration, unless they offered Heracles aid for which they received some kind of reward (as usual), perhaps in mutual reconciliation. Elsewhere Heracles could bury the hatchet with other comic adversaries such as the Cercopes, notorious tricksters who were eventually released by him after they had attempted to steal his weapons ([Apollod.] 2.6.3; Zenobius 5.10; Pausanias Atticista μ 17 Erbse) just as the satyrs themselves did (see KPS pls 20a–b, 30a). Heracles and Oeneus must have dominated the end of the play (Conrad (1997) 159).

In F 1130 the satyrs present their credentials to Oeneus with racy insouciance; their boasting contrasts interestingly with the abuse for their cowardice which Silenus throws at them in *Trackers* F 314.145–68. Moreover, vv. 8–18 are generally interpreted as Sophocles' satire upon the pretensions of contemporary Sophists to be 'jacks of all trades', both practical and intellectual: see Carden (1974) 145–6 and n. 8 below, C. W. Marshall in Harrison (2005) 103–17 and cf. P. O'Sullivan *ibid.* 119–59, at 121–9. The apparently overt criticism of real-life contemporaries is more typical of Comedy, but occasional in satyric: see *e.g.* Pratinas 4 F 3 above, and on Lycophron, *Menedemus* F 2–3; for various reflections of 'civic reality' see M. Griffith in Harrison (2005) 161–99, at 161–5 and 172–9. So Oeneus is invited to choose any 'technique' he deems appropriate in a worthy suitor (vv. 17–18: Conrad (1997) 156–7; see n. 8 below).

F **1130

<ΧΟΡΟΣ?>   ... κυρεῖν δρῶντα δηλοῦν τί; χρη[
       ἐργάτην τοιοῦδ᾽ ἀγῶνος αἰχμαλ[ωτ
<ΟΙΝΕΥΣ>   ἀλλ᾽ ἐξεροῦμεν. ἀλλὰ πρῶτα βούλομ[αι
       γνῶναι τίνες π[ά]ρεστε καὶ γένους ὅ[του
       βλαστόντες· οὐ γ[ὰρ] νῦν γέ πω μαθ[ὼν ἔχω. (5)
ΧΟ.   ἅπαντα πεύσῃ· νύμφιοι μὲν ἥ[κομε]ν,
       παῖδες δὲ νυμφῶν, Βακχίου δ᾽ ὑπηρέται,
       θεῶν δ᾽ ὅμαυλοι· πᾶσα δ᾽ ἥρμοσται τέχνη
       πρέπουσ᾽ ἐν ἡμῖν· ἔστι μὲν τὰ πρὸς μάχην
       δορός, πάλης ἀγῶνες, ἱππικῆς, δρόμου, (10)

P. Oxy. 1083 ed. A. S. Hunt (1911) fr. 1
1 τί followed by a mark breaking sense or metre read in P. Oxy by Carden: τί; Radt; χρὴ [Hunt
3 ΟΙΝΕΥΣ: see on 19
6 χορ[*3 let.*]ατυ[P. Oxy., *i.e.* ΧΟΡ[ΟΣ Σ]ΑΤΥ[ΡΩΝ

Notes

[1] The voice-part against v. 19 begins immediately after a hole in the papyrus. Maas had once suggested reading it as originally '[Sch]oeneus', because this man too, like Oeneus, had held a competition for his daughter's hand; but she was the splendid runner Atalanta, and the contest stipulated for aspirants was with herself, not between them. See Carden (1997) 136–7.

[2] The unassigned Soph. F 756 has a satyr wishing 'If only I might jump on the middle of (Heracles') neck when he's inflamed', and was suggested by W. Dindorf for the play – an attribution more likely if 'neck' is a euphemism for 'penis', as it may well be at *Cyc.* 184 and Ar. *Lysistrata* 681. To replace '(when he's) inflamed' the conjecture 'lying back' has been made, because the fragment's source is discussing variant terms for 'reclining'; but the resulting sense is as tame as it is unlikely.

F **1130 (P. Oxy. 1083 fr. 1)

\<CHORUS?\>	... to make clear that ... was doing ... to achieve (?) what? (*or* was actually doing what?) ... ought (?) ... agent of such a contest captive ...[3]
\<OENEUS\>	Well, I'll tell you! But first I want to know who you are here, and from what race you are sprung; for now (I've) not yet learned this. (5)
CHO.	You shall find out everything! We (come) as bridegrooms[4] and we're the sons of nymphs, and servants of Bacchus, and lie down with gods.[5] Every suitable technique has been accommodated among us with distinction: there's what makes for fighting with spears, wrestling-contests, horsemanship, running, (10) boxing, biting, (*and there's*) twisting testicles;[6] we've got musical songs

[3] The interpretation and punctuation of vv. 1–2 are wholly uncertain.

[4] 'bridegrooms': that is, they hope to become so; this word (Greek *numphioi*), rather than 'suitors', is used for a play upon 'sons of nymphs' in v. 7 (so Carden (1974) 135–6; cf. Apollo's description of them at Soph. *Trackers* F 314.41); nymphs are part of satyrs' association with Dionysus, *e.g.* Pratinas 4 F 3.2 and n. 3, *Trackers* F 314.228 *etc.*; Aesch. *Prometheus the Fire-Kindler* F 204b; Achaeus, *The Fates* F 28; *Adespota* F 646a n. 7; Seaford (1984) 115, 135. Nymphs even as satyrs' mothers, Hesiod F 10(a).18; see also Gen. Intro. p. 9 n. 32.

[5] 'servants of Bacchus' (lit. 'the Bacchic one'): cf. Eur. *Cyc.* 76, where the chorus collectively describes itself as the 'servant' (πρόπολος) of Dionysus; in the play's final line the chorus relish the prospect of becoming 'slaves' to 'the Bacchic one' (*Cyc.* 709). 'lie down with gods': ambiguous, both 'share their lodging' and 'sleep with them', carnally.

[6] 'twisting testicles': Ar. *Birds* 442, *Clouds* 713. This last item, like 'biting', is perhaps more appropriate for the *pankration*, a form of fighting that could include not only wrestling

πυγμῆς, ὀδόντων, ὄρχεων ἀποστροφαί,
ἔνεισι δ᾽ ᾠδαὶ μουσικῆς, ἔνεστι δὲ
μαντεῖα παντάγνωτα κοὐκ ἐψευσμένα,
ἰαμάτων τ᾽ ἔλεγχος, ἔστιν οὐρανοῦ
μέτρησις, ἔστ᾽ ὄρχησις, ἔστι τῶν κάτω　　　　(15)
λάλησις· ἆρ᾽ ἄκαρπος ἡ θεωρία;
ὧν σοι λαβεῖν ἔξεστι τοῦθ᾽ ὁποῖον ἂν
χρῄζῃς, ἐὰν τὴν παῖδα [π]ροστιθῇς ἐμοί.

OIN.　　　ἀλλ᾽ οὐχὶ μεμπτὸν τὸ γένος. ἀλλὰ βούλομαι
καὶ τόνδ᾽ ἀθρῆσαι πρῶτο[ν] ὅστις ἔρχεται.　　　(20)

13 παντάγνωτα Maas: πάντα γνωτὰ Hunt
19 ΟΙΝΕΥΣ Hunt, eds:]οινευς P. Oxy., with possible trace of a preceding letter: ΣΧ]ΟΙΝΕΥΣ
Maas (see introductory discussion, n. 1)

among us, and we've got completely unknown and unfalsified oracles too,[7] and (a) test (for) cures; there's measuring the sky, there's dancing, there's chatter from our nether regions:[8] (15) is our study unprofitable?[9] You can take whatever of these you desire, if you award your daughter to me!

OEN.   Well, your lineage is not to be faulted! But first I wish to have a look also at this man who is coming. (20)[10]

and boxing, but kicking, strangling and bone-breaking (even though biting was technically illegal). So 'wrestling' perhaps suggests that for 'real' fighting 'with spears' (v. 9) they are wholly useless. Similar denigration of athletes at Eur. *Autolycus A* F 282.16–23 (see n.).

[7] 'completely unknown (oracles)': so Maas, but text and meaning are in doubt (possibly an implied boast in itself, 'indecipherable to all except satyrs'): 'all known', Hunt and Carden (1974) 144. The satyrs here claim expertise in Apollo's provinces, prophecy and music; they denounce Polyphemus' ignorant unmusicality at Eur. *Cyc.* 488–93; it may be satyrs who object to the intrusive music of the pipe at Pratinas 4 F 3.4–14.

[8] *i.e.* farting (so Maas, cf. A. López Eire in Sommerstein (2003) 404, who compares Ar. *Knights* 1381 'the chatter (*of a backside?*)'; see nn. 23 and 33 on *Trackers* F 314.128 and 168) – a surprise final item like the testicles of v. 11. Some editors however take the meaning to be 'chatter about things under the earth', as a complement of 'measuring the sky' in the 'study' of vv. 15–16, just as it is paired with astronomy in the activities of 'Socrates' in Ar. *Clouds* 184–94 and in the prosecution of the historical Socrates at Plato, *Apology* 18b7; in that case these lines are a swipe at contemporary 'science'. Both nuances may coexist, when the satyrs will be lampooning their own self-importance. The satyrs' admitted predilection for chatter (λάλησις) undercuts their claims on another level: Aristophanes denounces Socrates for this very quality (*Frogs* 1491), and has Euripides make the vain boast that his dramas had taught his audience to 'chatter' (*Frogs* 954); Eupolis in his *Demes* (F 116 *PCG*) pillories Alcibiades for being 'best at chatter (λαλεῖν), most inept at speaking (λέγειν)' and Demosthenes similarly contrasts chatter and speaking (21.118); elsewhere satyrs admit to liking a good chat (Eur. *Cyc.* 175). Satyric claims to versatile skills could also be a parody of mythic 'culture heroes' such as Prometheus (cf. *Prometheus Bound* 454–506) or Palamedes (Gorgias 82 B 11a *Palamedes* DK), but a more obvious contemporary target would be Hippias, whose alleged claims to versatility receive typically tongue-in-cheek treatment from Plato at *Hippias Minor* 368b–e; Plato, *Protagoras* 318e presents that most famous of all sophists as indifferent, if not hostile, to such versatility. For such contemporary references in satyric see the end of our introductory discussion to Python's *Agen*.

[9] The term 'study' (or 'contemplation', Carden (1974) 146) too is disputed, since its commoner meaning is 'sacred delegation' – on which the satyrs might well pompously claim to have come (cf. above on Aeschylus' *Sacred Delegates*). The use of *theoria* – a word associated with fifth century intellectuals such as Anaxagoras (59 A 1.7, 10; 29 DK) – here seems to sum up the grandiose opinion the satyrs have of their own achievements.

[10] Presumably Heracles: see introductory discussion.

EURIPIDES

(active 455–406 BC)

Autolycus A and B (ΑΥΤΟΛΥΚΟΣ Α, Β)

TrGF 5.342–7 (T iiia–*vb, F 282–4).

Texts etc. Diggle (1998) 96–7 (F 282 only); Pechstein (1998) 39–122, 287–343; H. Van Looy in Budé VIII.1 (1998) 329–40; N. Pechstein, R. Krumeich in KPS 403–12; Voelke (2001) 264–7 (F 282); I. Mangidis, *Euripides' Satyrspiel Autolykos* (Frankfurt am Main, 2003); Collard and Cropp (2008) I.278–87.

Discussions. Sutton (1980) 59–60; D. G. Kyle, *Athletics in Ancient Athens* (Leiden, 1987) 128–30; V. Masciadri, 'Autolykos und der Silen. Eine übersehene Szene des Euripides bei Tzetzes', *MH* 44 (1987) 1–7; R. Kannicht, 'De Euripidis *Autolyco* vel *Autolycis*', *Dioniso* 61.2 (1991) 91–9; F. d'Angiò, 'Euripide, *Autolico* Fr. 282 N²', *Dioniso* 62.2 (1992) 83–94; Gantz (1993) 109–10, 176; Z. P. Ambrose in Harrison (2005) 30–1; J. P. Harris, 'Xenophanes, Euripides, and Socrates', *AJP* 130 (2009) 157–94, esp. 163–6; D. M. Pritchard, 'Athletics in Greek Drama', *G&R* 59 (2012) 1–16, esp. 11–16.

Art. LIMC III.1.55–6 'Autolykos I' no. 2 = I.1.828–30 'Antikleia' no. 2 = VII.1.783 'Sisyphos' no. 3, cf. 'Sisyphos' nos 2a, b; Pechstein (1998) 93–113 and figs 2, 3; KPS (1999) 408–9 and fig. 25b; Mangidis (2003, above) pls 1–4.

Athenaeus 10.413c cites F 282 from 'the first *Autolycus*' (T iiia). The implication, that there was therefore a second play, was long doubted but confirmed by a papyrus scrap (P. Vindob. 19766.6–9 = P. Rainer 3.32; = T iiib): ... Euripides' play ... the first *Autolycus* ... Autolycus the son of Hermes ...; cf. Tzetzes, *Chiliades* 8.435 (from T iv below).

Autolycus was the thieving and deceitful son of Hermes who was the patron of all thieves (their skills were attributed to Hermes' teaching: Homer, *Odyssey* 19.395); his entire mythography is reviewed by Mangidis (2003) 71–107. The plot of Athenaeus' 'first' play (now *Autolycus A* in *TrGF*) has been conjectured on the basis of Hyginus, *Fables* 201 (= T *va):

Mercury (Hermes) gave his son Autolycus ... this gift: he was to be the greatest of thieves but never to be detected thieving, such that he had the power of changing whatever he stole into any guise he wished:[1] from white to black and from black to white, to horned from hornless, to hornless from horned. When Autolycus continually raided Sisyphus' cattle but could never be caught, Sisyphus realised that it was Autolycus who was thieving from him, because his number of cattle was increasing while his own was decreasing. To catch him, he put a mark into the hooves of his animals. When Autolycus raided in his usual way, Sisyphus went to him and detected his own animals by their hooves .... While Autolycus was delaying there (i.e. *in returning Sisyphus' cattle*), Sisyphus violated his daughter Anticleia, who was later given in marriage to Laertes and became Ulysses' (*Odysseus '*) mother.

A now lost 2nd century AD cup (T *vb) with all four of Autolycus, Sisyphus, Anticleia and Laertes named in a succession of scenes – but without satyrs – has been associated with this story, but contentiously: see *LIMC* III. 1 'Autolykos' no. 2 in 'Art' above. If the plot was in accord with Hyginus' narrative, its ending is hard to see, except in some kind of reconciliation.

After the confirmation of a second play (*Autolycus B* in *TrGF*), its differing plot was conjectured by Masciadri (1987) on the basis of Tzetzes, *Chiliades* 8.435–8, 442–53 (= T iv):

Autolycus the son of Hermes, father of Laertes and grandfather of Odysseus, being in extreme poverty, was granted by Hermes the art of thieving (437) ... to surpass every thief (442): for when stealing he would interchange some things and give back others in their place. Those who took them thought they were taking back their own property, not that they were being deceived by him and taking different things. (445) For instance, when stealing an excellent horse he gave back an ass,[2] one of the mangy ones, and made it seem that he had given back the horse; and when he kidnapped a nubile young girl, he gave in return either a silen or satyr, some decrepit little old man,[3] snub-nosed, toothless and bald, snot-ridden, one of the uglies (450) – and her father considered him his daughter. In a satyric drama *Autolycus* Euripides accurately records everything about this character.

Masciadri's hypothetical plot has as its essence Autolycus stealing a girl from her father (who is a traveller), and substituting Silenus (who may have been complicit with the deception) for her; perhaps he had already shown this skill by giving back an ass for the father's horse. Masciadri has been in the main supported by Kannicht (1991) and in *TrGF,* and by Pechstein

(1998) 51–3 *etc.* and (in) KPS 410–12, cf. Collard and Cropp (2008) I.279; Van Looy (1998) 332–5 is non-committal.

The long F 282 has become the focus of an associated problem. Its topic of athletics is much at home in satyric drama (see *e.g.* the introductory discussion on Aesch. *Sacred Delegates*; Voelke (2001) 264–72; n. 6 below, and Index of Motifs);[4] and its rhetorical style is well possible too in the genre (cf. esp. *Cyc.* 314–40 and notes, Sophocles, *Lovers of Achilles* F 149 and *Oeneus* F **1130.8–16, and perhaps Critias (?) 43 F 19;[5] the latter three passages are all in our selection). Yet d'Angiò (1992) in particular has argued that the matter and style suggest rather tragic provenance, and Pechstein has asked whether one of the two plays was therefore a 'light' tragedy substituted for a satyr-play, like Euripides' *Alcestis* (Pechstein (1998) 39–40, 114 and (in) KPS 403: see n. 3 on our Introductory Note). F 282 is still very hard to place in the supposed plot of either play, satyric or not; Harris (2009) 163 n. 23 regards it as from *Autolycus A*. Pechstein (1998) 82–5 and (in) KPS 411, endorsed by Z. P. Ambrose in Harrison (2005) 30–1, suggests that if it came from the 'Tzetzes' plot, *Autolycus B*, then Autolycus himself may be the speaker, demonstrating the clever rhetoric which helps him deceive his victims and arguing humorously from the example of useless belly-slaves, the satyrs themselves (see v. 5). Pritchard (2102) 2 rather assumes that the speaker is indeed Autolycus (Athenaeus contains no hint of identity), and makes no mention of two plays rather than one; but Pritchard discusses at useful length the likely impact upon the 'vast majority of theatre-goers', *i.e.* the majority of the *demos*, of this 'broadened ... traditional attack' upon athletes 'by associating them with pre-existing prejudices against the

---

F 282

κακῶν γὰρ ὄντων μυρίων καθ' Ἑλλάδα
οὐδὲν κάκιόν ἐστιν ἀθλητῶν γένους·
οἳ πρῶτον οἰκεῖν οὔτε μανθάνουσιν εὖ

Athenaeus 10.413c; 1–6 beg P. Oxy. 3699 (2nd c. AD), remnants of a possible 4th c. BC protreptic dialogue, fr. d col. ii; 1–9, 16–22 Galen, *Protreptic* 10; 12 Diogenes Laertius 1.56; 22 Plutarch, *Moralia* 581f and 803b
3 πρῶτον οἰκεῖν P. Oxy., Galen: πρῶτα μὲν ζῆν Athenaeus
3–4 οὔτε ... οὔτ' ἂν P. Oxy., Athen.: οὐδὲ ... ὅταν Galen

wealthy' (see esp. his pp. 13–15). Mangidis (2003, 110–18) however has revived an older idea that Athenaeus (and therefore P. Vindob.) reflected not two separate plays, but a record of two performances of one play, or its revival; and he reconstructs a single plot on the basis of both Hyginus and Tzetzes (65–70, 109–202, with a schematic reconstruction 206–8); he cites two further disputedly relevant painted vessels: see 'Art' above *LIMC* 'Sisyphos' nos. 2a, b (= Mangidis pls 3, 4). All these issues are likely to remain unresolved.

The three, tiny, other book fragments (all below) seem more appropriate to the Tzetzes story, *Autolycus B*: F 282a a mention of 'an ugly little man'; F 283 and F 284 mention of asses and horses.

Notes

[1]   The archetype for such switching of goods lies in Hermes' own actions in the *Homeric Hymn to Hermes* 516–17.

[2]   Cf. perhaps F 283 below.

[3]   Cf. F 282a below.

[4]   The place of this fragment in the long history of 'athletics' as a literary and dramatic motif is surveyed by Mangidis 41–63 and most recently by Pritchard (2012); earlier, cf. Pechstein (1998) 70–85. See also nn. 6, 8, 10, 11 below. Eupolis wrote a comedy entitled *Autolycus,* probably in 422 BC (F 48–75 *PCG*: see I. C. Storey, *Eupolis* (Oxford, 2003) 84–6), which parodied the victory of a pancratiast of that name, but its relation to our play in terms of date or influence (if any) is irrecoverable.

[5]   Indeed Pechstein (1998) 117, cf. 318, and (in) KPS 561, suggests that the Critias-fragment, whose authorship is disputed between Critias and Euripides and which is attributed in a part-source to Euripides' character (not, play) Sisyphus (see p. 441 below), may in fact stem from one or other of the *Autolycus*-plays; he favours *A*.

F 282 (Athenaeus 10.413c; 1–6 P. Oxy. 3699; 1–9, 16–22 Galen, *Protreptic* 10; other briefer citations)

> Now of the countless evils throughout Greece none is worse than athletes as a kind.[6] Firstly they neither learn well how to

[6]   An equally powerful condemnation of athletes, from the late 6th century, was much cited in antiquity, Xenophanes 21 B F 2.11–24 DK, some of it echoed in Euripides' criticisms here, chiefly the favouritism shown to athletes through civic meals (F 282.13–15), the false equation of physical prowess with true soldierly courage (16–23), and the consequential neglect of 'good' citizens who alone can prevent feuding (23–8); cf. also esp. Eur. *Electra* 386–90. Earlier still, Tyrtaeus F 12.1–20 *IEG* praised patriotic courage above all other qualities, including athletic prowess; later came *e.g.* Isocrates, *Panegyricus* 1–2. Cf. n. 4 above, and n. 11 below.

οὔτ' ἂν δύναιντο· πῶς γὰρ ὅστις ἔστ' ἀνὴρ
γνάθου τε δοῦλος νηδύος θ' ἡσσημένος   (5)
κτήσαιτ' ἂν ὄλβον εἰς ὑπερβολὴν πατρός;
οὐδ' αὖ πένεσθαι κἀξυπηρετεῖν τύχαις
οἷοί τ'· ἔθη γὰρ οὐκ ἐθισθέντες καλὰ
σκληρῶς μεταλλάσσουσιν εἰς τἀμήχανον.
λαμπροὶ δ' ἐν ἥβῃ καὶ πόλεως ἀγάλματα   (10)
φοιτῶσ'· ὅταν δὲ προσπέσῃ γῆρας πικρόν,
τρίβωνες ἐκβαλόντες οἴχονται κρόκας.
ἐμεμψάμην δὲ καὶ τὸν Ἑλλήνων νόμον,
οἳ τῶνδ' ἕκατι σύλλογον ποιούμενοι
τιμῶσ' ἀχρείους ἡδονὰς δαιτὸς χάριν.   (15)

5]μενος P. Oxy.: ἡσσώμενος Herwerden
6 εἰς ὑπερβολὴν πατρός Athen.: εἰς ὑπεκτροφὴν πάτρας Galen: P. Oxy. defective
7 κἀξυπηρετεῖν Galen: καὶ ξυνηρετ(μ)εῖν Athen.
8 οἷοί τ' om. Galen
9 μεταλλάσσουσιν Galen: διαλλάσσουσιν Athen.: τἀμήχανον Jamot, Bothe: τἀμήχανα Athen.
12 ἐκβαλόντες Athen.: ἐκλ(ε)ιποντες Diog. L.

manage house and family, nor would they be able to do so.[7] For
how would a man who is a slave to his jaws and a minion to
his belly[8] (5) acquire wealth to exceed his father's?[9] Still less
are they able to endure poverty or to cope with misfortunes.
Since they have not cultivated good habits, they meet a change
to troubles with difficulty. In their prime they are glorious and
go about as ornaments to a city, (10) but when bitter old age
falls upon them, they fade away (*like*) worn-out garments that
have lost their thread.[10] I blame too the custom of the Greeks
who assemble in crowds because of these men, and value useless
pleasures in order to enjoy a feast.[11] (15) For who that has been

[7] 'manage house and family': as only the well-born can, Eur. *El.* 386–7. This ability was
a major aspect of the εὐβουλία (*euboulia*) or 'good management of one's affairs' which the
contemporary sophist Protagoras aimed to teach, Plato, *Prot.* 318e. The application of such
good management in a city reappears in vv. 18 and esp. 25–8.

[8] 'slave ... belly': athletes with an 'undisciplined habit of the belly' Eur. *Antiope* F 201; for
the contemptuous phrase cf. *Alexander* F 49 'the race of slaves, all belly', and the Muses'
denunciation of shepherds as 'mere bellies' (Hesiod, *Theogony* 26). The most famous 'athlete-
glutton' was Milo of Croton, champion Olympic wrestler from 535–16 BC; his prodigious
strength and matching appetites are described at Athenaeus 10.412f. For Heracles' satyric
gluttony see Eur. *Syleus* F 691, and Ion, *Omphale* F 29–30.

[9] Athenaeus' text, 'to exceed his father's (wealth)', is disputed but emphasizes duty to
secure prosperity for one's own family (vv. 3–4); Galen's 'to ensure the future generations
of his fatherland' exposes athletes' inability to ensure sufficient wealth for their own old age
(vv. 11–12).

[10] 'ornaments to a city', ἀγάλματα (*agalmata*), a common Euripidean metaphor (*e.g.*
Suppliants 632–3), if perhaps also a critical allusion to the real statues (also *agalmata*) often
erected to honour athletes (*e.g.* Pindar, *Nemeans* 5.1–2); cf. Eur. *Electra* 387–9 '(men all
brawn and no brains) ornamenting the *agora*'. On these and other sources which tend to
denigrate visual artworks, see P. O'Sullivan 'Victory Statue, Victory Song: Pindar's Agonistic
Poetics and its Legacy' in *Sport and Festival in the Ancient Greek World*, eds D. Phillips and
D. Pritchard (Swansea, 2003) 77, 79–93.

'(*like*)': 'identification instead of comparison', J. Diggle, *CQ* 47 (1997) 102–3, comparing
for this idiom Aesch. *Seven* 835–6, *Ag.* 394.

[11] Victors were 'dined' in the Prytaneion at Athens, the official residence of the Council's
'presidents' (Plato, *Apology* 36d) – an ironic pendant to the criticism of athletes' gluttony in
v 5. In Eupolis' *Demes* F 129 *PCG* a character complains that a victorious runner is awarded
a hand-basin, while a good and useful citizen goes unrewarded.

τίς γὰρ παλαίσας εὖ, τίς ὠκύπους ἀνὴρ
ἢ δίσκον ἄρας ἢ γνάθον παίσας καλῶς
πόλει πατρῴᾳ στέφανον ἤρκεσεν λαβών;
πότερα μαχοῦνται πολεμίοισιν ἐν χεροῖν
δίσκους ἔχοντες ἢ δι' ἀσπίδων χερὶ   (20)
θείνοντες ἐκβαλοῦσι πολεμίους πάτρας;
οὐδεὶς σιδήρου ταῦτα μωραίνει πέλας
†στάς†. ἄνδρας χρὴ σοφούς τε κἀγαθούς
φύλλοις στέφεσθαι, χὤστις ἡγεῖται πόλει
κάλλιστα σώφρων καὶ δίκαιος ὢν ἀνήρ,   (25)
ὅστις τε μύθοις ἔργ' ἀπαλλάσσει κακὰ
μάχας τ' ἀφαιρῶν καὶ στάσεις· τοιαῦτα γὰρ
πόλει τε πάσῃ πᾶσί θ' Ἕλλησιν καλά.

16 τίς ... τίς Galen: τί ... τί Athen.
17 παίσας Athen.: πλήξας Galen
20–1 χερὶ | θείνοντες Athen.: ποσὶ | θέοντες Galen
23 †στάς†: ἰστάμενος Pechstein: σπασθέντος Collard: στάς· ἄνδρας <οἶμαι> Mekler
26 τε Musgrave: γε Athen.

F 282a

                    μηδὲν τῷ πατρὶ
μέμφεσθ' ἄωρον ἀποκαλοῦντες ἀνδρίον.

Photius α 1760 Theodoridis

F 283

        τοὺς ὄνους τοὺς λαρκαγωγοὺς ἐξ ὄρους οἴσειν ξύλα ...

Pollux 10.111
ἐξ ὄρους οἴσειν ξύλα Musgrave: οἴσειν ἐξ ὄρους ξύλα Pollux

F 284

        †σχοινίνας γὰρ ἵπποισι φλοΐνας ἡνίας πλέκει.†

Pollux 10.178; the words yield no metre; either σχοινίνας or φλοΐνας is a gloss upon the
other.

a good wrestler or sprinter or discus-thrower, or who has struck a good blow to the jaw – what use to his ancestral city was his winning a crown? Will they fight enemies with discus in hand or drive enemies out of their fatherland by punching through shields? (20) Nobody is this stupid when standing(?)[12] close to a sword! It is wise and good men we ought to crown with leaves,[13] and whoever leads a city best as a prudent and just man, (25) and who rids it of evil acts through his words, and by ending faction and feuding.[14] These are the kind of things good for every city and for all Greeks.

[12] 'standing': Pechstein's conjecture, with the same sense, restores metre; similarly Mekler's supplement '(I think,) it is wise ...' Collard's '(when in the face of) drawn (sword)' is bolder, when the enjambed Greek participle 'drawn' gives emphasis to the idea; for this verb cf. *IT* 322; for 'close to a sword' cf. *Med.* 265. The criticism probably develops the Spartan elegist Tyrtaeus' condemnation of athletic ability, specifically running and wrestling (F 12.2 *IEG*), as unworthy of comparison with military prowess.

[13] Deliberate irony: victorious athletes were ceremoniously wreathed, or pelted or showered, with leaves of bay in the ritual φυλλοβολία, *phyllobolia* (Pindar, *Pythians* 9.124), or sometimes those of other trees or plants ('pine-leaves' at Aesch. *Sacred Delegates* F 78c.39–40: see n. 21) – and the same congratulation rewarded any brave or significant act: see commentators on Eur. *Hec.* 574, Polyxena's voluntary death.

[14] 'feuding': see on Xenophanes in n. 6 above.

F 282a (Photius α 1760 Theodoridis)

Don't deride my father at all, in calling him an ugly little man![15]

[15] or 'your (father)': is Autolycus is speaking to the satyrs, warning them not to reveal his tricks? See Z. P. Ambrose in Harrison (2005) 29–30.

F 283 (Pollux 10.111)

... (*that*) asses that carry charcoal baskets will bring logs from the mountain ...[16]

[16] The Greek words happen to make a trochaic tetrameter, but may represent the end of an iambic trimeter followed by a complete one (τοὺς ὄνους | τοὺς ...)

F 284 (Pollux 10.178)

†... for he's weaving harness for horses out of sedge-rushes.†[17]

[17] The text is metrically corrupt, and 'sedge-rushes' translates two words in the Greek one of which appears to be a gloss upon the other; but the sense is clear.

Eurystheus (ΕΥΡΥΣΘΕΥΣ)

TrGF 5.419–24 (F 371–80).

Texts etc. Pechstein (1998) 145–76; N. Pechstein, R. Krumeich in KPS 422–30; H. Van Looy in Budé VIII.2 (2000) 133–41; Collard and Cropp (2008) I.403–11.

Discussions. Sutton (1980) 61–2; Gantz (1993) 413–16, cf. 389–90.
Art. LIMC .V.1.92 'Herakles' no. 2616, cf. VIII.1.580 'Eurystheus'.

The few fragments are all brief, but the play's plot may be surmised from F 371 and 379a, and perhaps 372 and 377.

   Heracles is ordered by Eurystheus to enter Hades (F 371; the one-word F 380 'Tartarean', not reproduced here, alludes to Hades). This must be his twelfth and last 'Labour', to fetch the monstrous dog Cerberus. Then the corrupt F 379a, if correctly interpreted, refers to recovery and restoration to life of the dead. Now the fetching of Cerberus is part of the background to Euripides' tragedy *Heracles* (vv. 22–5, 610–17, 1274–8 *etc.*); and both there and in myth generally this quest is linked with another feat of Heracles: when he gets to Hades he finds his living friend Theseus there together with a living Pirithous (they were trying to bring back to the world Pirithous' intended bride Persephone, who had been abducted by Hades). Heracles recovers Theseus (*Heracles* 1169–70) – but not Pirithous – as well as capturing Cerberus, and asks Theseus to help him bring the dog to Eurystheus (1386–7). Further, if F 377 refers not to the ambiguous parentage of Heracles, son of Zeus and Amphitryon (see n. 7 below), but of Theseus (in some accounts he was 'jointly' the son of both Poseidon and Aegeus), then Theseus may have had a role in *Eurystheus* too (but not also Pirithous, probably, given the usually short cast-list of satyr-plays).[1] F 379a is likely then to be about Heracles, as having miraculously brought up from Hades either or both of Theseus and Cerberus; and it was perhaps spoken by Silenus or the satyrs ('very great' suggests their approval), rather than by Eurystheus (but see n. 9 on the fragment).

Satyrs were unlikely to be shown in Hades itself, but may at least have been shown at an entrance to the Underworld, *e.g.* in Aeschylus' *Sisyphus*, as well as Sophocles' satyric *Cerberus* and *On Taenarum* — this latter drama was located before a mountain-cave through which Heracles descended to Hades. In any event, Euripides' play was almost certainly set at Eurystheus' palace at Argos (or Mycenae); and no doubt the satyrs were serving him in some way. Heracles would go off to Hades amid suitable stage-business; dramatic time would be shortened so that he returned quickly with Cerberus, terrifying both Eurystheus and the satyrs. F 372 is interesting here ('They aren't real, old man; don't be afraid of them. Figures made by Daedalus seem to move and see, so clever is that man'): presumably the 'old man' who is addressed is Silenus (as at *e.g. Cyc.* 145), and perhaps he is frightened by 'Cerberus', a creature fabricated for the theatre (cf. Seaford (1984) 36). It may well have terrified Eurystheus too: myth had it that he was frightened when Heracles brought him the Erymanthine boar (or the Nemean lion: see Gantz (1993) 389–90); a late 6th century Caeretan vase paints him hiding from Cerberus in a huge jar (see *LIMC* no. 2616; but KPS 427 n. 21 rejects the association). Be that as it may, F 372 attests yet another comic encounter in satyric drama between an unsophisticated character and a dismaying marvel, as in Aeschylus' *Sacred Delegates* (portrait-masks) or Sophocles' *Trackers* (music).

We cannot guess much more about the play from the remaining fragments. F 373 is a boast of past courage by the satyrs; F 374 and F 379 ('a large drinking-cup': not reproduced below) may relate to past violence. There are four gnomic book fragments, F 375, 376, 377 and 378, none of which comes with a hint of its dramatic context.

The play would end with Eurystheus being forced to release Heracles from further labours; and no doubt the satyrs would gain their freedom too.

Note

[1] The interwoven Hades-episode of Heracles, Theseus and Pirithous provided the plot for the fragmentary tragedy *Pirithous*; its attribution was disputed in antiquity, and still is, between Euripides and Critias (*TrGF* 1². 171–8 prints it as Critias 43 F 1–16), and the issue is bound up with the attribution of the 'Sisyphus(?)' play-fragment to Critias (?) 43 F 19: see there.

F 371

ΗΡΑΚΛΗΣ   πέμψεις δ' ἐς Ἅιδου ζῶντα κοὐ τεθνηκότα,
                 καί μοι τὸ τέρθρον δῆλον οἷ πορεύομαι.

Erotian τ 29 Nachmanson
2 οἷ πορεύομαι Erfurdt: εἰσπορεύομαι Erotian

F 372

<ΗΡΑΚΛΗΣ>   οὐκ ἔστιν, ὦ γεραιέ, μὴ δείσῃς τάδε·
                 τὰ Δαιδάλεια πάντα κινεῖσθαι δοκεῖ
                 βλέπειν τ' ἀγάλμαθ'· ὧδ' ἀνὴρ κεῖνος σοφός.

Scholia on Euripides, *Hecuba* 838
<ΗΡΑΚΛΗΣ> Musgrave
3 βλέπειν Grotius: βλέπει Stobaeus

F 373

<ΣΙΛΗΝΟΣ?>   πᾶς δ' ἐξεθέρισεν ὥστε πύρινον <στάχυν>
                 σπάθῃ κολούων φασγάνου μελανδέτου.

Pollux 10.145
<ΣΙΛΗΝΟΣ?> Steffen
1 Pierson, Heath: πᾶς δὲ φασγάνῳ ἐξεθέρισεν ὥστε πύρινον Pollux

F 374

                      ἢ κύαθον ἢ χαλκήλατον
                 ἠθμὸν προσίσχων τοῖσδε τοῖς ὑπωπίοις.

Pollux 10.108

F 375

                 †πιστὸν μὲν οὖν εἶναι χρὴ τὸν διάκονον
                 τοιοῦτον εἶναι† καὶ στέγειν τὰ δεσποτῶν.

Stobaeus 4.19.26

F 371 (Erotian τ 29 Nachmanson)

HERACLES   (*to Eurystheus*) You'll send me to Hades while I'm alive and not
dead, and the end to which I'm travelling is clear to me.

F 372 (Scholia on Euripides, *Hecuba* 838)

<HERACLES>   They aren't real, old man, don't be afraid of them. Figures made
by Daedalus seem to move and see, so clever is that man.[2]

[2]   On this fragment see the introductory discussion. For Daedalus' figures see Aesch. *Sacred
Delegates* F 78a.7 and n. 7; commentators on Eur. *Hecuba* 838; Morris (1992) 220–7. The
Daedalus of myth, however, became more and more a key for laughter by the later 5th Century
in that Daedalus' statues were considered outmoded by that time, *e.g.* Cratinus F 75 *PCG*,
Aristophanes, *Daedalus* F 191–204 *PCG*; cf. Plato, *Hippias Major* 282a, Plato Comicus
F 293 *PCG* (if genuine). The humour, then, in F 372 may be (doubly) against Silenus, as
lacking in the sophistication of the spectators. 'clever', Greek σοφός, with the inventive and
practical skills of the artisan; Minos of Crete kidnapped Daedalus for his σοφία, Xenophon,
Memorabilia 4.2.33.

F 373 (Pollux 10.145)

<SILENUS?>   Everyone mowed *(them*?) like an (ear) of corn, cutting with the
blade of a black sword.[3]

[3]   Braggadocio typical of the satyrs (cf. Silenus at Soph. *Trackers* F 314.153–8), here a
claim to have helped Heracles in killing the many-headed Hydra of Lerna, rather as they
claim, or at least Silenus claims, to have helped Dionysus extinguish the giant Enceladus and
then ordinary pirates at *Cyc.* 5–12.

F 374 (Pollux 10.108)

     ... holding either a wine-cup or a strainer made of beaten
bronze up against my black eyes here ...[4]

[4]   *i.e.* to reduce contusion (scholia on Ar. *Peace* 541–2): got during a drunken brawl (cf. the
satyrs at Achaeus, *Linus* F 26), or by Heracles himself struggling with Cerberus?

*The next four fragments are gnomic, of which only F 377 may help
reconstruction.*

F 375 (Stobaeus 4.19.26)

     †Such an attendant must be loyal† and conceal his masters'
affairs.[5]

[5]   Text so corrupt that translation can be only approximate.

F 376

οὐκ οἶδ' ὅτῳ χρὴ κανόνι τὰς βροτῶν τύχας
ὀρθῶς ἀθρήσαντ' εἰδέναι τί δραστέον.

Stobaeus 4.34.41
2 τί Meineke, West: τὸ Pollux

F 377

μάτην δὲ θνητοὶ τοὺς νόθους φεύγουσ' ἄρα
παῖδας φυτεύειν· ὃς γὰρ ἂν χρηστὸς φύῃ,
οὐ τοὔνομ' αὐτοῦ τὴν φύσιν διαφθερεῖ.

Stobaeus 4.24.44

F 378

νῦν δ' ἤν τις οἴκων πλουσίαν ἔχῃ φάτνην,
πρῶτος γέγραπται τῶν τ' ἀρειόνων κρατεῖ·
τὰ δ' ἔργ' ἐλάσσω χρημάτων νομίζομεν.

Stobaeus 4.31.42
1 οἴκοι Grotius
2 τῶν τ' ἀρειόνων (ἀρειόνων Erfurdt) κρατεῖ Weil: τῶν κακιόνων κράτει Stobaeus

F 379a

βάσκανον μέγιστον ψυχαγωγόν

Lexicon Vindobonense ψ 6 Nauck, and possible allusions in some late authors; the wording is unmetrical, and the quotation probably condensed, if not corrupt.

F 376 (Stobaeus 4.34.41)

    I do not know by what yardstick I should consider the fortunes of mortals in a true light and know what is to be done.[6]

[6]   The unpredictable but certain mutability of fortune was one of the commonest puzzles for the Greeks; the 'classic' instance is in Solon's words to Croesus, Herodotus 1.32.7, echoed in 86.3–6.

F 377 (Stobaeus 4.24.44)

    It is foolish then that mortals flee from getting bastard children, because anyone who is born virtuous will not have that name corrupt his nature.[7]

[7]   More likely said to (if not by) Heracles, illegitimate son of Zeus, in contrast to the cowardly Eurystheus, than to Theseus (see introductory discussion). Euripides elsewhere suggests that bastards are inferior to legitimate sons only in name, *e.g. Andromache* 638, *Andromeda* F 141. The issue relates to the famous contemporary speculation upon 'culture vs. nature' (νόμος, φύσις; *nomos, physis*), pioneered by the Sophists: see the magisterial treatment by Guthrie (1969) 55–134, 152–5.

F 378 (Stobaeus 4.31.42)

    Now if someone keeps a rich table at(?) his(?) house, his name is written first and he overcomes his betters; and we consider actions to be inferior to money.[8]

[8]   The genitive translated 'at(?) his(?) house' is questionable, as is also 'belonging to (his?) house'; an easy correction that gives similar sense is Grotius (locative). 'table' translates 'manger', a half-colloquial idiom which is apparently not depreciatory ('rich table', also *And.* 295–6). 'and he overcomes his betters' (Erfurdt, Weil; the idea at *e.g. IA* 449–50) improves Stobaeus' 'on the authority of his inferiors'.

F 379a (*Lexicon Vindobonense* ψ 6 Nauck)

    ... a sorcerer, a very great conjuror-up of souls ...[9]

[9]   A problematic fragment (see introductory discussion). It is textually insecure; the word translated 'sorcerer' is usually pejorative, a 'malign caster of spells', and may also be translated as 'a slanderer' (but its relevance to the plot is then hard to see).

Sciron (*ΣΚΕΙΡΩΝ*)

TrGF 5.660–4 (T iia, b; F 674a–81).

Texts etc. Pechstein (1998) 218–42; N. Pechstein, R. Krumeich in KPS 449–56; H. Van Looy in Budé VIII.3 (2002) 39–49, cf. 35–8; Collard and Cropp (2008) II.148–57.

Discussions. Sutton (1980) 62–5; Gantz (1993) 252, cf. 249–50; Conrad (1997) 189–95, 293–5; Voelke (2001) 225–8.

Art. LIMC VII.1.931–2 'Theseus' nos 97–122.

A typical plot – the destruction of an 'ogre' – like that of Euripides' vestigial *Busiris* (Heracles kills this tyrant of Egypt), *Syleus* (our next fragmentary play) – and *Cyclops* itself. Like the latter two, the play almost certainly employed the frequent motif of release from slavery of the satyrs. Here they are serving Sciron by luring passers-by, on the coastal road from Athens to Corinth, to the cliff-tops west of Megara named for him as the Scironides. These men were made to wash Sciron's feet when he himself returned from journeying, and while they did this he kicked them into the sea to be eaten by a huge turtle, at a place commemorated in its name Chelone (Greek 'Turtle'): thus [Apollod.], *Epitome* 1.2 and Diodorus 4.59. 4 (together = T iib; different maltreatment of travellers by the ogres Syleus and Lityerses in Sositheus' *Daphnis* below). The turtle is depicted in *LIMC* nos 105–7 under 'Art' above; the other representations are of the mythical incident in general. This action of the play is confirmed by a fragmentary hypothesis from the famous 'alphabetical' collection of such Euripidean pieces P. Oxy. 2455; fr. 6 (T iia), which preserves half of the play's first line, 'Hermes, for it is you who hold ...' (F 674a), a formulaic invocation of the god perhaps voiced by Silenus, and the following defective plot-summary:

> Sciron ... occupied a ravine (5) and got a ... livelihood from robbery; he was (a son) of Poseidon. He did not himself keep watch on the entrance ... (but had Silenus as his watchman) and servant of his violent assaults: he entrusted him

with (guarding the path?) (10) while he himself had gone away ... the satyrs imported (revels with) prostitutes (into the) solitude ...[1]

The preceding fr. 5 of the same papyrus has a few legible words including 'Heracles appeared'. It is thought unlikely, however, that Euripides would have included Theseus' friend Heracles in a mythical episode which universally had Theseus as its sole hero (Conrad (1997) 193–4; contrast the much greater possibility that Theseus supported Heracles in the *Eurystheus*, above); so fr. 5 is assigned by many to Euripides' satyric *Sisyphus*, for the hypothesis to this play is likely to have stood alphabetically before that of *Sciron* in the papyrus. Similarly the following fr. 7 has been considered for *Sciron*, but apart from purely physical and technical issues in ordering fragments of papyrus, its (damaged) content looks foreign to the Sciron-story. So fr. 7 too is therefore generally assigned to the *Sisyphus*, but tentatively, for that play's plot is totally irrecoverable; fr. 7 tells how Hermes after an apparently mischievous episode (cf. his characteristics in Sophocles, *Trackers*) appears and terrifies the satyrs and perhaps puts them up to some further mischief. On the ascriptions of frs. 5 and 7 see esp. Pechstein (1998) 199–204, Van Looy (2002) 35–8, and *TrGF* 5.658.

The fragments of the play itself are very few. Most noteworthy, and nicely illustrative of satyric drama's racier moments (Voelke 225–7), are F 675 and 676, two fragments revealing how the satyrs lured the passers-by, no doubt lining their own pockets in doing so (Conrad (1997) 191–3); cf. the mercenary Silenus of *Cyc.* 138 (n. 2 below), and the satyrs of Ion, *Omphale* F 31 and n. 15 below, and Soph. *Trackers* F 314.50–6. F 677–81 are very brief and hardly give further clues to content (all stand below, except F 680, a one-word lexicographic fragment 'to accompany').

Note

[1] Text as in the first edition (E. G. Turner, 1962), except the supplements '(a son)' Snell; '(but had ... as his watchman)' Barrett; '(Silenus)' Lloyd-Jones; '(guarding the path'?), '(revels with)' and '(into the)' Barrett.

F 674a

<ΣΙΛΗΝΟΣ?> Ἑρμῆ, σὺ γὰρ δὴ [   ] ἔχεις

P. Oxy. 2455 fr. 6. 2–3
<ΣΙΛΗΝΟΣ?> Kassel, Steffen

F 675

<ΣΙΛΗΝΟΣ?> καὶ τὰς μὲν ἄξῃ, πῶλον ἢν διδῷς ἕνα,
τὰς δ᾽ ἢν ξυνωρίδ᾽· αἳ δὲ κἀπὶ τεσσάρων
φοιτῶσιν ἵππων ἀργυρῶν. φιλοῦσι δὲ
τὰς ἐξ Ἀθηνῶν παρθένους ὅταν φέρῃ
πολλάς <τις> ...   (5)

Pollux 9.75
<ΣΙΛΗΝΟΣ?> Kannicht
5 <τις>Snell

F 676

<ΣΙΛΗΝΟΣ> σχεδὸν χαμεύνῃ σύμμετρος Κορινθίας
παιδός, κνεφάλλου δ᾽ οὐχ ὑπερτενεῖς πόδα.

Pollux 10.35
2 ὑπερτενεῖς Meineke: ὑπερτείνεις Pollux

F 677

οὐδὲ κωλῆνες νεβρῶν

Athenaeus 9.368d

F 674a (P. Oxy. 2455 fr. 6. 2–3)

<SILENUS?>   Hermes, for it is you who hold …

F 675 (Pollux 9.75)

<SILENUS?>   You can take these women with you if you pay one 'colt', and those if you give 'a teamed pair'; but these go in fact for four 'silver mares'. Men like the 'girls from Athens', when someone has plenty (*of such coins*?) with him.[2]

[2] Silenus offers a selection of girls to a passer-by, almost certainly Theseus; he is similarly on the make when bartering his master's cheese and meat for wine from Odysseus, *Cyc.* 136–92. One 'colt', a 'teamed pair (of colts)', four 'silver mares', 'girls from Athens': images stamped on coins, Corinthian or Athenian, put here in order of ascending value; 'men like the girls from Athens' has two meanings, both that they like paying this top price and that they like such girls. '(*of such coins*?)': the now isolated feminine plural (adjective) 'plenty' may refer to 'owls' (γλαύκας), a noun idiomatically omitted, the names of silver coins with an owl, Athena's emblematic bird, on the reverse of the goddess's head: see Dunbar on Aristophanes, *Birds* 1106, citing Plutarch, *Lysander* 16.4 where the pairing πολλὰς γλαύκας actually occurs.

    The names also reflect sexual activity ('horse-riding', whether by prostitutes (cf. Ar. *Thesm.* 153) or men: see Henderson (1991) 164–6). Nearby Corinth was famous for its prostitutes (F 676; temple-prostitutes *e.g.* Pindar F 122.18–19), and their pandering to very rich clients is noted at Ar. *Wealth* 149–52. 'Coins' and 'pay' are here anachronisms, as in *e.g. Cyc.* 160. For buying sex in satyric drama see also Achaeus' *Aethon*, introductory discussion.

F 676 (Pollux 10.35)

<SILENUS>   (*As you're*) almost the same size as a Corinthian girl's mattress, your foot won't stretch beyond the cushion.[3]

[3] An allusion to another ogre exterminated by Theseus, Procrustes, who 'tailored' passers-by to the beds he offered them. 'mattress': the Greek word χαμεύνη, lit. 'bed on the ground', is defined as a pallet of low quality in the lexicographic source of Soph. F 175, where it occurs without context; the word itself hints its cognate χαμαιτύπη, a low word for a prostitute (English 'a bang on the ground'; for the metaphor see n. on *Cyc.* 180).

F 677 (Athenaeus 9.368d)

     … and not the thigh-bones of fawns …[4]

[4] A reference to the satyrs' diet (Aesch. *Net-Fishers* F 47a.52); they wear the fawn-skins for Dionysus' worship (Soph. *Trackers* F 314.225). On another level, there may have been actual human bones left by the turtles, those of Sciron's victims, alluded to with understated foreboding by the satyrs.

F 678

ἔστι τοι καλὸν
{τοὺς} κακοὺς κολάζειν

678 Stobaeus 4.5.6
{τοὺς} Grotius

F 679

... ἢ προσπηγνύναι
κράδαις ἐρινaῖς ...

Athenaeus 3.76c

F 681

ἔμβολα

Hesychius ε 2307 Latte

F 678 (Stobaeus 4.5.6)

I tell you, it is a fine thing to punish evil men.[5]

[5] Theseus speaking? – see the next fragment. 'To punish evil men' is a cliché, found also in Eur. F 953a.17, varied at *Hel.* 1172, *Supp.* 341; the idea, incorporating the word 'justice', in satyric also *e.g. Cyc.* 422 (see n.), 693, *Syleus* F 692, and Aeschylus' 'Justice'-play F 281a.15–21.

F 679 (Athenaeus 3.76c)

... or fix (*them*) to the branches of fig-trees ...[6]

[6] From a narration, how Theseus destroyed another ogre who menaced passers-by, Sinis, who killed them by tying them to bent-over trees which he then let spring apart; cf. Aeschylus, 'Justice'-play F 281a.28–34 and n. 13; also n. 3 above on F 676.

F 681 (Hesychius ε 2307 Latte)

door-bars[7]

[7] 'door-bars' is the pedestrian translation, but '(ships') rams' is well possible, as a metaphor for the satyrs' phalluses in brandishing their sexual prowess (*e.g.* Soph. *Trackers* F 314.366–8 and nn.), just as Peisetairos boasts of his at Ar. *Birds* 1256 when menacing Iris, who elsewhere is menaced by lustful satyrs (*LIMC* V.2 107, 110, 113, 114, 116); for such nautical metaphors see Henderson (1991) 161–6.

Syleus (ΣΥΛΕΥΣ)

TrGF 5.671–8 (T ii, iiia, b, c; F 686a–94).

Texts etc. Pechstein (1998) 243–83; N. Pechstein, R. Krumeich in KPS 457–73; H. Van Looy in Budé VIII.3 (2002) 75–90; Collard and Cropp (2008) II.169–83.

Discussions. B. A. van Groningen, 'De Syleo Euripideo', *Mnem* 58 (1930) 293–9; Chourmouziades (1974) 120–57 (*passim*, with 'reconstruction' at 156–7), 230–47; Sutton (1980) 66–7; Gantz (1993) 440–1, cf. 434–7; Conrad (1997) 196–7; Voelke (2001) 330–8 and *passim*; C. Jourdain-Annequin, 'Héraclès chez Syleus ou le héros entre soumission et résistance', *Studia Historica. Historia Antigua (Salamanca)* 25 (2007) 147–161: résumé in *APh* 78 (2007) 234.

Art. LIMC VII.1.825–7 'Syleus', nos 1–7, esp. 5–7.

Another 'ogre' play: Syleus' name means 'Despoiler, Bandit'. His story is well attested in Attic vase-paintings of the later 5th century, which do not necessarily relate, even loosely, to Euripides' play, and not one shows satyrs. The play was known (but almost certainly not read first-hand) well into the Byzantine period (see Tzetzes in T iiia below); we have more extensive book fragments from it than from any other Euripidean satyr-play, and much more secondary evidence.

A fragmentary hypothesis to the play (P. Strasb. 2676 fr. A = T ii.1–12) begins:

(Syleus, saty)ric ... [*three letters from the play's first line,* = F 686a]. (Its) plot is ... Zeus (ordered Heracles, who had killed) his own (guest-friend Iphitus, the son) of Eurytus, to be sold away ... If ... the labour ... for the duration of a year ...

For this killing Heracles had been, in the fullest account ([Apollod.] 2.6.2–3 = T iiic), afflicted by madness; an oracle of Apollo (by definition at Zeus' 'order') told him he would be cured if he were sold into slavery for a period (the varying versions of the myth are analyzed by Gantz (1993) 434–7; compare the god Apollo in slavery to the mortal Admetus, also for bloodshed, *Alcestis* 1–7). The mortal is usually named as Omphale queen of Lydia; but for this play Euripides developed (or devised) an association between that servitude and Heracles' destruction of Syleus during it (see introductory discussion to Ion of Chios' *Omphale*): Heracles now serves the monstrous Syleus himself, who is located not in Lydia but in mainland Greece (in Aulis, according to [Apollod.] 2.6.3, but this name is almost certainly corrupt and is usually emended to Phyllis, a place in N. Greece).

The play is set outside Syleus' farmhouse (cf. F 689.1, 694). We get a good idea of its opening, very probably its prologue-scene, in which Hermes sells Heracles to Syleus, from an account by the 1st century AD philosopher Philo in his *Every Good Man Is Free* §§ 98–104 (T iiib: below), which includes four fragments in close dramatic order (F 687–90): Philo is illustrating the contrast between the 'free' nature of a virtuous man and the repression which characterizes an ignoble one (conceivably Euripides touched on a similar theme in his *Eurystheus*: see above on F 377). Jourdain-Annequin (2007: see *Discussions*) writes that *Syleus* reflects contemporary social reality, through symbolic aspects of slavery, submission and resistance.

The very few other fragments can be fitted easily into the play's ending as it is surmised from Philo's further summary (§§ 103–4, which includes F 691) and from the other book-fragments (F 692–4) and secondary evidence (T ii.13–17: below). Heracles' instinct for 'freedom' causes him to rebel against his vicious master (F 690; contrast his possibly amicable relationship with Omphale in Ion of Chios). He refuses to work in Syleus' vineyard; instead, as we learn from Tzetzes, *Prolegomena on Comedy* XIa II Koster, who is discussing the nature of satyric as productive of enjoyment and laughter (= T iiia, cf. Philo on F 691 below),

> Heracles, after being sold to Syleus as a farm-slave, was sent to the field to work the vineyard, but he dug up all the vines by the roots with a double-fork; he carried them on his back to the farmhouse, made them up into great heaps, and after sacrificing the better of (Syleus') bulls feasted on it. He broke into the cellar and, after removing the lid from the finest jar and setting the doors down as a table, 'began to eat and drink',[1] singing the while. Then he looked fiercely in the face of the field's overseer and ordered him to bring him the fruits of the season and flat cakes. Lastly the 'slave' diverted the whole river to the farmyard and flooded everything – that most accomplished farmer![2]
>
> That's what satyr-plays are like.

Then, Syleus comes angrily to remonstrate, and Heracles challenges him to a drinking contest (F 691 itself). Finally, Heracles emboldens himself to kill Syleus with his great club (F 693: cf. the earlier mention of his club at F 688.4 – but another meaning may underlie F 693: see n. 11 there). Heracles is acting in absolute hostility to an evil man (F 692; again cf. Philo after his quotation of F 691). He does not however kill Syleus' daughter Xenodoce, as we learn from the second brief fragment of the papyrus hypothesis, the now separated P. Oxy. 2455 fr. 8 (= T ii.13–17):

> ... and Syleus ... the daughter of the above-mentioned ... when she was being pursued ... These (he)... but saved her (Xenodoce).[3]

– indeed he takes her to bed (F 694). This last fragment is addressed to her, and it is possible that she had a considerable part in the play. In some reconstructions (discussed by Van Looy (2002) 81–2), she earlier narrates Heracles' destruction of the vineyard, perhaps also the flooding, and even the killing of her father; then she would be like Deianeira at the start of Sophocles' *Women of Trachis* (1–48, esp. 19–25) outlining how Heracles won her hand by overcoming the bestial river-god Achelous (cf. also Sophocles' *Oeneus* F 1130). The play therefore seems to have had a longish cast-list: Hermes, Heracles, Syleus and Xenodoce for certain, possibly also Silenus if he acted as the 'foreman' of the satyrs (Tzetzes, *Prolegomena*, T

T iiia

Ἡρακλῆς πραθεὶς τῷ Συλεῖ ὡς γεωργὸς δοῦλος ἐστάλη εἰς τὸν ἀγρὸν τὸν ἀμπελῶνα ἐργάσασθαι, ἀνεσπακὼς δὲ δικέλλῃ προρρίζους τὰς ἀμπέλους ἁπάσας νωτοφορήσας τε αὐτὰς εἰς τὸ οἴκημα τοῦ ἀγροῦ θωμοὺς μεγάλους ἐποίησε τὸν κρείττω τε τῶν βοῶν θύσας κατεθοινᾶτο καὶ τὸν πιθεῶνα δὲ διαρρήξας καὶ τὸν κάλλιστον πίθον ἀποπωμάσας τὰς θύρας τε ὡς τράπεζαν θεὶς "ἦσθε καὶ ἔπινεν" ᾄδων, καὶ τῷ προεστῶτι δὲ τοῦ ἀγροῦ δριμὺ ἐνορῶν φέρειν ἐκέλευεν ὡραῖά τε καὶ πλακοῦντας· καὶ τέλος ὅλον ποταμὸν πρὸς τὴν ἔπαυλιν τρέψας τὰ πάντα κατέκλυσεν ὁ δοῦλος. ἐκεῖνος ὁ τεχνικώτατος γεωργός.

τοιαῦτα τὰ σατυρικὰ δράματα ...

Tzetzes, *Prolegomena on Comedy* XIa II Koster
This testimony is translated in the introductory discussion.

iia above, writes of 'the field's overseer', unless this means Syleus himself). Heracles would have found them already working in the vineyard and later he freed them; Conrad (1997) 196–7 suggests that they would have joined gleefully in the wrecking and drinking.

Syleus thus contained many elements typical of satyric: servitude (here of two kinds); an ogre, humiliated and violently killed; feasting, drinking and sex.

Notes

1   Tzetzes uses a common Homeric phrase, e.g. *Iliad* 24.476. Heracles' gluttony is widespread in satyric drama, *e.g.* F 691 here (see n. 9).

2   In the ms. of Tzetzes a later hand has substituted for 'that most accomplished farmer' the statement 'There is such a play by Euripides.' Compare Heracles' compulsory and wholly menial 'Labour' of cleansing the stables of Augeas by diverting rivers through them ([Apollod.] 2.5.5).

3   This hypothesis must be taken to report Euripides' ending more accurately than [Apollod.] 2.6.3 and Tzetzes, *Chiliades* 2.435–8 (both = T iiic), who after narrating the uprooting of the vines state that Heracles killed Xenodoce. Her name occurs in the secondary sources both in this form ('Guest-Hostess') and as Xenodice ('Guest-Justice'); *TrGF* prefers the former, and we adopt it as playing ironically upon the girl's intercourse with Heracles, F 694.

F 687–91 all come from Philo, *Every Good Man is Free* §§ 98–104 (T iiic)
(98) Τῆς δὲ σπουδαίων ἐλευθερίας μάρτυρές εἰσι ποιηταί ...
(99) ... ἴδε γοῦν οἷα παρ' Εὐριπίδῃ φησὶν ὁ Ἡρακλῆς·

F 687

ΗΡΑΚΛΗΣ   πίμπρη, κάταιθε σάρκας, ἐμπλήσθητί μου
πίνων κελαινὸν αἷμα· πρόσθε γὰρ κάτω
γῆς εἶσιν ἄστρα, γῆ δ' ἄνεισ' ἐς αἰθέρα,
πρὶν ἐξ ἐμοῦ σοι θῶπ' ἀπαντῆσαι λόγον.

The four verses of F 687 are cited with mostly slight variations by Philo three other times, and are cited in part by, or are known to, some later authors. Van Groningen (1930) however assigned this fragment to *Eurystheus*.

(100) πάλιν τὸν αὐτὸν σπουδαῖον οὐχ ὁρᾷς, ὅτι οὐδὲ πωλούμενος θεράπων εἶναι δοκεῖ, καταπλήττων τοὺς ὁρῶντας, ὡς οὐ μόνον ἐλεύθερος ὢν ἀλλὰ καὶ (101) δεσπότης ἐσόμενος τοῦ πριαμένου; ὁ γοῦν Ἑρμῆς πυνθανομένῳ Συλεῖ εἰ φαῦλός ἐστιν, ἀποκρίνεται·

101 πυνθανομένῳ Συλεῖ εἰ Kannicht: πυνθανομένῳ μὲν εἰ Philo

F 688

ΕΡΜΗΣ   ἥκιστα φαῦλος, ἀλλὰ πᾶν τοὐναντίον·
τὸ σχῆμα σεμνὸς κοὐ ταπεινὸς οὐδ' ἄγαν
εὔογκος ὡς ἂν δοῦλος, ἀλλὰ καὶ στολὴν
ἰδόντι λαμπρὸς καὶ ξύλῳ δραστήριος.

(Philo continues directly into)

From the beginning of the play, almost certainly from a prologue-scene, in which Hermes brings Heracles to be sold (Philo §§ 98–104 summarises it, citing F 687–91):

> (98) Poets are witness to the freedom of virtuous men ... (99) At any rate, look at the sort of things Heracles says in Euripides:

F 687

HERACLES   (*to Hermes*) Set fire to me, burn my flesh up, glut yourself in drinking my black blood! For the stars will go down below the earth, and the earth go up into the sky, before a grovelling word from me greets you.[4]

(Philo continues in § 100)

> Again, don't you see that the same virtuous man doesn't appear to be a lackey even when being sold, but astonishes the onlookers, as being not only free but about to become the master of the one who buys him? Anyway, Hermes answers Syleus'[5] question whether Heracles is weak:

4   Van Groningen (1930) assigned F 687 to *Eurystheus* because he judged it to convey a hero's defiance, not that of a slave as in F 688–90, and because he thought that Philo's 'again' in § 100 (below) implied citation from a different play.

5   The insertion of Syleus' name by Kannicht in *TrGF* heals a damaged and unclear text in Philo.

F 688

HERM.   Least of all is he weak – everything opposite to that! His demeanour is proud, and he is not humble at all; nor is he too well-padded as a slave would be, but in his attire he is splendid to look at,[6] and he knows how to use a club.

6   'attire': Heracles for stage-purposes is still dressed in his lion-skin (iconic, *e.g. Heracles* 360–3); for his similarly iconic club see F 693 and n. 11.

For the ellipse of an optative with ὡς ἄν see Sositheus, *Daphnis* F 2 n. 6.

(Philo continues directly into the next fragment)

F 689

EPM.

οὐδεὶς δ' ἐς οἴκους δεσπότης ἀμείνονας
αὐτοῦ πρίασθαι βούλεται· σὲ δ' εἰσορῶν
πᾶς τις δέδοικεν· ὄμμα γὰρ πυρὸς γέμεις,
ταῦρος λέοντος ὡς βλέπων πρὸς ἐμβολήν.

εἶτ' ἐπιλέγει·

F 690

EPM.

... τό <γ'> εἶδος αὐτὸ σοῦ κατηγορεῖ
σιγῶντος ὡς εἴης ἂν οὐχ ὑπήκοος,
τάσσειν δὲ μᾶλλον ἢ ἐπιτάσσεσθαι θέλοις.

689 was separated from 688 by Grotius, and attached to the beginning of 690 by Musgrave
689.1 δεσπότης Musgrave: δεσπότας Philo
690.1 <γ'> Elmsley; εἶδος αὐτὸ σοῦ Mangey, Elmsley: εἶδος αὐτοῦ οὗ Philo, most mss.;
some omit αὐτοῦ

(102) ἐπεὶ δὲ καὶ πριαμένου Συλέως εἰς ἀγρὸν ἐπέμφθη, διέδειξεν ἔργοις τὸ
τῆς φύσεως ἀδούλωτον· τὸν μὲν γὰρ ἄριστον τῶν ἐκεῖ ταύρων καταθύσας Διὶ
πρόφασιν εὐωχεῖτο, πολὺν δ' οἶνον ἐκφορήσας ἀθρόον εὖ μάλα κατακλιθεὶς
ἠκρατίζετο. (103) Συλεῖ δὲ ἀφικομένῳ καὶ δυσανασχετοῦντι ἐπί τε τῇ βλάβῃ
καὶ τῇ τοῦ θεράποντος ῥαθυμίᾳ καὶ τῇ περιττῇ καταφρονήσει μηδὲν μήτε τῆς
χρόας μήτε ὧν ἔπραττε μεταβαλὼν εὐτολμότατά φησι·

F 689

HERMES   No master wants to buy men better than himself for his household. And everybody who looks at *you* is frightened: for your eye is full of fire, like a bull watching for the onset of a lion.[7]

[7]   In v. 1 Musgrave's change to '(No) master' improved Philo's 'No one wants to buy masters better than himself'. Heracles' bull-like glare equates him with such raging figures as Ajax (Soph. *Ajax* 322), Medea (Eur. *Med.* 92: see Mastronarde's n.), or the seething Aristophanic Aeschylus (*Frogs* 804). Here 'the onset of a lion' may allude to his Labour in killing the lion of Nemea, Eur. *Heracles* 359–60.

Then (Hermes) continues:

F 690

HERM.   ... your very appearance, though you are silent, indicates that you would not be subservient, but would want rather to give orders than be given them.[8]

[8]   Inference of inner nature from outward appearance or demeanour in drama *e.g.* Eur. *Ion* 237–8, *Hypsipyle* F 757.854–5, Soph. *El.* 663–4; emotions inferred and translated into expression by painters or sculptors Xenophon, *Memorablia* 3.10.3–5, 8.

(Philo jumps to a later point in the action)

(102) And then when Syleus had bought him and he was sent to work the land, he showed by his actions that there was nothing slavish about his nature. For he feasted sumptuously on the finest bull there, on the pretext of sacrificing it to Zeus, and then he brought out a vast quantity of wine, and reclining well at his ease he drank it neat. (103) When Syleus arrived and became angry at the damage and the laziness of his servant and his exceedingly contemptuous attitude, Heracles changed neither his colour at all nor any of the things he was doing, but said with the greatest boldness:

F 691

HP.   κλίθητι καὶ πίωμεν· ἐν τούτῳ δέ μου
τὴν πεῖραν εὐθὺς λάμβαν' εἰ κρείσσων ἔσῃ.

(104) τοῦτον οὖν πότερον δοῦλον ἢ κύριον ἀποφαντέον τοῦ δεσπότου, μὴ μόνον ἀπελευθεριάζειν ἀλλὰ καὶ ἐπιτάγματα ἐπιτάττειν τῷ κτησαμένῳ καὶ εἰ ἀφηνιάζοι τύπτειν καὶ προπηλακίζειν, εἰ δὲ καὶ βοηθοὺς ἐπάγοιτο, πάντας ἄρδην ἀπολλύναι τολμῶντα;

Book-fragments from the play's final scenes:

F 692

τοῖς μὲν δικαίοις ἔνδικος, τοῖς δ' αὖ κακοῖς
πάντων μέγιστος πολέμιος κατὰ χθόνα.

Stobaeus 4.5.1

F 693

HP.   ... εἶα δή, φίλον ξύλον,
ἔγειρέ μοι σεαυτὸ καὶ γίγνου θρασύ.

Choeroboscus in Eustathius, *Iliad* 107.31 (on Book 1.302); cited in part by, or known to, later grammarians

F 694

HP.   βαυβῶμεν εἰσελθόντες· ἀπόμορξαι σέθεν
τὰ δάκρυα.

'Antiatticist' 85.10 Bekker, cf. Aristophanes of Byzantium fr. 15 Slater

F 691
HER.   Lie down and let's drink! And then test me right away to see if you'll be better at this than I am!⁹

⁹ A comic counterpart to Heracles' usual means of overcoming opponents, physical violence (*e.g.* Achelous in Soph. *Oeneus* F 1130). His gross eating too (Philo, above) is regular in satyric drama (Ion, *Omphale* F 29–30 and notes; cf. the servant's complaints about Heracles' gluttony in Eur. *Alcestis* 747–72); but the ogre Syleus is not presented as gluttonous (at least in the admittedly sparse remains of the play) as are other satyric ogres, *e.g.* Euripides' Polyphemus in *Cyc.* 327 and Lityerses in Sositheus, *Daphnis*).

(Philo completes his moral example from Heracles in the play)

(104) So is this man to be declared the slave or the lord of his master, in that he not only acts freely but gives orders to his owner and, if he refuses to be reined in, beats him and abuses him, and if his master calls for people to help him, dares to destroy all of them utterly?

Book-fragments from the play's final scenes:

F 692 (Stobaeus 4.5.1)
        (Heracles) … just to the just, but the greatest of all enemies on earth to the wicked.¹⁰

¹⁰ A staunch statement of the straightforward satyric ethic of retributive justice: see on *Cyc.* 421–2, *Sciron* F 678.

F 693 (Choeroboscus in Eustathius, *Iliad* 107.31 on Book 1.302)
HER.   Come on there, my dear club, rouse yourself, please, and be bold!¹¹

¹¹ One uncertainly interpreted lexicon-entry, and likely allusions to these lines, or adaptations, also in late authors (set out in *TrGF* 5.678), open the possibility that Heracles is preparing not to kill Syleus but to rape his daughter Xenodoce (cf. F 694), and is addressing his penis. Van Looy (2002) 83 regards it as certain; Heracles' sexual appetite enabled him to bed all but one of Thestius' 'fifty' daughters in one night (Paus. 9.27.6). KPS 472 suggests that it is Silenus who is aroused (typically of satyrs: Aesch. *Net-Fishers* F 47a.23–4, Soph. *Trackers* F 314.368).

F 694 ('Antiatticist' 85.10 Bekker)
HER.   (*to Xenodoce*) Let's go to bed¹² inside: wipe away your tears!

¹² 'go to bed': a 'low' word, a colloquial euphemism, in Greek, as in English. The Greek word-stem provided a term for a 'dildo', *e.g.* Herodas 6.19.

ION OF CHIOS

(active from about 450 BC; died before 421)

Omphale (ΟΜΦΑΛΗ)

TrGF 1².101–5, 113 (19 F 17a–33a, *59), 346; cf. 5.1106.

Texts etc. A. von Blumenthal, *Ion von Chios* (Stuttgart-Berlin, 1939) 35–43; Page (1942) 136–7 (F 17a only); Gauly (1991) 68–73, 276; N. Pechstein, R. Krumeich in KPS 479–90; L. Leurini, *Ionis Chii Testimonia et Fragmenta* (Amsterdam, 2000²) frs 22–38, 73a; Cipolla (2003) 106–38.

Discussions. Chourmouziades (1974) 139–41; Sutton (1980) 73–4; Lloyd-Jones (1990, orig. 1957) 385–6 (on F 17a); L. Leurini, 'Il βόρειος ἵππος di Ione di Chio (19 F 17a Sn.)', *QUCC* 9 (1981) 155–61 (on F 17a), cf. L. Lehnus, 'Ancora Ione di Chio *TrGF* 19 F 17a', *ibid.* 17 (1984) 137–9; N. Loraux, 'Herakles: The Super-Male and the Feminine', in D. Halperin, J. Winkler, F. Zeitlin (eds), *Before Sexuality: the Construction of Erotic Experience in the Ancient World* (Princeton, 1990) 21–52, at 25–6, 35–6; Gantz (1993) 439–42; B. Marzullo, 'Ione, fr. 59 Sn. (ex Ὀμφάλη)', *Museum Criticum* 30/31 (1995/96) 127–35; Voelke (2001) 333–4; P. E. Easterling, 'Looking for *Omphale*', in V. Jennings, A. Katsaros (eds), *The World of Ion of Chios. Mnemosyne Supplement* 288 (Leiden, 2007) 282–92, cf. J. Maitland, 'Ion of Chios, Sophocles and Myth', *ibid.* 266–81, at 274–80.

Art. LIMC VII.1.45–50 'Omphale' nos 1–42 (Omphale with Heracles in various contexts; depictions mostly from 1st century BC and later, but nos 1–7 from the late 6th to the 4th century).

All but two of the play's nineteen likely fragments are book-fragments (F 17a and 33a are from papyri, the latter a bare reference not reproduced here); all are brief, the two longest having only three lines each (F 18, 24); all but one (F 18) are lexicographic in source; all except F 17a come without dramatic context – but eleven (F 20–30) attest words or phenomena from a feast. This is confidently assumed to be one where Heracles demonstrated his huge capacity for eating and drinking (F 30 has 'Heracles has his teeth in three rows'). The character of these eleven fragments is enough by itself to mark the play as satyric; otherwise there is only one express statement of its genre, in the source of F 18. All known evidence for the play, and all that can be conjectured or asked from it, has recently been set out with judicious concision by Easterling (2007); earlier surveys were by KPS 480–3, 488–90, and Cipolla (2003) 122–3.

The plot is safely enough inferred to be Heracles' servitude, for a predetermined period, to Omphale queen of Lydia. This episode is well attested (Gantz 439–42), from the 5th Century by Pherecydes (below), in allusion by Sophocles, *Women of Trachis* 248–79 (see esp. Maitland 2007), and as the plot also of Achaeus' *Omphale* (below; but his play's scanty fragments give no help in determining either his plot or Ion's);[1] from the 4th Century in comedies by Aristophanes and Cratinus II; from later antiquity by Diodorus, [Apollodorus] and Lucian (all summarised below). Details in these last three suggest expansion of the story over time, as well as contamination with the episode involving Heracles and the ogre Syleus which provided a whole satyr-play for Euripides.

Thus Pherecydes 3 F 82b *FGrH* (= F 82b 9–12 Fowler 319): Heracles killed Iphitus the son of Eurytus while the former was his guest, for he thought both had played him false:

In anger at the killing of a guest Zeus ordered Hermes to take Heracles and to sell him (i.e. *into slavery*) as penalty for the bloodshed; Hermes took him to Lydia and gave him to Omphale the queen of those parts; his price was set at three talents.

Much later Diodorus 4.31.5–8 gives a version in which Heracles becomes mad as a result of the guest-killing; learning from Apollo that he will recover sanity if he allows himself to be sold and pays his selling price as recompense to Eurytus, he becomes Omphale's slave and is healed (see the start of our introductory discussion to Euripides' *Syleus*). During his servitude he rids Omphale's land of various pests including Syleus (above); Omphale admires his valour and learns his identity; she frees him and has a son by him. [Apollod.] 2.6.3 differs slightly, including Syleus but omitting the sexual liaison. Lucian 59.10 (cf. 79.15.2) writes of a painting in which Omphale bullies Heracles physically while he cards wool wearing a woman's purple garment, and she herself wears his lionskin and carries his club; in this Lucian seems heir to a good deal of 4th century art (see *LIMC* under 'Art' above), and the subject was depicted in later art as well, *e.g.* by Annibale Caracci (1560–1609) in the Farnese Gallery in Rome.

The fragments do not reveal how far, or how widely, Ion had taken this progressively more elaborate story, which in its various versions was potentially rich in familiar satyric elements like slavery, ogres, festivity and sexual fun. F 17a certainly, and therefore probably F 18 and 19, begin the play with Hermes and Heracles arriving in Lydia, presumably at Omphale's palace near the River Pactolus (cf. F 27). The play's dramatic time may however not have spanned Heracles' entire period of slavery, his release and the celebration: F 21 has him saying 'I must keep the festival all year long', and in F 22 he is Omphale's 'guest': it is fairly inferred that the year is the period for which he must serve, and that it is not yet over, even if nearly so (but other accounts say that it was three years: see on F 21). These two fragments in particular, and the eleven 'feasting' fragments collectively (F 20–30), have prompted suggestions (see especially Easterling (2007) 286) that Heracles' 'servitude' was an endurance test of his appetite – a contradiction of 'punishment' but perhaps not surprising in a satyr-play, and certainly entertaining. Again, Euripides' *Syleus* is comparable: it too has Heracles sold into slavery by Hermes, and Heracles' huge appetite is a weapon he uses against his master Syleus (F 690 and Philo § 102 there).

So there is much room for guess-work: did Ion 'anticipate' 4th Century art and comedy by showing an Omphale almost literally wearing the trousers, both bullying and indulging Heracles, plying him all the time with food, wine and music while humiliating him with female dress? On this assumption F *59, otherwise unattributed to any play, has been brought in: hesitantly by Snell in *TrGF* (1971[1], 1986[2]) and KPS, earlier but more confidently by (Meineke and) von Blumenthal (1939) 42 and later by Marzullo (1995/96), cf. Leurini (1981), Cipolla (2003), Maitland (2007) 277–8; the attribution is resisted by Easterling (2007) 291, who does however concede that the hero may have been made to wear 'a luxurious costume that looks more feminine than masculine' (287). The issue goes unmentioned by Gauly (1991).

In all, however, there is insufficient evidence for the span, outcome and character of the plot; and one big question remains: what role did the satyrs have? The single fragment feasibly attributable to them is the one-word F

F 17a
<ΗΡΑΚΛΗΣ> ὅρων μὲν [ἤ]δη Πέλοπος ἐξελαύ[νο]μεν,
             Ἑρμῆ, βόρειον [ἵπ]πον, ἄνεται δ' ὁδός.

P. Oxy. 1611 fr. 2 col. i.124–7

31 'we were dealing in petty wares', and their wares perhaps included the women's cosmetics of F 24 and 25. In F 20 Omphale (?) orders 'girls' to bring out drinking vessels, and in F 22 she addresses Lydian (women) harpists. Were these real females, mute 'extras', or satyrs got up as women-musicians (and wearing the cosmetics of F 24 and F 25), to form a transvestite 'male' chorus? – for unless Ion's was an extremely unconventional satyr-play, the satyrs would certainly have formed the main chorus, not a 'secondary' female one (a similar problem arises in *Adespota* F 667a below: see our introductory discussion there). If Heracles appeared 'in drag' (F *59 above), the satyrs may also have been compelled to dress up, and transvestism perhaps became a comic theme of the play (for transvestite satyrs on painted vases see the references in Easterling (2007) 287–8). Thus it is very possible that the satyrs were once again cast as slaves, like Heracles, this time in Omphale's household, and destined as so often for 'freedom' at play-end, when they might well form again into Dionysus' 'sacred troop' (F 32).

Note

[1] In doubt still is the reality of a satyr-play of about 400 BC ascribed to a Demetrius under the title *Hesione* (*TrGF* I².39 DID B 4, and 189; T. H. Carpenter in Harrison (2005) 222–6, at 225) but increasingly held to be an *Omphale* illustrated in the famous 'Pronomos' vase of that date: see E. Simon, *Arch.Anz.* (1971) 199–206 (*Beiblatt* of *JDAI* 86), *TrGF* I² (1986) 351 and KPS (1999) 562–5; suggested for Sophocles' *Oeneus* by I. C. Storey in Harrison (2005) 205. On this entire question see now O. Taplin, R. Wyles (eds), *The Pronomos Vase and its Context* (Oxford, 2010).

F 17a (P. Oxy. 1611 fr. 2 col. i.124–7)
<HERACLES> We are already riding Boreas' horse out of Pelops' boundaries, Hermes, and our journey nears its end.[2]

[2] Possibly the play's opening lines, making clear the remoteness of the play's setting, typical of satyr plays. 'Boreas' horse': seemingly an allusion to the mares of Erichthonius the son of Dardanus of Troy, which Boreas the North Wind so coveted, that he changed himself into a stallion and sired twelve colts upon them (Homer, *Iliad* 20.219–25). They could run across the tops of cornfields and over the sea (226–9), so that Heracles might ride one easily from the Peloponnese to Lydia (while Hermes would 'fly' unmounted) – credibly enough in myth if the horse's father was himself a wind. This explanation by Lloyd-Jones (1990) 385–6 is followed by Leurini (1981) and Lehnus (1984), who have made it clear that 'Pelops' boundaries' are therefore not of those lands in Phrygia-Lydia itself with which he is credited by some authors, *e.g.* Pindar, *Olympians* 1.24. That Heracles and Hermes started their flight from the Peloponnese is strongly implied by the localities in F 18 and 19, successively eastward in direction; cf. n. 4 on F 19.

F 18

<ΕΡΜΗΣ?>   Εὐβοῖδα μὲν γῆν λεπτὸς Εὐρίπου κλύδων
                  †Βοιωτίας ἀκτῆς ἐχώρισεν ἐκτέμνων
                  πρὸς Κρῆτα πορθμόν†

Strabo 1.3.19
1 <ΕΡΜΗΣ?> von Blumenthal

F 19

                  σπίλον Παρνασσίαν

Hesychius σ 1515 Hansen

F 20

<ΟΜΦΑΛΗ>   ἴτ᾽ ἐκφορεῖτε, παρθένοι, κύπελλα καὶ μεσομφάλους ...

Athenaeus 11.501f
<ΟΜΦΑΛΗ> von Blumenthal

F 21

<ΗΡ.>   ἐνιαυσίαν γὰρ δεῖ με τὴν ὁρτὴν ἄγειν.

Athenaeus 6.258f

F 18 (Strabo 1.3.19)

<HERMES?>   The gentle billowing of Euripus †separates† Euboea's land †from the shore of Boeotia, cutting it off in the direction of the Cretan crossing.†[3]

[3] The text is badly corrupt, and still without convincing emendation or interpretation. The description may be part of a narrative of Hermes' and Heracles' journey eastward to Lydia (see also F 19). Mention of Euboea suggests an allusion to Oechalia on the island, the home of Eurytus whose son Iphitus Heracles had killed; for the strait of Euripus see also Aeschylus, *Glaucus the Sea-god*, introductory discussion, at start.

F 19 (Hesychius σ 1515 Hansen)
                    crag of Parnassus[4]

[4] Parnassus would logically have preceded mention of Boeotia in any account of the journey to Lydia, since Parnassus lay to the west of it.

F 20–30 describe feasting, drinking, music-making and dancing in which Heracles is prominent, no doubt with the satyrs in attendance; and in which there may be an element of cross-dressing (see F 24, 25 and 59).

F 20 (Athenaeus 11.501f)

<OMPHALE>   Go, you girls, bring out beakers and (bowls) with central bosses ...[5]

[5] 'Central bosses': raised inside a vessel; the description does not necessarily imply bowls of metal rather than pottery. 'bosses' translates Greek *omphal-* ('navel'); the part-word here is taken by Maitland (2007) 277 as (Ion's) playful allusion to the queen's name; cf. Loraux (1990) 25 n. 17.

The metre of this line is iambic tetrameter, which suggests a lively scene: see n. 54 on Sophocles, *Trackers* F 314.298–327.

For the 'girls' see also n. 7 on F 22 below.

F 21 (Athenaeus 6.258f)

<HER.>   For I must keep the festival all year long.[6]

[6] Cf. introductory discussion and esp. Soph. *Women of Trachis* 252–3, 'Heracles after being sold to the barbarian Omphale completed a year'; but Herodorus F 26.1 Müller in Scholia to Soph. *Trach.* 253 puts the period at three years. Easterling (2007) 286 notes the irony that Heracles, Doric hero *par excellence*, uses the Ionic ὁρτήν instead of ἑορτήν ('festival') as if he is adopting the local dialect; see also n. 9 on F 24.

F 22

<OM.>

ἀλλ᾽ εἶα, Λυδαὶ ψάλτριαι, παλαιθέτων
ὕμνων ἀοιδοί, τὸν ξένον κοσμήσατε.

Athenaeus 14.634e

F 23

<OM.>

Λυδός τε μάγαδις αὐλὸς ἡγείσθω βοῆς.

Athenaeus 14.634c; Hesychius μ 3 Latte cites the words μαγάδης (*sic*) αὐλός from the play
{Λύδος} ... τε μάγαδις Λύδος ἡγείσθω βοῆς M. L. West, *BICS* 30 (1986) 79.

F 24

βακκάρις δὲ καὶ μύρα
καὶ Σαρδιανὸν κόσμον εἰδέναι χροὸς
ἄμεινον ἢ τὸν Πέλοπος ἐν νήσῳ τρόπον.

Athenaeus 15.690b

F 25

καὶ τὴν μέλαιναν στίμμιν ὀμματογράφον

Aristophanes of Byzantium fr. 23 Slater

F 26

οἶνος οὐκ ἔνι
ἐν τῷ σκύφει

Athenaeus 11.498e

F 22 (Athenaeus 14.634e)

<OM.>   Come on there, women-harpists of Lydia, singers of anciently made odes: honour our guest![7]

[7] Like F 20, possibly addressed to the chorus of satyrs dressed as women-musicians: see introductory discussion. Omphale may be pandering to Heracles' sensual appetites (see on Eur. *Syleus* F 688, 691), just as in Ar. *Frogs* 502–18 Dionysus' servant Xanthias, disguised as Heracles, is lured by a 'hostess'.

F 23 (Athenaeus 14.634c)

<OM.>   ... and let the Lydian *magadis* pipe lead with its voice![8]

[8] Athenaeus names alternative musical authorities, whether the *magadis* was a blown or plucked instrument, and whether the name applied to both; its origin in Lydia was also disputed. These insoluble questions are reviewed by West (1992) 72–3, cf. Maitland (2007) 272–3, with bibl.; Kaimio (2001) 47 favoured a harp, noting F 22. West had already suggested that 'pipe' was an error in the Greek for 'Lydian' (the words are visually alike), and that 'Lydian' itself was an intrusion: if so, West argued, Athenaeus was employing an incorrect and empty 'reference', originally 'let the Lydian *magadis* lead ...'

F 24 (Athenaeus 15.690b)

It is better to know perfumed salves and myrrh, and Sardian cosmetics for the skin, than the way of the Peloponnese.[9]

[9] That is, total avoidance of all pampering, Spartan austerity being notorious; Lydian effeminacy, such as Omphale would typify, was proverbial, *e.g.* Xenophanes 21 B 3.1 DK; Aesch. *Persians* 41–2 and scholia. For 'perfumed salves' see Achaeus, *Aethon* F 10 below. In the Greek the plural of 'salves' is an Ionian-'Lydian' word-form, while in F 25 'mascara' is a loan-word from Egypt (cf. A. López Eire in Sommerstein (2003) 389–90): Ion is using evocative exoticisms.

The fragment appeals to reconstructors who think that Omphale may have compelled Heracles to wear female dress: cf. F *59 and n. 18.

F 25 (Aristophanes of Byzantium fr. 23 Slater)

... and black mascara to line the eyes ...

F 26 (Athenaeus 11.498e)

There is no wine in the cup.[10]

[10] Possibly a complaint by Heracles, cf. Polyphemus' boorish demands for more wine as he drains one cup after another (*Cyc.* 556, 558); see also the next note. The satyrs may also be waiting on Heracles here, and like Silenus in the same passage of *Cyc.*, helping themselves to the wine behind his back.

F 27

ἔσπεισας· ἀλλὰ πῖθι Πακτωλοῦ ῥοάς.

Anecdota Oxoniensia 2.250.8 Cramer without attribution; πῖθι ... ῥοάς *Etymologicum Magnum* 671.41 Gaisford with attribution

F 28

ἐξανθρακώσας πυθμέν' εὔκηλον δρυός

Etymologicum Magnum 392.12 Gaisford, cf. Photius ε 2224 Theodoridis

F 29

ὑπὸ δὲ τῆς εὐφημίας
κατέπινε καὶ τὰ κᾶλα καὶ τοὺς ἄνθρακας.

Athenaeus 10.411b

F *30

εἶχεν ... τοὺς ὀδόντας ... τριστοίχους Ἡρακλῆς

Pollux 2.95, whence Tzetzes, *Chiliades* 3.957

F 31

ἐρρωπίζομεν

Hesychius ε 6050 Latte

F 27 (*Anecdota Oxoniensia* 2.250.8 Cramer and *Etymologicum Magnum* 671.41 Gaisford)

> You poured a libation – but you are to drink stream-water from Pactolus![11]

[11] 'Pactolus': a Lydian river. Normally at a feast wine would first be poured in libation, then drunk mixed with water. For this practice (unpopular with satyrs: Achaeus, *Aethon* F 9; Lycophron, *Menedemus* F 2–3), cf. *Cyc.*149 and n.; see Voelke (2001) 194–6. This fragment may be part of a scene in which Heracles, although no stranger to wine, is prepared for a symposium of sorts – including possible instructions about cross-dressing (see F 24 and 25); cf. *Cyc.* (519–75) when Odysseus and Silenus induct the oafish Polyphemus into the rites of sympotic etiquette (esp. 541–3, 558–9, 561–3, *etc.*; cf. also Achaeus F 17). I. Lada-Richards, *Initiating Dionysus* (Oxford 1999) 195–7 suggests that Heracles is becoming 'civilised' in Lydian terms in learning the local sympotic norms; see above on F 21.

F 28 (*Etymologicum Magnum* 392.12 Gaisford, cf. Photius ε 2224 Theodoridis)

> ... having reduced the easily burnt stump of an oak to cinders ...[12]

[12] Possibly to eat it: see Heracles in F 29 and F 30. Both sources of the fragment offer an alternative translation, 'easily split'.

F 29 (Athenaeus 10.411b)

> During the reverent silence (Heracles) continued to gulp down the logs and the cinders.[13]

[13] In Eur. *Alcestis* 747–72, esp. 751–2, 761–4, Heracles' gluttony similarly offends propriety, but during mourning. His greed here is gross, sub-human: see note on F 30.

F *30 (Pollux 2.95, a testimony)

> Heracles has his teeth in three rows.[14]

[14] An enormity borrowed from Homer's description of the Scylla, *Odyssey* 12.91. The 'fragment' is a paraphrase, not a quotation.

F 31 (Hesychius ε 6050 Latte)

> We were dealing in petty wares ...[15]

[15] Spoken by Silenus or the satyrs: they were mercenary and 'on the make', perhaps portrayed like the pimping satyrs in Euripides' *Sciron* F 675 and 676; see the last paragraph of our introductory discussion here. Silenus similarly shows avarice at *e.g. Cyc.* 138 (but see 161, 192); Soph. *Trackers* F 314.51–6.

F 32

θίασος

Harpocration θ 25 Keaney

F 33

Ἴων ἐν Ὀμφάλῃ (τοὺς) βαρβάρους ... χελιδόνας ἀρσενικῶς φησιν.

Scholia to Aristophanes, *Birds* 1680

F *59

βραχὺν λίνου κύπασσιν ἐς μηρὸν μέσον
ἐσταλμένος

Pollux 7.60; first attributed to the play by Meineke

F 32 (Harpocration θ 25 Keaney)
... sacred troop ...[16]

[16] The satyr-chorus might well form into Dionysus' troop, if as in other plays they are liberated at the end – but since Harpocration states that Ion uses the word of 'every gathering', it may have no specific reference here.

F 33 (Scholia to Aristophanes, *Birds* 1680, a testimony)
Ion in *Omphale* uses 'swallows' in the masculine gender of non-Greeks.[17]

[17] This is a scholar's gloss. Ion is describing how non-Greeks speak, sounding like swallows, a comparison as old as Aesch. *Ag*.1050.

F *59 (Pollux 7.60)
... (*a man*) dressed in a short linen garment reaching mid-thigh ...[18]

[18] Taken by some to be Heracles made by Omphale to dress as a woman, and attributed by them to the play, because the Greek word for 'garment' here is often applied to a female 'frock' (cf. the cosmetics of F 24, F 25); and (Snell) when worn by a tall male it would reach only to mid-thigh – but the fragment's source names only Ion, not this play. Others translate with 'tunic', and take Heracles to be clad simply as a slave: see introductory discussion.

ACHAEUS I

(born before 480?, died after 405 BC)

Selected fragments

TrGF 1².115–28 (20 F 1–[56]), 347–8, cf. 5.1106.
Texts etc. Gauly (1991) 80–9, 277–80; J. Schloemann, R. Krumeich, N. Pechstein in KPS 490–545; Cipolla (2003) 142–223.
Discussions. Sutton (1980) 69–74; Voelke (2001) 206–7.

We include some of the scrappy fragments of Achaeus because antiquity ranked him highly among dramatists (*TrGF* 1².53–4, CAT A 2 and 3); the learned Menedemus in the 3rd century (the subject of Lycophron's satyr-play, below) put Achaeus second only to Aeschylus as a poet of satyr-drama (*TrGF* 1².115 T 6, Diogenes Laertius 2.133). Although Achaeus' fragments are brief, and we possess so little firm information about their source-plays, we select those which exemplify some recurrent motifs and topics of satyr-drama; see, for athletics, *The Games* F 3, 4; eating, *Aethon* F 6–8, *Alcmeon* F 12, 13, *Hephaestus* F 17; drinking *Aethon* F 9, *Hephaestus* F 17, *Linus* F 26, *Omphale* F 33; dress and bodily ornament *Aethon* F 10; sex *Aethon* F 6, *Linus* F 26, *Fates* F 28. For some other plays of Achaeus see the Appendix.

F 3

<A> πότερα θεωροῖς εἴτ᾽ ἀγωνισταῖς λέγεις;
<B> πόλλ᾽ ἐσθίουσιν, ὡς ἐπασκούντων τρόπος.
<A> ποδαποὶ γάρ εἰσιν οἱ ξένοι; <B> Βοιώτιοι.

Athenaeus 10.417f

F *4

γυμνοὶ γὰρ †ὤθουν† φαιδίμους βραχίονας
ἥβῃ σφριγῶντες ἐμπορεύονται, νέῳ
στίλβοντες ἄνθει καρτερὰς ἐπωμίδας·
ἄδην δ᾽ ἐλαίου στέρνα καὶ πλευρῶν κύτος
χρίουσιν ὡς ἔχοντες οἴκοθεν τρυφήν.   (5)

Athenaeus 10.414d
4 πλευρῶν Emper: ποδῶν Athenaeus

The Games (*AΘΛA* or *AΘΛOI*, *Ludi*)

The plot of the play is wholly unknown, but F 3 suggests that the satyrs may have been aspirant competitors like those in Aeschylus' *Sacred Delegates* (above). If they were the 'Boeotians' of F 3.3, they would be cast as crude rustics (the Athenians' unkind image of that people). Athenaeus cites the fragment to illustrate the Boeotians' notorious gluttony; it is inferred that the play had a setting in Boeotia/Thebes, a chief site of Dionysus' cult. F 3 and F 4 both mock the gluttony and the arrogance of athletes.

F 3 (Athenaeus 10.417f)

<A>   Do you mean (*to?*) spectators or competitors?[1]
<B>   (*To?*) great eaters, as is the way of those in training.[2]
<A>   So where are the strangers from? <B> They're Boeotians.

[1]   This seems the likely meaning of the two nouns, *i.e.* categories of persons attending the Games, not '(the) spectators (watching the play)' and 'actors'; but as in Aeschylus, *Sacred Delegates* 'spectators' may hint an official, religious delegation to the games: see n. 1 on that play; P. Cipolla, *RFIC* 126 (1998) 259–67 and (2003) 172.

In vv. 1–2 the loss of the preceding lines makes the point of '(*to?*: dative case)' irrecoverable.
[2]   Another instance of athletes presented as gluttons, for which see n. 5 on Euripides, *Autolycus A* F 282; cf. Voelke (2001) 267–8.

F *4 (Athenaeus 10.414d)

                   Stripped off, they †were thrusting forward†(?) gleaming arms,
                   bursting with their prime as they make their entry, mighty
                   shoulders glistening in youth's bloom. Their torsos and hollowed
                   trunks are anointed with plenty of oil, such is the luxury they
                   have (*brought*) with them from their homes.[3]

[3]   Young athletes a superb sight Pindar, *Olympians* 8.19, 10.99–104, *etc.*: Voelke (2001) 271 n. 30. Even the critical speaker in Eur. *Autolycus A* F 282.10 concedes that athletes are 'in their prime ... glorious'.

In v. 1 'were thrusting forward' is a very insecure translation – athletes marching, perhaps? The text of 1–2 is suspect to most editors because of discrepant tenses and faulty syntax.

In v. 4 'trunks' (Emper) seems the most likely emendation of impossible 'feet', and gains support from the description of a veteran pancratiast at Ar. *Wasps* 1192–4 'already old and greying, but with a very deep chest (πλευρά), and the flanks (λαγών) of a Heracles ('of a Heracles' is Starkie's emendation: 'and hands and flanks' mss.), and a splendid torso (θώραξ)'; 'hollowed' is a metaphor from a rounded container, here suggesting a tautly muscled abdomen beneath a bulging chest.

Aethon (*ΑΙΘΩΝ*)

Athenaeus 10.416b records 'Aethon' ('Blazing, Blazer') as a by-name of Erysichthon, a grandson of Poseidon: it was given to him because of his 'insatiable (i.e. *burning*) hunger' (this is Achaeus F **5a); cf. Hesiod F 43a.5–6 M-W (below). This man had destroyed a grove sacred to Demeter, and she punished him by inflicting perpetual hunger upon him; so great did it become that he was forced to sell his daughter Mestra into prostitution to pay for his appetite, and in the end he died from eating his own flesh. According to Ovid, *Metamorphoses* 8.738–878 and the scholion on Lycophron, *Alexandra* 1393, Mestra is able to change shape (see F 8 below) and to return to her father to be resold to a new buyer; for the myth generally

---

F 6

> ... ἐν κενῇ γὰρ γαστρὶ τῶν καλῶν ἔρως
> οὐκ ἔστι· πεινῶσιν γὰρ ἡ Κύπρις πικρά.

Athenaeus 6.270b

F 7

> κεκερματίσθω δ' ἄλλα μοι παροψίδων
> κάθεφθα καὶ κνισηρὰ παραφλογίσματα.

Athenaeus 9.368a

F 8

>   πεταλίδων δέ τοι συῶν
> <   > μορφαῖς ταῖσδε πόλλ' ἐπάϊον.

Athenaeus 9.376a
2 μορφαῖς (at least) deemed corrupt by Snell

see Gantz (1993) 68–9, and on Ovid Z. P. Ambrose in Harrison (2005) 31–3. Hesiod's version seems to have Sisyphus as one of the buyers, who, having been cheated, remonstrates with Erysichthon only to have an arbitration go against him (Hes. F 43a.18–43 M-W: see I. Rutherford in R. Hunter (ed.), *The Hesiodic Catalogue of Women: Constructions and Reconstructions* (Cambridge, 2005) 103–11 (*Aethon* at 111)). As Sutton (1980) 70 notes, the general story of Erysichthon is grim, but the episode with Sisyphus seems to present a lighter aspect of the tale whereby the famous satyric trickster gets his come-uppance; nothing of this, however, is suggested in Achaeus' meagre fragments. It would nevertheless provide a further apt theme for satyr-drama (for cheating cf. especially Euripides' *Autolycus B* with its theme of shape-shifting, T iv); for buying sex, cf. his *Sciron* F 675 and 676).

F 6 (Athenaeus 6.270b)

> ... for there is no desire for beauty on an empty belly: Cypris is cruel to the starving![4]

[4] Most likely spoken by Erysichthon. Cf. Euripides F 895 'Cypris exists upon plenty, not in a starving man'; a widely attested attested saying; cf. Achaeus, *Cycnus* F 25 'To a hungry man bread is more precious than gold and ivory.' While gluttony is a frequent theme of satyric drama (*e.g.* Eur. *Autolycus A* F 282, *Syleus* F 691, Ion *Omphale*, esp. F 20, 21, 26–30), here the focus is darker, on the pangs of hunger itself.

F 7 (Athenaeus 9.368a)

> Let me have other well-minced and boiled side-dishes, and savoury-smelling roasts![5]

[5] See above on F 6.

F 8 (Athenaeus 9.376a)

> Indeed I have heard much of fully-grown sheep ... with(?) these forms.[5a]

[5a] 'fully grown', lit. 'with (horns) spread wide'. The Greek dative '(with) forms' has no syntax in the defective text, and the word itself may be corrupt; but Snell suggests a possible reference to Mestra's changes of shape alluded to in the Scholion of Lycophron, *Alexandra* 1393 (cited in the introductory discussion), which writes of Mestra 'changing into every kind of animal'.

F 9

<A>　　　　　　μῶν Ἀχελῷος οὑγκεκραμένος πολύς;
<B>　　　　　　ἀλλ' οὐδὲ λεῖξαι τοῦδε τῷ γένει θέμις.
<A>　　　　　　καλῶς μὲν οὖν ἂν ἐγχέοις Σκύθῃ πιεῖν.

Athenaeus 10.427c
1 οὑγκεκραμένος West: ἦν κεκραμένος Athenaeus
3 ἂν ἐγχέοις Σκύθῃ Meineke (-οις Snell: -αις Meineke): ἄγειν σκύθη Athenaeus

F 10

... βακκάρει χρισθέντα καὶ ψυκτηρίοις
πτεροῖς ἀναστήσαντα προσθίαν τρίχα ...

Athenaeus 15.690b

F 11

ΣΑΤΥΡΟΙ　　　χαῖρ' ὦ Χάρων, χαῖρ' ὦ Χάρων, χαῖρ' ὦ Χάρων.
　　　　　　　　ἦ που σφόδρα θυμοῖ;

Scholia on Aristophanes, *Frogs* 184

F 9 (Athenaeus 10.427c)

<A>   The mixed-in river-water isn't much, is it?

<B>   Our sort aren't permitted even a lick of that!

<A>   Then you'd do well to pour it for a Scythian to drink![5]

[5] An exchange between satyrs, discontented (so Athenaeus) with wine watered in the way most Greeks drank it – as Scythians would be, who drank it undiluted (Herodotus 6.84.3), cf. *Cyc.* 558 and n., Ion, *Omphale* F 27 and n. 11, Lycophron, *Menedemus* F 2–3: see Voelke (2001) 194–6, 198–200 etc. In v. 3 a corrupt text has been emended to make this implication clear.

In v. 1 'river-water' translates the name of a major river, the Achelous (see on Soph. *Oeneus* F 1130); it was used in metonymy for any pure water (see Garvie on Aesch. *Pers.*868). Also in v. 1: KPS 500 n. 21 suggests that West's conjecture is apter to drinking already begun than Athenaeus' 'There wasn't much river-water mixed in, was there?'

F 10 (Athenaeus 15.690b)

              ... (*a male*) anointed with perfumed salve, his hair above his forehead lifted by cooling fans.[6]

[6] A satyr masquerading as a luxurious diner?

F 11 (Scholia on Aristophanes, *Frogs* 184)

SATYRS   Greetings, Charon! Greetings, Charon! Greetings, Charon! You're of course very angry?[7]

[7] A pun at the expense of the ferryman of the dead, whose perpetual bad temper (*e.g.* Aristophanes, *Frogs* 188–200) is at odds with his ironically euphemistic name 'Happy'. Achaeus' tripling of the greeting was mocked by Aristophanes at *Frogs* 184, although such threefold salutation of a corpse was customary, *Frogs* 1176, cf. Homer, *Odyssey* 9.65.

Alcmeon (ΑΛΚΜΑΙΩΝ)

The naming of Delphi in the source for F 12 and 13 makes it almost certain that the play travestied Alcmeon's visit to Apollo's temple there to obtain purification for killing his mother Eriphyle to avenge his father Amphiaraus (Gantz (1993) 522–7); this story was a very popular tragic plot, but visible to us only from Euripides' fragmentary *Alcmeon in Psophis*.

F 12
ΣΑΤΥΡΟΙ　　καρυκκοποιοὺς προσβλέπων βδελύσσομαι
　　　　　　* * *

F 13

　　　　τίς ὑποκεκρυμμένος μένει,
　　　　†σαραβάκων† κοπίδων συνομώνυμε;

Athenaeus 4.173d

F 12 (Athenaeus 4.173d)

SATYRS   I am revolted when I watch (*the Delphians*) making blood-sauces
                    ...[8]

* * *

F 13 (also Athenaeus 7.173d)
          ... Who stays hidden, you name-sake of dirty(?) choppers?[9]

[8]   That is, they scavenge from the shambles of 'sacrifices and feasts' (Athenaeus, who cites the two fragments as evidence for the gluttony and greed of the Delphians). Clearly feasting was a theme of the play, with the satyrs either hopeful or frustrated participants.

  The verse comes probably from a stichomythic exchange.

[9]   Probably a play upon the name Machaereus ('Chopperman'), possibly a historical person, possibly one invented to reflect the disproportionate time which the Delphians gave to feasts and sacrifices (to increase local revenues from visitors); the 'Delphic chopper' became proverbial, Macarius III.22 (*CPG* II.155).

  The adjective translated 'dirty' has a rare spelling (but cf. Herodian I.139.2 Lentz) and is probably unmetrical (the two verses appear to be lyric); and it may be a noun used adjectivally, conveying an obscene insult, for other forms are glossed with 'a woman's *pudendum*', *e.g.* Hesychius σ 191 Hansen, Photius II. 495.1 (cf. 500.5) and 500.2 Porson, attesting them at Telecleides F 70 *PCG* and *Adespota* F 536 PCG, cf. Herodian I. 346.30 Lentz.

  We lack a dramatic context to explain 'Who stays hidden?'.

Hephaestus (ΗΦΑΙΣΤΟΣ)

Hephaestus was a son of Hera (although not certainly also of Hera's husband Zeus; cf. Hesiod, *Theogony* 927–9 who says that Hera conceived the god on her own as a likely response to the birth of Athena from the head of Zeus). In apparent disgust with his lameness, however, she hurled him from Olympus (Homer, *Iliad* 18.395–7 – but at 1.589–91 it is Zeus who threw him – although this act may have been poetic invention to 'aetiologize' the lameness). There was a much-told and much-painted incident where this artificer-god retaliated upon Hera by tricking her with the gift of a chair in which when she sat she was held immobile (*e.g. Homeric Hymn to Dionysus* (C) 5–9 West); Hephaestus then disappeared. She was freed only when Dionysus found him and made him drunk (cf. F 17 below), and so was able to bring him back to Olympus (Gantz (1993) 75–6) to release Hera; for

---

F 17

<ΔΙΟΝΥΣΟΣ> θοίνῃ σε πρῶτον τέρψομεν· πάρεστι δέ.
<ΗΦΑΙΣΤΟΣ> τὸ δεύτερον <δὲ> τῷ με κηλήσεις τρόπῳ;
<ΔΙ.>   μύρῳ σε χρίσω πάμπαν εὐόσμῳ δέμας.
<ΗΦ.>   ὕδωρ δὲ νίψαι χεῖρας οὐ πρόσθεν δίδως;
<ΔΙ.>   ἡνίκα τράπεζά γ' ἐκποδὼν ἀπαίρεται.   (5)

Athenaeus 14.641d
<ΔΙΟΝΥΣΟΣ> and <ΗΦΑΙΣΤΟΣ> Welcker
1 θοίνῃ σε Casaubon: θοίνην δὲ Athenaeus
2 <δὲ> Casaubon
5 ἡνίκα Kaibel: ναί· Athenaeus

painted vases showing their return see *TrGF* 2.10, on *Adespota* F 3f; *LIMC* IV.1.637–45 'Hephaistos' nos 103–72, and KPS 519–21 (with bibl.); with satyrs KPS figs 28a (= *LIMC* 'Hephaistos' no. 171b) and 28b (not in *LIMC*?). In fact, the earliest known depiction of satyrs (named as 'Silenoi') in art is of this scene on the famous Attic volute-krater called the 'François Vase' of *c.* 570 BC (*LIMC* IV.1.638 'Hephaistos' no. 114 = VIII.1.1113 'Silenoi' no. 22 = KPS fig. 1a).

This tale afforded excellent material for a satyr-play (cf. Sutton (1980) 70–1); and Hephaestus had been a comic figure since archaic poetry (at *Iliad* 1.599–600 his ungainliness is mocked), as well as a trickster (Alcaeus F 349 L-P; Pindar F 283) and a cuckold avenged (*Odyssey* 8.266–358, with a virtually satyric exchange between Apollo and Hermes at 335–42).

The one fragment of the play shows Dionysus preparing the feast and drinking-party (Voelke (2001) 206–7).

F 17 (Athenaeus 14.641d)

<DIONYSUS>   First we will delight you with a feast. It's ready.

<HEPHAESTUS>   And how will you entice me next?

<DI.>   I'll anoint you all over your body with fragrant myrrh.

<HE.>   But aren't you giving me water beforehand to wash my hands?

<DI.>   When the table is moved out of the way, yes.[10]   (5)

[10] The Greeks washed their hands both before and after a formal meal, the second time to purify themselves for libations to the gods, as vv. 4–5 imply: see *e.g.* Ar. *Wasps* 1216–17 and the many quotations in Athenaeus 9.408b–9f. But Hephaestus must eat with dirty ones, and this hints his offence in the gods' eyes. Such scenes would accommodate satyrs' mischief very well. Cf. *Cyc.* 519–75 and Ion, *Omphale* F 21–7 for similar incidents of managing a guest before eating and drinking.

Linus (ΛΙΝΟΣ)

Linus, a son of Apollo, was appointed to teach the boy Heracles music (or his letters: Theocritus 24.105); he struck Heracles as punishment for his poor learning, and the boy struck back in anger, his abnormal strength killing Linus. The incident was not rare in 5th century Attic vase-painting: *LIMC* IV.1.833 'Herakles' nos 1666 Heracles with Linus and 1667–73 with Heracles killing him, esp. 1671. It formed presumably the plot of Achaeus' play (or at least its background: would Linus' death have been shown?), and was later told in Diodorus 3.67.2 and [Apollod.] 2.4.9: see Gantz (1993) 379.

F 26 (below) suggests boisterous drinking; the 'smashing' begins during a game of *kottabos*: full description in F. Lissarague, *The Aesthetics of the Greek Banquet*, trans. A. Szegedy-Maszak (Princeton, 1990) 80–6 with figs 67–71 and in Olson's commentary on Aristophanes, *Peace* 343; cf. n. 28 on Sophocles, *Inachus* F 277. The satyrs toss drops of wine at a target, aiming to score both a hit and in consequence a success with the 'lover' they name

---

F 26

<ΗΡΑΚΛΗΣ>   ῥιπτοῦντες ἐκβάλλοντες ἀγνύντες, τί μ' οὐ
λέγοντες· ὦ κάλλιστον Ἡρακλεί<διον> ...
λάταξ ...

Athenaeus 15.668a
2 Ἡρακλεί<διον> Methner

as they throw. Here he is the handsome young Heracles, whom they address as 'little darling' (satyrs similarly name him with a diminutive in *Adespota* F 590, a lexicographic fragment).

Achaeus' rowdy scene seems to have been prompted by one in Aeschylus: in his *Bone-Gatherers* (*Ostologoi*; probably a tragedy: see our Appendix), F 179 has Eurymachus, the most violent of Penelope's suitors in the *Odyssey*, aiming at the head of the disguised Odysseus, first with wine, as if in the game of *kottabos* (he aims a wine-jug in Homer, *Odyssey* 18.396–7), then with a chamber-pot which breaks and splashes its odorous contents over him (F 180). Aeschylus' incident is reflected verbally in Sophocles' *Fellow-Diners* (*Syndeipnoi*) F 565 (a satyr-play for Voelke (2001) 349–53, but a tragedy for Sommerstein (2006) 124–7). In Euripides' tragedy *Oeneus* F 562 an old man's bald head is the target; in Sophocles' satyric *Salmoneus* F 537 it is the head of a bronze statue.

(Discussions of the play: Gantz (1993) 379; Voelke (2001) 203–4 (F 26), 349–53. Alexis' mid-4th Century comedy *Linus* is the only other play known with this title.)

F 26 (Athenaeus 15.668a)
\<HERACLES\>   ... (satyrs) hurling, letting fall, smashing – what did they not say
           of me? 'O most handsome, darling little Heracles ... (*my?*) drop
           ...!'[11]

[11]   The satyrs variously throw wine or break cups (?) accidentally or deliberately. Satyrs elsewhere display homoerotic lust: for Heracles also in Sophocles F 756 (see introductory discussion on his *Oeneus*, n. 2); for Achilles in his *Lovers of Achilles* (above); cf. n. on *Cyc.* 498. The homoerotic nuances of the game of *kottabos* are elegantly and humorously depicted on the fresco of *c.* 470 BC known as 'The Tomb of the Diver' (Museo Nazionale, Paestum: see *e.g.* J. G. Pedley, *Paestum* (1990) 89–94 and pls 54–5). Silenus' address to Polyphemus at *Cyc.* 266 ὦ κάλλιστον, ὦ Κυκλώπιον is phrased like F 26.2, but is not erotic.

Athenaeus' quotation is damaged at the end of v. 2 and defective in 3, the word 'drop' being without syntax, unless it begins the main clause after the vocative.

The Fates *(MOIRAI)*

The content and plot of this play are totally unknown.

F 28

<ΣΙΛΗΝΟΣ ?> βαβαὶ βαβαί, βήσομαι γυναῖκας.

Hesychius v 722 Latte

Omphale *(ΟΜΦΑΛΗ)*

In default of all evidence for the plot, it is generally assumed that Achaeus dramatised essentially the same story as did Ion of Chios (cf. Sutton (1980) 72–3): see the introductory discussion on Ion's play.

F 33

ΣΑΤΥΡΟΙ   ὁ δὲ σκύφος με τοῦ θεοῦ καλεῖ πάλαι
τὸ γράμμα φαίνων· δέλτ᾽, ἰῶτα καὶ τρίτον
οὗ, νῦ τό τ᾽ ὗ πάρεστι, κοὐκ ἀπουσίαν
ἐκ τοὐπέκεινα σὰν τό τ᾽ οὗ κηρύσσετον.

Athenaeus 11.466e; 1 also 11.498d

F 34

ἡλίσκετ᾽ ἆρα καὶ πρὸς ἀσθενῶν ταχὺς
καὶ πρὸς χελώνης αἰετὸς βραχεῖ χρόνῳ.

(Antigonus of Carystus p. 97 Wilamowitz in) Diogenes Laertius 2.133

F 28 (Hesychius v 722 Latte)

\<SILENUS?\>   Hurrah, hurrah! I'll be mounting women![12]

[12]   Achaeus F 52 (also cited by Hesychius, with no play named) describes Silenus as 'mounter of nymphs': for such congress cf. Aesch. *Prometheus the Fire-Kindler* F 204b.4–8 and Soph. *Oeneus* F 1130.8 (both in this volume). Silenus' exclamation is consistent with his lecherous fantasies elsewhere: Eur. *Cyc.* 169–71, Aesch. *Net-Fishers* F 47a.60–8, Soph. *Trackers* F 314.154–5. 'Mount' is a metaphor from animals, *e.g.* Plato, *Phaedrus* 250e.

F 33 (Athenaeus 11.466e)

SATYRS   The god's cup has long been inviting me, showing its inscription: 'd', 'i' and thirdly 'o'; 'n' and 'y' are there, and 's' and 'o' following them proclaim their presence.[13]

[13]   The 'Greek' spelling has the god's name in the possessive case, as was usual upon inscribed vessels, that is, as Athenaeus explains, with the case-ending 'ου' written as 'o' (a final 'ς' is not missing). Comparable descriptions of spelling, all of the name Theseus (in the nominative case), are found at Euripides, *Theseus* F 382 and Agathon 39 *Telephus* F 4, both from tragedies; and at Theodectas 72 F 6 (lyric), of unknown genre.

F 34 (Diogenes Laertius 2.133)

Just as the speedy man proves to be overtaken by the weak, so is the eagle by the tortoise, in a short time.[14]

[14]   A favourite quotation of Lycophron's contemporary Menedemus: see our introductory discussion to the name-play below. With v. 1 compare Homer, *Odyssey* 8.329 'the slow man catches the fast.'

CRITIAS (?)

(born after 460?, died 403 BC)

Sisyphus (?) (*ΣΙΣΥΦΟΣ?*)

TrGF I².180–2 (43 F 19), 351; cf. 5.1107–8.

Texts etc.: M. Davies, 'Sisyphus and the Invention of Religion', *BICS* 36 (1989) 16–32; Gauly (1991) 108–9, 120–3, 284; Diggle (1998) 177–9; Pechstein (1998), 319–43 (see also *Discussions*) and in KPS 552–61; Voelke (2001) 358–62; Cipolla (2003) 228–68; Collard and Cropp (2008) II.672–7.

Discussions. U. von Wilamowitz, *Analecta Euripidea* (Berlin, 1875) 161–6 and repeatedly in articles until 1929; Lesky (1983) 396 = (1972) 525–6; A. Dihle, 'Das Satyrspiel *Sisyphus*', *Hermes* 105 (1977) 28–42; D. F. Sutton, 'Critias and Atheism', *CQ* 31 (1981) 33–8; R. Scodel, *The Trojan Trilogy of Euripides* (Göttingen, 1982) 124–8; W. Burkert, *Greek Religion* (trans. J. Raffan, Oxford, 1985) 311–17 ('The Crisis. Sophists and Atheists'), at 314–15; Davies (above); M. Winiarczyk, 'Nochmals das Satyrspiel des Sisyphos', *WS* 100 (1987) 35–45; H. Yunis, 'The debate on undetected crime and an undetected fragment from Euripides' *Sisyphus* (F 1007c N–Sn)', *ZPE* 75 (1988) 39–46 (on v. 11); D. Obbink, *Philodemus on Piety. Part I* (Oxford, 1996) 353–5; Pechstein (1998) 185–92, 289–318; J. Hesk, *Democracy and Deception in Classical Athens* (Cambridge, 2000) 179–88; Cipolla (2003) 225–6, 247–68; E. Kearns, *Ancient Greek Religion* (Oxford, 2010) 36; P. O'Sullivan, 'Sophistic Ethics, Old Atheism and 'Critias' on Religion', *Classical World* 104 (2012) 167–85 (= O'Sullivan 2012b).

For our purposes in this volume the unresolved dispute whether Critias or Euripides was the author of this fragment is not important; it stems from conflicting testimonies and rests upon conflicting interpretations of a badly corrupt text, such that verbal style, metre and 'atheistic' content are claimed or disallowed for either poet.[1] It is however relevant here to state that none of the sources quoting this fragment, in whole or part, attributes it either to a named play or to a satyr-play. That the play was satyric is therefore merely a claim; it was made chiefly because Aëtius (who cites only part of the fragment) attributes the words to the mythical trickster Sisyphus, who would be more suitably at home in satyr drama than tragedy (see our introductory discussions on Aeschylus' *Sisyphus* and Euripides' *Autolycus A* and *B*) – indeed the fragment has been attributed to *Autolycus A*, rather than to Euripides' *Sisyphus*, by Pechstein (1998) 289–318, cf. (1999) 554, 561. For a possible lexical indication of satyric status see n. 12 on 'spot' in v. 39.

We include the fragment for its interest, and as analogous to other extended serious disquisitions which may seem intrusive in the satyric genre but are in fact quite well attested for Euripides at least, *e.g.* the argument between Odysseus and Cyclops about the gods and the laws of hospitality in *Cyc.* 285– 340, esp. 315–40, and about the status of athletes in *Autolycus A* F 282.[2]

Notes

[1] For summaries of the evidence and arguments, with full bibliography, see most recently C. Collard, *Tragedy, Euripides and Euripideans* (Exeter, 2007) 55–68 (revised from an original publ. of 1995) and Collard and Cropp (2008) II.629–35; cf. G. Alvoni, 'Ist Critias fr. 1 Sn.–K. Teil des *Perithous*?', *Hermes* 139 (2011) 120–8. See also n. 5 below.

[2] Readers interested primarily in the 'atheism' may study the 'state of the question' through the 20th century authors listed in *Discussions* above, most of them with full bibliography; see in particular O'Sullivan (2012b), who argues that the fragment's avowedly atheistic stance need not be reducible to an anti-religious one. It is too large a topic for our space; for the general content of the fragment, however, we have supplied limited illustrative matter.

F19

<ΣΙΣΥΦΟΣ>   ἦν χρόνος ὅτ' ἦν ἄτακτος ἀνθρώπων βίος
                 καὶ θηριώδης ἰσχύος θ' ὑπηρέτης,
                 ὅτ' οὐδὲν ἆθλον οὔτε τοῖς ἐσθλοῖσιν ἦν
                 οὔτ' αὖ κόλασμα τοῖς κακοῖς ἐγίγνετο.
                 κἄπειτά μοι δοκοῦσιν ἄνθρωποι νόμους   (5)
                 θέσθαι κολαστάς, ἵνα δίκη τύραννος ᾖ
                 <γένους βροτείου> τήν θ' ὕβριν δούλην ἔχῃ·
                 ἐζημιοῦτο δ' εἴ τις ἐξαμαρτάνοι.

Sextus Empiricus, *Against the Mathematicians* 9.54, attributed to Critias, with no speaker or play named, and noting after v. 40 'his continuation after a few details' with vv. 41–2; 1–2, 17–18, with 3–16 in brief summary, Aëtius, *Doctrines* 1.7, attributed to Euripides' Sisyphus (character-name, not play-name); 33–4, 34 separately, and 35 are also cited in antiquity, 33–4 and 35 with attribution to Euripides.

7 <γένους βροτείου> Grotius
12 <πρῶτον> Enger
13 θεῶν Wecklein: γνῶναι Sextus; δέη Diggle: δὲ ὃς or δεοση Sextus

F 19 (Sextus Empiricus, *Against the Mathematicians* 9.54, attributed to Critias; 1–2, 17–18 Aëtius, *Doctrines* 1–2, 17–18, with 3–16 in brief summary, attributed to Euripides' (character) Sisyphus; other partial quotations, with no attribution, or to Euripides)

<SISYPHUS>   There was a time when the life of humans was disordered, and beast-like and subject to mere strength,[3] when there was no prize for those who were upright, nor again any punishment for wrong-doers. Then, I think, men established laws (5) for purposes of punishment, so that justice might be sovereign (over the human race) and keep wanton outrage in slavery;[4] and if someone did

---

[3] In the 5th century the generally improving condition of human life was gradually rationalised as man's own achievement, sometimes displacing archaic views of it as the gift of the gods: see *e.g.* Guthrie (1969) 60–84, esp. 60–3, and A. J. Podlecki, *Aeschylus. Prometheus Bound* (Oxford, 2005) 16–27 (bibl.); the chief passages are Soph. *Antigone* 332–70 (men's own material and cultural advance, including city-law); *Prometheus Bound* 442–506 (where, however, the Titan demi-god Prometheus still claims to be the first general benefactor of humanity); Eur. *Suppliants* 196–215 (development from bestial chaos to cultured plenty still seen as god's gift); Plato, *Protagoras* 322a–d (Plato recalls the famous sophist of the later 5th century: gods already existed, men had practical but not political skill and so were subject to violence; law came as Zeus' gift). Often an anonymous individual is credited as the 'first inventor' of this or that 'advance', as here in vv. 12–13; cf. esp. Palamedes, the inventor of writing and other skills which helped the Greeks at Troy (Eur. *Palamedes* F 578) and who was therefore the facilitator of written law (Gorgias 82 B 11a.30 DK): see next n. Our fragment seems to operate on many levels: to some it seems to pass from congratulation (1–8) through disillusion (9–11) to sardonism or even cynicism (11–15, 15–6, 25–8); but, as has also been recognised, the invention of religion (vv. 11ff.) comes across as a 'benign swindle that produced the advance of human culture': thus, for instance, Sutton (1980) 38. For a full analysis of the fragment's presentation of religion as a socially useful fiction, see O'Sullivan (2012b).

[4] Codification (and publication) of the law, for 'equal' justice: see *e.g.* Guthrie (1969) 117–31; T. C. W. Stinton in C. Collard, *Euripides Supplices* (Groningen, 1975) II.440–2; M. Gagarin, *Early Greek Law* (Berkeley, 1986) 51–2 and *Writing Greek Law* (Cambridge, 2008). 'so that justice might be sovereign': lit. '... be a tyrant', *i.e.* have absolute power. The metaphor, which is not rare in 'rhetorical' emphasis, seems not to be pejorative here, since Critias(?) says that laws are to 'keep wanton outrage in slavery' (v. 7); cf. persuasion ruefully acknowledged as man's only sovereign Eur. *Hec.* 816, Love *Hipp.* 538, *Andromeda* F 136 – but at Plato, *Protagoras* 337d the sophist Hippias condemns law as a tyrant that builds artificial barriers between men who are akin by nature. The more common metaphor 'king' (βασιλεύς) is regularly approving, moreover, or at least neutral, after Pindar's F 169a.1–3 'law, the king of all mortals and immortals, guides them'; and *e.g.* the sophistic Anonymus Iamblichi says that law and justice 'rule as a king' as an agent of civilisation, 89.6.1 DK. See also nn. 5 and 6 below.

ἔπειτ' ἐπειδὴ τἀμφανῆ μὲν οἱ νόμοι
ἀπεῖργον αὐτοὺς ἔργα μὴ πράσσειν βίᾳ,   (10)
λάθρᾳ δ' ἔπρασσον, τηνικαῦτά μοι δοκεῖ
<πρῶτον> πυκνός τις καὶ σοφὸς γνώμην ἀνὴρ
θεῶν δέη θνητοῖσιν ἐξευρεῖν, ὅπως
εἴη τι δεῖμα τοῖς κακοῖσι, κἂν λάθρᾳ
πράσσωσιν ἢ λέγωσιν ἢ φρονῶσί <τι>.   (15)
ἐντεῦθεν οὖν τὸ θεῖον εἰσηγήσατο,
ὡς ἔστι δαίμων ἀφθίτῳ θάλλων βίῳ
{νόῳ τ' ἀκούων καὶ βλέπων, φρονῶν τε †καὶ
προσέχων τε ταῦτα† καὶ φύσιν θείαν φορῶν,}
ὃς πᾶν τὸ λεχθὲν ἐν βροτοῖς ἀκούσεται,   (20)
<τὸ> δρώμενον δὲ πᾶν ἰδεῖν δυνήσεται.
ἐὰν δὲ σὺν σιγῇ τι βουλεύῃς κακόν,
τοῦτ' οὐχὶ λήσει τοὺς θεούς· τὸ γὰρ φρονοῦν
ἔνεστι<ν αὐτοῖς>. τούσδε τοὺς λόγους λέγων
διδαγμάτων ἥδιστον εἰσηγήσατο   (25)
ψευδεῖ καλύψας τὴν ἀλήθειαν λόγῳ.
ναίειν δ' ἔφασκε τοὺς θεοὺς ἐνταῦθ' ἵνα
μάλιστ' ἂν ἐξέπληξεν ἀνθρώπους ἄγων,
ὅθενπερ ἔγνω τοὺς φόβους ὄντας βροτοῖς
καὶ τὰς ὀνήσεις τῷ ταλαιπώρῳ βίῳ,   (30)
ἐκ τῆς ὕπερθε περιφορᾶς, ἵν' ἀστραπὰς
κατεῖδεν οὔσας, δεινὰ δὲ κτυπήματα
βροντῆς τό τ' ἀστερωπὸν οὐρανοῦ σέλας,

15 <τι> Grotius
18–19 del. Blaydes and (with *obeli*) Diggle: 18 ὃς ταῦτ' ἀκούει καὶ βλέπει φρονεῖ τ' ἄγαν
Aëtius; 19 τὰ πάντα Grotius: τε πάντη West
21 <τὸ> Normann
24 ἔνεστι<ν αὐτοῖς> Heath
25 ἥδιστον suspect: κύδιστον Haupt, Diggle
27 ναίειν Pierson: αἰεὶ Sextus
28 μάλιστ' ἂν Toup: μάλιστα Sextus; ἐξέπληξεν Sextus: ἐκπλήξειεν Grotius; ἄγων suspect:
λέγων Grotius
30 ὀνήσεις Musgrave: πονήσεις Sextus
33 σέλας Chrysippus fr. 1009 *SVF* von Arnim: δέμας Sextus

wrong, he was punished. Then, since the laws prevented men from doing violent deeds openly, (10) they continued to do them in secret.[5] I think that it was then (for the first time) that some clever man of shrewd mind invented[6] fears of the gods for mortals, so that the evil ones would have some fear, even if they were acting or saying or thinking (something) in secret. (15) Then he introduced religion, saying: 'There is a divinity, flourishing with eternal life {who with his mind hears and sees, both pondering and attending to (?) these things, and bearing a divine nature}, who will hear everything that was said among mortals, (20) and be able to see everything that is done.[7] If ever you plan some evil in silence, this will not escape the notice of the gods: for the power of thought is in (them).' Saying these words, he introduced the most pleasant (?) of lessons, (25) concealing the truth with falsehood.[8] He then claimed that the gods lived where he would most have terrified men by leading (?) them – the source, he knew, of mortals' fears as well as of benefits for their wretched life: (30) from the revolving sky above, where he saw there were lightning and terrible rumblings of thunder[9] and the starry brightness of heaven, the beautiful artwork of Time, a

[5] 'since the laws ... in secret': a fact of man's behaviour recognized by Democritus 68 B 181 DK and Antiphon 87 B 44 A col. 2 1–20 DK. Yunis (1988) adduces Eur. F 1007c <A> 'If these things are done secretly, whom do you fear?' <B> 'The gods, whose view is greater than men's', and assigns this fragment and our F 19 to the satyric *Sisyphus* of Euripides.

[6] 'clever ... shrewd mind ... invented': see n. 3 above. Contempt for the framers of laws as 'weak men' intending to 'frighten the stronger' is found in the views of Callicles in Plato's *Gorgias* (483a–e) comparable to Euripides' Polyphemus (see *Cyc.* 338–40 and n.). But such contempt is nowhere evident in our F 19; nor is it certainly to be read into vv. 5–15 and 40 from the notion of 'fear' attending the introduction of religion, vv. 13–14, 28–9.

[7] 'divinity ... will hear everything *etc.*': divine omniscience is already a concept in Homer, *e.g. Odyssey* 4.379, cf. (Zeus at) Hesiod, *Works and Days* 267–9, Xenophanes 11 B 24 DK; cf. our n. on Aesch F 281a.21, where 'Justice' records and reports all transgressions to Zeus. Similarly, that the divine can detect unspoken thoughts (our vv. 22–3, 'in silence') is claimed by Xenophon's Socrates, *Memorabilia* 1.1.19, and at *e.g.* Demosthenes 19.239–40.

[8] 'most pleasant ... concealing truth with falsehood': deceit on such a scale is not necessarily seen as bad *per se*: the social order of Plato's *Republic* is (in)famously predicated on a 'noble lie' (414bc). Yet 'most pleasant', if correct, may be sardonic (as perhaps is 'beautifully' in 38); so too Haupt's and Diggle's 'most glorious'.

[9] 'the source ... rumblings of thunder': Democritus 68 A 75 DK remarks that 'men of old' feared the gods, believing them responsible for such celestial phenomena. Thunder, like lightning, is associated with Zeus (the 'sky-god') from Homer onward (*e.g. Iliad* 8.133).

Χρόνου καλὸν ποίκιλμα, τέκτονος σοφοῦ,
ὅθεν τε λαμπρὸς ἀστέρος στείχει μύδρος   (35)
ὅ θ' ὑγρὸς εἰς γῆν ὄμβρος ἐκπορεύεται.
τοίους πέριξ ἔστησεν ἀνθρώποις φόβους,
δι' οὓς καλῶς τε τῷ λόγῳ κατῴκισεν
τὸν δαίμον' οὗτος ἐν πρέποντι χωρίῳ,
τὴν ἀνομίαν τε τοῖς νόμοις κατέσβεσε.   (40)

καί ὀλίγα προσδιελθὼν ἐπιφέρει·

οὕτω δὲ πρῶτον οἴομαι πεῖσαί τινα
θνητοὺς νομίζειν δαιμόνων εἶναι γένος.

37–40 deleted by Pechstein (40 only, Luppe)
[*Notes on the text*. Editors have either tried to emend vv. 18–19 because the Greek expression is very questionable (even with Grotius' suggestion 'attending to (*or* 'applying') all these things' and West's 'attending in every way'), or condemned them because they are tautologous and duplicate ideas in 17, 20–1 and 23–4; it is unfortunate that Aëtius cites only 1–2 and 17–18, and only paraphrases 3–16. In v. 28 Grotius proposed 'would most terrify', a Greek potential Optative with ἄν; the phrase 'by leading them' (Greek ἄγων), *i.e.* in their imaginations, seems very flat. But the abilities to induce ἔκπληξις ('terror', 'astonishment') and ψυχαγωγία ('leading, conjuring of the soul') were seen in the 5th Century as typical of some poetic and rhetorical styles (see O'Sullivan 2012b for references) and may be relevant here; and Grotius' 'by telling them' (λέγων) may not seem much of an improvement on 'leading' (ἄγων), but is at least consistent with Thucydides' favourable reference (2.65.9) to Pericles' ability to induce ἔκπληξις in his hearers 'by (*or* in) speaking' (λέγων). In v. 30 the 'benefits' (Musgrave) are those of heaven's sun and rain (33–6); but some editors prefer Sextus' 'ordeals', the endurance of what heaven sends (lightning and thunder, 31–3). In v. 33 'brightness' (Aëtius) seems preferable to 'structure' (Sextus), although some editors defend the latter for its aptness to 34 'architect'. Vv. 37–40 are deleted by Pechstein and Luppe as an interpolated and muddled summary of vv. 1–36 (note that Sextus recorded his omission of matter between 40 and 41). See also n. 8 on v. 25.]

clever craftsman;[10] from there comes the (*sun*–)star's brilliant hot mass,[11] (35) and the drenching rain travels to earth. Such were the fears this man set up on all sides for men; by their means in his argument he beautifully established the divinity in a suitable spot;[12] and he extinguished lawlessness with laws.[13] (40) (*Sextus then has 'after adding a few details Critias continues'*) Thus, I think, someone first persuaded mortals to believe that a race of gods exists.

[10] 'beautiful artwork of Time': cf. Critias (?), *Pirithous* F 3.1–3 'Time is unwearying ... it goes its round begetting (i.e. *perpetuating*) itself'. Time as a cosmogonical god appeared first in the 6th Century mythographer Pherecydes of Syros, 7 A 8 DK. 'clever craftsman': the adjective *sophos* is used of any excellent artisan, *e.g.* of Daedalus at Eur. *Eurystheus* F 372.2 and n. 2. Since the celestial phenomena of vv. 31–6 are invoked to deceive and frighten mortals into thinking they are evidence of the divine, the phrase 'clever craftsman' may carry an overtone of cunning (as it does at Eur. *Medea* 409; cf. the n. on 'architects' at *Cyc.* 477), just as 'clever' recalls the 'inventor' of the gods in v. 12.

[11] '(the (*sun*–)star's brilliant) hot mass': a metaphor from the smithy for the sun's blazing heat, Pre-Socratic in origin, *e.g.* Anaxagoras 59 A 1.8, 12 *etc.*, Gorgias 82 B 31 (and n.) DK.

[12] 'beautifully established': the invention of the divine is again described in ostensibly favourable language: cf. nn. 3 and 8 above.

'spot': the Greek word χωρίον is in form a diminutive, from an everyday linguistic register very rare in Greek tragedy but not in satyric drama (*e.g.* Eur. *Cyc.*185, *Autolycus A* F 282a.2); its occurrence is taken by some to indicate by itself satyric status for F 19 (*e.g.* Scodel (1980) 126, Davies (1986) 29). The word however is so frequent in 5th century prose (and in Aristophanes), and used simply to locate something rather than to indicate a place's smallness, that it can provide no sure criterion of genre. The regular diminutive is χωρίδιον, *e.g.* Lysias 19.28, Men. *Dyscolus* 23.

[13] 'extinguished lawlessness with laws': the thought seems to revert to law as the guarantor of justice, the curber of outrage and violence, vv. 5–10. Herodotus 1.96.2–97.3 presents justice as the foil to lawlessness; among the sophists Antiphon 87 B 61 DK and Anonymus Iamblichi 89.7.7–14 DK denounce anarchy and lawlessness respectively as the greatest of evils.

PYTHON

(active 325 BC)

Agen (ΑΓΗΝ)

TrGF 1².259–60 (91 F 1); cf. 5.1113.

Texts etc.: B. Snell, *Szenen aus griechischen Dramen* (Berlin, 1971) 104–37 (revised from *Scenes from Greek Drama* (Berkeley, 1970) 119–38); Gauly (1991) 194–7, 294; T. Günther in KPS 594–601; Cipolla (2003) 336–47; L. Sbardella, 'La megalomania di Arpalo e la scena dell' Ἀγήν. Una proposta di emendamento al testo di *TrGF* 91 Python fr. 1, 2 Snell', in Martina (2003) 177–90.

Discussions. Lloyd-Jones (1990) 214–17 (orig. 1965); Sutton (1980) 75–81; Lesky (1983) 402–3 (= (1972) 534–5); Gallo (1992) 102–3; P. Cipolla, 'La datazione del dramma satiresco dell' Ἀγήν', *Eikasmos* 11 (2000) 135–54 (cf. his (2003) 347–60); Conrad (1997) 212–13, 301–2; R. Pretagostini, 'La rappresentazione dell' Ἀγήν e la nuova drammaturgia', in Martina (2003) 161–75.

Python, from Catane in Sicily, is unrecorded except as the author of this play.[1] He is said to have accompanied Alexander the Great during his Eastern campaigns, in particular that to the Indus river around the year 326 BC, and to have produced the play to mock and stigmatise Alexander's campaign-treasurer Harpalus.[2] This man, disabled and unable to fight himself (Arrian, *Anabasis* 3.6.6), milked huge sums in Babylon (where he stayed behind the army) to fund his indulgence in prostitutes, especially one called Pythionice; he gave her an extravagant funeral and founded a temple to Pythionice Aphrodite in her honour (F 1.2–4).[3] These details are in Theopompus 115 F 253, 254b *FGrH*, preserved by Athenaeus 13.595d–6b, where the text of F 1 is given and the play described as satyric (see the end of this introductory discussion). Harpalus tried to anticipate Alexander's punishment by securing a future refuge in Athens (F 1.4; cf. n. 9 below), and through hiring a further prostitute Glycera from there and sending the hungry Athenians corn in exchange (F 1.14–18). The majority of scholars agree that events gradually overtook Harpalus, and that the play was subsequently composed and performed, remarkably enough, in a military camp (Conrad (1997) 213), probably in or near Babylon, in 324 BC.[4]

F 1 indeed unlocks this *drame à clef*: Agen ('Leader'; Greek participle ἄγων 'leading') disguises Alexander (see vv. 14–16), but Pretagostini (2003) 165–6 ingeniously suggests that Agen 'Leader' connotes also the god Dionysus, who in myth led an expedition near the Indus river, and founded the city of Nisa (Arrian, *Anabasis* 5.1–2; Alexander there on this campaign, 5.25.3–26.8): thus Agen is implicitly Alexander-Dionysus, acting as his own *deus ex machina* exacting justice from Harpalus at play-end. Harpalus, whose name's meaning 'Grabber' Python possibly exploited, is named expressly in v. 14 but disguised in 3 as Pallides, that is, either 'Son of Pallas' *i.e.* 'Son of Athens' (cf. 9), or, more likely, 'Son of P(h)allos', which suggests his sexual appetite (Pretagostini (2003) 169 notes that the collocation in 3 of 'whore' with 'Pallides' strengthens this play upon 'Harpalus'). The prostitutes Pythionice and Glycera are both named, 8, 17.

The fragment is almost certainly from the prologue-scene, but not from its very beginning, for line 1 starts with a connective particle (Snell (1971) 109–10; KPS 599; Pretagostini (2003) 166 n. 20). It reveals that the stage-setting is near Pythionice's 'temple' in Babylon (3), and possibly also near her tomb, if not near an entrance to Hades itself (see n. 5 on v. 2); here Harpalus has been persuaded to summon up her ghost for advice: for such action compare Aeschylus' tragedies *Persians*, with the summoning of the dead King Darius, and *Ghost-Raisers (Psychagogi)*, with Odysseus raising ghosts as in Homer's *Odyssey* 11; for actions set at Hades' door see on Aeschylus' *Sisyphus* (above) and Sophocles, *On Taenarum* (Appendix). 'Magi' (Persian 'wise men, wizards', 5) do the summoning; most scholars think that they would have been the satyrs, no doubt bizarrely dressed as Persians (Conrad (1997) 213: see n. 6 below). The second part of F 1, which must come later in the scene or play, gives details of Harpalus' dealings with Athens; it is a dialogue, the speakers unidentified, but probably one of them had delivered the prologue-speech proper; Snell (1971) 116 thought of a servant of Harpalus speaking subsequently to a Macedonian. The play's development and ending can be guessed: Pythionice's ghost advised Pallides-Harpalus about the arrival of her successor Glycera, which was imminent, or had occurred (F 1.17 '(paid) for Glycera' hints this); Agen-Alexander(-Dionysus?) appeared and restored order to the chaos which had no doubt been created by the satyrs around the embezzler and his whore-ghost (and perhaps later around Glycera, if she was a stage-character). Harpalus was more likely punished by Alexander (Pretagostini (2003) above), than forgiven (*e.g.* Snell (1971) 116–17); this corresponds with the regular pattern of satyr-plays ending with punishment of the 'ogre', often depicted as greedy (*e.g.* Aeschylus' Sisyphus, above; Polyphemus in *Cyc.* 316–46, *etc.*). Harpalus' lechery would endear him to a figure like Silenus, who might also have acted as a pimp to him (like the satyrs in Euripides' *Sciron* F 675).

Athenaeus (dependent upon Theopompus?) describes the *Agen* as 'a satyric drama' (2.50f), and Theopompus (in Athenaeus) twice as 'the little satyr-play' (13.586d, 595e). The latter may mean simply that it was altogether very short, or that the raising of Pythionice's ghost may have been the chief or indeed only 'satyric' scene, set between a conventional dramatic exposition (note the narrative past tenses of vv. 4 'condemned', 7 'persuaded', 16 'sent', 17 'was') and a similarly styled epilogue. Satyric features of the fragments other than greed and sexuality, and the ludicrous casting of the satyrs (above), are the raising of dead and the metrical licence in the dialogue trimeter ('Porson's Law' is broken in 3, 16 and 18). Pretagostini (2003) 170–1 emphasizes the latter, as well as the sexuality, as two elements typical of Old Comedy, like the criticism in F 1 of named historical persons; he suggests however that Harpalus and Pythionice (and Glycera) were styled upon character-types of New Comedy, and that the play exemplifies the appropriation by satyric drama from comedy of 'contemporary-historical' satire of living persons whose behaviour and story afforded a whole plot. In this respect *Agen* stands beside Lycophron's *Menedemus* (below) and perhaps Sositheus' *Cleanthes* (see the introductory discussion to his *Daphnis*, first paragraph). For such incidental criticism, overt or allusive, in the genre see also Soph. *Oeneus* F 1130.8–16 and n. 8, Eur. *Eurystheus* F 377 and n. 7, and for criticism of other poets and performers Pratinas 4 F 3 and *Adespota* F 646a with our notes. On all these 'contemporary' aspects of satyric drama see Sutton (1980) 76–86, 176–7; Seaford (1984) 18–19; Gallo (1992) 102, 119–23; KPS 10, 11, 33–4, 595, 601, 623; I. C. S. Storey in Harrison (2005) 204–9.

Notes

[1] Theopompus (or Athenaeus) refers to the author three times as Python of Catane (2.50f, 13.586d, 13.595e, but in 50f and 595e adds 'or of Byzantium') – but in all three places he names as an alternative author 'the king himself', *i.e.* Alexander. It is likely then that Alexander at least authorised the play, if he did not actually devise it, but wished to hide his hand; and the political message was clear: Harpalus was treacherous and justly punished, and the Athenians at fault for protecting him: see Pretagostini (2003) 164, 174.

[2] On Harpalus' 'megalomania' in this and other respects see Sbardella (2003), esp. 187–90.

[3] A prostitute Pythionice is mocked for her gluttony for fish at Timocles, *Icarian Satyrs* F 16 *PCG*, a play so titled in the fragments' sources, but almost certainly a comedy: see our Appendix. It is not certain that she is the same woman, although the dates of both Timocles and Python make this possible; nor is it certain that only one Timocles is in question: for discussion see E. Constantinides, *TAPA* 100 (1969) 49–61 (arguing for the play's comic nature); Cipolla (2003) 313–14, 326–31; I. C. S. Storey in Harrison (2005) 205–8.

[4] For the historical evidence and its analysis see E. Badian, 'Harpalus', *JHS* 81 (1961) 15–43; W. Heckel, *The Marshals of Alexander's Empire* (London and NY, 1992) 213–21. For the dating, Snell (1971) had suggested 326, followed by Sutton (1980) 77–81 and Cipolla (2000, 2003); for 324 Lloyd-Jones (1990) followed Badian (1961), cf. I. Worthington, 'The Chronology of the Harpalus-Affair', *SO* 61 (1981) 63–76, Gauly (1991) 194, KPS 594, Voelke (2001) 22, Pretagostini (2003) 163–5.

F 1

<A>   ἔστιν δ' ὅπου μὲν ὁ κάλαμος πέφυχ' ὅδε
         †φέτωμ'† ἄορνον, οὐξ ἀριστερᾶς δ' ὅδε
         πόρνης ὁ κλεινὸς ναός, ὃν δὴ Παλλίδης
         τεύξας κατέγνω διὰ τὸ πρᾶγμ' αὐτοῦ φυγήν.
         ἐνταῦθα δὴ τῶν βαρβάρων τινὲς μάγοι   (5)

(Theopompus 115 F 254 *FGrH* in) Athenaeus 13.595d–6b.; 14–18 also Athenaeus 13.586d;
a bare reference to the play at 2.50f

2 πέτρωμ' Sbardella (2003): στόμωμ' Erbse
3 ναός Casaubon: λαός Athenaeus

F 1 (Theopompus 115 F 254 *FGrH* in) Athenaeus 13.595d–6b; 14–18 also Athenaeus 13.586d

<A>   Where these reeds are growing there is a birdless †(*a meaningless word*)†;[5] and here on the left is the famous temple of the whore, the one which Pallides built, of course, and (*so*) condemned himself to exile because of the affair. Here, some barbarian

---

[5] Two good conjectures have been made for the meaningless word †φέτωμα† which follows 'birdless'. First, Sbardella's πέτρωμα yields '(there is) a large stone building (where there are no birds)'; this very rare noun describes a distinctive building at Pausanias 8.15.1. The conjecture is palaeographically straightforward but depends upon supposing a rich but difficult complex of historical and literary allusions. Sbardella starts from Arrian, *Anabasis* 7.22.2, where the Assyrians are said to have built their royal tombs in marshes; he identifies his conjectured building 'where these reeds are growing' (v. 1) with the 'extravagant tomb' which Harpalus erected for Pythionice (Athenaeus 13.594e); and he identifies the 'famous temple of the whore' (vv. 2–3) as that dedicated to Pythionice Aphrodite (see the introductory discussion). In the adjective 'where there are no birds' (ἄορνος, *aornos*), Sbardella finds reinforcement for his conjecture in allusions (a) to a massive stone fortress known to Alexander's army near the Indus river as 'Aornos' (Ἄορνος πέτρα, 'birdless rock', Arrian, *Anabasis* 4.28.1, Diodorus 17.85.1) and (b) to Sophocles' description (F 748) of an entrance to Hades as a 'birdless marsh' (cf. 'reeds' in our v. 1 again; a link appears to have been supposed between this Greek adj. *aornos* and the Latin name for the Underworld, *Avernus*). Sbardella argues that this second allusion compounds the long-noted ironic echo in 'here on the left is the famous temple of the whore' (vv. 2–3) of another Sophoclean passage, *Electra* 7–8 'here on the left is the famous temple of Hera' (cf. Pretagostini (2003) 171–2).

The second conjecture is Erbse's στόμωμα '(birdless) gaping entrance'; the word is used of the 'mouth' to the Pontic sea, *i.e.* the Bosporus, at Aesch. *Persians* 877. In Erbse's conjecture the allusion to Sophocles F 748 is no less clear than in Sbardella's, like interdependence with the allusion to *Electra* 7–8; but the corruption is harder to explain palaeographically.

Which conjecture to prefer? Sbardella's multiple allusions are attractive because they would have had immediate impact upon Alexander's men familiar both with Harpalus' extravagance and with the campaign near Aornos. Erbse's conjectured noun is more direct, and aptly suggests that the satyr-magi offered to summon up Pythionice's ghost (vv. 5–6) directly from Hades itself, rather than above her tomb.

ὁρῶντες αὐτὸν παγκάκως διακείμενον
ἔπεισαν ὡς ἄξουσι τὴν ψυχὴν ἄνω
τὴν Πυθιονίκης ...

        ... ἐν δὲ τοῖς ἑξῆς ...

        ... ἐκμαθεῖν δέ σου ποθῶ
μακρὰν ἀποικῶν κεῖθεν, Ἀτθίδα χθόνα
τίνες τύχαι μένουσιν ἢ πράττουσι τί.   (10)

<B>   ὅτε μὲν ἔφασκον δοῦλον ἐκτῆσθαι βίον,
ἱκανὸν ἐδείπνουν· νῦν δὲ τὸν χέδροπα μόνον
καὶ τὸν μάραθον ἔσθουσι, πυροὺς δ᾽ οὐ μάλα.

<A>   καὶ μὴν ἀκούω μυριάδας τὸν Ἅρπαλον
αὐτοῖσι τῶν Ἀγῆνος οὐκ ἐλάττονας   (15)
σίτου διαπέμψαι καὶ πολίτην γεγονέναι.

<B>   Γλυκέρας ὁ σῖτος οὗτος ἦν, ἔσται δ᾽ ἴσως
αὐτοῖσιν ὀλέθρου κοὐχ ἑταίρας ἀρραβών.

6 παγκάκως Jacobs: παγκάλως Athenaeus
10 μένουσιν Collard: καλοῦσιν Athenaeus
16 διαπέμψαι Athenaeus 596b: παραπέμψαι 586d

magi,[6] (5) seeing him in utter distress, persuaded him that they would summon up the soul of Pythionice[7] ... (*further*) ... I long to hear from you, as I live far away from Athens, what fortunes await[8] that land, or how the people are faring. (10)

<B>   When – so they asserted – they had a life of slavery, they had enough to eat; now they have only peas and fennel to eat, and no wheat at all.

<A>   And yet I hear that Harpalus sent them countless bushels of grain, no fewer than Agen had done, (15) and became a citizen![9]

<B>   That grain was (*paid*) for Glycera, and maybe it will be a down-payment on their death and not the prostitute's.[10]

[6]   The chorus of satyrs; see introductory discussion. Compare their possible costuming as women in Ion's *Omphale* F 22, and their appearance as white-haired old men or 'sages' confronting the Sphinx on the well-known Attic vessel of *c.* 460 BC (*LIMC* VIII. 1.1125 'Silenoi' no. 160 = KPS fig. 22b).

[7]   So the satyrs were able to bring a female figure on stage, like Danae hauled ashore in the chest in Aesch. *Net-Fishers* and Cyllene provoked into coming from her cave in Soph. *Trackers*. A closer parallel for a female brought up from below the ground (actually, manufactured from its soil) lay in Sophocles' satyric *Pandora* or *Hammerers* (see esp. F 482 'begin first upon kneading the clay'; our Appendix): this mythical incident, if not Sophocles' play, has been seen behind an Attic crater of *c.* 450 BC (Trendall-Webster (1971) II.7–8, cf. *LIMC* VII.1.164 'Pandora' no. 4) in which satyrs cavort round a crowned female figure emerging from the earth.

[8]   For the Athenians' future 'fortunes' cf. 17–18, whence Collard's 'await'; also n. 9. Athenaeus' 'call (that land)' is clearly impossible.

[9]   Hyperbole, an example of how satyric drama could be a distorting mirror for historical events. No other ancient source tells us that Harpalus sent the Athenians grain or won Athenian citizenship; in fact when he arrived he was at first turned away and, on returning as a suppliant, was put under house arrest (Plutarch, *Demosthenes* 25.3); initially he was believed to have 700 talents with him, which were stored on the Acropolis, but as it turned out the amount was 350 talents (Hyperides, *Demosthenes* VIII. 10; Plut. *Mor.* 846b). Harpalus eventually escaped from Athens but was killed in Crete (Diod. Sic. 17.108.8; cf. Paus. 2.33.4–5); those who had dealings with him in Athens were put on trial for taking bribes, including Demosthenes (Dinarchus 1.6; cf. Plut. *Mor.* 846c). See also the modern analyses noted in n. 4 above.

[10]   In the Greek the ends of line 13 and of 3 show satyric drama's indifference to 'Porson's Law' of the final cretic in the imabic trimeter: see the General Index.

SOSITHEUS

(active first part of 3rd century BC)

Daphnis or Lityerses (ΔΑΦΝΙΣ Η ΛΙΤΥΕΡΣΗΣ)

TrGF 1².269–73 (99 T 1–2, F 1a–3), 356.

Texts etc. Gauly (1991) 208–11, 296–7; T. Günther in KPS 602–13; Voelke (2001) 302–3 (F 2); Cipolla (2003) 381–420, at 386–92, 406–415; Cozzoli (2003, below) 283–91.

Discussions. Sutton (1980) 86–7; Gallo (1992) 121–3; G. Xanthakis-Karamanos, 'The *Daphnis* or *Lityerses* of Sositheus', *AC* 63 (1994) 235–50 (= G. X.-K., *Dramatica* (Athens, 2002) 313–28) and 'Echoes of Earlier Drama in Sositheus' *Daphnis* and Lycophron's *Menedemus*', *AC* 66 (1997) 121–43, at 121–31 (= *Dramatica* 359–83, at 361–71); Conrad (1997) 209–12, 300–1; Voelke (2001) 23–4 (date); Cipolla (2003) 398–406; A.-T. Cozzoli, 'Sositeo e il nuovo dramma satiresco', in Martina (2003) 265–91.

Sositheus, of the early 3rd century BC and a native probably of Alexandria, was a member like Lycophron of the literary 'Pleiad' active there (*TrGF* 99 T 1; Lycophron 100 T 1). He appears to have led a revival of satyr-drama: 'the man wore ivy worthy of Phliasian Satyrs' (*i.e.* worthy of the celebrated satyr-playwright Pratinas, a native of Phlius): so *TrGF* 99 T 2.3–4, lines from an 'epitaph' upon Sositheus by Dioscorides, *Anthologia Palatina* 7.707, analysed most recently by Cozzoli (2003) 278–81, cf. now M. Fantuzzi, 'Epigrams on the Theater', in P. Bing, J. S. Bruss (eds), *Brill's Companion to Hellenistic Epigram* (Leiden-Boston, 2007) 477–96, at 490–3, and A.K. Petrides, *CQ* 59 (2009) 502–3. Diogenes Laertius 7.173 records the hostile reception given in the theatre to another satyr-play which Sositheus directed against the philosopher Cleanthes and named for him (F 4, *TrGF* 1².272; KPS 614–16; I. Gallo, *QUCC* 27 (1978) 161–79 (= *Teatro ellenistico minore* (Roma, 1981) 157–78) argues that a trace of it survives in P. Herc. 1018 col.24.3–9 (= *TrGF* I².356 F 4a??).

It is not absolutely certain that *Daphnis* was indeed satyric, for there is no hard evidence: it is assessed by Xanthakis-Karamanos (1994) and (2002), cf. KPS 605–6, 611–13. Xanthakis-Karamanos argues that what can be guessed of the plot, especially the reunion of lovers, encourages the idea that it was light-hearted, suspended between tragedy and satyr-play; and that two surviving fragments (F 2, 3) in their general style and fairly strict metre (T. B. L. Webster, *Gnomon* 44 (1972) 739) would suit a 'romantic tragedy' like Euripides' *Alcestis* (see n. 3 on our Introductory Note). Cipolla (2003) 404–6 agrees, and suggests that the rather elevated style of F 2 (also, there are no metrical resolutions in its trimeters) indicates its speaker as Daphnis, who in this regard was marked off from the cruder register of the satyrs (or of Lityerses), as Odysseus is from them (or from Polyphemus) in Euripides' *Cyclops*. Cozzoli (2003) 283 nevertheless well counters Xanthakis-Karamanos by observing that three things all mark the play as satyric, (1) the play's setting in Phrygia, (2) the nature of Lityerses (on which see below) as a son of the ass-eared Midas (who from 560 BC onward was frequently painted together with Silenus, who had first been brought to him in bonds: see *LIMC* VIII.1.846–8 'Midas' nos 7–32), and (3) the adventurous tale of Daphnis and Thalia.

The play is titled *Daphnis* in two of the sources for F 2, and *Daphnis or Lityerses* in the third. The plot can be confidently reconstructed from the story told, but without ascription, by Servius Auctus on Vergil, *Eclogues* 8.68 (= *TrGF* F 1a.III; for ascription to Sositheus see the Scholia to Theocritus 8, on the 'argument' to that poem, and on its line 93 [= F 1a.I, II]). Sositheus brought together and contrasted the figures of Daphnis, a young, good-looking, musical, and amorous rustic traditional in poetry since the 6th century (first at Stesichorus F 279 *PMG*) and popular in the more refined Hellenistic pastoral (*e.g.* Theocritus 8), and of the rougher Lityerses, an ogre (cf. Euripides' Cyclops and Syleus); the play's alternative titles may reflect this contrast (cf. Cipolla (2003) 399).[1] Daphnis' sweetheart Thalia (or Pimplea, according to Servius) was abducted by robbers; after long searching he found her in servitude to Lityerses, in central Asia Minor. Heracles came along during the course of his Labours, as often in satyr-drama (see our Index of Motifs), and was forced by Lityerses, like all strangers, to compete with him in reaping his crops (compare Syleus in Euripides, above). Lityerses invariably fed his 'guests' well before outstripping them in the fields, and towards evening cut off their heads and rolled their bodies up in the sheaves (vv.12–20 of F 2; cf. the Scholia to Theocritus 10.41c [= *TrGF* F 2a.I]). Heracles was however superior to Lityerses (just as he overcame Euripides' Syleus), freed Thalia, and restored her to Daphnis.

The role of the satyrs can nevertheless only be conjectured (Conrad (1997) 211–12). Possibly they were in servitude to Lityerses and attended him during the meal and the harvesting; Cozzoli (2003) 283 n. 63 suggests that the satyrs had been enslaved by Lityerses, who was illegitimate and degenerate (F 2.4–5), and who probably reversed the friendly relationship they had developed with his father Midas (on whom see above).

The resemblances between Sositheus' play and Euripides' *Syleus* remarked above are striking, and can be extended. Both Lityerses and Syleus, the 'ogres', are located in distant Asia Minor. Behind 'Daphnis' is a story of separated and then reunited lovers comparable with Admetus and Alcestis reunited (by Heracles) in Euripides' pro-satyric *Alcestis*; Sositheus' young lovers are also comparable with couples reunited and saving themselves from barbarians, in remote places, in Euripides' lighter tragedies, in particular Menelaus and Helen in *Helen*, and the siblings Orestes and Iphigenia in *Iphigenia in Tauris*. There is speculation that Euripides' wholly lost satyr-play *Harvesters* (*Theristae*, accompanying his *Medea* in 431: see our Appendix) told essentially the same story as *Daphnis*: see *e.g.* KPS 476, Voelke (2001) 23, 43. There is also one striking lexical link between the

---

F 2

τούτῳ Κελαιναὶ πατρίς, ἀρχαία πόλις
Μίδου γέροντος, ὅστις ὦτ᾽ ἔχων ὄνου
ἤνασσε καὶ νοῦν φωτὸς εὐήθους ἄγαν.
οὗτος δ᾽ ἐκείνου παῖς παράπλαστος νόθος,
μητρὸς δ᾽ ὁποίας ἡ τεκοῦσ᾽ ἐπίσταται.   (5)
ἔσθει μὲν ἄρτους, τρεῖς ὅλους κανθηλίους,
τρὶς τῆς βραχείας ἡμέρας· πίνει δ᾽, ἕνα
καλῶν μετρητήν, τὸν δεκάμφορον πίθον.

Mythographus Anonymus 346.11ff. Westermann; 4–9 Tzetzes, *Chiliades* 2.599–604, with paraphrase preceding in 591–8; 6–8 Athenaeus 10.415b

two poets: see n. 4 below. If Sositheus was indeed a 'classicizing' reviver of satyric, it seems that his play(s) owed more to Euripides than to other 5th or 4th century dramatists, notwithstanding other literary elements detectable in his work, such as Hellenistic pastoral (for these, see Xanthakis-Karamanos (2002) 320–2).

M. Di Marco in Martina (2003) 68–74 has suggested that *Adespota* F 646a may come from Sositheus' play: see our introductory discussion there.

Note

[1] Since 'Lityerses' is recorded as the title of a well-known harvesting 'work-song' in the century before Sositheus (Menander, *The Carthaginian* F 3 Sandbach), KPS 607–8 suggests that its narrative content may have afforded Sositheus much of his plot. A version is sung in Theocritus 10.41–55 (see R. Hunter's commentary, Cambridge 1998); cf. the Scholia on Theocr. 10.41e (F 3 below), 'After Heracles killed (Lityerses) he threw him into the river Meander; as a result harvesters in Phrygia even to this day sing of (Lityerses), extolling him as an excellent harvester.' See further n. 8 on F 2.21 below.

F 2 (Mythographus Anonymus p. 346.11ff. Westermann; 4–9 Tzetzes, *Chiliades* 2.599–604)

> Celaenae is Lityerses' homeland,[2] the ancient city of old Midas, who was king although he had the ears of an ass[3] and the mind of an exceedingly simple man. Lityerses is bogus, a bastard son of Midas, but from what sort of mother, (*only*) that mother knows (5). He eats loaves of bread, three whole pack-ass loads of it, three times within the short space of a day; he drinks a storage jar as big as ten amphorae,[4] calling it one measure. He works briskly

[2] The setting is on the fringes of the Greek world, as in many satyr-plays (cf. General Introduction and our Index of Motifs) – Euripides depicts even Sicily in *Cyclops* as a barbaric dystopia (see O'Sullivan 2012a). Celaenae (the later Apamea) lay on the river Meander (v. 16), the archetypal tortuous river which near the sea divided Lydia from Caria in Asia Minor; Celaenae was a long way inland, in Phrygia (Herodotus 7.26.3).

This fragment is almost certainly from the play's orientatory prologue, and the speaker may be Daphnis (Webster) or Silenus (Snell).

[3] Cf. Ar. *Wealth* 287.

[4] Perhaps borrowed from *Cyc.* 388 'a mixing bowl as big as ten amphorae'; in fact Sositheus and Euripides are the only two known authors who use this adjective δεκάμφορος. For gluttony in satyric drama see *e.g.* n. 8 on Euripides, *Autolycus A* F 282 above, and our Index of Motifs.

ἐργάζεται δ' ἐλαφρὰ πρὸς τὰ σιτία
ὄγμον θερίζων· τῇ μιᾷ δ' ἐν ἡμέρᾳ　　　　　　　　(10)
τὰ δράγματ' ἔμπης συντίθησιν εἰς τέγος.
χὥταν τις ἔλθῃ ξεῖνος ἢ παρεξίῃ,
φαγεῖν τ' ἔδωκεν εὐθὺ κἀπεχόρτασεν
καὶ τοῦ ποτοῦ προύτεινεν ὡς ἂν ἐν θέρει
πλέον· φθονεῖν γὰρ τοῖς θανουμένοις ὀκνεῖ.　　　(15)
ἔπειτ' ἄγων εἰς λῆα Μαιάνδρου ῥοαῖς
κηπεύματ' ὡς ἀρδευτὰ δαψιλεῖ ποτῷ
τὸν ἀνδρομήκη πυρὸν ἠκονημένῃ
ἅρπῃ θερίζει· τὸν ξένον δὲ δράγματι
αὐτῷ κολούσας κρατὸς ὀρφανὸν φέρει　　　　　(20)
γελῶν θεριστὴν ὡς ἄνουν ἠρίστισεν.

11 τὰ δράγματ' Gauly (and Kannicht): δαινυσίτ' Mythogr.; (δράγνυσί τ' ἔμπης συντίθησί τ' εἰς) τέγος Walker: συντίθησιν εἰς τέλος Mythogr.
13 εὐθὺ Steffen: εὖ Mythogr.
16 ἔπειτ' ἄγων εἰς λῆα Nauck, Headlam: ἐπιστατῶν †οἴδηα† Mythogr.
17 κηπεύματ' ὡς Headlam: καρπευμάτων Mythogr.
20 κολούσας Schramm: κυλίσας Mythogr.
21 γελῶν … ἠρίστισεν Casaubon: γέρων … ἠρίστησεν Mythogr.

F 3

θανὼν μὲν οὖν Μαίανδρον ἐρρίφη ποδὸς
σόλος τις ὥσπερ· ἦν δ' ὁ δισκεύσας ἀνὴρ
†πυθιο† < … >· τίς γὰρ ἀνθ' Ἡρακλέους;

Mythographus Anonymus 347.9 Westermann, after citation of F 2; there is an allusion to Heracles' throw, without attribution, in the Scholia to Theocritus 10.41e (= F 2a.II; see n. 1 above).
2 σόλος Casaubon: σοφός Mythogr.; after ὥσπερ Mythogr. has the gloss δίσκος, deleted by Casaubon.
1–2 voice A, ending ἀνήρ …, 3 voice B <τίς δή;>, voice A πύθοι' (πύθοιο one ms. of Mythogr.) ἄν; τίς γὰρ ἀνθ' Ἡρακλέους; Hermann

at his corn, reaping the furrow; and within the one day (10) he puts the sheaves together completely under a roof.[5] Whenever some stranger arrives or passes by, he straightway gives him good fodder to eat, and keeps offering him more drink, as (*one*) would in summer,[6] for he shrinks from begrudging it to those who are about to die. (15) Then he leads the stranger into his ripe crops by Meander's streams, like gardens[7] watered with abundant drink, and reaps his man-high corn with whetted sickle. The stranger he docks of his head and carries him off in the very sheaf, (20) laughing how he had given lunch to a stupid reaper.[8]

[5] 'he puts together ... under a roof' is the text implicitly approved by Snell-Kannicht in *TrGF* 1[2] and by Kannicht in Gauly (1991) 208–9; Walker's full conjecture produces 'he makes (his corn, 9) completely into sheaves and puts (them) together under a roof'. The transmitted text is corrupt at the start, the rest meaning 'finally puts them together.'

[6] 'more drink': τοῦ ποτοῦ is partitive genitive, Smyth § 1341; for ὡς ἄν in 'as (*one*) would' (Greek idiom omits the pronoun, and relies on the particle ἄν to imply a potential optative) cf. Eur. *Syleus* F 688.3; Smyth § 1766.a. In 13 the transmitted text is metrically deficient; we print the most economical conjecture (Steffen), but the sense is clear from 21, and the metaphor in 'good fodder' from fattening cattle is common in Comedy, *e.g.* Eubulus F 6.5 *PCG*. There is perhaps black humour in giving 'fodder', from a field-crop, to the doomed reaper.

[7] In 16–17 'Then he leads ... gardens': we again follow the text (Nauck and Headlam) suggested by Kannicht in Gauly (1991) 208–9.

[8] 'laughing ... a stupid reaper': 12–15. Cozzoli (2003) 286–9 shows how such mockery was a traditional part of merry harvest-songs (it is well attested too from English countryside lore); cf. n. 10 on F 3 below. Beyond that, compare Polyphemus' cruel parody of hospitality in *Cyc.* 342–4; on the motif in satyr-plays see Voelke (2001) 301–14, esp. 302–3.

F 3 (Mythographus Anonymus p. 347.9 Westermann)

So once he was dead he was thrown by the foot[9] into the Meander, like some lump of iron. The man who flung him was ... (*text corrupt and defective*) Who if not Heracles?[10]

[9] For the Greek partitive genitive 'by the foot' cf. Homer, *Iliad* 1.591, 17.289; Smyth § 1346, and cf. *Cyc.* 400 and n. At *Il.* 21.120 Achilles seizes Lycaon by the foot to throw him into the river Scamander – probably the model for our passage.

[10] Gauly (1991) 210 favours Hermann's text and division among two voices, <A> 'So once ... who flung him was ...' <B> <'Who then?'> <A> 'You wish to ask? Who if not Heracles?' Only Heracles had sufficient physical strength; and such contemptuous punishment of an ogre is unproblematic for the simple ethic of satyric drama (see *e.g.* Eur. *Cyc.* 693–5, *Sciron* F 678); Hesychius λ 1161 Latte describes Lityerses with the single adjective 'most unjust' (ἀδικώτατος).

LYCOPHRON

(active first quarter of 3rd century BC)

Menedemus (*ΜΕΝΕΔΗΜΟΣ*)

*TrGF*1².276–7 (100 F 2–4), 356; 5.1116.

Texts etc. Gauly (1991) 212–17, 297–8; G. Xanthakis-Karamanos, 'The *Menedemus* of Lycophron', *Athena* 81 (1996) 339–65 (= G. X.-K., *Dramatica* (Athens, 2002) 329–57); T. Günther in KPS 617–23; Cipolla (2003) 365–76.

Discussions. I. Wikarjak, 'De Menedemo a Lycophrone in fabula satyrica irriso', *Eos* 43 (1949) 127–33; C. A. Van Rooy, *Studies in Classical Satire* (Leiden, 1965) 124–43, esp. 127–34 (older bibl. at 141 n. 25); Sutton (1980) 81–2; Conrad (1997) 202–9, 297–300; G. Xanthakis-Karamanos, 'Echoes of Earlier Drama in Sositheus' *Daphnis* and Lycophron's *Menedemus*', *AC* 66 (1997) 121–43, at 131–43 (= *Dramatica* [above] 359–83, at 371–83); Voelke (2001) 22–3; Cipolla (2003) 377–9.

The early 3rd century BC philosopher Menedemus, of Eretria in Euboea, was what Jane Austen would have called 'an odd mixture of quick parts' (and in some ways indeed like her Mr Bennet: *Pride and Prejudice*, Ch. 1): clever, both private and open as a person, literary, a quixotic host (Diogenes Laertius 2.126–39); (Antigonus of Carystus in) Athenaeus 10.419e–20c describes his manner of entertaining guests; Van Rooy (1965) 128–30 surveys the biographical details offered by these two and other, minor sources. Among his intellectual pursuits was satyric drama, in which he rated Aeschylus as supreme, and Achaeus second; Diog. L. 2.133 records that he used to apply

Achaeus, *Omphale* F 34 to political opponents, 'Just as the speedy man proves to be overtaken by the weak, so is the eagle by the tortoise, in a short time.'

Lycophron, Menedemus' fellow Euboean, but from Chalcis (Athenaeus 2.55c), was a member of the same literary 'Pleiad' as Sositheus (*TrGF* 100 T 1). He was the not quite securely identified poet of the surviving dramatic monologue *Alexandra* (called 'obscure' at Suda λ 827 Adler: Alexandra is the riddling prophetess Cassandra, sister of Alexander-Paris). Lycophron is stated by (Antigonus of Carystus in) Diog. L. 2.139 to have composed his *Menedemus* 'in praise of' the philosopher – but Athenaeus 2.55c records that he wrote this satyr-play to 'tease' the philosopher, by 'mocking his dinner-parties' (cf. Athenaeus 10.419e above). This contradiction is discussed at length by Van Rooy (1965) 130–4, giving some credence to both judgements, but favouring Athenaeus; he suggests that Lycophron wrote the play 'in a mocking fashion as a paradoxical tribute to the philosopher' – perhaps also to his taste for satyric? This would not be the first time that a philosopher was linked with satyrs. Plato famously has Alcibiades compare Socrates to the satyrs Marsyas and Silenus (*Symp.* 216c–217a; 221d, 222d) on the basis of the playful and paradoxical nature of each figure.

The three fragments which survive all relate to one dinner-party and its meagre and poor fare. Lycophron may have chosen satyric form precisely for this easy contrast between Menedemus' ascetic frugality and satyrs' gluttony – but gently hits his personal target in two ways: first, he characterises his title-figure as an extreme opposite of the gluttonous ogre frequent in satyr plays; second, Van Rooy (1965) 134 and others before him (he cites esp. T. Sinko, *Eos* 43 (1949) 28) suggest that the entire piece was a monologue like the *Alexandra*, and that as there the name-figure did not appear; Silenus delivered the monologue to the satyrs. For us the principal interest of the play is its depiction of historical figures: like Python's *Agen* (above), it used the satyric genre as satirical, in mocking contemporary persons.

F 2

ΣΙΛΗΝΟΣ   παῖδες κρατίστου πατρὸς ἐξωλέστατοι,
ἐγὼ μὲν ὑμῖν, ὡς ὁρᾶτε, στρηνιῶ·
δεῖπνον γὰρ οὔτ᾽ ἐν Καρίᾳ, μὰ τοὺς θεούς,
οὔτ᾽ ἐν Ῥόδῳ τοιοῦτον οὔτ᾽ ἐν Λυδίᾳ
κατέχω δεδειπνηκώς· Ἄπολλον, ὡς καλόν.   (5)

και προελθών·

ἀλλὰ κυλίκιον
ὑδαρὲς ὁ παῖς περιῆγε τοῦ πεντωβόλου,
ἀτρέμα παρεξεστηκός· ὅ τ᾽ ἀλιτήριος
καὶ δημόκοινος ἐπεχόρευε δαψιλὴς
θέρμος, πενήτων καὶ τρικλίνου συμπότης.   (10)

(Antigonus of Carystus p. 100B Wilamowitz in) Athenaeus 10.420b–c; 9–10 2.55d
1 πατρὸς Canter: παιδὸς Athenaeus
9 δημόκοινος Casaubon: δημόνικος Athenaeus 10.420c: δημόκριτος 2.55d

F 2 ((Antigonus of Carystus p. 100B Wilamowitz in) Athenaeus 10.420b–c;
9–10 2.55d)

SILENUS   You most abominable sons of a most excellent father,[1] I've had
a wild time, I can tell you, as you see: for I know perfectly well[2]
that I've not eaten such a dinner either in Caria, by Heaven, or
in Rhodes or in Lydia.[3] By Apollo (*gritting his teeth*), it was
splendid![4] (5)

and further:

    ... but the boy was taking round a watery little cup of five-obol
(*wine*),[5] gone sour from standing still; and then came dancing in
those vile common-or-garden beans in rich plenty, the fellow-
guests of paupers and a three-couch dinner-party![6] (10)

[1] Cf. Silenus' abuse of his sons, amid extravagant self-praise, at Soph. *Trackers* F 314.145–
68, esp. 153; abuse goes both ways at *Cyc.* 268–72.

[2] So translated by A. K. Petrides, *CR* 55 (2005) 40–1 (reviewing Cipolla 2003); alternatively,
'I don't recall that I've eaten', Snell.

[3] 'Lydia': a by-word for luxury, *e.g.* Ion, *Omphale* F 24 and n.

[4] Vv. 6–10 make it clear that 1–5 are sarcastic. Images in comedy of frugal and austere
intellectuals provide a running gag from Aristophanes, *Clouds* 102–3, 175–90 onward (the
pale, unshod Socrates and Chaerephon), *e.g.* Antiphanes F 120.2–4 and Alexis F 24 *PCG*.
Such images have endured: see R. Barthes, 'Poujade and the Intellectuals' in *The Eiffel Tower
and Other Mythologies*, tr. R. Howard (Berkeley-London, 1979) 127–35.

[5] 'watery ... wine': wine was normally drunk (heavily) diluted, but satyrs and Silenus liked
it neat: *Cyc.* 149–50, cf. Achaeus, *Aethon* F 9 and n. Silenus points out that Menedemus has
gone too far with water and cheap wine, as he has with the smallness of the cup (F 3.1). There
is disgust at a single cup of wine costing one obol at Menander, *Men at Arbitration* 130.

[6] 'vile (beans)': the Greek adjective ἀλίθριος is used of accursed or offensive persons (*e.g.*
Thuc.1.126.11). Silenus engages in bathetic rage when using it of a bean, just as 'beans in
rich plenty' employs oxymoron for sarcasm – so too perhaps the locution 'came dancing in',
although it occurs elsewhere, *e.g.* Diphilus F 43.1 *PCG* 'a choice breakfast came dancing in',
cf. F 64.4. 'common-or-garden': beans are emblematic of poor diet, in Middle Comedy *e.g.*
Timocles F 20.4 *PCG*. The Greek term translated as 'common-or-garden' (δημόκοινος) is also
used for 'the public executioner', *i.e.* connoting here 'lethal (beans)'; Casaubon's correction
yields fine sense, and both 'variants' in Athenaeus are plainly errors of transcription. 'a three-
couch dinner party': only a possible translation, implying that Menedemus was as mean with
invitations as with fare. The words may however mean just 'a (paupers') dinner-couch' (Van
Rooy (1965) 131), or the text may be incomplete (Gauly, 1991).

F 3

<ΣΙΛ.>   ὡς ἐκ βραχείας δαιτὸς ἡ βαιὰ κύλιξ
             αὐτοῖς κυκλεῖται πρὸς μέτρον, τράγημα δὲ
             ὁ σωφρονιστὴς πᾶσιν ἐν μέσῳ λόγος ...

(Antigonus of Carystus p. 99A Wilamowitz in) Diogenes Laertius 2.139; 2 τράγημα ... 3
(Antigonus of Carystus p. 100B Wilamowitz in) Athenaeus 10.420c
3 πᾶσιν ἐν μέσῳ Athenaeus: τοῖς φιληκόοις ('for glad listeners') Diog. L., perhaps a deliberate
alteration.

F 4

                                      πολλάκις
             συνόντας αὐτοὺς
                 ἐπὶ πλεῖον ὁ ὄρνις κατελάμβανε
                                      τὴν ἔω καλῶν
             ... τοῖσι δ' οὐδέπω κόρος ...

(Antigonus of Carystus p. 100B Wilamowitz in) Athenaeus 10.420c.

F 3 ((Antigonus of Carystus p. 99A Wilamowitz in) Diogenes Laertius 2.139; 2 end-3 Athenaeus 10.420c)

<SIL.>   As (*or* When?) after a brief meal the little cup goes round them in moderation, and dessert is moralising discussion in which all join ...[7]

[7] Silenus continues his anger with Menedemus' dinner, loathing the 'moralising discussion' as much as the meagre wine and food: *e.g.* *Cyc*.164–74 gives Silenus' own idea of after-dinner amusement (which he would not want replaced by 'chastening (discussion)', an alternative meaning of σωφρονιστής).

F 4 ((Antigonus of Carystus p. 100B Wilamowitz in) Athenaeus 10.420c)

        ... when they were often together the fowl generally overtook them as it summoned the dawn ... but they were not yet sated ...[8]

[8] 'not yet sated': a further allusion to Menedemus' stinginess, which denied his guests a normal satiety with food and drink? Symposiasts are overtaken by cock-crow in Plato, *Symposium* 223c2, a passage probably recalled by Lycophron.

ANONYMOUS

Adespota F 646a
(undated)

TrGF 5.1134–7 (revising and amplifying 2.217–20).

Texts etc. P. Köln 242 ed. K. Maresch, *Kölner Papyri* VI (1987) and P. Fackelmann 5 ed. B. Kramer, *ZPE* 34 (1979) 1–14; W. Luppe, 'Zu den Kölner anapästischen Tetrametern', *ZPE* 72 (1988) 35–6; Bierl (1990, below) 354–6, with 2 Plates; Gauly (1991) 250–3, 302; P. Kruschwitz, L. Lehmann, J. Schloemann in KPS 635–8; L. Battezzato (2006, below) 21–5.

Discussions. A. Bierl, 'Dionysus, Wine and Tragic Poetry: A Metatheatrical Reading of P. Köln VI.242A = *TrGF* F 646a', *GRBS* 31 (1990) 353–91; Gallo (1992) 114–17; Conrad (1997) 216–20, 303–4; Voelke (2001) 21, 47, 393; Cipolla (2003) 17 n. 72; M. Di Marco, 'Poetica e metateatro in un dramma satiresco di età ellenistica', in Martina (2003) 41–74; L. Battezzato, 'La fatica dei canti: tragedia, commedia e dramma satiresco nel frammento adespoto 646a *TrGF*', in E. Medda and others (eds), ΚΩΜΩΙΔΟΤΡΑΓΩΙΔΙΑ. *Intersezioni del tragico e del comico nel teatro del V secolo a.c.* (Pisa, 2006) 19–68 (with excellent bibl.); G. D'Alessio in Perusino and Colantonio (2007) 120–1.

There is no evidence whatever for the content and plot of the source-play, but the fragment is of remarkable historical interest. Its stylistic and metrical character compares with that of Attic comedy of the very late 5th century, but its complaint that satyric drama is being 'side-lined' (vv. 24–5) suits the period of its apparent decline in status, from a little before 400 BC, or may be part of the archaizing revival which began from about 340 (see above Gen. Intro. pp. 5–6). This seeming contradiction has led to still unresolved dispute about both date and genre of the fragment; the lack of a sure date prevents confident interpretation of much of its content (Gauly (1991) 251).

Before a second papyrus text (P. Köln 242, publ. 1987) was found to overlap and amplify the first (P. Fackelmann 5, publ. 1979), scholars inclined to treat the fragment as comic: see *TrGF* 2 (1981) 217 and the commentary by Bierl (1990) 359–61, 371–3.[1] The enlargement of the text confirmed both its Dionysiac content and the identification of its speaker as Silenus; and the inference that the fragment is satyric is now shared by most scholars. It was hesitantly so described by Snell-Kannicht in *TrGF* 2.217 (1981); cf. Gallo (1992), Gauly (1991) 250, Conrad (1997) 216, KPS 637 and Voelke (2001) 21 n. 19, 393. Di Marco (2003) 42–3 surveyed all previous attributions, and datings, and rebutted in particular Bierl's attribution to comedy (43–7); he himself favoured satyric, and of the Hellenistic period, like D'Alessio in Perusino and Colantonio (2007) 120–1; Cipolla (2003) 17 n. 72 was non-committal, and Battezzato (2006: see below) very guarded. The fragment was not discussed by I.C.S. Storey in his paper 'But Comedy has satyrs too' (in Harrison (2005) 201–9), but his evidence shows that a presence and speaking role for Silenus do not of themselves exclude comic origin.

The fragment begins at the end of what appears to be a 'hymn' (v. 4)[2] to Dionysus (1–18): Silenus recounts how he fled (8) with the infant god from Hera's anger at his birth; how he kept him safe in the mountains, where he was proud to bring up the infant into his youth (7–12; cf. n. 3 on Sophocles, *Lovers of Achilles* and e.g. *Little Dionysus* F 171; n. 11 on Aeschylus, *Net-Fishers* F 47a.23–4); and how he instituted the god's celebration through wine (13–15) and the ecstatic revel-band of initiates or *thiasos* (15–18: cf. e.g. Pratinas 4 F 3.2, 15–17).

In 19–27, the remainder of the fragment, Silenus laments the fallen status of 'his' genre, the result of 'deceptions' (20, *i.e.* betrayal?), by (apparently: the text of 20–3 is defective) tragic poets (23). He pleads with the Muses not to permit the 'side-lining' of his art into 'third place' in the dramatic competition presided over by Dionysus (25–7); this 'contest' (27: see n. 22 there) may be the real-life one in which the play is being performed, or it may be one within the play itself (particularly if it is after all a comedy: Battezzato (2006) and Storey (personal communication) below). The transition between the 'hymn' and this 'metatheatrical' passage is made in v. 18 over the words 'I was taught (*or* trained) to vaunt such things', which may be significant: with 'taught' Silenus is using the official term at Athens for a dramatic poet first rehearsing and then producing a play, so 'I was taught' may be self-referential, Silenus speaking of his role in this play.

Luppe (1988) 36 suggested that our passage is possibly the 'epilogue' of a play, although it resembles a 5th century comic poet's direct address to his audience in a choral parabasis within a play (this view was endorsed by Kannicht in Gauly (1991) 250, not least because the metre here, anapaestic tetrameters, is characteristic of such passages). Battezzato (2006) has subjected these 'parabatic' or 'metatheatrical'[3] elements, so suggestive of Old Comedy, to the most detailed appraisal yet (26, 39–60); he shows that the anapaests approximate in style to those of 5th century tragedy rather than comedy (27–36); and he reviews all similar phenomena from known satyric fragments. He concludes that our fragment's genre is not certainly identifiable, let alone its poet's identity and date: if it is satyric, there is no parallel for its rupture of the theatrical illusion with these 'metatheatrical' elements, unless the genre had now become assimilated to comedy (61); if it is comic, such a rupture is unproblematic, but then the fragment may well be a Hellenistic 'recreation' of a 'classical' comedy (with the anapaests imitating tragic style) as if from the 5th century itself; and Battezzato himself inclines to 5th century comic authorship (62). His paper constitutes the current 'state of the question'.

[Prof. Storey has since given us personally his 'instinctive reaction' that the fragment is comic rather than satyric; he favours its origin in a parabasis not an *agon* (for *agon* 'contest' see our n. 22 on v. 27), since 'the anapaests are very much in the comic manner'. He notes the self-referential passage Aristophanes, *Acharnians* 504 'Our *agon* is at the Lenaea' (the Athenian dramatic festival in very early spring) and that the word 'trash' (our v. 25) is used of inferior comedy by Aristophanes at *Clouds* 524, *Wasps* 66. In particular, he adduces Eupolis, *Marikas* F 205 *PCG* (anapaestic like our fragment) 'today's nonsense from poets' as probably a reference to tragic poets, comparing the term 'nonsense' abusing Aeschylus at Aristophanes, *Frogs* 1005 (but the text is insecure) and Euripides at 1497 (cf. I. C. S. Storey, *Eupolis* (Oxford, 2003) 212). In thinking of a 'late 5th Century comedy' Prof. Storey thus offers the same judgement as Battezzato (2006; see below).]

The fragment certainly reads as if it stems from a performance-text, rather than one for a literary readership alone: for this issue cf. Lycophron's *Menedemus* above, and *Adespota* F 655 and F 667a below. The combative stance is like that of the probably satyric Pratinas 4 F 3, where a performer complains and appeals to his patron deity (Dionysus) very emphatically; and its 'metatheatrical' address to the audience resembles that of the mid-4th century Astydamas II 60 *Heracles* F 4 (satyric: see our Appendix), 'The wise poet must offer the spectators varied good cheer, like that of a rich dinner, so that a man may go away after eating and drinking what he enjoys taking, and there is no one kind of musical performance provided' (on this 'one clear example of audience address' in satyric drama see Kaimio (2001) 59–60, cf. 36–8);[4] cf. also the comedian Metagenes of about 400 BC, *The*

Lover of Sacrifices F 15 *PCG* 'I change my style episode by episode, so that I may feast the spectators with many novel dishes.'[5] Conversely, a would-be dramatist is frustrated by the laxity of his tragic Muse in the comic *Adespota* F 1051 *PCG* (reproduced as a testimony, *Adespota* F 727, in *TrGF* 2.310).

Lastly, Di Marco (2003) 68–74 boldly hazards that the author may be Sositheus, and the play his *Daphnis or Lityerses*. His arguments rest chiefly on Sositheus' reputation as reviver of satyric (see our introductory discussion to the play); on the severe metrical style of both F 646a and of *Daphnis* F 2; and on Silenus' prominence as the speaker, as in the *Menedemus* of Sositheus' contemporary Lycophron (above). Di Marco suggests that in F 646a.22 'the (*a noun is missing*) from a foreign land' is not a person, or the god Dionysus himself, but the popular ditty 'Lament for Lityerses', introduced from abroad into an Alexandrian setting. Di Marco's arguments go hand in hand, however, with widespread and extremely speculative supplements of the text of vv. 19–27.[6]

Notes

[1] Gauly (1991) 250 suspects that the mere fact, that two papyri survive, indicates wide circulation and possible influence of this text; similarly Conrad (1997) 220. P. Köln is the older papyrus (c. 2 BC), and clearly from an anthology (in which F 646a is followed by a different hymn); P. Fack. is younger by a century, and probably from an originally complete play-text: see Battezzato (2006) 21–3.

[2] The 'hymn' is finely analysed by Di Marco (2003) 48–54. Battezzato (2006) 60 n. 137 compares the god's progress from babyhood to full stature with accounts in tragedy of 'human progress': see n. 3 on Critias' (?) *Sisyphus* (?).

[3] Battezzato's (2006, 40–1) suggestion of the alternative terms 'metaliterary, metadiscursive, metaperformative' shows how difficult it is to describe this text satisfactorily.

[4] This F 4 of Astydamas is constantly adduced: most recently by Di Marco (2003) 63–4 and Battezzato (2006) 44, 47–50. The latter notes the opinions of D. Bain, *CQ* 25 (1975) 23–5 and of O. Taplin, *JHS* 106 (1986) 166 n.16 that its 'parabatic' character requires its attribution to comedy; but satyric (and Hellenistic) origin has again been argued by A. Barbieri, *Eikasmos* 13 (2002) 121–31. Cf. Storey's reference to Eupolis, *Marikas* F 205, introductory discussion above.

[5] The culinary metaphor is best known from Aeschylus' supposed comment that his plays were 'slices from Homer's great dinners', Athenaeus 8.347d = *TrGF* 3.69 T 112a, which is a commonplace in Plato: see Dodds on *Gorgias* 447a5. Such metaphors are illustrated by E. Gowers, *The Loaded Table* (Oxford, 1993), esp. 79–87 (with Astydamas II 60 F 4 and Metagenes F 15 on p. 80).

[6] We do not report them: they can be assessed only as part of his own lengthy discussion of the entire fragment.

F 646a

<ΣΙΛΗΝΟΣ>

remnants of 6 line-ends (1–6), *in which the following words are read*:

1 ε]ἲς οἶδμ' ἀπολίσθο[ι, 4] Σεμέλης [τέ]κ[ο]ς ὕμνον, 5]
θεὸς Ἀρκάς, 6]σκεπτομεν[,

then ends of 21 lines (7–27), *with perhaps 15 to 20 letters missing from the start of most:*

].υλε…δησ 9 *let.* ει παρέδωκεν	(7)
] πεφευγὼς ἤθυρον ἐγὼ νέος ἄντροις	
]ουργος ἁπλοῦς, πάσης κακίας ἀμίαντος	
].οσισου καρπὸν μὲν ἑλὼν τὸν ὄρειον	(10)
]αι τὸ πάλαι θηρῶν ἐφόδοις ἀκόμιστον	
] παιδεύσας ὥριον ἥβην ἐφύλαξα	
καρπὸ]ν ὀπώρας ἦρα βαθείας ἐπὶ λήνους	
]ν εἰς θνητοὺς ἀνέφηνα ποτὸν Διονύσου	
]σος ὁ μύστης οὔποτε λήγων ἐπὶ Βάκχῳ	(15)

P. Köln 242 (2nd c. BC) ed. K. Maresch, *Kölner Papyri* VI (1987) fr. a col. i (line-ends only, varying between about 10 and 20 letters and some defective); 7–25 P. Fackelmann 5 (1st c. BC) ed. B. Kramer, *ZPE* 34 (1979) 1–14 fr. b (line-ends, many slightly defective, esp. 21, 24, 25), re-ed. Kannicht-Snell in *TrGF* 2 (1981) 217–19; combined text ed. (Kannicht in) Gauly (1991) 250–3 and Kannicht in *TrGF* 5.1134–7. Thus only P. Köln has parts of 1–6 and 26–7; and it helps restore the line-ends of P. Fack. in 7, 9, 11, 14, 15–18, 20, 22–5. Our *apparatus* does not give full details of the overlaps between the two papyri: for these see *TrGF* vols. 2 and 5.

1 (μὴ) … ἀπολίσθο[ις Maresch
4 τὸν δ' εἰς] Σεμέλης Luppe
8–9 αντροι[ς P. Fack., αντρ`ασ´ων *i.e.* ἄντρων P. Köln, whence ἄντρων | φρουρὸς Di Marco
9 ὑπ]οὖργος Di Marco
13 καρπὸ]ν Maresch
15 επι βακχωι P. Köln: ἐπ' Ἰά[κχῳ read and supplemented in P. Fack. by Parsons

F 646a (P. Köln 242 fr. a col. i; 7–25 P. Fackelmann 5 fr. b)
<SILENUS>
remains of 6 line-ends (1–6) *including the following words*:

> 1 (*lest he*?) slip off into the swell,[7] 4 the hymn (to?) Semele's
> son (i.e. *Dionysus*), 5 the Arcadian god (i.e. *Hermes, or possibly
> Pan*), 6 (examining?), *then centres and ends of 21 lines* (7–27):
>
> ... (Hermes?) handed over (Dionysus) ... after my escape I played
> as a youngster in the cave ... a simple ...-worker,[8] untainted
> by every vice ... taking the mountain's harvest[9] (10) ... what
> anciently had not been gathered because of wild beasts' attacks
> ... I educated and guarded (*Dionysus'*) youthful prime[10] ... I bore
> autumn's (harvest?) to deep vats ... I revealed Dionysus' draught
> to mortals[11] ... the initiate never ceasing ... for Bacchus[12] (15) ...

[7] '(*lest he*?) slip off into the swell': whether expressing a purpose or a fear, often taken to allude to the young Dionysus' taking refuge with the sea-goddess Thetis when pursued by Lycurgus (Homer, *Iliad* 6.135–7); but the suggestion also suits very well Hermes' transportation by air of the infant Dionysus, handed over (7) for upbringing to the nymphs of Mt. Nysa (Eur. *Cyc.* 4, cf. 68; also *Iliad* 6.132–3, *Homeric Hymn to Dionysus* XXXVI 2–5 Allen, Diodorus 3.70.7, 4.2.3; in art *e.g. LIMC* VIII.1.1130 'Silenoi' no. 215 (late 4th century); cf. G. Hedreen *JHS* 114 (1994) 49–54) – just as the infant Hermes is given to the nymph Cyllene in Sophocles' *Trackers* F 314.271. Maresch's supplement makes the verb 'slip' 2nd person, and into a wish or even (Di Marco (2003) 73) a curse upon another character.

[8] Vv. 8–9: 'cave' can refer only to Silenus' mountain refuge; but the case of the Greek word differs between the two papyri, and the genitive in P. Köln may go with the beginning of v. 9 (Di Marco (2003) 49, conjecturing '(as guardian) of the cave'). The simplest supplement of '-worker' is Di Marco's (50), 'under-worker', *i.e.* a 'servant': the verb occurs in 21.

[9] Grapes, to make wine, 13–14.

[10] 'educated ... youthful prime': the satyrs' guardianship of the infant and young Dionysus is well-attested (n. 7 above); they offer similar care to the infant Perseus, Aesch. *Net-Fishers* F 47a.41–56. There may be a play on meanings in Greek 'youthful prime': Silenus tends not only the god of the vine (who was frequently held to personify wine: see on *Cyc.* 123–4, 519), but the vine itself; for the role of the educator as cultivator or gardener, see Antiphon 87 B 60 D-K; Plato, *Rep.* 491d–e; cf. Pindar, *Nem.* 8.40–2. The word 'youthful prime' may be a metaphor for a young plant (Gauly (1991) 302), or a name for a species of fine grape (see Gow on Theocritus 5.109).

[11] Similarly Astydamas II 60 F 6 (genre unknown), with revelation by the god himself; cf. n. 8 on Pratinas 4 F 3.15. In Soph. *Little Dionysus* F 171–2 the satyrs seem to be present at the invention of wine.

[12] So P. Köln; P. Fack.'s reading had suggested 'Iacchus', a cult-name of Dionysus local to Eleusis, the site of the famous Mysteries; it is used of the god's association with Mt. Nysa at Sophocles F 959. Silenus indeed uses the term 'initiate' here; for allusions in satyric drama to the mysteries see Seaford (1984) on *Cyc.* 495–502.

Βάκχη] δὲ θεοῦ πρώτη πλοκάμοις ἀνέδησεν
]ων λήθη χάρισιν κείναις ἀνέλαμψεν
]αι θίασος· τοιάδε κομπεῖν ἐδιδάχθην.
]. μέγας φησὶν ἀοιδὸς Σαλαμῖνος
]ης ταμίας, νῦν δ' εἰς ἀπατὰς κεκύλισμαι   (20)
]ας παῦρος ὑπουργῶν ταῖς ψευδομένα[ις] …[
]αραπέμψει τὸν ἀπ' ὀθνείας ἐπεγείρων
]γνωτε, θεαί· τραγικῶν ὁ παρὼν πόνος ὕμνων

16 Βάκχη] δὲ Kannicht
17 κακ]ῶν Lloyd-Jones: πόν]ων Parsons;
19 μέγας, φῆσιν ἀοιδός, Σαλαμῖνος punct. Kannicht
20 γνώμ]ης ταμίας Kannicht; κεκυλισμαι P. Köln: κεκυλ[P. Fack.
21 ψευδομένα[ις] Snell: ψευδομε`να[ (an incomplete addition, perhaps `να['ις) P. Köln: ψευδομε[P. Fack.
22 π]αραπέμψει Kannicht; επεγειρων P. Köln: επιγ[P. Fack.
23 εὖ] γνῶτε Kannicht: σύγ]γνωτε West, Austin; end P. Köln: ο (*i.e.* δ) παρωσ`ι' (*i.e.* παρῶσι) πο[P. Fack.

and the first (Bacchant?) of the god tied ... up in her locks[13] ...
forgetfulness (of?)[14]... shone out in those delights ... the sacred
troop: I was taught (*or* trained) to vaunt such things.
... says the great bard of Salamis[15] ... steward ...;[16] but now I have
been rolled headlong into deceptions (20) ... a little (...?), serving
the lying[17] ... will stir and escort(?) the ... from a foreign land(?)[18]
... know (well?) (*or* show pardon?), you goddesses:[19] the present

[13] 'tied ... up in her locks', *i.e.* wool, probably, as Eur. *Bacc.* 111–13; bay-leaves, Pindar, *Pythians* 10.40 *etc.*

[14] 'forgetfulness (of?)': probably 'of evils' (Lloyd-Jones), cf. *Cyc.* 172; wine cures 'grief' *e.g.* Soph. *Little Dionysus* F 172. However, 'toils' (Parsons) is a possibility; in Ar. *Frogs* (1321) the grape vine is described as 'ending toil'; see also on n. 20 below.

[15] A possible allusion to Euripides (for the island of Salamis as his birth-place see *TrGF* 5.45 T IA.1); if so, the fragment is almost certainly to be dated after his death. More likely Homer is meant, since the Greek word 'bard' suggests an epic poet (Battezzato (2006) 50–3); and Salamis on Cyprus was among many cities which claimed Homer's birth – or a lyric poet is meant, for whom Di Marco (2003) 57–8 suggests Simonides. But the Greek may be punctuated alternatively as '"... great ... of Salamis", says the bard', when the latter 'bard' may denote the poet himself (suggested by Kannicht, following West).

[16] 'steward (with good judgement)' supplemented by Kannicht, comparing the expression at Theognis 504.

[17] 'deceptions ... lying': reference unclear, but 'lying' is a recognized feature of poetry as far back as Hesiod, *Theogony* 27; and 'deception' was considered intrinsic to tragedy generally, Gorgias 82 B 23 DK (with approval), Plato, *Republic* 10.598d–e, *etc.* (without approval); see n. 8 on Critias(?), *Sisyphus*(?). Aristophanes' Euripides accuses Aeschylus of 'deceiving' the spectators, *Frogs* 911. Further material and discussion in Bierl (1990) 365–8, 384–6.

[18] 'the ... from a foreign land': 'god' is suggested; Dionysus' arrival in Greece from the East is evoked in Eur. *Bacc.* 13–20. See however the last paragraph of our introductory discussion.

[19] 'you goddesses': the Muses; cf. Pratinas 4 F 3.4.

].ος ὁρίζει· μὴ τὰ δικαίως καλὰ μόχθῳ
]φθέντα μόλις θῆτε παρέργου τρίτα φόρτου   (25)
]αδεν ὀρθῇ Διόνυσος
β]ραβεύσας γ᾽ ἐν ἀγῶνι.

24 καλα μοχθωι P. Köln: καλαμ[P. Fack.
25 end P. Köln: παρεργου .[P. Fack.

effort of tragic songs[20] ... sets a limit ... Don't put what is justly
beautiful ... (*and?*) has been hard (*won?*) ... with toil ... in third
place ... among incidental trash[21] (25) ... with upright ... Dionysus
... adjudicating in the contest.[22]

[20] 'the present effort of tragic songs': meaning obscure and possibly the key phrase of vv.
19–27; it is the title of Battezzato's 2006 paper. Both he (53–6) and Di Marco (2003) 45
interpret 'effort' as poetic activity, Di Marco as Hellenistic 'code' for artistic elaboration
in general. Probably the sentence continues the hostility towards tragic poetry explicit in
vv. 20–1. πόνος denotes the 'labour' or 'toil' that a poet has in making his creations (LSJ
Suppl. s.v. III; see also Pindar, *Nem.* 3.12, *Dith.* 3.16; Callimachus, *Epigr.* 6.1 Pfeiffer, *etc.*);
in Ar. *Frogs* (1370) Aeschylus and Euripides are both described as ἐπίπονοί ('painstaking').
The connotations of πόνος in F 646a, then, may thus also be stylistic, which suggests that
the criticism may be directed at certain poets of the day ('present effort') because of the
laboriousness or πόνος of their hymns. This would be fitting if it comes from Silenus, since
he, even more than Dionysus, is averse to πόνος in any form (cf. *Cyc.* 1–2, *etc.*).
    The translation 'the present effort' is of P. Köln, the older papyrus; P. Fack., the younger,
is strikingly different and difficult (and the word 'effort' incomplete), for its text yields
'which (*a relative clause apparently to be governed by* 'sets a limit (*to*)' *in the next line*) ...
(*no subject survives for the following verb*) neglect'.
[21] 'in third place': the last in many poetic and dramatic contests (cf. 27). In the Greek 'trash'
is a partitive genitive of value, Smyth § 1373, cf. LSJ τίθημι B.II.4. (Our interpretation of
these lines coincides with Battezzato (2006) 25 n. 16, cf. 56–7.)
[22] 'upright': the missing noun was something like 'mind' or '(good) judgement' (cf. n. 16
on v. 20). 'adjudicating': for this word see Soph. *Trackers* F 314a.26; for a poetic 'contest'
(*agon*) within a play see above all that between Aeschylus and Euripides in Ar. *Frogs* –
which Dionysus 'judges' (873); also in Cratinus' *Dionysalexandros* F 39–51 *PCG* Dionysus
played the role of Alexander (Paris) in judging the beauty contest between Hera, Athena and
Aphrodite (F 41); in Soph. *Inachus* F 288 and F 295 references are made to possible voting
equipment to decide what may be a musical contest in that play (see Lloyd-Jones (1996)
116). On vv. 24–7 see also our introductory discussion.

Adespota F 655: an 'Atlas' play

(3rd/2nd century BC?)

TrGF 2.231–5.

Text etc. E. G. Turner, 'P. Bodmer XXVIII: A Satyr Play on the Confrontation of Heracles and Atlas', *MH* 33 (1976) 1–23; Gauly (1991) 256–61, 302–3; T. Günther, R. Krumeich in KPS 624–31.

Discussions. M. L. West, 'The Asigmatic Atlas', *ZPE* 22 (1976) 41–2; W. Luppe, *APF* 27 (1980) 246–7; Sutton (1980) 87–8; Gallo (1992) 43 n.1, 104; Gantz (1993) 410–13; G. Xanthakis-Karamanos, 'A Survey of the Main Papyrus Texts for Post-Classical Tragedy', *Akten des 21. Internationalen Papyrologen-Kongress, Berlin 1995.* II (Stuttgart 1997) 1034–48, at 1039–41 = G. X.-K., *Dramatica* (Athens, 2002) 385–401, at 392–4; Conrad (1997) 213–16, 302–3; Voelke (2001) 23–4; Cipolla (2003) 17 n. 92; Luz (2010) 234–40.

Art. Gallo (1992) 23–41 and figs 1–6; *LIMC* V.1.100–2 'Herakles' nos 2676–89, esp. 2687 = Trendall-Webster (1971) II.13, Gallo (1992) 35–6 with fig. 6, KPS 624–5 and fig. 30b, T. H. Carpenter in Harrison (2005) 229–31 with fig. 7, Taplin (2007) 34 with fig. 14.

Heracles' 'Eleventh Labour' in servitude to Eurystheus (the eponym of the Euripidean satyr play F 371–80, above) was to fetch the golden apples of the Hesperides. On his way to attempt this he passed near Prometheus, fettered to a mountain in the Caucasus as punishment for his theft of fire from heaven to give to men (see on Aeschylus, *Prometheus the Fire-Kindler*, above). Prometheus was daily tormented by an eagle tearing at his liver, which Heracles shot with his bow; in gratitude Prometheus gave him advice how to succeed in fetching the apples by getting the help of Atlas (who bore the sky on his shoulders); Gantz (1993) 410–13 analyses the varied mythography. What happened is recounted by Pherecydes 3 F 17.2–14 *FGrH* (= F 17.15–25 Fowler 287):

> Heracles went to Atlas and explained his task, and ordered him to take three of their apples from the Hesperides and bring them. Atlas put the sky on Heracles' shoulders and went off to the Hesperides. He got the apples from them; returning to Heracles he said he would take the apples back to Eurystheus, and ordered Heracles to hold the sky in his place. After promising this Heracles put the sky back on to Atlas by means of a trick: for Prometheus had suggested he should order Atlas to take the sky back until he made a

cushion for his shoulders. So Atlas put the apples on the ground and took over the sky. Heracles picked the apples up and bade Atlas farewell; he went off to Mycenae to Eurystheus and showed him the apples.

The only documented 'Atlas' play was produced at Athens in 255/4 BC (inscriptional record: *TrGF* I². 31 DID II A 4a.12 and 14 = *TrGF* 2.7 *Adespota* F 1f). It was satyric (DID 12); but its poet's name is lost, it is unknown whether it was a new play or a revival, and its plot is a blank. The papyrus text of F 655 was written in the 2nd century AD.

An Apulian bell-crater of *c.* 390/80 BC depicts satyrs having stolen Heracles' weapons while he supports the sky on his shoulders (see *LIMC* no. 2687 in 'Art' above). This depiction may just vary a not uncommon motif of older art in which satyrs rob Heracles of his weapons while he is (drunkenly) asleep (*e.g.* an Attic kalpis of *c.* 460 BC, *LIMC* V.1.156 'Herakles' no. 3234 = KPS figs 20a, b); but scholars have inevitably been tempted, in the light of Pherecydes, to relate the crater to F 655; for in the fragment Heracles accuses Atlas of having broken an oath (v. 2), to which Atlas replies that he swore only to bring the apples (4), not to take back the sky (6–7). The rest of the papyrus continues their argument, with Heracles bitter at his deception and promising retaliation (8–13, 19–25); both he and Atlas claim that their divine ancestry deserves respect by the other, while Atlas adds that his release from bearing the sky was foretold in an ancient oracle (35–7), at the hands of a 'helper' (37, perhaps also 59), whom he identifies in Heracles.

Even if the 4th century crater reflects in some degree the mythical incident known to us from the 5th Century Pherecydes, it may not depend upon a satyr-play of that or any period. Similarly there is no inevitable link between F 655 and the satyric 'Atlas' play of 254 BC, still less any putative earlier satyr-play (see Gallo (1992) under 'Art', Conrad (1997) 215–16). Most importantly, the fragment yields no certain internal indication that it was satyric, although:

(1) the word 'sons' (or 'boys') in 43 has seemed to some (first to Turner (1976) 15) to echo Silenus' common address to his satyrs (*e.g.* Lycophron, *Menedemus* F 2.1);

(2) the word 'coward' in 21 translates a metaphor from the name for a kind of eagle, 'white-tail' (cf. English 'white feathers'). Its component '-tail' is the common (or vulgar), but also medical, word for 'buttock' which is not found in Lyric or Tragedy, and is very rare in Epic; the metaphorical compound occurs also in the one-word Sophocles F 1085, of unknown genre; but it is not safe to infer that both fragments are therefore satyric (on the

pedigree of the word and metaphor see Fraenkel on Aesch. *Ag.* 115, where the brave Agamemnon is 'black behind' and the implicitly timid Menelaus is 'white behind'). See also our n. 9 below;

(3) while the words 'escape from the labours' in 42 suggest this common motif of satyric (*e.g. Cyc.* 442), they are no less appropriate to the simple predicament of either Heracles or Atlas. As with other fragments of doubtful attribution, the part played by the satyrs or Silenus can only be guessed, but they might well encourage, if not share in, any deception. There may well have been a comic opportunity for them to make off with Heracles' weapons while he was incapacitated (above).

The fragmentary play's genre is thus not established (so Cipolla (2003) 17). Its subject matter may seem satyric rather than tragic, especially with the deception charged to Atlas (v. 8) and Heracles' intention to retaliate in kind (13, 21?; cf. Pherecydes): the triumph of the Greek hero over a threatening giant is consistent with, for instance, Odysseus' triumph over Polyphemus in *Cyclops*. West (1976) argues nevertheless that such a ruse is not incompatible with tragedy; cf. KPS (1999) 624.

There may be greater hope of establishing the fragment's pedigree than its genre, however (even the late date of the papyrus is not conclusive), for it has one distinctive feature: the poet has eschewed the letter *sigma* entirely. Similar virtuoso compositions omitting individual letters ('lipogrammatic') are known throughout antiquity (D. Clayman, 'Sigmatism in Greek Poetry', *TAPA* 117 (1987) 69–84; KPS 625 n. 8 also cites the 6th century BC poet Lasus of Hermione, named by Athenaeus 10.455c; for his asigmatic *Hymn to the Demeter of Hesione* (F 702 *PMG*) see now Luz 2010 *passim*). This

---

F 655
col. i fr. A
<ΑΤΛΑΣ>   μόχθων· ἐπ' ἄτην δευτέρα[ν
<ΗΡΑΚΛΗΣ>   εἶτ' οὐκ ἐπαίδη τὴν μεθ' ὁρκ[ίων φάτιν
            αἴρων παλαιόν τ' ἀφθίτων [

P. Bodmer XXVIII (2nd c. AD) ed. E. G. Turner, *MH* 33 (1976) 1–23; our text reproduces *TrGF*

1 at least one line from Atlas preceded μόχθων
2 end Snell

virtuosity strongly suggests the Hellenistic age, in which such literary 'trifles' or 'games' (*paignia*, παίγνια) were common: see our discussion of the 'new (2007) *adespoton*', below. This dating is also indicated by the avoidance in our fragment of metrical resolution, a feature shared with Sositheus' *Daphnis* (above). Again, however, West (1976) 42 thinks chiefly on this metrical basis that the piece is more likely to be tragic than satyric.

Such a Hellenistic dating for the fragment opens two further questions. First, did the papyrus contain merely a scene or an entire play: again, see on the 'new (2007) *adespoton*'. Second, was either the scene or the play a literary 'version' of a much older 'traditional' one, or an original composition, prompted perhaps either by scholarly knowledge of the 3rd Century *Atlas* from Athens, or part of the 3rd century enthusiasm at Alexandria for satyric of which Sositheus' *Daphnis* and Lycophron's *Menedemus* are examples? Recent opinion has hardened in support of Sutton's view (1980, 87–8) that the play was a new work of this time; cf. esp. Conrad (1997) 214–16. Luz (2010) 234 offers answers to both questions: that an entire play, not just one scene, was possible without *sigma*s; and that the 'Atlas' play stems from any time between the 3rd century BC and the 2nd century AD, the date of the papyrus.

Some kind of theatrical performance is conceivable: even if Atlas and Heracles are shown alternating in their support of the sky, the latter could be symbolically represented or even painted on a backcloth. It must remain speculative whether the cast-list extended beyond Atlas, Heracles and satyrs, but some action and diversion for a theatre audience would be needed while Atlas was absent recovering the apples.

F 655 (P. Bodmer XXVIII)

col. i fr. A

<ATLAS>   ... of (my?) labours: ... to a second fatal error.[1]

<HERACLES>   Then have you no shame in reneging upon (?) your (word given) on oath and ... the ancient ... of the immortal gods?

[1] 'second fatal error': if he now takes the sky back from Heracles. His first error was sharing the Titans' attempt to overthrow Zeus (23, cf. n. 10), for which he was punished with holding up the sky for eternity (Hesiod, *Theogony* 517–20; *Prometheus Bound* 348–50; cf. Gantz (1993) 46): thus Atlas and his brother Titan, Prometheus, were both punished with immobility, in the case of Atlas perpetually.

<AT.>   μήλων ἐπώμνυν δεῦρ[(ο)

            ἰδού, φέρου τόνδ᾽· ἄλλο δ᾽ οὐ[(5)

            ὅρκοι διεῖπαν· οὔτε τόνδ[(ε)

            νώτῳ βαρύν μοι μόχθον [*traces*

<HP.>   διηπάτημαι· τἆλλα δ᾽ εὐγενεῖ δόλ[ῳ

            κλέπτων ἐπ᾽ ἄλλην πημάτων ἵξῃ .[

            μαρτύρομαι δὲ τὴν κατ᾽ οὐρανὸν Θέμιν   (10)

            ὀθούν[ε]χ᾽ εὑρὼν οὐ δίκαιον Ἡρακλεῖ

            Ἄτλαντα, κεἰ πέφυκεν ἀφθίτων ἄπο,

            μέτειμ[ι·] κεἰ γὰρ θνητά μοι τὰ μητρό[θεν,

            Δίων γ᾽ ἂ[ν] εἶμεν ἄξιοι γεννητόρων.

<AT.>   ἄλλων [τὸ] ταρβεῖν, οὐκ ἐμόν· ῥώμη τε γ[ὰρ   (15)

            πρῶτόν με μήτηρ Γαῖα Τιτάνων τεκ[εῖν

            αὐχεῖ Κρόνου θ᾽ ὅμαιμον, ᾧ ποτ᾽ εἴχομ[εν

            κοινὴν Ὀλύμπου τὴν ἄνω μοναρχίαν.

<HP.>   ἥ τοι πάρ[ε]δρον θεῶν δρόμον κεκτημένη

4 *e.g.* δεῦρ[ο φορμὸν (Handley) αὖ φέρειν Turner
9 end *e.g.* β[ολήν Turner
13 end Handley
14 the letters α[.]ειμ in ἂ[ν] εἶμεν are uncertainly read in P. Bodmer
19 θρόνον suggested but rejected by Turner

<ATL.> I swore ...[2] of the apples to this place. Look, take this for yourself; but (my?) oath spoke clearly of no other ... (5), nor ... this heavy burden (*or* burden heavy?) on my back ...

<HER.> I have been wholly deceived! – but while you cheat in other things with a noble[3] trick, you'll come to a second (throw?) of suffering.[4] I swear, by Themis high in heaven, (10) that now I have found Atlas unjust to Heracles, I will pursue him for revenge even if he is the son of immortal gods; for even if my mother's side was mortal, I'd prove worthy of my father Zeus' line.[5]

<AT.> Fear is for others: it's not for me! (15) My mother Earth can vaunt my birth as first in strength of the Titans, as well as brother to Cronus, with whom we once shared the monarchy above of Olympus.[6]

<HER.> Justice who possesses a course that sits alongside the gods[7] has

[2] 'swore *etc.*': he defends his refusal to take back the sky by presenting his oath to Heracles as relating only to fetching the apples. The missing sense: *e.g.* '(to bring the) basket', Turner, Handley.

[3] 'noble': sardonic; cf. Critias(?), *Sisyphus*(?) 43 F 19.25 and Lycophron, *Menedemus* F 2.5.

[4] 'throw' Turner, a metaphor from dicing. Heracles appears to mean, Atlas may cheat him now, but his luck will change again for the worse.

[5] Heracles was jointly the son of Zeus and of the mortals Amphitryo and (see the introductory discussion to Eur. *Eurystheus* on F 377) Alcmene. In the Greek the author uses a plural periphrase in 'my father Zeus' line' in order to avoid the *sigma* which ends the singular possessive form of 'Zeus'. Similarly in 'I'd prove worthy' the Greek has a 'royal' plural to avoid the singular form of the adjective ending in *sigma* – but the plural also adds a certain pomposity to Heracles' words (cf. *Cyc.* 96–8 and n.). Heracles' invocation of Themis resonates on more than one level: not only is Themis 'Right' (see next note), she is, in another tradition, the mother of Prometheus (*Prometheus Bound* 18, 209–10, 874) who, according to Pherecydes (see introductory discussion above), gave Heracles the idea of how to trick Atlas into giving up the apples and taking back the sky.

[6] Cronus and his brother Atlas are here the sons of Earth and Uranus, the first ruler of all the gods; our poet, like that of *Prometheus Bound* 205, abandons Hesiod's version (Atlas the son of Iapetus and Clymene, *Theogony* 507–9), perhaps to heighten a contrast between Olympian and chthonian values appropriate for satyric drama. Heracles as son of Zeus invokes Themis ('Right', v. 10; see previous n.) as well as Justice (see nn. 7, 8), while Atlas vaunts his connections with the Titans and justifies his actions from his brute strength, as if he were a satyric ogre; and so in his lack of fear of Zeus (v. 15) he is like Polyphemus, *Cyc.* 320–1 and n.

[7] The contradictory expression in 'course that sits' is remarkable, but perhaps alludes to Justice's course as a star crossing the heaven (Aratus, *Phaenomena* 96–136; she is 'untroubled' at 100). Indeed the Greek word 'that sits alongside' regularly connotes an official or judicial capacity: LSJ s.v. πάρεδρος II. At Aeschylus F 281a.10 Justice sits by Zeus's throne, so that Turner suggested but himself rejected a simple scribe's error of 'course' for 'throne' here.

Δίκη δέδορκεν ὀξύ, κἂν ἀπῇ μακ[ράν·   (20)
κα]ὶ δὴ τό[δ'] ἂν πράξαιμεν· ἢ π[ύ]γαργο[ν
...].[.]ναπ[.]λλων κοιράνων ὁρμωμε[ν
..]. τἀπὶ Φ[λ]έγρα γηγενῶν φρονήμ[ατα
....].λ[....]η· καὶ τὸν ἐγγελῶντ' ἐ[μοὶ
ἐ]λθοιμ'· εἶτα δαιμ[ον   (25)

*single words and some letters from 5 further lines (26–30), into which the
tiny frs B and C (perhaps also from col. i) have been fitted (see n. 11 on the
translation)*

col. ii fr. D
*beginnings of 30 lines (31–60), the first (31) with only a few letters; letters
from the ends of some lines but no meaningful words perhaps remain in the
very scrappy frs F and E.*

ὅπου γὰρ ὧδεχ[(32)
πέποιθεν ἀλκ[..].[
θυμὸν καθημ[...]χθ[
ἐγὼ δὲ Μοιρῶν [.]ν..[(35)
οὕτω γε γραμμα[.]ων[
ἀρωγὸν εὕρω κ..τιδ[
φρούρημ' ['Ολ]ύμπου τη[
παῦλάν τιν' ἥξειν π[
ἀλλ' εἶα· μήλων ἐξοχ[(40)
δώρημα θνητῶν οὐκ[
φυγὴν δὲ μόχθων ων[
παίδων γὰρ οἶμαι π.[

HP. ὦ δαῖμον, εἰ χρὴ τὴν [
τάξιν μ' Ὀλυμπο[(45)
AT. οὕτω πατρῴων ἐλπ[
νεύων ἐπ' ἄτην μᾶλ[λον

21 τό[δ'] West
22 ἀπ' [ἄ]λλων Snell-Kannicht
24 -λων- uncertainly read
35 Μοιρῶν Snell-Kannicht: μοιρων P. Bodm.
41 δώρημ' ἀθνήτων Turner
44 and 46 full speaker-names were added only here by a second hand in the papyrus (the first
hand used only paragraphi here and everywhere else)

sharp sight,[8] I tell you, even if she is far away. (20) In truth I
might take this revenge ...; either (?) ... a coward[9] ... setting out ...
(from other?) rulers ... the arrogant intentions of the earth-born
at Phlegra[10] ...; and I would pursue (?) the one who mocks (me);
then ... god(s?) ... (25), *then:*

remnants of 5 lines (26–30) into which the very scrappy frs. B *and* C *have
been fitted, but still with no clear sense;*[11]

   then follows col. ii fr. D, *with the beginnings of 30 lines (31–60). At some
point between 29 or 30 and 43 Atlas resumes speaking, for the papyrus
makes* Heracles *the speaker of 44–5:*

<ATL.>	... *a few letters only* ... for where ... he has trust (in his?) strength ... (I?) sit ... anger (?) ... But I ... of the Fates[12] (35) ... Thus the writing[13] ... (if?) I find a helper ... protection of Olympus ... that some respite will come ... But – here! ... the finest of the apples ... (40) ... the gift of mortals (*or* immortals?) ... escape from the labours ... for I think ... of the sons.[14]
HER.	O deity! If (I?) must ... the ordinance (of?) Olympus ... (45)
ATL.	(If you?) ... hopes (from your) father's ... in this way ... (you will?) ... inclining more to ruin ...

[8]   Justice's 'sharp sight': Hesiod, *Works and Days* 267 etc.

[9]   'coward': for the register of this metaphor in the Greek, lit. 'white-buttocked, *or* -tailed',
and its converse, 'black-buttocked', *i.e.* 'brave', see the introductory discussion (2). For other
associations of cowardice and 'having a white tail', or being λευκόπυγος, see Alexis F 322
PCG and its lexicographic sources. Heracles was nicknamed 'black-buttocked', *i.e.* 'hairy-
arsed' and virile, as proverbially formidable (Ar. *Lysistrata* 802; Zenobius 5.10.5; Suda μ 449
Adler *etc.*; for 'hairy-arsed' in this sense cf. also Plato Comicus F 3.1 *PCG*), and there may
be an unspoken such allusion here.

[10] 'Phlegra' (historical Pallene): on the westernmost of the three peninsulas of the Chalcidice
in the north Aegean, east of Macedonia; it was where Heracles helped Zeus overthrow the
Titans (kinsmen of Atlas; cf. n. 1 above), *e.g.* Aesch. *Eum.* 295; [Apollod.] 1.6.1.

[11] A bold reconstruction of these lines (by M. L. West in *TrGF* 2.233) begins 'I would (still)
pursue the one who mocks (me), if (my father) has won the rule (over) the gods (above, and
brings me) honour ever (to be proclaimed).'

[12] 'Fates': associated and almost identified with the Erinyes ('Furies'), Aesch. *Eum.* 335,
724, 961.

[13] 'writing (i.e. *an oracle*) ... helper': see introductory discussion.

[14] 'sons' has no clear reference: see introductory discussion.

<HP.>   ὦ δεινὰ τολμῶν .δ..[
                ξένων τ᾽ ἐπόπτην ου[
<AT.>   μὴ κάμνε μόχθον κα[(50)
                παλαιόν, ἐξ οὗ τήνδεκ.[
<HP.>   ἀλλ᾽ εἰ τόδ᾽ "Ηρᾳ τερπνὸ[ν
                παρ᾽ οὐδὲν οὕτω τἀμὰ [
                ἐκεῖ]νο δ᾽ ἡμῖν λ[υ]πρ[ὸν
                ... τ]όλμαν ἔργω[ν] τῶ[ν   (55)
                ...]δε κάμνων [ο]υ πυ[
                ...]μῃ· πάρεργον τοῦ[το
                ...].τα· ἔρημοι δ[
                ...]νδ᾽ ἀρωγὸν το..[
                τὸ]ν οὐ δίκαιον ο.[(60)

49 κακ(ων) written above ξενων P. Bodm.
55 end, 57 end, 60 beg Kannicht

\<HER.\>	Your audacity is terrible! ... observer of strange(rs?)[15] ...
\<ATL.\>	Don't weary with the burden ... (50) ... ancient, from the time when ...
\<HER.\>	But if this is pleasing to Hera[16] ... my (condition?) like this at nothing ... That is however painful to me ... the audacity of (your?) actions ... (55) ... (as I?) weary ... This (is?) incidental[17] ... abandoned (*plural*) ... a helper ... the unjust (*singular*) ... (60)

[15] The papyrus has 'evil' above 'strange(rs?)', but whether as adjective or noun is unclear through textual damage.

[16] 'Hera': the goddess who relentlessly persecuted Heracles received the first apple-tree as a wedding gift from Earth (Pherecydes 3 F 16 abc *FGrH* = F 16 abc Fowler 286); so his present 'condition' (v. 53?) is 'pleasing' to her.

[17] 'incidental': perhaps an allusion to Heracles' counter-trick, to punish Atlas (v. 8–9: so Gauly (1991, 303 n. 7); the word translates πάρεργον, a term used to denote Heracles' heroic achievements done 'beside, incidentally to' his journeys upon famous labours (Philostratus, *Imagines* II.398.3 Kayser), which included, among other things, defeating satyric ogres such as Busiris and Syleus. Perhaps it also alludes to Atlas' 'audacity' (v. 55) as a side-issue to completing the Labour itself, but one nevertheless with which Heracles must deal (cf. Heracles in a different context at Eur. *Heracles* 1340, Theseus' offer to him of sanctuary, 'incidental' to the effects of his infanticide).

Adespota F 667a: a 'Medea' play
(undated)

TrGF 5.1137–42.

Text etc. P. Lit. Lond. 77 ed. H. J. Milne (1927), after the first edition by W. Crönert, *APF* 3 (1906) 1–5; C. Austin, *Comicorum Graecorum Fragmenta in Papyris Reperta* (Berlin, 1973) 347–53 (F 350), an edition adopted for *TrGF* by Kannicht, with acknowledgement; D. F. Sutton, 'P. Lit. Lond. 77: a Post-Classical Satyr-Play', in his *Papyrological Studies in Dionysiac Literature* (Oak Park ILL, 1987) 9–60.

Discussion. R. L. Hunter, 'P. Lit. Lond. 77 and Tragic Burlesque', *ZPE* 41 (1981) 19–24.

The naming in this fragment of Creon (39, 91), Aegeus (42), Jason (48) and women of Corinth (113), and the mention of a woman's dishonour (22) and then of someone's flight (46: see n. 5 below), at once identify the play as a '*Medea*', and suggest that its plot resembled that of Euripides' tragedy. The first editor and students of the fragment had inclined to assign it to Neophron's *Medea* (*TrGF* 1¹.92–4; 15 F 13), but later ones to comedy (Austin, cf. *TrGF* 1².346). Not long after them Hunter (1981) suggested that it is a post-classical burlesque of tragedy. Sutton (1987) argued however from the linguistic register of 88 and 94 (see n. 7 below) and the (homo)sexual explicitness of 85 and 96–7 that it was probably a satyr-play in the form of a mythological travesty (see his pp. 19–28); but it is worth noting that the distinctive words are grouped in a short passage and are the only ones suggestive of satyric origin in the more than 120 fragmentary lines which survive (see nn. 9 and 10 below). Subsequently the fragment has not been included in *PCG* by Kassel-Austin (see Vol. VIII.518, which refers to Sutton 1987) nor by KPS, but Kannicht has taken it into *TrGF* as from a 'satyric (?) *Medea*' (5.1137).[1]

So the argument for satyric status depends largely upon surmise from the register of a few verses, while the rest of a fairly long text savours of 'a reasonable approximation' to the 'metrical and verbal style' of 'classical Tragedy': thus Hunter (19–21), concluding his detailed analysis of the fragment before arguing (21–4) that the few parodies of tragedy known from comedy offer nothing sustained at such length as F 667a. Against parodic provenance too may be the striking fact that 667a divides over a choral interlude at v. 112 (see on fr. 3 below).

Medea's grim story, especially her deliberate infanticide in Euripides' version, moreover, seems to offer unlikely material for a satyr-play which disguises parody or burlesque of tragedy – unless the myth was turned completely on its head and both she and the children escaped in a conventional happy ending; and a miraculous chariot imitating that of Euripides' play would suit satyric or comic ambience very well (cf. the sea-chariot in Aeschylus' *Glaucus the Sea-god* F 25e and the aerial flight of Heracles and Hermes in Ion's *Omphale* F 17a – even if both were 'narrated').

What, though, might satyrs have been doing in a royal palace which was so preoccupied with Medea's presence, and would Silenus have had any independent role? The play is set at Corinth, notorious for sexual licence and so opportune for satyric fun. Corinthian prostitutes appear in Euripides' satyric *Sciron* F 675, 676, but there is nothing of them in F 667a; both Sutton (1987) 51–3 and Kannicht (5.1141) have nevertheless suggested that the Corinthian women addressed in v. 103 are 'extras', perhaps forming a secondary chorus and perhaps comparable with the prostitutes of *Sciron* (on the main chorus, see n. 12 on fr. 3 below). In any case, the human characters would be numerous enough for a satyr-play, with Medea, both Jason and the (probable) servant attested in fr. 1.39–52, and possibly Aegeus and even Creon (cf. fr. 1.38–53).

Dr Doreen Innes (independently of Sutton (1987) 52–3) ingeniously wonders whether in a satyric *Medea* echoing Euripides' tragedy Silenus might credibly, and ludicrously, be cast as the children's Tutor (Euripides, *Medea* 49–88), and be, as so often, in involuntary servitude, possibly to Creon. At fr. 1.60 'slave' is perhaps self-description by the same person who apparently names himself 'well-disposed' in fr. 1.49 when addressing Jason; compare the Nurse and Tutor at the start of Euripides' play, 1–95 (see Hunter (1981) 20). The satyrs would be as eager for the children's survival and escape as for their own; cf. Silenus' selfish attention to the castaways Danae and the baby Perseus in Aeschylus' *Net-Fishers* F 47a.22–56. Further: Dr Innes's suggestion makes a Tutor-Silenus into a plausible speaker of the obscene lines fr.2.85–97, with their homosexual content; he would fear for the boys' safety in this respect, either with no father to protect them, or even from the father (96–7, with n. 9). Conversely, Silenus may be himself accused in these lines of assaulting the boys (for satyric homosexuality see *Cyc.* 498 and n., 584, and our introductory discussion to Sophocles' *Lovers of Achilles*) and somehow imperilling Medea's hopes of 'justice' (84–90) – but there is too much uncertainty about the speaker and possible interruption of the long speech 84–109/12: see n. 6 below on fr. 2.

The four fragments are put in the same order by editors. They contain successively 78, 31, 7 and 10 lines, almost all very badly damaged. The first editor of the papyrus was uncertain about both the papyrological and the dramatic order of the fragments, however; and Sutton (1987) 41–4 both repeated that uncertainty (fr. 2 may precede fr. 1) and suggested (49) that fr. 4 may cohere with fr. 1 (see below, and cf. fr. 1.43).

Fr. 1 col. i describes the situation at Corinth, one of wretchedness for Medea's children and dishonour for her (21–2); either she is herself speaking, or a different but sympathetic voice (above). In col. ii Jason reports Aegeus' arrival (41–3); note '(for talk) shared with (my?) wife', Snell's conjecture in 43, with which compare Eur. *Medea* 663–758 where Aegeus' arrival and conversation with Medea remain unknown to (or are not mentioned by) Jason, even at 1384–5. Jason is addressed in 48, but the very fragmentary state of the rest of this column yields nothing definite about how the scene developed; it is possible, but unlikely, that the same voice continued until the fragment ends (78), or even beyond.

Fr. 2, whether following or preceding fr. 1, is baffling, not least because no indications of voice-parts survive. The suddenly vituperative and obscene tone of its vv. 85–94 hardly suggests a woman (although Snell thought of Medea abusing Jason for his love of Creon's daughter) – but who else at Corinth would abuse Jason – Silenus (above) – or abuse Silenus (also above)? Indeed the obscenity is extraordinary, especially the possible charge of pederasty (see n. 9 below); it is extreme, in any form of comic or satyric drama, as well as in burlesque, the more so because the rest of the (admittedly damaged) fragments afford nothing comparable and no plausible motive for the charge.

The tiny fr. 3 is equally difficult for notional reconstruction. It bestrides the end and beginning of episodes, the papyrus merely marking the presence of an intervening choral ode at 112 and not giving its text.[2] Who addresses the 'women who inhabit this plain of Corinth' at the new episode's start? – may the next words 'under this land's ancestral laws' have an implication we cannot catch (113–14)? Such a form of address almost certainly comes from a foreigner, Aegeus or Medea (less probably, Jason) – or, again, Silenus; but it is impossible to say to whom of the first three the phrase 'deprived of children' in 116 refers (if it is correctly read and understood: see n. 13 below). Also, are these women the play's main or secondary chorus? In a satyr-play the chorus would have to comprise the satyrs, and thus here be disguised as women (above).[3] If the play is not satyric, there is no problem.

In fr. 4 only the words 'child' and 'of your wife' are legible: the unidentified speaker must be addressing Jason, but does he mean Medea or Jason's intended new wife, the daughter of Creon?

The nature, purpose and occasion of this play and its fragments therefore remain uncertain. In favour of a burlesque, or of some kind of parody, are: the many echoes of Euripides' play; the sudden (but limited) intrusion of non-tragic vocabulary and obscenity into what otherwise is acceptable tragic style; the apparent composition of the chorus from women; and the absence from the fragment of certainly satyric elements or ambience. These features seem to exclude a satyr-play, unless Dr Innes' and Sutton's (1987) suggestion of Silenus as the speaker of the obscenities (or as their object) is right and the satyrs pose as the female chorus. Can this text be anything other than a paper exercise, although put together in normal dramatic manner (compare *Adespota* F 655, the 'Atlas' play, introductory discussion, and almost certainly the new *adespoton*, below)? The late date of the papyrus (2nd/3rd century AD) means little to that question (the papyrus of Sophocles' *Trackers*, for example, is also of that time), but if this 'Medea' is either a 4th century or a Hellenistic composition, its survival and later recopying are remarkable.

Notes

[1] Gauly (1991) omitted the fragment altogether (despite Kannicht's participation in *Musa Tragica*); Gallo (1992), Conrad (1997), B. Seidensticker in KPS (see p. 4 there), and Voelke (2001) do not mention it. In our own discussion we are especially grateful to Dr. Doreen Innes, who persuaded us to rethink and reformulate this introductory discussion.

[2] Such omission does not necessarily imply that no lyrics survived for the scribe to copy (or that none had ever been composed), for the terse signal 'Choral (song)' is found in papyri from plays, both tragic and comic, where lyrics are omitted; cf. particularly P. Sorb. 2252 at Eur. *Hippolytus* 58–72, where there is a gap but in fact no signal. Dio of Prusa ('Chrysostom'), *Oration* 19.5 tells us that in later times some copies of classical plays omitted the choral passages.

[3] For a similar problem see Ion of Chios, *Omphale* above, introductory discussion.

F 667a

fr. 1 col. i

38 extremely damaged lines (1–38), *in which the following words are confidently read:*

> 21 ταλ]αιπωροῦντες 22 ἀτ]ιμασθεῖσα, 25 end κατεῖχε μυρία πρόσω

col. ii

40 line-beginnings (39–78), *in which the following words are read with varying confidence:*

<IAΣΩN>   .]εν[.].[. Κ]ρέοντος ω[

                ἐνταῦθ' ἀνεῖται π[(40)

                καὶ νῦν τριταῖον ἦμ[αρ

                Αἰγεὺς λιπὼν γὰρ η[

                δάμαρτι κοινοὺς [

                ταῦτ' οὖν ἀθρῶν δυσ.[

                κοὐκ οἶδ' ὅπῃ .η..[(45)

                ὁμοῦ φυγὴ γὰρ ἀπορ..[

                κακοῖς ἐγὼ τὰς ευμι.[

< – >   ἄναξ 'Ιᾶσον *remnants*

                εὔνουν *remnants*

                κέκευθε φροντὶς ..[(50)

                αἰεὶ ματα[*remnants*

                καίει γὰρ [*remnants*

and then some words are intermittently legible:

> 59 διεκπερ[α, 60 δοῦλον [, 61 χρυσ[, 62 καὶ προσθ[, 63 νῦν δ' εισ[, 65 κακῶν, 67 ἔθηκε[, 70 τὰ πρῶτα, 72 ἔχοις, 73 εἰ μὴ, 76 δηλο[

fr. 2

top of the single column lost, then 5 badly damaged lines (79–83) *in which the following words are legible:*

> 81 πρὶν 'ξίδης, 82 δοκεῖς;

P. Lit. Lond. 77 (2nd–3rd c. AD) ed. H. J. Milne (1927), after the first edition by W. Crönert, *APF* 3 (1906) 1–5

43 κοινοὺς [εἰς λόγους Snell   44 δύστ[ηνός εἰμι Snell
46 ἄπορος [Snell   51 μάτα[ιο]ι Snell

F 667a (P. Lit. Lond. 77)
fr. 1 col. i
38 extremely damaged lines (1–38), including the following words:

> 21 suffering miserably (*masc. plural, i.e. Medea with her and Jason's sons?*), 22 after (my?) dishonour (*fem. singular, i.e. Medea herself?*), 25 limitless ... seized (me?) thereafter ...

col. ii
40 line-beginnings (39–78), of which the following yield sense:

<JASON>
> 39 ... of Creon, 40 then (Then?) ... has been relaxed[4] ..., 41 And now (for?) a third day ..., 42 ... because Aegeus after (*or* on) leaving ..., 43 ... (for talk?) shared with (my?) wife ..., 44 When I consider this, therefore, (I am in misery?) ..., 45 and I do not know, (how?) ..., 46 ... for together ... flight (is impossible?)[5] ..., 47 ... I ... by troubles ...
> (*change of speaker*) 48 Lord Jason, ..., 49 ... (me?) well-disposed ..., 50 ... anxiety has hidden (*or* lies hidden)..., 51 ... always (useless?) ..., 52 because ... kindles ...

then, only intermittent words yield sense, perhaps from the same speaker:

> 59 pass through, 60 slave, 61 gold(en?), 62 and previously(?), 63 but now, 65 of (your?) troubles, 67 (s)he put (*or* made), 70 the first thing(s) (*or* those in power), 72 you would (?) have, 73 unless, 76 clear

fr. 2
probably one (abusive) speaker throughout;[6] the top of the single column is missing, then come 5 damaged lines (79–83) in which the following words give sense:

> 81 before (you see?) clearly, 82 you seem (*or* think);

---

4   Possibly the extension of Medea's leave to stay in Corinth for a further day (Eur. *Med.* 340, 352); 'third day' of 41 may however relate not to this but to the duration of Aegeus' stay.
5   Jason rejecting the idea of his own flight from Corinth? Cf. Eur. *Med.* 604, Medea's 'I'll flee this land on my own.'
6   The speaker abuses Jason for his betrayal – and in 85–97 seems to accuse him of surrender to his lust (85), perhaps for both his new bride, Creon's daughter, and even for his own sons (96–7) – unless Silenus is being accused: see introductory discussion. These lines may be a counterpart to Jason's words in Euripides, when he claims that Aphrodite was his real saviour, since Medea was guided by love in aiding him (*Med.* 527–31); he had earlier asserted that married women care only about having a good sex life (569–73).

then right-centres and a few ends of 22 lines (84–105), with greatly varying numbers of letters missing from their beginnings:

remnants κωλύσων δίκ[η]ν

remnants εὐτόνῳ φλεβί   (85)

]πώπ[ο]τ' 7 *let.* δεδεγμ[.]..

].....οἱ λελεγμένοι λ[ό]γοι

]δοξαι καταπιεῖν δ' ορφανα

]. εἰσορᾶν ἃ χρὴ

]η δ[ια]σφάλλει νόον   (90)

]ν τῆσδε γῆς Κρέων ποεῖ

] φῶς πᾶσι κηρύχθη πάλαι

]οῦντες ὡς καλῶς ἐγνωκότες

]εσι τυφεδόνος εὐδόξου δέ· υ.[.]ου

]παντι τοὔμπαλιν σάφ' οἶδ' ἐγὼ   (95)

]υσω παῖδας ἐν μηροῖς ἔχε[

]. θέλοντος εὐφλεβὲς κέρας

remnants πώπ[ο]τ' ἀθλίας δόξης κρι[

οὐ]δ' [ἃ]ν δυναίμην εἰσορᾶν ὅσσοισι [

]ον. κοίμιζε σὰς κόρας ..[(100)

ἐ]κεῖ γε ταὐτὸ γὰρ πραχθή[σεται

]..δη[..]ον νοσεῖν ἔφυ τέκνον [

]ν μὴ κεκρυμμένων ομ[

]εν τῶνδε δωμάτων ἄπο

]ν κοίμησον ἠρεθισμ[(105)

words from 4 further lines (106–9), including:

106 κακῶν, 107 ταῦτα … φέρει[ν, 108 οὐθαμῶς

88 δ' ορφανα P. Lond., for which Snell conjectured *e.g.* δ' οὐ ῥᾴδιον
91 νοει, with π(οει) above the line, P. Lond.
92 σα]φῶς Snell
96 ἔχε[ιν Austin
97 κεαρ, with (κε)ρας above the line, P. Lond.
99 the letters –νδυναιμ- are insecurely read

then, with greater completeness, but with all line-beginnings and some line-ends damaged or lost, 84–109:

> ... with the intention of preventing justice ... (with?) stiffened member (85) ... (n)ever yet ... having received ... the spoken words (*grammatical subject*) ... opinions (?), but (it is not easy?) to swallow[7] ... to see what ... ought ... ruins (my?) intention ... (90) ... Creon ... of this land is doing (*or* intends) ... was long ago proclaimed (openly *or* clearly) to all[8] ... as well realising (*plural*) ... nonsense, but specious ... (all?) the opposite I know for certain (95) ... (to take?) the boys between (your?) thighs[9] ... wishing ... horn well-filled with blood[10] ... never ... judge(ment?) of a sorry reputation (?) ... and I'd (not) be able to look upon ... with ... eyes ... put (*imperative, sing.*) your eyes to sleep ... (100) ... for there the same will be done ... a child is born ... to suffer ... (of things?) unless hidden ... away from this house ... in anger (?) lay ... to rest ... (105)[11] *then:*

words from 4 further lines (106–9) *including*

106 (of?) troubles, (107) (to?) bear this, (108) in no way

[7] 'swallow': possibly a colloquialism in the sense of 'be forced to accept'; certainly the word is not tragic, and occurs with the plain meaning 'gulp greedily down' in the satyric *Cyc.* 219 and Ion, *Omphale* F 29, and as 'overcome' in Aeschylus' satyric *Ixion* F 91. 'Nonsense' too, in 94, is not a tragic word.

[8] Cf. Eur. *Med.* 70–4, the Tutor: 'that Creon this land's sovereign (cf. v. 91 here) intends to expel these boys with their mother; but whether this report is definite, I do not know.' The Greek verb 'was ... proclaimed' in 92 lacks the temporal augment, a usage found in 5th century tragedy only in messengers' reports; so it is here 'hard to explain even if this is a tragic text', Hunter (1981) 20.

[9] 'boys ... between ... thighs': if this is the correct text and translation, the expression is not in itself a sure indication of satyric status, but its application to pederasty would be (cf. Soph. *Lovers of Achilles*, esp. F 153, above): the intercrural coupling implied in Aeschylus' tragedy *Myrmidons* F 135 and 136 is between adult males (Achilles and Patroclus).

[10] 'horn': Greek κέρας. In the papyrus this metaphor for 'penis' (*e.g.* Archilochus F 247 *IEG*; shared with *e.g.* Latin *cornu* and with English) has been written above 'heart' (κέαρ), to which the unique Greek adjective 'well-filled with blood' (εὐφλεβές), is inappropriate; cf. 85 'stiffened member' (εὐτόνῳ φλεβί). The word φλέψ 'vein, (vein full of) blood' occurs incomplete in Soph. *Trackers* F 314a.32 and may refer to the satyrs' sexual excitement, for example their masturbation at F 314.368. Hunter (1981) 20–1 observes that the metaphor in 'horn' appears to be found in Euripides' tragedy *Auge* F 278 (remarkably – but the meaning is disputed).

[11] 'lay ... to rest': probably the same metaphor as 100 'put your eyes to sleep', *i.e.* 'forget your anxiety'; but some interpreters take it as euphemistic here for 'put to death'.

fr. 3

*letters from 3 lines (110–12) which end a speech and episode, the last line
ending with the word* λόγους; *then follow:*

] ΧΟΡΟΥ

γ]υναῖκες, αἳ Κορίνθιον πέδον   (113)
οἰκε]ῖτε χώρας τῆσδε πατρῴοις νόμοις,
]δα τοῦτο κἀξεπίσταμαι φρενί   (115)
letters from one further line (116), including ορφανι

fr. 4

only letters from the centres of 10 lines (117–26), including 119 τέκνον *and*
120 δ]άμαρτος σῆς [

113 probably ΜΕΛΟΣ] ΧΟΡΟΥ (cf. *e.g.* Astydamas II 60 F **1h.10 ΧΟΡΟΥ ΜΕΛΟΣ)
115 beg ἐγῷ]δα Snell (δα insecure); end the letters -ιστ-, -μαι and φρ are insecurely read

fr. 3

3 badly damaged lines (110–12), *the end of a speech and episode, finishing with* 112 *words, then:*

<SONG OF?> CHORUS

then the start of a new episode:

<−>   ... you women[12] who (inhabit) this plain of Corinth (113) under this land's ancestral laws ... (I myself know) and understand in my mind (115) ... deprived (of children? *or* being made orphan?)[13]

letters from one further line (116), *including the noun or verb* orphan

fr. 4

10 lines (117–26), *in which only* 119 child *and* 120 of your wife[14] *are legible*

---

12   For the identity of the 'women' see the end of the introductory discussion. It is tempting to think of Medea as the speaker, since in Euripides (214) she begins her address to the chorus with 'Women of Corinth'; but here the beginning is more grandiose, and Hunter (1981) 20 aptly compares Phaedra's address to the chorus at Eur. *Hipp.* 373–4, 'Women of Trozen, whose home this is, the furthest promontory of the Peloponnese'.

13   'deprived (of children?)' *or* 'being made orphan'? (the damaged wording permits either): strongly resonant with Euripides' play, in which not only Jason loses the children by threatened expulsion (70–2) and actual infanticide (792, 1325–6 *etc.*) but also Creon loses his daughter poisoned by Medea's wedding gift (1209), and Aegeus is childless (669–71). As to 'being made orphan': conversely the children may lose both parents (a fear found at *e.g.* Eur. *Her.* 546–7) or just their father if they are expelled with their mother (*Med.* 70–2 *etc.*); the word 'orphan' is used mostly when a father dies (*e.g.* Hom. *Iliad* 6.342) but not rarely also a mother (*e.g.* Eur. *Alc.* 165).

14   'your wife': see on fr. 4 in the introductory discussion.

A new (2007) *adespoton* (P. Köln XI 431): almost certainly not satyric
(undated)

Text. P. Köln 431 ed. M. Gronewald, 'Alphabetisches Akrostichon mit 24 trochäischen Tetrametern', *Kölner Papyri* XI (Paderborn, 2007) 20–37, with plate.

Discussions. C. Collard, 'P. Köln XI 431 and its 'Genre'. A Suggestion', *ZPE* 171 (2009) 9–14; P. Parsons, 'P. Köln XI 431. A Further Note', *ibid.* 15–16; Luz (2010) 67–9.

Prof. M. Gronewald, the first editor of this text, suggested on the basis of its content and acrostic form that it is satyric in nature but also that it stems from a play of the mid-4th century BC, the *Centaur* of Chaeremon (see our Appendix). Collard (2009) however has argued that the text is most likely a Hellenistic literary 'game' or 'fun-piece', a *paignion*; we draw below upon his arguments, which Gronewald has himself generously accepted (Collard 14 n. 12); see also Parsons (2009) 15 and Luz (2010) 67–9. We nevertheless discuss the text because it raises general issues of attribution (cf. our Introductory Note), and because it is still of interest for *Centaur*.

The papyrus, dated by Gronewald to the 2nd century BC, has only one fragment of any extent (fr. 1), a single column with the heavily damaged beginnings of 24 trochaic tetrameters. They derive it would seem from a play, for vv. 1–2 resemble the start of a messenger's report; but any speaker-note has been lost (if indeed there ever was one). The initial letters of about half the verses survive intermittently and reveal the alphabetic-acrostic form. The fragment is subscribed, and its verses numbered as 24; these features, and its frequent errors, some self-corrected, suggest that it was a copying-exercise (or an amateur production), and confirm that the 24 verses were the entire content of the column.

Enough is left of vv. 3–19 to show that they 'reported' a divinely beautiful and alluring woman; she is likely to have been Helen if her brother Castor's name can be securely read in 3. Then in vv. 20–3 a man is described apparently 'toasting' his hopes of winning her during a game of *kottabos*; the man may be Achilles, if 'the (son of Peleus)' is supplemented in v. 24 (but this is precarious); in some mythography Achilles is an early suitor of Helen: see *Cyc.* 181–2n.

[The papyrus-text as edited and in part supplemented by Gronewald translates as: '… I am here to report … (and) I wish (to …) to you from the beginning. (Castor! ?) … totally desirable (and?) conspicuous … well(-

shaded?) ... (5) ... (child?) of Zeus ... was beautiful ... godlike ... (and? exhaling ... divine ... inflaming ... outstanding beauty ... (10) ... white among (women?) .. hand ... foreign ... with a fair breeze ... (15) rhythm ... pouring in (*or* upon; *masculine or feminine participle*) ... (20) of love ... raising (*masculine*) his right arm ... and drops were thrown to the gound ... the (son of Peleus?) ...']

Among the difficult issues of provenance complicated by the fragment's form, physical condition and subscribed length, two are paramount for us here: (1) necessarily, its association by Gronewald with Chaeremon's satyr-play, and (2) its dramatic origin at all, and in a 'real', performable play.

(1) For the scanty evidence and few fragments of Chaeremon's *Centaur* see *TrGF* 1².71 F 9a, 10, 11 and possibly 14b, cf. 5.1112; T. Günther in KPS 581–90 provides a commentary and appreciation; see also our Appendix. Aristotle, *Poetics* Ch. 1.12, 1447b21ff. (= F 9a) describes the play as a 'mixed rhapsody of all the metres' – mixed, it may well be, because the name-figure was himself 'mixed', a hybrid creature: he would have been Chiron, the principal Centaur, famous for educating the young Achilles ('the (son of Peleus?)' in v. 24 of our fragment?). Gronewald pursued a hint of Snell (in *TrGF* 2.12, on *Adespota* F 5g) that the satyrs in *Centaur* formed a chorus of Chiron's pupils, and supposed that if P. Köln 431 belonged to the play, Achilles (as their class-mate) had a speaking part, and that Silenus was the 'messenger' (vv. 1–2) who read the narrative verses out as a copying exercise. Now F 14b of Chaeremon is an acrostic upon the poet's name composed from (damaged) dactylic hexameters, each of which is a one-line moral *gnome*; and F 14b is plausibly associated with (but not certainly attributed to) *Centaur* in the light of Chiron's role as tutor and of the play's attested mixture of metres.[1] It fits this association that trochaic tetrameters such as stand in P. Köln 431 might well feature in a 'mixed rhapsody', like dactylic hexameters.

There are however big obstacles to Gronewald's suggestions: the fragment contains not a hint of satyric provenance (the presence of *kottabos* is not a determinant: see our introductory discussion to Achaeus, *Linus* F 25); and trochaic tetrameters in narrative are so far unattested for any dramatic genre. Furthermore, the acrostic on Chaeremon's name (F 14b) did not certainly occur in the play-text itself of *Centaur*, and if it did, the presence of a second acrostic, let alone also an exactly complete 'abc', is very unlikely.

(2) Origin in a 'real' play, at all: would not an acrostic be missed by a live audience – and perhaps by readers – unless it was signalled to them in advance? Remarkably, there survives one analogous fragmentary and also

seemingly 'real' dramatic text in which a warning is indeed given that an alphabetic acrostic is coming. This is *Adespota* F 53 *PCG*, from P. Sorb. 72, 3rd century BC; it is a comic prologue which begins

> ... I ... am Aphrodite; I have come here to explain an incident which happened in this very place at my doing ... To prevent my seeming unpractised in poetry (v. 5), I'll both tell the incident and in doing so make use of (a game?: *only the first letter of this word at verse-end survives, Greek pi (π); if the supplement of a form of* paignion *(i.e.* π[αίγνιον) *were correct, this would be very much like a 'metapoetic' or 'intertextual' allusion to the piece's own 'genre'*); each of the verses I am about to speak will begin with the written sounds we are used to calling letters, written one after the other continuously and in their natural (v. 10) and harmonious sequence. But let's have no delay, and I'll begin with the letter alpha first ...'

(*only the start of the next verse survives; its first word begins with alpha*).

The care taken in *Adespota* F 53 *PCG* to guide the audience before the alphabet-acrostic begins – exactly what is missing from (and may never have preceded) the acrostic in P. Köln 431 – is in turn illuminated by the passage Athenaeus 10.453a–5a. Here, Athenaeus (or his source Clearchus, a pupil of Aristotle) describes three separate parts of the 'so-called letter- (*or* 'alphabet-') tragedy' of Callias, now housed putatively as a 'comedy' at T 7 *PCG* IV.39–40): a prologue recounting the letters of the alphabet, some choral antistrophic lyrics comprising paired letter-names and phonetic variation on their syllables, and a dialogue between an actor and the chorus enumerating and pronouncing the vowels; for the prologue and dialogue Athenaeus (Clearchus) records instruction to the performers how to speak the letters and vowels 'divided according to the punctuation'. In short, the audience was to be given the greatest possible help towards quick intelligibility and appreciation.

While it appears that Callias' play was performable (and performed? – one wonders, where and on what occasion?),[2] and that it had conventional formal elements, a prologue, choral lyrics and at least one episode, it must have been a bizarre composition, reliant it would seem on repeated fun with letters. In this respect, one other singular text may be adduced to the question of origin in a 'real' drama, the single fragment from an anonymous 'Atlas' play, *Adespota* F 655 *TrGF* (P. Bodmer XXVIII, 2nd century BC: above). It is unique as the only surviving dramatic text which eschews one letter of the alphabet entirely (*sigma*). Was this fragment part of an entirely asigmatic play, or part of a single such scene, and was it from a 'real' play?

Would the audience or, again, its readers have been expected, or been able, to perceive this character, and how quickly? We have no way to answer these questions. As to the possible length of its original: note our remarks upon Python's *Agen,* described as a 'little satyr-play' by Athenaeus (or his source Theopompus) and perhaps no more than an episode.

Now the comic *Adespota* F 53 looks like the beginning of a whole and indeed 'real' play; if so, its acrostic was a remarkable (and very deliberate) beginning – and for us the fragmentary papyrus breaks off as soon as the acrostic starts. Both the 'Atlas' play and the comic prologue differ from P. Köln 431 in one important way, therefore: we cannot know the extent of the texts from which they derive, and both may in any case have been copied from anthologies. The survival of P. Köln, a text implicitly complete in its subscribed 24 verses, and its metrical singularity as a trochaic narrative, together make strongly for its being just an individual, self-contained *paignion,* a literary (and metrically experimental) type well represented (like the visual *technopaignion*) among Hellenistic remains: see the references attached to F 996 in H. Lloyd-Jones, P. Parsons, *Supplementum Hellenisticum* (Berlin, 1983). As such it may well have been a paper exercise, and no more, employing dramatic form (again, see our discussion of the 'Atlas' play). This suggested 'classification' of P. Köln 431 is taken further (and with aptly ingenious playfulness) by Parsons (2009); he hazards a partial but very different reconstruction of its acrostic as an approximate narrative summary of the *Iliad,* each alphabetically ordered verse reflecting a chief theme or element of each of the epic's alphabetically numbered 24 books: not just a *jeu,* but a *tour de force!*

The problems in classifying P. Köln 431 add interestingly to those we have discussed in treating Python's *Agen* and *Adespota* F 646a, 655 (the 'Atlas' play) and 667a earlier in our volume.

Notes

[1] This acrostic is the earliest surviving poetic example (if it was part of Chaeremon's original text); the device is first regularly traced in Hellenistic poetry. The most recent general surveys of the topic are *Reallexikon für Antike und Christentum* 1 (1950) 235–8 and its *Supplement* 1 (2001) 11–13, and Luz (2010) 1–77, esp. 7–15 on Chaeremon F 14b.

[2] Collard (2009) should have noted some recent major articles on Callias' play which appear to accept as fact its performability (and indeed performance), R. A. Rosen, *CPh* 94 (1999) 147–67, esp. 148, and C. J. Ruigh, *Mnem* 54 (2001) 261–339, esp. 269–71. A third and later article on Callias raises precisely the questions about differing intelligibility for (unwarned) audience and readers, and therefore performability, which we ask here: J. A. Smith, *CPh* 98 (2003) 313–29, esp. 317–29.

APPENDIX

Summary description of some other satyr-plays

Authors are arranged in chronological order.

Plays of each author are given almost always in the alphabetical order of their 'English' titles, with the Greek titles transliterated or Latinised in brackets. After a play-name (A) = attested in antiquity as satyric, (B) = confidently identified by modern scholars as such, (C) = diffidently conjectured as such. An asterisk signals a play or fragmentary text 'selected' and treated in detail in this volume.

Pratinas (*Hyporchema**): *Suda* π 2230 Adler (*TrGF* 1².79 T 1) counts 50 plays for him, 32 of them satyric; he and his son Aristias (separate entry below) were the most celebrated satyric playwrights of their day, second only to Aeschylus (Pausanias 2.13.6, *TrGF* T 7). Yet only **Wrestlers** (**Palaestae**) (A) is named by antiquity, produced by Aristias in 467 BC (*TrGF* 1².43–4 II DID C 4b). The title (all that survives: 4 F 2) suggests that the satyr-chorus were at a mythical wrestling contest such as that between Theseus and Cercyon (Gantz (1993) 252–3: cf. Aeschylus' *Cercyon* below) or between Heracles and the giant Antaeus (Gantz (1993) 416–17; Aristias is credited with a satyric *Antaeus*); both possibilities, KPS 77–80. Cf. also Heracles wrestling Achelous in Sophocles' *Oeneus**, and the satyrs' aspirations to wrestle in Aeschylus' *Sacred Delegates**.

Aeschylus (for whom see esp. Podlecki in Harrison (2005) 1–19): 14 plays in category (A), *Amymone, Cercyon, Circe, Glaucus the Sea-God**, *Heralds* (*Kerykes*), *Leon, Lycurgus, Net-Fishers** (*Dictyulci*), *Prometheus the Fire-Kindler**, *Proteus, Sacred Delegates** (*Theoroi*), *Sisyphus**, *Sphinx* and a 'Justice' play, F 281a*; 7 plays in category (C), some known only by title, *Argo, Bridal-Suite-Makers* (*Thalamopoioi*), *Cabiri, Escorts* (*Propompoi*), *Ixion, Nurses* (*Trophoi*), and *Phorcides. Bone-Gatherers* (*Ostologoi*) and *Ghost-Raisers* (*Psychagogoi*) were probably tragedies from one trilogy, not satyr-plays: see *e.g.* KPS 205–7, Sommerstein (2008) 178–81, (2010) 250–2.

Amymone (A): the satyr-play accompanying the Danaid-trilogy (460s BC?) which included the extant *Suppliant Women*: 3 short book-fragments. Silenus or the satyrs attempted the rape of Danaus' daughter Amymone, only for the god Poseidon to rescue and rape her himself (Gantz (1993) 207–8), but also to reward her. KPS 91–7, Sommerstein (2008) 8–11.

Cercyon (A): 6 lexicographic fragments; for the background story see on Pratinas' *Wrestlers* (above). KPS (1999) 149–51, Sommerstein (2008) 116–17.

Circe (A): 3 lexicographic fragments. The plot was no doubt founded upon Book 10 of the *Odyssey*; perhaps the satyrs had been bewitched, or transformed, by Circe (like Odysseus' crew), and he secured their release (cf. Euripides' *Cyclops*); see KPS 157–60, Sommerstein (2008) 121. A vase-painting of about 460 BC showing a woman recoiling from an apparently farting monkey-satyr (*LIMC* III.1.493 'Dionysos' no. 833 = VI.1.56 'Kirke' no. 57) has been related to this possible plot: see our n. 22 on Soph. *Trackers* F 314.128, cf. KPS 159.

Heralds (Kerykes) (A): 6 lexicographic fragments: a 'Heracles' play. After killing the lion of Cithaeron, and taking its skin and mane as his emblematic dress (F 109, 110), Heracles encountered 'heralds' from a certain Erginus demanding tribute from the Thebans; Heracles mutilated them and sent them back to Erginus in lieu (Gantz (1993) 379–80). It is guesswork whether the satyrs were among, or accompanied, the 'heralds', and that Heracles perhaps released them. KPS 152–6, Sommerstein (2008) 118–19.

The Lion (Leon) (A): 1 book-fragment; possibly dramatising Heracles' conquest of the Lion of Nemea (Gantz (1993) 383–4, KPS 161–3, Sommerstein (2008) 124–5), no doubt in a rural setting apt for satyrs.

Lycurgus (A): 3 book-fragments. The play would have presented as light entertainment some episode belonging to the grim stories forming Aeschylus' tragic trilogy *Lycurgeia*, in which Dionysus destroyed his human opponent, this king of Thrace (Gantz (1993) 113–14); the satyrs may have been captive victims of Lycurgus, and saved by the god. KPS 164–8, at 168, Sommerstein (2008) 126–9.

Nurses (Trophoi) (C): only 3 lexicographic fragments but one important testimony (F 246a) which compares Medea's rejuvenation of Jason by boiling him with her similar rejuvenation of Dionysus' 'nurses' and their husbands (Gantz (1993) 112–13, KPS 197–202, Sommerstein (2008) 248–9). If these husbands were played, or impersonated, by the satyrs, then their escape from the pot might have provided the farce.

Proteus (A): 1 book-fragment and 5 lexicographic. The play complemented the celebrated and surviving *Oresteia*-trilogy of 458 BC. Sailing home from Troy, Menelaus encountered Proteus, the 'Old Man of the Sea' (as foretold in *Agamemnon* 617–21, 674–9), from whom he learned his own future miseries and those of other Greeks, including Agamemnon: Gantz (1993) 663–4, KPS 179–81, Sommerstein (2008) 220–3; on the play see M. Griffith, *ClAnt* 21 (2002) 237–54. The role of the satyrs cannot be known, but together with the metamorphosing Proteus they would have created much stage-fun.

Sphinx (A): 2 book-fragments and 1 lexicographic. This satyr-play completed the 'Theban' trilogy of 467 BC, of which the final play survives, the *Seven against Thebes*. The plot is likely to have been the satyrs' ludicrous aspiration to King Laius' widow Jocasta if they could solve the Sphinx's riddle. KPS 189–96, Sommerstein (2008) 238–43 and (2010) 89–90; cf. Gantz (1993) 494.

Aristias, son of Pratinas (above), active from the 460s, date of death not known.

Fates (***Keres***) (B): 1 book-fragment. Named for the malignant female underworld 'demons', drinkers of human blood (Gantz (1999) 8–9). In the play Heracles may have rescued the satyrs from them (cf. his capture of Cerberus in many satyr-plays, and struggle with Death in *Alcestis*); whether the satyrs formed the chorus of demons, or acted as themselves in a secondary chorus, is discussed by KPS 214–17.

Cyclops (A): Probably later than Epicharmus' comedy of this title and certainly earlier than Euripides' play; from its single book-fragment 9 F 4 unwatered wine appears to have been as important to subduing Polyphemus as at Eur. *Cyc.* 556–8. KPS 218–21.

Sophocles (for whom see esp. Radt (1982 = 1991 = 2002) in Bibliographical Guidance p. 239). 10 documented satyr-plays (A; including *Lovers of Achilles**, *Inachus**, *Trackers**, and *Oeneus**), another 4–5 more or less certainly identified by inference and conjecture (B), and up to a further 10 whose identification is much less confidently conjectured (C).

Amphiaraus (A): 9 book-fragments, 4 of them lexicographic. The plot cannot be confidently conjectured (KPS 236–42, esp. 240–2, Lloyd-Jones (1996) 46–7), but Amphiaraus, the seer who accepted his destiny of dying in the expedition of the 'Seven Against Thebes', was a very popular figure in all drama, for his myth was rich in extraordinary incidents (Gantz (1993) 506–19, 522–8, cf. 191–3).

Amycus (A): 2 book-fragments, one of which (F 112) suggests that the play portrayed this famous boxer in the only known mythological incident, his fight with Polydeuces the Argonaut ([Apollod.] 1.9.20; Gantz (1993) 348–9). Lloyd-Jones (1996) 44–5, KPS 243–9.

Daedalus (C): 6 fragments, 3 of them lexicographic, and 2 testimonies; plot indeterminable.

Little Dionysus (A): 3 lexicographic fragments; they confirm that the plot was the infancy of the god and his 'invention' of wine (cf. *Adespota* F 646a* vv. 12–14 and introductory discussion). Lloyd-Jones (1996) 66–7, KPS 250–8.

Three '*Heracles*'-plays (all A). *On Taenarum*: 5 book-fragments, 4 lexicographic. Since a chasm of Mt. Taenarum was an entrance to the Underworld, the plot was almost certainly Heracles' descent to fetch Cerberus (cf. Euripides, *Eurystheus**; Gantz (1993) 413–16): so KPS 261–5. The satyrs were cast as Spartan helots, *i.e.* in their frequent role as slaves. One other fragment survives attributed to a *Cerberus* (C), which some scholars think has 'escaped' from *On Taenarum*: see KPS 275–6. *Little Heracles*: 2 book-fragments. As in *Little Dionysus* the name-character was an infant, and probably either or both of the best-known incidents of Heracles' infancy and childhood were depicted, his strangling of the snakes (Gantz (1993) 377) or killing of his music-teacher Linus (see Achaeus' *Linus**; Gantz (1993) 379, cf. KPS 266–9, at 269). *Heracles*: 3 lexicographic fragments, which permit no association with any mythological incident. KPS 270–4.

Three plays titled for personified 'abstractions': *Hybris* (A): 2 book-fragments, plot indeterminable. KPS 277–8. *Momus* ('Blame') (B): 5 lexicographic fragments, plot indeterminable (KPS 363–7, at 367); but Gantz (1993) 567–8, on the basis of the Scholia to Homer, *Iliad* 1.5, notes Momus' opposition to Zeus' destruction of Troy, or to Zeus' causation of the Trojan War, as a 'wrong' attempt to reduce the world's population (cf. KPS 364). *Eris* ('Strife') (C): 1 book-fragment; plot indeterminable but the quarrel between the Lapiths and the Centaurs at the wedding of Peleus and Thetis would make a good satyric subject (Gantz (1993) 9, 230).

Cedalion (B): 5 book-fragments, 3 of them lexicographic: possibly featuring (i) this famous blacksmith's guidance of Orion, blinded by Oenopion, until his sight was cured, or (ii) his teaching his skills to the lame artificer-god Hephaestus (cf. Hesiod F 148a Merkelbach-West; Gantz (1993) 271–2, KPS 344–8, Lloyd-Jones (1996) 182–5 and n. on *Cyc.* 213). The satyrs would have made clumsy assistant 'smiths'.

The Deaf (*Kophoi*) – or ?*The Dumb* or ?*The Stupid* (B): 5 assorted testimonies and fragments. The title indicates the characterisation of the satyrs, but the plot is indeterminable. Lloyd-Jones (1996) 194–5, KPS 349–55, at 353–5.

The Judgement (*Krisis*) (A): 1 book-fragment and 3 probable testimonies: almost certainly a burlesque of the famous Judgement of Paris (Gantz (1993) 567–71, KPS 356–62), with much opportunity for satyrs' lubricity. So too *Helen's Marriage* (*Helenes Gamos*) (C), if by this was meant Paris' abduction of Helen from her husband Menelaus (Gantz (1993) 571–6, Lloyd-Jones (1996) 194–5, KPS 391–3): 1 book-fragment, 1 possible papyrus-fragment.

Pandora or *Hammerers* (*Sphyrokopoi*) (B): 5 book-fragments, 4 of them lexicographic. F 482 'begin first upon kneading the clay' and the alternative title suggest that the play's essence was Hephaestus' 'construction' of Pandora from clay (Hesiod, *Works and Days* 60–4; Gantz (1993) 155–8 etc., cf. Lloyd-Jones (1996) 250–3, KPS 375–80, at 379–80: see on *Prometheus the Fire-Kindler**); the satyrs would be his 'assistants' (cf. *Cedalion* above). See also Voelke (2001) 228–30.

Salmoneus (A): 6 book-fragments, 2 of them lexicographic. Salmoneus was a magical artificer who contrived thunder and lightning, and demanded worship as a god (cf. e.g. Euripides F 929b.3–4); Zeus destroyed him with the real things (F 538 and 539 suggest appropriate stage-effects): Gantz (1993) 171–3. The satyrs may have been Salmoneus' slave-assistants (again cf. *Cedalion* and *Pandora*). Lloyd-Jones (1996) 370–3, KPS 381–7.

Also 'C': *Nausicaa* or *Laundry-Maids* (*Plyntriai*), *Sisyphus*, both names suited to satyric plots. For *Fellow-Diners* (*Syndeipnoi*), of disputed genre (KPS 396–8) but almost certainly tragic, see now A. Sommerstein, D. Fitzpatrick, D. Talboy (eds), *Sophocles. Selected Fragmentary Plays.* I (Oxford, 2006) 84–140, at 100–3.

Euripides (for whom see esp. Pechstein 1998). 10 or 11 plays are known in title and/or fragments: *Autolycus A** and *B** (both A), *Busiris*, *Epeus* (?), *Eurystheus**, *Harvesters*, *Cyclops**, *Lamia*, *Sisyphus*, *Sciron** (A), *Syleus** (A). See our Introductory Note.

Busiris (A): a tiny papyrus fragment from a *hypothesis*; 1 book-fragment and 2 lexicographic fragments. Busiris was an 'Egyptian' ogre who sacrificed strangers to the gods. He captured Heracles, who was passing through his land; but he broke free and killed both the ogre and his sons, perhaps releasing the satyrs from slavery to Busiris. The plot is inferred from Pherecydes 3 F 17.25–7 *FGrH* (= F 17.3–6 Fowler 287) and [Apollod.] 2.5.11: Gantz (1993) 418, Pechstein (1998) 122–40, KPS 413–9, at 418–19, Jouan and Van Looy VIII.2 (2002) 37–45, at 43, Collard and Cropp (2008) I.320–1.

Epeus (?: C): only a disputed title in an inscriptional list of Euripides plays, with no fragments or other testimony. Since Epeus devised the Wooden Horse at Troy (Homer, *Odyssey* 8.493) but was no warrior (*Iliad* 23.670; cf. Gantz (1993) 223–4, 641), the play would have provided amusement for the satyrs marvelling at the Horse and being eager to enter it, no doubt with Odysseus as usual thwarting them. KPS 420–1, Collard and Cropp (2008) I.361.

Harvesters (***Theristai***) (A): the satyr-play complementing Euripides' tragedies of 431 BC (*Medea, Philoctetes, Dictys*); now only a title, and uncertain because already lost to the 3rd/2nd century Alexandrian scholars. The plot is indeterminable (KPS 476, Collard and Cropp (2008) I.413); but see on Sositheus*.

Lamia (B): the title is attested only by Varro fr. 56a Cardauns, and there is only 1 book-fragment. The beautiful Lamia was seduced by Zeus; his jealous wife Hera doomed all her children to die. In her bitterness she became hideous, a killer of others' children – an ogre tailor-made for a satyr-play. 'One can imagine Heracles as her opponent', KPS 476. Pechstein (1998) 177–84, Jouan and Van Looy VIII.2 (2002) 333–5, Collard and Cropp (2008) I.557–9.

Sisyphus (A): the satyr-play completing the so-called 'Trojan trilogy' of 415 BC, *Alexander, Palamedes* and *Trojan Women*. A very fragmentary papyrus *hypothesis* reveals that Heracles was the 'hero': he is greeted in the single surely attributed book-fragment. The plot is not known (conjectures are reviewed by KPS 445–8), and Sisyphus figured in many plays: see on Aeschylus, *Sisyphus** and Euripides, *Autolycus A* and B**. It cannot be established whether the much-disputed book-fragment Critias(?) 43 F 19* belonged to any satyr-play, let alone a *Sisyphus* by Critias or Euripides: see there. Pechstein (1998) 185–217; Jouan and Van Looy VIII.3 (2003) 29–38, at 31–3; Collard and Cropp (2008) II.142–3.

Astydamas II (active from 372 BC, died after 340). *Heracles* (A): 1 book-fragment, 60 F 4, which we have cited in full in our introductory discussion to *Adespota* F 646a*; plot not determinable. *Hermes* (B): 1 book-fragment, describing drinking-vessels, probably associated with the worship of Dionysus; plot indeterminable (Krumeich (1999) 574–9, at 577–9). Hermes was always close to the satyrs, and even putatively their father (Gantz (1993) 135); for his roles in satyr-plays cf. *e.g.* Sophocles, *Inachus** and *Trackers**, Euripides' *Syleus** and Ion's *Omphale**.

Chaeremon (active in mid-4th Century). *Centaur (Kentauros)* (C): 7 varied testimonies and fragments, including F 14b, an acrostic on Chaeremon's name (see Luz (2010) 7–15). The title in itself suggests a 'hybrid' plot, just as Aristotle, *Poetics* 1447b22 says that the play was 'a mixed rhapsody of all metres'. The name-figure was almost certainly Chiron, the principal Centaur (Gantz 144–7, 390–2 *etc.*, cf. KPS 581–90, at 585ff.); he may have been in the background of Sophocles' *Lovers of Achilles**. G. Morelli, 'Per la ricostruzione del *Centauro* di Cheremone', in Martina (2003) 12–27. On this play see further our introductory discussion to 'A new (2007) *adespoton*'.

For complete lists of satyr-plays or fragments by minor poets, or unattributed fragments, see *TrGF* 2.414 and KPS 661–2; of play-characters KPS 663–5.

Also: (*TrGF* 1²) **Achaeus**, *Iris* (A) 20 F 19–23, *Momus* (A) F 29; unattributed fragments (C) F 40–2, 47, 49–52, 54. **Iophon**, *Singers to the Pipe (Aulodoi)* (A) 22 F 1. **Xenocles**, *Athamas* (A) 33 F 1. **Demetrius**, *Hesione* (?; C), 49 F (see n. 1 to our introductory discussion to Ion, *Omphale**; T.H. Carpenter in Harrison (2005) 222–6, at 225). **Dionysius**, *Hunger* (B) 76 F 3a. **Timocles**, *Lycurgus* (A) 86 T 2 (title only), *Phorcides* (A) T 4 (title only; for his *Icarian Satyrs,*, almost certainly a comedy despite its name, see *PCG* VII.766–9 and *TrGF* 1².252, and our n. 3 on Python's *Agen**). **Sositheus**, a play 'against Cleanthes' (A) 99 F 4, 5 (see our introductory discussion to his *Daphnis or Lityerses**). **Alexander the Aetolian**, *Dice-Players* (C) 101 F 1, 2 (testimonies only). **Theodorus**, *The Sacrificer* (B) 134 F 2 (title only). **Polemaeus of Ephesus**, *Ajax* (A) 155 F 2 (title only). **Harmodius of Tarsus**, *Protesilaus* (A) 156 (title only). **Theodo(tus**?: name damaged), *Palamedes* (A) 157 (title only). **Anaxion**, *Persians* (A) 202 (title only).

INDEX OF MOTIFS AND CHARACTERS

ADDENDA

General Introduction

p. 14 Heracles and the Apples of the Hesperides: see *Adespota* F 655 (an 'Atlas'-play) pp. 478–9.

p. 39 a 'classroom setting': see 'A new *adespoton* ...' p. 499, a suggestion by the papyrus' first editor that a classroom of satyrs is there *copying a text*.

Cyclops

p. 157 185–6n. end, Menelaus a coward: Aesch. *Ag.* 115 is to be found also in introductory discussion (2) and n. 9 to *Adespota* F 655, pp. 479–80 and 485.

p. 166 283n.: αἰσχρὸν στράτευμά γ(ε) is exclamatory, and probably nominative; it is much more difficult to take it as 'accusative in apposition to the whole sentence' (296 may afford an example), discussed by Barrett on Eur. *Hipp.* 752–7.

p. 211 *Cyc.* 608–23 and pp. 217–18 *Cyc.* 656–62, astrophic verses: see on Fragments p. 349 below.

Fragments

pp. 238 General Surveys and 503 Appendix: note D. F. Sutton, 'A Handlist of Satyr Plays', *HSCPh* 78 (1974) 107–43 (this is Sutton (1974d) in our General Bibliography).

Sophocles, *Trackers*
p. 336 *Discussions*: E. K. Borthwick, 'The Riddle of the Tortoise and the Lyre', *Music and Letters* 51 (1970) 373–87; C. Piraino, 'Per una ricostruzione della parte mancante degli *Ichneutai* Sofoclei', *Helikon* 18/19 (1978/79) 141–60; M. Hillgruber, '"Ohne das Hinterteil kann der Pudel nicht laufen." Zur Aufführung der *Spürhunde* des Sophokles unter der Regie Carl Roberts im Goethe-Theater Bad Lauchstädt', *APF* 57 (2011) 241–60, with 3 photographs; A. P. Antonopoulos, 'The Metre of the Parodos of Sophocles' *Ichneutai*', *ZPE* 184 (2013) 51–3; 'Marginal Variants on the Papyrus of Sophocles' *Ichneutai* (P. Oxy. 1174) and their Attribution', *ibid.* 55–7; 'An Extraordinary Insult in Sophocles' *Ichneutai*', *Hermes* 141 (2013) 83–7.

p. 341, second paragraph, lines 145–8: Antonopoulos (2013) *Hermes* 84 adds 2–*Frogs* 465–6 and *Knights* 247–9 to the passages deemed inferior, in extent and 'picturesque' quality, to 145–50 as 'a single lengthy asyndeton ... a breathless flood of abusive language'.

p. 343: Hillgruber (2011) gives a a documented account and discusses aspects of the first (and amazingly quick) modern performance of the play in 1913, only one year after the papyrus was first published. It was directed by the eminent classical scholar Carl Robert, together with excerpts from his German text and supplement of the play's lost ending; three photographs are reproduced, of Silenus being rewarded by Apollo (our p. 341), of the satyr-chorus dancing (lines 64–78), and of a child acting Hermes with the lyre.

p. 344 first paragraph, Theon (in the Apparatus to lines [31, not cited by us], 72, [88, 89], 99, 135, 143, [186], 230, 260, 310, 374, 452): see now Antonopoulos (2013) *ZPE* 55–6; on other attributions, to Nicanor/Nicander ([79], 108, 156, [221]), to Aristonicus (146: not Aristophanes) and Aristophanes/Aristarchus (143) see his 56–7.

p. 349 n. 12: Antonopoulos (2013) *ZPE* 51–3 offers a tentative analysis into mixed cretics, iambics, anapaests and dochmiacs, with particular attention to 76–8, where he suggests dividing 77–8 over χρυ|σοῦ. On p. 54 he notes the resemblance of this astrophic parodos to the later astrophic system 176–202, observing 'that the use of astrophic songs, esp. short ones, must have been typical of Satyr Play': *Inachus* F 269a.51–5 and 269c.1–7; Aesch. *Sacred Delegates* F 78a.5–17 and 78c.43–8; Eur. *Cyc.* 608–23 and 656–62.

p. 355 n. 26, on 146 'wax': Antonopoulos (2013) *Hermes* 84 argues that the allusion is to plastic art, to 'wax likenesses' such as those described by Plato, *Laws* 933b as apotropaic at doors and cross-roads, and on tombs; he compares Aesch. *Sacred Delegates* F 78a.1ff. for 'likenesses' as temple-antefixes.
pp. 85–6 he sees the point of the metaphor in (soft) wax in 146 as the 'ineffectiveness, stillness, brainlessness and faint-heartedness' of the satyrs.
pp. 86–7 also in line 146 he finds the adjective 'impure, unholy' suggestive of its weight in tragedy (see esp. Soph. *OT* 823 and 1323, of Oedipus' incest); so it gives an extravagant contrast with the inconsequential tone of our passage, perhaps in deliberate paratragedy? Compare the abusive colloquialism 'bastard' (lit. 'polluted, polluting') at *Cyc.* 677, with n. Cf also Soph. *Trackers* 197 and n. 36.

p. 367 n. 53 Borthwick (1970), a Greek scholar and noted student of ancient and modern music, traces the riddle of a dead creature acquiring a voice (*Trackers* 292–3) from its earlier (?) occurrence in the *Homeric Hymn to Hermes* (line 38), through its constant reappearance in literature and its adaptation as an inscription for various musical instruments into the modern period.

Sophocles, *Oeneus*
p. 379: for speculation that the play may have dealt with or alluded to Oeneus' receipt (as 'Wine-Man') of wine from Dionysus as the god's gift to mankind, see n. on *Cyc.* 39, at 'Althaea'.

GENERAL INDEX

This index is to the principal phenomena of satyric drama: its remains and their nature; issues of attribution to the genre; primary texts and the most important secondary evidence or testimonies; characteristics of the genre and its plots and figures, motifs and ethos; dramatic and theatrical aspects; and representation in art and especially vase-painting. The index is thus selective. Users may find it helpful to look first at the consecutive headings **Satyric**, **Satyr Plays**, **Satyrs** and **Silenus**. References are to numbered pages alone; a comma separates page-numbers when a lemma continues; when a colon separates items it is a page-number which follows.

There is also an Index of Motifs and Characters on pp. 509–12.

This index ignores very many matters of Greek language, especially grammar and syntax, and almost all individual words and phenomena of style: there are excellent indexes to these for *Cyclops* in the editions by Ussher (1978) and Biehl (1986).

Menedemus, philosopher 426, 462–3, 467
Mestra 30, 428–9
Metagenes F 15 *PCG*: 470–1
metatheatre 133, 245, 373, 470
metre
  iambic trimeter
  2nd foot anapaest 164, 3rd 161, 4th 283
  Porson's Law not observed *e.g.* 250, 273, 450, 455
  strict in some dialogue 457
  antilabe x 4 in one line 361
  and date of *Cyclops* 39–41
  iambic tetrameter 271, 357, 419
  trochaic tetrameter 259, 273, 323, 391, 498, 499
  anapaestic 263
    tetrameter 469–70
  dochmiac 325
  lyric 138, 139, 142, 176, 192, 211, 217, 244, 285, 331, 363, Addenda, mixed with iambic 321
  and stage-activity 341–2, 359

Midas 19, 457
milk 149, 171
Milo of Croton 389
minor satyric dramatists, Contents-page, 241 (bibl.), 502, 504, 508
misogyny 12, 157
mockery of enemies 222
moderation 12, 20, 173, cf. *sôphrosynê*
money 152, cf. Coinage
Muses 475
music 35–6, 184, 243–5, 247, 316, 338, 369, 371, 383
  'New Music' 186–7

Mysteries 473
  Aeschylus and 290, 294–5

Naiads 185, 244, 247;
  see also Nymphs
Neophron, *Medea* 488
Nicander/Nicanor Alexandrian scholar 344, Addenda
Nietzsche, F., and satyric 18, 19, 25, 26
'Nobody' (Homer, *Odyssey* 9) 199, 201, 219, 220
nymphs 12–13, 140, 154, 185, 247, 285, 347, 357, 363, 381, 439, 473; cf. Naiads
Nysa 131–2, 141, 285, 473

oaths 277, 479, 483
obscenity 263, 265, 271, 275, 433, 489, 490
Odysseus, in *Cyclops* 44–57, 143, 144, 145, 148, 158, 175, 179, 182, 183, 187, 188, 197–8, 207, 210, 214, 216, 224
  elsewhere 457, 480, 503, 507
Oeneus 136, 378–80, Addenda
ogres 29–30, 49–50, 130, 398, 404, 413, 450, 457, 458, 463, 507
  female 507
Omphale 307, 379, 404, 415–17, 438
  play on name 419
oracles 224, 479, 485, cf. Prophecy
Orion 159–60, 505–6
Ovid, *Metamorphoses* 1. 671–721: 316, 8.738–884: 30–1, 9. 1–97: 379, 13.867–9, 877
  Tristia 2. 411–12: 308–9

paean 219

costumes 331, of satyrs 142, 161,
(phallos) 154, 275, 403, of
Heracles 409
mask 219, disguise 317
'props' 135, 222, 481, (back-cloth)
481, (animals?) 137, (baby?)
256, eccyclema 259, cf. Settings
in this entry
stage-business 283, 291–2, 315,
340, 359, 435, 436, farcical 219–
24, 307, 311, 503, 504

Satyrs
parentage 9, cf. Hermes, as Silenus'
sons 164–5, 479; contrasted with
him 47–8, 165, 341 physical
characteristics 7–8, 10, 249, 263,
289, goat-like (in behaviour) 3, 35,
142, 289, 373; as θῆρες 'beasts,
creatures' 54, 211, 213, as men 209,
contrasted with mankind 341
cultural status 8–9
costume 7–8, 10, 263, 359, 449, 452,
ithyphallic 7–8, 11–12, 263, 335,
365, 373, cf. Erections, Phallos
immortal 18–19
'nonentities' 220
nature, sexual behaviour 8–17, stupid
506, inept 347, but intelligent
19–22, 38–9, 383, lazy 9–10, 31–3,
42–3, boastful 52, 190, 202, 269,
379, 395, ridiculous quests 504,
507, bibulous 33–4, 51, 140, 395
etc., gluttonous 33–4, 51, 459, 463
etc., noisy 363, crude 373, raped 15,
violent against goddesses 12–13,
206, 301, paradoxical aspects 17–22
in art, esp. vase-paintings 6–8, 8–11

Silenus
and satyrs 7, and his sons 164–5
aged 131, 135, white-haired 249
characterized 146, cowardly 153,
inconstant 161, braggart 132, 265,
357, venal, mercenary 150, 347,
401, 423, and wine 152, sings well
20, wise and didactic 18–19, 20, 39
and Dionysus 181–9, cares for the
infant 150, complaining servant 131
and Midas 19
in *Cyclops* 42, and Polyphemus 165,
raped by 15, 17, 207, cf. Ganymede
in *Trackers* 54
dramaturgy: as coryphaeus or actor 7,
prologuist 130, 315, prominence
135, 200, 268, 318
also in Comedy 469
other 15, 38, 46, 50, 51, 198, 201, 202,
204, 208, 209, 249, 255–6, 295,
337, 340–1, 347, 357, 385, 393,
394, 395, 398–9, 401, 406, 413,
450, 457, 463, 465, 469, 473, 477,
480, 489, 490

scholia on Aristophanes, *Assembly-
Women* 79–81: 331
on Hesiod, *Works and Days* 59:
283–4
on Homer, *Iliad* 6.153: 291, 21.194
(= Pindar F 249a): 378–9
on Theocritus 10.41: 457, 459
Sciron 24, 398–9
Scyros 306, 307
Servius Auctus on Vergil, *Eclogues*
6.13–26: 20, 8.68: 457
sex, sexuality 8–10, 11–13, 14, 26, 33,
46, 141, 154, 191, 200, 255, 308–9,